**From the Perspective Of . . .** are located in every chapter. These incorporate short, question-based overviews that tie management concepts to real-world career examples and chapter concepts in depth.

### From the PERSPECTIVE OF...

**A City Planner**

For cities large and small, growth is a fact of life, and without a detailed plan for that growth, the city's infrastructure—roads, utilities, water, schools, and police and fire services—would be unable to keep up. What other factors would be important in the development of raw land?

**Progress Check Questions** provide assessments of comprehension throughout each chapter.

### [PROGRESS] ✓questions

1. What is an organization chart?
2. Explain the stages an organization goes through as it grows and matures.
3. What are the four most important factors affecting organization structure?
4. Explain the differences between mechanistic and organic organizational systems.

**Ethical Management** dilemmas present students with a scenario that requires a decision but that may not provide an immediately obvious solution. These underline the likelihood of difficult "right vs. right" decisions that people face at some point in their management career.

**Cases** appear at the end of every chapter. These detailed case studies, featuring well-known companies, present management situations that encourage students to focus on the impact of "big picture" decisions on the lower levels of the organizational pyramid.

#### WHAT'S IN A NAME?

Before the arrival of Internet-based stock trading, financial services companies such as Merrill Lynch would award brand new stockbrokers the title of "vice president" to convey to prospective clients that they were dealing with a person of significance and seniority within the organization.

In teaching hospitals, first-year residents still carry the title of "doctor" even though they have years of practical training ahead of them. In many companies, HR generalists reporting to HR managers have now become HR managers reporting to HR directors, often with no increase in salary or any significant change in responsibilities. This practice is referred to as *title inflation*. Does it really matter what your title is within an organization? Why?

ETHICAL
MANAGEMENT
Does your job title accurately reflect your position and responsibilities within the company?

### Case 4.3

#### >> Planning a Future for Metro Mercy

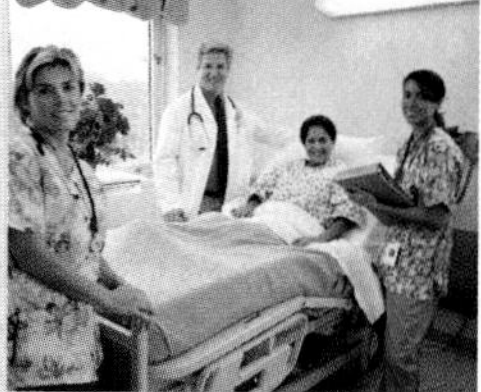

Metro Mercy Hospital (MMH) has been in a downward spiral, resulting in losses in the past few years and a tenuous cash position. Although a new management team has recently been put in place and a turnaround begun, the board of directors is unclear as to whether the hospital can and should remain independent now and in the future.

MMH is a Catholic-sponsored, freestanding, 200-bed hospital with annual operating revenues of $125 million, located in the western end of a city in a large metropolitan area. The hospital is a relatively undifferentiated, general acute care facility with the typical range of medical, surgical, obstetric and gynecologic, and pediatric services. It has a very busy emergency department and owns a network of physician practices in the area it serves; these practices provide mainly primary care services and constitute a significant portion of the primary care medical staff of the hospital.

MMH is located in a rapidly changing community. The population it has historically served, primarily second- and third-generation Italian and Polish Americans, has moved to the suburbs and/or aged. These groups have been replaced by African Americans and, more recently, Hispanics, particularly immigrants from Mexico. Although the service area population was expected to decrease from 1990 to 2000, Census Bureau data indicate that the population—especially Hispanic—actually grew. Recent estimates suggest continued slow growth and a transformation of service area demographics.

MMH faces very stiff competition due in part to the number of competitors in and around its service area and the general "overbeddedness" in the region. Its main competitors include St. Luke's Hospital, the 600-bed flagship of a very successful multihospital system, located a few miles west of MMH in an affluent suburban area; a nationally recognized teaching hospital located within five miles of MMH; a number of other tertiary teaching hospitals located in and around the downtown area of the city; and one large for-profit community hospital and two large system-affiliated community hospitals all located within three to five miles of MMH.

MMH has experienced downward trends in utilization and financial performance since 2004. In 2006, the hospital had an operating loss of $10.9 million (total loss of $10.6 million) after an operating loss of $10 million (total loss of $10.2 million) in 2005. The financial situation led to the resignation of the previous CEO and an interim management arrangement for about 12 months until a new CEO was named and who began work in early 2007. The board was also reorganized, and a new board chair and other board members with strong business skills were added in 2006–07.

The new management team's first priority was to restore the organization to financial health. By fall 2007, operating losses had been trimmed substantially to $6 million, and the organization was on target to be at break-even on a monthly basis by the end of fiscal year 2008.

As the turnaround proceeds, the new CEO and board leadership believe it is imperative that the hospital develop a new strategic plan. Although much of the financial improvement that is occurring is a result of internal operating changes and managed care contract revisions, and leadership believes that tighter operations and financial management can bring the hospital to break even, the hospital needs to make significant improvements on the market and revenue side if it is to become truly viable. Therefore, while management continues its operational changes, a strategic planning effort needs to commence to help position MMH for long-term success. A key question to be answered in the strategic planning process is whether MMH should remain freestanding, become an affiliate, or join a system.

94 • MANAGEMENT NOW

### Thinking Critically 7.1

#### >> Who Dropped the Ball?

In October 2006, Industrial Water Treatment Company (IWT) introduced Kelate, a new product that was 10 times more effective than other treatments in controlling scale buildup in boilers. The instantaneous demand for Kelate required that IWT double its number of service engineers within the following year.

The sudden expansion caused IWT to reorganize its operations. Previously, each district office was headed by a district manager who was assisted by a chief engineer and two engineering supervisors. In 2007, this structure changed. The district manager now had a chief engineer and a manager of operations. Four engineering supervisors (now designated as group leaders) were established. They we assignments through the manager of operations, while all engineering-related problem by the chief engineer. Each group leader supervised 8 to 10 field service engineers (see

Bill Marlowe, district manager for the southeast district, has just received a letter f large customer, Sel Tex, Inc. The letter revealed that when Sel Tex inspected one of its found the water treatment was not working properly. When Sel Tex officials contacte service engineer for the area, they were told he was scheduled to be working in the Jacks of the week but would get someone else down there the next day. When no one showed were naturally upset; after all, they were only requesting the engineering service they h

Bill Marlowe, upset over the growing number of customer complaints that seemed desk in recent months, called Ed Jones, chief engineer, into his office and showed hin received from Sel Tex.

**Ed:** Why are you showing me this? This is a work assignment foul-up.

**Bill:** Do you know anything about this unsatisfactory condition?

Conti

**Thinking Critically** exercises reinforce key learning outcomes with challenging management scenarios.

# Management Now

VICE PRESIDENT/EDITOR IN CHIEF **Elizabeth Haefele**
VICE PRESIDENT/DIRECTOR OF MARKETING **Alice Harra**
SPONSORING EDITOR **Barbara Owca**
DIRECTOR OF DEVELOPMENT **Sarah Wood**
DEVELOPMENTAL EDITOR **Danielle McCumber**
EXECUTIVE MARKETING MANAGER **Keari Green**
LEAD DIGITAL PRODUCT MANAGER **Damian Moshak**
DIGITAL DEVELOPMENT EDITOR **Kevin White**
DIRECTOR, EDITING /DESIGN /PRODUCTION **Jess Ann Kosic**
PROJECT MANAGER **Jean R. Starr**
BUYER **Kara Kudronowicz**
SENIOR DESIGNER **Anna Kinigakis**
LEAD PHOTO RESEARCH COORDINATOR **Keri Johnson**
PHOTO RESEARCHER **Agate ProBooks**
MEDIA PROJECT MANAGER **Cathy L. Tepper**
OUTSIDE DEVELOPMENT HOUSE **Agate ProBooks**
COVER DESIGN **Alexa R. Viscius**
INTERIOR DESIGN **Kay Lieberherr**
TYPEFACE **11/13 Minion Pro**
COMPOSITOR **Agate ProBooks**
PRINTER **Quad/Graphics-Dubuque**
CREDITS **The credits section for this book begins on page 363 and is considered an extension of the copyright page.**

**Management Now**
Published by McGraw-Hill, a business unit of The McGraw-Hill Companies, Inc., 1221 Avenue of the Americas, New York, NY, 10020. 

This book is printed on acid-free paper.

1 2 3 4 5 6 7 8 9 0 QDB/QDB 1 0 9 8 7 6 5 4 3 2 1

ISBN 978-0-07-337729-2
MHID 0-07-337729-5

**Library of Congress Cataloging in Publication Data**

Library of Congress Control Number: 2010939985



www.mhhe.com

To Princess Megan

# ABOUT THE AUTHOR

**Dr. Andrew W. Ghillyer** is the Vice President of Academic Affairs for Argosy University in Tampa, Florida. His operational management experience spans over 25 years across a wide range of industries, including Chief Operating Officer (COO) of a civil engineering software company and Director of International Business Relations for a global training organization. Dr. Ghillyer also served on the Board of Examiners for the Malcolm Baldrige National Quality Award for the 2007 award year. He received his doctorate in Management Studies from the University of Surrey in the United Kingdom. His first McGraw-Hill textbook, *Business Ethics: A Real World Approach*, was published in January 2007.

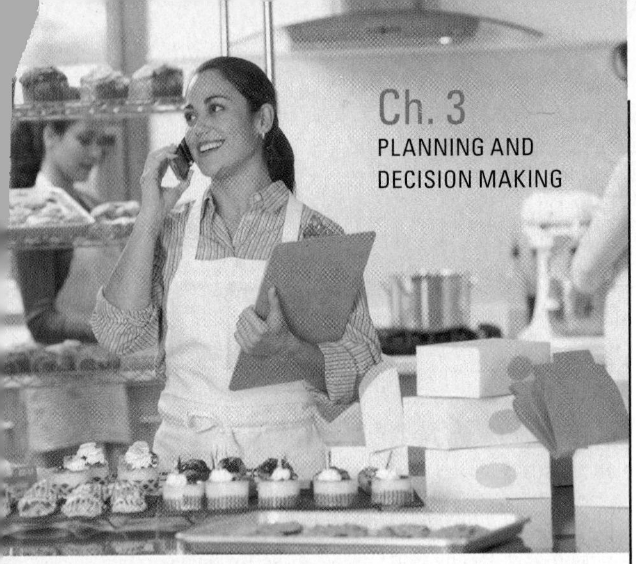

Ch. 3
PLANNING AND DECISION MAKING

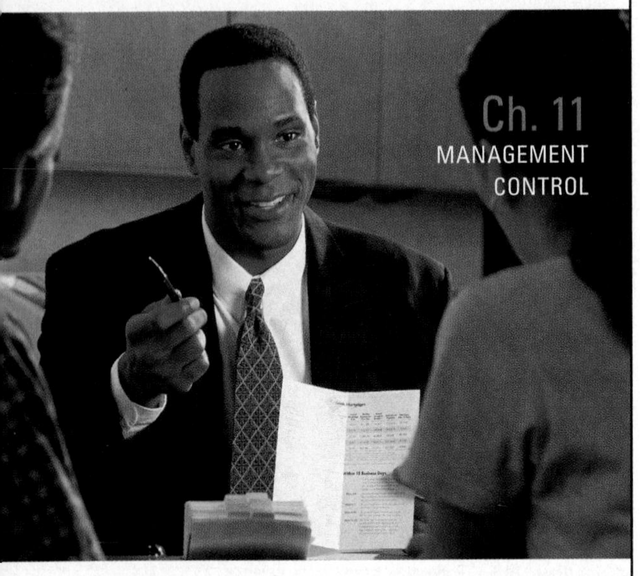

Ch. 11
MANAGEMENT CONTROL

Ch. 5
GLOBAL MANAGEMENT

Ch. 14
MANAGEMENT IN THE 21ST CENTURY

>

# ManagementNow

## BRIEF TABLE OF CONTENTS



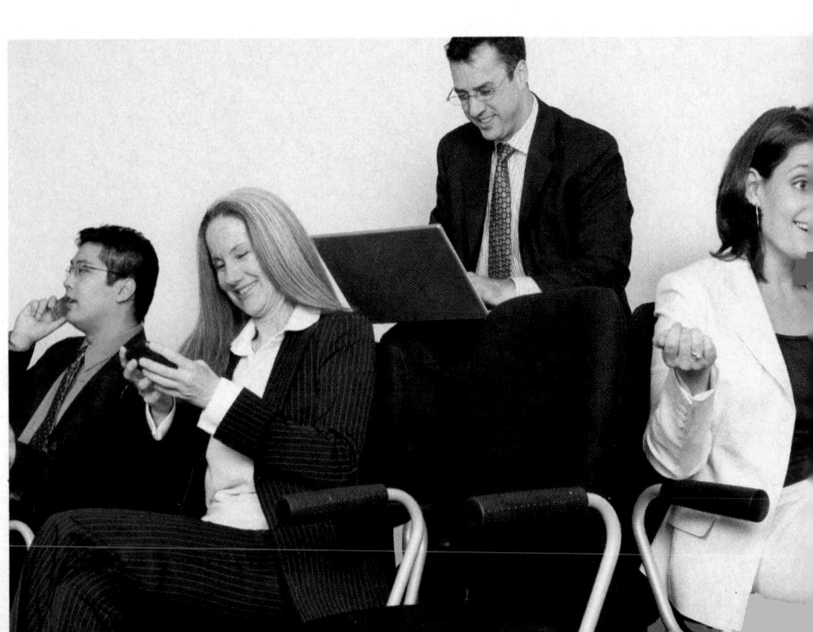

Table of Contents



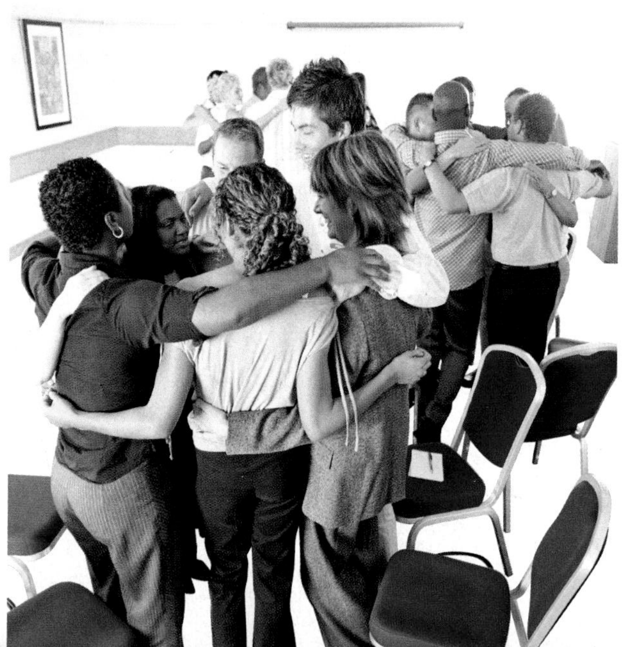

## 3 > Planning and Decision Making 48

## 4 > Strategic Management 72

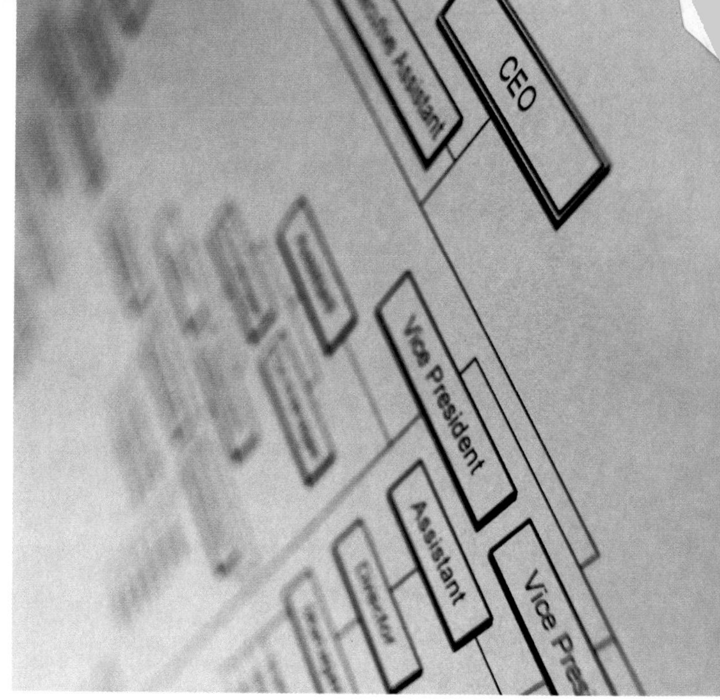
CEO
Vice President
Assistant
Vice Pres

SEARS

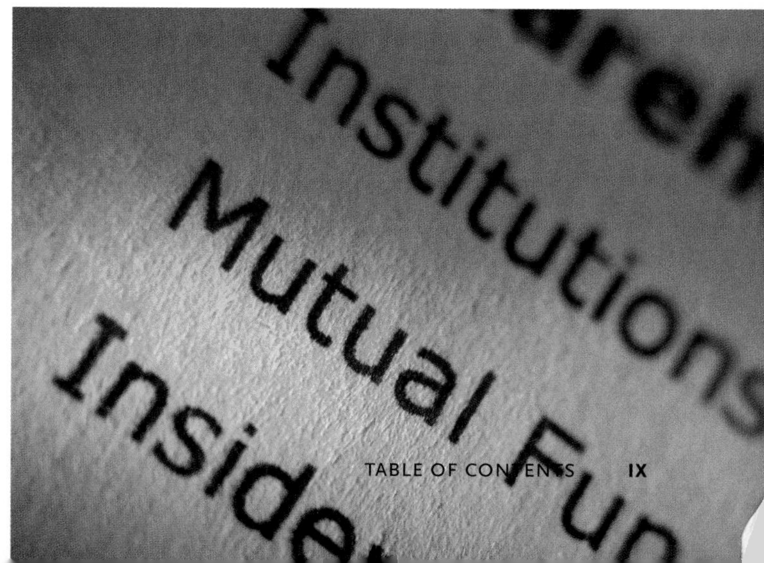
Institutions
Mutual

C

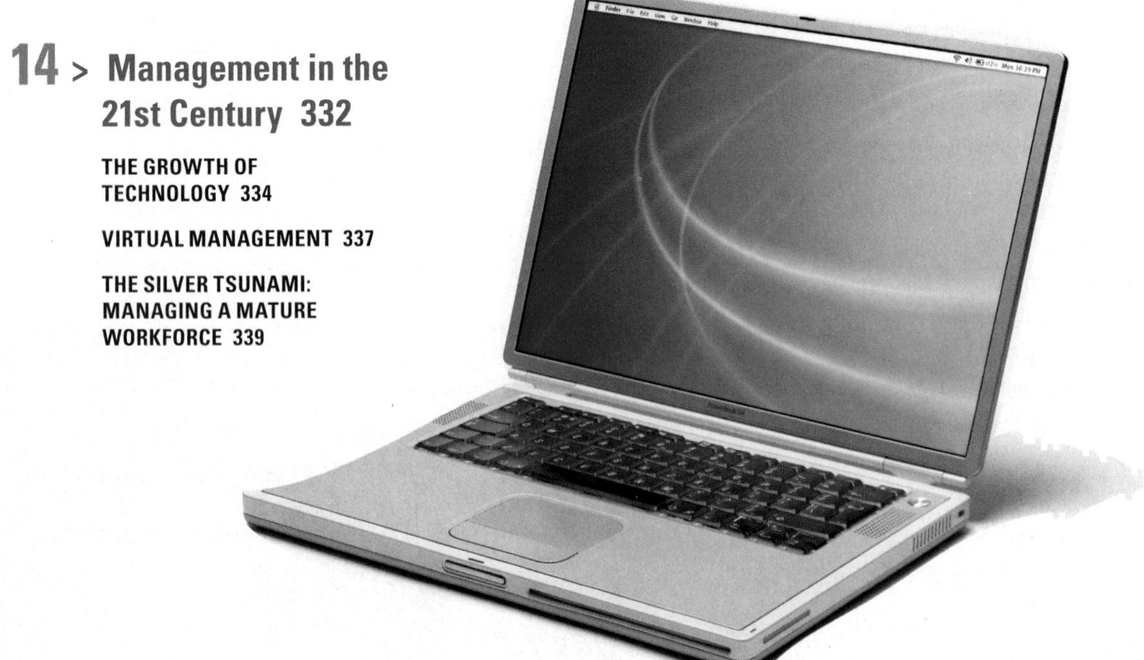

# What's New

## Chapter 1: What is Management
- New 'For Review' section to summarize Learning Outcomes.
- New "Thinking Critically" chapter component
- Updated case studies
- New ethical dilemmas

## Chapter 2: Communication
- New 'For Review' section to summarize Learning Outcomes.
- Updated "Thinking Critically" chapter component
- New ethical dilemmas
- Updated case studies

## Chapter 3: Planning & Decision Making
- New 'For Review' section to summarize Learning Outcomes.
- Updated "Thinking Critically" chapter component
- New ethical dilemmas
- Updated case studies

## Chapter 4: Strategic Management
- Updated "Thinking Critically" chapter component
- New ethical dilemmas
- New 'For Review' section to summarize Learning Outcomes.
- Updated case studies
- Reduced length

## Chapter 5: Global Management
- New 'For Review' section to summarize Learning Outcomes.
- Updated "Thinking Critically" chapter component
- New ethical dilemmas
- Updated case studies

## Chapter 6: Organizing Work
- New 'For Review' section to summarize Learning Outcomes.
- Updated "Thinking Critically" chapter component
- New ethical dilemmas
- Updated case studies

## Chapter 7: Organizing Structure
- New 'For Review' section to summarize Learning Outcomes.
- Updated "Thinking Critically" chapter component
- New ethical dilemmas
- Updated case studies

## Chapter 8: Organizing People
- New 'For Review' section to summarize Learning Outcomes.
- Updated "Thinking Critically" chapter component
- New ethical dilemmas
- Modified Internet Exercises
- Updated case studies

## Chapter 9: Leadership & Culture
- New 'For Review' section to summarize Learning Outcomes.
- Updated "Thinking Critically" chapter component
- New ethical dilemmas
- Updated case studies
- Modified Internet Exercises

## Chapter 10: Motivation
- New 'For Review' section to summarize Learning Outcomes.
- Updated "Thinking Critically" chapter component
- New ethical dilemmas
- Updated discussion of Frederick Herzberg's 'Motivation-Maintenance' theory

## Chapter 11: Management Control
- New 'For Review' section to summarize Learning Outcomes.
- Updated "Thinking Critically" chapter component
- New ethical dilemmas
- Updated case studies

## Chapter 12: Operations Control
- New 'For Review' section to summarize Learning Outcomes.
- Updated "Thinking Critically" chapter component
- New ethical dilemmas
- Updated case studies

## Chapter 13: Legal & Ethical
- New 'For Review' section to summarize Learning Outcomes.
- Updated "Thinking Critically" chapter component
- New ethical dilemmas
- Expanded coverage of Foreign Corrupt Practices Act

## Chapter 14: 21st Century
- New 'For Review' section to summarize Learning Outcomes.
- Updated "Thinking Critically" chapter component
- New ethical dilemmas

CHAPTER 1

"Good management is the art of making problems so interesting and their solutions so constructive that everyone wants to get to work and deal with them."

**Paul Hawken,** ***Growing a Business***

# WHAT IS MANAGEMENT?

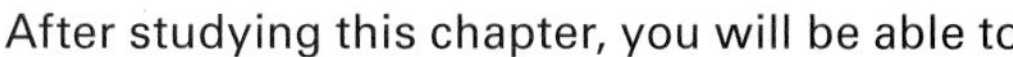

LEARNING OUTCOMES

After studying this chapter, you will be able to:

1 Define *management.*

2 Identify and explain the levels of management.

3 Explain the management process.

4 Understand the different perspectives of scientific management and the human relations movement.

## THE WORLD OF WORK **Tony gets a promotion**

Tony Davis had been an employee of Taco Barn, Inc., for four years, and today he had a feeling that his 11 o'clock appointment with Dawn Williams, the regional manager for the area, would be his reward for his years of dedication and hard work.

Tony had started working in his local Taco Barn after school and decided to stay on after he graduated high school. Over the four years he had been trained in every area in the restaurant, from the correct use of cleaning supplies to food preparation and service, to working the cash register and taking the cash receipts to the bank at the end of the day. They had a good crew at this Taco Barn location—one of the best in the region, Tony thought. Their manager, Jerry Smith, "ran a tight ship," as he liked to say, but he treated his people well and was willing to work with them on their schedule if they had any special requests for things like evening classes or sports practice or family commitments.

Since Taco Barn preferred to employ young people on a part-time basis, the rest of the crew added up to 18 people working a variety of hours and shifts. For the most part, everybody got on okay—no big fights or dramas—and everybody could be counted on to show up for his or her shift on time and ready to work. From what Jerry had told them about other locations in the Taco Barn chain, such productivity and reliability were rare.

At 11:05 the receptionist told Tony that Ms. Williams was ready for him and that he should go into her office. Meeting him at the door, Dawn shook his hand and asked him to take a seat.

"Tony, we've had our eye on you for a while now. Jerry tells me that you've become his right-hand man at the restaurant, and he sees a great future for you with Taco Barn."

Tony mumbled, "Thank you," and tried not to blush in response to the glowing praise.

"As you know," Dawn continued, "Taco Barn is a growing company, and we are always looking for locations to build new units. We built over 100 new units last year alone, and there are plans for us to start opening international units in the next few years. It's an exciting time to be with the organization, Tony."

"As we continue to grow," continued Dawn, "we need more regional managers to oversee new groups of restaurants, and new managers for both the new restaurants and the existing restaurants where managers have been promoted—and that, Tony, is where you come into the picture. Your team knows what a great job Jerry has done in building up that unit, and Taco Barn is finally recognizing that by giving him a regional management position across the other side of the state. He and his wife will be moving to the same city as their daughter and grandkids, so it's working out well for everybody."

"Of course," Dawn continued with a broad grin on her face, "that leaves an opening for a unit manager, and both Jerry and I think you're ready for the job—what do you think?"

### QUESTIONS

1. Do you think Tony is ready for this promotion? Why or why not?
2. The team at Tony's location is performing well. Is there anything that he needs to change?
3. What skills do you think Tony will need to succeed in his new role? Refer to the section "Management Roles" on page 6 for guidance.
4. What should Tony do in his first week as manager?

# >> What is Management?

Organizations today operate in a world of constant change. Technology and society are changing more rapidly than ever before. Concern for the environment has forced companies to think about how their actions affect the quality of the air, land, and water. Competition is fiercer than ever, because organizations from all over the world must now try to sell their products and services to the same customers in order to meet the aggressive growth expectations of the investors that purchase their shares. Workplaces have become increasingly diverse, with an ever more litigious environment for those organizations that fail to acknowledge the diverse needs of their employees and their customers. Business is now conducted on a global stage, and with that global emphasis comes a mix of challenges that traditional managers who have "worked their way up the ranks of the organization" find themselves woefully unprepared to handle.

To help managers prepare for this harsh new world, we must begin at the beginning with a clear understanding of what management is.

## DEFINING MANAGEMENT

**Management** is the process of deciding the best way to use an organization's resources to produce goods or provide services. An organization's resources include its employees, equipment, and money. Although the definition is simple, the job of management is quite complex. Management must make good decisions, communicate well with people, make work assignments, delegate, plan, train people, motivate people, and appraise employees' job performance. The varied work of management is extremely difficult to master. Yet mastery of management is vital to organizational success.

**Figure 1.1 • The Management Pyramid**

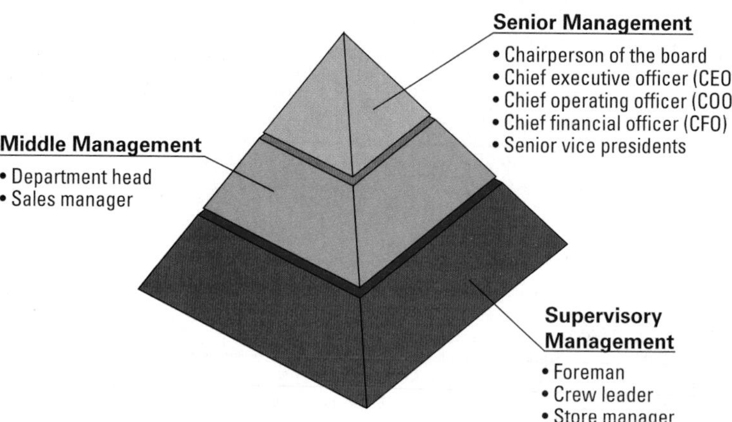


## LEVELS OF MANAGEMENT

All organizations, from one-person businesses to giant corporations, need managers. Small businesses may be managed by one or just a few managers. Large and medium-size companies may have many levels of management.

**Senior Management** The highest level of an organization is known as **senior management**. Senior management has several important functions. First, it establishes the goals, or objectives, of the organization.* Second, it decides which actions are necessary to meet those goals. Finally, it decides how to use the organization's resources. This level of management usually includes the chairperson of the company's board of directors, the chief executive officer (CEO), the chief operating officer (COO), the chief financial officer (CFO), and the company's senior vice presidents. Senior managers are not involved in the company's day-to-day problems. Instead, they concentrate on setting the direction the company will follow.

**Middle Management** **Middle management** is responsible for meeting the goals that senior management sets. Middle managers can include department heads and district sales managers. This level of management sets goals for specific areas of the organization and decides what the employees in each area must do to meet those goals. For example, senior management might set a goal of increasing company sales by 15 percent in the next year. To meet that objective, middle management might develop a new

*Throughout this book, the terms *objectives* and *goals* will be used interchangeably.

advertising campaign for one of the organization's products or services.

**Supervisory Management** The front-line level of management is **supervisory management**. Supervisory managers make sure that the day-to-day operations of the organization run smoothly. They are in charge of the people who physically produce the organization's goods or provide its services. Forepersons, crew leaders, and store managers are all examples of supervisory managers.

Large companies usually have all three kinds of management. At Walmart, for example, supervisory or general managers run stores and departments within stores. These managers are responsible for making sure that the daily operations of the store run well. Middle or area managers oversee districts. These managers are responsible for making sure that all store managers within their district are performing well. Middle managers also may suggest ideas for increasing sales, improving service, or reducing costs within their districts. Senior managers include Walmart's CEO and senior vice presidents. These managers make decisions about the company's policies, products, and organizational strategy. A decision to increase salaries throughout the company or modify the employee benefit plan would be made by senior management, for example.

The three levels of management form a *hierarchy*, or a group ranked in order of importance. As can be seen in Figure 1.1, the management hierarchy is shaped like a pyramid, with very few senior managers at the top and many supervisory managers at the bottom.

## >> The Management Process

There are several ways to examine how management works. One way is to divide the *tasks* that managers perform into categories. A second way is to look at the *roles* that different types of managers play in a company. A **role** is a set of behaviors associated with a particular job. A third way is to look at the *skills* that managers need to do their jobs. Each way of thinking about management will help you understand the management process.

### MANAGEMENT TASKS

Managers in all organizations—from small businesses to large companies—engage in basic activities. These activities can be divided into five categories:

1. *Planning.* A manager decides on goals and the actions the organization must take to meet them. A CEO who sets a goal of increasing sales by 10 percent in the next year by developing a new software program is engaged in planning.
2. *Organizing.* A manager groups related activities together and assigns employees to perform them. A manager who sets up a team of employees to restock an aisle in a supermarket is organizing.
3. *Staffing.* A manager decides how many and what kind of people an organization needs to meet its goals and then recruits, selects, and trains the right people. A restaurant manager's staffing duties include interviewing and training waiters.
4. *Leading.* A manager provides the guidance employees need to perform their tasks. This helps ensure that organizational goals are met. A manager leads by keeping the lines of communication open. Holding regular staff meetings where employees can ask questions about their projects and responsibilities is a good example of leading.

**Management** The process of deciding the best way to use an organization's resources to produce goods or provide services.

**Senior Management** The highest level of management; establishes the goals, or objectives, of the organization, decides which actions are necessary to meet those goals, and decides how to use the organization's resources.

**Middle Management** Managers responsible for implementing and achieving organizational objectives and for developing departmental objectives and actions.

**Supervisory Management** Managers responsible for the day-to-day operations of an organization and who supervise operative employees; considered the first level of management.

**Role** Set of behaviors associated with a particular job.

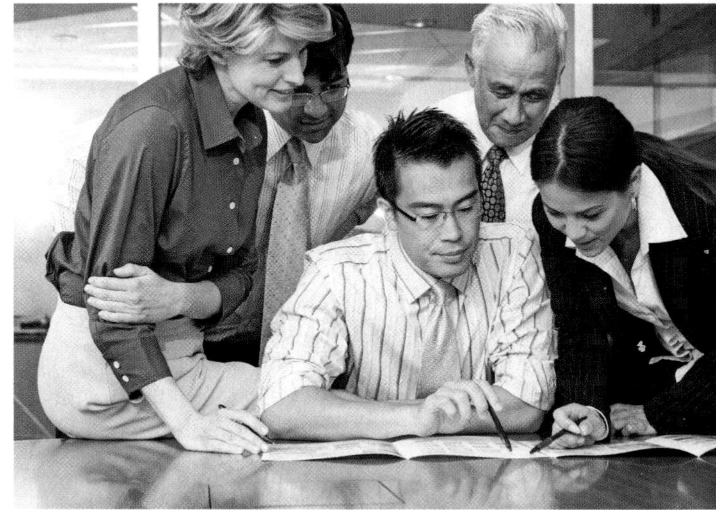

5. *Controlling.* A manager measures how the organization performs to ensure that financial goals are being met. Controlling requires a manager to analyze accounting records and to make changes if financial standards are not being met.

### Figure 1.2 • Relative Amount of Emphasis Placed on Each Function of Management

1. **Senior Management**

   Senior management is responsible for setting objectives for the organization, deciding what actions are necessary to meet them, and determining how best to use resources. This level of management usually includes the chairperson of the board of directors, the CEO, the COO, the CFO, and the organization's senior vice presidents.

2. **Middle Management**

   Middle management is responsible for achieving the goals set by senior management. Middle management includes department heads and district sales managers.

3. **Supervisory Management**

   Supervisory management is responsible for the people who physically produce the organization's products or provide its services. Crew leaders and store managers are all examples of supervisors.

Many management activities overlap. Organizing, for example, is difficult without a plan. Keeping good employees on the job is difficult if a workplace is poorly organized and lacks leadership.

**Conceptual Skills** Skills that help managers understand how different parts of a company relate to one another and to the company as a whole.

**Human Relations Skills** Skills that managers need to understand and work well with people.

**Technical Skills** Specific abilities that people use to perform their jobs.

Figure 1.2 shows how different levels of management focus on different activities. Senior managers divide their time about equally among the five activities. Middle managers spend most of their time leading and controlling. Supervisory managers spend little time planning and a lot of time controlling.

## MANAGEMENT ROLES

Managers have authority, or power, within organizations and use it in many ways. To best use their authority, managers take on different roles. In the early 1970s Henry Mintzberg delivered a series of research reports that were based on the question, "How can management be improved and the skills of managers appropriately developed, without first understanding how managers spend their time?"

Mintzberg's research led him to identify ten key managerial roles split into three categories.[1] Figure 1.3 provides a summary of Mintzberg's ten roles and examples of how managers can perform those roles.

By spending time with five organizations and analyzing how their chief executives spent their time, Mintzberg identified one of the biggest challenges of managerial research.[2] His observations revealed that managers were more often called upon to be "in the moment" rather than focused on farsighted strategic plans. He found that their work often placed them as hostages to constant interruptions, jumping from subject to subject and problem to problem, rarely being allowed to give their undivided and uninterrupted attention to anything for any length of time.

## MANAGEMENT SKILLS

A third way of looking at the management process is by examining the kinds of skills required to perform a particular job.[3] Three types of skills have been identified.

1. **Conceptual skills** are those that help managers understand how different parts of a company relate to one another and to the company as a whole. Decision making, planning, and organizing are managerial activities that require conceptual skills.
2. **Human relations skills** are those that managers need to understand and work well with people. Interviewing job applicants, forming partnerships with other companies, and resolving conflicts all require good human relations skills.
3. **Technical skills** are the specific abilities that people use to perform their jobs. Operating a word processing or financial spreadsheet program, designing a brochure, and training people to use a

### [PROGRESS] ✓questions

1. What is management?
2. Describe the three levels of management.
3. Describe the five categories of management tasks.
4. Which of the management tasks is most important for a first-line manager? Why?

## Figure 1.3 • Management Roles

| Category | Role | Definition | Example of manager performing the role |
|---|---|---|---|
| Interpersonal | **Figurehead** | Performs symbolic duties as head of the organization | Greeting visitors or introducing keynote speakers |
| | **Leader** | Establishes the work atmosphere and motivates subordinates to act | Directing, counseling, and motivating subordinates; authorizing training if needed |
| | **Liaison** | Develops and maintains webs of contacts outside the organization | Attending chamber of commerce or Rotary groups |
| Informational | **Monitor** | Collects all types of information relevant and useful to the organization | Reading industry journals and attending conferences where needed |
| | **Disseminator** | Gives other people the information they need to make decisions | Summarizing data in reports; giving presentations to superiors and/or subordinates |
| | **Spokesperson** | Transmits information to the outside world | Giving keynote speeches at conferences and media interviews |
| Decisional | **Entrepreneur** | Initiates controlled change in the organization to adapt to the changing environment | Identifying new ideas with potential and delegating implementation; initiating improvement projects |
| | **Disturbance handler** | Deals with the unexpected changes | Resolving disputes; initiating crisis management plans |
| | **Resource allocator** | Makes decisions on the use of organizational resources | Setting and scheduling priorities; controlling resources via the budgeting process |
| | **Negotiator** | Deals with other organizations and individuals | Representing departmental interests in negotiations with unions, vendors, and customers |

Based on H. Mintzberg, *The Nature of Managerial Work* (New York: Harper & Row, 1973).

new budgeting system are all examples of technical skills that a manager would need to possess or train others to possess in order for the department to function effectively.

Not all management skills are easy to place in a single category. Most fall into more than one. In order to develop a company advertisement, for example, a manager must have conceptual, human relations, and technical skills. Managers would need conceptual skills to develop the advertisement's message. They would need human relations skills to assemble and motivate the team of people who would create the advertisement. Training the team by teaching them a computer graphics program would require technical skills.

All levels of management require a combination of these skills. Different skills are more important at different levels of management, as Figure 1.4 shows. Conceptual skills are most important at the senior management level. Technical skills are most important at supervisory levels of management. Human relations skills are important at all levels of management.

## >> The History of Management

Knowledge of the history of any subject is necessary to understanding where the subject came from, where it is now, and where it is going. Management is no exception. The development of management as we know it is a relatively modern concept. The age of industrialization in the nineteenth century and the subsequent emergence of large corporate organizations called for new approaches to management. Appendix A on page 350 shows a brief history of management thought that has brought us to our current management philosophies, and we will examine some of the key concepts in greater detail.

**Study Alert!**

Document your activities for one full workday in as much detail as possible. How many of Mintzberg's ten roles did you fulfill in that one day? How many times did you fulfill a role more than once? Is management "in the moment" more productive or just a necessary evil?

## SCIENTIFIC MANAGEMENT

**Scientific Management** Philosophy of Frederick W. Taylor that sought to increase productivity and make the work easier by scientifically studying work methods and establishing standards.

**Study Alert!** Understanding the difference between tasks, roles, and skills will help you better prepare for success in your management career. Don't just think of your responsibilities in terms of the job description that the human resource (HR) department uses to hire for the position.

In the late 1880s, a young mechanical engineer named Frederick Winslow Taylor noticed that workers in the rapidly expanding factories of the new Industrial Revolution had little or no reason to increase productivity; most wage systems of that time were based on attendance and position. Piece-rate systems had been tried before but generally failed because of poor use and weak standards. Taylor believed a piece-rate system would work if the workers believed the standard had been fairly set and management would stick to that standard. Taylor wanted to use scientific and empirical methods rather than tradition and custom for setting work standards. Taylor's efforts became the true beginning of what would become known as **scientific management**.

### Figure 1.4 • Mix of Skills Used at Different Levels of Management

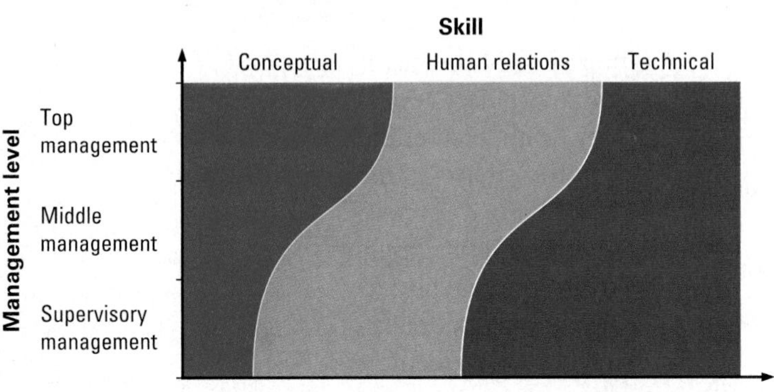


**From the PERSPECTIVE OF...**

**A Call Center Manager** When you are managing customer service reps (CSRs) who are on the phone all day helping customers (and often dealing with very upset customers), are you using your conceptual skills, your human relations skills, or your technical skills?

**PROGRESS ✓questions**

5. Describe and provide an example of each of the three categories of managerial roles.
6. Describe and provide an example of each of the three managerial skills.
7. Think of a manager you work for currently (or have worked for in the past). How would you describe his or her combination of managerial skills?
8. If you were interviewing for a management role, how would you describe your managerial skills?

Scientific management, as developed by Taylor, was based on four main principles:

1. *The development of a scientific method of designing jobs to replace the old rule-of-thumb methods.* This involved gathering, classifying, and tabulating data to arrive at the "one best way" to perform a task or a series of tasks.
2. *The scientific selection and progressive teaching and development of employees.* Taylor saw the value of matching the job to the worker. He also emphasized the need to study worker strengths and weaknesses and to provide training to improve employee performance.
3. *The bringing together of scientifically selected employees and scientifically developed methods for designing jobs.* Taylor believed that new and scientific methods of job design should not merely be put before an employee; they should also be fully explained by management. He believed employees would show little resistance to changes in methods if they understood the reasons for the changes and saw a chance for greater earnings for themselves.
4. *A division of work resulting in interdependence between management and workers.* Taylor believed if they were truly dependent on each other, cooperation would naturally follow.[4]

For both management and employees, scientific management brought a new attitude toward their respective duties and toward each other.[5] It was a new philosophy about the use of human effort. It emphasized maximum

# Thinking Critically 1.1

## >> A Typical Morning

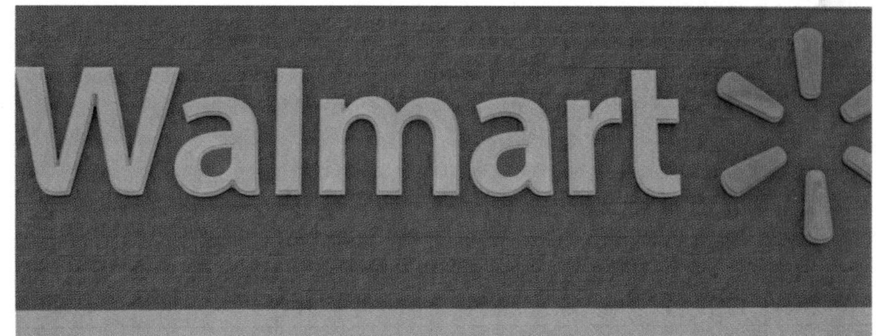


Mike King manages a Walmart Supercenter in southern Indiana. His store covers more than 150,000 square feet and employs over 500 people. His morning routine begins at 7 A.M., as he walks through the store with his third-shift managers. The walk-through allows him to see the entire store and identify areas that may need attention during the coming workday.

After scanning the summary reports from the previous day, he meets briefly with his morning shift at exactly 8 A.M. The morning meeting lasts less than 15 minutes and is broken into two parts. The first part of the meeting is an update on current promotional activities in the store. This update will help the crew quickly answer customer questions. In the second half of the meeting, Mike recognizes departments that exceeded sales goals in the previous day.

Because the store is so large, it is impossible to succeed without a dedicated team. Mike believes in the importance of delegating tasks to his team members, right down to assigning responsibility for cleaning the tops of the soda machines.

Delegating tasks gives Mike time to return to his office to look through the summary reports in more detail. These reports list sales data for all departments, as well as the number of payroll hours used in each department. By reading the sales data, Mike can begin to identify trends in his store. The summary report includes other information that is not related to sales. The first list shows employees who have a birthday during the workweek, and the second lists associates who are celebrating an anniversary as a Walmart employee. He often uses this information as an icebreaker when interacting with his associates during the workweek.

Mike recognizes the importance of the three major skill areas: conceptual, human relations, and technical. His efforts in all three categories have allowed his store to thrive.

### QUESTIONS

1. List the tasks that Mike completes in a typical morning, and identify them as conceptual tasks, human relations tasks, and technical tasks. In which category do you think Mike devotes the most time?
2. What information could a manager gather in a store walk-through?
3. What reasons would Mike have to serve doughnuts and fresh fruit at the shift meeting?
4. Why would Mike choose to delegate simple tasks, such as cleaning the top of a soda machine?

output with minimum effort through the elimination of waste and inefficiency at the operational level of the organization.[6] A methodological approach was used to study job tasks. This approach included research and experimentation (i.e., scientific methods). Standards were set in the areas of personnel, working conditions, equipment, output, and procedures. The managers planned the work; the employees performed it. The result was closer cooperation between managers and employees.

The scientific study of work also emphasized specialization and division of labor. Thus, the need for an organizational framework became more and more apparent. The concepts of line and staff emerged. In an effort to motivate employees, wage incentives were developed in most scientific management programs. Once standards were set, managers began to monitor actual performance and compare it with the standards. Thus began the managerial function of control.

Scientific management is a philosophy about the relationship between people and work, not a technique or an efficiency device. Taylor's ideas and scientific management were based on a concern not only for the proper design of the job but also for the worker. This aspect has often been misunderstood. Taylor and scientific management were (and still are) attacked as being inhumane and aimed only at increasing output. In this regard, scientific management and Taylor were the targets of a congressional investigation in 1912.[7] The key to Taylor's thinking was that he saw scientific management as benefiting management and employees equally: Management could achieve more work in a given amount of time; the employee could produce more—and hence earn more—with little or no additional effort.

**Fordism** An economic model that features mass production, low prices, above-average wages, and workers becoming customers; named after Henry Ford.

## Taylor's Most Famous Disciple—Henry Ford

Henry Ford, the founder of the Ford Motor Company, is attributed with realizing the full economic potential of Taylor's work on labor and task specialization in the creation of assembly lines to manufacture the Model-T automobile. Mass production at the new Highland Park, Michigan plant allowed Ford to achieve much lower production costs, which, in turn,

**Study Alert!**

Examine the basic premise of Henry Ford's Fordism model. Do you think the reason he paid such a high salary ($5 a day at the time) was because he wanted more customers or because stories of numerous injuries on the assembly line made it hard to find people to work there?

*Timekeeping was fundamental to Frederick Winslow Taylor's theories on management.*

allowed him to price the car at a low enough level to attract a broader segment of consumers. Every part was counted and every task measured and timed in the production of the "Tin Lizzies." This practice, combined with the payment of above-average wages to his workers, allowed his workers to become customers—an economic model that became known as **Fordism**.[8]

However, the success of the Model-T came with a price. Constant experimentation with the speed of the assembly line, combined with boring and repetitive work for nine-hour shifts, produced low morale and a large number of injuries. In 1916, the Highland Park plant documented almost 200 severed fingers and over 75,000 cuts, burns, and puncture wounds from a workforce of only 14,000. Stories of dangerous working conditions and employee burnout contributed to high levels of turnover. In 1913 the plant hired 53,000 workers to keep a staffing level of 14,000.[9]

To combat low morale and high turnover, Ford announced a daily wage of $5, at a time when the average wage for a nine-hour shift was only $2.25. The wage was actually half-wage and half-performance bonus (including specific requirements of employee "character," such as no drinking or gambling and learning English for immigrant workers), but it was arguably a stroke of genius in creating a new

THE WHOLE TRUTH

The XYZ Corporation has been growing rapidly over the past three years. To help manage this growth, the CEO decides to create a new director level position. The position requires extensive business expertise, an understanding of the XYZ Corporation's industry, and exemplary people skills.

Two candidates remain after the final interviews: Lara Kempton, an external candidate with a strong business background, and Michelle Lopane, a candidate from within the company, who also has the required skills. After two rounds of interviews, the vice president for human resources decides to offer the position to Lara. Lara considers the offer for several days but decides to turn it down.

The vice president then meets with Michelle and offers her the position. On hearing the offer, Michelle pauses. She looks the VP straight in the eye and asks, "Was the job offered to Lara first?"

How should the vice president respond?

ETHICAL
MANAGEMENT
If a job candidate asks you a question you don't want to answer, what do you do?


*Source:* Adapted from "The Second Choice Asks a Hard Question," Institute for Global Ethics, **www.globalethics.org**.

population of customers for his Model-T and, at the same time, placing pressure on competing automobile manufacturers to match the pay scale.[10]

**Fayol's Theory of Management** Henri Fayol, a Frenchman, was the first to issue a complete statement on a theory of general management. Though popular in Europe in the early 1900s, the theory did not really gain acceptance in America until the late 1940s. Today, Fayol's greatest contribution is considered to be his theory of management principles and elements. Fayol identified the following fourteen principles of management:

*Division of work:* Concept of specialization of work.

*Authority:* Formal (positional) authority versus personal authority.

*Discipline:* Based on obedience and respect.

*Unity of command:* Each employee should receive orders from only one superior.

*Unity of direction:* One boss and one plan for a group of activities having the same objective.

*Subordination of individual interests to the general interest:* A plea to abolish the tendency to place individual interest ahead of the group interest.

*Remuneration:* The mode of payment of wages was dependent on many factors.

*Centralization:* The degree of centralization desired depended on the situation and the formal communication channels.

*Scalar chain* (line of authority): Shows the routing of the line of authority and formal communication channels.

*Order:* Ensured a place for everything.

*Equity:* Resulted from kindness and justice.

*Stability of tenured personnel:* Called for orderly personnel planning.

*Initiative:* Called for individual zeal and energy in all efforts.

*Esprit de corps:* Stressed the building of harmony and unity within the organization.

Fayol developed his list of principles from the practices he had used most often in his own work. He used them as general guidelines for effective management but stressed flexibility in their application to allow for different and changing circumstances.

Fayol's real contribution, however, was not the fourteen principles themselves but his formal recognition and combination of these principles. In presenting his principles of management, Fayol was probably the first to outline what today are called the **functions of management**. In essence, he identified planning, organizing, commanding, coordinating, and controlling as elements of management. He most heavily emphasized planning and organizing because he viewed these elements as essential to the other functions. Recent translations and interpretations of some of Fayol's very early papers have further reinforced the fact that Fayol was ahead of his time in recognizing the role of administration (management) in determining the success of an organization.[11]

The works of Taylor and Fayol are essentially complementary. Both believed proper management of personnel and other resources is the key to organizational success. Both used a scientific approach to management. The major difference is in their orientation. Taylor stressed the management of work, whereas Fayol emphasized the management of organization.

**Figure 1.5 • Significant Pro-Union Legislation During the 1920s and 1930s**

| | |
|---|---|
| Railway Labor Act of 1926 | Gave railway workers the right to form unions and engage in collective bargaining; established a corresponding obligation for employers to recognize and collectively bargain with the union. |
| Norris–La Guardia Act of 1932 | Severely restricted the use of injunctions to limit union activity. |
| National Labor Relations Act of 1935 (Wagner Act) | Resulted in full, enforceable rights of employees to join unions and to engage in collective bargaining with their employer, which was legally obligated to do so. |
| Fair Labor Standards Act of 1938 | Established minimum wages and required that time and a half be paid for hours worked over 40 in one week. |

## THE HUMAN RELATIONS MOVEMENT

The Great Depression of 1929–32 saw unemployment in excess of 25 percent. Afterward, unions sought and gained major advantages for the working class. In this period, known as the Golden Age of Unionism, legislatures and courts actively supported organized labor and the worker. The general climate tended to emphasize understanding employees and their needs (as opposed to focusing on the methods used to conduct work). Figure 1.5 summarizes several of the most important pro-union laws passed during the 1920s and 1930s. A major research project, known as the Hawthorne studies, is generally recognized as igniting the interest of business in the human element of the workplace.[12]

**The Hawthorne Studies** The Hawthorne studies began in 1924 when the National Research Council of the National Academy of Sciences began a project to define the relationship between physical working conditions and worker productivity. The Hawthorne plant of Western Electric in Cicero, Illinois, was the study site. First, the researchers lowered the level of lighting, expecting productivity to decrease. To their astonishment, productivity increased. Over the next several months, the researchers repeated the experiment by testing many different levels of lighting and other variables. Regardless of the variables, output was found to increase.

Baffled by the results, in early 1927 the researchers called in a team of psychologists from Harvard University led by Elton Mayo. Over the next five years, hundreds of experiments were run involving thousands of employees. In these experiments, the researchers altered such variable elements as wage

### [PROGRESS] ✓questions

9. Explain the four main principles of Taylor's scientific management.
10. Why did the application of Taylor's principles lead to a congressional investigation?
11. Explain the business model developed by Henry Ford that later became known as Fordism.
12. Why do Fayol's five functions of management still apply today?

*Cicero, Illinois, home of the Hawthorne Plant of Western Electric, was the backdrop for studies that would revolutionize the interaction between management and employees.*

**Functions of Management** Elements of management that include planning, organizing, commanding, coordinating, and controlling.

**Hawthorne Effect** Phenomenon that employees respond positively to the attention paid to them by the researchers.

The researchers also discovered that the employees responded positively to the attention paid to them by the researchers. This phenomenon has since become known as the **Hawthorne effect**. Yet another finding was the significance of effective supervision to both productivity and employee morale. While the methods used and the conclusions reached by the Hawthorne researchers have been questioned, they did generate great interest in the human problems in the workplace and focused attention on the human factor.[13]

payments, rest periods, and length of workday. The results were similar to those obtained in the lighting experiments: Production increased, but with no obvious relationship to the environment. After much analysis, the researchers concluded that other factors besides the physical environment affected worker productivity. They found that employees reacted to the psychological and social conditions at work, such as informal group pressures, individual recognition, and participation in decision making.

Researchers repeated the experiment by testing many variables. Regardless of the variables, output was found to increase.

**The Professional Manager** The career manager, or professional manager, did not exist until the 1930s. Until this time, managers were placed into one of three categories: owner-managers, captains of industry, or financial managers. The owner-managers dominated until after the Civil War. The captains of industry controlled organizations from the 1880s through the turn of the century. The financial managers operated in much the same ways the captains of industry did, except that they often did not own the enterprises they controlled and operated. The financial managers dominated from around 1905 until the early 1930s,

**Professional Manager** Career person who does not necessarily have a controlling interest in the enterprise for which he or she works.

**Open System** An organization that interacts with its external environment.

**Closed System** An organization that has no interaction with its external environment.

**Theory X** Managerial belief that most employees don't like to work and will only work at the required level of productivity if they are forced to do so under the threat of punishment.

**Theory Y** Managerial belief that employees can be trusted to meet production targets without being threatened and that they will often seek additional responsibilities because they enjoy the satisfaction of being creative and increasing their own skills.

when the Great Depression severely weakened public confidence in business organizations.

In the late 1930s, the professional manager emerged. The **professional manager** is a career person who does not necessarily have a controlling interest in the enterprise for which he or she works. Professional managers realize their responsibility to three groups: employees, stockholders, and the public. With expanded technology and more complex organizations, the professional manager became more and more widespread.

## THE SYSTEMS APPROACH

The fragmentation period of the late 1950s and early 1960s was followed by an era of attempted integration. Many management theorists sought to use a systems approach to integrate the various management schools. A *system* is a set of connected elements that function as a whole.

The systems approach to management was viewed as "a way of thinking about the job of managing . . . [which] provides a framework for visualizing internal and external environmental factors as an integrated whole."[14] Under this approach, the organization can be seen as either an **open system**, where it interacts with its external environment, or a **closed system**, where it has no interaction with its external environment. Most organizations are run as open systems, but even then they can make the mistake of ignoring their environment and acting as though they can operate independently of the world around them.

### First Line Focus

*At some point in your early management career you are going to make a mistake—it's not a question of "if"; it's a matter of "when," and, more importantly, how you react when it happens. Everything you learn in this book, and the other management courses in your degree program, will go a long way toward preparing you for success in your management career, but the true test comes in how you handle your day-to-day responsibilities—the specific elements of your job and all the many variables that contribute to effective performance in that job.*

*Consider the tale of a young IBM executive who was called to appear before CEO Tom Watson Jr. after making a mistake that cost the company several million dollars. The young man presented himself to Watson with the statement: "I suppose after that set of mistakes you will want to fire me." Watson is attributed with a reply that has since become part of management lore: "Not at all, young man. We have just spent a couple of million dollars educating you."*

*The lesson here? Mistakes are learning opportunities, and a smart manager uses them as such.*

THEORIES CAN ONLY GET YOU SO FAR . . .

**From the** PERSPECTIVE OF . . .

**An Emergency Room (ER) Manager** How do you manage quality of work life for your team in a fast-paced and stressful environment like an ER?

## THEORY X AND THEORY Y

In his 1960 book *The Human Side of Enterprise*, American social psychologist Douglas McGregor proposed a simple division of management styles that captured what he argued were fundamentally different ways of managing people:[15]

**Theory X**: The controlling or authoritative manager believes that most employees don't like to work and will only work at the required level of productivity if they are forced to do so under the threat of punishment.

**Theory Y:** The democratic or participative manager believes that employees can be trusted to meet production targets without being threatened and that they will often seek additional responsibilities because they enjoy the satisfaction of being creative and increasing their own skills.

Theory X and Theory Y managers have now become featured players in many management-training videos as the direct opposition of these management styles is reviewed. However, as managerial research progressed in the twentieth century, this division of styles was considered to be too simplistic, and a broader approach to management was proposed.

13. Summarize the Hawthorne experiments, and explain the Hawthorne effect.
14. Explain the differences between Theory X and Theory Y managers.
15. Why would Douglas McGregor's theory be considered too simplistic?
16. Are you a Theory X or Theory Y manager? Why?

WHAT BUG?

You manage the tech-support call center for a financial software manufacturer. Your director informs you that a bug has been found in the software that will take several weeks to fix. You are instructed to "handle" all calls without admitting the existence of the bug. Specific examples are provided to "fob off" the customer with suggestions of user error and concerns about hardware problems and conflicts with other software packages. The bug, you are told, causes rounding errors after three decimal places in calculations. The plan is to fix it in a scheduled version upgrade without any admission of its existence. Could you do that?

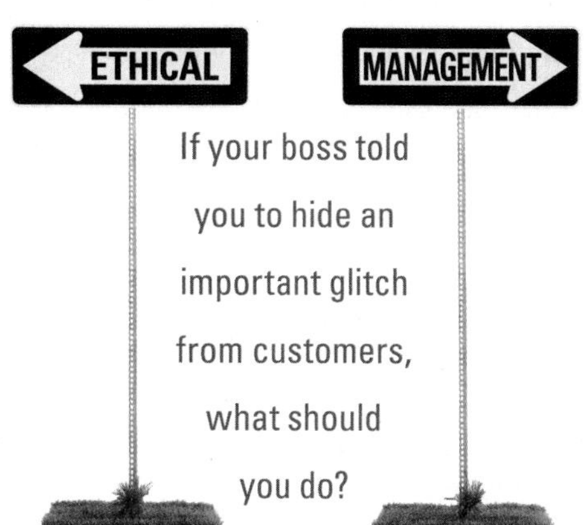

ETHICAL
MANAGEMENT
If your boss told you to hide an important glitch from customers, what should you do?


## >> Chapter Summary

Management is a complex subject. This chapter presented a series of alternative templates that can be used to better understand what management is and to analyze the management process in terms of the different roles, tasks, and skills needed to succeed. In addition, we reviewed some the major events and theories that affected the management discipline from the nineteenth century to the present.

In Chapter 2 we'll begin to examine the challenging mix of tasks and responsibilities that a manager needs to succeed in the modern business environment. Ironically, as we will see, many of those tasks and responsibilities are fundamentally the same as those identified by the management scholars of a century ago.

# Thinking Critically 1.2

## >> Managing Things Differently

After selling his low-cost airline Morris Air, which served the northwest, to Southwest Airlines for a personal profit of $25 million, entrepreneur David Neeleman managed to last only five months as a Southwest employee before being asked by Southwest Chairman Herb Kelleher to seek other opportunities elsewhere. His clear and often-shared dissatisfactions with Southwest led him to the formation of a competing low-cost carrier called JetBlue Airways in 2004. Offering such advances as e-ticketing, automatic ticket machines, in-flight cable, and leather seats with more legroom, JetBlue became known for offering better services than the major airlines at a price low enough to compete directly with Southwest, the founding champion of no-frills flights, often derided by business travelers as "the cattle airline."

While leveraging technology allowed JetBlue to improve customer service, especially in the area of transactional convenience, Neeleman's key objective was cost containment. He approached the issue of flight reservations in the same manner. Rather than leasing expensive office space and managing a complex call center operation for 700 reservation agents, Neeleman chose to leverage technology by hiring agents to work from their homes. Using a VoIP (voice over Internet protocol) phone system, JetBlue could route calls to available agents and reach them via e-mail, phone, and the Web in order to provide maximum contact with customers with minimal overhead for the organization.

However, JetBlue's reliance, or some would argue dependence, on technology proved to be a major obstacle when a freak ice storm struck its home base of New York City in February 2007. Flight delays in its tightly managed fleet resulted in stranded passengers at airports throughout its service area, with horror stories of passengers remaining stuck on planes for three hours or more as the planes waited for backup takeoff slots in its busiest airports.

Neeleman took full and very public responsibility for the service disaster, making numerous public appearances as the repentant CEO and crafting a recovery package of refunds and vouchers to satisfy angry customers. JetBlue also championed a "customer's bill of rights" that clarified refund and voucher entitlements in delayed flight situations, even though JetBlue's delays had been much less than those of competing airline American, which held the record for keeping passengers stranded on a plane for over eight hours in December 2006.

In the months that followed, JetBlue made a concerted effort to build up its operational bench strength by hiring several experienced flight operation executives from competing airlines. Neeleman's role as the public face of the service debacle prompted the board of directors to ask him to step aside in favor of a new president, David Barger, who was also known for his operations experience. Neeleman took on the role of nonexecutive chairman of JetBlue. Deeply shocked by the board's decision, he turned his attention to a new project—founding a low-cost Brazilian airline named Azul (Portuguese for "blue"), on the same operational model as JetBlue, and launching it in January 2009.

*Source:* Jena McGregor, "JetBlue's Winter Blues," *BusinessWeek*, November 27, 2007; and Jessie Scanlon, "Innovation: Braving Brazil's 'Airline Graveyard,' " BusinessWeek Online, May 6, 2008.

QUESTIONS

1. What was different about Neeleman's approach to managing JetBlue?
2. Will hiring executives with more operational experience help prevent another service disaster? Why or why not?
3. Why do you think the board of directors asked Neeleman to step aside after the February 2007 service disaster?
4. Based on his track record with Morris Air and JetBlue, do you think Neeleman will be successful in his Brazilian venture? Why or why not?

# For REVIEW >>

1. Define *management*.

   Management is the process of deciding the best way to use an organization's resources (employees, equipment, and money) to produce goods or provide services. Although the definition is simple, the job of management is quite complex. Management must make good decisions, communicate well with people, make work assignments, delegate, plan, train people, motivate people, and appraise employees' job performance. The varied work of management is extremely difficult to master. Yet mastery of management is vital to organizational success.

2. Identify and explain the levels of management.

   At the highest levels of an organization, senior managers establish the long-term strategic goals and objectives and identify the actions needed to achieve those goals and objectives. Middle managers at the next level of the organization (department or division heads) are responsible for implementing the actions identified by senior managers and assigning the organizational resources needed to achieve departmental goals and objectives. At the front line of management, supervisors oversee the day-to-day operations of the organization and manage the employees who produce the organization's goods or provide its services.

3. Explain the management process.

   The process of management can be examined by reviewing the tasks performed, the roles that managers play in the organization, and the skills those managers need to be effective. Managerial tasks can be classified as planning, organizing, staffing, leading, and controlling. The exhaustive list of managerial roles was documented by Henry Mintzberg under three groups: interpersonal, informational, and decisional. Management skills can be classified in three ways: conceptual, human relations, and technical.

4. Understand the different perspectives of scientific management and the human relations movement.

   Proponents of scientific management pursue the identification of "one best way" of performing a job. By quantifying the maximum productive capacity of a job, the company can ensure that labor dollars are being used efficiently, and employees, it is argued, can earn the maximum income possible (assuming they are paid on a "piece rate"). The perspective of the human relations movement is that employees offer a greater resource to the organization than just their productive capacity. Data from the Hawthorne studies led researchers to conclude that worker productivity was impacted by other factors than just the physical environment. Individual recognition, the opportunity to participate in decision making, and greater awareness of informal group pressures by their managers can all affect how employees contribute to the organization.

# THE WORLD of Work >>

**TONY GETS SOME ADVICE** *(continued from page 3)*

Tony's manager, Jerry Smith, was waiting for him when he got back to the restaurant." So, how are you doing, son?" asked Jerry. "Has it sunk in yet?"

"Not really," said Tony. "I really appreciate your confidence in me, Jerry, and I want you to know that I won't let you down."

"I know," said Jerry, who paused for a moment and then continued. "While you were gone, I received a call from corporate—there's been a change of plan. The company needs me to start in my new region at the beginning of next week instead of next month, as we originally planned, so you and I only have this week to manage the transition from me to you as the new manager.

"You'll be able to reach me on my cell phone," Jerry said, reacting to the surprise in Tony's eyes. "But my new region has some challenges so I'll be pretty busy. Dawn Williams will be your boss now, and she'll be there to help you too.

"Let's talk about staffing," continued Jerry. "I'll go over the payroll paperwork with you tomorrow. It hasn't changed much since you covered for my vacation earlier this year, so you should be okay there. I'm more concerned about the schedule." Jerry paused and took a deep breath. "Because Tanya gave her two weeks' notice this morning while you were at your meeting with Dawn."

"What?" shouted Tony, not believing what he was hearing. "She's our most experienced shift leader, our best trainer, and she's the best closer we've got. Why is she leaving? Can we persuade her to stay?"

"Believe me, son, if there was a way to keep her, I would have done it," said Jerry, "but her husband just got offered a new job out of state, and they're moving in a couple of weeks. So we need to find a replacement for Tanya ASAP and then decide who she's going to train to take over her responsibilities over the next two weeks."

"Okay," said Tony, trying very hard to treat this bombshell like it was an everyday thing for the manager of a Taco Barn. "That sounds like a plan. What else do we have going on with the schedule?"

"Well," continued Jerry, "don't forget that the schools go back in a couple of weeks and the new athletic schedules will start, so some of the kids—Matt, William, Paul, Kate, Susan, Jennifer, Megan, and others—will want to cut back their hours and change their shifts so that they can make it to their practice and meets. The good news is you have some good applications on hand, but you'll need to start interviewing right away so that you can get these new people trained and ready to go."

"Okay," said Tony absentmindedly. He was already thinking about how he was going to get all these replacements trained after his best trainer had left. "What else?"

"That about covers the schedule," said Jerry, "so let's move on to the new menu items that the company is launching."

**QUESTIONS**

1. What do you think the team's reaction to Tony's promotion will be?
2. Do you think a week will be enough time for Tony to get all the information from Jerry that he needs to run the restaurant? Why or why not?
3. What else can Jerry do to better prepare Tony for success in his new role?
4. If you were in Tony's shoes, what would you do now?

## Key Terms >>

closed system 14
conceptual skills 6
Fordism 10
functions of management 13
Hawthorne effect 13
human relations skills 6
management 5
middle management 5
open system 14
professional manager 14
role 5
scientific management 8
senior management 5
supervisory management 5
technical skills 6
Theory X 14
Theory Y 14

## Think << AND DISCUSS

1. Management has often been described as a universal process, meaning that basic management skills are transferable and applicable to almost any work environment. Do you believe that a good manager in an insurance company could be equally as effective in a restaurant? Explain your reasoning.
2. Do you think management can be learned through books and study or only through experience?
3. Consider your own personality, skills, and work experience. What makes you (or will make you) a good manager?
4. What are the benefits of understanding how management theory and practice have changed over the past 100 years? How could you use this information as a manager?
5. What are the key differences between the principles of scientific management and the core elements of human relations management?
6. What do you see as the most challenging part of being a manager? Explain your reasoning.

## INTERNET In Action >>

1. Visit the Web site for the American Management Association (**www.amanet.org**). Find a course on supervisory skills and summarize the content of that course: What does the training include? What will it do for the skills of the course participants?
2. Visit the Web site of the National Academies (comprised of four organizations: the National Academy of Sciences, the National Academy of Engineering, the Institute of Medicine, and the National Research Council) at **www.nationalacademies.org**.
   a. Describe the history of the National Academy of Sciences and its expansion into the National Academies.
   b. List the six major divisions of the National Academies.
   c. What are the objectives of the Division of Behavioral and Social Sciences and Education (DBASSE)?
   d. Select the "Featured Reports in Behavioral Sciences" page, and summarize the description of one of the reports relating to a business topic.

1. **Finding the One Best Way**

   Suppose you have been assigned the simple task of stuffing 1,000 two-page flyers (8½″ × 11″) into a normal-size envelope (4″ × 9½″). The envelopes come in boxes of 250, and the flyer pages are in stacks of 1,000 each. The flyers must first be stapled together, folded, and then placed into the envelopes.

   a. Get a stapler, a few envelopes, and several 8½″ × 11″ sheets of paper, and determine how you might accomplish this task. Identify where each component will be positioned and exactly how you will perform the task.

   b. After you have tried your first method, see if you can determine any ways in which it might be improved.

   c. Compare your method with others in your class.

   d. Vote as a group on the "one best way" to perform the task.

   **Questions**

   1. Were you able to improve your first method in step *b*?
   2. Did you pick up further improvements from others in your class (step *c*)?
   3. Were you able to agree on one best way (step *d*)?
   4. How different was your original method from the final one best way?

2. **Theory X or Theory Y?**

   Divide into two groups, one taking the Theory X perspective and one taking the Theory Y perspective, and prepare a response to the following scenario:

   Your company produces widgets, which are high-tolerance components that must be manufactured within a tolerance of 0.5 microns to function effectively within a large piece of machinery that costs several million dollars to manufacture and that costs the customer $100,000 for every day the machine is down if the widgets need to be replaced.

   Your manufacturing plant runs on an assembly-line configuration with detailed production targets that are monitored per hour, per shift, and per day. The plant director has noticed that production levels are erratic with evidence of a slow decline in production quantity and quality. There are no apparent issues in raw materials or equipment, so the director has determined that it is a people problem. What are you going to do?

# Case 1.1

## >> Face Time: The New Assembly Line

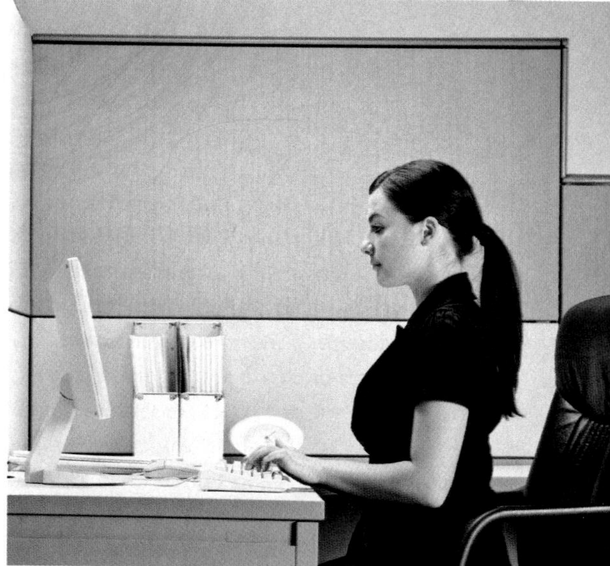

When Frederick Winslow Taylor first proposed his theories of scientific management, he believed that breaking down a task into its component parts would facilitate the measurement of a maximum productivity level for that task. However, the fruits of Taylor's labor produced a dramatically different harvest. Vivid accounts of the abysmal working conditions in Chicago's meatpacking plants, documented in Upton Sinclair's *The Jungle*, illustrated how the "specialization of labor" was adapted in a manner that Taylor probably never envisioned. Monotonous work in hazardous conditions, whether cutting up beef carcasses or assembling cars, became the normal work environment of the day.

A century later, our access to sophisticated information technology has supposedly replaced graft labor with the "knowledge worker"—a person whose chief contribution to a company is intellectual rather than physical. However, this dramatic improvement in work design has not been matched by an equal shift in management philosophy. Admittedly, the cubicles of a nondescript office building are certainly more comfortable than a slaughterhouse, but the way in which employees are managed in those environments hasn't really changed much.

We now have the technology to work literally from anywhere with an Internet connection, and yet work performance is still linked to physical presence in the office, where your manager can keep an eye on you and make sure you are working hard through measurable "face time."

Consider this office example: One evening, a young man meets the Chinese restaurant delivery person at the side entrance of his office building. He returns to his office, opens the container, sticks a fork in the chicken chow mein, turns up his desk radio, and arranges his jacket over the back of his chair. Then, leaving his light on, the dinner on his desk, and his office door ajar, he goes to his car.

A carton of food wasted! Well, not in his mind: He had bought himself an extra hour or two of face time, because if a higher-up walked by that open door he'd be likely to think the employee was still working (just at the copier or in the men's room).

In this instance, the productive capacity of this knowledge worker was devoted to working around the system rather than contributing to it. If that reflects your corporate culture, how far have your managers really come from those meatpacking days?

### QUESTIONS

1. Assembly lines are commonly found in the automotive industry. Provide examples of two other industries that use the same manufacturing process.
2. What kind of face time does your boss expect at your current job (or a job you have held in the past)?
3. Have you ever felt pressure to put in more face time to keep up with your coworkers? How did you handle that pressure?
4. Is there a solution to the pressure of face time? How could you reassure your boss that you are being productive even when he can't see you every minute of the working day?

*Source:* Liz Ryan, "Employment Trends," BusinessWeek Online, April 22, 2005; and David A. Hounshell, *From the American System to Mass Production, 1800–1932: The Development of Manufacturing Technology in the United States* (Baltimore, MD: Johns Hopkins University Press, 1984).

# Case 1.2

## >> Efficient Creativity

When James McNerney, after falling short in the race to succeed Jack Welch at General Electric, was hired to run 3M in 2000, he was the first outsider to lead the inward-looking St. Paul, Minnesota company in its 100-year history. He took a classic GE approach to running 3M, axing 8,000 workers (about 11 percent of the workforce), intensifying the performance-review process, and tightening the purse strings at a company that had become an extravagant spender. He also brought in GE's famous Six Sigma program—a series of management techniques designed to decrease production defects and increase efficiency. Thousands of staffers became trained as Six Sigma "black belt" specialists. Under McNerney, the research and development (R&D) function at 3M was organized in ways that were unheard of in St. Paul, even though the guidelines would have looked familiar at many other organizations. After a couple of months on a research project, researchers would have to fill in a "red book" with scores of pages worth of charts and tables, analyzing everything from the potential commercial application to the size of the market and to possible manufacturing problems.

The plan appeared to work: McNerney brought 3M's declining stock back to life and won rave reviews for bringing discipline to an organization that had become clumsy, inconsistent, and slow. Then, four and a half years after arriving, McNerney abruptly left for a bigger opportunity, the top job at Boeing. Now his successors faced a challenging question: whether the relentless emphasis on efficiency had made 3M a less creative company. That was a vitally important issue for a company whose very identity is built on innovation. After all, 3M is the birthplace of Scotchguard, Scotch tape, Thinsulate, and the Post-it Note.

Nothing captures 3M's traditional approach to creativity more than the story of the discovery of the Post-it Note

Nothing captures 3M's traditional approach to creativity more than the story of the discovery of the Post-it Note:

How many Six Sigma–driven organizations would allow a researcher to dabble with a product that had been shelved over a decade before? In our modern pay-for-performance business culture, managers are expected to deliver on targets or quotas against previously established metrics—sales increased, costs reduced, profits generated. Thomas J. Watson Sr., the legendary manager who drove the growth of International Business Machines (IBM) from the 1920s to the 1950s, took a different view. He is quoted as saying, "The fastest way to succeed is to double your failure rate."

QUESTIONS

1. Why would the use of "exact statistical analysis" reduce creativity?
2. Is it appropriate to expect a researcher to document the potential commercial application and market size of every breakthrough?
3. Would 3M's Post-it Note have ever been created under a Six Sigma management process? Why or why not?
4. Does your organization encourage experimentation and support failures? Why or why not?

*Source:* Robert Weisman, "In Some Cases, Nothing Succeeds Like Failure," *The Boston Globe*, December 10, 2006; Brian Hindo, "Inside Innovation: 3M: A Struggle between Efficiency and Creativity," *BusinessWeek*, June 11, 2007; and J. C. Collins and J. I. Porras, *Built to Last: Successful Habits of Visionary Companies* (New York: HarperBusiness, 1994).

# Case 1.3

## >> Health Care: Managing Treatment and Administration

The traditional model of health care management divides roles along functional lines: Doctors and nurses look after patients, and administrators manage the organizations that treat those patients. However, if we examine the extent to which this conventional model works effectively, we find some disturbing data. For example, there are about 90,000 avoidable deaths every year in U.S. health care alone, and after years of double-digit increases, the average U.S. household spends more on health insurance than on mortgage payments.

Initiatives are in place to begin to address the cost issue through better information management. The Obama administration committed $19 billion in 2009 to promote the use of health information technology (HIT) and, in particular, electronic health records (EHRs). However, fewer than 2 percent of hospitals in a recent survey by the *New England Journal of Medicine* had completely abandoned paper-based medical records in favor of digital records. Justification for the lack of progress included potential capital investments of anywhere from $20 million for small hospitals to $200 million for larger medical centers, the high cost of system maintenance, and physician resistance to the change.

Fortunately, there is a growing body of evidence to support the argument that greater clinical involvement in administrative decisions can result in better operational efficiency and patient care. Kaiser Permanente's Colorado affiliate, for example, increased annual net income from $0 to $87 million while dramatically increasing patient satisfaction and reducing staff turnover after a systemwide commitment to redefining the role of a physician as "healer, leader, and partner." In the same manner, the Veterans Health Administration (VHA) was able to recover from performance levels in the mid-1990s that were so poor as to prompt calls for privatization and/or closure of many hospitals. Involving physicians in critical decisions on the provision of clinical services contributed directly to dramatic improvements in the quality of patient care. In the last decade, the risk of death for men over 65 in the care of the VHA was 40 percent lower than the U.S. average. Patient satisfaction has risen to 83 percent, 12 percent above the national average, during a period in which patient enrollment doubled.

To be clear, greater physician involvement in the management of patient care has not been achieved with a few business classes, modified job descriptions, and committee assignments. Success has been achieved by starting with the responsibility doctors feel for their patients' well-being and broadening that responsibility to the organization as a whole. This involved both a clearer sense of accountability for the overall patient experience and a change in professional identity. With the provision of real-time data to track the performance of each department, and a systemwide commitment to detailed examination of service failures as lessons for future improvement, doctors were encouraged to shift their focus beyond clinical outcomes to overall quality.

### QUESTIONS

1. Describe the traditional model of patient care in health care.
2. Why would doctors be resistant to a switch to digital medical records?
3. Should hard data be enough to change doctors' minds? Why or why not?
4. As a new hospital administrator, how would you initiate the discussion of greater physician involvement in administrative decisions?

*Source:* D. Blumenthal, "Stimulating the Adoption of Health Information Technology," *New England Journal of Medicine*, April 9, 2009; J. Mountford and C. Webb, "When Clinicians Lead," *The McKinsey Quarterly*, February 2009; and Institute of Medicine, *Crossing the Quality Chasm*, 2001.

CHAPTER 2

"The most important thing in communication is hearing what isn't said."

Peter F. Drucker

# COMMUNICATION SKILLS

LEARNING OUTCOMES

After studying this chapter, you will able to:

1 Define *communication.*

2 Explain why effective communication is an important management skill.

3 Explain the significance of networking and social media in management communications.

4 Understand why it's still possible to communicate poorly.

5 Understand the challenges of communication in international business activities.

## THE WORLD OF WORK Under new management

Tony's transition week with Jerry Smith went very quickly. They spent time covering payroll, banking, and food orders and planning out the schedule for the next month. Tony had covered a lot of these duties before when Jerry was on vacation, but it felt different to be doing them as the new unit manager.

The schedule was the worst—trying to cover everybody's individual requests (only this many hours; only these days; wanting to be scheduled together because they car pool; needing time off for sports practice; canceling at the last minute because the babysitter didn't show)—all these headaches made staffing the biggest block of Jerry's time, and Tony started to think that there had to be a better way to handle scheduling. Jerry was a nice guy and did his best to accommodate requests, but Tony felt that people were beginning to take advantage of Jerry's flexibility.

After the fifth attempt at completing the schedule, Tony had decided that this would be the first opportunity for him to make some real changes and to show Jerry and his new boss Dawn Williams that he wasn't afraid to step up and put his stamp on this Taco Barn. Jerry ran a great unit, which was why he was being promoted to regional manager, but that didn't mean there wasn't room to improve. Tony believed that by setting a tougher standard on the schedule, he could simplify the process and free up some time to work on other things in the restaurant. Plus, he thought, running the daily operations would be a lot easier if he didn't have to deal with schedule changes every time the shift changed. In addition, it would send a clear message to his staff that just because they used to be co-workers didn't mean that he was going to be easier on them than Jerry was.

The next morning, as the lunch crew started clocking in for their shift, they noticed a new sign on the staff notice board on bright yellow paper:

Effective immediately, there will be no changes to the schedule once posted. It is your responsibility to show up for your designated shift or find someone to cover for you if a problem or emergency prevents you from showing up.—**Tony Davis, Unit Manager**

### QUESTIONS

1. Why is it so important for Tony to "put his stamp" on the Taco Barn as the new manager?
2. Did Tony make the right choice here? Why or why not?
3. What do you think the team's reaction will be?
4. What could Tony do differently here?

# >> Communication

**Communication** is the act of exchanging information. It can be used to inform, command, instruct, assess, influence, and persuade other people. Communication skills are important in all aspects of life, including business.

**Communication** The act of exchanging information.

Managers use communication every day. In fact, they spend over three-quarters of their time communicating (see Figure 2.1). Good managers develop effective communication skills. They use these skills to absorb information, motivate employees, and deal effectively with customers and co-workers. Good communication can significantly affect a manager's success.

**Figure 2.1 • Communicating in the Business World**

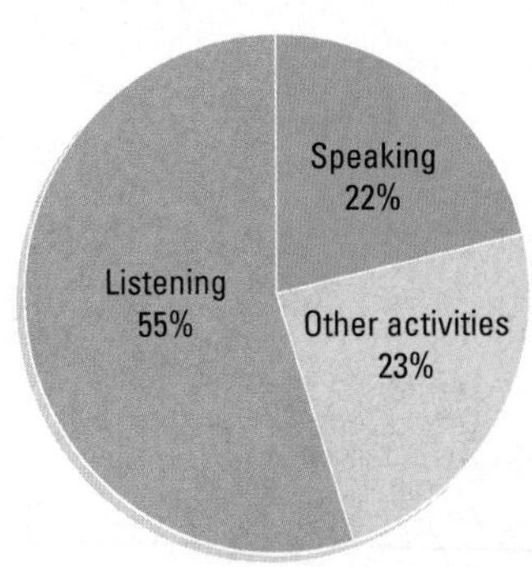


## COMMUNICATION AS A MANAGEMENT SKILL

Study Alert !

Why are communication skills so critical to a manager's success? What is an example of a manager effectively managing a team through good communication? Is your manager an effective or ineffective communicator? Provide an example.

Communicating effectively is an important management skill for several reasons:

- *Managers must give direction to the people who work for them.* Managers who fail to give clear guidance often find that employees perform their jobs poorly because they do not understand what is expected of them.
- *Managers must be able to motivate people.* Good managers use their ability to communicate to get other people excited about their jobs.
- *Managers must be able to convince customers that they should do business with them.* Effective communication is the key to convincing a customer to purchase a product or service. Without good communication skills, managers will find it difficult to attract customers, even if their companies' products or services meet the customers' needs.
- *Managers must be able to absorb the ideas of others.* Business managers interact with many people, including co-workers, customers, and suppliers. To be effective, they must be able to understand and accept other people's viewpoints.
- *Managers must be able to persuade other people.* Managers often have ideas that others oppose. To persuade other people to accept their ideas, managers must be able to communicate effectively.

## INTERPERSONAL COMMUNICATION

Effective communication between individuals, especially between a manager and subordinates, is critical to achieving organizational objectives and, as a result, to managing people effectively. Estimates vary, but it is generally agreed that since managers spend much of their time with their subordinates, effective communication is critical to the wise and effective use of their time.

**Interpersonal communication** is an interactive process between individuals that involves sending and receiving verbal and nonverbal messages. The basic purpose of interpersonal communication is to transmit information so that the sender of the message is understood and understands the receiver. Figure 2.2 diagrams this dynamic and interactive process. An event or a condition generates information. The desire to share the information, or inform another person about it, creates the need to communicate. The sender then creates a message and communicates it both verbally and nonverbally. The receiver, in turn, perceives and interprets the message and (hopefully) creates a reply message as a response to it. This reply message may generate a response by the sender of the initial message, and the process continues in this fashion.

Often, however, many factors interfere and cause interpersonal communication to fail. Some causes of such failure are conflicting or inappropriate assumptions, different interpretations of the meanings of words (semantics), differences in perception, emotions either preceding or during communication, poor listening habits, inadequate communication skills, insufficient feedback, and differences in the interpretations of nonverbal communications.

### Conflicting or Inappropriate Assumptions

Have you ever thought you were being understood

## Figure 2.2 • Interpersonal Communication Process

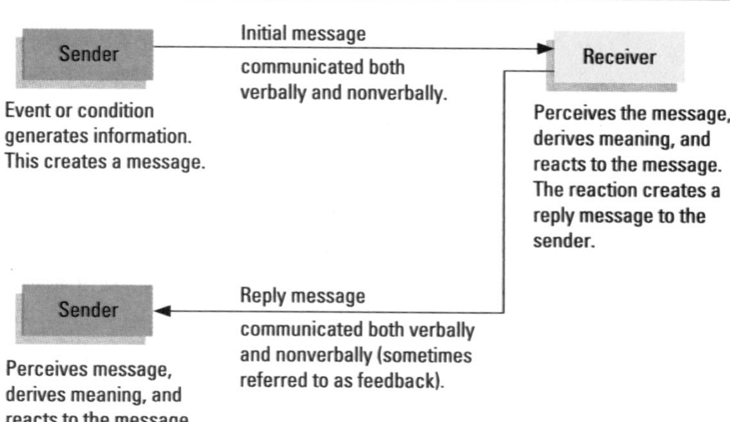

Sender
Initial message
communicated both verbally and nonverbally.
Receiver
Event or condition generates information. This creates a message.
Perceives the message, derives meaning, and reacts to the message. The reaction creates a reply message to the sender.
Sender
Reply message
communicated both verbally and nonverbally (sometimes referred to as feedback).
Perceives message, derives meaning, and reacts to the message.

when you were really not? This is a common mistake made by couples, teachers, superiors, and parents. If one assumes that communication is flowing as intended, one tends to move on with the dialogue without allowing feedback to indicate whether clarity of expression and communication has been achieved. Good managers and salespeople always seek verbal or nonverbal feedback, before continuing the communication process. Remember that interpretation of meaning can always be a problem when assumptions are involved. Messages such as "Stop," "Do this right now," and "Please don't" never seem to have the same meanings to children that the adult sender intended. Sound communication usually flows from ensuring that the sender and the receiver see and understand assumptions in the same way.

**Semantics** is the science or study of the meanings of words and symbols. Words themselves have no real meaning. They have meaning only in terms of people's reactions to them. A word may mean very different things to different people, depending on how it is used. In addition, a word may be interpreted differently based on the facial expressions, hand gestures, and voice inflections used.

The problems involved in semantics are of two general types. Some words and phrases invite multiple interpretations. For example, Figure 2.3 shows different interpretations of the word *fix*. Another problem is that groups of people in specific situations often develop their own technical language, which outsiders may or may not understand. For example, physicians, government workers, and military employees are often guilty of using acronyms and abbreviations that only they understand.

Words are the most common form of interpersonal communication. Because of the real possibility of misinterpretation, words must be carefully chosen and clearly defined for effective communication.

**Perception** deals with the mental and sensory processes an individual uses in interpreting information she or he receives. Since each individual's perception is unique, people often perceive the same situation in different ways.

Perception begins when the sense organs receive a stimulus. The stimulus is the information received, whether it is conveyed in writing, verbally, nonverbally, or in another way. The sense organs respond to, shape, and organize the information received. When this information reaches the brain, it is further organized and interpreted, resulting in perception. Different people perceive the same information differently because no two people have the same personal experiences, memories, likes, and dislikes. In addition, the phenomenon of selective perception often distorts the intended message: People tend to listen to only part of the message, blocking out the rest for any number of reasons.

**Interpersonal Communication** An interactive process between individuals that involves sending and receiving verbal and nonverbal messages.

**Semantics** The science or study of the meanings of words and symbols.

**Perception** The mental and sensory processes an individual uses in interpreting information received.

**Emotions Either Preceding or During Communication** Just as perception affects our cognitive

## Figure 2.3 • Interpretations of the Word *Fix*

An Englishman visits America and is completely awed by the many ways we use the word *fix*. For example,

1. His host asks him how he'd like his drink fixed. He meant *mixed*.
2. As he prepares to leave, he discovers he has a flat tire and calls a repairperson, who says he'll fix it immediately. He means *repair*.
3. On the way home, he is given a ticket for speeding. He calls his host, who says, "Don't worry, I'll fix it." He means *nullify*.
4. At the office the next day, he comments on the cost of living in America, and one of his colleagues says, "It's hard to make ends meet on a fixed income." She means *steady* or *unchanging*.
5. He has an argument with a co-worker. The latter says, "I'll fix you." He means *seek revenge*.
6. A colleague remarks that she is in a fix. She means *condition* or *situation*.

## [PROGRESS] ✓questions

1. What is communication?
2. Define *interpersonal communication.*
3. What is semantics?
4. What is perception, and what role does it play in communication?

processes during communication, emotions affect our disposition to send and receive the communication. Anger, joy, fear, sorrow, disgust, or panic (to mention only a few emotions) can all affect the way we send or receive messages. Emotional disposition is like the stage on which the communication piece plays its part: The stage can be perfectly prepared or in total disarray. The setting for the communication piece is obviously important. Communications during periods of high emotion usually have difficulty succeeding. Therefore, managers with good communication skills strive to manage the emotional as well as the physical communication environment.

# >> Learning to Communicate

Managers communicate in writing and verbally. Before they can master either form of communication, they must be able to identify the audience, develop good listening skills, and understand the importance of feedback and nonverbal communication.

### UNDERSTANDING THE AUDIENCE

Managers communicate with many different kinds of people. Hotel managers, for example, communicate with hotel guests, food and beverage managers, housekeepers, maintenance people, architects, travel agents, furniture salespeople, and many other types of people. They also may deal with senior management from the hotel's corporate office. Each group of people represents a different audience.

To communicate effectively, managers need to determine their audience. Specifically, they need to be able to answer the following questions:

- What does the audience already know?
- What does it want to know?
- What is its capacity for absorbing information?
- What does it hope to gain by listening? Is it hoping to be motivated? Informed? Convinced?
- Is the audience friendly or hostile?

Hotel managers communicate with the hotel's housekeeping staff about complaints by guests. In doing so, they must inform the staff of the problem and motivate them to work harder to prevent complaints in the future. They would not need to provide background material on the nature of the housekeeper's role. The audience already understands what that role includes.

If a lawsuit is filed against a hotel, managers of the hotel must inform senior management about the situation. In communicating with the hotel's senior management, they would describe what was being done to deal with the situation. They would also provide detailed background information that would allow the corporate officers to fully understand the situation.

### DEVELOPING GOOD LISTENING SKILLS

One of the most important skills a manager can develop is the ability to listen (see Figure 2.4). Good listening skills enable managers to absorb the information they need, recognize problems, and understand other people's viewpoints.

*If you are a hotel manager speaking to a bellhop, what can you determine about your audience?*

## TRIMMING FAT OR CUTTING CORNERS?

Your management team has just finished the operational plan for your division for the next three years. First action item will be layoffs to meet cost targets. After planning the human resource (HR) logistics of the layoffs—severance packages, outplacement support, and so forth—you move on to deciding how to communicate the news to the media. One of your colleagues suggests that you label the layoffs as "performance-based" to imply that the company is being fiscally responsible by "trimming the fat" rather than simply cutting heads to hit cost targets. Since each employee will receive a glowing reference as part of the outplacement package, your colleague argues, there's no real harm done. You know most of the people being laid off and have worked closely with several of them for a few years. They are all good people who worked hard for the company. Are you comfortable with labeling their unexpected departure as "performance-based"?

ETHICAL
MANAGEMENT
Is it fair to label layoffs as "performance-based," even when they are not?


*Source:* Inspired by Liz Ryan, "Commentary: Taking a Stand on Ethics," *BusinessWeek*, March 21, 2006.

Managers need to learn to listen actively. Active listening involves absorbing what another person is saying and responding to the person's concerns (see Figure 2.5). Learning to listen actively is the key to becoming a good communicator.

Most people do not listen actively. Tests indicate that immediately after listening to a 10-minute oral presentation, the average listener has heard, comprehended, accurately evaluated, and retained about half of what was said. Within 48 hours, the effectiveness level drops to just 25 percent. By the end of a week, listeners recall only about 10 percent or less of what they heard.

Managers need to work at being active listeners. Many people daydream or think about an unrelated topic when someone else is talking. Some people become angry by a speaker's remarks and fail to fully absorb what the person is saying. Others become impatient and interrupt, preferring to talk rather than listen.

### Figure 2.5 • Using Active Listening

1. **Listening**
   Knowing how to listen is an important part of dealing with customers. Using active listening skills helps managers understand why customers are dissatisfied.
2. **Responding**
   The way managers respond to complaints can be just as important as the way they solve a customer's problem. Businesspeople should always be courteous and friendly when dealing with customers. They should demonstrate interest in determining what went wrong and figuring out what they can do to solve the problem.
3. **Making Sure the Customers Are Satisfied**
   Managers need to determine whether they have satisfied the customers' needs. To do so, they must interpret the feedback they receive from the customers.

### Figure 2.4 • Are You a Good Listener?

- Are you open to what other people say to you, or do you make up your mind about things before you hear other people's views?
- Do you become bored when other people speak?
- Do you interrupt people when they are speaking?
- Do you daydream at meetings?
- Are you hesitant to ask clarifying questions?

Learning to listen actively involves the following steps:

- *Identify the speaker's purpose.* What is the speaker trying to achieve? Why is the speaker speaking?
- *Identify the speaker's main ideas.* Which of the points are the key points? Which points need to be addressed by the listener?
- *Note the speaker's tone as well as his or her body language.* Is the speaker angry? Nervous? Confident?
- *Respond to the speaker with appropriate comments, questions, and body language.* Use facial expressions and body language to express the emotions you want to express. Establish eye contact, sit up straight, and lean toward the speaker to show interest. Ask a question or make a comment from time to time to show that you are listening attentively.

## FEEDBACK

Effective communication is a two-way process. Information must flow back and forth between sender and receiver. The flow from the receiver to the sender is called *feedback*. It informs the sender whether the receiver has received the correct message; it also lets the receiver know if he or she has received the correct message. For example, asking a person if she or he understands a message often puts the person on the defensive and can result in limited feedback. Instead of asking if a person understands a message, it is much better to request that the receiver explain what he or she has heard.

**From the PERSPECTIVE OF...**

**A Licensed Mental Health Counselor**

Counselors by definition must have good listening skills if they are going to be able to help their patients. What elements of a manager's job might be compared to those of a counselor?

## UNDERSTANDING THE IMPORTANCE OF NONVERBAL COMMUNICATION

People have a great capacity to convey meaning through nonverbal means of expression. One form of nonverbal communication, called *paralanguage*, includes the pitch, tempo, loudness, and hesitations in the verbal communication. People also use a variety of gestures in nonverbal communication. In America, for example, one can raise an eyebrow to indicate disapproval, interest, concern, or attention. In Japan, however, that raised eyebrow would be considered an obscene gesture.

People communicate nonverbally by how close they stand to each other. Body posture and eye contact also communicate messages. For example, lack of eye contact can communicate indifference or shyness.

In summary, nonverbal communication is an important supplement to verbal communication and sometimes can change the meaning of verbal communication. Nonverbal communication is an effective way of conveying emotions. When combined with verbal communication, it gives managers powerful tools for transmitting information to employees.

# >> Written Communication

Managers communicate in writing every day. They send e-mails, write letters, and draft reports. To communicate effectively, managers must be able to write clearly, concisely, and persuasively.

Before actually writing a business document, managers need to think about what they want to achieve. They must identify the purpose of the document, the audience, and the main point they want to convey. Using a checklist like that shown in Figure 2.6 can help them work through this stage of the writing process.

## PRINCIPLES OF GOOD WRITING

Many business managers have difficulty writing well. To improve their writing, managers can apply three basic principles:

- *Write as simply and clearly as possible.* Avoid writing in a way that is difficult to understand.
- *Be sure that the content and tone of the document are appropriate for the audience.* Do not waste readers' time communicating information they already know. However, do not assume they are as familiar with the topic as you are. Always use a polite tone, especially when writing to customers.
- *Proofread the document.* If you are using a computer, use the spell-check function. If you are not using a computer, use a dictionary to check the spelling of words you do not know. Always read the document for incorrect grammar or usage.

## Figure 2.6 • Identifying the Purpose, Audience, and Main Point of a Document

**Purpose**
- Why am I writing this document?
- What action do I want the reader to take after reading it?

**Audience**
- Who will read this document?
- How much does the reader already know about the topic?
- How will the reader use the document?
- Are there any special sensitivities of which I should be aware?

**Main Message**
- What is the main message I want to convey in this document?
- How will I support that message?

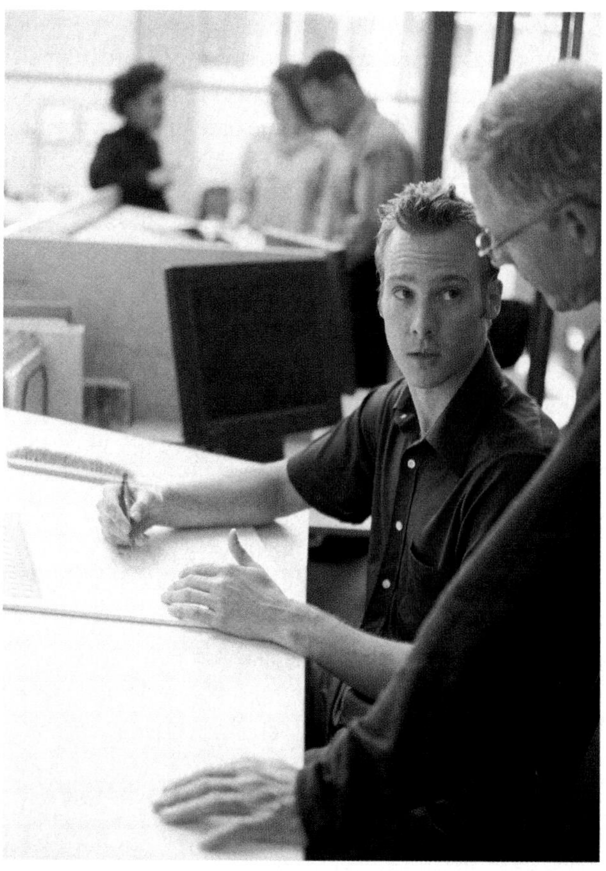

### [PROGRESS] ✓questions

5. What is feedback, and how does it affect the communication process?
6. What are the four key steps of active listening?
7. Explain the importance of nonverbal communication in interpersonal communication.
8. What are the three basic principles of good writing?

## >> Oral Communication

Not all business communication is in writing. In fact, most business communication is oral.

Some oral communication is formal and takes place at meetings or interviews. Most oral communication is informal. It takes place in offices and hallways, next to the water cooler, in the cafeteria, and over the telephone.

### THE IMPORTANCE OF ORAL COMMUNICATION

Communicating well verbally is important for managers. Successful managers use their oral communication skills to give clear instructions, motivate their staff, and persuade other people.

Being able to communicate effectively also is important because it can set the tone within a department or company. In some departments, managers say "good morning" to as many co-workers as they can. They invite their employees to discuss problems with them. In other departments, managers isolate themselves from lower-level employees and make no effort to communicate. These small differences can have a big effect on employee morale.

### DEVELOPING ORAL COMMUNICATION SKILLS

All businesspeople need to speak effectively. Whether they are talking to a colleague or presenting a keynote address before a large audience, businesspeople should follow the same rules of thumb:

- *Make emotional contact with listeners by addressing them by name where possible.* When talking face to face, establish eye contact.
- *Avoid speaking in a monotone.* Use your voice to emphasize important words within a sentence.
- *Be enthusiastic and project a positive outlook.* Focus on what is going right, rather than what is going wrong.

Stop and consider your body language right now—your posture and your facial expression. What nonverbal messages are you sending? Why is it important to understand the effects of nonverbal communication in a business environment?

- *Avoid interrupting others.* Even if you know what the other person is going to say, avoid cutting people off or finishing their sentences for them.
- *Always be courteous.* Avoid getting angry when other people are talking, even if you disagree with what they are saying.
- *Avoid empty sounds or words, such as "uh," "um," "like," and "you know."* Sprinkling your speech with empty fillers will make you sound unprofessional.

**PROGRESS ✓questions**

9. Explain the difference between formal and informal oral communication.
10. Successful managers use their oral communication skills in three primary ways. What are they?
11. List the six steps for effective oral communication.
12. How could you improve your oral communication skills?

## >> Choosing the Best Method of Communication

Managers need to master both written and verbal communication skills. They also need to understand when to use each. In general, verbal communication is most appropriate for sensitive communications, such as reprimanding or dismissing an employee (provided that communication is then confirmed in writing). Written communication is most appropriate for communicating routine information, such as changes in company policies or staff. Choosing the best method of communication will help you relay information in an appropriate and professional manner.

**Grapevine** Informal channels of communication within an organization.

**E-mail** Electronic mail; the system of sending and receiving messages over an electronic communications system.

## >> Communicating within the Organization

In order to be an effective manager, the importance of the grapevine and e-mail must be understood.

### THE GRAPEVINE

Many informal paths of communication exist in organizations. These informal channels are generally referred to as the **grapevine**. During the Civil War, intelligence telegraph lines hung loosely from tree to tree and looked like grapevines. Messages sent over these lines were often garbled; thus, any rumor was said to be from the grapevine. Grapevines develop within organizations when employees share common hobbies, hometowns, lunch breaks, family ties, and social relationships. The grapevine always exists within the formal organizational structure. However, it does not follow the organizational hierarchy; it may go from secretary to vice president or from engineer to clerk. The grapevine is not limited to nonmanagement personnel; it also operates among managers and professional personnel.

The grapevine has a poor reputation because it is regarded as the primary source of distorted messages and rumors. However, management must recognize that the grapevine is often accurate. Management must also recognize that information in the grapevine travels more rapidly than information in the formal channels of communication. Finally, management must recognize the resilience of the grapevine. No matter how much effort is spent improving the formal channels of communication, grapevines will always exist.

Because the grapevine is inevitable, management should use it to complement formal channels of communication. In utilizing the grapevine, honesty is always the best policy. Rumors and distorted messages will persist, but honest disclaimers by management will stop the spread of inaccurate information.[1]

### E-MAIL

Especially valuable to communication in today's organizations is the use of electronic mail systems, or **e-mail**, provided by networked and online systems. The e-mail system allows the high-speed exchange of written messages through the use of computerized text processing and computer-oriented communication networks. When e-mail first came to the business world, it appeared to hold much promise. Managers were told that it would save time, eliminate wasted effort (such as unanswered or repeat phone calls), provide written records (if necessary) of communications without the formality of memos, and enable communication among individuals who might not communicate otherwise. In reality, many would argue that e-mail has become both a blessing and a curse of management communication.

# Thinking Critically 2.1

## >> Starting a New Job

Jack Smythe, branch manager for a large computer manufacturer, had been told by his marketing manager, Linda Sprague, that Otis Brown had just given two weeks' notice. When Jack had interviewed Otis, he had been convinced of his tremendous potential in sales. Otis was bright and personable, an MIT honor graduate in electrical engineering who had the qualifications the company looked for in computer sales. Now he was leaving after only two months with the company. Jack called Otis into his office for an exit interview.

**Jack:** Come in, Otis. I really want to talk to you. I hope I can change your mind about leaving.
**Otis:** I don't think so.
**Jack:** Well, tell me why you want to go. Has some other company offered you more money?
**Otis:** No. In fact, I don't have another job; I'm just starting to look.
**Jack:** You've given us notice without having another job?
**Otis:** Well, I don't think this is the place for me!
**Jack:** What do you mean?
**Otis:** Let me see if I can explain. On my first day at work, I was told that formal classroom training in computers would not begin for a month. I was given a sales manual and told to read and study it for the rest of the day.

The next day, I was told that the technical library, where all the manuals on computers are kept, was in a mess and needed to be organized. That was to be my responsibility for the next three weeks.

The day before I was to begin computer school, my boss told me that the course had been delayed for another month. He said not to worry, because he was going to have James Crane, the branch's leading salesperson, give me some on-the-job training. I was told to accompany James on his calls. I'm supposed to start the school in two weeks, but I've made up my mind that this place is not for me.
**Jack:** Hold on a minute, Otis. That's the way it is for everyone in the first couple of months of employment in our industry. Any place you go will be the same. In fact, you had it better than I did. You should have seen what I did in my first couple of months.

**QUESTIONS**

1. What grade would you give Jack on this interview?
2. What suggestions do you have for Jack to help his company avoid similar problems of employee turnover in the future?
3. Should Jack find a way to make Otis change his mind? Why or why not?
4. Do you think Otis would change his mind and stay? Why or why not?

Study Alert

Examine your work e-mails for the last month. How many of them were truly effective in contributing to your productivity in your job? Why is it important to develop professional e-mail practices in a business setting?

Time is saved if managers can restrict answering e-mail to specific times in the day, but as managers get copied on multiple e-mails to "keep you in the loop," the inbox fills up with more and more messages that need nothing more than a cursory glance, and yet managers find themselves keeping the copies in case they might need them later. In addition, office politics now extends to e-mail where managers hold off responding to colleagues just to prove how busy they are, even if the response would require a simple one-line e-mail. Add to that the ease with which managers can "reply all," and the blessing of e-mail disappears.

The true blessing of e-mail is the speed with which you can communicate across the globe—so fast that the former wonders of fax machines now seem prehistoric by comparison.

### INTRANETS

An **intranet** is a private, corporate, computer network that uses Internet products and technologies to provide multimedia applications within organizations. An intranet connects people to people and people to information and knowledge within the organization; it serves as an "information hub" for the entire organization. Most organizations set up intranets primarily for employees, but they can extend to business partners and even customers with appropriate security clearance. Research has found that the biggest applications for intranets today are internal communications, followed by knowledge sharing and management information systems.[2]

**Intranet** A private, corporate, computer network that uses Internet products and technologies to provide multimedia applications within organizations.

## >> Networking

E-mail, cell phones, Blackberrys, and texting may have brought a whole new meaning to keeping in touch at work, but for most businesses the new disruptive technology is the change in social media represented by such tools as MySpace, Facebook, YouTube, and Twitter.

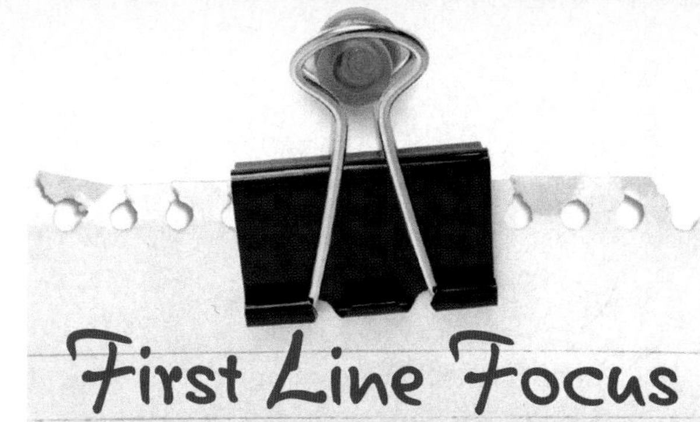

THINK BEFORE YOU CLICK . . .

### First Line Focus

*In October 2008, Google launched a new e-mail application called Mail Goggles.[3] Designed to protect you from sending e-mail while "under the influence," the application prompts you to solve math problems (at settings you can adjust) under a time limit as a means of testing your capacity to be sending e-mail at such a late hour (the software defaults to e-mail sent late on Friday and Saturday evenings but can be adjusted to any time frame). The "Jerry Maguire" lesson here? Poorly written or poorly thought-out e-mail can do irreparable harm to business relationships, your reputation, and sometimes even your career. If you find that e-mail is taking over your work life, block out time in your day to work on them, but never ever fire off a quick or emotionally charged response to someone who is ticking you off, unless you are prepared to live with the consequences. Remember, the "recall" function allows you to tell people that you want to recall the message you sent, but it's still in their inboxes, and now they're curious as to why you might want to recall it.*

### [PROGRESS] ✓questions

13. How do grapevines develop in organizations?
14. Why does the grapevine have a poor reputation?
15. Why might e-mail be considered both a blessing and a curse?
16. Why do managers set up intranets?

It seems that no sooner had managers figured out Web sites and blogs, than the playing field moved again, and customers suddenly got the upper hand with social media sites where they tell each other everything about everything—and often more than anyone could ever want to know. For businesses, this dramatic change in the environment has the potential to escalate customer satisfaction to a new level of connection—provided

*Social networking has completely altered the way consumers research products, as well as the way companies locate their target markets.*

those customers are happy. The old adage of a happy customer telling 3 or 4 people and an unhappy one telling 10 people must now be multiplied by 10 or 100. Happy customers not only tell associates but also have the technology to tell the world on their MySpace or Facebook pages.

## >> Getting It Wrong: The Problems of Poor Management Communication

It would seem that managers have more ways to communicate with their people and their customers than ever before. It is ironic therefore that even with all this new communication technology, managers do a poor job of what are considered basic skills.

Believing that information is power; keeping information on a need-to-know basis; delegating high-risk projects at the last minute in crisis mode with minimal explanation; making decisions and communicating those decisions with little or no input from the people affected by those decisions are activities that represent classic communications blunders. Such blunders take place every day in a business world where communication takes seconds rather than the days and weeks of what is now affectionately referred to as "snail mail." So if managers have all this technological wizardry at their disposal, how do they leverage it for maximum effect?

In his article "Six Secrets of Top Performers," John Finney referenced Watson Wyatt Worldwide's communication practice, and the six years' worth of data it had collected on the correlation between effective communication and financial performance for 750 companies around the world.[4] Companies that achieved the top scores in employee communication appeared to share the same six practices in common:

**Study Alert!**

**Does your company have a blog on its Web site? How about a Facebook page? Do you use Twitter? If these tools form a part of your company's communication strategy, research and document how each one contributes to your overall strategic plan. If your company doesn't use any of these tools, write a proposal showing your manager why they should be applied.**

- Focusing on the customer
- Engaging employees in business
- Improving managerial communication
- Managing change effectively
- Measuring the performance of communication programs
- Establishing a strong employee brand

We will return to these topics in subsequent chapters to see how these elements combine to produce truly effective organizational performance.

## >> Communication in International Business Activities

Communication in international business activities becomes more complicated in both the verbal and nonverbal communication processes. In verbal communication, the obvious problem of dealing with different languages exists. More than 3,000 languages are spoken, and about 100 of these are official languages of nations. English is the leading international language, and its leadership continues to grow. However, as anyone who has studied a modern language knows, verbally communicating with a person in another language complicates the communication process.

The nonverbal communication process is more complicated. Cultural differences play a significant role in nonverbal communication. For example, in the United States, people tend to place themselves about three feet apart when standing and talking. However,

# Thinking Critically 2.2

## >> Domino's Delivers a New Message

In these days of rapid technological advancement, most companies find themselves in a position of playing catch-up with the latest technology. This applies particularly to the world of social media. Companies that have just figured out how to use blogs and Facebook are now chasing Twitter and trying to figure out how to deal with "tweets" from their ever vigilant customers, as they increasingly crave closer and constant contact with their favorite brands.

On April 13, 2009, Domino's Pizza experienced a totally different side of the social media phenomenon when two now ex-employees posted a video on YouTube allegedly demonstrating some extremely unsavory food preparation practices on pizzas that they claimed were about to be delivered to loyal Domino's customers. Within two days the video "went viral" as viewers forwarded links to the video to friends, family members, group lists, and the like, reaching over one million views in less than two days.

On April 15, 2009, two days after the video was posted, Domino's responded by posting its own response on YouTube, a personal response from Patrick Doyle, president of Domino's USA. The attempt to reach the same mass audience fell short as the video had only been viewed 66,000 times by late the following day.

While the tone of the original video may have been in the same vein as the MTV show *Punk'd*, the fallout from the mass viewing has been considerable. Domino's originally elected to ignore the video, with the belief that giving any formal acknowledgment would only increase its popularity. That decision demonstrated a clear underestimation of the speed and power of social media mechanisms to spread a story—and particularly a story that would have mass appeal.

Once the extent of the damage was identified, Domino's response was classic crisis management—a personal apology from the company's senior executive, swift and firm action against the wrongdoers, and a sincere commitment to action with new processes to ensure that the event doesn't happen again. The key difference was the medium in which the crisis was addressed: no television or radio spots or newspaper ads. Since it was an online event, the response occurred online in the same forum in which the debacle first occurred—YouTube. Fortunately, someone in those crisis management meetings understood that the phrase "taking it to the streets" now has a whole new meaning.

QUESTIONS

1. Is there a general lesson for business managers here? What is it?
2. Was it reasonable to have expected Domino's senior management team to have a response plan in place for an event like this?
3. Did Domino's take too long to respond? Why or why not?
4. How would you have managed Domino's response to this media story? Why?

*Source:* B. L. Ochman, "Viewpoint: Lessons from the Amazon, Domino's Debacles," *BusinessWeek*, April 18, 2009; Stephanie Clifford, "Video Prank at Domino's Taints Brands," *The New York Times*, April 16, 2009; and Richard S. Levick, "Directorship: Domino's Discovers Social Media," *BusinessWeek*, April 21, 2009.

THE GRAPEVINE

You have worked at the same company with your best friend, Steven Tingelhoff, for the last ten years—in fact, he told you about the job and got you the interview. Steven works in the marketing department and is up for a promotion to marketing director—a position that he has been wanting for a long time. You work in sales, and on your weekly conference call, the new marketing director—someone recruited from outside the company—joins you. Your boss explains that although the formal announcement hasn't been made yet, the company felt it was important to get the new director up to speed as quickly as possible. He will be joining the company after completing his two weeks' notice with his current employer. Should you tell Steven what happened?

ETHICAL
MANAGEMENT
Who comes first:
your company or
your friend?

in the Middle East, individuals are likely to stand only a foot or so apart while conversing. This closeness obviously could intimidate an American manager.

There are no simple answers to the problems in communicating in international business activities. However, there are two things the manager should do: (1) learn the culture of the people with whom he or she communicates and (2) write and speak clearly and simply. Most people will have learned English in school and will not understand jargon or slang. As international business expands, these simple rules will become increasingly important.

From the PERSPECTIVE OF...

**A Taxicab Fleet Manager** New York City's 90,000 cab drivers are truly representative of the city's global population: African American, Colombian, Cuban, Dominican, Haitian, Iranian, Polish, Russian, and Salvadorian, to name just a few nationalities that deliver passengers safely around the city every day. With the modern taxi company representing multiple nationalities, what communication challenges does a manager face in working with such a diverse group of employees?

## >> Chapter Summary

Communication skills are critical to effective performance for any manager. Paying attention to the basics of good oral and written communication skills, as well as being able to respond to nonverbal communication is vital to productive relationships with all stakeholders—employees, colleagues, customers, and vendor partners. We have seen that top performance can have a positive effect on a company's bottom line just as poor communication can damage a reputation and a brand for months if not years. As we move closer to a truly global business world, the ability to communicate well across cultures and to leverage that ability through multiple social media tools will propel your career forward.

# For REVIEW >>

1. Define *communication.*

   Communication is the act of exchanging information. It can be used to inform, command, instruct, assess, influence, and persuade other people.

2. Explain why effective communication is an important management skill.

   It has been estimated that managers spend as much as 75 percent of their time communicating in one form or another. Effective communication is critical in every facet of a manager's role—for directing and motivating employees; for reporting to and updating supervisors; and for informing and persuading customers to purchase products or services.

3. Explain the significance of networking and social media in management communications.

   The availability of such tools as MySpace, Facebook, and Twitter has brought a new immediacy to personal and business communications. Messages to "friends" or "followers" can be sent almost immediately. This means that good news (sale prices, positive customer experiences) can be communicated to a much wider audience in a much shorter time frame. However, those tweets can also convey customer dissatisfaction and spread that dissatisfaction just as quickly and just as broadly.

4. Understand why it's still possible to communicate poorly.

   The increase in the number of available mechanisms to communicate (and the speed with which that communication can now take place) has, unfortunately, done little to improve the extent to which managers persist in communicating poorly with employees and customers alike. Examples of poor communication include believing that information is power; keeping information on a need-to-know basis; delegating high-risk projects at the last minute in crisis mode with minimal explanation; making decisions and communicating those decisions with little or no input from the people affected by those decisions.

5. Understand the challenges of communication in international business activities.

   There are no simple answers to the problems in communicating in international business activities. However, there are two things the manager should do: (1) learn the culture of the people with whom he or she communicates and (2) write and speak clearly and simply. Most people will have learned English in school and will not understand jargon or slang. As international business expands, these simple rules will become increasingly important.

## TONY GETS SOME FEEDBACK *(continued from page 25)*

Tony's new schedule policy started to create problems from the moment he posted the sign. First there were a few remarks about "Mr. Big" that Tony was sure were made deliberately as he walked by so that he could hear them. Then one or two employees started showing up late for their shifts with all kinds of excuses about buses being late, rides being late, or oversleeping, as if they had suddenly forgotten how to set their alarm clock!

The first test of the policy came when Matt Crocker, a track star from the local high school, failed to show for his shift altogether. When Tony confronted him the next day, the explanation Matt offered was, "I'm sorry Tony but my coach changed the times for our track practice at the last minute, and I couldn't get to a phone to call you or find someone to cover for me. You know coach has done this before, and Jerry used to work with me on my schedule, but with your new policy, I didn't have a lot of options."

Tony was left with a dilemma—should he make an example of Matt to enforce the policy? Or should he give the guy a break? "But," he thought, "if I give Matt a break, that will just encourage everyone else to ignore the policy, and I'll never cover my shifts. Pretty soon I'll be back to square one doing five versions of the schedule just like Jerry."

Tony decided to enforce the policy and took Matt off the schedule for the remainder of the week as a warning for not following the new policy. He felt bad about it but convinced himself that the tough decision would pay off in the long run.

The next morning two of the six folks scheduled for the morning shift failed to show up. Fortunately it was a slow morning, and the employees present were able to get the work done, but Tony was angry at what he saw as a direct challenge to his authority. As he sat angrily processing invoices in his office, Tanya, the shift leader, stopped by.

"Tony, can I talk to you for a minute?" Tanya asked.

"Sure," Tony said angrily.

"Look, I know it's my last week here and everything," continued Tanya, "but you have a real problem on your hands here, Tony. Being so strict about the schedule is really ticking some of your people off, and some are threatening to quit. They're even talking about calling Jerry to see if he can talk some sense into you. Did you ever think about asking them for suggestions or meeting with them to talk about the new schedule? Making such a dramatic change and then making an example of Matt like that looks to them like your new title is going to your head. He's been a good guy in the past, and it wasn't his fault that the coach changed the practice time."

### QUESTIONS

1. Should Tony have been surprised by the reactions of his crew?
2. Do you think the employees have the right to complain about the new schedule policy?
3. How could Tony have handled this differently?
4. What would you do now?

## Key Terms >>

**communication 26**

**e-mail 32**

**grapevine 32**

**interpersonal communication 27**

**intranet 34**

**perception 27**

**semantics 27**

1. Provide four reasons why effective communication is an important management skill.
2. What is active listening?
3. Describe some ways the grapevine can be used effectively in organizations.
4. Provide four examples of poor management communication.
5. Discuss why social media tools have such an important role to play.
6. Why is the ability to communicate across cultures so important?

## INTERNET In Action >>

1. Visit the National Communication Association (NCA) at **www.natcom.org**, and select the "Communication and the Workplace" community. Review the NCA member knowledge communities, and follow the link to the organizational communication division. Answer the following questions:
   a. What is the stated purpose of the organizational communication division?
   b. Follow the resources link, and explain what a "community of practice" is.
   c. Provide an example of a community of practice in a business environment.
   d. How would a business manager make use of the resources offered by this association?
2. Visit Toastmasters International at **www.toastmasters.org**. Answer the following questions:
   a. What is the Toastmasters Program, and how did it start?
   b. What are the vision and mission of Toastmasters International?
   c. Read the "Top 10 Tips for Public Speaking," and select the three tips that you found most useful.
   d. Would you ever consider joining the Toastmasters Program? Why or why not?

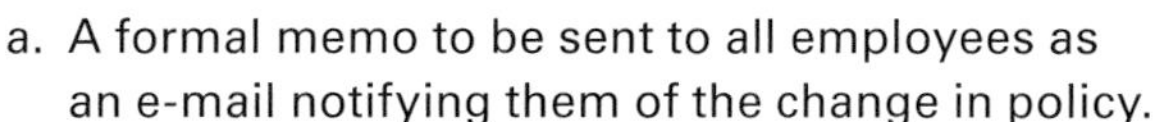

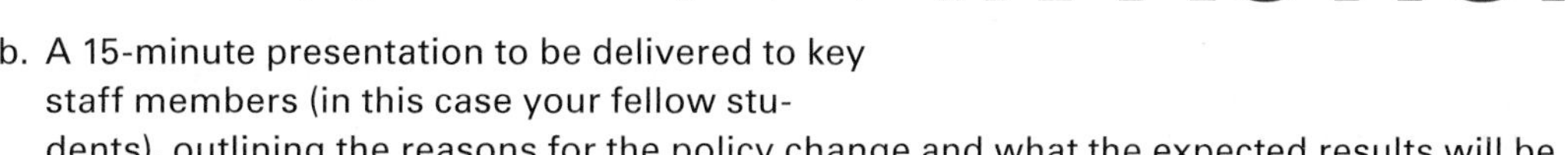

# << Team IN ACTION

1. **Communicating Management Policy**

   Divide into groups of two or three. Select a managerial policy change from the list below, and prepare the following:

   a. A formal memo to be sent to all employees as an e-mail notifying them of the change in policy.

   b. A 15-minute presentation to be delivered to key staff members (in this case your fellow students), outlining the reasons for the policy change and what the expected results will be.

   **Policy Change Topics**

   - The company on-site day care center is being closed to reduce costs.
   - Parking spaces in the front of the building are now reserved for senior managers only. Employees must now park at the far end of the parking lot.
   - Effective immediately, the entire company will be a nonsmoking area. No designated smoking areas will be provided.
   - The company health gym will be closed immediately because no one is using it.
   - The office cafeteria is being closed to make room for more office space.
   - Access to the building is being restricted to employees only. Family and friends will have to sign in and be issued visitor badges.

2. **The Gossip Game**

   This exercise is known by several names, including "telephone" or the "telephone game."

   Position the group in a line (or a circle) with each member standing close enough to the next so that he or she can whisper a phrase to his or her neighbor without players farther up or down the line overhearing that phrase. The first person in line may be given a phrase or be allowed to think of a phrase that is whispered quietly to the next person in line. The last person to receive the phrase announces it to the group, and a comparison is made with the original version of the phrase, often with hilarious results. If the class is big enough, use two groups with the same phrase and compare the outcomes.

   In January 2004, for example, Mac King, a magician-comedian at Harrah's Casino in Las Vegas, broke the world record for the longest game of telephone with 614 players. King started the game with the phrase, "Mac King is a comedy magic genius," and proceeded to predict the final whisper phrase that was locked in a briefcase before the game started. The final whisper prediction was "Macaroni cantaloupe knows the future," and King's prediction ended up being off by only one word.[5]

   *Key to success*: You cannot ask the person to repeat the phrase—pass on what you *thought* you heard.

   When you compare the original and final versions of the phrase, consider the following questions:

   **Questions**

   1. How distorted was the final version of the phrase when compared to the original?
   2. What would the likely consequences be if this were an important business communication?
   3. How can you prevent this kind of communication from happening at work?

# Case 2.1

## >> The Secret of BMW's Success

BMW's reputation for innovation can be traced to its equally innovative lateral management techniques.

BMW is one of a handful of global companies including Nokia and Raytheon that have turned to networks to manage day-to-day operations, overriding the classic management control pyramid. Those pioneering companies still turn to the management chain of command to set strategic goals, but workers have the freedom to forge teams across divisions and achieve targets in the best way possible—even if that way is unconventional. And they are encouraged to build ties across divisions to speed change.

Speed and organizational agility are increasingly vital to the auto industry, since electronics now make up some 20 percent of a car's value—and that level is rising. BMW figures some 90 percent of the innovations in its new models are electronics-driven. That requires once-slow-moving automakers to adapt to the lightning pace of innovation and change driving the semiconductor and software industries. Gone is the era of the 10-year model cycle. Now automakers must ram innovation into high gear to avoid being overtaken by the competition. That's especially true in the luxury-auto leagues, where market leaders must bring new innovations constantly onto the market, from podcasting for cars to infrared night vision systems. By shifting effective management of day-to-day operations to such human networks, which speed knowledge laterally through companies faster and better than old organizational models can, BMW has become as entrepreneurial as a tech start-up, consultants say.

How does BMW manage discipline with creativity and keep the anarchy of networks from careening out of control? Workers at the Bavarian automaker are encouraged from their first day on the job to build a network or web of personal ties to speed problem solving and innovation, be it in research and development (R&D), design, production, or marketing. Those ties run across divisions and up and down the chain of command.

When it comes to driving innovation, forget formal meetings, hierarchy, and stamps of approval. Each worker learns quickly that pushing fresh ideas is vital. BMW's complex customized production system, the polar opposite of Toyota's standardized lines, is easier to manage if workers feel empowered to drive change. Like Dell Computer, BMW configures its cars to customers' orders, so each auto moving down the production line is different.

Making sure the system works without a hitch requires savvy workers who continually suggest how to optimize processes. By contrast, companies that don't have lateral quickness are crippled in fast-moving technology-driven industries. Rigid hierarchies that stifle fresh ideas and slow reaction times are one problem facing General Motors and Ford. Once, giants like GM were king, dominating the market with their huge volume and purchasing muscle. Big is no longer the ticket to success, and the slow-moving bureaucracies that big companies are saddled with are now a major handicap.

Toyota's recent bloodied nose over product safety and delayed model recalls has further undermined the value of big bureaucracies, but with BMW's 2009 sales down around 30 percent in a poor market for luxury goods, it remains to be seen whether lateral agility will be enough to get the company through hard times.

### QUESTIONS

1. How is communication "across divisions and silos" different from communication "up and down the hierarchy"?
2. Define the term *boundaryless corporation*. You may want to do some research on Jack Welch and General Electric here.
3. If human networks "speed knowledge laterally through companies faster and better than old organizational models can," and employees are "encouraged from their first day on the job to build a network or web of personal ties to speed problem solving and innovation," how does BMW ensure that the right decisions are made?
4. Formal structures decide who to blame; informal structures decide how to get things done. What are the implications of this philosophy for a BMW manager?

*Source:* Gail Edmondson, "Innovation," BusinessWeek Online, October 16, 2006; Joseph R. Szczesny, "The Most Exciting Cars of 2010: Kia Soul," *Time*, August 17, 2009; and "Small Isn't Beautiful," *The Economist*, September 17, 2009.

# Case 2.2

## >> A Breakdown in Communication

David Walker was a senior attorney in a busy law practice, Finder, Minder, & Grinder (FMG). By fall 2009, he was well on his way to being made a partner, but during this especially busy time he became distracted by an office dispute between his trusted administrative assistant, Susan Emson, and a respected colleague, Ramya Kumar. He had already spent numerous hours listening to both sides tell their respective stories and was left with the growing sense that he had no answers. With two such polarized positions, he saw no immediate opportunity for compromise, and, more importantly, he was concerned as to how this dispute had been allowed to deteriorate this far without intervention.

### Susan Emson

Growing up as an army brat had been both difficult and exciting for Susan Emson. The family had moved frequently—so frequently that she had lived in many of the countries her geography teacher mentioned in class. Emson grew up with the understanding that she had the same mission in life as her father had in the military—do your work efficiently and with pride.

Most secretaries at FMG covered four or five lawyers, whose positions ranged from junior associates (who were with the firm less than three years), midlevel associates, senior associates, and perhaps one senior attorney (which meant being made partner was next and that meant there would be more work). Until Ramya Kumar was added, Emson's supervisors included two junior associates, one midlevel associate, one senior associate, and David Walker, a senior attorney. She also had to do some work for a former supervisor, who had become partner and had his own assistant, but still asked Emson to complete certain projects for him. Her favorite supervisor was Walker, who had an infectious personality and a seemingly breezy, lighthearted approach to both life and work. Despite his good-humored approach, Walker was a trailblazer and on the fast track—he was deadline-driven, and when he needed something from Emson, he generally wanted it right away. Emson had learned how to work with Walker, and they had come to a mutual understanding of how best to deal with Walker's work style and pace.

As the years went by, Emson began to feel that her extra effort was rewarded with an increased number of lawyers to work for. Given her contributions and growing responsibilities, however, Emson had the perception of inequity in the firm. New assistants were hired at higher wages, making the gap between Emson's pay and theirs increasingly smaller.

Emson's workload increased again in June 2009, when Kumar was added. Although Kumar and Emson knew who the other one was from working in the same organization, they really didn't know each other. Walker had heard through the grapevine that Kumar had had trouble with her former assistant and that she had specifically asked for Emson.

### Ramya Kumar

Ramya Kumar grew up in an affluent family from Delhi, India, and as an undergraduate attended the University of Calcutta, where she earned a BA in political science. She moved to Atlanta to work for an India-based information technology (IT) company, married a physician, and decided to go back to school. Kumar earned her doctor of law (JD) degree from Emory University's law school. After she spent two years as junior council for the city of Atlanta, she joined FMG as a junior associate.

With a mountain of documents piled on her desk, Kumar had gained a reputation for her ability to draft legal briefs and affidavits. She did acknowledge being somewhat disorganized when it came to paperwork, which made an organized assistant a critical part of her support team.

*Continued on next page*

Continued from page 43

Kumar would frequently write field notes and research on legal pads as well as banging out documents tying together challenging issues and arguments. A week after having Emson assigned as her assistant, Kumar took the combined notes and more formal documents for Emson to organize into one document or "brief." After making the same request with several other briefs, Kumar noticed that when she asked Emson to prepare the briefs in a couple of days, Emson always seemed to answer with a negative response like "if I have time," or "I need to finish David's editing first." Those responses were beginning to irritate Kumar.

### Black Line, Red Line

The strained relationship reached a breaking point when Kumar approached Emson with a particularly lengthy brief. The document had run through numerous drafts as it was being prepared for litigation. The law firm had software that allowed comparisons of two different documents, as well as a comparison of successive drafts of the same document. This process was referred to as "black lining" for different documents and "red lining" for drafts of the same document. Kumar wanted the lengthy brief cleaned up after spending several evenings working on it and then giving it to a junior associate to read and clarify some arguments. Time was getting short, and she needed to focus on other pressing issues, so Kumar took the old version of the brief, her version of the brief, and the junior associate's version to Emson. She asked Emson to compare the briefs and produce a clean final version. Emson immediately asked, "Should I be doing this?" Emson wondered if this task was a legal content issue, which was something administrative assistants were not qualified to judge. Kumar, frustrated that Emson never seemed to agree to do any work for her, asked: "Why am I always being pushed back? Why am I not getting what I need?"

Both Kumar and Emson confided in David Walker about issues that were upsetting them about each other. A skilled people person, Walker listened to what they both told him. He was very careful not to judge. Kumar felt that Emson always placed her requests in the "will do it if I have time" box and never seemed to give priority to Kumar's work. She told Walker that every time she asked Emson if her requests were completed, Emson developed a snippy attitude. Kumar asked Walker, "Why can't I ask her when I can get something done?" Although Walker treated the question as rhetorical, he smiled, since Emson had just told him that Kumar hounded her two or three times a week about items and had unreasonable deadlines. After hearing out Kumar's complaints, Walker encouraged her to take a leadership role and talk to Emson face to face about those issues. In the meantime, Emson went to see Jim Thomas, director of human resources (HR), about her problems with Kumar and asked to be reassigned.

> Given her contributions and growing responsibilities, Emson had the perception of inequity in the firm. New assistants were hired at higher wages, making the gap between Emson's pay and theirs increasingly smaller.

**QUESTIONS**

1. Summarize the work styles of the three key players here, and show how the differences contributed to the apparent communication breakdown.
2. What could David Walker have done differently to prevent this from happening?
3. Is there room for a compromise solution here? Why or why not?
4. What should David Walker do now?

***Source:*** Adapted from G. Yemen and M. N. Davidson, *Finder, Minder and Grinder: The Charges and Rebuttal* (University of Virginia Darden School Foundation, 2005).

# Case 2.3

## >> Better Health Care through Communication

Fairview Health Services is a comprehensive, regional medical system headquartered in Minneapolis and employing more than 19,000 people across 200 different facilities throughout the state of Minnesota. In fall 2005, Fairview launched a new benefit program called Ultimate Choice—the latest step in an ongoing attempt to engage Fairview employees in personal health consumerism.

Ultimate Choice included a create-your-own medical plan called MedChoice that offered employees more choices and flexibility in their health coverage. As part of this initiative, Fairview provided employees with an interactive tool that modeled the cost associated with the company's health plans. Employees were able to calculate various levels of copays, deductibles, coinsurance, and pharmacy benefits for themselves and the family members they cover. For employees not covered by a union contract, Ultimate Choice also included a Rewards Budget that employees could use to purchase benefits, including medical, dental, life insurance, disability insurance, paid time off, and other benefits. Fairview also provided a health risk assessment for employees that encouraged employees to learn more about their own personal health and how to manage their wellness. Together, these initiatives encouraged Fairview employees to take a greater role in assessing and using their benefits.

> Despite employees' desire for greater benefit flexibility, customizing a health plan and enrolling online were major changes for people accustomed to receiving medical benefits through standard prepackaged plans that carried minimal, if any, deductibles, copays, or coinsurance.

A significant culture shift accompanied the Ultimate Choice program–online benefits enrollment. Fairview facilitated this culture shift with a comprehensive communication campaign that provided remarkable results. More than 95 percent of the eligible workforce participated in the Ultimate Choice program and enrolled in their benefits via new online tools.

A workforce assessment revealed that many Fairview employees had minimal benefits and computer literacy. As a result, the key to ensuring the success of Ultimate Choice and enrolling virtually all Fairview's diverse employee workforce online was a comprehensive education and communication campaign that began in advance of the late fall enrollment period. The communication campaign was launched seven weeks prior to the enrollment period and was initiated by sending a newsletter to employees. The newsletter reinforced the connection between benefits and total compensation and shared information about health care trends. The newsletter was the first step in preparing employees for the coming changes. The communication campaign was ongoing throughout the enrollment period and continued 5 weeks beyond the end of the enrollment period, for a total of 18 weeks.

*Continued on next page*

Continued from page 45

Fairview recognized the need for different communication channels and methods to reach the entire workforce, from organizationwide e-mail announcements to personalized communication with employees. It also developed a volunteer program through which "benefit tutors" met with and assisted employees with diverse learning needs and from various ethnic communities, using materials in six different languages.

### Need for Flexibility

Because of varying needs, many Fairview employees asked for more flexibility in their benefit choices. And even though they had enjoyed first-rate coverage long after local competitors had adopted more restrictive plans, Fairview employees reported only moderate satisfaction with their benefits.

Through a range of communication methods—from one-on-one coaching to eye-catching, professionally designed newsletters and fact sheets with clear, consistent messages—Fairview introduced and positioned Ultimate Choice as the response to employees' desire for more choice. At the same time, employees were made aware that Fairview was working hard to stabilize rising benefit costs for both employees and the organization—and to continue as a leader in the health care market.

Despite employees' desire for greater benefit flexibility, customizing a health plan and enrolling online were major changes for people accustomed to receiving medical benefits through standard prepackaged plans that carried minimal, if any, deductibles, copays, or coinsurance.

To address that challenge, in the months preceding the enrollment period all employees were given individual e-mail accounts and 24-hour access to the company intranet. Basic computer courses were offered to employees at no charge. Computer labs across the health system were staffed to accommodate employees on all three shifts and provide instruction to employees, and 20 computer kiosks were set up throughout Fairview facilities for those without computer access.

Because of the assistance and communication provided throughout the enrollment period, employees came to accept and embrace the online plan selection and enrollment, which allowed them to create up to 52 unique MedChoice plan combinations.

A key component of the Ultimate Choice communication campaign was developing strong advocates and securing buy in from the Fairview System leadership team—600 clinical and administrative leaders from across the organization—as well as from human resource directors and staff.

### Advocates for Change

A key component of the Ultimate Choice communication campaign was developing strong advocates and securing buy-in from the Fairview System leadership team—600 clinical and administrative leaders from across the organization—as well as from human resource directors and staff. These leaders were provided tools and resources to promote the benefits of Ultimate Choice and to support employees.

Ultimate Choice was introduced by the chief executive officer and the senior vice president of human resources at a meeting of the Fairview System leadership team to ensure that all 600 leaders received the same message. The senior vice president of human resources presented the business case for Ultimate Choice to the leadership team. The senior vice president of human resources also presented the plan design and implementation plan during this briefing. The business case for change included data on increasing employer health costs and Fairview's need to respond to changing workforce demographics by providing more flexibility through innovative benefit options that helped employees not only to understand their benefits but to appreciate them as well. The business case also predicted that Ultimate Choice would better position Fairview as it competed for talent in an extremely tight labor market.

The process of creating advocates among Fairview leaders continued after the general meeting. The core planning team—led by the senior vice president of human resources and made up of Fairview experts in human resources, benefits, compensation, employee services, information technology, and communication—held eight briefings with front-line supervisors in each of Fairview's divisions during which the new health plan was presented in greater detail. The goal of these meetings was to help managers think through how the change would impact their employees and what it would mean for managers in terms of supporting employees through the changes. Managers were not expected to become benefits experts but to facilitate the change process.

Managers also were asked to be mindful that their employees might have complicated health care needs that weren't evident in the workplace. For example, an employee might have a chronic condition that they would like to keep private or a very ill child at home. Managers were encouraged to reach out to every employee so that each received the personal attention needed to make the right health plan decisions.

Throughout the communication campaign, the leadership group was given a commitment that there would be no surprises; they would be given specific details about benefit changes at least one week before they were announced to employees. The core planning team pledged to provide resources to managers as needed, to follow up with employees who had questions about the changes, and to readily accept managers' requests for a meeting or assistance.

The fundamental challenge to communicating this major change was that for the first time, employees would be required to understand and weigh the fundamentals of insurance. They needed to understand not only copays and deductibles but also what their employer must pay to provide each plan.

To educate employees in these fundamentals, three core documents were used throughout the campaign: an intranet e-mail guide, a benefits glossary with explanations of important terms, and a benefits overview. These documents were critical in alerting employees to the nature of the change, instructing them on how to access technology, and helping them understand the terminology in the newsletters and other communication materials.

### Continued Communication Support

Fairview's message to employees continues to be, "We are committed to providing you with the resources and information you need to make the most out of your benefits package." The success of Fairview's initiative in the face of many challenges—including the need to communicate to some of the most diverse audiences in the American workforce—demonstrates the effectiveness of a serious and thoughtful approach to benefits communication planning and execution.

As employers seek additional approaches and technologies to encourage health consumerism, it will become even more important to communicate new initiatives effectively. With more choices comes more responsibility, and it is easy to imagine employees being overwhelmed by new, complex changes. The key to successful introduction and support of leading-edge benefits programs will continue to be a well-thought-out communication strategy.

**QUESTIONS**

1. Why would Fairview want employees to "take a greater role in assessing and using their benefits"?
2. How important was the initial workplace assessment to the success of the communication campaign? What do you think would have happened if it had skipped that step of the process?
3. Which message do you think carried the greater impact for employees—that Fairview was working to control costs or that the company was responding to requests for greater choice in benefit options? Explain your answer.
4. What do you think was the most successful element of the communication campaign? Why?

*Source:* Adapted from Cindy Fruitrail and Valerie Wedin, "Creating Better Health Care Consumers: A Case Study," *Compensation and Benefits Review,* vol. 38, no. 5, 2006, p. 40.

CHAPTER 3

"I have to be wrong a certain number of times in order to be right a certain number of times. However, in order to be either, I must first make a decision."

Frank. N. Giampietro

# PLANNING AND DECISION MAKING

LEARNING OUTCOMES

After studying this chapter, you will be able to:

1 Define *planning,* and distinguish between formal and functional plans.

2 Contrast strategic planning with operational planning.

3 Understand different types of objectives.

4 Explain how decision making differs from problem solving, and compare and contrast rational and intuitive approaches to decision making.

5 Explain the decision maker's environment and the conditions for making a decision.

## THE WORLD OF WORK Tony tries another approach

Tony Davis's first attempt at putting his stamp on the Taco Barn hadn't gone well. All the time he had expected to gain by making the staff schedule less open to negotiation had been lost in finding coverage for employees who couldn't or didn't show for their assigned shifts. Tanya, his soon-to-be ex-shift leader had finally set him straight about the anger and frustration his new approach of "my way or the highway" was creating among his staff. His decision to make an example of Matt by keeping him off the schedule for a week after failing to show for his assigned shift was supposed to send a clear message of how serious Tony was about this scheduling issue. In reality, all he had succeeded in doing, as Tanya pointed out, was making the staff angrier. Everyone thought Matt was a good guy who was struggling to balance his school and sports commitments as well as his work shifts. Punishing him for not calling in because his coach changed the time of the practice was, in their eyes, too harsh. Some had even suggested calling Jerry, the former store manager, to see if he could talk some sense into Tony.

"Great," said Tony, "here I am trying to make this place more efficient by freeing some time from my schedule to be more available in the restaurant, and my staff is screaming for Jerry to come back. Now what do I do? If I go back on the new policy, they'll see me as being weak, and they'll complain about every new change from now on."

"Why do you feel the need to be in the restaurant more, Tony?" asked Tanya, who was doing her best to help Tony work through the unexpected negative feedback. "You've got a good crew here—they don't need to be watched every minute of the day."

"It's not about watching them every minute of the day," replied Tony. "I know this is a good crew—so good in fact that a few of them could really do well as future managers with Taco Barn. Plus you're leaving, and until I replace your position, I need to be out there helping them, not sitting in the office working on the schedule for hours at a time."

"Did you ever think about telling them that, instead of making such a dramatic change and then making an example of Matt?" said Tanya. "It looks to them like your new title is going to your head when all you want to do is be more available to help them."

### QUESTIONS

1. What assumptions did Tony make in introducing his new scheduling policy?
2. Which type of decision-making approach did Tony use here? Review the material on intuitive and rational approaches to decision making for help here.
3. How could Tony change his interpersonal skills to fix this communication breakdown?
4. What should Tony do now?

# >> The Planning Process

*Planning* is the process of deciding which objectives to pursue during a future time period and how to achieve those objectives. It is the primary management function and is inherent in everything a manager does. This chapter discusses the basics of the planning function and how this function relates to strategic management.

## WHY PLAN?

It is futile for a manager to attempt to perform any other management functions without having a plan. Managers who attempt to organize without a plan find themselves reorganizing on a regular basis. The manager who attempts to staff without a plan will be constantly hiring and firing employees. Motivation is almost impossible in an organization undergoing continuous reorganization and high employee turnover.

Planning enables a manager or an organization to actively affect rather than passively accept the future. By setting objectives and charting a course of action, the organization commits itself to "making it happen." This allows the organization to affect the future. Without a planned course of action, the organization is much more likely to sit back, let things happen, and then react to those happenings in a crisis mode.

**Study Alert !**

Consider your current job or a job you held in the past. How often does your company plan? How are those plans communicated to employees? How often do you track performance against that plan?

Planning provides a means for actively involving personnel from all areas of the organization in the management of the organization. Involvement produces a multitude of benefits. First, input from throughout the organization improves the quality of the plans; good suggestions can come from any level in the organization. Involvement in the planning process also enhances the overall understanding of the organization's direction. Knowing the big picture can minimize friction among departments, sections, and individuals. For example, through planning, the sales department can understand and appreciate the objectives of the production department and their relationship to organizational objectives. Involvement in the planning process fosters a greater personal commitment to the plan; the plan becomes "our" plan rather than "their" plan. Positive attitudes created by involvement improve overall organizational morale and loyalty.

**Formal Plan** A written, documented plan developed through an identifiable process.

**Functional Plan** Plan that originates from the functional areas of an organization, such as production, marketing, finance, and personnel.

Planning can also have positive effects on managerial performance. Studies have demonstrated that employees who stress planning earn high performance ratings from supervisors.[1] They have also shown that planning has a positive impact on the quality of work produced.[2] While some have proved inconclusive, several studies have reported a positive relationship between planning and certain measures of organizational success, such as profits and goals.[3] One explanation that would fit all the findings to date is that good planning, as opposed to the mere presence or absence of a plan, is related to organizational success.

Whether a business is locally owned or nationwide, management needs to create and implement formal plans.

A final reason for planning is the mental exercise required to develop a plan. Many people believe the experience and knowledge gained throughout the development of a plan force managers to think in a future- and contingency-oriented manner; this can result in great advantages over managers who are static in their thinking.

## FORMAL PLANNING

All managers plan. The difference lays in the methods they employ and the extent to which they plan. Most planning is carried out on an informal or casual basis. This occurs when planners do not record their thoughts but carry them around in their heads. A **formal plan** is a written, documented plan developed through an identifiable process. The appropriate degree of sophistication depends on the needs of the individual managers and the organization itself. The environment, size, and type of business are factors that typically affect the planning needs of an organization.

## FUNCTIONAL PLANS

Plans are often classified by function or use. The most frequently encountered types of **functional plans** are sales and marketing plans, production plans, financial plans, and personnel plans. Sales and marketing plans are for developing new products or services and selling both present and future products or services. Production plans deal with producing the desired

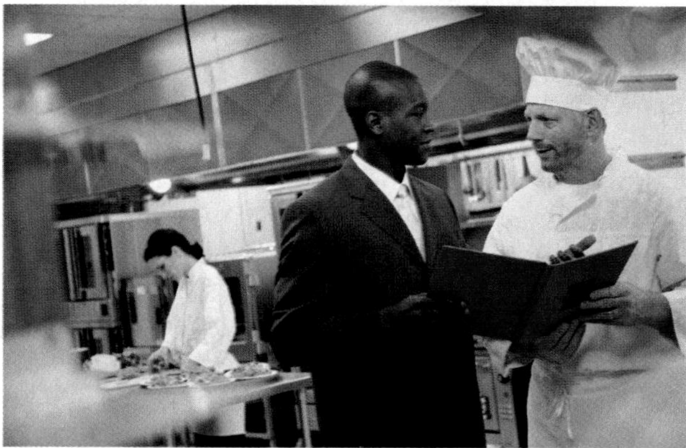

*Regardless of a person's occupation, long- and short-range objectives are essential. What are some of the differences in objectives for these two managers?*

products or services on a timely schedule. Financial plans deal primarily with meeting the financial commitments and capital expenditures of the organization. Personnel plans relate to the human resource needs of the organization. Many functional plans are interrelated and interdependent. For example, a financial plan would obviously be dependent on production, sales, and personnel plans.

## THE PLANNING HORIZON: SHORT RANGE, INTERMEDIATE, AND LONG RANGE

The length of the planning horizon is relative and varies somewhat from industry to industry, depending on the specific environment and activity. What may be long range when operating in a rapidly changing environment, such as the electronics industry, may be short range when operating in a relatively static environment, such as the brick manufacturing industry. In practice, however, **short-range plans** generally cover up to one year, whereas **long-range plans** span at least three to five years, with some extending as far as 20 years into the future. While long-range planning is possible at any level in the organization, it is carried out primarily at the top levels.

**Short-Range Plans** Plans that generally cover up to one year.

**Long-Range Plans** Plans that span at least 3 to 5 years; some extend as far as 20 years into the future.

**Strategic Planning** Top-level, long-range planning.

**Operations or Tactical Planning** Short-range planning that concentrates on the formulation of functional plans; done primarily by middle- to lower-level managers.

*Intermediate plans* cover the time span between short-range and long-range plans. From a pragmatic standpoint, intermediate plans generally cover from one to three or one to five years, depending on the horizon covered by the long-range plan. Usually, intermediate plans are derived from long-range plans, and short-range plans are derived from intermediate plans. For example, if the long-range plan calls for a 40 percent growth in sales by the end of five years, the intermediate plan should outline the necessary steps to be taken over the time span covering one to five years. Short-range plans would outline what actions are necessary within the next year.

## OPERATIONAL VERSUS STRATEGIC PLANS

**Strategic planning** is equivalent to top-level, long-range planning. It is the planning process applied at the highest levels of the organization, covering a relatively long period and affecting many parts of the organization. **Operations or tactical planning** is short-range planning and concentrates on the formulation of functional plans. Production schedules and day-to-day plans are examples of operations planning.

However, the distinctions between strategic and operations planning are relative, not absolute. The major difference is the level at which the planning is done. Strategic planning is done primarily by top-level managers; operational planning is done by managers at all levels in the organization and especially by middle- and lower-level managers.

## CONTINGENCY PLANS

Regardless of how thorough plans are, something will always go wrong. What goes wrong is often beyond the control of the manager. For example, the economy takes an unexpected dip, a machine breaks down, or the arrival of a new piece of equipment is delayed. When such things happen, managers must

## Thinking Critically 3.1

### >> Ryanair—The Little Airline That Could

On May 23, 1986, Tony Ryan's fledgling airline, Ryanair, made its first flight from Dublin to London's Luton airport for a round-trip price of £99, which was less than half the price of British Airways and competing Irish airline Aer Lingus. Two years later, Ryanair had lost £7 million and was on track to lose much more.

Twenty years later, Ryanair reported half-year profits of €408 million, up 24 percent on the same period for the preceding year, based on increased passenger traffic of 20 percent to 26.6 million passenger trips. The key to such an amazing change of fortunes? Detailed planning of every aspect of Ryanair's business. Borrowing best practices from American low-cost carriers such as Southwest and JetBlue, Ryanair's unwavering focus on revenue management and cost control has produced a business model that is far more robust that any of its closest competitors.

When Boeing stress-tested Ryanair's operations in 1998 as part of its due diligence process for the sale of 25 new planes, Boeing's auditors were unable to find any three-month period when Ryanair would not be profitable during the terms of the aircraft leases. Even with forecasted demand drops, fuel price fluctuations, and currency exchange volatility, Ryanair's operations were solid.

How cost conscious is the airline? Consider the story of CEO Michael O'Leary's foray into the World Wide Web. Persuaded that Web tickets would be free of travel agent commissions, O'Leary agreed that Ryanair would build a Web site. Quotes from conventional Web site companies came in at about £3 million. O'Leary chose an alternative option of two high school students who quoted him £15,500. After the site was delivered on time as agreed (and went on to become one of the highest-grossing e-commerce sites of the time), O'Leary attempted to negotiate the contract down to £12,000, even after the purchase order had been issued.

O'Leary's ferocious attention to cost control and revenue growth seems to be destined to propel Ryanair ever forward. In response to questions about the long-term viability of regional airlines in the face of volatile fuel prices, Finance Director Neil Sorahan revealed that Ryanair had plans to carry 87 to 100 million passengers in 2012, and 200 million in 2022, based on market share taken away from Alitalia in Italy and Iberia in Spain. The long-term objective? A transatlantic operation based on 31 bases in Europe providing a feeder network—provided it can get long-haul aircraft at the right price.

**QUESTIONS**

1. Is there a secret to Ryanair's success? What is it?
2. Can any regional airline do this? Why or why not.
3. How much of Ryanair's cost consciousness is based on O'Leary?
4. Do you think it will achieve its objectives? Why or why not?

*Source:* "Ryanair's Plans to Dominate Europe," *Travel Trade Gazette,* December 12, 2008, p. 23; A. Ruddock, *"In the slipstream of O'Leary," Management Today,* August 2007, p. 33; and J. Bain, "Ryanair—How a Small Irish Airline Conquered Europe," *Journal of Revenue and Pricing Management,* 2008, vol. 7, pp. 117–18.

be prepared with a backup, a contingency, plan. **Contingency plans** address the what-ifs of the manager's job. Contingency planning gets the manager in the habit of being prepared and knowing what to do if something does go wrong. Naturally, contingency plans cannot be prepared for all possibilities. What managers should do is identify the most critical assumptions of the current plan and then develop contingencies for problems that have a reasonable chance of occurring. A good approach is to examine the current plan from the point of view of what could go wrong. Contingency planning is most needed in rapidly changing environments.

## OBJECTIVES

If you don't know where you're going, how will you know when you get there? **Objectives** are statements outlining what a manager is trying to achieve; they give an organization and its members direction and purpose. Few managers question the importance of objectives, only what the objectives should be.

As discussed in Chapter 1, management is a process of coordinating an organization's resources—land, labor, and capital—in the attainment of organizational objectives or goals. Management cannot be properly conducted without pursuing specific objectives. Managers today and in the future must concentrate on where they and their organizations are headed.

It is also important to realize that managers and employees at all levels in an organization should have objectives; everyone should know what he or she is trying to achieve. One key for organizational success is for the objectives at all different levels to mesh together.

**Long-Range Objectives** generally go beyond the organization's current fiscal year. Long-range objectives must support and not conflict with the organizational mission. However, they may be quite different from the organizational mission, yet still support it. For instance, the organizational mission of a fast-food restaurant might be to provide rapid, hot-food service to a certain area of the city. One long-range objective might be to increase sales to a specific level within the next four years. Obviously, this objective is quite different from the organizational mission, but it still supports the mission.

**Short-Range Objectives** should be derived from an in-depth evaluation of long-range objectives. Such an evaluation should result in a listing of priorities of the long-range objectives. Then short-range objectives can be set to help achieve the long-range objectives.

Objectives should be clear, concise, and quantified when possible. Affected personnel should clearly understand what is expected. Normally, multiple objectives should be used to reflect the desired performance of a given organizational unit or person. From a top-level perspective, objectives should span all major areas of the organization. A problem with one dominant objective is that it is often achieved at the expense of other desirable objectives. For example, if production were the only objective, quality may suffer in attempts to realize maximum production. While objectives in different areas may serve as checks on one another, they should be reasonably consistent among themselves.

Objectives should be dynamic; that is, they should be reevaluated as the environment and opportunities change. Objectives for organizations usually fall into one of four general categories: (1) profit oriented, (2) service to customers, (3) employee needs and well-being, and (4) social responsibility. Even nonprofit organizations must be concerned with profit in the sense that they generally must operate within a budget. Another scheme for classifying organizational objectives is (1) primary, (2) secondary, (3) individual, and (4) societal. Primary objectives relate directly to profit. Secondary objectives apply to specific units of the organization (e.g., departmental objectives). Individual objectives directly concern the organization's employees. Finally, societal objectives relate to the local, national, and global communities. The following list outlines areas for establishing objectives in most organizations:[4]

1. *Profitability.* Measures the degree to which the firm is attaining an acceptable level of profits; usually expressed in terms of profits before or after taxes, return on investment, earnings per share, or profit-to-sales ratios.
2. *Markets.* Reflects the firm's position in its marketplace; expressed in terms of share of the market, dollar or unit volume in sales, or niche in the industry.
3. *Productivity.* Measures the efficiency of internal operations; expressed as a ratio of inputs to outputs, such as number of items or services produced per unit of time.

**Contingency Plans** Plans that address the what-ifs of a manager's job and that get the manager in the habit of being prepared and knowing what to do if something does go wrong.

**Objectives** Statements outlining what a manager is trying to achieve.

**Long-Range Objectives** Objectives that go beyond the current fiscal year and that must support and not conflict with the organizational mission.

**Short-Range Objectives** Objectives that are derived from an in-depth evaluation of long-range objectives and then set to help achieve the long-range objectives.

4. *Product.* Describes the introduction or elimination of products or services; expressed in terms of when a product or service will be introduced or dropped.
5. *Financial resources.* Reflects goals relating to the funding needs of the firm; expressed in terms of capital structure, new issues of common stock, cash flow, working capital, dividend payments, and collection periods.
6. *Physical facilities.* Describes the physical facilities of the firm; expressed in terms of square feet of office or plant space, fixed costs, units of production, or similar measurements.
7. *Research and innovation.* Reflects the research, development, or innovation aspirations of the firm; usually expressed in terms of dollars to be expended.
8. *Organization structure.* Describes objectives relating to changes in the organizational structure and related activities; expressed in terms of a desired future structure or network of relationships.
9. *Human resources.* Describes the human resource assets of the organization; expressed in terms of absenteeism, tardiness, number of grievances, and training.
10. *Social responsibility.* Refers to the commitments of the firm regarding society and the environment; expressed in terms of types of activities, number of days of service, or financial contributions.

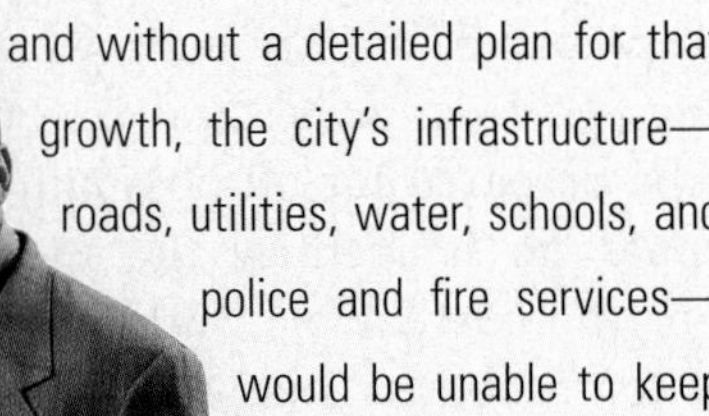

**From the PERSPECTIVE OF...**

**A City Planner**

For cities large and small, growth is a fact of life, and without a detailed plan for that growth, the city's infrastructure—roads, utilities, water, schools, and police and fire services—would be unable to keep up. What other factors would be important in the development of raw land?

**Management by Objectives (MBO)** A philosophy based on converting organizational objectives into personal objectives. It assumes that establishing personal objectives elicits employee commitment, which leads to improved performance.

**Policies** Broad, general guides to action that constrain or direct the attainment of objectives.

**Procedure** Series of related steps or tasks expressed in chronological order for a specific purpose.

## MANAGEMENT BY OBJECTIVES

One approach to setting objectives that has enjoyed considerable popularity is the concept of **management by objectives (MBO)**. MBO is a philosophy based on converting organizational objectives into personal objectives. It assumes that establishing personal objectives elicits employee commitment, which leads to improved performance. MBO has also been called management by results, goals and control, work planning and review, and goals management. All these programs are similar and follow the same basic process.

MBO works best when the objectives of each organizational unit are derived from the objectives of the next higher unit in the organization. Thus, the objective-setting process requires involvement and collaboration among the various levels of the organization; this joint effort has beneficial results. First, people at each level become more aware of organizational objectives. The better they understand the organization's objectives, the better they see their roles in the total organization. Second, the objectives for an individual are jointly set by the person and the superior; there are give-and-take negotiating sessions between them. Achieving self-formulated objectives can improve motivation and, thus, job performance. MBO is discussed in further depth in Chapter 11.

### [PROGRESS] ✓questions

1. Distinguish between formal and functional planning.
2. What is the difference between strategic planning and operational planning?
3. What are the four general categories of objectives for organizations?
4. What are the 10 areas for establishing objectives in most organizations?

## POLICIES

To help in the objective-setting process, a manager can rely to some extent on policies and procedures developed by the organization. **Policies** are broad, general guides to action that constrain or direct objective attainment. Policies do not tell organizational members exactly what to do, but they do establish the boundaries within which members

**THE CHIPS ARE DOWN**

The New England Potato Chip Company has been a well-respected food company for many years. Recently, the company has decided to expand into new markets to maintain an aggressive growth plan. To do this, it will need to attract new investors, and to accomplish that, it will need to show it is capable of producing a solid return on investments each year.

In keeping with these objectives, a policy has been introduced that reduces the finished products' inventory to a rock bottom level each June 30, which is the end of the company's fiscal year. Why? The lower the inventory, the less money tied up. This situation, in turn, tends to put the company in a better cash position at year-end, which means that more money can be passed on to the stockholders as dividends.

As the recently hired production manager, Pat Curl realizes there is a downside to this policy. With inventory levels on June 30 lower than at any other point during the year but with demand for potato chips higher than usual, the net result is an inability to meet the total customer demand for various types of potato chips. In fact, once inventory levels are reduced, it will take more than one month to get the process back to normal and running smoothly again.

ETHICAL
MANAGEMENT
How do you alert a supervisor to a potential problem?


The effect, Pat predicts, will be both lost sales at year-end and a number of operations problems associated with a low-inventory situation.

For Pat, the dilemma is whether or not to confront senior management with these problems. What should Pat do?

*Source:* "How the Chips Fall" copyright © 2010 Institute for Global Ethics®. All rights reserved. The Institute for Global Ethics®, a 501c(3) non-profit, provides ethics training, membership, and online downloadable resources. Founded by Dr. Rushworth M. Kidder (1990). Visit our website at **www.globalethics.org**

must operate. For example, a policy of "answering all written customer complaints in writing within 10 days" does not tell a manager exactly how to respond, but it does say it must be done in writing within 10 days. Policies create an understanding among members of a group that makes the actions of each member more predictable to other members.

Procedures and rules differ from policies only in degree. In fact, they may be thought of as low-level policies. A **procedure** is a series of related steps or tasks expressed in chronological order for a specific purpose. Procedures define in step-by-step fashion the methods through which policies are achieved. Procedures emphasize details. **Rules** require specific actions to be taken or not to be taken in a given situation. Rules leave little doubt about what is to be done. They permit no flexibility or deviation. Unlike procedures, rules do not have to specify sequence. For example, "No smoking in the conference room" is a rule. In reality, procedures and rules are subsets of policies. The primary purpose is guidance. The differences lie in the range of applicability and the degree of flexibility. A no-smoking rule is much less flexible than a procedure for handling customer complaints. However, a rule can have a clear relationship to an objective. For example, a no-smoking rule may help the organization reach a stated objective of "a cleaner and safer corporate environment."

**Rules** Require specific actions to be taken or not to be taken in a given situation.

## >> Making Decisions

Some authors use the term *decision maker* to mean *manager*. However, although managers are decision makers, not all decision makers are managers. For example, a person who sorts fruit or vegetables is required to make decisions, but not as a manager. However, all managers, regardless of their positions in the organization, must make decisions in the pursuit of organizational goals. In fact, decision making pervades all the basic management functions: planning, organizing, staffing, leading, and controlling. Although each function requires different types of decisions, all of them require decisions. Thus, to be a

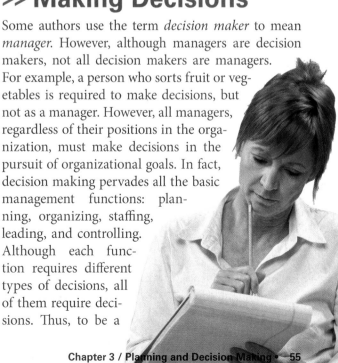

**Study Alert!**

How often do you receive a performance appraisal in your job? Does that appraisal include performance objectives from the previous appraisal? Do you agree on future performance objectives? If you don't, what do you think the reaction would be if you suggested it?

good planner, organizer, staffer, leader, and controller, a manager must first be a good decision maker.

Herbert Simon, a Nobel Prize winner, has described the manager's **decision process** in three stages: (1) intelligence, (2) design, and (3) choice.[5] The intelligence stage involves searching the environment for conditions requiring a decision. The design stage involves inventing, developing, and analyzing possible courses of action. Choice, the final stage, refers to the actual selection of a course of action.

The decision process stages show the difference between management and nonmanagement decisions. Nonmanagement decisions are concentrated in the last (choice) stage. The fruit-vegetable sorter has to make a choice regarding only the size or quality of the goods. Management decisions place greater emphasis on the intelligence and design stages. If the decision-making process is viewed as only the choice stage, managers spend very little time making decisions. If, however, the decision-making process is viewed as not only the actual choice but also the intelligence and design work needed to make the choice, managers spend most of their time making decisions.

**Decision Process** Process that involves three stages: intelligence, design, and choice.

**Decision Making** In its narrowest sense, the process of choosing from among various alternatives.

**Problem Solving** Process of determining the appropriate responses or actions necessary to alleviate a problem.

**Optimizing Approach** Decision-making process that includes the following steps: recognize the need for a decision; establish, rank, and weigh criteria; gather available information and data; identify possible alternatives; evaluate each alternative with respect to all criteria; and select the best alternative.

## DECISION MAKING VERSUS PROBLEM SOLVING

The terms *decision making* and *problem solving* are often confused and therefore need to be clarified. As indicated earlier, **decision making**, in its narrowest sense, is the process of choosing from among various alternatives. A *problem* is any deviation from some standard or desired level of performance. **Problem solving**, then, is the process of determining the appropriate responses or actions necessary to alleviate a problem. Problem solving necessarily involves decision making, since all problems can be attacked in numerous ways and the problem solver must decide which way is best. On the other hand, not all decisions involve problems (such as the person sorting fruit and vegetables). However, from a practical perspective, almost all managerial decisions do involve solving or at least avoiding problems.

5. What is management by objectives (MBO)?
6. Explain the three stages of a manager's decision process.
7. What is a nonmanagement decision? Give an example.
8. Explain the difference between decision making and problem solving.

## RATIONAL APPROACHES TO DECISION MAKING

Approaches to decision making that attempt to evaluate factual information through the use of some type of deductive reasoning are referred to as *rational approaches*. The following sections discuss two types of rational approaches.

**The Optimizing Approach** The physical sciences have provided a rational approach to decision making that can be adapted to management problems. The **optimizing approach** (sometimes called the *rational* or *scientific approach*) to decision making includes the following steps:

1. Recognize the need for a decision.
2. Establish, rank, and weigh the decision criteria.
3. Gather available information and data.
4. Identify possible alternatives.
5. Evaluate each alternative with respect to all criteria.
6. Select the best alternative.

Once the need to make the decision is known, criteria must be set for expected results of the decision. These criteria should then be ranked and weighed according to their relative importance.

Next, factual data relating to the decision should be collected. After that, all alternatives that meet the criteria are identified. Each is then evaluated with respect to all criteria. The final decision is based on the alternative that best meets the criteria.

### Limitations of the Optimizing Approach

The optimizing approach to decision making is an improvement over the intuitive approach (which is discussed in the section "The Intuitive Approach to Decision Making"), but it is not without its problems and limitations. The optimizing approach is based on the concept of the "economic person." This concept proposes that people behave rationally and their behavior is based on the following assumptions:

1. People have clearly defined criteria, and the relative weights they assign to these criteria are stable.
2. People have knowledge of all relevant alternatives.
3. People have the ability to evaluate each alternative with respect to all the criteria and arrive at an overall rating for each alternative.
4. People have the self-discipline to choose the alternative that rates the highest (they will not manipulate the system).

Consider the following difficulties with the above approach. First, these assumptions are often unrealistic; decision makers do not always have clearly defined criteria for making decisions. Second, many decisions are based on limited knowledge of the possible alternatives; even when information is available, it is usually less than perfect. Third, there is always a temptation to manipulate or ignore the gathered information and choose a favored (but not necessarily the best) alternative.

Due to the limitations of the optimizing approach, most decisions still involve some judgment. Thus, in making decisions, a manager generally uses a combination of intuitive and rational approaches.

**The Satisficing Approach** Believing the assumptions of the optimizing approach to be generally unrealistic, Herbert Simon, in attempting to understand how managerial decisions are actually made, formulated his **principle of bounded rationality**. This principle states, "The capacity of the human mind for formulating and solving complex problems is very small compared with the size of the problems whose solution is required for objectively rational behavior—or even for a reasonable approximation to such objective rationality."[6] Basically, the principle of bounded rationality states that human rationality has definite limits. Based on this principle, Simon proposed a decision model of the "administrative person," which makes the following assumptions:

1. A person's knowledge of alternatives and criteria is limited.
2. People act on the basis of a simplified, ill-structured, mental concept of the real world; this concept is influenced by personal perceptions, biases, and so forth.
3. People do not attempt to optimize but will take the first alternative that satisfies their current level of aspiration. This is called *satisficing.*
4. An individual's level of aspiration concerning a decision fluctuates upward and downward, depending on the values of the most recently identified alternatives.

**Principle of Bounded Rationality** Assumption that people have the time and cognitive ability to process only a limited amount of information on which to base decisions.

**Optimizing** Selecting the best possible alternative.

**Satisficing** Selecting the first alternative that meets the decision maker's minimum standard of satisfaction.

**Level of Aspiration** Level of performance that a person expects to attain; determined by the person's prior successes and failures.

The first assumption is a summary of the principle of bounded rationality. The second assumption follows naturally from the first. If limits to human rationality do exist, an individual must make decisions based on limited and incomplete knowledge. The third assumption also naturally follows from the first assumption: If the decision maker's knowledge of alternatives is incomplete, the individual cannot optimize but can only satisfice. **Optimizing** means selecting the best possible alternative; **satisficing** means selecting the first alternative that meets the decision maker's minimum standard of satisfaction. Assumption four is based on the belief that the criteria for a satisfactory alternative are determined by the person's current level of aspiration. **Level of aspiration** refers to the level of performance a person expects to attain, and it is affected by the person's prior successes and failures.

Figure 3.1 represents the satisficing approach to decision making. If the decision maker is satisfied that an acceptable alternative has been found, she or he selects that alternative. Otherwise, the decision maker searches for an additional alternative. In Figure 3.1, the double arrows indicate a two-way relationship: The value of the new alternative is influenced by the value of the best previous alternative; the value of the best previous alternative is in turn influenced by the value of the new alternative. As the arrows indicate, a similar two-way relationship exists between the value of the new alternative and the current level of aspiration. The net result of this evaluation determines whether or not the decision maker is satisfied with the alternative. Thus, the administrative person selects the first alternative that meets the minimum satisfaction criteria and makes no real attempt to optimize.

**Figure 3.1 • Model of the Satisficing Approach**

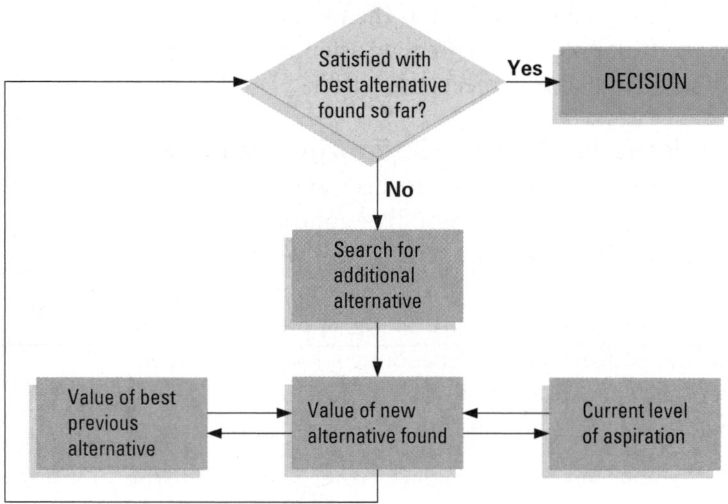


***Source:*** *Adapted from James G. March and Herbert A. Simon, Organizations, 1958, John Wiley & Sons.*

## THE DECISION MAKER'S ENVIRONMENT

A manager's freedom to make decisions depends largely on the manager's position within the organization and on its structure. In general, higher-level managers have more authority and operational freedom (autonomy) than lower-level managers. The patterns of authority outlined by the formal organization structure also influence the flexibility of the decision maker.

Another important factor in decision-making style is the purpose and tradition of the organization. For example, a military organization requires a different style of decision making than a volunteer organization does.

9. What are the six steps in the optimizing approach to decision making?
10. Explain the four assumptions of the optimizing approach.
11. Explain the principle of bounded rationality.
12. Which is the better approach—optimizing or satisficing? Explain your answer.

The organization's formal and informal group structures also affect decision-making styles. These groups may range from labor unions to advisory councils.

The culture of an organization can vary from militaristic or bureaucratic, where every decision is scrutinized and requires approval from a supervisor, to a more informal environment, where managers are trusted to make decisions in the best interests of the organization with limited supervision.

**Intuitive Approach** Decision-making process that relies on hunches and intuition.

**Situation of Certainty** Situation that occurs when a decision maker knows exactly what will happen and can calculate the precise outcome for each alternative.

The final subset of the environment includes all the decision maker's superiors and subordinates. The personalities, backgrounds, and expectations of these people influence the decision maker.

Figure 3.2 shows the major environmental factors within an organization that affect decision makers in an organization. In addition to these major organizational factors, there are always other factors in the general environment that can affect a decision. Some of these factors might include industry norms, the labor market, the political climate, and competition. The less information available to the manager, the greater the degree of uncertainty in making that decision. Successful managers must develop an appreciation for the different environmental forces that both influence them and are influenced by their decisions.

## THE INTUITIVE APPROACH TO DECISION MAKING

When managers make decisions solely on hunches and intuition (the **intuitive approach**), they are practicing management as though it were wholly an art based only on feelings. While intuition and other forms of judgment do play a role in many decision situations, problems can occur when managers ignore available facts and rely only on feelings. When this happens, managers sometimes become so emotionally attached to certain positions that almost nothing will change their mind. They develop the "don't bother me with the facts—my mind is made up" attitude. George Odiorne isolated the following emotional attachments that can hurt decision makers:

## Figure 3.2 • Environmental Factors Influencing Decision Making in an Organization

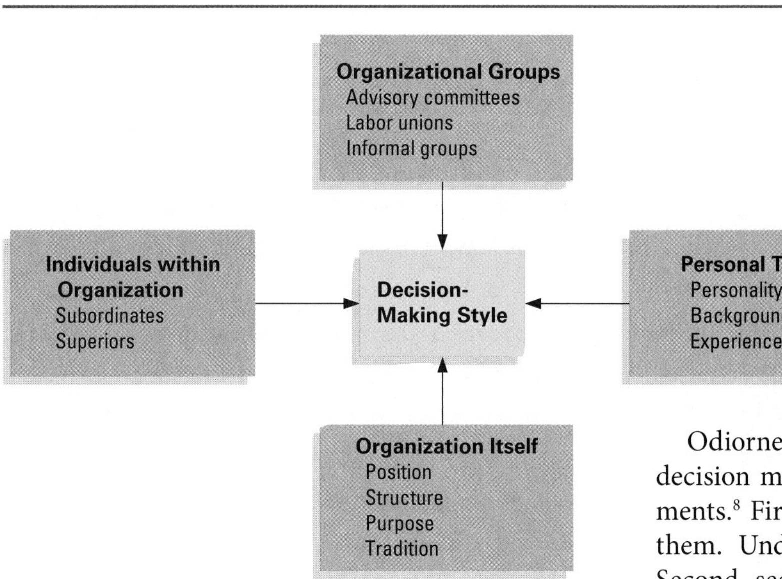


Study Alert!

Have you ever made a decision based purely on "gut instinct"? What prompted you to make that decision? What was the outcome? Did you tell your boss that it was a gut instinct decision? If not, why not? Do you think you put the company at risk by acting in that manner?

1. Fastening on unsubstantiated facts and sticking with them.
2. Being attracted to scandalous issues and heightening their significance.
3. Pressing every fact into a moral pattern.
4. Overlooking everything except what is immediately useful.
5. Having an affinity for romantic stories and finding such information more significant than any other kind, including hard evidence.[7]

Such emotional attachments can be very real and can lead to poor decisions. They most often affect managers or decision makers who are "living in the past" and either will not or cannot modernize their thinking. An example is the manager who insists on making decisions just as the founder of the company did 40 years ago.

*The inability to modernize can have serious consequences for a decision maker trying to make informed choices.*

Odiorne offers two suggestions for managers and decision makers overwhelmed by emotional attachments.[8] First, become aware of biases and allow for them. Undiscovered biases do the most damage. Second, seek independent opinions. It is always advisable to ask the opinion of a person who has no vested interest in the decision. Intuition does play a role in decision making. The key is not to ignore facts when they are available.

## CONDITIONS FOR MAKING DECISIONS

Decisions are not always made with the same amount of available information. The best decision often depends on what happens later. Consider the simple decision of whether to take an umbrella when going outside. The more desirable alternative is determined by whether or not it rains, but this is not under the control of the decision maker. Figure 3.3 gives combinations of alternatives and states of nature and their respective outcomes for the individual trying to decide whether or not to take an umbrella when going outside.

**Certainty** Knowing exactly what will happen places the decision maker in a **situation of certainty**. In such a situation, the decision maker can calculate the precise outcome for each alternative. If it is raining, the person knows the outcome of each alternative and therefore can choose the best alternative (take an umbrella). Rarely, however, are decisions made in today's organizations under a condition of certainty. A manager deciding between a delivery by air (taking a set time to arrive at a set cost) or one by truck (also taking a set time to arrive at a set cost) would be

# Thinking Critically 3.2

## >> Jerry Yang's Second Biggest Decision of His Career

If deciding to cofound Yahoo! was the biggest career decision Jerry Yang ever made, then his decision to turn down an offer of $44 billion from software giant Microsoft in 2008 must surely count as his second biggest.

The decision to turn down the deal, particularly from a suitor who is not known for being turned down, brought severe attacks on Yang's motives and overall business acumen. Critics argued that it was more about an emotional attachment to the company he helped to found, or his extreme hatred of Microsoft, or his need to be perceived as an Internet visionary in the same league as Google founders Larry Page and Sergey Brin. To make matters worse, the subsequent market decline added insult to the already injurious decision to turn down the 62 percent premium over Yahoo!'s stock price of $19.18 at the time of the Microsoft offer. By the time Yahoo! reached $10.63 a share, critics figured that Yang's decision had cost the company over $20 billion.

An aborted advertising deal with archrival Google that promised annual revenues from $250 to $450 million seemed to offer some hope of restoring Yang's reputation, but Google ultimately walked away from the deal under pressure from regulators' antitrust issues. In November 2008, Yang agreed to step down as CEO and resume his strategic post as "Chief Yahoo!" on the board of directors.

History may yet prove kinder to Yang than current critics. Many of his concerns about the Microsoft offer were valid. Supporters argue that he wasn't opposed to the deal in principle as was claimed. His demands during the negotiations were for more money and better terms that would guarantee long-term value for Yahoo! In particular, Yang had concerns over the half-cash, half-stock structure of the deal, which would expose Yahoo! shareholders to the mercy of Microsoft's stock price (which subsequently sank in the market decline along with all the others). He also wanted watertight guarantees for the yearlong approval process that he expected the deal would require—and with an 18 percent share of the search market as compared to Microsoft's paltry 10 percent, he perhaps thought he had the bargaining position. Whether or not he underestimated the tenacity of Microsoft CEO Steve Ballmer remains up for debate. What is clear is that Ballmer walked away, and Yang's legacy currently seems far removed from the Internet visionary he is reputed to have aspired to achieve.

### QUESTIONS

1. Do you think Yang's decision to turn down Microsoft's offer was a rational or intuitive one? What evidence do you have for your selection?
2. Do you think he made the right decision? Why or why not?
3. What do you think would have happened to Yahoo! if the deal had gone through?
4. Yang has since been replaced by Carol Bartz, the former CEO of billion-dollar software giant Autodesk, who was persuaded to come out of retirement to "fix" Yahoo! Research and summarize the key decisions implemented under her leadership.

*Source:* R. Hof, "Special Report: Why Yahoo's Yang Is Still Holding Out," *BusinessWeek*, June 3, 2008; "Technology: Jerry Yang's Letter to Stockholders," *BusinessWeek*, February 14, 2008; "Top Story: Letter from Microsoft CEO Steve Ballmer to Yahoo! CEO, Jerry Yang," *BusinessWeek*, May 3, 2008; and B. Stone and C. Cain Miller, "Jerry Yang, Yahoo Chief, Steps Down," *The New York Times*, November 17, 2008.

## Figure 3.3 • Umbrella Decision Alternatives and Outcomes

| Alternative | State of Nature | |
|---|---|---|
| | No Rain | Rain |
| Take umbrella | Dry, but inconvenient | Dry |
| Do not take umbrella | Dry, happy | Wet |

an example of a decision made under a condition of certainty.

**Risk** Unfortunately, the outcome associated with each alternative is not always known in advance. The decision maker can often obtain—at some cost—information regarding the different possible outcomes. The desirability of getting the information is figured by weighing the costs of obtaining the information against the information's value. A decision maker is in a **situation of risk** if certain reliable but incomplete information is available. In a situation of risk, some ideas of the relative probabilities associated with each outcome are known. If the weather forecaster has said there is a 40 percent chance of rain, the decision maker is operating in a situation of risk.

The precise probabilities of the various outcomes usually are not known. However, reasonably accurate probabilities based on historical data and past experiences often can be calculated.

When no such data exist, it is difficult to estimate probabilities. In such cases, one approach is to survey individual opinions.

Under conditions of risk, the decision maker can use expected value analysis to help arrive at a decision. With this technique, the expected payoff of each known alternative is mathematically calculated based on its probability of occurrence. One potential shortcoming of expected value analysis is that it represents the average outcome if the event is repeated many times. That is of little help if the act occurs only once. For example, airplane passengers are not interested in average fatality rates; rather, they are interested in what happens on their particular flight.

**Uncertainty** When having very little or no reliable information on which to evaluate the different possible outcomes, the decision maker is operating in a situation of uncertainty. Under a **situation of uncertainty**, the decision maker has no knowledge concerning the probabilities associated with different possible outcomes. For example, a person who is going to New York and has not heard a weather forecast for New York will have no knowledge of the likelihood of rain and hence will not know whether to carry an umbrella.

If the decision maker has little or no knowledge about which state of nature will occur, one of several basic approaches may be taken. The first is to choose the alternative whose best possible outcome is the best of all possible outcomes for all alternatives. This optimistic, or gambling, approach is called the **maximax approach.** A decision maker using this approach would not take the umbrella because the best possible outcome (being dry without being inconvenienced) could be achieved only with this alternative.

A second approach for dealing with uncertainty is to compare the worst possible outcomes for each alternative and select the one that is least bad. This pessimistic approach is called the **maximin approach**. In the umbrella example, the decision maker would compare the worst possible outcome of taking an umbrella to that of not taking an umbrella. The decision maker would then decide to take an umbrella because it is better to be dry than wet.

A third approach is to choose the alternative with the least variation among its possible outcomes. This is a **risk-averting approach** and results in more effective planning. If the decision maker chooses not to take an umbrella, the outcomes can vary from being dry to being wet. Thus, the risk-averting decision maker would take an umbrella to ensure staying dry.

Figure 3.4 summarizes the different approaches to making a decision under conditions of uncertainty.

**Situation of Risk** Situation that occurs when a decision maker has reliable but incomplete information.

**Situation of Uncertainty** Situation that occurs when a decision maker has very little or no reliable information on which to evaluate the different possible outcomes.

**Maximax Approach** Decision-making approach that involves selecting the alternative whose best possible outcome is the best of all possible outcomes for all alternatives; also known as the *optimistic* or *gambling approach*.

**Maximin Approach** Decision-making approach that involves comparing the worst possible outcomes for each alternative and selecting the one that is least undesirable; also known as the *pessimistic approach*.

**Risk-Averting Approach** Decision-making approach that involves choosing the alternative with the least variation among its possible outcomes.

## TIMING THE DECISION

To properly time a decision, the need for a decision must be recognized. That is not always easy. The manager may not be aware of what is going on, or the problem requiring a decision may be camouflaged. Some managers always seem to make decisions on the spot; others tend to take forever to decide even a simple matter. The manager who makes quick decisions runs the risk of making bad decisions. Failure to gather and evaluate available data, consider people's feelings, and anticipate the impact of the decision can result in a quick but poor decision. Just as risky is the other extreme: the manager who listens to problems, promises to act, but never does. Nearly as bad is the manager who responds only after an inordinate delay. Other familiar types are the manager who never seems to have enough information to make a decision, the manager who frets and worries over even the simplest decisions, and the manager who refers everything to superiors.

Knowing when to make a decision is complicated because different decisions have different time frames. For instance, a manager generally has more time to decide committee appointments than he or she has to decide what to do when three employees call in sick. No magic formula exists to tell managers when a decision should be made or how long it should take to make it. The important thing is to see the importance of properly timed decisions.

**Figure 3.4 • Possible Approaches to Making Decisions under Uncertainty**

| Approach | How It Works | Related to the Umbrella Example |
|---|---|---|
| Optimistic or gambling approach (maximax) | Choose the alternative whose best possible outcome is the best of all possible outcomes for all alternatives. | Do not take umbrella. |
| Pessimistic approach (maximin) | Compare the worst possible outcomes of each of the alternatives, and select the alternative whose worst possible outcome is least undesirable. | Take umbrella. |
| Risk-averting approach | Choose the alternative that has the least variation among its possible alternatives. | Take umbrella. |

## PARTICIPATION IN DECISION MAKING

Most managers have opportunities to involve their subordinates and others in the decision-making process. One pertinent question is, Do groups make better decisions than individuals? Another is, When should subordinates be involved in making managerial decisions?

*"Starbucks encourages its employees, who are called partners, to keep in mind its [six-point] mission statement, monitor management decisions, and submit comments and questions if they encounter anything that runs counter to any of the six points"—according to a 2003 workforce.com article at* **www.workforce.com/section/02/feature/23/52/96/.**

**Group or Team Decision Making** Everyone knows the old saying that two heads are better than one. Empirical evidence generally supports this view, with a few minor qualifications. Group performance is frequently better than that of the average group member.[9] Similarly, groups can often be successfully used to develop innovative and creative solutions to problems. Groups also often take longer to solve problems than does the average person.[10] Thus, group decisions are generally better when avoiding mistakes is more important than speed.

Group performance is generally superior to that of the average group member for two reasons. First, the sum total of the group's knowledge is greater. Second, the group has a much wider range of alternatives in the decision process.

One aspect of group or team decision making compares the risk people will take alone with the risk they will take in a group. Laboratory experiments have shown that unanimous group decisions are consistently riskier than the average of the individual decisions.[11] This is somewhat surprising, since group pressures often inhibit the members. Possibly people feel less responsible for the outcome of a group decision than when they act alone. More recent research has found that groups make decisions best described as more polar than do individuals acting alone.[12] "More polar" means that groups tend to make decisions that are more

THE DANGER OF GROUPTHINK . . .

# First Line Focus

*In 1972, Irving Janis, then a professor in the Psychology Department at Yale University, published a book,* Victims of Groupthink: A Psychological Study of Foreign-Policy Decisions and Fiascoes, *about many of the political decisions made in the Vietnam War. In writing that book, Janis gave a name to an area of research that captured the apparent willingness of groups to be swayed toward consensus out of conflict avoidance rather than seeking hard data or a firm conviction in an opposing position. The force of groupthink is not to be dismissed lightly. Even the NASA reports on the Columbia and Challenger shuttle disasters acknowledged the apparent tendency of NASA engineers to believe in the infallibility of their own processes and data rather than checking and double-checking the possible outcomes of the decisions they were making.*

*In a business environment, groupthink can be fatal. Just because something has worked in the past is no guarantee of success in the future. For the new or inexperienced manager, being the lone voice in the wilderness can be a tough role to play, but if you are convinced of your data and your argument, fight the tendency to "go along with the team"—the company's future may depend on it.*

*We will be examining groupthink in more detail in Chapter 8.*

extreme than those they would make as individuals. Figure 3.5 summarizes the positive and negative aspects of group decision making.

## BARRIERS TO EFFECTIVE DECISION MAKING

Although it is desirable to study how to make decisions, managers must also work to remove barriers that limit the effectiveness of those decisions. Daniel Wheeler and

## PROGRESS ✓questions

13. Explain the intuitive approach to decision making.
14. List the different conditions under which managers must make decisions.
15. What is the risk-averting approach to decision making?
16. Summarize the positive and negative aspects of group decision making.

Irving Janis identified four basic barriers to effective decision making. Barrier one is *complacency*: The decision maker either does not see danger signs or opportunity or ignores data from the environment that would affect decision making. Barrier two is called *defensive avoidance:* The decision maker denies the importance of danger, the opportunity, or the responsibility for taking action. *Panic* is the third barrier: Frantic attempts to solve a problem rarely produce the best results. The final barrier is *deciding to decide*: Accepting the responsibility and challenge of decision making is critical to overall effectiveness.[13] All these barriers must be dealt with to create an environment that stimulates effective and creative decision making.

**Management Information Systems (MISs)** Integrated approach for providing interpreted and relevant data that can help managers make decisions.

## >> Management Information Systems

**Management information systems (MISs)**, also called *management reporting systems,* support the day-to-day operational and tactical decision-making

**Figure 3.5 • Positive and Negative Aspects of Group (or Team) Decision Making**

| Positive Aspects | Negative Aspects |
|---|---|
| 1. The sum total of the group's knowledge is greater. | 1. One individual may dominate or control the group. |
| 2. The group possesses a much wider range of alternatives in the decision process. | 2. Social pressures to conform can inhibit group members. |
| 3. Participation in the decision-making process increases the acceptance of the decision by group members. | 3. Competition can develop to such an extent that winning becomes more important than the issue itself. |
| 4. Group members better understand the decision and the alternatives considered. | 4. Groups have a tendency to accept the first potentially positive solution while giving little attention to other possible solutions. |

ENVIRONMENTAL BACKLASH

You lead the Public Service Commission for a midwestern state. When natural gas prices were over $4 per thousand cubic feet, your commission voted in favor of the conversion of a generator from natural gas to petroleum coke. There was opposition from environmentalist groups, but with customers getting beaten up on their monthly utility bills, the vote was a popular one.

After an investment of over $300 million to convert, the utility company stopped work on the conversion since gas prices fell to such a low level that the cost savings promised by the conversion had evaporated. In addition, customers who had locked in long-term contracts in anticipation of even higher prices were still getting gouged while their neighbors paid lower market prices.

The utility company has now come before your commission to request your help in offsetting its "dire financial straits." It is asking for a one-time charge to be added to customer bills to recover the $300 million investment in the conversion and the right to delay the project for three years in anticipation of a return to higher natural gas prices.

What would you do?

ETHICAL | MANAGEMENT

Should customers pay for a company's financial troubles?

needs of managers. MISs are designed to produce information needed for the successful management of a process, department, or business. An MIS provides information that managers have specified in advance as adequately meeting their information needs. Usually the information made available by an MIS is in the form of periodic reports, special reports, and outputs of mathematical simulations.

In the broader sense, management information systems have existed for many years, even before computers. However, in most people's mind, the term *MIS* implies the use of computers to process data that managers will use to make operational decisions. The information an MIS provides describes the organization or one of its major parts in terms of what has happened in the past, what is happening now, and what is likely to happen in the future.

It is important to note that an MIS is not the same as data processing. **Data processing** is the capture, processing, and storage of data, whereas an MIS uses those data to produce information for management in making decisions to solve problems. In other words, data processing provides the database of the MIS.

**Data Processing** Capturing, processing, and storing data.

**Transaction-Processing Systems** Systems that substitute computer processing for manual record-keeping procedures.

**Transaction-processing systems** substitute computer processing for manual record-keeping procedures. Examples include payroll, billing, and inventory record systems. By definition, transaction processing requires routine and highly structured decisions. It is actually a subset of data processing. Therefore, an organization can have a very effective transaction-processing system and not have an MIS.

Many MISs have been developed for use by specific organizational subunits. Examples of MISs intended to support managers in particular functional areas include operational information systems, marketing information systems, financial information systems, and human resource information systems. Several specific MISs used by organizational subunits are discussed in later chapters.

**From the PERSPECTIVE OF...**

**An MIS Manager** MIS management often involves more equipment than employees to manage—desktop computers, laptops, printers, servers, network infrastructure, Web sites, and so forth—but the position carries considerable responsibility in the availability and accuracy of company data. What is meant by the acronym GIGO?

## >> Chapter Summary

Experienced managers are often most proud of the decisions they have made in their planning process on the basis of a hunch or gut instinct, without recognizing the important part played by experience in the development of that instinct that they trust so well. For new managers, decision-making skills often represent the most valuable asset they bring to the role. Product knowledge and job performance may win promotion to manager, but with that new title comes the responsibility to make decisions. As we have seen in this chapter, organizations would do well to establish consistent policies on how planning decisions should be made and to determine what constitutes an acceptable level of risk in making those decisions. In the next chapter, we review how those decision-making skills are put to work in making strategic choices for the management and future direction of a business.

1. Define *planning*, and distinguish between formal and functional plans.

   Planning is the process of deciding which objectives to pursue during a future time period and how to achieve those objectives. Beyond day-to-day managerial responsibilities, planning is the primary function of management and is inherent in everything a manager does. Formal plans are written documents that capture key strategic objectives for the future direction of the organization as a whole. Functional plans, as the term implies, focus on functional areas of the organization, such as sales and marketing, production, and finance.

2. Contrast strategic planning with operational planning.

   Strategic planning is a process that establishes long-range objectives for every department of an organization. Established at the highest levels of the organization, strategic plans are typically implemented by senior executives. In contrast, operational or tactical planning takes a more functional approach, focusing on individual departments over a shorter time period. Operational plans are implemented by middle- and lower-level managers.

3. Understand different types of objectives.

   Objectives outline specific achievement targets for the organization and provide management and employees at all levels of the organization with clear, concise, and quantifiable goals. Whether short- or long-term in design, objectives should be sufficiently detailed so that affected personnel clearly understand what is expected of them over the specified time period. Objectives should be dynamic in nature—they should be monitored and reevaluated as the environment and opportunities change.

4. Explain the difference between decision making and problem solving, and compare and contrast rational and intuitive approaches to decision making.

   Decision making requires that a choice be made among a range of alternatives. Managers make decisions many times every day, and it is their ability to make the correct decision in each instance that determines their future career path in the organization. Problem solving, by contrast, requires the identification of a problem and the selection of an appropriate solution to that problem. While problem solving requires that a decision be made in the selection of a solution, not all decisions involve problems. Often, decision making can involve a choice between two very positive outcomes.

   Rational decision making is data-driven and based on the evaluation of factual information collected in advance of the decision. The amount of data collected and the time period in which the decision must be made will determine whether a manager chooses an optimizing approach (where every element and variable is considered and scrutinized in detail) or the satisficing approach (where the manager selects the first choice that meets the minimum standards).

*Continued on next page*

Continued from page 65

Intuitive decision making, by contrast, involves hunches and intuition based on gut instinct developed over years of experience; in other words, managers are guided by feelings rather than data. Intuitive decisions have the advantage of speed, since managers are freed from the requirement to process data on multiple variables. However, emotional attachment to a decision can lead to bias and unwillingness to face the reality of an incorrect decision.

5. Explain the decision maker's environment and the conditions for making a decision.

   Manager's authority and freedom to make a decision is directly related to his or her position in an organization and the operational culture of that organization. Higher-level managers typically have more authority and operational freedom (autonomy) than lower-level managers. The culture of an organization can vary from militaristic or bureaucratic, where every decision is scrutinized and requires approval from a supervisor, to a more informal environment, where managers are trusted to make decisions in the best interests of the organization with limited supervision. The extent to which conditions are right for making a decision is determined by the amount of information available and the organization's risk tolerance. The less information available to the manager, the greater the degree of uncertainty in making that decision.

## THE WORLD of Work >>

**TONY SEES THINGS DIFFERENTLY** ***(continued from page 49)***

"It looks to them like your new title is going to your head when all you want to do is be more available to help them."

Tanya's statement opened Tony's eyes. He had automatically assumed that his staff would understand what he was trying to do by changing the scheduling policy, but now he realized that all they had seen was a new policy posted on the staff notice board without any discussion or warning. Making an example of Matt had been more about protecting Tony's ego than about sending a message to the rest of the staff—Tony didn't want word of him being a "pushover" reaching Jerry Smith or, worse still, Dawn Williams, his regional manager.

He might have had the best intentions in getting more time to work with his people, but their reaction showed that they didn't see it that way. Now Tony was stuck. He had been considering filling Tanya's position as shift leader as an internal promotion (there were a couple of good people who were ready), but now he wasn't sure if he could count on them sticking around long enough to apply for the position.

He had really wanted to put his stamp on this Taco Barn to reassure Jerry and Dawn for the faith that they had shown in him, but Tony was certain that this potential mutiny wasn't what he had in mind at all. He still felt sure that there was a better way to do the schedule every week, and he did want to free up more time to be in the restaurant with his staff, but all he had done was convince his staff—friends that he had worked with for years before his promotion—that he was on a power trip. How could he get the message across that he was on their side without that message being seen as an admission that he made a big mistake in his first major decision as unit manager?

**QUESTIONS**

1. Should Tony change the scheduling policy back to the way things were? Why or why not?
2. How do you think this new awareness will change Tony's management style?
3. Do you think he can rebuild his relationship with his staff? Why or why not?
4. What should Tony do now?

## Key Terms >>

contingency plans 53
data processing 64
decision making 56
decision process 56
formal plan 50
functional plan 50
intuitive approach 58
level of aspiration 57
long-range objectives 53
long-range plans 51
management by objectives (MBO) 54
management information systems (MISs) 63
maximax approach 61
maximin approach 61
objectives 53
operations or tactical planning 51
optimizing 57
optimizing approach 56
policies 54
principle of bounded rationality 57
problem solving 56
procedure 54
risk-averting approach 61
rules 55
satisficing 57
short-range objectives 53
short-range plans 51
situation of certainty 58
situation of risk 61
situation of uncertainty 61
strategic planning 51
transaction-processing systems 64

## Think << AND DISCUSS

1. Why is it necessary to plan? How is most planning conducted?
2. Describe the differences between objectives, policies, procedures, and rules.
3. How would you respond to the following question from a manager: "How can I plan for next year when I don't even know what I'm going to do tomorrow?"
4. What are the three stages in the decision-making process?
5. What criticisms can be made concerning the optimizing approach to decision making?
6. Should a manager make planning decisions on the basis of gut instinct? Why or why not?

## INTERNET In Action >>

1. Using multiple sources, research the Centers for Disease Control (CDC) response to the swine flu or H1N1 flu virus. From a management perspective, answer the following questions:
   b. Did the CDC have a plan in place for an event such as this?
   c. Should a business have a plan for an event such as this? Why?
   d. Given the extreme media attention to the virus and the subsequent reaction by the general public (closing schools, calls to close the border with Mexico), how should the CDC modify future plans for a similar event?
2. Research a business magazine (*BusinessWeek, Fast Company, Fortune,* or *Forbes*) or newspaper (*The Wall Street Journal* or *The New York Times*), and identify a significant business decision made by a major company:
   a. What business and/or economic factors prompted the decision?
   b. Did the managers involved satisfice or optimize?
   c. What was their risk approach to the decision they made?
   d. In your assessment, how creative was their decision?

# << Team IN ACTION

1. **Tesla Motors**

   Visit the Web site for Tesla Motors **(www.teslamotors.com)**, and review their vehicles, the Roadster and its new midpriced family saloon, the Model S. Your team has been asked to consult with Tesla Motors on their plans to ramp up capabilities for mass production of their vehicles. Using the four general categories of objectives outlined on page 53, divide into two groups and produce a three-year and five-year plan for Tesla. Approach this as a strategic rather than an operational planning exercise.

2. **Benjamin Franklin's "T-Chart"**

   When faced with making a tough decision, Ben Franklin used a simple but effective step to help him arrive at what he saw as the right decision. He would draw a large letter "T" on a piece of paper, with "+" over the left side of the crossbar of the T (indicating the points in favor of making the choice—the pros) and a "–" over the right side of the crossbar of the T (indicating the points against making the choice—the cons). Whichever side of the list contained the most items determined the choice to be made.

   Divide the group into two teams—one focusing on the pros and one on the cons of an important decision that the group as a whole selects. Take 10 minutes to fill your assigned side of the T-chart, and then answer the following questions:

   a. How hard was it to agree on the important decision you would use?

   b. What was the final verdict?

   c. If you could add a relative importance weighting to each of the pros and cons so that one pro could be treated as being more important than another, would that change the outcome?

   d. Should this be your only step in making an important decision? Why or why not?

# Case 3.1

## >> Avon: More Than Cosmetic Changes

Andrea Jung stopped the sag by getting smarter about the numbers.

In 2005, Avon Products Inc.'s success story turned ugly. After six straight years of over 10 percent growth and a tripling of earnings under CEO Andrea Jung, the company suddenly began losing sales across the globe. Developing markets such as Central Europe and Russia, the engine of Avon's amazing run, stumbled just as sales in the United States and Mexico stalled. The global diversity that had long propped up the company's performance suddenly began to weigh it down. This dramatic turn of events hit investors by surprise. In May, Jung had predicted Avon would exceed Wall Street's already high expectations. By September, problems in China, Eastern Europe, and Russia were mounting, and Jung was backpedaling at full speed. Angry shareholders bailed out. The stock price, which had risen 181 percent during Jung's first five and a half years at the helm, plummeted 45 percent between April and October.

Over the past five years, Jung has tried to figure out what went wrong and how to fix it. Avon sells Skin So Soft and Anew skin-care products, as well as makeup and other items, through a network of over 5.8 million independent representatives around the world. Jung's performance generated criticism from many representatives as well as analysts and shareholders. Her response? She listened to the pivotal advice of management consultant Ram Charan. He advised Jung to go home that Friday night and imagine she had been fired. Then, he said, return Monday morning with the mind-set of someone brought in from the outside. "If you can be that objective and blend in your institutional knowledge and relationships, you're going to have an advantage," he told her.

One of Jung's most important moves has been forcing managers to make decisions based on fact rather than intuition. She reorganized Avon's management structure, taking away much of the independence from country managers, in favor of globalized manufacturing and marketing. Previously, Avon managers from Poland to Mexico ran their own plants, developed new products, and created their own ads, often relying as much on gut as numbers. In Jung's words they were "king or queen of every decision."

Now Jung has trimmed out seven layers of management, bringing the total from 15 down to 8, and cut costs by $300 million. That analysis is directed from New York headquarters by an executive team stocked with more people from the outside. Recent recruits have come from larger, more analytical consumer-product companies such as Gillette, Procter & Gamble, PepsiCo, and Kraft.

Savings from centralized manufacturing and other initiatives are being put into advertising (up 95 percent since 2005) and research and development. Sales for fourth quarter of 2009 rose to $2.6 billion, up 9 percent compared to the same period in 2005.

**QUESTIONS**

1. Why would a new "outside" perspective help Andrea Jung manage the turnaround of Avon?
2. Is it always better for managers to make decisions based on fact rather than intuition?
3. What are the potential advantages for an organization becoming more data-centric?
4. Do you think that Andrea Jung has managed a successful turnaround? Why or why not?

*Source:* Nanette Byrnes, "The Corporation," *BusinessWeek*, March 12, 2007; Bill George, "Andrea Jung: Corporate Executive: A New Makeover for an Old Retail Face," *U.S. News & World Report*, November 12, 2007; and "Avon Regains Some Allure," *BusinessWeek*, February 24, 2010.

# Case 3.2

## >> GM: Lessons from the Alfred Sloan Era

Last year's historic bankruptcy filing by General Motors (GM) sent shock waves through the global automotive industry. The company that was, for most of the 20th century, the biggest company in the most important industry in the world was no more. Analysts and critics alike wrote obituaries and spouted alternative outcomes that were, it seemed, obvious to everyone except the executives of GM.

Critics who pointed to Toyota as the model for the future have seen that brash arrogance damaged with recent events, but if we are going to continue to offer alternative models for the leadership of the "new GM" to consider, here's another, less obvious model of managerial success to consider: General Motors.

It was the GM of 60 years ago, after all, that helped define the discipline of management, having served as the subject of Peter Drucker's landmark book, *Concept of the Corporation.* "When this book was being written . . . the corporation had barely been discovered and was totally unexplored—resembling somewhat the Africa of the medieval mapmaker, a big white space across which was written: 'Here elephants roam,' " Drucker remarked some four decades after the book's publication in 1946. "Books on the corporation itself and its management could have been counted on the fingers of one hand."

It is worth recalling that Drucker found many, many things to admire about GM—and especially its chairman, Alfred Sloan. In an introduction to Sloan's autobiography, *My Years with General Motors,* Drucker credited the no-nonsense executive with being "the first to work out systematic organization in a big company, planning and

*Continued on next page*

Continued from page 69

strategy, measurements, the principle of decentralization" and more. Sloan's role "as the designer and architect of management," Drucker added, "surely was a foundation for America's economic leadership in the 40 years following World War II."

Indeed, as Drucker saw it, Sloan was the pioneer who transformed management into a real profession, establishing the standard that the professional manager is duty-bound to put the interests of the enterprise ahead of his or her own. Sloan, Drucker wrote, also made clear that "the job of a professional manager is not to like people. It is not to change people. It is to put their strengths to work. And whether one approves of people or the way they do their work, their performance is the only thing that counts." Sloan's definition of performance, Drucker was quick to explain, meant much "more than the bottom line. It is also setting an example. And this requires integrity."

Of all the pointers Drucker picked up from observing Sloan, there is one in particular that today's GM might want to pay close attention to: Reaching difficult decisions (Hummer or hybrid?) demands healthy dissent.

David Garvin, a professor at Harvard Business School, says one of GM's fundamental problems over the years—an inability to make the right strategic calls—has been caused, at least in part, by a dearth of open debate among top managers. Rather than frankly and candidly working through various options, executives would often line up needed votes before meetings, like a group of political bosses, and gather privately at "pre-meetings" to eliminate any surprises at the regular session.

"All too many decisions were pre-cooked," says Garvin, who wrote a 2004 case study on GM's process for determining policy. Garvin points out that Sloan's basic challenge was in some ways the opposite of that faced by his successors. He had to take a collection of highly independent, entrepreneurial car companies and coordinate their actions. As time has rolled on, GM has had the burden of figuring out how divisions scattered all over the world could tailor their lines to meet varying customer needs.

But whether you're talking about the Alfred Sloan era or the future of the new GM, there are a couple of common denominators: First, the company must provide absolute clarity as to who is responsible for deciding what. This, says Garvin, got "fuzzier and fuzzier" at GM as the organization became "progressively more complex" and layered with bureaucracy. Second, when the time comes for a major decision to be made, such as which products to pursue and which to abandon, all the alternatives must be vetted honestly.

"Gentlemen, I take it we are all in complete agreement on the decision here," Drucker quotes Sloan as saying. After everyone around the table nodded affirmatively, Sloan is said to have continued: "Then I propose we postpone further discussion of this matter until our next meeting to give ourselves time to develop disagreement and perhaps gain some understanding of what the decision is all about."

Sloan, Drucker wrote in 1967's *The Effective Executive*, "was anything but an 'intuitive' decision-maker. He always emphasized the need to test opinions against facts and the need to make absolutely sure that one did not start out with the conclusion and then look for the facts that would support it. But he knew that the right decision demands adequate disagreement."

That said, perhaps we can all agree on this: The new GM would be wise to study up on the GM of old.

**QUESTIONS**

1. Why would insularity prove fatal to General Motors?
2. Alfred Sloan believed that "the job of a professional manager is not to like people." How should that perspective affect how decisions are made in an organization?
3. Why would "a dearth of open debate among top managers" be so damaging to General Motors' long-term success?
4. If Sloan believed that "the right decision demands adequate disagreement," whose responsibility should it be to determine when there has been enough discussion?

*Source:* Rick Wartzman, "GM: Lessons from the Alfred Sloan Era," *BusinessWeek*, June 12, 2009; Bill Vlasic, "After Bankruptcy, G.M. Struggles to Shed a Legendary Bureaucracy," *The New York Times*, November 12, 2009; and Joseph R. Szczesny, "Engine Troubles," *Time*, June 2, 2009.

# Case 3.3

## >> Who's Making Your Health Care Decisions?

A clinical decision support system (CDSS) is a computer program that utilizes knowledge management to assist doctors and other health professionals in making decisions related to your medical care. A CDSS is designed to assist at the "point of care," where a patient is seeking medical treatment. The primary objective of the program is to assist in the determination of both diagnosis and an appropriate treatment plan for the patient. Perrault and Metzger (1999) identified four key functions of a CDSS:

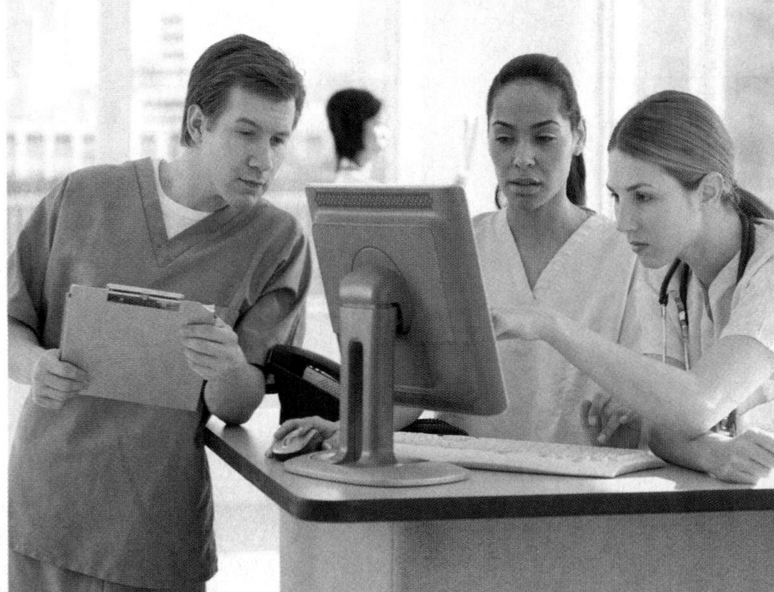

1. *Administrative:* Supporting clinical coding and documentation, authorization of procedures, and referrals.
2. *Managing clinical complexity and details:* Keeping patients on research and chemotherapy protocols; tracking orders, referrals, follow-up, and preventive care.
3. *Cost control:* Monitoring medication orders; avoiding duplicate or unnecessary tests.
4. *Decision support:* Supporting clinical diagnosis and treatment plan processes; promoting use of best practices, condition-specific guidelines, and population-based management.

It should come as no surprise in this era of escalating health costs that increasing attention is being paid to the implementation of a CDSS on the basis of function 3—cost control. Leveraging a detailed knowledge database allows the delegation of decisions to physician assistants as opposed to physicians. This, in turn, maximizes the use of the physician's time (which comes at a much higher cost per hour), but critics argue that this exposes patients to increased treatment by less qualified medical professionals.

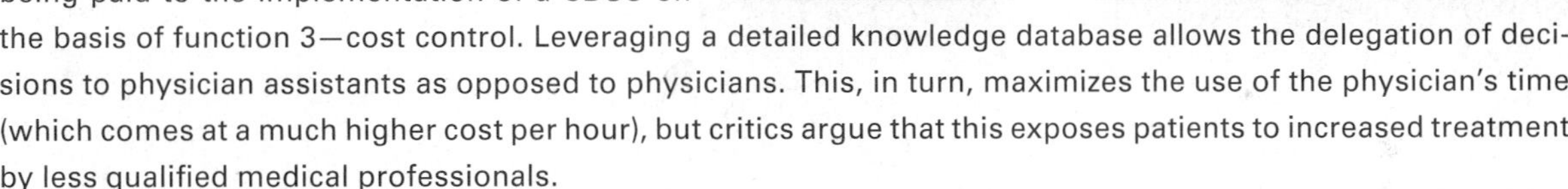

In addition, the dependence on a computer program leads to concern over the question of GIGO (i.e., garbage in, garbage out). Who compiles the database, who maintains and updates the data, and who takes responsibility for errors in that database? There is no doubt that the ability to track patient information, medical history, and response to pharmaceutical treatment over the long term is extremely valuable to clinical professionals in providing quality patient care. The ability to cross-reference that data with ongoing research on the patient's condition is equally valuable, but at some point in the patient care process, at prediagnosis, diagnosis, or postdiagnosis, a decision has to be made. Patients will inevitably be concerned as to who is making that decision—human or machine?

QUESTIONS

1. Summarize the arguments for and against the use of a clinical decision support system.
2. Should the doctor be required to disclose the use of a CDSS in making a health care decision? Why or why not?
3. How should the use of a CDSS be presented to a patient?
4. Who do you think should be held responsible if a diagnosis using a CDSS resulted in patient harm?

*Source:* L. Perrault and J. Metzger, "A Pragmatic Framework for Understanding Clinical Decision Support," *Journal of Healthcare Information Management,* vol. 13, no. 2, 1999, pp. 5–21; and M. E. Johnston, K. B. Langton, B. Haynes, and A. Mathieu, "Effects of Computer-Based Clinical Decision Support Systems on Clinician Performance and Patient Outcome: A Critical Appraisal of Research," *Annals of Internal Medicine,* vol. 120, no. 2, 1994, pp. 135–42.

# STRATEGIC MANAGEMENT

After studying this chapter, you will be able to:

1. Define *strategy*, and explain its importance to organizational success.
2. Explain the three levels of strategy that exist in an organization.
3. Discuss the stages of the strategic management process.
4. Define *organizational mission*, and explain how mission relates to long- and short-range objectives.
5. Discuss the components of a SWOT analysis.
6. Explain how strategic alternatives are identified and selected.

"Long range planning does not deal with future decisions, but with the future of present decisions."

Peter Drucker

## THE WORLD OF WORK Tony tries a new approach

Tanya had helped Tony see the situation at the Taco Barn in a different way, and he was ready to try a different approach—an approach that involved two stages.

In the first stage, rather than being rigid and refusing to make changes in the staffing schedule, Tony held a meeting of all the staff and explained that his fumbled attempt at improved efficiency was designed to give him more time to work with them in the restaurant, not just to make his life easier or theirs any harder. This admission seemed to calm everyone down, but it still left the problem of managing the individual scheduling needs of his crew. Tony knew he could play hardball and give his folks a "take-it-or-leave-it" choice on the shifts, but he was committed to these people and wanted them to continue to work for Taco Barn.

The second stage involved ordering "project planning" training material through the HR department at the head office and scheduling enough training sessions to make sure everyone was able to view the material. Tony waited until everyone had gone through the training before he made his announcement. The feedback on the training was very positive—people found the material interesting, and several of his crew started using some of the ideas in their jobs. However, no one questioned why the entire crew had been put through the training. Now they were about to find out.

Tony announced in a very matter-of-fact manner in the next staff meeting that he was handing responsibility for the staffing schedule over to them. Kevin, their most experienced team member and next in line for Tanya's position as shift leader, was appointed as project leader, but Tony emphasized that he wanted everyone involved in the project. More important, he expected them not only to work the schedule out among themselves but also to work as a team and cover each other in the event that they couldn't make it in for their assigned shift.

At first glance, this decision looked like Tony was just dumping the schedule headache in their laps. He was gambling that they would get a clearer picture of the situation if they reviewed everyone's requests as a team, rather than individual employees simply forwarding their scheduling issues to him and leaving him to figure out how to make it work.

Plus, Tony thought, the planning exercise would be good experience for them, and if they did it well, there would be lots of other opportunities for planning exercises in the future.

**QUESTIONS**

1. Do you think the employees will see this as a growth opportunity or as Tony dumping more work on them? Explain your answer.
2. Do you think the employees will be able to manage the schedule as a team? Why or why not?
3. What happens if their first attempt at a schedule doesn't work?
4. What type of strategy is Tony following here?

# >> Strategy

The word *strategy* originated with the Greeks about 400 B.C.; it pertained to the art and science of directing military forces.[1] A **strategy** outlines the basic steps that management plans to take to reach an objective or a set of objectives. In other words, a strategy outlines how management intends to achieve its objectives.

**Strategy** Outline of the basic steps that management plans to take to achieve an objective or a set of objectives.

**Corporate Strategies** Strategies that address which businesses an organization will be in and how resources will be allocated among those businesses; also known as *grand strategies.*

## LEVELS OF STRATEGY

Strategies exist at three primary levels in an organization and are classified according to the scope of what they are intended to accomplish. The three levels are corporate, business, and functional strategies.

### CORPORATE STRATEGIES

Strategies that address which businesses the organization will be in and how resources will be allocated among those businesses are referred to as **corporate strategies.** Corporate strategies are sometimes called *grand strategies.* They are established at the highest levels in the organization, and they involve a long-range time horizon. Corporate strategies are concerned with the overall direction of the organization, specifically tied to mission statements, and generally formulated by top corporate management. Four basic corporate strategy types are recognized: growth, stability, defensive, and combination.

**Growth strategies** are used when the organization tries to expand in terms of sales, product line, number of employees, or similar measures. Under this concept, an organization can grow through concentration of current businesses, vertical integration, and diversification. Kellogg and McDonald's use concentration strategies—focusing on extending the sales of their current products or services—very successfully. A. G. Bass (maker of the famous "preppie" shoe, Bass Weejuns) believes vertical integration, in which a company moves into areas it previously served either as a supplier to or as a customer for its current products or services, to be a superior growth strategy. The final growth strategy is exemplified by Coca-Cola's purchase of Minute Maid Orange Juice in the early 1980s and its more recent purchase of Dasani spring waters. Diversification can take several forms, but concentric (in related fields) is the most common.

**Growth Strategies** Strategies by which the organization tries to expand, as measured by sales, product line, number of employees, or similar measures.

**Stability Strategies** Strategies by which the organization maintains its present course (status quo strategies).

**Defensive or Retrenchment Strategies** Strategies by which a company reduces its operations.

**Stability strategies** are used when the organization is satisfied with its present course. Management will make efforts to eliminate minor weaknesses, but generally its actions will maintain the status quo. Stability strategies are most likely to be successful in unchanging or very slowly changing environments. Growth is possible under a stability strategy, but it will be slow, methodical, and nonaggressive. Most organizations elect a stability strategy by default rather than by any conscious decision or plan.

**Defensive** or **retrenchment strategies** are used when a company wants or needs to reduce its operations. Most often they are used to reverse a negative trend or to overcome a crisis or problem. The three most popular types are *turnaround* (designed to reverse a negative trend and get the organization back to profitability), *divestiture* (the company sells or divests itself of a business or part of a business), and *liquidation* (the entire company is sold or dissolved).

**Combination strategies** are used when an organization simultaneously employs different strategies

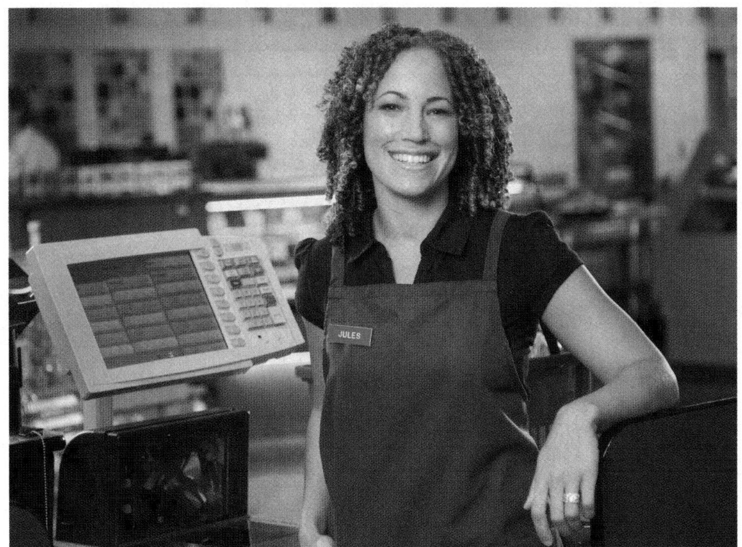

*Which corporate strategies might this business and the one shown on the previous page want to use?*

for different parts of the company. Most multibusiness companies use some type of combination strategy, especially those serving several different markets. Coca-Cola, for example, pursued a combination strategy in 1989 when it divested its Columbia Pictures division while expanding its soft-drink and orange juice businesses.

Figure 4.1 summarizes the major types and subtypes of corporate strategies.

## BUSINESS STRATEGIES

**Business strategies**, the second primary level of strategy formulation, are sometimes called *competitive strategies*. Business strategies focus on how to compete in a given business. Narrower in scope than a corporate strategy, a business strategy generally applies to a single business unit. Though usually situational in nature, most of these strategies can be classified as overall cost leadership, differentiation, or focus.[2]

### Figure 4.1 • Major Types and Subtypes of Corporate Strategies

| Corporate Strategies | Substrategies |
|---|---|
| 1. Growth strategies | Concentration<br>Vertical integration<br>Diversification |
| 2. Stability strategies | |
| 3. Defensive strategies | Turnaround<br>Divestiture<br>Liquidation |
| 4. Combination strategies | |

*Overall cost leadership* is a strategy designed to produce and deliver the product or service for a lower cost than the competition. Cost leadership is usually attained through a combination of experience and efficiency. More specifically, cost leadership requires close attention to production methods, overhead, marginal customers, and overall cost minimization in such areas as sales and research and development (R&D). Achieving an overall low-cost position usually requires that the company develop some unique advantage or advantages over its competitors. Examples include a high market share, favorable access to raw materials, use of state-of-the-art equipment, or special design features that make the product easy to manufacture. Walmart and Home Depot have adopted this strategy with great success.

*Differentiation* aims to make the product or service unique in its category, thus permitting the organization to charge higher-than-average prices. Differentiation can take many forms, such as design or brand image, quality, technology, customer service, or dealer network. The basic purpose of a differentiation strategy is to gain the brand loyalty of customers and a resulting lower sensitivity to price. Following a differentiation strategy does not imply that the business should have little concern for costs but that the major competitive advantage sought is through differentiation.

**Combination Strategies** Strategies by which an organization simultaneously employs different strategies for different parts of the company.

**Business Strategies** Strategies that focus on how to compete in a given business; also known as *competitive strategies*.

Depending on what is required to achieve differentiation, a company may or may not find it necessary to incur relatively high costs. For example, if high-quality materials or extensive research is necessary, the resulting product or service may be priced relatively high. When this is the case, the idea is that the uniqueness of the product or service will create a willingness on the part of the customers to pay the premium price. While such a strategy can be very profitable, it may or may not preclude gaining a high share of the market. For example, Rolex demands a very high price for its watches and makes a profit, but it has a very small market share.[3] Ralph Lauren Polo sportswear and Mercedes-Benz are other examples of products that used a differentiation strategy.

Differentiation can be achieved through a superior product (Microsoft), a quality image (Mercedes-Benz), or a brand image (Polo sportswear).

*Focus* is a third type of business strategy. Companies that use this method focus on, or direct their attention to, a narrow market segment. The segment may be a special buyer group, a geographic market, or one part of the product line. With a focus strategy, the firm serves a well-defined but narrow market better than competitors that serve a broader or less defined market. A "tall men's" clothing store is an example of a company following a focus strategy. Colgate-Palmolive, for example, has determined that to reach Hispanics successfully, it must capitalize on shared traits of this growing segment. Its 70 percent market share of toothpaste sold to Hispanics is largely attributed to understanding that three-quarters of Hispanics who watch TV or listen to radio do so with Spanish-language stations. Colgate-Palmolive has heavy sponsorship of favorite programs on these stations.[4]

**Figure 4.2 • Levels of Strategies**

**Corporate Strategy**
Addresses which businesses an organization will be in and how resources will be allocated among those businesses; describes the way the organization will pursue its objectives.

**Business Strategy**
Focuses on how to compete in a given business.

**Functional Strategy**
Concerned with the activities of the different functional areas of the organization, short-range step-by-step methods to be used (tactics).

1. What is the purpose of a business strategy?
2. Explain the three levels of strategy in an organization.
3. What are combination strategies?
4. How do functional strategies differ from business strategies?

*Colgate-Palmolive uses focus strategy to target specialized markets.*

## FUNCTIONAL STRATEGIES

**Functional Strategies**
Strategies that deal with the activities of the different functional areas of the business.

**Strategic Management**
Formulation, proper implementation, and continuous evaluation of strategic plans; determines the long-run directions and performance of an organization. The essence of strategic management is developing strategic plans and keeping them current.

The third primary level of strategy is functional strategies. **Functional strategies** are narrower in scope than business strategies and deal with the activities of the different functional areas of the business—production, finance, marketing, human resources, and the like. Functional strategies support the business strategies and are primarily concerned with how-to issues. Usually, functional strategies are in effect for a relatively short period, often one year or less. Figure 4.2 summarizes the different levels of strategies.

# >> The Strategic Management Process

## STRATEGIC MANAGEMENT

The rapid rate of change in today's business world is making it increasingly necessary that managers keep their plans current. **Strategic management** is the application of the basic planning process at the highest levels of the organization. Through the *strategic management process (SMP)*, top management determines the long-run direction and performance of the organization by ensuring careful formulation, proper implementation, and continuous evaluation of plans and strategies. The essence of strategic management is developing strategic plans and keeping them current as changes occur internally and in the environment. It is possible to prepare a formal plan with a well-defined strategy and not practice strategic management. In such a situation, the plan could become outmoded as changes occur in the environment. Practicing strategic management

# Thinking Critically 4.1

## >> Who Are We and What Do We Do?

The Department of Public Works (DPW) in Pinellas County, Florida, has approximately 515 employees and an annual operating budget of roughly $56 million. The DPW provides a wide range of services for the citizens residing in the county and for other county departments. About 60 percent of the staff and operating budget is related to the maintenance and operation of the county's road network, bridges, drainage systems, street lighting program, and traffic signs and signal systems. The remaining 40 percent of the department is involved with capital improvements and infrastructure reinvestment. Even though less than half of the county's activities focus on capital improvements, the primary measurement used to judge the performance and productivity of the DPW historically has been the percentage of capital projects completed.

Capital improvements are funded through the assessment of a penny per dollar sales tax, approved through referendum and identified by specific infrastructure improvement projects that are expected by citizens in the community. The DPW has come under fire because of the perception that the reported percentage completion of the past several years has been significantly lower than 100 percent. Questions have been asked: Why is the percentage completion so low? Is the goal too aggressive? Is the DPW inefficient? More recently, an even more compelling question has been asked: "How do we know that we [DPW] are competitive with the private sector?"

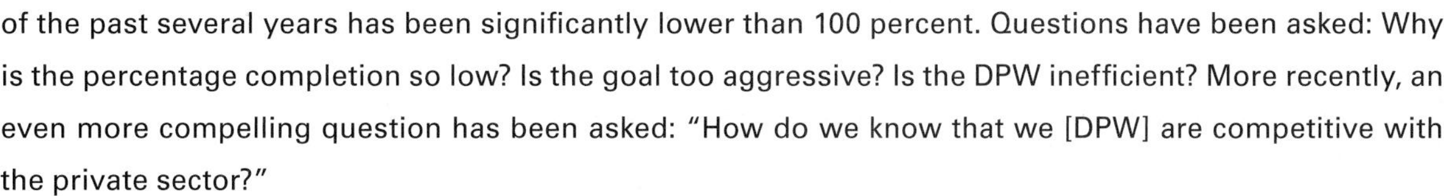

Working with a consulting company, the DPW undertook an extensive competitive assessment of the department's technical divisions that included financial services, real estate, contracting, and engineering services. A kickoff meeting was held to discuss the work plan and to prepare for interviews of key managers and supervisors within the department. More than 30 one-hour interviews were conducted over a four-day period. A facilitated, organizational self-assessment workshop for the DPW was conducted two months after the interviewing. More than 40 key managers and staff members participated in the daylong session during which participants:

1. Considered the key business objectives for the DPW.
2. Evaluated the way that work is typically performed.
3. Compared their work practices to behaviors that are characteristic of world-class public- and private-sector businesses.

During the workshop one of the exercises explored the department's mission by asking the questions, "Why does the DPW exist?" and "What is the primary business objective of the DPW?" To help answer these questions, workshop participants were asked to create a comprehensive list of activities performed by each of the DPW divisions. Participants were then asked to identify which of the tasks they considered to be the core and which to be support. A preliminary process model was then created that dramatically illustrated the following:

*Continued on next page*

Continued from page 77

1. The DPW performs a large number and wide variety of activities.
2. A significant number of those activities are performed for other departments in the county government.
3. More than one division performed the same or similar activity.
4. Focusing on a single measurement (such as the percentage of capital improvement projects completed) is inadequate for measuring the performance or productivity of the department.

After further organizational assessment at the division level, a benchmarking study of competitive business practices, and an analysis of employee interview data, a new listing of performance measures was created. Some of these measures included:

- The number of design starts this month and year to date, actual versus planned
- The number of preliminary engineering reports completed this month and year to date, actual versus planned
- The number of completed designs this month and year to date, actual versus planned
- The number of construction starts this month and year to date, actual versus planned

Managers recognized that these measures, and others like them, provided valuable insight into productivity, capacity, and demand. They could be used as management levers to make informed decisions for the corrective actions required to get things on the right track, such as decisions relating to resource allocation and workload redistribution.

**QUESTIONS**

1. Why is the "percentage of capital improvement projects completed" an inadequate measure of performance or productivity?
2. What difference does it make if the identified task is "core" or "support"?
3. Why would a benchmark study of competitive business practices be required?
4. How will these new performance measures affect the performance of the DPW?

*Source*: Adapted from David Mason, "The Long and Winding Road: Developing Useful Performance Measures," *OD Practitioner*, vol. 41, no. 2, 2009.

**Study Alert!**

Consider your current job or a job you held in the past. What is the company's mission statement? How easy is it to find? Does it reflect the business that you are in, or is it a generic statement?

does not ensure that an organization will meet all change successfully, but it does increase the odds.

Although guided by top management, successful strategic management involves many different levels in the organization. For example, top management may ask middle- and lower-level managers for input when formulating top-level plans. Once top-level plans have been finalized, different organizational units may be asked to formulate plans for their respective areas. A proper strategic management process helps ensure that plans throughout the different levels of the organization are coordinated and mutually supportive.

Organizations that consciously engage in strategic management generally follow a formalized process for making decisions and taking actions that affect their future direction. In the absence of a formal process, strategic decisions are made in a piecemeal fashion. An informal approach to strategy, however, does not necessarily mean the organization doesn't know what it is doing. It simply means the organization does not engage in any type of formalized process for initiating and managing strategy.

The strategic management process includes setting the organization's mission; defining what business or businesses the organization will be in; setting objectives; developing, implementing, and evaluating strategies; and adjusting these components as necessary. While the basic process is similar in most organizations, differences exist in the formality of the process, levels of managerial involvement, and degree of institutionalization of the process.

Although different organizations may use somewhat different approaches to the strategic management process, most successful approaches share several common components and a similar sequence. The strategic management process is composed of three major phases: (1) formulating the strategic plan, (2) implementing the strategic plan, and (3) evaluating the strategic plan. The **formulation phase** is concerned with developing the initial strategic plan. The **implementation phase** involves implementing the strategic plan that has been formulated. The **evaluation phase** stresses the importance of continuously evaluating and updating the strategic plan after it has been implemented. Each of these three phases is critical to the success of the strategic management process. A breakdown in any one area can easily cause the entire process to fail.

**Figure 4.3 • Objectives of the Company Mission**

1. To ensure harmony of purpose within the organization.
2. To provide a basis for motivating the use of the organization's resources.
3. To develop a basis, or standard, for allocating organizational resources.
4. To establish a general tone or organizational climate; for example, to suggest a businesslike operation.
5. To serve as a focal point for those who can identify with the organization's purpose and direction and to deter those who cannot do so from participating further in its activities.
6. To facilitate the translation of objectives and goals into a work structure involving the assignment of tasks to responsible elements within the organization.
7. To specify organizational purposes and the translation of these purpose into goals in such a way that cost, time, and performance parameters can be assessed and controlled.

## >> SMP: Formulation

The formulation stage of the strategic management process involves developing the corporate- and business-level strategies to be pursued. The strategies ultimately chosen are shaped by the organization's internal strengths and weaknesses and the threats and opportunities the environment presents.

The first part of the formulation phase is to obtain a clear understanding of the current position and status of the organization. This includes identifying the mission, identifying the past and present strategies, diagnosing the organization's past and present performance, and setting objectives for the company's operation.

### IDENTIFYING MISSION

An organization's mission is actually its broadest and highest level of objectives. The **mission** defines the basic purpose or purposes of the organization (for this reason, the terms *mission* and *purpose* are often used interchangeably). An organization's mission outlines why the organization exists. A mission statement usually includes a description of the organization's basic products or services and a definition of its markets or sources of revenue. Figure 4.3 outlines the objectives of a typical mission statement. Figure 4.4 has mission statements from three well-known companies.

Defining *mission* is crucial. It is also more difficult than one might imagine. Over 50 years ago, Peter Drucker emphasized that an organization's purpose should be examined and defined not only at its inception or during difficult

**Formulation Phase** First phase in strategic management, in which the initial strategic plan is developed.

**Implementation Phase** Second phase in strategic management, in which the strategic plan is put into effect.

**Evaluation Phase** Third phase in strategic management, in which the implemented strategic plan is monitored, evaluated, and updated.

**Mission** Basic purpose or purposes of the organization; why the organization exists; also known as *purpose*.

**Figure 4.4 • Examples of Mission Statements**

| Company | Mission Statement |
|---|---|
| FedEx | FedEx Corporation will produce superior financial returns for its shareowners by providing high value-added logistics, transportation, and related information services through focused operating companies. Customer requirements will be met in the highest quality manner appropriate to each market segment served. FedEx Corporation will strive to develop mutually rewarding relationships with its employees, partners, and suppliers. Safety will be the first consideration in all operations. Corporate activities will be conducted to the highest ethical and professional standards. |
| Harley-Davidson | We fulfill dreams through the experience of motorcycling, by providing to motorcyclists and to the general public an expanding line of motorcycles and branded products and services in selected market segments. |
| Pfizer | We will become the world's most valued company to patients, customers, colleagues, investors, business partners, and the communities where we work and live. |

times but also during successful periods.[5] If the railroad companies of the early 1900s or the wagon makers of the 1800s had made their organizational purpose to develop a firm position in the transportation business, they might hold the same economic positions today that they enjoyed in earlier times.

Drucker argues that an organization's purpose is determined not by the organization itself but by its customers. Customer satisfaction with the organization's product or service defines the purpose more clearly than does the organization's name, statutes, or articles of incorporation. Drucker outlines three questions that need to be answered to define an organization's present business. First, management must identify the customers: where they are, how they buy, and how they can be reached. Second, management must know what the customer buys. For instance, does the Rolls-Royce owner buy transportation or prestige? Finally, what is the customer looking for in the product? For example, does the homeowner buy an appliance from Sears because of price, quality, or service?

Management must also identify what the future business will be and what it should be. Drucker presents four areas to investigate. The first is market potential: What does the long-term trend look like? Second, what changes in market structure might occur due to economic developments, changes in styles or fashions, or competition? For example, how have oil prices affected the automobile market structure? Third, what possible changes will alter customers' buying habits? What new ideas or products might create new customer demand or change old demands? Consider the impact of the cell phone on the demand for pay telephones. Fourth, what customer needs are not being adequately served by available products and services? The introduction of overnight package delivery by FedEx is a well-known example of identifying and filling a current customer need.

## IDENTIFYING PAST AND PRESENT STRATEGIES

Before deciding if a strategic change is necessary or desirable, the past and present strategies used by the organization need to be clearly identified. General questions to be addressed include the following: Has past strategy been consciously developed? If not, can past history be analyzed to identify what inherent strategy has evolved? If so, has the strategy been recorded in writing? In either case, a strategy or a series of strategies, as reflected by the organization's past actions and intentions, can usually be identified.

## DIAGNOSING PAST AND PRESENT PERFORMANCE

To evaluate how past strategies have worked and determine whether strategic changes are needed, the organization's performance record must be examined. How is the organization currently performing? How has the organization performed over the last several years? Is the performance trend moving up or down? Management must address all these questions before attempting to formulate any future strategy. Evaluating an organization's performance usually involves in-depth financial analysis and diagnosis.

Once management has an accurate picture of the current status of the organization, the next step in formulating strategy is to decide what the long-, intermediate-, and short-range objectives should be in light of the current mission. However, these objectives cannot be accurately established without examining the internal and external environments. Thus, establishing the long- and intermediate-range objectives and analyzing the internal and external environments are concurrent processes that influence each other.

## SETTING OBJECTIVES

Once the mission of the organization has been clearly established, the guidelines offered earlier in this chapter should be followed to determine the specific long- and short-range objectives of the different organizational units. In general, long-range organizational objectives should derive from the mission statement. These long-range organizational objectives should then lead to the establishment of short-range performance objectives for the organization. Derivative objectives are subsequently developed for each major division and department. This process continues down through the various subunits to the individual level.

## SWOT ANALYSIS

**SWOT** is an acronym for an organization's strengths, weaknesses, opportunities, and threats. A SWOT analysis is a technique for evaluating an organization's

5. Define *strategic management.*
6. What are the three major phases of the strategic management process?
7. What is the purpose of an organization's mission?
8. Why is it important to diagnose past as well as present performance?

STAYING GREEN

Your company has seen a significant improvement in sales and market share on the basis of an aggressively advertised commitment to environmental responsibility. Media coverage of the use of solar power at your factory, increased use of recycled materials in your production processes, and tougher requirements for environmental responsibility from your suppliers have raised your public profile significantly, and other companies are coming to you for advice on making similar improvements in their operations. However, in this economic downturn, times have become much tougher. Several suppliers have either gone out of business or notified you that they can no longer maintain prices on your exacting environmental production standards. There are no alternative suppliers out there, and if you try sourcing products overseas, you are fairly certain that those suppliers will have even lower environmental standards. What do you do?

ETHICAL
MANAGEMENT
Can you relax a company's environmental standards and still advertise environmental responsibility?

internal strengths and weaknesses and its external opportunities and threats. A major advantage of using a SWOT analysis is that it provides a general overview of whether the organization's overall situation is healthy or unhealthy.[6] The underlying assumption of a SWOT analysis is that managers can better formulate a successful strategy after they have carefully reviewed the organization's strengths and weaknesses in light of the threats and opportunities the environment presents.

An organization's strengths and weaknesses are usually identified by conducting an internal analysis of the organization. The basic idea of conducting an internal analysis is to perform an objective assessment of the organization's current strengths and weaknesses. What does the organization do well? What does the organization do poorly? From a resource perspective, what are the organization's strengths and weaknesses?

The threats and opportunities presented by the environment are usually identified by methodically assessing the organization's external environment. An organization's **external environment** consists of everything outside the organization, but the focus of this assessment is on the external factors that affect its business. Such factors are classified by their proximity to the organization: they are either in its broad environment or in its competitive environment. Broad environmental factors are somewhat removed from the organization but can still influence it. General economic conditions and social, political, and technological trends represent major factors in the broad environment. Factors in the competitive environment are close to the organization and come in regular contact with it. Stockholders, suppliers, competitors, labor unions, customers, and potential new entrants represent members of the competitive environment.

Managers use many different qualitative and quantitative methods for forecasting broad environmental trends. Qualitative techniques are based primarily on opinions and judgments, whereas quantitative techniques are based primarily on the analysis of data and the use of statistical techniques. Both methods can be helpful depending on the circumstances and the information available.

The five forces model of competition is a tool developed by Michael Porter to help managers analyze their competitive environment. This model suggests that the competitive environment can be assessed by analyzing the import of and interactions among five major forces in the competitive or industry environment: (1) suppliers, (2) buyers, (3) competitive rivalry among firms currently in the industry, (4) product or service substitutes, and (5) potential entrants into the industry.[7] By using this tool to assess the competitive environment, managers can then better select the most appropriate business-level strategy to pursue. Figure 4.5 summarizes the five forces model of competition.

**SWOT** An acronym for strengths, weaknesses, opportunities, and threats. Business managers evaluate the performance of their department or the entire company using a SWOT analysis.

**External Environment** Everything outside the organization, with a focus on the external factors that affect the organization's business.

An assessment of the external environment emphasizes the fact that organizations do not operate in a vacuum and are very much affected by their surroundings. Figure 4.6 lists several factors that managers should consider when assessing an organization's strengths and weaknesses and the threats and opportunities posed by the environment. The most important result of a SWOT analysis is the ability to draw conclusions about the attractiveness of the organization's situation and the need for strategic action.

**Study Alert!** Make a SWOT analysis of your own strengths and weaknesses, then review the current job market – what challenges and opportunities are out there?

**Figure 4.5 • Five Forces Model of Competition**

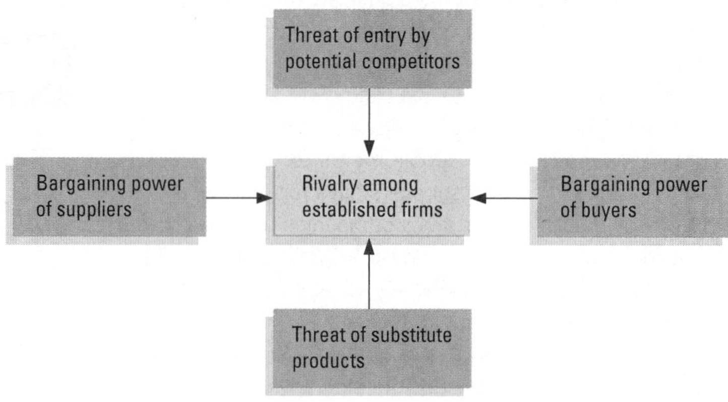


## COMPARING STRATEGIC ALTERNATIVES

The goal in this stage of the formulation process is to identify the feasible strategic alternatives (in light of everything that has been done up to this point) and then select the best alternative. Given the mission and long-range objectives, what are the feasible strategic alternatives? The results of the SWOT analysis limit the feasible strategic alternatives. For example, the results of an internal financial analysis could severely restrict an organization's options for expansion. Similarly, the results of an external analysis of population trends might also limit an organization's expansion plans. Once a set of feasible alternatives has been defined, the final strategic choice must be made.

The evaluation and final choice of an appropriate strategic alternative involve the integration of the mission, objectives, internal analysis, and external analysis. In this phase, management attempts to select the

**Figure 4.6 • SWOT Analysis**

**POTENTIAL INTERNAL STRENGTHS**
- Core competencies in key areas
- Adequate financial resources
- Well thought of by buyers
- An acknowledged market leader
- Well-conceived functional area strategies
- Access to economies of scale
- Insulated (at least somewhat) from strong competitive pressures
- Proprietary technology
- Cost advantages
- Better advertising campaigns
- Product innovation skills
- Proven management
- Ahead on experience curve
- Better manufacturing capability
- Superior technological skills
- Other?

**POTENTIAL EXTERNAL OPPORTUNITIES**
- Ability to serve additional customer groups or expand into new markets or segments
- Ways to expand product line to meet broader range of customer needs
- Ability to transfer skills or technological know-how to new products or businesses
- Integrating forward or backward
- Falling trade barriers in attractive foreign markets
- Complacency among rival firms
- Ability to grow rapidly because of strong increases in market demand
- Emerging new technologies

**POTENTIAL INTERNAL WEAKNESSES**
- No clear strategic direction
- Obsolete facilities
- Subpar profitability because . . .
- Lack of managerial depth and talent
- Missing some key skills or competencies
- Poor track record in implementing strategy
- Plagued with internal operating problems
- Falling behind in R&D
- Too narrow a product line
- Weak market image
- Weak distribution network
- Below-average marketing skills
- Unable to finance needed changes in strategy
- Higher overall unit costs relative to key competitors
- Other?

**POTENTIAL EXTERNAL THREATS**
- Entry of lower-cost foreign competitors
- Rising sales of substitute products
- Slower market growth
- Adverse shifts in foreign exchange rates and trade policies of foreign governments
- Costly regulatory requirements
- Vulnerability to recession and business cycle
- Growing bargaining power of customers or suppliers
- Changing buyer needs and tastes
- Adverse demographic changes
- Other?

THE IMPORTANCE OF "BEING REAL" . . .

## First Line Focus

*For a SWOT analysis to be truly effective, the appraisal must be honest and "real" on all four categories. Documenting strengths and opportunities is the easy part. Market leadership, new products in the pipeline, strong profit margins, and high customer satisfaction scores make for enjoyable reading in reports and presentations to your boss. However, acknowledging weaknesses and identifying serious external threats are often not so pleasant, because with those acknowledgments comes the expectation that you have a plan to address them. If you don't have such a plan, the temptation is to downplay the weaknesses and threats, thereby removing the need for the plan. That guarantees not only future problems for the company but also a very short career for you. Your plan may not be perfect, and it may need input and sign-off from other departments and managers, but it is better to have recognized the problem than to have pretended that it isn't there at all.*

corporate strategy that offers the organization its best chance to achieve its mission and objectives through actions that are compatible with its capacity for risk and its value structure. Once the corporate strategy has been identified, additional substrategies must be selected to support it.

**Strategic Business Unit (SBU)** Distinct business that has its own set of competitors and can be managed reasonably independently of other businesses within the organization.

In the case of diversified, multibusiness organizations, comparing strategic alternatives involves assessing the attractiveness of each business as well as the overall business mix. A **strategic business unit (SBU)** is a distinct business that has its own set of competitors and can be managed reasonably independently of other businesses within the organization.[8] The elements of an SBU vary from organization to organization but can be a division, a subsidiary, or a single product line. In a small organization, the entire company may be an SBU.

There must, inevitably, be some process of prioritization. With limited funding and resources, it would not be possible to address every element of a strategy at the same time and with the same degree of action. Therefore, specific choices must be made—is this an immediate problem that needs fixing or a longer-term initiative that needs to be started? How soon do we need to check back on progress in order to determine the need for a course correction? These are the responsibilities of a strategic manager.

### From the PERSPECTIVE OF...

**An SBU Planner** Running a division within a large corporation as a strategic business unit is very much like running your own business within a small competitive market. You must compete for resources and budget dollars and generate margins on a stand-alone basis, with no advantageous pricing from other departments or divisions within the corporation. What does the division gain from such an arrangement? How does that impact the role of the division manager?

### [PROGRESS] ✓questions

9. Explain the term SWOT analysis.
10. What are the five forces of competition?
11. What is an SBU?
12. Why must an organization prioritize strategic planning decisions?

## >> SMP: Implementation

After the corporate strategy has been carefully formulated, it must be translated into organizational actions. Given that the corporate strategy and business-level strategies have been clearly identified, what actions must be taken to implement them? Strategy implementation involves everything that must be done to put the strategy in motion successfully. Necessary actions include determining and implementing the most appropriate organizational structure, developing short-range objectives, and establishing functional strategies.

## Thinking Critically 4.2

### >> Transferring Responsibility for Food Safety

In January 2009, the peanut products produced at the Blakely, Georgia, plant of the Peanut Corporation of America (PCA) were found to be the source of a salmonella-poisoning outbreak that made almost 600 people sick and was implicated in the death of eight others. Once identified, the U.S. Food and Drug Administration's Center for Food Safety and Applied Nutrition ordered the recall of all the whole peanuts (dry and oil roasted), granulated peanuts, peanut meal, peanut butter, and peanut paste that had been produced at the plant since January 2007, making it one of the largest recalls the center had ever ordered.

With products distributed to 43 states through over 200 different products from 38 separate companies, the management of the recall presented logistical challenges in both communicating to consumers and in the recovery of physical inventory. By February 2009, the list of products identified for recall had exceeded 1,300, covering everything from ice cream to crackers, cereals, candy, trail mix, and dog biscuits. Media coverage of the story was so prominent that many other peanut product manufacturers, including Kraft Foods, the Hershey Company, Russell Stover Candies, and ConAgra, were prompted to take out prominent advertising messages to reassure their consumers that their peanut products were safe.

As the investigation of the Food and Drug Administration (FDA) continued, it became clear that PCA had an extremely poor track record of food safety, including the documented shipment of food products that were known to have tested positive for salmonella contamination. PCA was subsequently banned from doing business with the government, and the company was eventually forced into bankruptcy under a barrage of lawsuits.

Public outcry over the apparent lack of food safety measures prompted a comprehensive review of FDA operations ordered by President Barack Obama, in addition to a criminal investigation launched by the Justice Department into the operation of the Georgia plant.

ConAgra, one of the companies that rushed to advertise the safety of its peanut products, has had its own record of food safety issues, including a major Peter Pan peanut butter recall in 2006. In 2007, an estimated 15,000 people were sickened by salmonella poisoning from frozen pot pies under ConAgra's Banquet label—an event that prompted the company to examine the supply chain for ingredients in its processed food products.

The presence of lingering microbes in a supply chain that is becoming increasingly global as producers attempt to minimize ingredient costs is now taken as a given rather than a possibility. The key to food safety in processed foods is the "kill step" of cooking food to a sufficiently high temperature to kill any lingering microbes. While this may seem simple, food processors like ConAgra face the challenge of balancing that kill step with the knowledge that high cooking temperatures often turn the contents of those products—particularly vegetables—to mush before the products are frozen and shipped to retailers for sale to customers.

The solution? Shift the burden for food safety to consumers rather than trying to address it in the manufacturing process. General Mills, for example, which was forced to recall about 5 million frozen pizzas in 2007 after *an E. coli* outbreak, now instructs consumers to cook with conventional ovens rather than microwave ovens. ConAgra has taken this approach one step further by changing food safety instructions on it's Banquet pot pies to advise customers, "Internal temperature needs to reach 165°F as measured by a food thermometer in several spots."

According to the U.S. Department of Agriculture's Web site, less than half the U.S. population owns a food thermometer, and only 3 percent use it when cooking high-risk foods.

QUESTIONS

1. Is the need to keep ingredient costs down an acceptable justification to source those ingredients from lesser quality suppliers? Why or why not?
2. The public outcry over the peanut paste salmonella outbreak was directed at the FDA for failing to keep the food supply safe. Shouldn't companies be expected to deliver a safe product too?
3. From a strategic management perspective, how can you rationalize moving the burden for food safety to consumers?
4. What other steps could ConAgra have taken to address this issue?

*Source:* Steven Reinberg, "Executive Health: Seventh Salmonella Death Linked to Peanut Products," *BusinessWeek*, January 24, 2009; Steven Reinberg, "Executive Health: All Products at Georgia Peanut Plant Recalled," *BusinessWeek*, January 29, 2009; Michael Moss, "Food Companies Are Placing the Onus for Safety on Consumers," *The New York Times*, May 15, 2009; and E. J. Mundell, "Executive Health: FDA: Company Knowingly Shipped Tainted Peanut Products," *BusinessWeek*, February 7, 2009.

## ORGANIZATIONAL FACTORS

Not only does an organization have a strategic history; it also has existing structures, policies, and systems. Although each of these factors can change as a result of a new strategy, each must be assessed and dealt with as part of the implementation process.

Even though an organization's structure can always be altered, the associated costs may be high. For example, a reorganization may result in substantial hiring and training costs for newly structured jobs. Thus, from a practical standpoint, an organization's current structure places certain restrictions on strategy implementation.

The strategy must fit with current organizational policies, or the conflicting policies must be modified. Often, past policies heavily influence the extent to which future policies can be altered. For example, the A. T. Cross Company, manufacturer of world-renowned writing instruments, has a policy of unconditionally guaranteeing its products for life. Because customers have come to expect this policy, Cross would find it difficult to discontinue it.

Similarly, organizational systems that are currently in place can affect how the strategy might best be implemented. These systems can be either formal or informal. Examples include information systems, compensation systems, communication systems, and control systems.

## FUNCTIONAL STRATEGIES

As introduced earlier in this chapter, functional strategies are the means by which business strategies become operational. Functional strategies outline the specific short-range actions to be taken by the different functional units of the organization (e.g., production, marketing, finance, and human resources) to implement the business strategies. The development of functional strategies generally requires the active participation of many levels of management. In fact, input by lower levels of management at the development stage is essential to the successful implementation of functional strategies.

**Figure 4.7 • The Strategic Management Process**

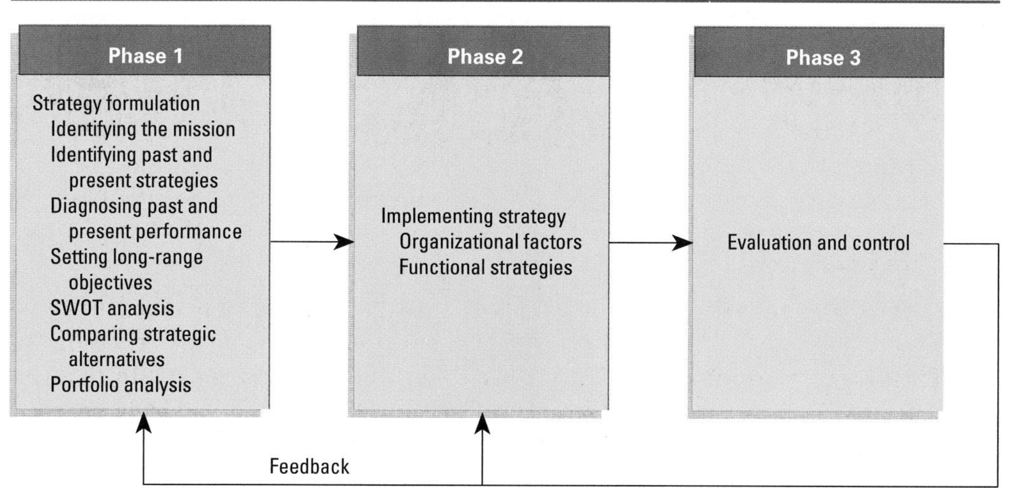

EMPLOYING ILLEGAL IMMIGRANTS

As a result of bad weather and supplier problems, you are behind schedule on a building project, and the owner of the company instructs you to hire some illegal immigrants to help get the project back on track. You are ordered to pay them in cash "under the table"; and the owner justifies the decision as being "a 'one-off'—besides, the INS [Immigration and Naturalization Service] has bigger fish to fry than a few undocumented workers on a building site! If we get caught, we'll pay the fine—it will be less than the penalty we would owe our client for missing our deadline on the project." What do you do?

ETHICAL
MANAGEMENT
Should you break the law to save your project's schedule?


## >> SMP: Evaluation and Control

After the strategic plan has been put into motion, the next challenge is to monitor continuously the organization's progress toward its long-range objectives and mission. Is the corporate strategy working, or should revisions be made? Where are problems likely to occur? The emphasis is on making the organization's managers aware of the problems that are likely to occur and of the actions to be taken if problems do arise. As discussed earlier in this chapter, continuously evaluating and responding to internal and environmental changes is what strategic management is all about.

On page 85, figure 4.7 summarizes the strategic management process and its major components.

### [PROGRESS] ✓questions

13. What is the difference between a functional strategy and a business strategy?
14. Which is more important, design or implementation? Why?
15. If the plan has been well designed, why should it need to be monitored?
16. Most effective managers have a "Plan B" to back up their strategy. Why would that be useful?

### From the PERSPECTIVE OF...

**An Army Officer** Business strategies are often implemented with the precision of military battle campaigns, and military bases are run with the same operational efficiency as for-profit businesses. From a management perspective, how different do you think the work environment of a military base would be? Would a military chain of command make a difference? Do you think your commanding officer would be open to the same input and feedback as a business manager? Why or why not?

## >> Chapter Summary

We have seen in this chapter that one of the keys to effective management is the ability to plan ahead and actively affect rather than passively accept the future. Strategic management allows managers to anticipate scenarios and to have responses in place, rather than leaving them exposed to crisis situations that may arise with no plan, and having to make decisions in the moment, often with little hard data. In the next chapter we examine how this situation is changed when management moves to the global stage.

1. Define *strategy*, and explain its importance to organizational success.

   A strategy outlines how management intends to achieve its objectives in the future. Without a clear and detailed strategy in place, management will lack the perspective and guidance needed to prioritize the allocation of resources—capital investment, new product development, marketing dollars, sales campaigns—to achieve future growth targets.

2. Explain the three levels of strategy that exist in an organization.

   Strategies can be classified according to the scope of what they are intended to accomplish. Corporate, or grand, strategies are developed at the highest levels of the organizational hierarchy and determine the overall direction for the organization, typically over a long-range time horizon. The position taken in these strategies can be categorized as growth, stability, defensive, or a combination for different markets or product lines.

   Business, or competitive, strategies represent a second level of strategic planning that typically focuses on competitive tactics in a single market or business unit. These strategies can categorized as overall cost leadership in the target market, product or service differentiation, or focus, where companies target a narrow market niche or specialty buyer group.

   The third primary level of strategy is the functional strategy, which is narrower in scope than business strategies and typically focuses on specific functional areas of the business—production, finance, marketing, human resources, and the like. Functional strategies support business strategies and are usually in effect for a short period, often one year or less.

3. Discuss the stages of the strategic management process.

   The strategic management process is composed of three major phases:

   a. Formulating the strategic plan based on a thorough assessment of the current condition of the organization and projected growth of the market, and prioritized objectives for the future that align with the corporate mission.
   b. Implementing the strategic plan, which involves everything that must be done to put the strategy in motion successfully, including establishing functional strategies, short-range objectives, and, if necessary, modifying the organizational structure.
   c. Evaluating the strategic plan to ensure progress against key objectives. To be effective, progress must be monitored continuously with special attention paid to key events and potential problems that were identified in the formulation stage.

4. Define *organizational mission*, and explain how mission relates to long- and short-range objectives.

   An organization's mission outlines why the organization exists (beyond the most common profit directive of making money for its shareholders). The statement of that mission typically includes a description of the products or services offered and the customers and/or markets served by the organization.

   Without a clear statement of why the organization exists and whom that organization exists to serve, management would have no benchmark by which to establish long- and short-range objectives. For example, tracking how customer expectations are changing requires that you have a clear idea of who those customers are, and to monitor your competition, you need a clear sense of the market in which you are competing.

5. Discuss the components of a SWOT analysis.

   SWOT is an acronym for a detailed assessment of an organization's internal strengths and weaknesses and external opportunities and threats. The underlying assumption of a SWOT

*Continued on next page*

Continued from page 87

analysis is that managers can better formulate a successful strategy after they have carefully reviewed the organization's strengths and weaknesses in light of the threats and opportunities the environment presents.

A truly effective SWOT analysis requires an honest assessment of both the organization and its environment. For the managers required to perform that analysis, there is a real temptation to overemphasize strengths and opportunities and minimize weaknesses and threats. A poorly formulated and implemented strategy can often be traced back to internal decisions that failed to address organizational weaknesses or underestimated threats in the marketplace.

6. Explain how strategic alternatives are identified and selected.

The evaluation and final choice of an appropriate strategic alternative involves the integration of the mission, objectives, internal analysis, and external analysis. In this phase, management attempts to select the corporate strategy that offers the organization its best chance to achieve its mission and objectives through actions that are compatible with its capacity for risk and its value structure.

Without the benefit of unlimited capital resources, objectives must be prioritized, and management must develop business and functional strategies to ensure the most effective implementation of those strategies based on assigned resources.

## THE WORLD of Work >>

**TONY FILLS A VACANCY** ***(continued from page 73)***

The scheduling project worked remarkably well. There were a few grumbles at first that Tony was simply dumping one of his headaches onto them, but once the crew rolled up their sleeves and started working on the schedule, some amazing things started to happen. First, the problems and challenges that prevented individual employees from working specific shifts on specific days suddenly became manageable outside the schedule. People started carpooling more; people traded babysitting duties for free to cover each other; the more experienced crew members swapped stations on their assigned shift—all to make the schedule work and to make sure every shift was covered. Tony was true to his word and spent every available minute in the restaurant working with new employees and helping others get cross-trained in other areas of the Taco Barn system.

Kevin had done a great job in leading the scheduling project, and he was hoping that this would clinch his promotion to shift leader once Tanya left. She was scheduled to leave at the end of the week, and so far no decision had been announced.

After the lunch rush was over, Kevin received the request he had been waiting for—a private meeting with Tony in his office.

"Kevin, you've been a great crew member here, and you did a good job on that scheduling project."

Just like Tony to get straight to the point thought Kevin. "Thanks, Tony," he replied.

"I'm putting your name forward to Dawn as Tanya's replacement," said Tony, "but to do that I will need some supporting information. Your work record here speaks for itself, but Dawn likes to get a sense of people outside their résumés, so I'd like you to write a little report for me."

"What kind of report?" asked Kevin, suddenly getting a little nervous.

"Taco Barn is always looking for future unit managers and regional managers, and I think you should be included in that group, Kevin. To convince Dawn of that, I'd like you to write a strategic planning document for this unit for the next three to five years. Nothing too complicated—where are we now and where you think we should go in the next few years. Can you do that?"

"Sure," answered Kevin, suddenly wishing he had paid more attention in his business classes at school.

"Great," said Tony. "If you can get it to me in a couple of days, I can have it on Dawn's desk in time to get you promoted before Tanya leaves at the end of the week."

**QUESTIONS**

1. Which should count more for Kevin's promotion: his leadership of the scheduling project or his length of employment with Taco Barn? Explain your answer.
2. Why is Tony making Kevin write the strategic planning report?
3. What information should Kevin put in his report?
4. Do you think Tony will be able to use any of the material in Kevin's report? Why or why not?

## Key Terms >>

**business strategies** 75

**combination strategies** 75

**corporate strategies** 75

**defensive or retrenchment strategies** 74

**evaluation phase** 79

**external environment** 81

**formulation phase** 79

**functional strategies** 76

**growth strategies** 74

**implementation phase** 79

**mission** 79

**stability strategies** 74

**strategic business unit (SBU)** 83

**strategic management** 76

**strategy** 74

**SWOT** 81

1. If strategic planning is an activity that originates from senior management, why should a front-line or middle manager be concerned with strategic planning?
2. Which should come first, the objectives or the strategy? Why?
3. Should a middle manager have a strategy? If so, what kind?
4. Under what circumstances would a company have a defensive strategy?
5. How often should a strategy be monitored? Provide examples.
6. What is the difference between actively affecting rather than passively accepting the future?

# INTERNET In Action >>

1. Select the mission statement of an organization of your choice, and identify the following components of the statement:
    a. Customer or market
    b. Product or service
    c. Geographic domain
    d. Technology
    e. Concern for survival
    f. Philosophy
    g. Self-concept
    h. Concern for public image
2. Research and identify a company that uses strategic business units as a method of corporate organization. Document how an individual SBU is managed. Does the SBU structure equate to strong business performance? Based on what criteria? Was the company built on SBUs from the beginning, or did it switch over time? Why?

1. **SWOT Analysis**

   Divide the class into four groups, with each one taking a component of the SWOT analysis: strengths, weaknesses, opportunities, and threats. Select a company, and produce an honest and detailed appraisal of that company's condition and future prospects based on your SWOT analysis.

2. **Strategic Plan**

   Based on the SWOT analysis completed in question 1, remain in your four separate groups and propose a strategy to address each issue identified. Once complete, decide as a group how you will prioritize your plan—which items will be addressed in what order and why?

   **Remember to answer the following questions:**

   What assumptions are you making?

   What happens if your assumptions are wrong?

   How soon will you know if your strategy is working?

   What is your plan B?

   How long before you need a course correction?

# Case 4.1

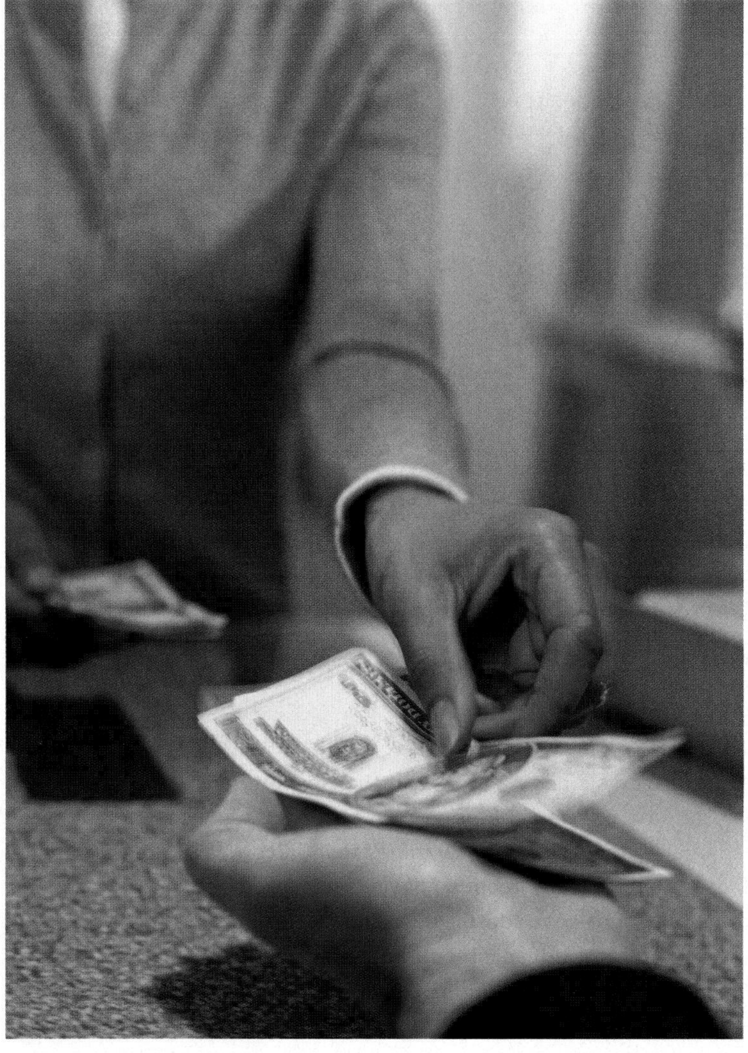

## >> The Long Road Back

Can Citigroup's Vikram Pandit lead the company back from a Troubled Asset Relief Program (TARP) bailout to anything resembling those former glory days of market dominance?

Formed in April 1998 from the merger of banking giant Citicorp and financial services giant Traveler's Group, Citigroup (which markets itself as "Citi") promoted a model of universal or one-stop banking and became a conglomerate of such size that when financial markets collapsed in 2008, Citi was one of only a few institutions deemed to be "too big to fail."

With a financial services network spanning over 140 countries, employing over 300,000 people at its peak, the size of Citi's operation was massive. At the time of the merger, the combined entity was valued at over $140 billion, with $700 billion in assets under management. However, that commitment to universal banking has seen the share price decline from a high of $57 per share in December 2006 to less than $1 per share in March 2009.

CEO Vikram S. Pandit was promoted to the office vacated by Charles O. Prince III in late 2007 with the task, at least initially, of making the wide range of companies under the Citi umbrella work efficiently and deliver on the promise of one-stop banking. With a troubled history of flawed deals followed by poor integration of the new acquisitions into the Citi corporate culture, the prospects for Pandit looked bleak. The collapse of the financial markets in 2008 changed priorities for Citi overnight, making survival the number one objective.

In October 2008 Citi received a bailout loan from the government's TARP of $25 billion, only to return one month later after a more detailed analysis of Citi's "bad assets" for an additional $20 billion loan. By March 2010, Citi was the only one of the "Big Four" banks in the United States (Bank of America, JP Morgan Chase, Wells Fargo, and Citi) to still owe money to taxpayers, having converted the TARP loans into stock in the company and giving the U.S. government a 36 percent stake in the company.

Pandit's strategy to restore Citi to some form of stability has come under severe criticism. In January 2009 it was announced that Citi would reorganize into two separate operating units: Citicorp (one-half of the original merger) would manage retail and investment banking, and Citi Holdings would manage stock brokerage and asset management services. With a reported loss of $7.6 billion for the final three months of 2009, it appears that Pandit still has a lot of work to do, even after cutting over a third of the organization's workforce (110,000 employees) and selling assets such as the commodity trading operation Phibro at what critics believed to be

*Continued on next page*

Continued from page 91

fire-sale prices. With a selling price of only $450 million (less than the division's annual net profit) and a highly disputed severance package of $100 million to senior trader Andrew Hall, critics are concerned that Pandit's urgency to right the sinking ship as quickly as possible could do long-term damage to the value of the assets Citi has left.

**QUESTIONS**

1. Many of the questionable investments that nearly destroyed Citi had been made before Pandit became CEO. Does that excuse him from any responsibility in fixing the problem? Why or why not?
2. Traveler's Group CEO Sandy Weil believed in the vision of one-stop banking and pushed for the merger with Citicorp to achieve that vision. Given what has happened since, and the criticism over banks being too big to fail, was the idea of one-stop banking doomed from the start? Why or why not?
3. Pandit has been criticized for his eagerness to unload assets at fire-sale prices. Research the company, and find two other deals that came under fire from critics.
4. Citi has lost over one-third of its workforce in cost-cutting measures. Analysts are now concerned that when financial markets do recover, many Citi employees will abandon the company for better opportunities elsewhere. Is that a valid concern? Why or why not?

*Source:* "A House Built on Sandy," *The Economist,* January 15, 2009; Eric Dash, "Pandit Is Running Out of Time to Clean Up Citigroup," *The New York Times,* January 20, 2010; and "Pandit and the Playthings," *The Economist,* October 15, 2009.

# Case 4.2

## >> Taking Hewlett-Packard in a New Direction

In the four years since he took over the Hewlett-Packard (HP) CEO role from Carleton S. "Carly" Fiorina, Mark V. Hurd has won recognition in Silicon Valley for doing the very things that Silicon Valley does not enjoy doing: running fiscally responsible businesses based on performance metrics and tight cost control (as opposed to amazing the world with new technological advancements and then figuring out how to make businesses out of them). As one of the largest buyers of computer system components (HP buys about one-fifth of Intel's chips), Hurd has devoted a great deal of time and attention to leverage the company's size in playing suppliers off one another to keep costs as low as possible.

Hurd's first major challenge was to manage the integration of the $20 billion purchase of Compaq Computer initiated by Fiorina. Add to that the unpopular $13 billion purchase of Electronic Data Systems (EDS) in 2008, and it becomes apparent that the majority of Hurd's attention in the last four years has been, of necessity, internally focused. One of his first acts as CEO was to cut 15,000 jobs—10 percent of the workforce at that time. The EDS deal brought a totally different set of challenges. EDS's $22 billion in annual sales as number two in the market, added to HP's $16.6 billion as number three, allowed HP to jump into second place behind IBM's $54 billion in annual sales, but the deal remained unpopular because EDS's operating margin of 6 percent was significantly lower than HP's 10 percent. In addition, EDS's workforce is primarily U.S.-based at a time when technology outsourcing has moved overseas to leverage lower employee costs in places like India.

Hurd's legendary cost-cutting capabilities can probably be counted on to tighten up EDS's operating costs, but there is a growing concern that the internal focus on costs may leave HP behind in the race for new game-changing products and technology. In particular, Hurd's approach to research and development at HP has generated concern that while operations at the company are definitely leaner and tighter than they have ever been, which has been a tremendous asset in this economic downturn, when demand does return, HP may come up short in new products to meet that new demand.

HP uses a metric called "R&D productivity," where the research spending is tracked as a percentage of gross margin. In practice, this means that a low-margin product such as a desktop computer will get less R&D funds for new features than a high-margin product like a laptop. This approach has allowed HP's multi-touch screen technology to push the company past Dell as the world's largest PC maker. However, critics have also argued that this metric-driven approach contributed to HP's late arrival with a line of netbooks, the low-cost laptops that have diverted a lot of sales from the traditional laptop market, allowing Acer to gain a significant market share advantage.

HP Labs, historically one of the company's most admired divisions, has seen dramatic changes ensue since Hurd's arrival. Traditionally run in the freewheeling style of Xerox's Palo Alto Research Center (PARC)—the R&D shop credited with the development of the mouse and the graphical user interface (GUI) technology that so dramatically impacted the development of Apple's Macintosh—HP Labs has reduced the number of active projects from 150 down to 30 on the basis of a new Darwinian selection process. The projects with the most commercial potential get the funds rather than the projects with the potential for the greatest technological advancement. Researchers now find themselves submitting business plans based on customer focus groups rather than research proposals based on abstract theoretical propositions.

What makes critics nervous about this performance-driven approach is how different this path looks from those of the true game changers in the market. HP may have a tight rein on costs in the computer component market, but it was Apple that produced the iPod, iPad, and iPhone, and Amazon that produced the Kindle. Similarly, the purchase of EDS was designed to cement HP's long-term presence in the data-mining and information analysis market, but IBM and Oracle have the leading software packages.

Hurd has recognized that businesses face a future of ever-increasing data management and storage, and HP has provided hardware and printer products to meet that need. Indeed, the expensive printer ink division remains HP's cash cow. However, now that companies are examining the potential of web-based "cloud computing" for the virtual management of data, HP has yet to carve out a clear brand in that market.

Cost containment has given HP the funds to thrive in an economic downturn and a war chest of cash to make even more acquisitions in the future, but to do that, the company must have a clear sense of not only where it sees the market going but also the role it intends to play in that new market. Critics argue that this will require a dramatically different skill set than the impressive performance displayed by Mark Hurd in his tenure as CEO thus far.

## QUESTIONS

1. Summarize a SWOT analysis of Mark Hurd's performance at Hewlett-Packard.
2. R&D is a creative function. Is it a good idea to make it metric-driven? Explain your answer.
3. Is HP positioned to be successful over the long term? Why or why not?
4. What would you advise Hurd to do now?

*Source:* Adam Lashinsky and Doris Burke, "Mark Hurd's Moment," *Fortune Magazine*, vol. 159, no. 5, pp. 90–100; Cliff Edwards, "The Return on Research," *BusinessWeek*, March 23, 2009; Ashlee Vance, "Does H.P. Need a Dose of Anarchy," *The New York Times*, April 26, 2009; and Conrad de Aenlle, "Weighing Prospects for H.P.," *The New York Times*, May 24, 2009.

# Case 4.3

## >> Planning a Future for Metro Mercy

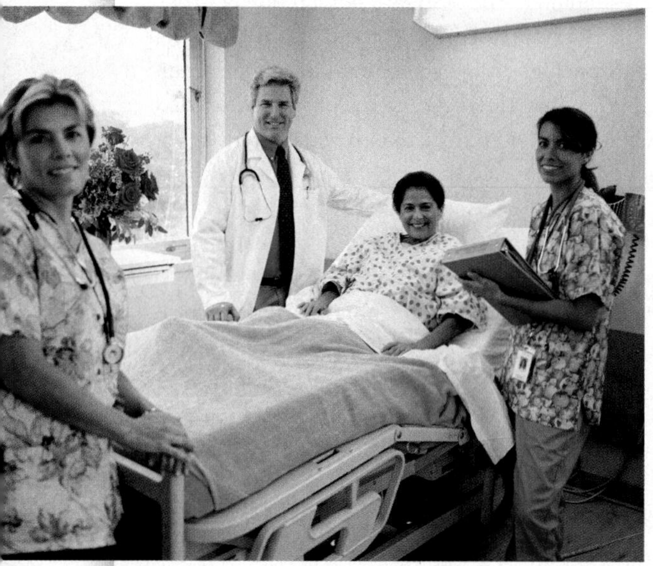

Metro Mercy Hospital (MMH) has been in a downward spiral, resulting in losses in the past few years and a tenuous cash position. Although a new management team has recently been put in place and a turnaround begun, the board of directors is unclear as to whether the hospital can and should remain independent now and in the future.

MMH is a Catholic-sponsored, freestanding, 200-bed hospital with annual operating revenues of $125 million, located in the western end of a city in a large metropolitan area. The hospital is a relatively undifferentiated, general acute care facility with the typical range of medical, surgical, obstetric and gynecologic, and pediatric services. It has a very busy emergency department and owns a network of physician practices in the area it serves; these practices provide mainly primary care services and constitute a significant portion of the primary care medical staff of the hospital.

MMH is located in a rapidly changing community. The population it has historically served, primarily second- and third-generation Italian and Polish Americans, has moved to the suburbs and/or aged. These groups have been replaced by African Americans and, more recently, Hispanics, particularly immigrants from Mexico. Although the service area population was expected to decrease from 1990 to 2000, Census Bureau data indicate that the population—especially Hispanic—actually grew. Recent estimates suggest continued slow growth and a transformation of service area demographics.

MMH faces very stiff competition due in part to the number of competitors in and around its service area and the general "overbeddedness" in the region. Its main competitors include St. Luke's Hospital, the 600-bed flagship of a very successful multihospital system, located a few miles west of MMH in an affluent suburban area; a nationally recognized teaching hospital located within five miles of MMH; a number of other tertiary teaching hospitals located in and around the downtown area of the city; and one large for-profit community hospital and two large system-affiliated community hospitals all located within three to five miles of MMH.

MMH has experienced downward trends in utilization and financial performance since 2004. In 2006, the hospital had an operating loss of $10.9 million (total loss of $10.6 million) after an operating loss of $10 million (total loss of $10.2 million) in 2005. The financial situation led to the resignation of the previous CEO and an interim management arrangement for about 12 months until a new CEO was named and who began work in early 2007. The board was also reorganized, and a new board chair and other board members with strong business skills were added in 2006–07.

The new management team's first priority was to restore the organization to financial health. By fall 2007, operating losses had been trimmed substantially to $6 million, and the organization was on target to be at break-even on a monthly basis by the end of fiscal year 2008.

As the turnaround proceeds, the new CEO and board leadership believe it is imperative that the hospital develop a new strategic plan. Although much of the financial improvement that is occurring is a result of internal operating changes and managed care contract revisions, and leadership believes that tighter operations and financial management can bring the hospital to break even, the hospital needs to make significant improvements on the market and revenue side if it is to become truly viable. Therefore, while management continues its operational changes, a strategic planning effort needs to commence to help position MMH for long-term success. A key question to be answered in the strategic planning process is whether MMH should remain freestanding, become an affiliate, or join a system.

## SWOT Analysis

| Strengths | Weaknesses | Opportunities | Threats |
|---|---|---|---|
| Catholic base, caring organization | Limited response to neighborhood diversity | Differentiation through Catholic identity | Continued erosion of volumes and market share |
| Strong history | Declining volumes, weak market position | Community outreach | Significant number of providers in the market |
| Neighborhood growth, economic revitalization | Aging medical staff | Medical staff development | Inability to compete as a stand-alone provider |
| Several younger, well-trained, entrepreneurial physicians on staff | Medical staff–hospital relations | Program development/ enhancement in key service lines | Payer mix |
| Primary care base | Poor financial performance | Partnerships (other Catholic hospitals, physicians, niche players) | "Outsiders" skimming business from local hospitals |
| | Large proportion of admissions through the emergency department (few patients choosing MMH) | Niche programs (occupational medicine, wound care, pain management, sleep lab) | Medical staff |
| | | Prevention and health promotion | |

## Options Being Considered for MMH

| | Freestanding | Affiliate | Merge |
|---|---|---|---|
| Pros | Proud tradition<br>Growing Catholic area<br>Good book of business | Attractive to two or three organizations<br>Strong clinical management complementarity<br>Transitional step to merger | Would provide support needed to thrive<br>Potential Catholic and non-Catholic options<br>Likely anyway in 3–5 years |
| Cons | Weak cash position<br>Capital needs<br>Formidable competition | Does not address capital needs<br>Hard to get/keep partners' attention<br>Probably not long-term solution | Better deal possible if stabilized<br>Wrenching decision for sponsor<br>Potential loss of community focus |

### QUESTIONS

1. Review the SWOT analysis for MMH, and identify the top two issues for each category. Explain your selection.
2. What does the focus on business skills for the new leadership team suggest about the leadership history of MMH?
3. Based on the SWOT analysis and options chart, what is your recommendation for MMH? Explain your answer.
4. Is there a fourth alternative other than to remain freestanding, affiliate, or merge? Why or why not?

*Source:* Adapted from A. M. Zuckerman, "Affiliate, Merge, or Stay Independent?" *Healthcare Financial Management*, August 2008, pp. 118–20.

# CHAPTER 5

"The World has become small and completely interdependent."

**Wendell L. Wilkie, Republican presidential nominee defeated by Franklin D. Roosevelt in 1940**

# GLOBAL MANAGEMENT

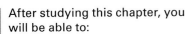

LEARNING OUTCOMES

After studying this chapter, you will be able to:

1 Define *global management.*

2 Compare and contrast importing and exporting.

3 Explain the advantages and disadvantages of protectionism.

4 Discuss the challenges of doing business globally.

## THE WORLD OF WORK

### Taco Barn takes customer service offshore

Tony was looking forward to reading Kevin's strategic planning report, but, as was often the case, a project from corporate headquarters gave Tony a new priority. Dawn Williams announced a new customer service initiative called "Taco Barn To Go," as an attempt to reach customers who didn't want to sit and eat in the restaurant. With a toll-free central ordering number, customers could call in their order from the Taco Barn menu and pick up their food at their local restaurant within 30 minutes.

Tony was introduced to this new initiative at the regular monthly regional meeting for unit managers. His first reaction was very positive. Their competition had been offering a similar service for months now, and Tony felt that Taco Barn's response was long overdue. However, when the regional information technology (IT) specialist began his presentation to explain why the launch had taken so long to get off the ground, Tony found his enthusiasm for the new project rapidly disappearing.

Because there were so many choices on the Taco Barn menu—particularly side items—the company had decided not to use a Web site for the new "To Go" service. It felt it would be more customer-friendly to have a live person on the phone taking your order, just like the waiter would if you ate in the restaurant. Further research had shown that taking telephone orders at each restaurant would disrupt running the restaurant and that developing a central reservations center would be too expensive to build and maintain. The company then looked at contracting with a service to take orders on a per call basis, but even that was expensive.

The solution had been found after the regional IT specialist had returned from a conference on outsourcing manufacturing and service functions overseas (a trend now referred to as "offshoring"). The IT specialist had attended a presentation by an Indian company that could maintain a call center for Taco Barn to take telephone orders during U.S. business hours, transmit those orders by computer to the closest Taco Barn, and do all that at less than half the cost quoted by U.S. vendors offering the same service.

The general reaction in the regional meeting was very positive. Corporate executives were pleased with both the potential cost savings and the prospect of a few magazine articles on how Taco Barn was using cutting-edge technology to serve their customers. Regional and unit managers were pleased not to have to handle the calls in the local restaurants. Tony, however, was not so sure.

#### QUESTIONS

1. Do you think cost savings should be the primary decision factor for any new company initiative? Why or why not?
2. What are the potential benefits and challenges of outsourcing? Review the material on pages 147–148 for help on this.
3. Which issues will have to be addressed before this service will be ready to launch?
4. What do you think Tony's concerns are here?

## >> Global Management

In the last decade we have seen the Soviet Union replaced by 15 independent republics and the rise to prominence of large economic trading blocs: the European Union (EU); the Southern Common Markets (SCCM) of Brazil, Argentina, Paraguay, and Uruguay; the Association of Southeast Asian Nations (ASEAN); and the North American Free Trade Agreement (NAFTA) between the United States, Canada, and Mexico. In China, the transformation from third-world country to economic superpower appears to be taking place in decades rather than generations. Global business analysts now recognize the "BRIC" nations (Brazil, Russia, India, and China) as future economic superpowers that will dominate the provision of both raw materials and manufactured goods and services over the next 50 years.

**International Trade** The exchange of goods and services by different countries.

The business opportunities in this new world appear to be phenomenal, even with the current global recession, but with those opportunities come risks of political instability, erratic currency exchange rates, and a global economic interdependence that ties the fortunes of formerly isolated countries more closely together than they have ever been.

Managing on a global stage demands a new set of skills, since "knowing your customer" takes on a whole new meaning when that customer is in a country with a different culture, political system, legal framework, and economic standard of living. To complicate things even further, that customer is now comfortable with purchasing goods that were designed in one country, manufactured in another, and serviced after sale in a third. In addition, the global scale of technology and information availability means that national or territorial borders are now exclusively political rather than economic. National economies are being replaced by an interdependent global economic system.

In this chapter we examine the terminology and operating practices required in the management of an international business in this global economic system.

**International trade** consists of the exchange of goods and services by different countries. Most of the world today depends on international trade to maintain its standard of living. American manufacturers sell automobiles, heavy machinery, clothing, and electronic goods abroad. Argentine cattle ranchers ship beef to consumers in dozens of foreign countries. Saudi Arabian oil producers supply much of the world with oil. In return, they purchase food, cars, and electronic goods from other countries.

Countries trade for several different reasons. One country may not be able to produce a good it wants. France, for example, cannot produce oil because it has no oil fields. If it wants to consume oil, France must trade with oil-producing countries. Countries also may trade because they have an advantage over other countries in producing particular goods or services.

*Florida's climate is perfect for growing oranges; over what states would Florida have an absolute advantage in orange juice production?*

## ABSOLUTE ADVANTAGE

Different countries are endowed with different resources. Honduras, for example, has fertile land, a warm and sunny climate, and inexpensive labor. Compared with Honduras, Great Britain has less fertile soil, a colder and rainier climate, and more expensive labor. Given the same combination of inputs (land, labor, and capital), Honduras would produce much more coffee than Great Britain. It has an absolute advantage in the production of coffee. An **absolute advantage** is the ability to produce more of a good than another producer with the same quantity of inputs.

## COMPARATIVE ADVANTAGE

Countries need not have an absolute advantage in the production of a good to trade. Some countries may be less efficient at producing *all* goods than other countries. Even countries that are not very efficient producers are more efficient at producing some goods than others, however. The **law of comparative advantage** states that producers should produce the goods they are most efficient at producing and purchase from others the goods they are less efficient at producing. According to the law of comparative advantage, individuals, companies, and countries should specialize in what they do best.

**Absolute Advantage** The ability to produce more of a good than another producer with the same quantity of inputs.

**Law of Comparative Advantage** Axiom that producers should produce the goods they are most efficient at producing and purchase from others the goods they are less efficient at producing.

# >> Exporting and Importing

International trade takes place when companies sell the goods they produce in a foreign country or purchase goods produced abroad. Goods and services that are sold abroad are called **exports**. Goods and services that are purchased abroad are called **imports**.

**Exports** Goods and services that are sold abroad.

**Imports** Goods and services purchased abroad.

The United States is the largest exporter in the world, exporting about $700 billion worth of goods and services a year. It also is the world's largest importer, purchasing about $900 billion worth of

### ACCEPTABLE CHARITY

The 2004 tsunami that devastated the shorelines of several countries around the Indian Ocean prompted fast and aggressive fund-raising by all relief organizations that were in a position to provide aid to survivors in the region. The relief group Doctors Without Borders made the unique decision to stop fund-raising for the disaster once sufficient funds had been donated to complete the relief mission it had planned for the region. Other organizations faced criticism for continuing to raise money for as long as the story of the disaster held the media spotlight and then spending a portion of that money elsewhere in their operations once the worst of the disaster was over.

As a fund-raising manager for a relief organization, what would you do in this situation? Is enough money for the planned relief mission enough? Or does the ability to do good work elsewhere with the money, even if it was donated specifically for the tsunami victims, make the decision acceptable?

ETHICAL
MANAGEMENT
Can a charity reappropriate funds that were donated for a specific cause?

foreign goods and services annually.

**Study Alert!** Under the law of comparative advantage, just because a company can produce a certain good doesn't mean that it should. Companies should focus on producing goods that reflect the most efficient use of the resources available to them.

## EXPORTS

Exports represent an important source of revenue for many companies. Northwest Airlines, for example, earns about a third of its revenues outside the United States. IBM earns more than 50 percent of its revenues abroad.

**Why Do Companies Export?** About 95 percent of the world's consumers live outside the United States. Companies that sell their products exclusively within the United States miss out on the opportunity to reach most of the world's consumers. To increase their sales, companies like Procter & Gamble spend millions of dollars trying to identify what customers in foreign countries want.

*When GE bought NBC Universal, it was diversifying its operations.*

Companies also seek out export markets in order to diversify their sources of revenue. **Diversification** is engaging in a variety of operations. Businesses like to diversify their sales so that sluggish sales in one market can be offset by stronger sales elsewhere.

**How Do Companies Identify Export Markets?** To determine if there is sufficient demand for their products or services overseas, companies analyze demographic figures, economic data, country reports, consumer tastes, and competition in the markets they are considering. Business managers contact the International Trade Administration of the U.S. Department of Commerce, foreign consulates and embassies, and foreign and international trade organizations. They also visit the countries they are considering and conduct surveys in order to assess consumer demand.

Businesses also need to find out what restrictions they may face as exporters. All countries require exporters to complete certain documents. Some countries also insist that foreign companies meet specific requirements on packaging, labeling, and product safety. Some also limit the ability of exporters to take money they earn from their exports out of the country.

## IMPORTS

American companies import billions of dollars worth of goods and services every year. They import consumer goods, such as television sets and automobiles, and industrial goods, such as machines and parts. They import raw materials, such as petroleum, and food products, such as fruits and vegetables. They import these goods in order to use them to produce other goods or to sell them to customers.

**Imports of Materials** Many companies import some or all of the materials they use in order to reduce their production costs. Manufacturers of appliances, for example, import steel from Japan because it is less expensive than steel manufactured in the United States.

Some companies use imports because domestically made materials are not available or their quality is not as good as that of imported goods. Jewelry designers import diamonds and emeralds, which are not produced in the United States. Fashion designers use imported cashmere wool, which is softer than domestic wool.

**Imports of Consumer Goods** Companies also import products that they can resell in their own countries. Automobile dealers in the United States used to import cars and trucks from Europe and Asia. Today, those automobile manufacturers have U.S. assembly plants. Wholesalers and retailers import clothing from Thailand, electronic goods from Japan, and cheese from France.

Companies import these goods because consumers want to purchase them. Some of these goods, such as garments from Asia, are less expensive than domestically manufactured products. Others, such as Saabs and Volvos, are popular despite costing more than domestically produced goods.

*Due to foreign exchange rates, the same sweater will cost the buyer different amounts depending on whether it is purchased at Harrod's in London or Macy's in New York. What are some possible benefits to money carrying different values in different countries?*

## THE TRADE BALANCE

The **balance of trade** is the difference between the value of goods a country exports and the value of goods it imports. A country that exports more than it imports runs a *trade surplus.* A country that imports more than it exports runs a *trade deficit.*

For many years the United States has run a trade deficit. This means that the value of the goods and services it buys from other countries exceeds the value of the goods and services it sells to other countries. Other countries, such as China, have run huge trade surpluses. In these countries, the value of exports exceeds the value of imports.

## FOREIGN EXCHANGE

Companies that purchase goods or services from foreign countries may be asked to pay for them with foreign currency, depending on the contract governing the purchase. For example, if a U.S. company purchases goods from Japan, it may be asked to pay for them in yen. If it purchases goods from Switzerland, it must pay for them in Swiss francs.

**Diversification** Process by which a company engages in a variety of operations.

**Balance of Trade** Difference between the value of goods a country exports and the value of goods it imports.

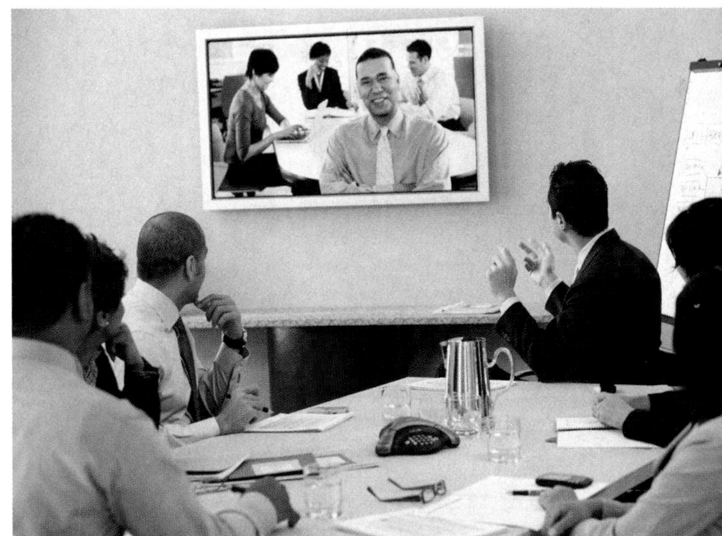

Companies purchase foreign currency from banks, which convert each currency into dollars. The value of one currency in terms of another is the foreign exchange rate.

Exchange rates can be quoted in dollars per unit of foreign currency or units of foreign currency per dollar. The exchange rate for the Swiss franc, for

*Always learn the customs of the country in which you are doing business. In China one can shake hands, bow, or nod; in Japan it would be rude not to bow slightly from the waist when meeting someone.*

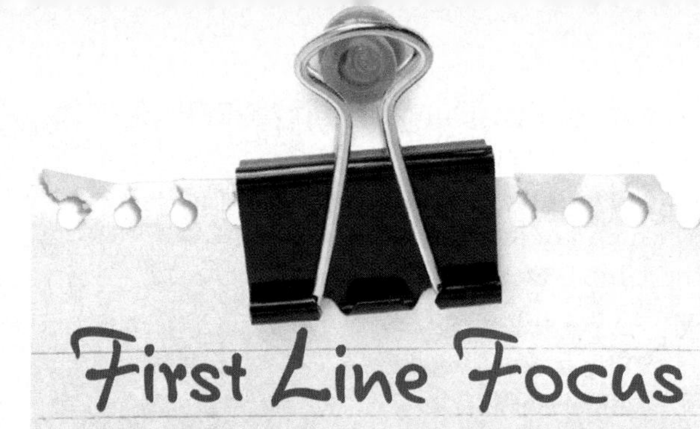

BEING A GLOBAL MANAGER . . .

## First Line Focus

*Taking on managerial responsibilities for another country or geographic region doesn't change your job in the ways you might think. From an operational perspective, your accountability is the same: to manage the resources you have been given in the most efficient manner possible, ensuring cost control, product or service quality, and customer satisfaction. What does change is the world in which you fulfill those obligations. Countries, to be blunt, are different. They have different legal, economic, and political systems and from a western perspective have differing levels of economic development. For a manager "in the trenches," your greatest concern should be the cultural differences that can make or break a successful business relationship. The way it is done here does not automatically work the same way over there. The features and benefits of your product or service can quickly become irrelevant in the face of rude or culturally insensitive behavior. Don't just buy the phrase book and think you can get by. Respect the culture of the country you are working in, demonstrate that respect in your business dealings, and let the other managers embarrass themselves. See the section "Understanding Foreign Cultures" for more information.*

## [PROGRESS] ✓questions

1. How might a country's standard of living affect international trade?
2. What is the law of comparative advantage?
3. Provide three examples why companies would import materials.
4. Explain the difference between a trade *surplus* and a trade *deficit*.

example, might be 1.5 to the dollar. This means that 1 dollar is worth 1.5 Swiss francs and 1 Swiss franc is worth 0.67 dollar.

Most exchange rates fluctuate from day to day. Managers involved in international trade must follow these fluctuations closely, because they can have a dramatic effect on profits. Consider, for example, an American electronics store that wants to purchase 10 million yen of Japanese stereos, camcorders, and cameras. If the exchange rate of the yen is 115 to the dollar, the U.S. company must pay 86,956 dollars to purchase 10 million yen worth of Japanese equipment (10 million yen divided by 115 yen per dollar). If the value of the yen rises so that a dollar is worth 100 yen, the company would have to spend $100,000 to purchase the same value of Japanese goods (10 million yen divided by 100 yen per dollar).

# >> Protectionism

International trade can benefit all trading partners. It also may hurt some domestic producers. A U.S. manufacturer of watches may find it difficult to compete with a Taiwanese producer, which pays workers a fraction of what workers in the United States earn. Competition from the Taiwanese producer may force the U.S. company out of business.

To help domestic manufacturers compete against foreign companies, governments sometimes impose protectionist measures, such as tariffs, quotas, and other types of restrictions. All these measures reduce the volume of international trade.

## TARIFFS

A **tariff** is a tax on imports. The purpose of a tariff is to raise the price of foreign goods in order to allow domestic manufacturers to compete. The United States imposes tariffs on many goods. This means that a Korean company that sells men's shirts in the United States must pay an import tax on every one of its shirts that enters the country. U.S.-imposed tariffs make it more difficult for foreign manufacturers to compete with American companies in the United States.

Tariffs fall into two classifications: a *specific tariff* levied per unit imported ($3 per barrel of oil, for example) and an *ad valorem tariff* levied as a percentage of the value of the imported good. For example, the former colonies of Great Britain and France are given preferential treatment in exporting bananas to the EU over competing producers in Latin America. Up to 875,000 tons of bananas from the Caribbean and Africa can enter the EU duty-free each year, whereas banana imports from Latin America are levied a tariff of 15 to 20 percent on the first 2.5 million tons.[1]

## QUOTAS

**Quotas** are restrictions on the quantity of a good that can enter a country. The United States imposes quotas on many kinds of goods. For example, it allows just 1.6 million tons of raw sugar to enter the country from abroad in comparison to a U.S. Department of Agriculture domestic production forecast of 7.2 million tons for 2009–2010. This quota raised the price of raw sugar, making goods that use sugar, such as candy and cold cereal, more expensive. It hurt American companies and individuals that consume sugar, but it helped American companies and individuals that produce sugar.

**Tariff** Government-imposed tax on goods imported into a country.

**Quotas** Restrictions on the quantity of a good that can enter the country.

**Embargo** A ban on exports to or imports from a foreign country.

## EMBARGOES

An **embargo** is a total ban on the import of a good from a particular country. Embargoes usually are

*Cuban goods have been banned in the United States since 1961.*

imposed for political rather than economic reasons. Since 1961, for example, the United States has imposed an embargo on Cuba, whose regime it opposes. This embargo bans the importation of goods from Cuba and the export of U.S. goods to Cuba.

## FREE TRADE AREAS

To promote international trade and limit protectionism, countries create free trade areas. A **free trade area** is a region within which trade restrictions are reduced or eliminated.

The largest free trade area in the world is North America. Under the terms of the **North American Free Trade Agreement (NAFTA)** of 1994, businesses in the United States, Mexico, and Canada can sell their products anywhere in North America without facing major trade restrictions.

**Study Alert !**

Trade embargoes are political. For example, the Cuban embargo started as a result of Fidel Castro's willingness to work with communist Soviet Union; in 1992 however, with communism no longer a concern to the U.S., the embargo was renamed the Cuban Democracy Act to reflect the country's poor economic and political record.

Consumers in all three countries have benefited from lower prices on North American imports. The price of a blouse imported from Canada or a pair of shoes imported from Mexico, for example, is lower than it used to be, because the price no longer includes a tariff.

Many producers have also benefited from NAFTA by increasing their exports within North America. American grain farmers, for example, have increased their sales to Mexico as a result of NAFTA. U.S. automobile sales to Mexico have also risen.

**Free Trade Area** A region within which trade restrictions are reduced or eliminated.

**North American Free Trade Agreement (NAFTA)** Treaty that allows businesses in the United States, Mexico, and Canada to sell their products anywhere in North America without facing major trade restrictions.

NAFTA has forced American workers to lose their jobs, however. Sara Lee laid off more than 1,000 American workers after it moved some of its operations to Mexico. Many other companies have also reduced their workforces in this country to take advantage of lower labor costs south of the border.

Created with the signing of the Maastricht Treaty in 1993, the European Union (EU) is a union of 27 European countries, known as member states, with other countries (Croatia, Macedonia, and Turkey) recognized as candidate countries (i.e., future members) and others (such as Albania, Serbia, and Iceland) recognized as potential candidates (i.e., considering national referenda to apply for membership).[2] As an economic bloc, the EU generates over 22 percent of the world's gross domestic product, and 16 member countries utilize a single currency—the euro. Figure 5.1 has a list of the member states by date when they joined. A key activity of the EU is the establishment of a common single market within the member states.

### Figure 5.1 • Member States of the EU and Date of Joining

| Year | Country |
|---|---|
| 1952 | Belgium, France, West Germany, Italy, Luxembourg, the Netherlands (founding members) |
| 1973 | Denmark, Ireland, United Kingdom |
| 1981 | Greece |
| 1986 | Portugal, Spain |
| 1990 | East Germany (reunites with West Germany and becomes part of the EU) |
| 1995 | Austria, Finland, Sweden |
| 2004 | Cyprus, Czech Republic, Estonia, Hungary, Latvia, Lithuania, Malta, Poland, Slovakia, Slovenia |
| 2007 | Bulgaria, Romania |

## [PROGRESS] ✓questions

5. Why would a government consider imposing protectionist measures?
6. Explain the difference between *specific* and *ad valorem* tariffs.
7. Evaluate the statement, "NAFTA has benefited American companies but punished American workers who have seen their jobs move south of the border."
8. What are the benefits of a free trade area?

# Thinking Critically 5.1

## >> "Buy American?"

On February 17, 2009, President Barack Obama signed a $787 billion spending bill designed to stimulate the flagging U.S. economy. As is typical of the political process, the final version of the bill represented a series of compromises among numerous interested parties. After aggressive lobbying, the final language included a "buy American" provision that required only U.S. iron, steel, and other manufactured goods to be used for public buildings and public works funded by the bill.

In anticipation of cries of "Protectionism!" the language included several caveats—the policy could not violate any existing U.S. obligations under international trade agreements, nor would it apply if American goods were in short supply, of insufficient quality, or of such a high cost that the overall project cost was going to increase by more than 25 percent. With those caveats in place, the final language ended up being very similar to buy American requirements that have been applied in the past for federal highway, transit, and airport projects.

Advocates of the language argued that it provided much needed support to the U.S. construction and manufacturing sectors at a critical time for the country's economy. Critics were not convinced, raising concerns of the potential for retaliatory requirements by other countries that would, in effect, reduce U.S. exports and, they argued, dilute the power of the stimulus package.

One company that was featured prominently during this period was Caterpillar, the world's largest heavy equipment manufacturer. The CEO, James Owens, is a member of President Obama's Economic Advisory Board. During a series of speeches intended to promote the stimulus package, Obama stopped in Peoria, Illinois, Caterpillar's headquarters, to promise that stimulus-funded public works projects would benefit Caterpillar directly and help the company hire back some of the 22,000 people that were being laid off in response to the global recession.

The buy American provision presented Owens with a quandary. "Shovel-ready" projects in the United States would, hopefully, mean new construction equipment orders at a time of falling global demand. However, if that provision was perceived as being protectionist, Caterpillar's largest customer, China, might retaliate with a similar "buy Chinese" policy, which would shut Caterpillar out of a lucrative economic rebound in the Far East.

Owens's concerns proved to be well founded. By June 2009, many of the American shovel-ready projects were still several months from starting, whereas the Chinese government had begun initiating new construction projects four months earlier. To make matters worse, when a Chinese economic stimulus package of 4 trillion yuan ($586 billion) was announced, it was accompanied with a clear directive to award government contracts to local firms.

### QUESTIONS

1. If the U.S. government wants to stimulate the U.S. economy, doesn't it make sense to ensure that those dollars are spent with U.S. companies? Why or why not?
2. Were the caveats enough to silence critics of the buy American policy? Explain your answer.
3. How could the Obama administration have approached this differently?
4. What would you advise James Owens to do now?

*Source:* Moira Herbs, "Jobs and Protectionism in the Stimulus Package," *BusinessWeek,* February 16, 2009; David Greising, "Caterpillar's Lessons from China Useful in US Too," *Chicago Tribune,* May 1, 2009; Reuters, "Caterpillar Moves to Cut 20,000 Jobs," *The New York Times,* January 27, 2009; and Vivian Wai-yin Kwo, "The 'Buy Chinese' Trade Dispute," *Forbes,* June 18, 2009.

# >> Doing Business Globally

Thousands of U.S. businesses, large and small, participate in the global marketplace. Some companies, such as Benetton, build factories in foreign countries or set up retail outlets overseas. Others, such as Harley-Davidson, export their products throughout the world and import materials from other countries.

**Foreign Intermediary** A wholesaler or agent that markets products for companies wanting to do business abroad.

**Licensing Agreement** An agreement that permits one company to sell another company's products abroad in return for a percentage of the company's revenues.

**Strategic Alliance** An agreement by which companies pool resources and skills in order to achieve common goals.

## FORMS OF INTERNATIONAL OPERATIONS

Companies can sell their products or services in foreign countries in various ways. Small companies often work through local companies, which are familiar with local markets. Large companies often establish sales, manufacturing, and distribution facilities in foreign countries.

## WORKING THROUGH A FOREIGN INTERMEDIARY

Companies that are not willing or able to invest millions of dollars in operations abroad often export their products through foreign intermediaries. A **foreign intermediary** is a wholesaler or agent that markets products for companies wanting to do business abroad. In return for a commission, the agent markets the foreign company's product.

Working through a foreign intermediary saves a company the expense of setting up facilities in a foreign country. It also ensures that the company is represented by someone familiar with local conditions. Foreign intermediaries usually work for many foreign companies at a time, however. Thus, they are not likely to devote as much time to a single company's products as the company's own sales force would.

## SIGNING A LICENSING AGREEMENT WITH A FOREIGN COMPANY

Another way companies can reach foreign consumers is by licensing a foreign company to sell their products or services abroad. A **licensing agreement** is an agreement that permits one company to sell another company's products abroad in return for a percentage of the company's revenues.

TGI Friday's, a Dallas-based restaurant company, has used licensing agreements to expand its operations overseas. Signing such agreements has enabled it to open branches in Singapore, Indonesia, Malaysia, Thailand, Australia, and New Zealand. Without such agreements, it might not have been able to penetrate those markets.

## FORMING A STRATEGIC ALLIANCE

Some companies can expand into foreign markets by forming strategic alliances with foreign companies. A **strategic alliance** involves pooling resources and skills in order to achieve common goals. Companies usually form strategic alliances to gain access to new markets, share research, broaden their product lines, learn new skills, and expand cross-cultural knowledge of management groups.

**Figure 5.2 • Multinational Corporations**

1. **Imported Materials**
   Multinational corporations may import materials used to manufacture their products. General Motors (GM), the largest automobile producer in the United States, works with more than 30,000 suppliers worldwide. Many of these suppliers are overseas.
2. **International Production**
   Multinational companies may produce their products in other countries. GM has manufacturing, assembly, or component operations in 50 countries. It operates abroad in order to improve service or reduce costs.
3. **International Sales**
   Multinational companies sell their products in other countries. GM cars and trucks are sold in Africa, Asia and the Pacific, Europe, the Middle East, and North America. Foreign sales represent a significant share of the company's total sales.

**From the** PERSPECTIVE OF...

**An MNC Regional Manager**

When you are responsible for managing the Latin American market for your organization, what are your primary responsibilities and challenges? How do they differ for a manager responsible for the production of goods in that region as opposed to selling goods?

[PROGRESS] questions

9. List the four options available to a company seeking to sell its products and services internationally.
10. Which of the above options would best suit a small company?
11. Which option offers the greatest risk and why?
12. What is a Multinational Corporation (MNC)?

One of the largest strategic alliances in recent years has been the Star Alliance between major airlines started in 1997 by Air Canada, Lufthansa, Scandinavián Airlines, Thai Airways, and United Airlines. By 2006 the alliance had grown to 38 members divided among full, regional, and alliance membership categories, running almost 17,000 daily flights to over 800 airports in more than 150 countries worldwide.

## BECOMING A MULTINATIONAL CORPORATION

Companies willing to make a significant financial commitment often establish manufacturing and distribution facilities in foreign countries. A business with such facilities is known as a **Multinational Corporation (MNC)** (see Figure 5.2).

Businesses become multinational corporations for several reasons. Some do so in order to sell their products or services in other countries. McDonald's, for example, maintains restaurants in 116 countries. Sales to customers in these countries represent half the company's total revenue.

**Multinational Corporation (MNC)** Business that maintains a presence in two or more countries, has a considerable portion of its assets invested in and derives a substantial portion of its sales and profits from international activities, considers opportunities throughout the world, and has a worldwide perspective and orientation.

Companies also expand abroad in order to take advantage of inexpensive labor costs. For example, Tarrant Apparel, a U.S. manufacturer of blue jeans, weaves most of its fabric in Mexico. It also has most of

## Thinking Critically 5.2

### >> Management by a Modern Steel Magnate

When you think of the term "steel magnate," the first name that comes to mind is Andrew Carnegie, the Scottish-born American industrialist who built Pittsburgh's Carnegie Steel Company to a position of market dominance before selling out to J.P. Morgan's U.S. Steel Corporation for over $225 million (approximately $150 billion in today's dollars) in 1901.

By contrast, Lakshmi Mittal, chairman and chief executive of ArcelorMittal, the world's largest steel company, presents a very different picture. Carnegie started with nothing and built a fortune based on strict personal values that he later captured in his *Gospel of Wealth* that outlined what he saw as his obligation to give all his wealth away before his death. Mittal's career as an industrialist began with a trip to

*Continued on next page*

Continued from page 107

Indonesia in the 1970s to sell a piece of land that his father had purchased for a steel mill. After examining the situation in detail and convincing his father that the obstacles to successful construction and operation of the mill that had prompted the sale could be overcome, Mittal entered the steel business in 1976, overseeing the construction of the mill from the ground up.

Fast-forward to 2006 and an extended hostile $33 billion takeover of Arcelor, the world's second largest steelmaker. In planning a deal that would give the combined operation a global market share of 11 percent and sales of over $60 billion, Mittal saw an opportunity to eliminate a future competitor and give the new organization greater pricing power. However, his comfort with the standard tactics of strategic acquisitions should not convince you that Mittal is a standard businessman. For example, the Arcelor acquisition was not a traditional expense reduction venture with massive layoffs in the name of economies of scale. As Mittal acknowledged: "Mittal Steel had a very lean organization; Arcelor did not have a lean organization. We needed to strengthen our middle management at Mittal Steel. Arcelor provided the opportunity to strengthen our middle management. Arcelor had very good people with a lot of experience."

In a similar manner, Mittal's involvement with a Caribbean steel venture (his first international deal after Indonesia) brought a nontraditional response. After agreeing to lease the Iron & Steel Company of Trinidad & Tobago with an option to purchase after five years in 1989, Mittal succeeded in turning around a "government-owned company that was hemorrhaging money" by bringing in his operational team, keeping the best local workers, and making whatever capital investments were necessary to produce a stable venture.

Such business practices have brought Mittal global recognition. He was awarded the Dwight D. Eisenhower Global Leadership Award in 2007 and was awarded the Padma Vibhushan, India's second highest civilian honor, by the president of India in 2008.

## QUESTIONS

1. Research Andrew Carnegie's management philosophy, and provide three examples of key decisions that reflected his style.
2. Do you think Mittal's different economic background (following his father's business success) made his success easier to achieve? Why or why not?
3. What would have been a more traditional outcome for Mittal's hostile takeover of Arcelor?
4. What do the decisions to keep people on and make long-term capital investments tell you about Mittal's management philosophy?

*Source:* Julia Werdigier, "New Board Member Reflects Global Influence on Goldman," *The New York Times,* June 30, 2008; Stanley Reed, "Q&A with Lakshmi Mittal," *BusinessWeek,* April 16, 2007; "Global Business: Mittal: Blood, Steel, and Empire Building," BusinessWeek Online, February 13, 2006; and James C. Robinson, "A Case Study of Mittal Management," *BusinessWeek,* May 7, 2007.

**Figure 5.3 • Examples of Foreign Business Practices**

| Country | Business Practice |
|---|---|
| China | Food is extremely important. All business transactions require at least one and usually two evening banquets. The first banquet is given by the host, the second by the guest. |
| Indonesia | Even foreigners are expected to arrive late to social occasions. It is generally appropriate to arrive about 30 minutes after the scheduled time. |
| Singapore | Businesspeople exchange business cards in a formal manner, receiving the card with both hands and studying it for a few moments before putting it away. |
| Saudi Arabia | Businesspeople greet foreigners by clasping their hand, but they do not shake hands. |
| Switzerland | Business is conducted very formally. Humor and informality are inappropriate. |

its jeans sewn in Mexico, where labor is cheaper than in the United States.

## CHALLENGES OF WORKING IN AN INTERNATIONAL ENVIRONMENT

Working for a multinational corporation presents many challenges. Managers must learn to deal with customers, producers, suppliers, and employees from different countries. They must become familiar with local laws and learn to respect local customs. They must try to understand what customers and employees want in countries that may be very different from the United States.

**Understanding Foreign Cultures** Business managers from different countries see the world differently. Japanese managers, for example, tend to be more sensitive to job layoffs than American managers. Asian and African managers often have different views about the role of women in the workplace than American managers do.

Managers who work in foreign countries need to be aware of different cultural attitudes. They also need to understand business customs in different countries (see Figure 5.3). Not knowing how to act in a foreign country can cause managers embarrassment, and it can cause them to miss out on business opportunities. Showing up for a business meeting without a tie might be acceptable in Israel, for example, but it would be completely out of place in Switzerland. Demonstrating great respect to a superior would be appreciated in Indonesia, but it would send the wrong signal in the Netherlands, where equality among individuals is valued.

**PROGRESS ✓questions**

13. How would a U.S.-based manager go about addressing his or her lack of knowledge about another country's business culture?
14. Why would an MNC want to do business in a politically unstable country?
15. If an MNC chooses to do business in a politically unstable country, should it have different obligations to its employees in that country? Explain your answer.
16. You are an employee of an American MNC based overseas. In negotiating a large contract with a local company, your client contact makes it clear that he expects a finder's fee for awarding the contract to your company. The request is a common practice in this country but goes against your company's published code of ethics. What do you do?

**Political Changes** One of the most dramatic illustrations of how political changes influence the international business environment was the breakup of the Soviet Union and the fall of communist governments in Eastern Europe in the early 1990s. In addition, the political and economic upheavals in Bulgaria, Hungary, Poland, Romania, and the countries formerly known as Czechoslovakia and Yugoslavia have caused significant changes in how these countries conduct their own international business activities and how they relate to businesses from foreign countries.

**Human Rights and Ethics** Should multinational firms close their plants in countries where human rights abuses are common and accepted ethical boundaries are violated? This is a valid issue, but U.S. managers must remember that business ethics have not yet been globalized; the norms of ethical behavior continue to vary widely even in Western capitalist countries. Thus, questions such as, "Should Coca-Cola establish minimum labor standards for all

UP IN SMOKE

You have been building a successful management career in the United States. You get a call from a recruiter who encourages you to consider a senior position with a newly formed international tobacco company. Formed when the U.S. parent company rebranded and spun off its international division into a separate company, the new operation is based in Switzerland. Your job will be to manage the global growth of the parent company's most famous cigarette brand. In the United States the brand holds over 40 percent of the market, but in the global market, the share is less than 16 percent.

Financial analysts have high expectations of the growth of the new international company—with no cigarette taxes, smoking bans, or antitobacco activist ads, the brand has a lot of potential, particularly in the Far East. In response to criticism, the CEO has conceded that his product is "very harmful," but he points out that the new company isn't recruiting new customers around the world, just convincing existing smokers to switch to a better-quality cigarette. Would you take the job? Why or why not?

ETHICAL
MANAGEMENT
Would you work for a company that sells products harmful to one's health?


Study Alert!

Maintaining a global standard of ethical business practices is much easier said than done. The norms of ethical behavior continue to vary widely around the world. Practices such as bribes and "finder's fees" are common in some countries even though they are considered illegal under the Foreign Corrupt Practices Act of 1977 here.

of its bottlers around the world to prevent abuses of workers in certain countries?" seem highly appropriate in the United States. However, such questions present dilemmas for multinational firms that are accompanied by ethical predicaments and hard choices. In each situation, the multinational firm must strike a balance among the values and ideals of all its various publics. No clear and easy choices exist.

**From the PERSPECTIVE OF . . .**

**A Textile Factory Manager** Your company manufactures clothes for Walmart—a very cost-conscious and demanding customer. Lately the Walmart buyers have focused on your labor practices. What policies and procedures should you have in place to reassure them that your company takes good care of its workers?

## >> Chapter Summary

The topic of global management is worthy of a course all its own, and we are seeing an increasing number of business degrees specializing in international or global management. In this chapter we have examined a few of the key differences between domestic management and global management.

In the next chapter we return to the fundamental responsibilities: organizing work to achieve the operational efficiency that a manager will always be accountable for, no matter what part of the world he or she may be working in.

1. Define *global management*.

Global management means managing the operations of a business that increasingly embrace multiple countries. Managing on a global stage demands a new set of skills since "knowing your customer" takes on a whole new meaning when that customer is in a country with a different culture, political system, legal framework, and economic standard of living. To complicate things even further, that customer is now comfortable with purchasing goods that were designed in one country, manufactured in another, and serviced after sale in a third. In addition, the global scale of technology and information availability means that national or territorial borders are now exclusively political rather than economic. National economies are being replaced by an interdependent global economic system.

2. Compare and contrast importing and exporting.

Goods and services purchased from overseas are called imports. Those imports can be finished goods to be resold or raw materials purchased at lower prices than could be achieved domestically. When raw materials are imported, the finished goods can then be sold domestically or sold abroad as exports.

Exports represent sales outside of a company's domestic market that are sold as a diversification strategy and as part of a long-range growth strategy.

If a country imports more goods and services than it exports, like the United States, it is said to be running a trade deficit. If a country exports more than it imports, like China, it is said to be running a trade surplus.

3. Explain the advantages and disadvantages of protectionism.

To help domestic manufacturers compete against foreign companies, governments sometimes impose protectionist measures such as charging an import tax or tariff on overseas goods in order to bring their prices more in line with domestic prices. As an alternative, quotas may be implemented to limit the amount of a raw material, such as sugar, rice, or steel, that can be imported from a specific country.

Protectionist measures can protect domestic manufacturers, but they typically lead to retaliatory measures from other countries that then impact exporters and bring down the overall volume of international trade.

4. Discuss the challenges of doing business globally.

Conducting business on a global platform requires managers to learn to deal with customers, producers, suppliers, and employees from different countries. They must become familiar with local laws and learn to respect local customs. They must try to understand what customers and employees want in countries that may be very different from the United States.

As companies constantly expand their markets in search of revenue growth, the move into international and global markets becomes inevitable. While the core responsibilities for managers may be the same—manage the resources you have been given in the most efficient manner possible, ensuring cost control, product or service quality, and customer satisfaction—the environment is significantly more complex.

# THE WORLD of Work >>

**"TACO BARN TO GO"** ***(continued from page 97)***

Tony had not been convinced that the new "Taco Barn To Go" project would live up to everyone's high expectations. There were a couple of trade magazine articles featuring Taco Barn's use of cutting-edge technology to deliver superior customer service, but they were printed when the project was still in the development stage. "Probably a good thing," thought Tony, since the implementation wasn't delivering the promised cost savings, at least not yet.

The "To Go" project had been all about costs savings, which was why the idea of using an Indian call center had been so attractive. The quoted cost per order processed had been less than half the number quoted by U.S. providers of the same service. However, as the project had progressed, it became clear that many setup costs to get the service off the ground had not been included in that quoted cost per order processed. Suddenly everything was going to cost more—sending Taco Barn personnel overseas to train the call center people on the Taco Barn restaurant concept and the intricacies of the menu from which customers would be ordering and bringing Indian call center managers to the United States to see Taco Barns in operation. All of this had to be paid for before the first order was taken.

To make sure costs were minimized, most of these expenses were scaled back. Call center managers were shown internal Taco Barn training videos rather than visiting the U.S. units. Training of the call center personnel was handled by conference calls where Indian trainers were walked through the menu so that they could then train their people on how to take telephone orders. Call center managers assured Taco Barn executives that this would not be a problem, since they handled calls for many U.S. manufacturers and their products—computers, cell phones, tech support, and many other services.

A few weeks later, Tony received notice in an e-mail that his region had been selected as the pilot region for testing the "To Go" project and that it would start the following Friday. "Great," Tony said to himself, "start it on a busy night. Why not start it on Saturday night and really cause some confusion?"

Tony had never considered himself to be a pessimist, but the first night's trial run performed even worse than he had expected. Some customers called the central ordering number and then called the restaurant to make sure the order had come through. Other customers called the restaurant to complain that the "girl on the phone had a strange accent and didn't understand her." Still more customers complained that they couldn't switch around menu items like they did in their local Taco Barn.

On the restaurant's side of this experiment, orders came through with incorrect items or wrong numbers of items or items the restaurant didn't serve. Some orders never arrived at all, which caused much confusion and scrambling when the customer showed up 30 minutes after placing the order and expecting to drive away with a freshly prepared meal.

After two weeks of trials, the "To Go" project was pulled from Tony's region, and all parties involved went back to the drawing board. Tony was left with a 15-page assessment report to fill out.

"Where do I start?" thought Tony.

**QUESTIONS**

1. Where does Tony start here? What went wrong with the implementation of "Taco Barn To Go"?
2. Could these mistakes have been anticipated? Why or why not?
3. How do you think Tony's local customers have been affected by this project?
4. What should Taco Barn do now? Explain your answer.

## Key Terms >>

absolute advantage 99
balance of trade 101
diversification 101
embargo 103
exports 99
foreign intermediary 106
free trade area 104
imports 99
international trade 98
law of competitive advantage 99
licensing agreement 106
multinational corporation (MNC) 107
North American Free Trade Agreement (NAFTA) 104
quotas 103
strategic alliance 106
tariff 103

1. Why should a U.S.-based manager be concerned with globalization?
2. Research an example of an *ad valorem* tariff, and defend the reason for its implementation.
3. Which is better, a trade *surplus* or a trade *deficit?*
4. "The expectations of shareholders for continued growth make the risks of doing business in politically unstable countries a necessary cost of operating effectively." Do you agree with this statement? Why or why not?
5. Under what conditions would the Cuban embargo be removed? Who stands to benefit from such a decision?
6. You are offered a promotion with the choice of a three-year posting to an overseas division of your company or a U.S.-based position with 50 percent international travel. Which position would you take and why?

1. Free trade agreements, such as the North American Free Trade Agreement and the General Agreement on Tariffs and Trade (GATT), may reduce trade restrictions within a designated region, as well as allow increased sales and lower-priced goods. However, much criticism has also been voiced by consumer, labor, health, and environmental groups, such as the Alliance for Democracy, Public Citizen in Washington, D.C., and the Fair Trade Network. They believe that unrestricted, "corporate-managed" trade will do more harm than good. Do research on the Internet to answer the following questions:
   a. Be prepared to discuss either the positives or negatives of NAFTA and GATT.
   b. Document the purpose of either Alliance for Democracy or the Fair Trade Network.
2. Review the Web site of Transparency International (TI) at **www.transparency.org**, and answer the following questions:
   a. When was TI founded, and what does the organization do?
   b. How does TI define *corruption?*
   c. Explain the differences between TI's Global Corruption Barometer and Bribe Payers Index.

1. **International Blunders**

   Divide into teams of two or three, research an example of an international business blunder made by a Western organization, and prepare a 10-minute presentation on how the company could have approached the situation differently.

2. **Which Country?**

   As part of its long-term growth plan, your organization is contemplating global expansion. Divide into teams of two or three, and research the business culture of a country of your choice. Pay particular attention to its economy, political system, language, cultural issues, religious practices, and any other information you deem to be relevant for a successful business venture. Prepare a 10-minute presentation for your group, concluding with whether or not your chosen country would be a viable candidate for your organization's global expansion plans.

# Case 5.1

## >> A Company in Crisis • Sony's comeback may ride on its ability to break from tradition and embrace a global mentality.

SONY®

For the company that gave the world the first pocket transistor radio and the Walkman—and as a result owned the personal audio business for years—Sony boasts no real category killers today. Its portable digital audio and video players haven't come close to the market dominance of the iPod. The PlayStation 3 video game console has yet to match the buzz or sales of rival machines from Microsoft and Nintendo, and despite being the second largest LCD television maker in the world (behind Korea's Samsung Electronics), Sony has lost money on every set it has sold. Chairman Howard K. Stringer, the former chief of Sony Corp. of America—and the first Westerner to lead the entire company—is two years into a push to revitalize Sony and restore its reputation as the leader of the cutthroat consumer electronics business, which still accounts for nearly 70 percent of the company's revenues.

Since Stringer's appointment, Sony has been reorganized into two groups—a networked media products group (games, computers, music players, new mobile products, and related services) and a television, camera, and component group. In Stringer's attempt to manage the high value of the yen (half of Sony's products are made in Japan, but only 15 percent of sales are domestic), 16,000 jobs have been cut, 6 of its 57 factories around the world have been closed, and plans are in place to cut the company's budget for factories and chip-making equipment by a third by 2010—all planned to generate costs savings of around $2.5 billion per year.

Stringer sees outsourcing as a key element in cost containment for Sony, which marks a major culture shift for an organization that has historically preferred state-of-the-art production facilities to remain in Japan. Competitors like Apple and Cisco have focused on product design, left manufacturing to others, and earned significantly higher profit margins as a result. For Sony, a weak yen was a bonus while overseas demand was strong, but as the yen strengthened and the global economy faltered, the company was left badly exposed with falling sales and higher costs of production than its competitors.

Sony is not an outsourcing novice, but less than 8 percent of the company's overall TV production was handled by outside vendors in 2008. Even then the process was managed with military-level component security so that vendors got design specs for specific parts without knowing anything about the entire assembly process, which was handled in-house.

Given the constant pressure for new product development, Sony's concern for innovation design leaks is understandable, but for the company to fully leverage the cost benefits of outsourcing, there will need to be more collaboration and information sharing between designer and manufacturer. Sony's culture will need to make that adjustment in short order if the company is to regain lost market share. For Stringer, the turnaround of Sony may be his greatest success or his swan song. It is highly likely that if he is unable to implement his planned overhaul of the company, his job will join the ranks of the 16,000 positions already cut from payroll.

QUESTIONS

1. What factors led to Sony's current financial issues?
2. Why is Howard K. Stringer's appointment as chairman of Sony Corporation significant?
3. Why is outsourcing seen as a critical component of Sony's revival?
4. Do you think Stringer's strategy will work? Why or why not?

*Source:* "Game On," *The Economist,* March 5, 2009; Cliff Edwards and Kenji Hall, "Global Business," *BusinessWeek,* May 7, 2007; Kenji Hall, "Can Outsourcing Save Sony?" *BusinessWeek,* January 30, 2009; and "Unplugged," *The Economist,* February 5, 2009.

# Case 5.2

## >> Siemens' Commitment to "Clean Hands" • After CEO Klaus Kleinfeld put Siemens back on the road to recovery, a bribery scandal threatened to undo all the progress made.

SIEMENS

If things had turned out a little differently, Siemens CEO Klaus Kleinfeld might already be on his way to executive stardom, like his role model Jack Welch. Just two years after Kleinfeld took over the Munich electronics and engineering behemoth in January 2005, Siemens was on track to hit its aggressive internal earnings targets for the first time since 2000. In fact, it was expanding both sales and profits faster than Welch's former domain, General Electric. The 2006 sales rose by 16 percent and profits by 35 percent, and the future was looking very positive.

Transforming Siemens was never going to be easy. With branches in 190 countries and over $100 billion in sales, the company has long been respected for its engineering expertise but criticized for its sluggishness. And Germany, with its long-standing tradition of labor harmony and powerful workers' councils, is highly resistant to the kind of change Kleinfeld tried to implement.

Against the odds, in just two years Kleinfeld had managed a major restructuring. He pushed Siemens' 475,000 employees to make decisions faster and focus as much on customers as on technology. He spun off underperforming telecommunications businesses and simplified the company's structure. When one group of managers failed to deliver, he broke up an entire division—at the end of 2005, it became clear that the Logistics & Assembly Systems Division, which made products such as sorting equipment used by the U.S. Postal Service, would deliver only a 2 percent profit margin. Most unpardonable in Kleinfeld's eyes was that the unit's managers waited too long to alert him to the problem. So Kleinfeld transferred the most profitable parts of the division, such as baggage-handling systems for airports, to other parts of Siemens. The rest was sold. Within weeks, an entire Siemens division with $1.9 billion in annual sales was vaporized.

Such aggressive tactics would inevitably lead to criticism of Kleinfeld's "American" style of leadership, but his eventual departure from Siemens (he is now CEO of aluminum giant Alcoa) came not, as many suspected,

*Continued on next page*

Continued from page 115

as a result of secret boardroom maneuvers. It came as a result of a need for a fresh start for the company after a scandal over bribery and corruption practices by senior managers to the tune of an estimated $2.5 billion.

In December 2008, Siemens announced that it would pay fines and other penalties totaling $800 million after pleading guilty in U.S. federal court to violations of the Foreign Corrupt Practices Act. The company also agreed to pay $540 million to German authorities in addition to a $274 million fine already levied for evidence of systematic bribery and corruption, including the use of airline tickets that could be exchanged for cash, which executives in Siemens' medical division used to bribe clients in contract negotiations.

Thanks to full cooperation and transparency in the investigation, in addition to a multibillion-dollar internal investigation in which Siemens provided most of the evidence for its own prosecution, the company did not receive a ban from competing for future government contracts. However, having clearly demonstrated that much of its commercial prowess was achieved through a willingness to "grease the appropriate palms" to win large government contracts from Nigeria to Norway, Siemens faced the challenge of rebuilding its reputation and proving that it can win business honestly (with "clean hands")—even when competitors may continue to acquiesce to demands for bribes in order to win contracts.

Kleinfeld's eventual departure from Siemens came not, as many suspected, as a result of secret boardroom maneuvers, but as a result of a need for a fresh start for the company after a scandal over bribery and corruption practices by senior managers to the tune of an estimated $2.5 billion.

The responsibility for rebuilding the company's reputation fell to Peter Löscher, as a designated (and untainted) outsider who previously headed divisions at GE (Siemens' greatest rival) to draw a line under the scandal and start a new era for the company. One of his first acts was to declare an amnesty for all managers to come forward and share what they knew about the bribery practices—110 managers came forward and provided multiple new leads to internal and external investigators.

With Löscher's arrival and the need to wipe the slate clean, there was a dramatic housecleaning in the executive offices in addition to a cosmetic restructuring of the organization into three main divisions: industry, energy, and health care. It remains to be seen whether the restructuring is designed to improve operational efficiency or to make units more attractive to potential buyers.

## QUESTIONS

1. How would you describe the culture of Siemens before Kleinfeld's appointment as CEO?
2. Kleinfeld's leadership style was criticized as being "brash" and "American." Is that a fair assessment? Why or why not?
3. Do you think the decision to "clean house" in the Siemens executive offices was the right one? Why or why not?
4. What challenges does Peter Löscher face in restoring the company's reputation?

*Source:* "Unfair and Amateurish," *The Economist,* April 26, 2007; Jack Ewing, "Global Business," BusinessWeek Online, January 29, 2007; "Stopping the Rot," *The Economist,* March 6, 2008; and Jack Ewing, "Siemens Settlement: Relief, but Is It Over?" *BusinessWeek,* December 15, 2008.

# Case 5.3

## >> The Demographics Challenge • What happens when a country gets old before it gets rich?

India's favorable demographics are often touted as one of the major reasons behind the country's growth. Millions of educated Indians under the age of 30 act as the pistons firing in a multicylinder economic system, which continues to expand at enviable rates despite the global recession. There's no doubt that this confers upon India an enormous demographic advantage, an upper hand that will continue to fuel growth for decades to come.

What happens, however, to the Indian economy when the country's demographics tilt higher, as today's youth begin to retire? The Indian workforce is on pace to transform into an enormous health care burden for the country as workers age, live longer, and demand more medical services, as well as pensions and other correlated elements of social security. India will have no choice but to spend more of its gross domestic product (GDP) on health care. India's soaring birthrates will expound this dilemma. By 2050, the United Nations expects India to boast the world's largest population. While India cannot impose draconian rules such as China's "one child" policy, the sheer scale of these numbers places tremendous pressure on the country's ability to succeed in innovation in medical science and delivery models to help India avoid the burdens of health care costs that countries, such as the United States, carry today.

For China, 2010 will be celebrated as a golden year: the moment when the demographic dividend realized by the one child per family policy imposed in the 1970s will finally reach its peak. With the low birthrate, the number of dependent children has been falling, whereas the number of elderly people in the population has only risen gradually, producing a low "dependency ratio"—the number of dependents compared to the working population.

A high dependency ratio in the United States has already raised alarm bells about the long-term viability of the Social Security program as fewer and fewer workers are around to pay into the program as compared to an increasing number of retirees withdrawing checks from it. Demographics are expected to turn against China also, as an increasing number of retirees become dependent on an increasingly smaller working population (the downside of the one child policy). From a ratio of 0.4 dependents per worker in 2010, forecasters expect the ratio to jump to 0.6 or more by 2050.

In addition to the same health care burden issues that India is already planning for, Chinese companies are anticipating a dramatic shift in employment policies as middle managers and technical workers become increasingly scarce commodities in the workforce. Salaries are expected to rise as companies endeavor to attract the best talent, and companies are beginning to reexamine their training programs as it becomes harder to justify extensive training for managers only to see them leave for higher salaries elsewhere.

### QUESTIONS

1. Why should a country be concerned about getting old before it gets rich?
2. What is a *dependency ratio,* and why is it significant?
3. Why wouldn't the one child policy provide a workable solution for India?
4. How can companies prepare for a shrinking workforce?

*Source:* "Old-Age Dependency Ratios," *The Economist,* May 7, 2009; Semil Shah, "Conversation Starter," BusinessWeek Online, May 29, 2009; "Peak Labor," *The Economist,* November 13, 2009; and Christopher Power, "Davos: Demographics, Economics, Destiny," *BusinessWeek,* January 27, 2007.

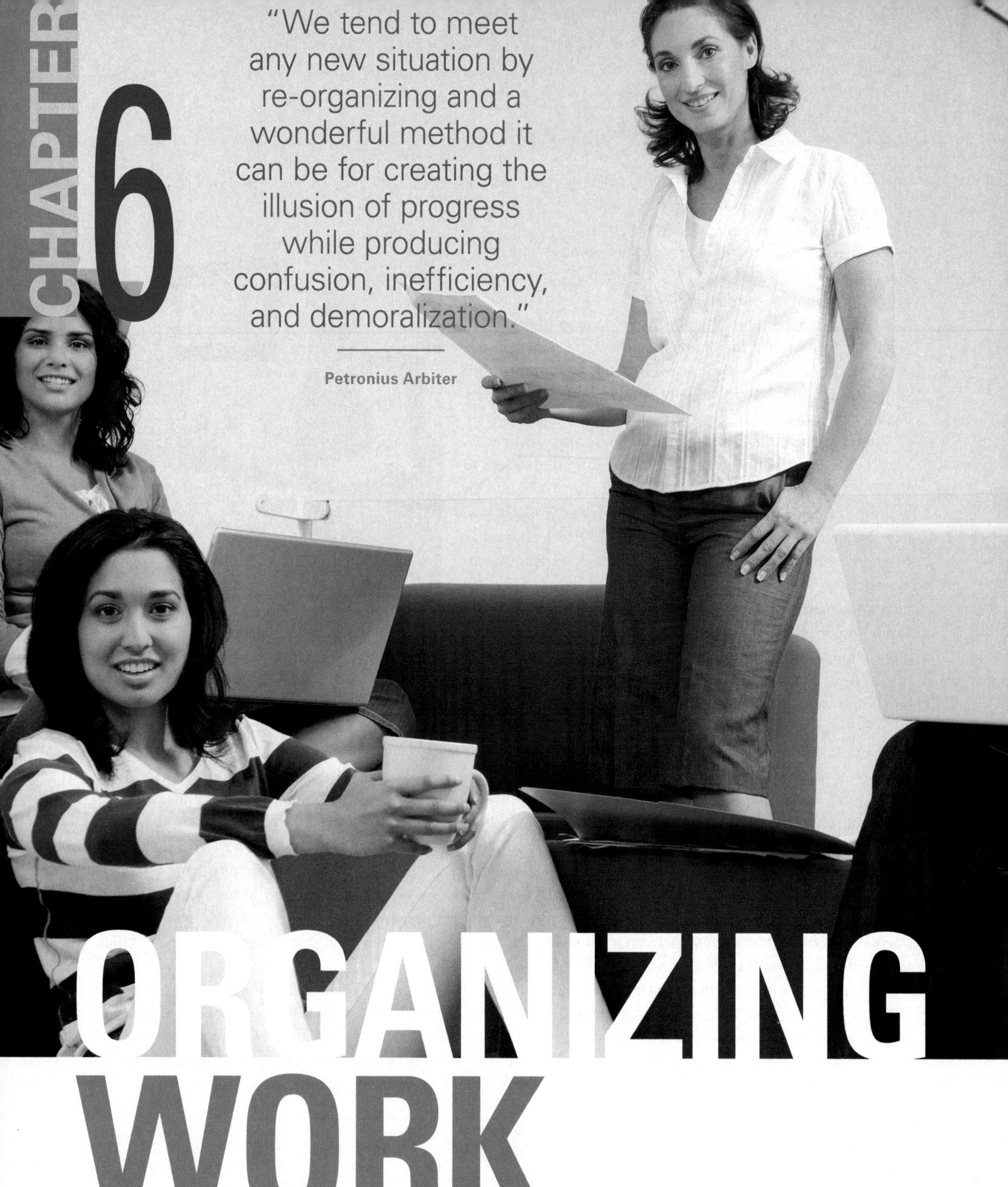

CHAPTER 6

"We tend to meet any new situation by re-organizing and a wonderful method it can be for creating the illusion of progress while producing confusion, inefficiency, and demoralization."

Petronius Arbiter

# ORGANIZING WORK

LEARNING OUTCOMES

After studying this chapter, you will be able to:

1 Define *organization,* and differentiate between a formal and an informal organization.

2 Distinguish between power, authority, and responsibility.

3 Explain the concept of centralization versus decentralization.

4 Define *empowerment.*

5 Identify several reasons why managers are reluctant to delegate authority.

6 Explain flextime, telecommuting, and job sharing, and discuss their respective impact on the organization of work.

## THE WORLD OF WORK Tony tries to delegate

All the time Tony had spent on the "Taco Barn To Go" project was stretching his schedule to the point where he was falling behind in his responsibilities at the restaurant. He didn't want to admit to Dawn that he couldn't manage all this extra work, but he was smart enough to realize that he needed some help, and so he called a few of his fellow unit managers for some advice.

That advice ranged from asking for another assistant manager (not an option!) to simply letting the work pile up and getting to it when he could. In the end he took the advice of Fred Thompson, one of the veteran unit managers, who suggested that he "offload some of the work onto his people."

"HR calls it 'delegation,' " continued Fred, "but don't give them anything they can mess up because it'll be your job to clean it up. Stop trying to run everything, and give them some of the easier tasks to do: ordering, menus, time sheets. They'll appreciate the break in their regular routine, and if they do a good job, you know you've found some future shift leaders."

Tony liked Fred's idea, but he admitted to himself that he had gotten this far in his career by always being better than the folks he worked with—working harder, longer, and always being willing to take on extra work from Jerry to learn more about how he ran the restaurant. Did he have anyone he could count on to do it as well as he could do it himself?

In the end, the decision was made for Tony. One day, Katie, one of his waitresses, reminded him that they were running low on stuff for the restaurant: napkins, condiments, and menu holders. Tony, distracted by a fast-approaching deadline for something he needed to give to Dawn, snapped back at Katie:

"Look Katie I'm really busy here—why don't you make up a list of what we need and call it in to our supplier, okay? Kevin can give you the number. Just don't spend too much."

**QUESTIONS**

1. Why wouldn't Tony just withdraw from the survey project if it was affecting his work at the Taco Barn?
2. What's wrong with Fred's interpretation of "delegation"? Review pages 126 to 128 for guidance here.
3. Did Tony give Katie clear directions? Why or why not?
4. What should Tony have done here?

# >> Organizing Work

Most work today is accomplished through organizations. An **organization** is a group of people working together in some type of concentrated or coordinated effort to achieve objectives. As such, an organization provides a vehicle for implementing strategy and accomplishing objectives that could not be achieved by individuals working separately. The process of **organizing** is the grouping of activities necessary to achieve common objectives and the assignment of each grouping to a manager who has the authority required to supervise the people performing the activities.[1] Thus, organizing is basically a process of division of labor accompanied by appropriate delegation of authority. Proper organizing results in more effective use of resources.

**Organization** A group of people working together in some concerted or coordinated effort to attain objectives.

**Organizing** Grouping activities, assigning activities, and providing the authority necessary to carry out the activities.

**Formal Organization** Organization structure that defines the boundaries of the organization and within which the organization operates.

**Informal Organization** Aggregate of the personal contacts and interactions and the associated groupings of people working within the formal organization.

The framework that defines the boundaries of the **formal organization** and within which the organization operates is the organization structure. A second and equally important element of an organization is the informal organization. The **informal organization** refers to the sum of the personal contacts and interactions and the associated groupings of people working within the formal organization.[2] The informal organization has a structure, but it is not formally and consciously designed.

# >> Reasons for Organizing

One of the primary reasons for organizing is to establish lines of authority. Clear lines of authority create order within a group. Absence of authority almost always leads to chaotic situations where everyone is telling everyone else what to do.

**Study Alert!**

How is your company organized? Have you experienced synergism at any organizations you've worked for? What are some examples of synergism and communication?

Second, organizing improves the efficiency and quality of work through synergism. *Synergism* occurs when individuals or groups work together to produce a whole greater than the sum of the parts. For example, synergism results when three people working together produce more than three people working separately. Synergism can result from division of labor or from increased coordination, both of which are products of good organization. Two organizations that appear to be very similar can experience very different levels of performance due to the synergism resulting from their organizational structures. Highly successful organizations generally achieve a high level of synergism as a result of the manner in which they are organized.

A final reason for organizing is to improve communication. A good organization structure clearly defines channels of communication among the members of the organization. Such a system also ensures more efficient communications.

Historically, the desire to organize led to the development of an organization. The use of an organization allows people to jointly (1) increase specialization and division of labor, (2) use large-scale technology, (3) manage the external environment, (4) economize on transaction costs, and (5) exert power and control.[3] When designed and coordinated effectively, these characteristics help the organization serve its customers with a high degree of productivity.

# >> Division of Labor

Organizing is basically a process of division of labor. The merits of dividing labor have been known for centuries. Labor can be divided either vertically or horizontally. Vertical division of labor is based on the establishment of lines of authority and defines the

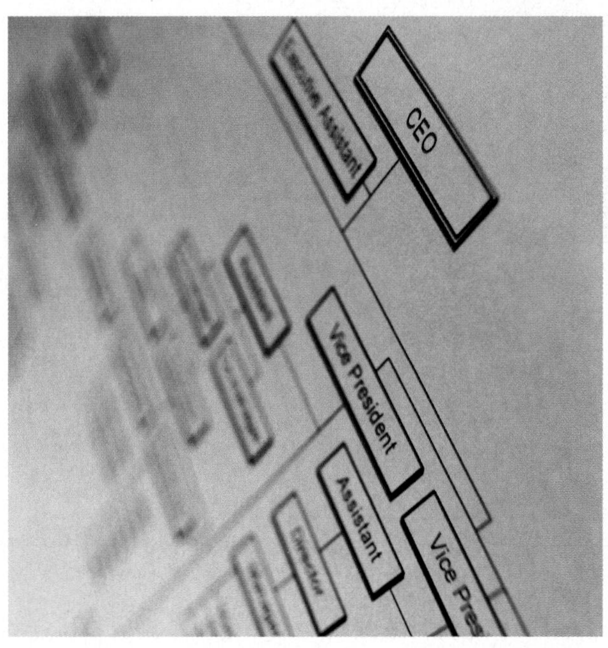

levels that make up the vertical organization structure. In addition to establishing authority, vertical division of labor facilitates the flow of communication within the organization. To illustrate how vertical division of labor can vary from company to company, consider the automobile industry in the early 1980s. At that time, Toyota had 5 levels between the chairperson and the first-line supervisor, whereas Ford had over 15.[4]

Horizontal division of labor is based on specialization of work. The basic assumption underlying horizontal division of labor is that by making each worker's task specialized, more work can be produced with the same effort through increased efficiency and quality. Specifically, horizontal division of labor can result in the following advantages:

1. Fewer skills are required per person.
2. The skills required for selection or training purposes are easier to supply.
3. Practice in the same job develops proficiency.
4. Primarily utilizing each worker's best skills promotes efficient use of skills.
5. Simultaneous operations are made possible.
6. More conformity in the final product results when each piece is always produced by the same person.

The major problem with horizontal division of labor is that it can result in job boredom and even humiliation of the employee. An extreme example of horizontal division of labor is the automobile assembly line. Most people working on an automobile assembly line do a small number of very simple tasks over and over again. It usually doesn't take long for these employees to become bored. Once employees become bored, their productivity often declines, absenteeism and lateness increase, and the quality of work goes down. Solutions to the problems created by horizontal division of labor include a reexamination of job scope, implementing job rotation, and balancing job simplification with job depth, often referred to as *job enrichment.*

**Job scope** refers to the number of different types of operations performed. In performing a job with narrow scope, the employee performs few operations and repeats the cycle frequently. The negative effects of jobs lacking in scope vary with the person performing the job, but they can include more errors and lower quality. Often job rotation, wherein workers shift in the planned sequence of activities, eliminates boredom and monotony and encourages multiple skills and cross training.

**Job depth** refers to the freedom of employees to plan and organize their own work, work at their own pace, and move around and communicate as desired. A lack of job depth can result in job dissatisfaction and work avoidance, which in turn can lead to absenteeism, lateness, and even sabotage.

Division of labor is not more efficient or even desirable in all situations. At least two basic requirements must exist for the successful use of division of labor. The first requirement is a relatively large volume of work. Enough volume must be produced to allow specialization and keep each employee busy. The second requirement is stability in the volume of work, employee attendance, quality of raw materials, product design, and production technology.

**Job Scope** Number of different types of operations performed on the job.

**Job Depth** Freedom of employees to plan and organize their own work, work at their own pace, and move around and communicate as desired.

**Power** Ability to influence, command, or apply force; a measure of a person's potential to get others to do what he or she wants them to do, as well as to avoid being forced by others to do what he or she does not want to do.

**Authority** Legitimate exercise of power; the right to issue directives and expend resources; related to power but narrower in scope.

**Responsibility** Accountability for the attainment of objectives, the use of resources, and the adherence to organizational policy.

### PROGRESS questions

1. What is an informal organization?
2. Explain the term synergism.
3. What are the six advantages and disadvantages of horizontal division of labor?
4. Explain the terms job scope and job depth.

## POWER, AUTHORITY, AND RESPONSIBILITY

**Power** is the ability to influence, command, or apply force. Power is usually derived from the control of resources. **Authority** is power derived from the rights that come with a position and represents the legitimate exercise of power. Thus, authority is one source of power for a manager. Lines of authority link the various organizational components. Unclear lines of authority can create major confusion and conflict within an organization.

**Responsibility** is the accountability for the achievement of objectives, the use of resources, and the adherence to organizational policy. Once responsibility is accepted, performing assigned work becomes an obligation. The term *responsibility* as used here should not be confused with the term *responsibilities* as in the context of defining job duties.

CHAIN OF RESPONSIBILITY

A group of civil engineers are involved in a major construction project. Their duties include liaison with the architects and builders and advice on appropriate structural materials for different parts of the building. Unfortunately, the software package they are using to run the numbers has two major flaws—a bug that produces arithmetic errors in some calculations, and some incorrect information on the load-bearing properties of some of the materials being used in the construction project. The project is behind schedule, and the developers are putting pressure on the builders to catch up.

Halfway through the construction process, the building is unable to support the loads being placed on it. A crane on the top floor crashes through several floors and kills a number of workers in the process. An analysis of the disaster shows that the arithmetic bug and the incorrect information on material strength combined to bring about the failure. In these circumstances, who has the greater ethical responsibility for the accident? The engineers who failed to recognize that the material information was incorrect? The developers whose tight schedules made checking the stress calculations impossible? Or the software developers who supplied a faulty product?

ETHICAL
MANAGEMENT
Who is to blame when accidents happen on the job?


*Source*: T. Forester and P. Morrison, *Computer Ethics: Cautionary Tales and Ethical Dilemmas in Computing,* 2nd ed. (Cambridge, MA: MIT Press, 2001), pp. 233–36.

## SOURCES OF AUTHORITY

As just mentioned, authority can be viewed as a function of position, flowing from top to bottom through the formal organization. According to this view, people hold authority because they occupy a certain position; once removed from the position, they lose their authority. Taking this theory one step further, one can say the American people, through the Constitution and laws, represent the ultimate source of authority in this country. The Constitution and laws guarantee the right of free enterprise. The owners of a free enterprise organization have the right to elect a board of directors and top management. Top management selects middle-level managers. This process continues down to the lowest person in the organization. This traditional view of authority is also called the *formal theory of authority.*

A second theory of authority was first outlined in 1926 by Mary Parker Follett and popularized in 1938 by Chester Barnard.[5] Called the *acceptance theory of authority,* this theory maintains that a manager's source of authority lies with his or her subordinates because they have the power to either accept or reject the manager's command. Presumably, if a subordinate does not view a manager's authority as legitimate, it does not exist. Both Follett and Barnard viewed disobeying a communication from a manager as a denial of authority by the subordinate. In summary, the acceptance theory of authority recognizes that subordinates play an active role in determining lines of authority and are not merely passive recipients in the process. This idea is somewhat similar to the contention that without followers you can have no leaders. Both elements must be present and mutually recognized for true structure to exist. Companies with a high degree of employee involvement, responsibility, and accountability appear to recognize acceptance theory as being beneficial for mutual support and encouragement between labor and management.

**Study Alert!**

In the position you hold in your company, what are you responsible for? How much power and authority do you have to meet that responsibility?

*Power, authority, and responsibility are all part of the equation when factoring effective versus ineffective management. What are some potential problems for a manager lacking power, authority, or responsibility?*

# >> Centralization Versus Decentralization

There are limitations to the authority of any position. These limitations may be external, in the form of laws, politics, or social attitudes, or they may be internal, as

# Thinking Critically 6.1

## >> A Good Manager?

Janet Lieb is assistant general manager and sales manager for Webb Enterprises. At the moment, this self-styled perfectionist is sitting up in bed, checking her TTD (things to do) sheet for tomorrow. The TTD itemizes daily activities, placing them on an exact time schedule. Never one to browbeat subordinates, Janet has her own special way of reminding people that time is money. Ever since the days when she was the best salesperson the company ever had, she has worked harder than the rest. It had paid off too, because in only two years (when old Tom DiPietropolo retires), she would be heir apparent to the general managership. As this thought crosses Janet's mind, her immediate pride is replaced with a nagging problem. Where is she going to find the time to do all the things the position required? She certainly couldn't afford to maintain the status quo. Then her mind forces her to plan tomorrow's activities, and the problem is pushed into the background for future consideration.

Following is a portion of Janet's well-planned day.

**TTD–October 16**

7:15 Breakfast with Mei Lynn D'Alessandro (Purchasing). Get information on cataloging system.

Maybe combine with sales department and avoid duplication.

8:30 Meeting with Rick Fritzinger (assistant sales manager). Tell him exactly how the sales meeting for out-of-state representatives should be conducted. Caution—he's shaky on questions.

9:15 Discuss progress on new office procedures manual with Stacey Kaiser (general manager). (She's irritated because I've dragged my heels on this. Let her know I've got Jeannie Newman working on the problem.)

9:45 Assign Jeannie Newman the job of collecting data and sample copies regarding office manuals in other companies in our industry. Set up a system for her to use in analysis.

10:45 Call on Acliff Printing. A potentially big customer. [*As Janet jots down some information on this client, she reflects that it is a shame no one else on her staff could really handle the big ones the way she could. This thought is pleasing and bothersome at the same time.*]

12:00 Lunch with Adam Rooke (reservations at Black Angus).

3:00 Meet with Manny Washington (advertising assistant), and check his progress on the new sales campaign. [*Janet thinks about Washington's usual wild ideas and hopes that he has followed the general theme and rough sketches he had prepared.*]

7:30 Chamber of Commerce meeting. (Look up Randall Swift—he may be able to help on the Acliff account.)

**QUESTIONS**

1. Do you think Janet is a highly motivated employee trying to do a good job? Explain your answer.
2. What problems do you see concerning Janet's effectiveness as a manager?
3. What options are available to help Janet?
4. Assuming you were Tom, the general manager, what solutions would you recommend?

delineated by the organization's objectives or by the job description. The tapered concept of authority states that the breadth and scope of authority become more limited as one descends the scalar chain (see Figure 6.1).

The top levels of management establish the shapes of the funnels in Figures 6.1 and 6.2. The more authority top management chooses to delegate, the less conical the funnel becomes. The less conical the funnel, the more decentralized the organization. **Centralization** and **decentralization** refer to the degree of authority delegated by upper management. This is usually reflected by the numbers and kinds of decisions made by the lower levels of management. As they increase, the degree of decentralization also increases. Thus, an organization is never totally centralized or totally decentralized; rather, it falls along a continuum ranging from highly centralized to highly decentralized. In Figure 6.2, the organization represented by the diagram on the left is much more centralized than that represented by the right-hand diagram.

The trend in today's organizations is toward more decentralization. Decentralization has the advantage of allowing more flexibility and quicker action. It also relieves executives from time-consuming detail work. It often results in higher morale by allowing lower levels of management to be actively involved in the decision-making process. The major disadvantage of decentralization is the potential loss of control. Duplication of effort can also accompany decentralization.

## [PROGRESS] ✓questions

5. Explain the terms power, authority, and responsibility.
6. What is the formal theory of authority?
7. What is the acceptance theory of authority?
8. What are the advantages and disadvantages of a decentralized structure?

**Figure 6.1 • Tapered Concept of Authority**

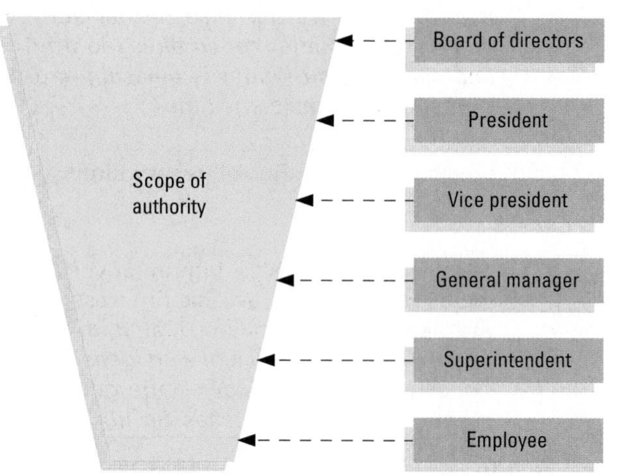


**From the PERSPECTIVE OF...**

**An HR Manager** In a decentralized organization you balance the potential loss of managerial control with the advantage of greater operational flexibility. As an HR manager at the corporate headquarters, what challenges would you face in running a team of HR generalists at regional locations?

**Figure 6.2 • Centralized versus Decentralized Authority**

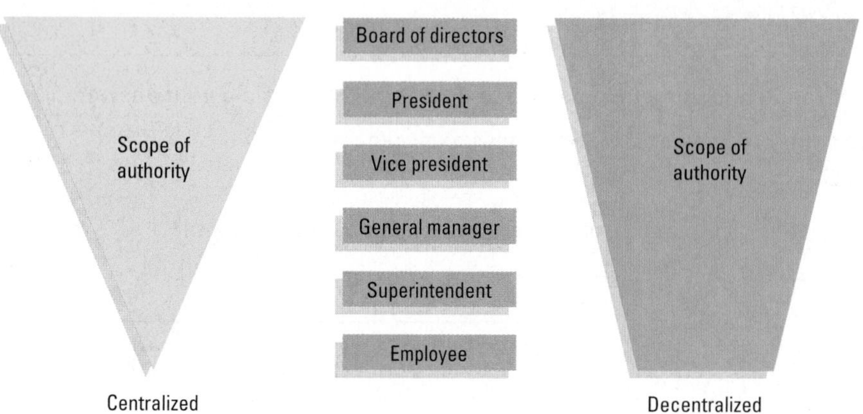


## >> Empowerment

**Empowerment** is a form of decentralization that involves giving subordinates substantial authority to make decisions. Under empowerment, managers express confidence in the ability of employees to perform at high levels. Employees are also encouraged to accept personal responsibility for their work. In situations where true empowerment takes place, employees gain confidence in their ability to perform their jobs and influence the organization's performance. Under true empowerment, employees can bend the rules to do whatever they have to do to take care of the customer.[6] One result of empowerment is that employees demonstrate more initiative and perseverance in pursuing organizational goals. In order for empowerment to take root and thrive, the following four elements must be present:[7]

- *Participation.* Employees must be actively and willingly engaged in their respective job. They must want to improve their work processes and work relationship.
- *Innovation.* Employees must be given permission and encouragement to innovate and not do things the way they have always been done.
- *Access to information.* Employees at every level in the organization should make decisions about the kind of information they need to perform their job. This is different from traditional organizations where senior managers decide who gets what information.
- *Accountability.* Employees must be held accountable for their actions and the results achieved.

While the concept of empowerment looks relatively simple, it can be difficult to implement—especially in organizations where authority has traditionally flowed from top to bottom. Organizations can take several actions to help implement empowerment:[8]

- Whenever possible, restructure organizational units to be smaller, less complex, and less dependent on other units for decision making and action.
- Reduce to a minimum the number of hard rules for the organization.
- Emphasize a change throughout the organization that focuses on empowerment and personal accountability for delivering results.
- Provide the education and training necessary to enable people to respond to opportunities for improvement.

**Centralization** Little authority is delegated to lower levels of management.

**Decentralization** A great deal of authority is delegated to lower levels of management.

**Empowerment** Form of decentralization in which subordinates have authority to make decisions.

Accompanying the trend toward more decentralization in today's organizations is a trend toward increased empowerment of today's workforce. While some people believe that empowerment is praised loudly in public but seldom implemented, companies have experienced very positive results from having empowered their employees.

## SELF-MANAGED WORK TEAMS

One method for empowering employees is through the use of *self-managed work teams.* Self-managed work teams (also called *self-directed* or *self-regulated work teams*) are work units without a frontline manager that are empowered to control their own work.[9] The philosophy behind any type of work team is that teams can contribute to improved performance by identifying and solving work-related problems. The basic idea is to motivate employees by having them participate in decisions that affect them and their work. Self-managed work teams are teams of

### RISING TO THE OCCASION

You have been assigned to a companywide strategic planning project for a month. The e-mail that was sent to your manager clearly stated, "Representation from all departments is seen as a precursor to success." You're not sure why you were picked for the project, but you suspect that your primary value was that you wouldn't be missed in your department. You're not the top producer on your team, and you've been around long enough to realize that your boss doesn't hold you in the highest regard as a valued member of her team, even though you are a consistent, solid, and dependable worker.

As the project proceeds, it becomes clear that your manager has miscalculated the importance of this strategic planning initiative. Several key decisions are being made that will directly affect your department. The question is, Should you perform to the low expectations that your manager apparently has for you and do as little

ETHICAL
MANAGEMENT
Should you meet expectations, however negative, or exceed them?

as possible on this project, or should you fulfill that mandate of representation and speak out for your peers and colleagues in your department by making sure that their interests and concerns are truly represented?

employees who accomplish tasks within their area of responsibility without direct supervision. Each team makes its own job assignments, plans its own work, performs equipment maintenance, keeps records, obtains supplies, and makes selection decisions of new members into the work unit.

There is no doubt that the use of self-managed work teams has grown dramatically over the last several years and will continue to grow in the future. Self-directed work teams are discussed further in Chapter 8, which is devoted to understanding all forms of work teams.

## >> Principles Based on Authority

Because authority is a key element in managing organizations, several key concepts are relevant. Delegation, unity of command, the scalar principle, and the span of management historically have been the most important of these concepts.

### DELEGATION: THE PARITY PRINCIPLE

According to Herbert Engel, "As an abstract idea, delegation must be as old as the human race itself."[10] The allocation of specific duties to members of a group by a leader seems almost as natural as it is necessary. Delegation normally occurs when one needs something done that one either cannot or chooses not to do oneself. The decision may be based on situations, skills, time, established order, or the expansion and growth of responsibilities as dictated by the group or the organization. Managers can delegate responsibility to subordinates in the sense of making subordinates responsible to them. However, this delegation to subordinates makes managers no less responsible to their superiors. Delegation of responsibility does not mean abdication of responsibility by the delegating manager. Responsibility is not like an object that can be passed from individual to individual.

The **parity principle** states that authority and responsibility must coincide. Management must delegate sufficient authority to enable subordinates to do their jobs. At the same time, subordinates can be expected to accept responsibility only for those areas within their authority.

Subordinates must accept both authority and responsibility before the delegation process has been completed. Management sometimes expects employees to seek and assume responsibility they have not been asked to assume and then bid for the necessary authority. Such a system leads to guessing games that do nothing but create frustration and waste energy.

A manager's resistance to delegating authority is natural. There are several reasons for this reluctance:

- Fear that subordinates will fail in doing the task.
- The belief that it is easier to do the task oneself rather than delegate it.
- Fear that subordinates will look "too good".
- Humans' attraction to power.
- Comfort in doing the tasks of the previous job held.
- Preconceived ideas about employees.
- Desire to set the right example.

Despite all the reasons for not delegating, there are some very strong reasons for a manager to delegate. Several things occur when a manager successfully delegates. First, the manager's time is freed to pursue other tasks, and the subordinates gain feelings of belonging and being needed. These feelings often lead to a genuine commitment on the part of the subordinates. Second, delegation is one of the best methods for developing subordinates and satisfying customers. Pushing authority down the organization also allows employees to deal more effectively with customers. In its mid-1990s reengineering effort, Hallmark Cards, Inc., found that when you drive something from the top, you have to articulate clearly and communicate why it is being done.[11] By converting delegation to a shared vision, the organization has a much better chance of accomplishing its

**Figure 6.3 • Steps in the Delegation Process**

1. Analyze how you spend your time.
2. Decide which tasks can be assigned.
3. Decide who can handle each task.
4. Delegate the authority.
5. Create an obligation (responsibility).
6. Control the delegation.

goals and objectives without resorting to adverse persuasion. Similarly, Taco Bell went from a $500 million regional company in 1982 to a $3 billion national company today because it recognized that the way to ultimately reach and satisfy customers was to empower its lower-level employees to make changes in operational strategies and tactics.[12] Successful delegation involves delegating matters that stimulate subordinates.

## HOW TO DELEGATE

To successfully delegate, a manager must decide which tasks can be delegated. Figure 6.3 indicates the steps the manager can follow to analyze and improve the delegation process. Clearly defining objectives and standards, involving subordinates in the delegation process, and initiating training that defines and encourages delegation tend to improve the overall delegation process. Controlling the delegation requires that the delegating manager periodically check to ensure that things are going as planned. The frequency of these checks should be cooperatively decided by the delegating manager and the employees. Checks should not be so frequent as to stifle the employees, but they should be frequent enough to provide necessary support and guidance.

Probably the most vague part of the delegation process centers around the question of how much authority to delegate. As mentioned previously, management must delegate sufficient authority to allow the subordinate to perform the job. Precisely what can and cannot be delegated depends on the commitments of the manager and the number and quality of subordinates. A rule of thumb is to delegate authority and responsibility to the lowest organization level that has the competence to accept them.

Failure to master delegation is probably the single most frequently encountered reason managers fail. To be a good manager, a person must learn to delegate.

The **exception principle** (also known as *management by exception*) states that managers should concentrate their efforts on matters that deviate significantly from normal and let subordinates handle routine matters. The exception principle is closely related to the parity principle. The idea behind the exception principle is that managers should concentrate on those matters that require their abilities and not become bogged down with duties their subordinates should be doing. The exception principle can be hard to comply with when incompetent or insecure subordinates refer everything to their superiors because they are afraid to make a decision. On the other hand, superiors should refrain from making everyday decisions that they have delegated to subordinates. This problem is often referred to as *micromanaging*.

**Parity Principle** Principle that authority and responsibility must coincide.

**Exception Principle** Principle that managers should concentrate on matters that deviate significantly from normal and let subordinates handle routing matters; also called *management by exception*.

## UNITY OF COMMAND

The **unity of command principle** states that an employee should have one, and only one, immediate manager. The difficulty of serving more than one superior has been recognized for thousands of years. Recall the biblical quote, "No man can serve two masters." In its simplest form, this problem arises when two managers tell the same employee to do different jobs at the same time. The employee is thus placed in a no-win situation. Regardless of which manager the employee obeys, the other will be dissatisfied. The key to avoiding problems with unity of command is to make sure employees clearly

**Unity of Command Principle** Principle that an employee should have one, and only one, immediate manager.

understand the lines of authority that directly affect them. Too often managers assume employees understand the lines of authority when in fact they do not. All employees should have a basic understanding of the organization chart for their company and where they fit on it. An organization chart frequently clarifies lines of authority and the chain of command.

**Study Alert!** Under the unity of command principle, do you report to only one manager at your company? Or do you have a "dotted line" in the organization chart to other managers?

More times than not, problems relating to the unity of command principle stem from the actions of managers rather than the actions of employees. This happens most often when managers make requests of employees who do not work directly for them.

# First Line Focus

WHEN TO DELEGATE . . .

*Delegating responsibility to one of your people can offer a multitude of positive outcomes—less work on your plate (or, more likely, more time to put toward other responsibilities) and an opportunity for that team member to expand his or her skill set and corresponding value to the organization. However, the same act of delegation also has the potential to offer a multitude of negative outcomes—when poorly planned and executed, that work can come back around to your plate to be fixed or redone; and for a poorly prepared and supported team member, a nightmare experience that can undermine confidence and handicap future career advancement.*

*Delegation should be carefully planned and monitored. Unfortunately, in many instances, delegation is instituted when your plate is already full and in danger of overflowing with projects and responsibilities. Reassigning projects under time pressure with little, if any, time devoted to careful selection, thorough explanation, and regular monitoring, will more than likely just delay those projects for future rework later on down the road.*

## SCALAR PRINCIPLE

The **scalar principle** states that authority in the organization flows through the chain of managers one link at a time, ranging from the highest to the lowest ranks. Commonly referred to as the *chain of command*, the scalar principle is based on the need for communication and the principle of unity of command.

**Scalar Principle** Principle that authority in the organization flows through the chain of managers one link at a time, ranging from the highest to the lowest ranks; also called *chain of command.*

The problem with going around the scalar principle is that the link bypassed in the process may have very important information. For example, suppose Jerry goes directly above his immediate boss, Ellen, to Charlie for permission to take his lunch break 30 minutes earlier. Charlie, believing the request is reasonable, approves it, only to find out later that the other two people in Jerry's department had also rescheduled their lunch breaks. Thus, the department would be totally vacant from 12:30 to 1 o'clock. Ellen, the bypassed manager, would have known about the other rescheduled lunch breaks.

A common misconception is that every action must painstakingly progress through every link in the chain, whether its course is upward or downward. This point was refuted many years ago by Lyndall Urwick, an internationally known management consultant:

> Provided there is proper confidence and loyalty between superiors and subordinates, and both parties take the trouble to keep the other informed in matters in which they should have a concern, the "scalar process" does not imply that there should be no shortcuts. It is concerned with authority, and provided the authority is recognized and no attempt is made to evade or to supersede it, there is ample room for avoiding in matters of action the childish practices of going upstairs one step at a time or running up one ladder and down another when there is nothing to prevent a direct approach on level ground.[13]

As Henri Fayol stated years before Urwick, "It is an error to depart needlessly from authority, but it is an even greater one to keep to it when detriment to the business ensues."[14] Both Urwick and Fayol are simply saying that in certain instances one can and should

# Thinking Critically 6.2

## >> The Vacation Request

Randall Swift has a week's vacation coming and really wants to take it the third week in May, which is the height of the bass fishing season. The only problem is that two of the other five members of his department have already requested and received approval from their boss, Lisa Portz, to take off that same week. Afraid that Lisa would not approve his request, Randall decided to forward his request directly to Eugene Kivett, who is Lisa's boss and who is rather friendly to Randall (Randall has taken Eugene fishing on several occasions). Not realizing that Lisa has not seen the request, Eugene approves it. Several weeks pass before Lisa finds out, by accident, that Randall has been approved to go on vacation the third week of May.

The thing that really bugs Lisa is that this is only one of many instances in which her subordinates have gone directly to Eugene and gotten permission to do something. Just last week, in fact, she overheard a conversation in the washroom to the effect that "if you want anything approved, don't waste time with Lisa; go directly to Eugene."

**QUESTIONS**

1. What should Eugene have done?
2. Who is at fault, Eugene or Randall?
3. Should Randall get his vacation? Why or why not?
4. What should Lisa do to make sure this doesn't happen again?

**[PROGRESS] questions**

9. What are the four elements that must be present for empowerment to thrive?
10. What is a self-managed work team?
11. What are the seven reasons for a manager's reluctance to delegate authority?
12. What is the exception principle?

shortcut the scalar chain as long as not doing so in a secretive or deceitful manner.

## SPAN OF MANAGEMENT

The **span of management** (also called the *span of control*) refers to the number of subordinates a manager can effectively manage. Although the British World War I general Sir Ian Hamilton is usually credited for developing the concept of a limited span of control, related examples abound throughout history. Hamilton argued that a narrow span of management (with no more than six subordinates reporting to a manager) would enable the manager to get the job accomplished in the course of a normal working day.[15]

In 1933, V. A. Graicunas published a classic paper that analyzed subordinate-superior relationships in terms of a mathematical formula.[16] This formula was based on the theory that the complexities of managing increase geometrically as the number of subordinates increases arithmetically.

Based on his personal experience and the works of Hamilton and Graicunas, Lyndall Urwick first stated the concept of span of management as a management principle in 1938: "No superior can supervise directly the work of more than five, or at the most, six subordinates whose work interlocks."[17]

**Span of Management** Number of subordinates a manager can effectively manage; also called *span of control*.

A span of five or six subordinates is a rule of thumb at best. How many people report directly to you? How many people, including you, report directly to your manager?

## Figure 6.4 • Factors Affecting the Span of Management

| Factor | Description | Relationship to Span of Control |
|---|---|---|
| Complexity | Job scope<br>Job depth | Shortens span of control |
| Variety | Number of different types of jobs being managed | Shortens span of control |
| Proximity | Physical dispersion of jobs being managed | Lengthens span of control |
| Quality of subordinates | General quality of the employees being managed | Lengthens span of control |
| Quality of manager | Ability to perform managerial duties | Lengthens span of control |

Since the publication of Graicunas's and Urwick's works, the upper limit of five or six subordinates has been continuously criticized as being too restrictive. Many practitioners and scholars contend there are situations in which more than five or six subordinates can be effectively supervised. Their beliefs have been substantiated by considerable empirical evidence showing that the limit of five or six subordinates has been successfully exceeded in many situations.[18] Urwick has suggested these exceptions can be explained by the fact that senior workers often function as unofficial managers or leaders.[19]

In view of recent evidence, the span of management concept has been revised to state that the number of people who should report directly to any one person should be based on the complexity, variety, and proximity of the jobs, the quality of the people filling the jobs, and the ability of the manager.

While much effort is given to ensuring that a manager's span of management is not too great, the opposite situation is often overlooked. All too frequently in organizations, situations develop in which only one employee reports to a particular manager. While this situation might very well be justified under certain circumstances, it often results in an inefficient and top-heavy organization. The pros and cons of flat structures (i.e., organizations having wide spans of management with few levels) versus tall structures (i.e., organizations having narrow spans of management with many levels) are discussed at length in the next chapter. Figure 6.4 summarizes the factors affecting the manager's span of management.

# >> Workplace Changes in Organizations

Several changes are occurring in the workplace environment that can affect how an entity might best be organized. Flextime, telecommuting, and job sharing are three such practices that are growing in popularity.

*Flextime,* or flexible working hours, allows employees to choose, within certain limits, when they start and end their workday. Usually the organization defines a core period (such as 10 A.M. to 3 P.M.) when all employees will be at work. It is then left to each employee to decide when to start and end the workday as long as the hours encompass the core period. Some flextime programs allow employees to vary the hours worked each day as long as they meet some specific total, which is usually 40 hours. The percentage of organizations offering flextime has increased dramatically over the last 15 years. A recent study by the Society for Human Resource Management found that 56 percent of employers offered some type of flextime in 2005.[20]

Flextime has the advantage of allowing different employees to accommodate different lifestyles and schedules. Other potential advantages include avoiding rush hours and having less absenteeism and tardiness. From the employer's viewpoint, flextime can have the advantage of providing an edge in recruiting new employees and also retaining hard-to-find qualified employees. Also, organizations with flextime schedules have reported an average increase of 1 to 5 percent in productivity, as well as improved recruiting and retention.[21] On the downside, flextime can create communication and coordination problems for supervisors and managers.

*Telecommuting* is the practice of working at home, while traveling and being able to interact with the office, or working at a satellite office. Today's information technology (PCs, the Internet, cellular phones, etc.) has made telecommuting a reality for many companies. According to the International Telework Association and Council (ITAC), over 45 million Americans were working from their home in 2005 and over 20 million were working from their cars.[22] The earlier referenced survey by the Society for Human Resource Management found that 37 percent of its respondents offered some type of telecommuting.[23] Advantages of telecommuting include lower turnover, less travel time, avoiding rush hour, avoiding distractions at the office, being able to work flexible hours, and lower real estate costs for employers. Potential disadvantages of telecommuting are insurance concerns relating to the health and safety of employees working at home. Another drawback is that some state and local laws restrict the type of work that can be done at home. The dramatic rise in the price of gasoline has made telecommuting even more attractive to millions of Americans.

*Job sharing* is a relatively new concept whereby two or more part-time employees perform a job that would normally be held by one full-time employee. Job sharing can be in the form of equally shared responsibilities or split duties, or a combination of both. Approximately 19 percent of major firms in the United States offer some type of job sharing, according to the 2005 survey by the Society for Human Resource Management. Job sharing is especially attractive to people who want to work but not full-time. A critical factor relating to job sharing is how benefits are handled. Often benefits are prorated between the part-time employees. Some organizations allow job-sharing employees to purchase full health insurance by paying the difference between their prorated benefit and the premium for a full-time employee.

**From the PERSPECTIVE OF...**

**A Sales Manager**

What are the challenges in running a team of telecommuting salespeople who only meet as a team once per quarter?

**[PROGRESS] ✓questions**

13. Explain the span of management (span of control).
14. Think of an organization you work for (or have worked for in the past). What is the span of management at your company?
15. Explain the following terms: flextime, telecommuting, and job sharing.
16. Would it be possible to introduce telecommuting at your company? Why or why not?

## >> Chapter Summary

Organizing work is the process of dividing labor resources according to assigned tasks and delegating the necessary authority to perform those tasks. Managers should be directly involved in all aspects of that process but, most importantly, in establishing the lines of authority because without those clearly defined lines the organization can collapse into chaos very quickly. In the next chapter we review the options available to managers in defining the formal boundaries of an organization in order to establish the environment in which the work of the organization takes place.

# For REVIEW >>

1. Define *organization*, and differentiate between a formal and an informal organization.

   An organization is a group of people working together in some type of concentrated or coordinated effort to achieve objectives. As such, an organization provides a vehicle for implementing strategy and accomplishing objectives that could not be achieved by individuals working separately. The process of organizing is the grouping of activities necessary to achieve common objectives and the assignment of each grouping to a manager who has the authority required to supervise the people performing the activities. A formal organization represents the documented structure of each of those respective assignments of responsibility, typically presented graphically as an organization chart. Separate from this formal structure is an informal organization that represents the sum of the personal contacts and interactions and the associated groupings of people working within the formal organization. The informal organization has a structure, but it is not formally and consciously designed.

2. Distinguish between power, authority, and responsibility.

   Power is the ability to influence, command, or apply force. Power is usually derived from the control of resources. Authority is power derived from the rights that come with a position and represents the legitimate exercise of power. Thus, authority is one source of power for a manager. Lines of authority link the various organizational components. Unclear lines of authority can create major confusion and conflict within an organization. Responsibility is accountability for the achievement of objectives, the use of resources, and the adherence to organizational policy. Once responsibility is accepted, performing assigned work becomes an obligation.

3. Explain the concept of centralization versus decentralization.

   Centralization and decentralization refer to the degree of authority delegated by upper management. This is usually reflected by the numbers and kinds of decisions made by the lower levels of management. As they increase, the degree of decentralization also increases. Thus, an organization is never totally centralized or totally decentralized; rather, it falls along a continuum ranging from highly centralized to highly decentralized.

   The trend in today's organizations is toward more decentralization. Decentralization has the advantage of allowing more flexibility and quicker action. It also relieves executives from time-consuming detail work. It often results in higher morale by allowing lower levels of management to be actively involved in the decision-making process. The major disadvantages of decentralization are the potential for duplication of effort and loss of control.

4. Define *empowerment*.

   Empowerment is a form of decentralization that involves giving subordinates substantial authority to make decisions. Under empowerment, managers express confidence in the ability of employees to perform at high levels. Employees are also encouraged to accept personal responsibility for their work. In situations where true empowerment takes place, employees gain confidence in their ability to perform their jobs and influence the organization's performance. Under true empowerment, employees can bend the rules to do whatever they have to do to take care of the customer. One result of empowerment is that employees demonstrate more initiative and perseverance in pursuing organizational goals.

5. Identify several reasons why managers are reluctant to delegate authority.

   A manager's resistance to delegating authority is natural. There are several reasons for this reluctance:

   - Fear that subordinates will fail in doing the task.
   - The belief that it is easier to do the task oneself rather than to delegate it.
   - Fear that subordinates will look "too good."
   - Humans' attraction to power.
   - Comfort in doing the tasks of the previous job held.
   - Preconceived ideas about employees.
   - Desire to set the right example.

6. Explain flextime, telecommuting, and job-sharing, and discuss their respective impact on the organization of work.

   Flextime, or flexible working hours, allows employees to choose, within certain limits, when they start and end their workday. Some flextime programs allow employees to vary the hours worked each day as long as they meet some specific total, which is usually 40 hours. Flextime has the advantage of allowing different employees to accommodate different lifestyles and schedules. Other potential advantages include avoiding rush hours and having less absenteeism and tardiness. From the employer's viewpoint, flextime can have the advantage of providing an edge in recruiting new employees and also retaining hard-to-find qualified employees. On the downside, flextime can create communication and coordination problems for supervisors and managers.

   Telecommuting is the practice of working at home, while traveling and being able to interact with the office, or working at a satellite office. Today's information technology (PCs, the Internet, wireless technology, etc.) has made telecommuting a reality for many companies. Advantages of telecommuting include lower turnover, less travel time, avoiding rush hour, avoiding distractions at the office, being able to work flexible hours, and lower real estate costs for employers. Potential disadvantages of telecommuting are insurance concerns relating to the health and safety of employees working at home.

   Job sharing refers to two or more part-time employees performing a job that would normally be held by one full-time employee. Job sharing can be in the form of equally shared responsibilities or split duties, or a combination of both. Job sharing is especially attractive to people who want to work but not full-time. On the downside, the arrangement shares the same potential for communication and coordination problems for supervisors and managers.

## THE WORLD of Work >>

**BE CAREFUL WHAT YOU WISH FOR ... (*continued from page 119*)**

Katie really liked working at the Taco Barn. Several of her friends worked there, and Tony had followed in Jerry's footsteps by being really flexible on her schedule so that she could meet her cheerleading and AP course commitments. So when Tony asked her to make up a list of things they needed in the restaurant and to place the order, Katie decided that she would show Tony what a smart choice he had made in giving her the task.

She had originally gone to him to remind him that they needed napkins, condiments (salt and pepper), and some new tabletop menu holders to replace the ones that were cracked and chipped. Since Tony wanted her to make a list of everything they needed, Katie decided to make a detailed inspection of the restaurant before putting the order together. She came in half an hour before her regular shift and checked the restaurant from top to bottom. Not only did they need napkins, condiments, and a few menu holders, she noted, but they could also use some more silverware (they were always running so low on teaspoons that waiters and waitresses started hoarding them at their stations to make sure they had enough). Plus, several of the trays were cracked, and a couple of the tray stands were wobbly. (What would Tony say if a tray full of food fell on the floor because the tray stand broke?) And so it went on—a few water jugs here, a couple of candleholders there—all designed to make the restaurant look as good as it possibly could.

Katie asked Kevin for the number and catalog for their vendor and placed the order—an order that was several hundred dollars more than their regular weekly order—as the salesperson was kind enough to point out to Katie. She replied: "Tony is very busy on a project for our regional office right now, and he asked me to place the order. When will these items be delivered?"

**QUESTIONS**

1. What was Katie's mistake here?
2. What contribution did Tony make to this situation?
3. How do you think Tony will react?
4. How would you have handled this situation?

TACO BARN

## Key Terms >>

authority 121
centralization 125
decentralization 125
empowerment 125
exception principle 127
formal organization 120
informal organization 120
job depth 121
job scope 121
organization 120
organizing 120
parity principle 127
power 121
responsibility 121
scalar principle 128
span of management 129
unity of command principle 127

## Think << AND DISCUSS

1. What is the difference between horizontal and vertical division of labor?
2. Discuss two approaches to viewing the sources of authority.
3. Which is more valuable to a national organization with regional offices—flexibility to respond to local market issues or standardized controls based at headquarters? Why?
4. What is the unity of command principle?
5. As a manager, would you prefer a relatively large (more than seven subordinates) or small (seven or fewer subordinates) span of management? Why? What are the implications of your choice?
6. When would it be appropriate to "shortcut" the chain of command when seeking approval for a decision?

## INTERNET In Action >>

1. Visit the Web site of the Telework Coalition at **www.telcoa.org.**
   a. What are the mission and vision of TelCoa?
   b. How does telecommuting relate to "business continuity planning"?
   c. Why would TelCoa take such a vocal role in addressing the H1N1 virus?
   d. What would an organization like Avaya gain from sponsoring TelCoa?
2. Search the Web for a generic template that would guide your organization in the development of a policy for the delegation of authority.
   a. What types of templates are out there?
   b. To which industries do most of these templates apply?
   c. How applicable are they to general management policies?
   d. Based on these templates, draft a one-page delegation of authority policy.

**The New Sales Manager**

The assistant sales manager of ABC Company has been in that job for six months. Due to poor sales over the past 18 months, the sales manager (his or her boss) has just been fired. The president of ABC then offers this job to the assistant sales manager subject to the following stipulations:

- You cannot increase the advertising budget.
- You must continue to let Metro-Media, Inc., handle the advertising.
- You cannot make any personnel changes.
- You will accept full responsibility for the sales for this fiscal year (which started two months ago).

Divide into two teams. Team 1 is in favor of taking the job offer. Team 2 wants to pass. Each team will have 15 minutes to prepare a presentation outlining its reasons for its decision.

**Decentralization versus Centralization**

The organization you work for is struggling financially in this tough economy. External consultants have assessed that your work processes need to be revamped. They have decided that your organization is "slowed by unnecessarily bureaucratic and inconsistent work procedures" and "lacks the responsiveness needed to compete in your market."

Divide into two teams. Team 1 decides that the answer is clearer and more direct control from headquarters with standardized policies and procedures. Team 2 decides that the answer is greater operational flexibility at the local level to increase responsiveness. Each team will have 15 minutes to prepare a presentation outlining its case and the steps it intends to take.

# Case 6.1

## >> Cisco: The Plumber Branches Out

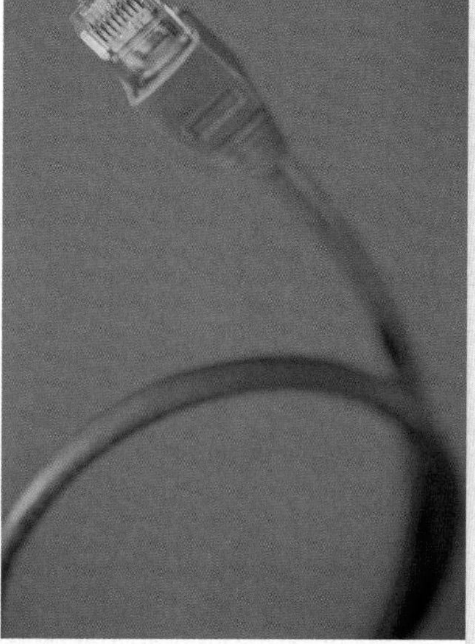

At the peak of the dot-com boom, Cisco owned and provided the backbone of the rapidly expanding Internet. Its range of routers and switches were required purchases to enter the world of electronic commerce, and as a result, growth was astronomic in the early days, rising from revenues of $1.2 billion in 1994 to $18.9 billion in 2002. However, as the market matured and new competitors arrived, Cisco's role changed from "gatekeeper" to "plumber," and the key metric of the Internet changed from access points to "the information superhighway" to how much traffic now travels on that highway.

At a peak valuation of $550 billion in 2000, Cisco appeared to be living up to its reputation as the leading light of the "new economy," but when the dot-com bubble burst less than a year later, Cisco was almost stopped in its tracks. In an event that CEO John Chambers refers to as the "hundred year flood," the company's valuation plummeted to $100 billion, and critics began to question whether Cisco had what it took to reclaim its former glory.

Labeling the company as the plumber of the Internet is perhaps unfair. Routers and switches did generate the largest portion of Cisco's revenue, and traffic still needs to be routed through networks; but from its earliest days Cisco saw the need for a service component to support that hardware revenue—helping companies to set up and maintain their networks and developing the operating system for the components to talk to each other.

The growth of competition relegated networking gear to the status of a commodity that rose or fell on the wave of economic activity. Profitable companies had money to stay on the cutting edge of technology, but as soon as profits started to fall, capital expenditures were deferred or postponed indefinitely, and Cisco's sales suffered as a result. Chambers saw a way out of the boom-and-bust cycle by pursuing what he termed "market adjacencies"—ancillary or complementary products and services built on the concept of a connected network. Niche markets such as "cloud computing," "virtual health care," and "smart grid technology" to improve the transmission of electricity are now on Cisco's play sheet, and Chambers expects these adjacencies to be generating as much as 25 percent of the company's revenues within 5 to 10 years.

Are adjacencies just another word for diversification? Is Chambers just following the path of 3M and GE and reducing his dependence on networking gear? Not at all. The networking market continues to generate Cisco's highest gross margins, and Chambers has every intention of remaining as a major player in a market where the amount of Internet traffic is expected to increase tenfold by 2013. Cisco's newest router, the Nexus 7000, handles 15 trillion bits of information every second—that's equivalent to 1,350 feature-length movies, every second.

The question then arises as to how all of these adjacencies will operate. If they're not separate divisions like GE, what are they? Rather than following the traditional path of an organization chart built around lines of business with subordinate organizations overseeing each line, Cisco uses committees made up of managers from different functions, with each committee labeled according to its target market. "Councils" manage markets that are expected to reach $10 billion in sales, and "boards" manage smaller ($1 billion) markets. Membership of these entities rarely exceeds 15 people, and they are expected to operate with a cooperative management style. Managers, who serve both a functional role and a council-board role, are expected to manage collaboratively—the performance of their respective team represents 30 percent of their annual bonuses. Not surprisingly, not every manager fits this operating style, and as a result, one-fifth of Cisco's leadership has left the company since this plan was initiated.

While the departure of talented people is a concern, the commitment to a new managerial system represents a significant step for Cisco that mirrors its own product lines. If your future is tied to a vision of a new data-rich corporate model based on Web-based collaboration, wikis, and social networking, it seems natural that the vendor that aspires to be number one should model the potential of all that communication power. Whether the capacity to communicate cultivates rapid decision making rather than endless meetings and consensus management remains to be seen.

QUESTIONS

1. Why would Cisco be referred to as "the gatekeeper of the Internet"?
2. What is the significance of networking gear becoming "a commodity"?
3. How does Cisco define a "market adjacency"?
4. Why would a collaborative managerial model cause such a large departure of Cisco's leadership?

*Source:* "The World According to Chambers," *The Economist*, August 27, 2009; Ashlee Vance, "Cisco's Profit Surges 23 Percent," *The New York Times*, February 4, 2010; and Aaron Ricadela, "Cisco's EMC Venture: Better Than a Buyout?" *BusinessWeek*, November 3, 2006.

# Case 6.2

## >> The Wiki Workplace

Thanks in part to younger workers, more companies are using social computing tools to aid collaboration and to foster innovation and growth.

When Robert Stephens graduated from the University of Minnesota with a degree in computer science in 1994, he wanted to start a business consultancy. But hiring a staff of good consultants takes a lot of money, and Stephens had little, so he founded Geek Squad, a cheekily branded computer repair company that helps consumers navigate the increasing complexity of electronic gadgetry.

From humble origins, Geek Squad grew and grew. In 2002, after nearly a decade of profitable operations, the company was acquired by consumer electronics giant Best Buy.

At the time, Stephens had 60 employees and was booking $3 million in annual revenue. Today, working out of 700 Best Buy locations across North America, Geek Squad's service agents are generating growth rates twice those achieved by the rest of Best Buy.

For Stephens, Geek Squad's meteoric success was exhilarating and challenging. How, for example, would he recruit and train an ever-growing number of employees, let alone keep them in the loop and gather their input into the business?

One day, Stephens asked his deputy director for counterintelligence at headquarters how things were going in the field. "I worry about those agents in Anchorage, Alaska," he said. "There are about 20 of them there, and I worry about them staying connected to the mission."

"Oh, those Anchorage guys, I talk to them all the time," the deputy director replied.

Prodded for details, he sheepishly told Stevens that they all play Battlefield 2 online. "With each server, you can have 128 people simultaneously fighting each other in a virtual environment," said the director. "We wear headsets and use Ventrilo software so that we can talk over the Internet while we are running around fighting."

Stephens, who now joins in from time to time, says: "The agents taunt each other, saying, 'Hey, I see you behind the wall.' But then, while we're running along, rifles in our hands, one of the agents behind me will be like,

*Continued on next page*

Continued from page 137

'Yeah, we just hit our revenue to budget,' and somebody else will be like, 'Hey, how do you reset the password on a Linksys router?'"

Welcome to the wiki workplace.

**Rise of the Wiki Workplace**

The information and communication technologies that are transforming media, culture, and the economy are also reshaping how companies and employees function. New social computing tools such as wikis and blogs put unprecedented communication power in the hands of employees.

Some companies worry about the risks of uncontrolled communications leaking out. But a growing number believe the new collaboration tools are good for innovation and growth—they help employees connect with more people, in more regions of the world, with less hassle and more enjoyment, than earlier generations of workplace technology.

Much of this is due to a younger generation of workers who embrace Web-based tools in a way that often confounds older workers. Nourished on instant messaging, blogs, wikis, chat groups, playlists, peer-to-peer file sharing, online multiplayer video games, and most recently the ubiquitous Twitter, the Net Generation will increasingly bring a heightened comfort with technology, inclination toward social connectivity, more emphasis on creativity and fun, and greater diversity to the companies they work for and to the companies they found themselves.

**Bottom-Up Knowledge Creation**

Some companies, like Geek Squad, are already finding that internal blogs and wikis help stimulate creative thinking and capture knowledge. One example is webworks.com.:

Another trailblazer is IBM, which from October 5 to 9, 2008, invited employees in more than 160 countries—along with their clients, business partners, and even family members—to join in a massive, wide-open brainstorming session it called the InnovationJam.

**Ready or Not**

Wikis, blogs, and other tools will arrive in the workplace whether companies are ready or not, as younger employees tend to develop their own self-organized networks that cut across traditional corporate divisions. Increasingly, these employees will be capable of interacting as a global, real-time workforce. Indeed, if Linux, Wikipedia, and other collaborative projects are any indication, it will often be easier and less expensive for workers to self-organize productively than to squeeze them into more traditional business units.

Could too much openness and self-organization in the workplace lead to disorganization, confusion, and lack of focus and direction? Not according to Google CEO Eric Schmidt, whose employees are allowed plenty of self-direction.

Clear goals, structure, discipline, and leadership in the organization will remain as important as ever and perhaps more so as self-organization and peer production emerge as organizing principles for the workplace. The difference today is that these qualities can emerge organically as employees seize the new tools to collaborate across departmental and organizational boundaries, and, yes, "the power of human capital" can be unleashed.

**QUESTIONS**

1. Why are these new collaboration tools "good for innovation and growth"?
2. What are the potential benefits of "unleashing the power of human capital"?
3. Is there a downside to so much openness and self-organization?
4. Would blogs, wikis, and Twitter work at your company? Why or why not?

*Source:* Don Tapscott, and Anthony D. Williams, "The BusinessWeek Wikinomics Series," *BusinessWeek*, March 26, 2007; "InnovationJam 2008," www.ibm.com/ibm/jam; Alan J. Porter, "Wikis in the Workplace: A Practical Introduction," *ars technica*, November 16, 2009; and Ezra Goodnoe, "Wikis in the Workplace," *InformationWeek*, February 27, 2006.

# Case 6.3

## >> The Debate Over Rapid Response Teams

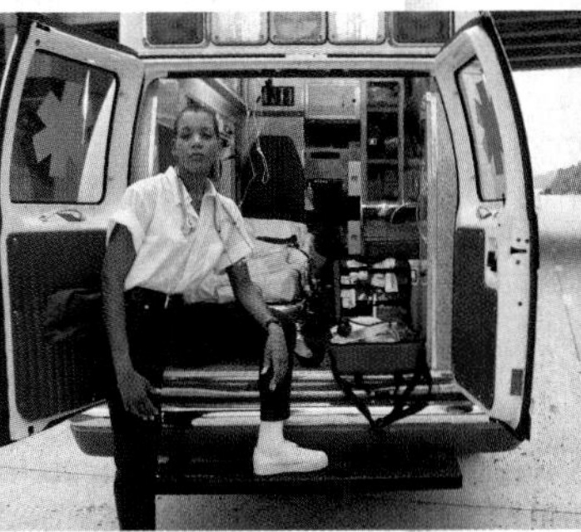

Studies present conflicting opinions on the effectiveness of rapid response teams.

Hospital rapid response teams (RRTs), created to prevent cardiac arrest and deaths in critically ill patients, are not universally effective, according to two conflicting studies from the *Journal of the American Medical Association (JAMA).*

Originally pioneered in Australia, RRTs are usually made up of doctors, nurses, and respiratory therapists, whose primary role is to care for patients in the intensive care unit (ICU). The teams are also called to help evaluate patients who are not in the ICU.

Strongly endorsed by the Institute for Healthcare Improvement (IHI) in its "100,000 Lives Campaign" (subsequently renewed as the "Five Million Lives Campaign"), RRTs are based on the premise that patients can exhibit signs of medical instability for several hours prior to a cardiac event. As such, there is a need for action before the "code blue" team is called to address an arresting patient—a task that falls to the RRT.

However, the data presented by the IHI to endorse the concept of the RRT have since been undermined by conflicting studies on the effectiveness of RRTs in reducing mortality rates for hospital patients.

A 2007 study led by Dr. Paul J. Sharek at Lucile Packard Children's Hospital in Palo Alto, California, showed an 18 percent decrease in the monthly mortality rate after the implementation of an RRT. As the study concludes: "Based on our findings, we found that 33 children's lives were saved in 19 months as a direct result of the RRT implementation."

A 2007 study led by Dr. Paul S. Chan at St. Luke's Hospital in Kansas City, Missouri, came to a very different conclusion. Tracking the implementation on January 1, 2006, of a nurse-led RRT consisting of two experienced ICU nurses and a respiratory therapist (supported by a consulting ICU physician when requested by the RRT), the study came to the following conclusion: "Implementation of a rapid response team in our tertiary care adult hospital was not associated with lower rates of either hospital-wide cardiopulmonary arrests or mortality."

"Many hospitals have implemented these teams over the past decade," said lead researcher Dr. Paul S. Chan, a cardiologist at the Mid America Heart Institute in Kansas City, Missouri. "Earlier studies had shown that rapid response teams may decrease code [cardiac arrest] rates for patients in the hospital."

"The goal of these teams was to get called, usually by nurses, to patients who are declining and do a rapid assessment and treatment to try to prevent cardiac arrest and deaths," Chan said. Before the rapid response team was in place, there were 11.2 cardiac arrests per 1,000 patients. After the team was started, the cardiac arrest rate was 7.5 per 1,000 patients. While there was a reduction in cardiac arrests after the team was in place, the reduction was not statistically significant, Chan said.

In addition, overall hospital deaths did not change after the team was in place. Before the rapid response team, in-hospital deaths were 3.22 per 100 patients, and after intervention the death rate was 3.09 per 100 patients.

"Our findings raise questions whether or not hospitals should be investing huge financial and personnel resources in these teams without a demonstrable benefit," Chan said.

One expert thinks hospitals should use their resources in areas of proven value.

"The evidence supporting any benefits of rapid response teams has been tenuous at best," said Dr. Gregg C. Fonarow, director of the Ahmanson-UCLA Cardiomyopathy Center at the University of California, Los Angeles. "Yet, based on recommendations to implement rapid response teams by the Institute for Healthcare Improvement, hospitals across the country have diverted substantial resources and personnel to create and staff such teams."

**QUESTIONS**

1. Which data were utilized to justify the creation of these rapid response teams?
2. Which data were offered as evidence to question the value of the rapid response teams?
3. Are there other factors that should be considered when making this decision? Or is the data-driven approach appropriate?
4. As a hospital administrator, what would you do with this information?

*Source:* P. S. Chan et al., "Hospital-wide Code Rates and Mortality before and after Implementation of a Rapid Response Team," *Journal of the American Medical Association,* December 3, 2008; P. J. Sharek et al., "Effect of a Rapid Response Team on Hospital-wide Mortality and Code Rates Outside the ICU in a Children's Hospital," *Journal of the American Medical Association,* November 21, 2007; Steven Reinberg, "Executive Health," *BusinessWeek,* December 2, 2008; and "Rapid Response Teams: The Case for Early Intervention," Institute for Healthcare Improvement, www.ihi.org/IHI/Topics/CriticalCare/IntensiveCare/ImprovementStories/RapidResponseTeamsTheCaseforEarlyIntervention.htm.

# CHAPTER 7

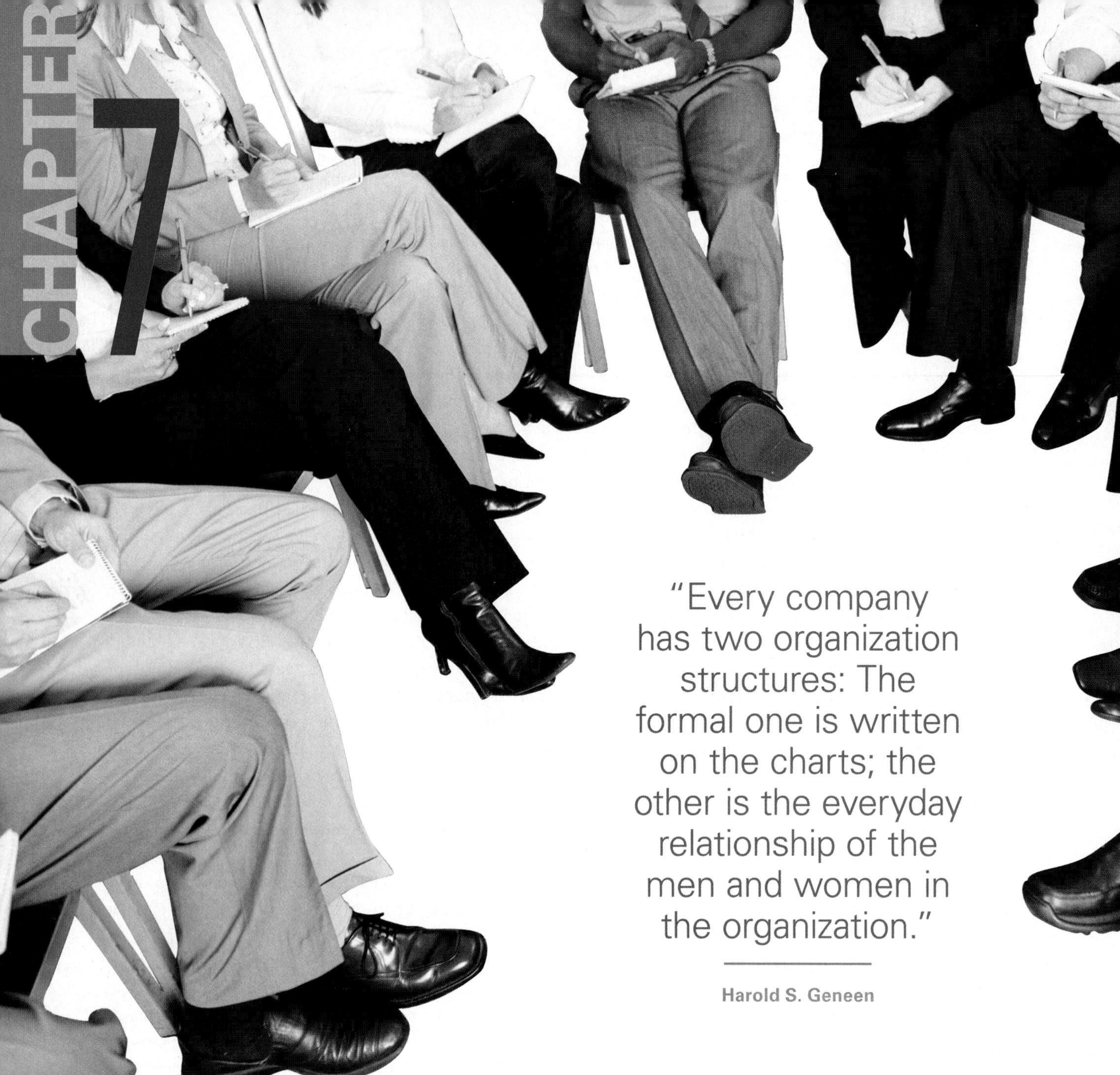

"Every company has two organization structures: The formal one is written on the charts; the other is the everyday relationship of the men and women in the organization."

Harold S. Geneen

# ORGANIZING STRUCTURE

LEARNING OUTCOMES

After studying this chapter, you will be able to:

1 Explain the purpose of an organization chart.

2 Describe factors and changes that affect an organization's structure.

3 Define a contingency approach.

4 Identify the different types of departmentalization.

5 Describe the different types of organization structure, and explain why companies choose one structure over another.

6 Discuss the types and effective use of committees.

## THE WORLD OF WORK Kevin makes his move

After his success with the scheduling project, Kevin had won Tony's confidence that he would be the logical choice to fill Tanya's position as shift leader. To support that proposal, Tony had asked Kevin to write a strategic planning report outlining where he thought the Taco Barn unit was now and where it should go over the next three to five years. Kevin had been given only a couple of days to do it, and he had put every spare moment into producing a report that he hoped would convince Tony and Dawn Williams that he was the right person for the shift leader position.

He went back to his business course textbooks and decided that the best place to start was a SWOT analysis summarizing the unit's strengths, weaknesses, opportunities, and threats. Based on that, Kevin outlined some menu theme and marketing plan ideas and documented his concerns about increasing competition in their market—while remembering to stay at the big picture strategic level rather than drilling down to individual operational issues. Always a positive thinker, Kevin felt that if the report met Tony's expectations, he could provide more detail later.

Much to Kevin's surprise, he found that the area of the report that interested him the most was how the departments in the restaurant were organized. Looking at the organization chart, he found himself questioning why they worked on the basis of shift crews with designated shift leaders and "openers" and "closers." Having one unit manager made sense, and having a team of unit managers in a geographic area report to a regional manager also made sense, but within the individual unit, arranging everything around hours of operation rather than the work being performed seemed confusing.

Kevin returned to his business textbooks. Most organizations used a functional organization chart with presidents and vice presidents and divisional leaders, so why should Taco Barn be different? "Why, for example, instead of a shift leader, couldn't we have an assistant unit manager?"

**QUESTIONS**

1. What is the benefit of using a SWOT analysis in a strategic planning document?
2. Why would organizing the restaurant around its hours of operation be confusing?
3. Review pages 148 to 149, and summarize the advantages of a functional organization chart.
4. How would the responsibilities of a shift leader be different from those of an assistant manager?

# >> Organizing Structure

**Organization structure** is the framework that defines the boundaries of the formal organization and within which the organization operates. The structure of an organization reflects how groups compete for resources, where responsibilities for profits and other performance measures lie, how information is transmitted, and how decisions are made. Many people believe a good manager or a competent employee should be able to perform well regardless of the organization structure and environment. They believe that if managers or employees are good enough, they can overcome any obstacles the organization structure presents. Others believe that given the right organization structure, anyone should be able to perform in an acceptable fashion. The truth lies somewhere in between. An appropriate organization structure certainly helps foster good performance.

**Organization Structure** The framework that defines the boundaries of the formal organization and within which the organization operates.

## ORGANIZATION GROWTH STAGES

Figure 7.1 shows in general terms the stages an organization goes through as it grows and matures. The craft or family stage is characterized by the absence of formal policies, objectives, and structure. The operations of the organization at this stage generally center on one individual and one functional area. During the entrepreneurial stage, the organization grows first at an increasing and then a decreasing rate. An atmosphere of optimism spreads through the entire organization as sales and profits rise rapidly. By the third stage of growth, the entrepreneur has been replaced by or evolved into a professional manager who performs the processes of planning, organizing, staffing, motivating, and controlling.[1] Profits are realized more from internal efficiency and less from external exploitation of the market. At this stage, the organization becomes characterized by written policies, procedures, and plans.

**Study Alert !** Lines on an organization chart can be solid, to reflect a direct reporting relationship, or *dotted*, to reflect an indirect reporting relationship to another manager. For example, in the human resource department of a regionally structured organization, you might report directly to your office or store manager but also have a dotted-line reporting relationship to the HR director at the head office. When it comes time for your annual performance appraisal, both managers would contribute to that review.

**Figure 7.1 • Organization Growth and Change**

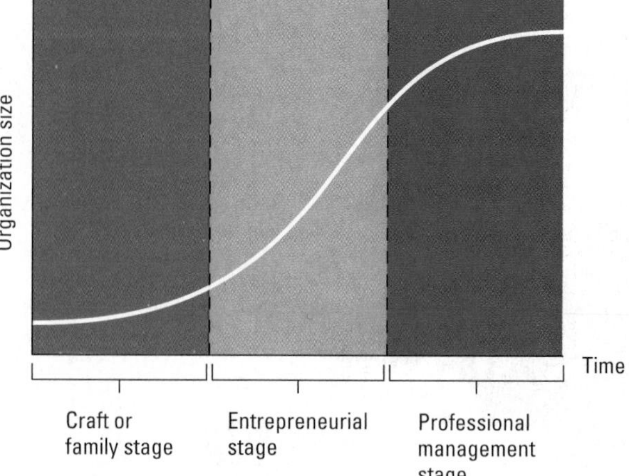


As the organization moves through the craft stage and into the entrepreneurial stage, an organization structure must be developed. This is a critical point for the organization. If an appropriate structure is not established and utilized, the entrepreneur may lose control and the entire organization may collapse. An organization structure must be developed that allows the organization to adapt to change in its environment.

## ORGANIZATION CHARTS

An organization chart uses a series of boxes connected with one or more lines to graphically represent the organization's structure. Each box represents a position within the organization, and each line indicates the nature of the relationships among the different positions. The organization chart not only identifies specific relationships but also provides an overall picture of how the entire organization fits together. As organizations become larger and more complex, it becomes increasingly difficult to represent all the relationships accurately.

## FACTORS AFFECTING ORGANIZATION STRUCTURE

Several factors can affect which structure is the most appropriate for a given organization. A structure that is appropriate for a high-tech company that employs 50,000 people in eight countries will probably not be appropriate for a small retail business with just a dozen employees. Strategy, size, environment, and

technology are some of the important factors found to be most closely related to organization structure.

**Strategy** A major part of an organization's strategy for achieving its objectives deals with how the organization is structured. An appropriate structure will not guarantee success, but it will improve the organization's chances for success. Business leaders, athletic coaches, and military leaders all stress that to succeed one must not only have a good strategy but also be prepared to win (mentally and structurally). In addition to clarifying and defining strategy through the delegation of authority and responsibility, the organization structure can either help or hinder strategy implementation.

In a groundbreaking study of organizational strategy, Alfred D. Chandler described a pattern in the evolution of organization structures.[2] The pattern was based on studies of Du Pont, General Motors, Sears, and Standard Oil Company, with supporting evidence from many other firms. The pattern Chandler described was that of changing strategy, followed by administrative problems, leading to decline in performance, revised structure, and a subsequent return to economic health. In summary, Chandler concluded that structure follows strategy; in other words, changes in strategy ultimately lead to changes in the organization's structure. Chandler's work related particularly to growth and to the structural adjustments made to maintain efficient performance during market expansion, product line diversification, and vertical integration.

Although subsequent research has supported the idea of a relationship between strategy and structure, it is clear that strategy is not the only variable that has an impact on structure.[3] The process of matching structure to strategy is complex and should be undertaken with a thorough understanding of the historical development of the current structure and of other variables, including size, environment, and technology.

**Size** There are many ways to measure the size of an organization, but sales volume and number of employees are the most frequently used factors. While no hard-and-fast rules exist, certain characteristics generally relate to an organization's size. Small organizations tend to be less specialized (horizontal division of labor), less standardized, and more centralized. Larger organizations tend to be more specialized, more standardized, and more decentralized. Thus, as an organization grows in size, certain structural changes naturally occur.

**Environment** A landmark study relating organization to environment was conducted by Tom Burns and G. M. Stalker in the United Kingdom.[4] By examining some 20 industrial firms in both a changing industry and a more stable, established industry, Burns and Stalker focused on how a firm's pattern of organization was related to certain characteristics of the external environment. The researchers identified two distinct organizational systems. **Mechanistic systems** are characterized by a rigid definition of functional duties, precise job descriptions, fixed authority and responsibility, and a well-developed organizational hierarchy through which information filters up and instructions flow down. **Organic systems** are characterized by less formal job descriptions, greater emphasis on adaptability, more participation, and less fixed authority. Burns and Stalker found that successful firms in stable and established industries tended to be mechanistic in structure, whereas successful firms in dynamic industries tended to be organic in structure. See Figure 7.2 for a more complete evaluation of the structural differences between mechanistic and organic systems.

**Mechanistic Systems** Organizational systems characterized by a rigid delineation of functional duties, precise job descriptions, fixed authority and responsibility, and a well-developed organizational hierarchy through which information filters up and instructions flow down.

**Organic Systems** Organizational systems having less formal job descriptions, greater emphasis on adaptability, more participation, and less fixed authority.

Paul Lawrence and Jay Lorsch conducted a later study dealing with organization structure and its environment.[5] Their original study included 10 firms

## Figure 7.2 • Structural Differences between Mechanistic and Organic Systems

| Characteristics of Mechanistic and Organic Organizations | |
|---|---|
| **Mechanistic** | **Organic** |
| Work is divided into narrow, specialized tasks. | Work is defined in terms of general tasks. |
| Tasks are performed as specified unless changed by managers in the hierarchy. | Tasks are continually adjusted as needed through interaction with others involved in the task. |
| Structure of control, authority, and communication is hierarchical. | Structure of control, authority, and communication is a network. |
| Decisions are made by the specified hierarchical level. | Decisions are made by individuals with relevant knowledge and technical expertise. |
| Communication is mainly vertical, between superior and subordinate. | Communication is vertical and horizontal, among superiors, subordinates, and peers. |
| Communication content is largely instructions and decisions issued by superiors. | Communication content is largely information and advice. |
| Emphasis is on loyalty to the organization and obedience to superiors. | Emphasis is on commitment to organizational goals and possession of needed expertise. |

in three different industrial environments. Reaching conclusions similar to those of Burns and Stalker, Lawrence and Lorsch found that to be successful, firms operating in a dynamic environment needed a relatively flexible structure, firms operating in a stable environment needed a more rigid structure, and firms operating in an intermediate environment needed a structure somewhere between the two extremes.

**Organization and Technology** Numerous studies have also been conducted investigating potential relationships between technology and organization structure. One of the most important of these studies was conducted by Joan Woodward in the late 1950s.[6] Her study was based on an analysis of 100 manufacturing firms in the southeast Essex area of England. Woodward's general approach was to classify firms along a scale of "technical complexity" with particular emphasis on three modes of production: (1) unit or small-batch production (e.g., custom-made machines), (2) large-batch or mass production (e.g., an automotive assembly plant), and (3) continuous flow or process production (e.g., a chemical plant). The unit or small-batch production mode represents the lower end of the technical complexity scale, while the continuous flow mode represents the upper end.

After classifying each firm into one of the preceding categories, Woodward investigated a number of organizational variables. Some of her findings follow:

1. The number of levels in an organization increased as technical complexity increased.
2. The ratio of managers and supervisors to total personnel increased as technical complexity increased.
3. Using Burns and Stalker's definition of organic and mechanistic systems, organic management systems tended to predominate in firms at both ends of the scale of technical complexity, while mechanistic systems predominated in firms falling in the middle ranges.
4. No significant relationship existed between technical complexity and organizational size.

A few years later, Edward Harvey undertook a similar study.[7] Rather than using Woodward's technical complexity scale, Harvey grouped firms along a continuum from technical "diffuseness" to technical "specificity." Technically diffused firms have a wider range of products, produce products that vary from year to year, and produce more made-to-order products. Harvey's findings were similar to Woodward's in that he found significant relationships between technology and several organizational characteristics.

The general conclusion reached in the Woodward and Harvey studies was that a relationship clearly exists between organizational technology and a number of aspects of organization structure. Many additional studies have investigated the relationship between technology and structure. While they have reported some conflicting results, most studies have found a relationship between technology and structure.

### [PROGRESS] ✓questions

1. What is an organization chart?
2. Explain the stages an organization goes through as it grows and matures.
3. What are the four most important factors affecting organization structure?
4. Explain the differences between mechanistic and organic organizational systems.

WHAT'S IN A NAME?

Before the arrival of Internet-based stock trading, financial services companies such as Merrill Lynch would award brand new stockbrokers the title of "vice president" to convey to prospective clients that they were dealing with a person of significance and seniority within the organization.

In teaching hospitals, first-year residents still carry the title of "doctor" even though they have years of practical training ahead of them. In many companies, HR generalists reporting to HR managers have now become HR managers reporting to HR directors, often with no increase in salary or any significant change in responsibilities. This practice is referred to as *title inflation*. Does it really matter what your title is within an organization? Why?

ETHICAL
MANAGEMENT
Does your job title accurately reflect your position and responsibilities within the company?


# Thinking Critically 7.1

## >> Who Dropped the Ball?

In October 2006, Industrial Water Treatment Company (IWT) introduced Kelate, a new product that was 10 times more effective than other treatments in controlling scale buildup in boilers. The instantaneous demand for Kelate required that IWT double its number of service engineers within the following year.

The sudden expansion caused IWT to reorganize its operations. Previously, each district office was headed by a district manager who was assisted by a chief engineer and two engineering supervisors. In 2007, this structure changed. The district manager now had a chief engineer and a manager of operations. Four engineering supervisors (now designated as group leaders) were established. They were to channel all work assignments through the manager of operations, while all engineering-related problems were to be handled by the chief engineer. Each group leader supervised 8 to 10 field service engineers (see Figure 7.3).

Bill Marlowe, district manager for the southeast district, has just received a letter from an old and very large customer, Sel Tex, Inc. The letter revealed that when Sel Tex inspected one of its boilers last week, it found the water treatment was not working properly. When Sel Tex officials contacted Wes Smith, IWT's service engineer for the area, they were told he was scheduled to be working in the Jacksonville area the rest of the week but would get someone else down there the next day. When no one showed up, Sel Tex officials were naturally upset; after all, they were only requesting the engineering service they had been promised.

Bill Marlowe, upset over the growing number of customer complaints that seemed to be crossing his desk in recent months, called Ed Jones, chief engineer, into his office and showed him the letter he had received from Sel Tex.

**Ed:** Why are you showing me this? This is a work assignment foul-up.

**Bill:** Do you know anything about this unsatisfactory condition?

*Continued on next page*

Continued from page 145

**Ed:** Sure, Wes called me immediately after he found out. Their concentration of Kelate must have gone up, since they're getting corrosion and oxygen on their tubes. I told Peter Adinaro, Wes's group leader, about it, and I suggested he schedule someone to visit Sel Tex.

**Bill:** OK, Ed, thanks for your help. [*Ed leaves, and Bill calls Peter Adinaro into his office.*] Peter, two weeks ago Ed asked you to assign someone to visit Sel Tex because of a tube corrosion problem they are having. Do you remember?

**Peter:** Oh, sure! As usual, Wes Smith called Ed instead of me. I left a message for Dick to assign someone there because my whole group was tied up and I couldn't spare anyone. I thought Dick would ask another group leader to assign someone to check it out.

## Figure 7.3 • Partial Organization Chart for IWT

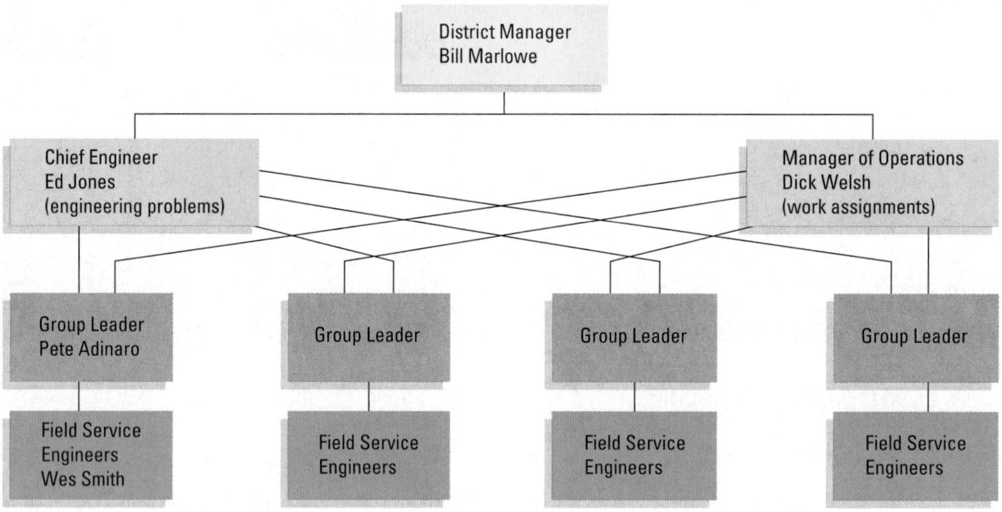

District Manager
Bill Marlowe

Chief Engineer
Ed Jones
(engineering problems)

Manager of Operations
Dick Welsh
(work assignments)

Group Leader
Pete Adinaro

Group Leader

Group Leader

Group Leader

Field Service
Engineers
Wes Smith

Field Service
Engineers

Field Service
Engineers

Field Service
Engineers

**Bill:** Well, thanks for your help. Tell Dick to come on in here for a second.

*[Dick Welsh, manager of operations, comes into Bill's office about 20 minutes later.]*

**Bill:** Dick, here's a letter from Sel Tex. Please read it, and tell me what you know about the situation.

**Dick:** [Dick reads the letter.] Bill, I didn't know anything about this.

**Bill:** I checked with Pete, Wes's group leader, and he tells me he left a message for you to assign someone since his group was all tied up. Didn't you get the message?

**Dick:** Have you taken a look at my desk lately? I'm flooded with messages. Heck, I'm the greatest message handler of all times. If I could schedule my people without having all the engineering headaches unloaded on me, I wouldn't have all these messages. Sure, it's possible that he left a message, but I haven't seen it. I will look for it, though. Anyway, that letter sounds to me like they've got an engineering problem, and Ed should contact them to solve it.

**Bill:** I'll write Sel Tex myself and try to explain the situation to them. You and I will have to get together this afternoon and talk over some of these difficulties. See you later, Dick.

**QUESTIONS**

1. How has IWT's structure changed?
2. What problems does Bill Marlowe face?
3. Are the problems related to the way IWT is organized, or are they related to the employees?
4. How could these problems be resolved?

CONTROL OR COMMUNICATION . . . ?

## First Line Focus

*An organization chart is designed to graphically represent the structure of each department in the company and the respective operational relationships between those departments, along with indicating the relative seniority of the leadership team of the company.*

*From an operational perspective, the chart conveys a command and control model—who is responsible for which function and who reports to that person within that function. However, an organization chart can also be considered to reflect an alternative perspective—a communications model. The array of boxes, solid lines, and dotted lines offer a road map to productive and frequent communication. The organization chart shows the communication path not only from the front line employees up the chain to the leadership team but also from the leadership team back down, so that all employees are kept up-to-date on the fortunes of the organization and are then able to better understand their contribution to those fortunes.*

**From the** PERSPECTIVE OF . . .

**A Tech Support Specialist**

In an outsourced call center, tech support specialists often support multiple products from several different client organizations. How would this be reflected in an organization chart?

## CHANGES AFFECTING ORGANIZATION STRUCTURE

In recent years, dramatic improvements in communication technology have introduced new ways of conducting business. These new practices have affected the structure of many organizations. Outsourcing has resulted from improved communication technology and is having an effect on the structure of many organizations. **Outsourcing** is the practice of subcontracting certain work functions to an outside organization. Whether outsourcing is a response to downsizing, an attempt to cut costs, or an effort to increase service, it is a practice that will significantly affect the workplace and organization charts. Work functions that are frequently being outsourced include accounting and finance functions, human resources, information technology, and contract manufacturing. Dun and Bradstreet estimates that outsourcing, which began a mere 30 years ago, is now a $4 trillion a year business worldwide.[8] Outsourcing in the United States grew from $21.5 billion in 2004 to over $30 billion in 2008.[9] It has been estimated that over 25 percent of the typical executive's budget goes to outsourcing supplies or services, and that is expected to grow considerably.[10] Outsourcing is a practice utilized by both large and small companies.

**Outsourcing** Practice of subcontracting certain work functions to an outside organization.

**Study Alert!**

The cost advantage of outsourcing organizational functions to overseas vendors—referred to as *offshoring*—is achieved by leveraging the available technology (satellites and thousands of miles of fiber-optic cable strung across the world's oceans) combined with lower labor costs in the vendor country. Failure to plan beyond that cost advantage has generated operational problems (e.g., lack of training and poor cultural adaptation) and prompted some organizations, such as Dell Computers, to bring "offshored" call centers back to the United States.

The International Association of Outsourcing Professionals estimates that almost 30 percent of all outsourcing in the United States is conducted by companies with less than $500 million in annual revenues.[11]

Outsourcing has numerous potential benefits, including the following:[12]

- Allowing the organization to emphasize its core competencies by not spending time on routine areas that can be outsourced.
- Reducing operating costs by utilizing others who can do the job more efficiently.

**Figure 7.4 • Variables Affecting Appropriate Organization Structure**

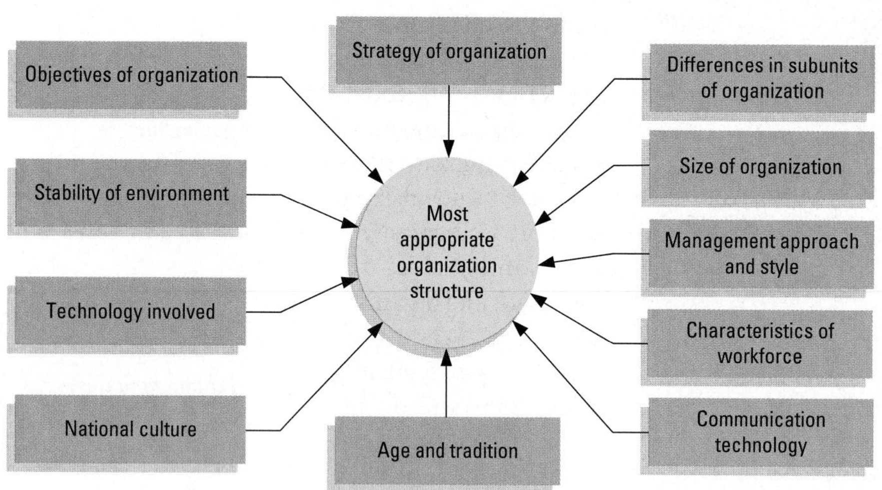


- Accessing top talent and state-of-the-art technology without having to own it.
- Fewer personnel headaches.
- Improving resource allocation by allowing growth to take place more quickly.

Of course, there are potential drawbacks to outsourcing.[13] One overriding concern is that a large number of jobs are being lost to other countries through outsourcing. For example, it has been estimated that more than 3 million jobs will leave the United States by 2015.[14] Other specific drawbacks include:

- Loss of control and being at the mercy of the vendor.
- Loss of in-house skills.
- Threat to the morale of the workforce if too many areas are dominated by outside vendors.
- No guarantee that it will save money or provide higher service standards.

**Contingency (Situational) Approach** The process of assessing relevant variables that affect an organization's structure and then choosing the most appropriate structure for the situation.

**Departmentalization** Arrangement of jobs into related work units.

**Functional Departmentalization** Categorization of organization units in terms of the nature of the work.

As with most management approaches, outsourcing is not a cure-all. Care must be taken that a long-term strategy evolves out of the use of outsourcing, not just a short-term fix to reduce costs. In the right situations, outsourcing can work well; but it almost always requires good management, good contracts, and realistic expectations.

### A CONTINGENCY APPROACH

The previous discussions emphasize the fact that several factors affect an organization's structure. The knowledge that there is no one best way to organize (i.e., the design is conditional) has led to a **contingency (situational) approach** to organizing. Figure 7.4 shows the previously discussed variables and others that can help determine the most appropriate organization structure. The contingency approach should be viewed as a process of assessing these relevant variables and then choosing the most appropriate structure for the situation. Because most of the relevant variables are dynamic, management should periodically analyze and appraise the organization's structure in light of any relevant changes.

## >> Departmentalization

While thousands of different organization structures exist, almost all are built on the concept of departmentalization. **Departmentalization** involves grouping jobs into related work units. The work units may be related on the basis of work functions, product, geography, customer, technique, or time.

### WORK FUNCTIONS

**Functional departmentalization** occurs when organization units are defined by the nature of the work. Although different terms may be used, most organizations have four basic functions: production, marketing, finance, and human resources. Production refers to the actual creation of something of value, either goods, services, or both. Marketing involves product or service planning, pricing the product or service with respect to demand, evaluating how to best distribute the good or service, and communicating information to the market through sales and advertising. Any organization, whether manufacturing or service, must provide the financial structure necessary for carrying out its activities. The human resource function is responsible for securing and developing the organization's people.

Each of these basic functions may be broken down as necessary. For instance, the production department may be split into maintenance, quality

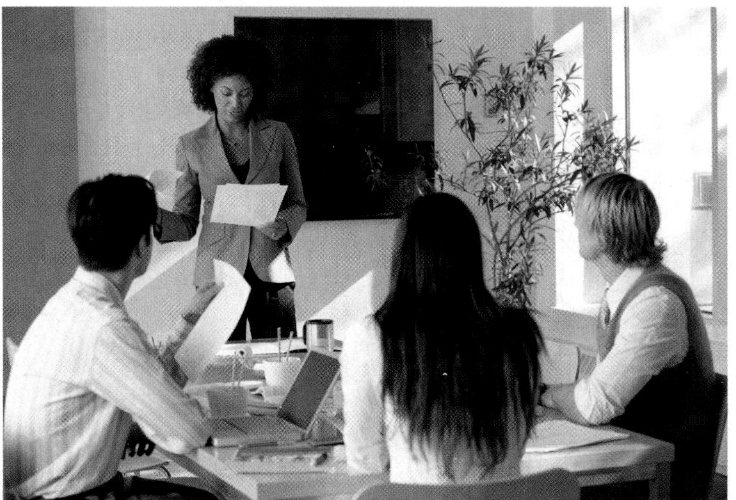

*These two groups of employees work for the same company, but they serve very different functions.*

control, engineering, manufacturing, and so on. The marketing department may be grouped into advertising, sales, and market research. Figure 7.5 charts a typical functional departmentalization.

The primary advantage of functional departmentalization is that it allows specialization within functions. It also provides efficient use of equipment and resources, potential economies of scale, and ease of coordination within the function itself. However, functional departmentalization can have negative effects, such as when members of a functional group develop more loyalty to the functional group's goals than to the organization's goals. For example, the marketing department might be overzealous in selling products even when production cannot meet any additional demand. If the group's goals and the organization's goals are not mutually supportive, such activity can lead to problems. Conflict may also develop among different departments striving for different goals. In addition, employees who are locked into their functions have a restricted view of the organization. Finally, the rather narrow functional scope of managers may be a disadvantage when a multidisciplinary approach would be more advantageous.

## Figure 7.5 • Functional Departmentalization

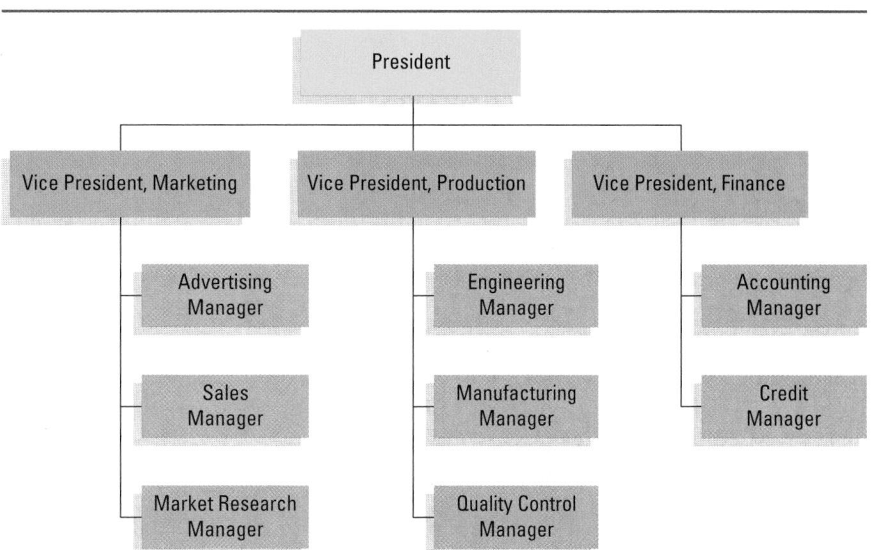


## PRODUCT

Under **product departmentalization,** all the activities needed to produce and market a product or service are usually under a single manager. This system allows employees to identify with a particular product and thus develop esprit de corps. It also facilitates managing each product as a distinct profit center.

**Product Departmentalization** Placement of all activities necessary to produce and market a product or service under one manager.

Product departmentalization provides opportunities for training executive personnel by letting them experience a broad range of functional activities. Problems can arise if departments become overly competitive to the detriment of the overall organization. A second potential problem is duplication of facilities and equipment.

## Figure 7.6 • Product Departmentalization

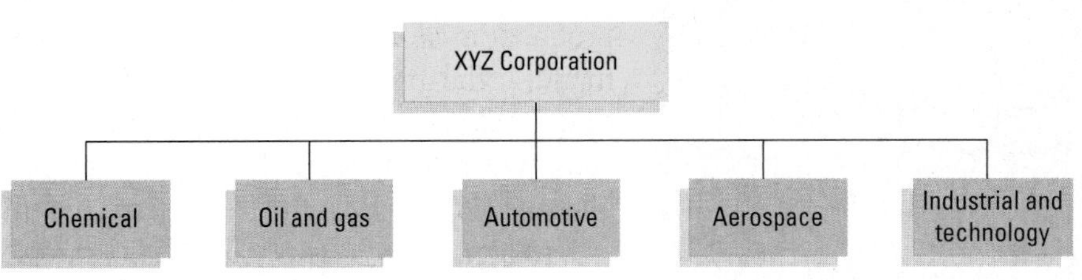


Product departmentalization adapts best to large, multiproduct organizations. Figure 7.6 illustrates how a company might be structured using product departmentalization.

### GEOGRAPHIC

**Geographic departmentalization** is most likely to occur in organizations that maintain physically isolated and independent operations or offices. Departmentalization by geography permits the use of local employees or salespeople. This can create customer goodwill and an awareness of local feelings and desires. It can also lead to a high level of service. Of course, having too many locations can be costly.

**Geographic Departmentalization** Organizational units that are defined by territories.

**Customer Departmentalization** Organizational units that are defined by customers served.

**Hybrid Departmentalization** Use of multiple types of departmentalization within the organization.

*What kind(s) of departmentalization does a police force use?*

### CUSTOMER

**Customer departmentalization** is based on division by customers served. A common example is an organization that has one department to handle retail customers and one department to handle wholesale or industrial customers. Figure 7.7 shows departmentalization by customer for Johnson & Johnson. This type of departmentalization has the same advantages and disadvantages as product departmentalization. For example, if the professional group and the pharmaceutical group in Figure 7.7 became too competitive with each other for corporate resources, the organization's overall performance could suffer.

## Figure 7.7 • Customer Departmentalization

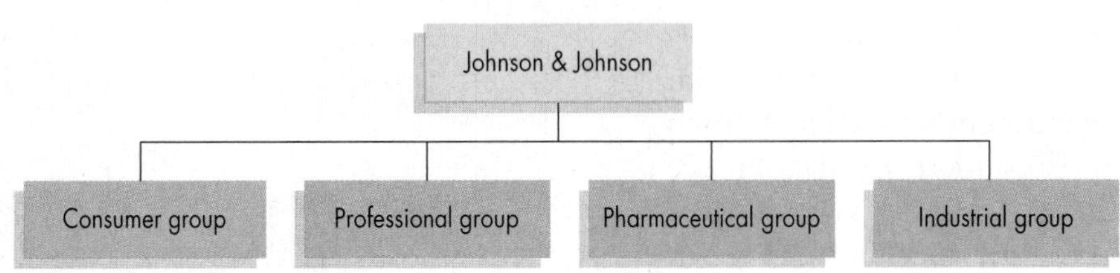


### OTHER TYPES

Several other types of departmentalization are possible. Departmentalization by simple numbers is practiced when the most important ingredient for success is the number of employees. Organizing for a local United Way drive would be an example. Departmentalization by process or equipment is another possibility. A final type of departmentalization is by time or shift, by which organizations operate production shifts around the clock and wish to monitor productivity and quality according to shift teams.

### HYBRID DEPARTMENTALIZATION

Typically, as an organization grows in size, it adds levels of departmentalization. A small organization may have no departmentalization at first. As it grows, it may departmentalize first on one basis, then another, and then another. For example, a large sales organization may use product departmentalization to create self-contained divisions; then each division might be further divided by geography and then by type of customer. **Hybrid departmentalization** occurs when an organization simultaneously uses more than one type of departmentalization. As Figure 7.8 illustrates, many different department mixes are possible for a given organization. Which one is best depends on the specific situation.

## Figure 7.8 • Possible Departmentalization Mixes for a Sales Organization

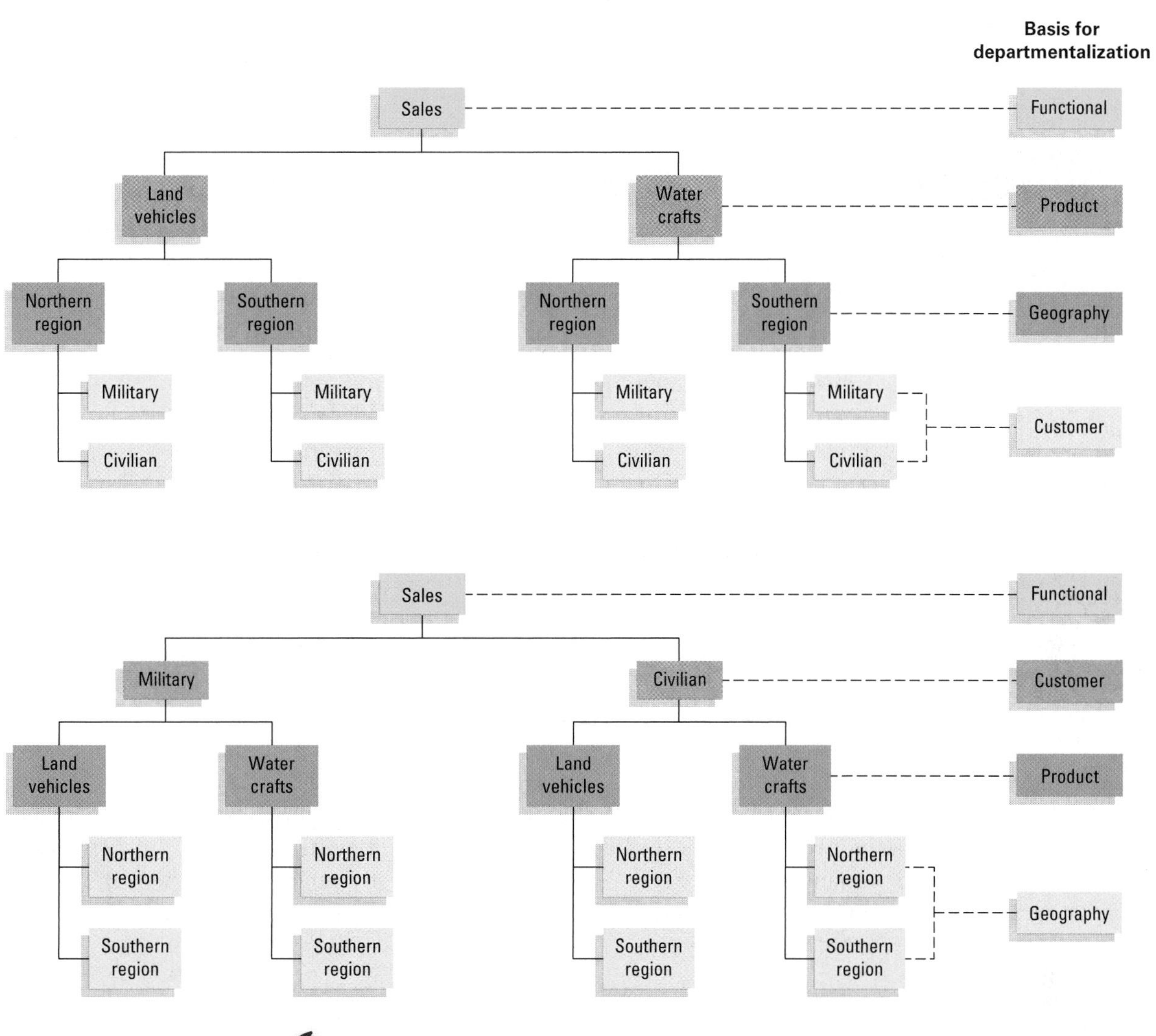


### [PROGRESS] ✓questions

5. What are the potential benefits and drawbacks of outsourcing?
6. Explain the contingency (situational) approach to organizing.
7. Explain the process of departmentalization.
8. Define the terms *geographic, customer,* and *hybrid departmentalization.*

# >> Types of Organization Structures

There are several basic types of structures that organizations may use. Traditionally, these have been the line structure, the line and staff structure, or the matrix structure. Recently, new types of structures and organizations have evolved and are evolving to take advantage of the new communication and logistical technology available. These new structures include the horizontal structure and the virtual organization. Each type of structure is discussed in the following sections.

## LINE STRUCTURE

In a *line organization,* authority originates at the top and moves downward in a line. The most important aspect of the **line structure** is that the work of all organizational units is directly involved in producing and marketing the organization's goods or services. This is the simplest organization structure and is characterized by vertical links between the different levels of the organization.

**Line Structure** Organization structure in which authority originates at the top and moves downward in a line and in which all organizational units are directly involved in producing and marketing the organization's goods or services.

## Figure 7.9 • A Simplified Line Structure

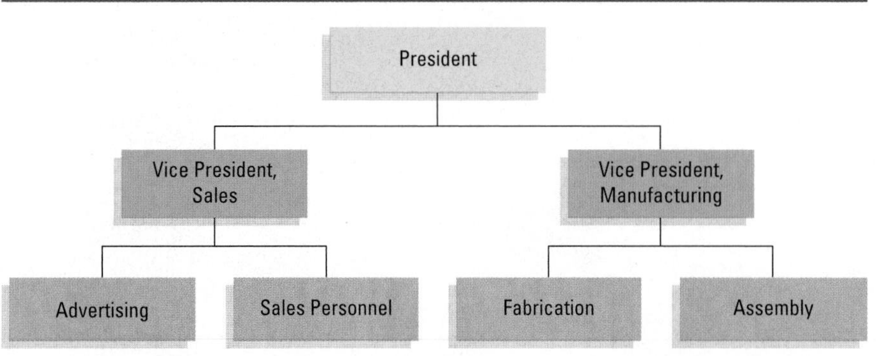


**Line and Staff Structure** Organization structure that results when staff specialists are added to a line organization.

**Staff Functions** Functions that are advisory and supportive in nature; designed to contribute to the efficiency and maintenance of the organization.

**Line Functions** Functions and activities directly involved in producing and marketing the organization's goods or services.

All members of the organization receive instructions through the chain of command. One advantage is a clear authority structure that promotes rapid decision making and prevents "passing the buck." A disadvantage is that it may force managers to perform too broad a range of duties. It may also cause the organization to become too dependent on one or two key employees who are capable of performing many duties. Because of its simplicity, line structure exists most frequently in small organizations. Figure 7.9 represents a simplified line structure.

## LINE AND STAFF STRUCTURE

The addition of staff specialists to a line-structured organization creates a **line and staff structure.** As a line organization grows, staff assistance often becomes necessary. **Staff functions** are advisory and supportive in nature; they contribute to the efficiency and maintenance of the organization. All managers perform **line functions**, which are directly involved in producing and marketing the organization's goods or services. Examples of line functions include production managers, sales representatives, and marketing managers. They generally relate directly to the attainment of major organizational objectives, while staff functions contribute indirectly. Staff people are generally specialists in one field, and their authority is normally limited to making recommendations to line people. Typical staff functions include research and development, personnel management, employee training, and various "assistant to" positions. Figure 7.10 shows a simplified line and staff organization structure.

## LINE AND STAFF CONFLICT

The line and staff organization allows much more specialization and flexibility than does the simple line organization; however, it sometimes creates conflict. Some staff specialists resent the fact that they may be only advisers to line personnel and have no real authority over the line. At the same time, line managers, knowing they have final responsibility for the product, are often reluctant to listen to staff advice. Many staff specialists think they should not be in a position of having to sell their ideas to the line. They believe the line managers should openly listen to their ideas. If the staff specialist is persistent, the line manager often resents even more that the staff "always tries to interfere and run my department." The staff specialist who does not persist often becomes discouraged because "no one ever listens."

## MATRIX STRUCTURE

The matrix (sometimes called *project*) form of organization is a way of forming project teams within the traditional line and staff organization. A project is "a combination of human and nonhuman resources pulled together in a temporary organization to achieve a specified purpose."[15] The marketing of a new product and the construction of a new building

## Figure 7.10 • A Simplified Line and Staff Structure

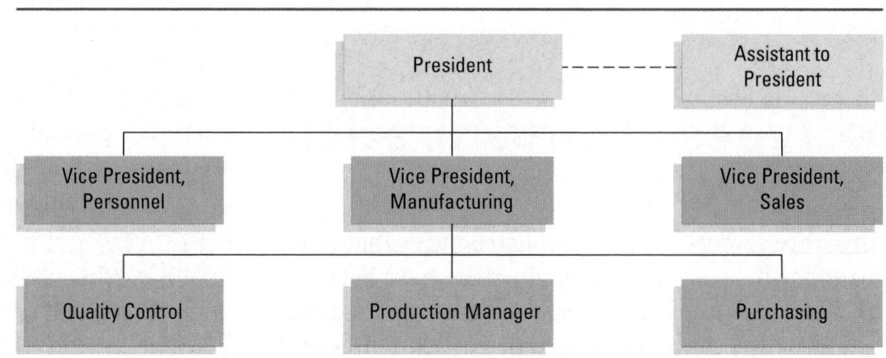

## Figure 7.11 • Illustrative Matrix Structure

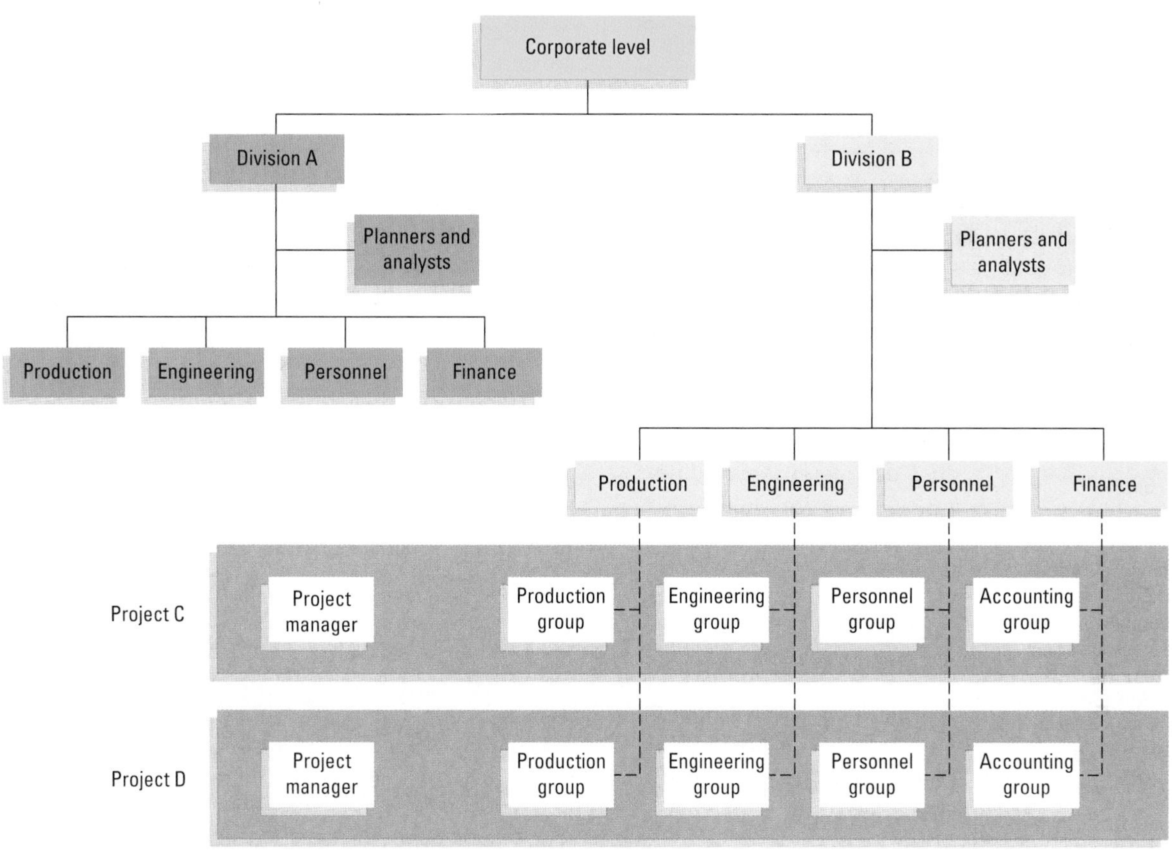


*Source:* From David Cleland and William King, *Systems Analysis and Project Management,* 3rd ed. (New York: McGraw-Hill, 1983). Reproduced with permission of the McGraw-Hill Companies.

are examples of projects. Because projects have a temporary life, a method of managing and organizing them was sought so that the existing organization structure would not be totally disrupted and would maintain some efficiency.

Under the **matrix structure**, those working on a project are officially assigned to the project and to their original or base departments. A manager is given the authority and responsibility to meet the project objectives in terms of cost, quality, quantity, and time of completion. The project manager is then assigned the necessary personnel from the functional departments of the parent organization. Thus, a horizontal-line organization develops for the project within the parent vertical-line structure. Under such a system, the functional personnel are assigned to and evaluated by the project manager while they work on the project. When the project or their individual work on it is done, the functional personnel return to their departments or begin a new project, perhaps with a new project team. Figure 7.11 shows a matrix structure.

A major advantage of matrix structure is that the mix of people and resources can readily be changed as project needs change. Other advantages include the emphasis placed on the project by use of a project team and the relative ease with which project members can move back into the functional organization once the project has ended. In addition, employees are challenged constantly, and interdepartmental cooperation develops along with expanded managerial talent due to the multitude of roles the project manager must undertake.

**Matrix Structure** Hybrid organization structure in which individuals from different functional areas are assigned to work on a specific project or task.

One serious problem with the matrix structure is that it can violate the principle of unity of command. A role conflict can develop if the authority of the project manager is not clearly delineated from that of the functional managers. In such a case, the people assigned to the project may receive conflicting assignments from the project manager and their functional managers. A second problem occurs when the personnel assigned to a project are still evaluated by their functional manager, who usually has little opportunity to observe their work on the project. Third,

**Figure 7.12 • Horizontal Structure**

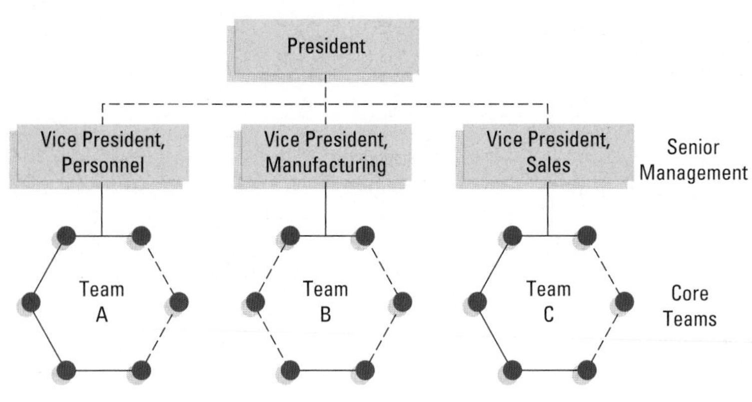


**Horizontal Structure** Organization structure consisting of two groups: the first composed of senior management responsible for strategic decisions and policies and the second composed of empowered employees working together in different process teams; also known as *team structure*.

**Virtual Organization** Temporary network of independent companies—suppliers, customers, and even rivals—linked by information technology to share skills, costs, and access to one another's markets.

they defy tradition, and put undue stress on communication networks.

## HORIZONTAL STRUCTURE

A relatively new type of structure is the **horizontal structure** (also called *team structure*). The pure form of a horizontal structure consists of two core groups. One group is composed of senior management responsible for strategic decisions and policies. The second group is composed of empowered employees working together in different process teams. Figure 7.12 illustrates a basic horizontal structure. Characteristics of a horizontal organization include the following:

- The organization is built around three to five core processes, such as developing new products, with specific performance goals assigned. Each process has an owner or champion.
- The hierarchy is flattened to reduce supervision.
- Teams manage everything, including themselves. They're held accountable for performance goals.
- Customers, not stock appreciation or profitability, drive performance.
- Team performance, not just the individual, is rewarded. Staffers are encouraged to develop multiple skills and are rewarded for them.
- Customer contact is maximized with employees.
- Emphasis is on informing and training all employees. "Don't just spoon-feed information on a 'need to know' basis."[16]

As suggested above, the horizontal structure emphasizes customer satisfaction, rather than focusing on financial or functional goals. Information is processed at the local level by process teams. Local problems can often be resolved quickly by the process team, thus permitting the organization to operate with flexibility and responsiveness.[17]

Additional advantages of the horizontal structure include increased efficiency, improved work culture and morale, and more satisfied customers. Kraft Foods, Ford Motor Company, General Electric, British Airways, AT&T, Motorola, Saab, Tesco, and American Express Financial Advisors have all made efforts to implement a horizontal structure in at least a part of their organizations.

9. How is a line and staff structure created?
10. Explain how the matrix organization structure works.
11. What is the major advantage of the matrix structure?
12. What are the seven characteristics of the horizontal organization structure?

# >> The Virtual Organization

A **virtual organization** is one in which business partners and teams work together across geographic or organizational boundaries by means of information technology.[18] In a virtual organization, co-workers often do not see each other on a regular basis. Three common types of virtual organizations have been identified.[19]

One type exists when a group of skilled individuals form a company by communicating via computer, phone, fax, and videoconference. A second type occurs when a group of companies, each of which specializes in a certain function such as manufacturing or marketing, partner together. A third type occurs when one large company outsources many of its operations by using modern technology to transmit

**Figure 7.13 • Virtual Organization**

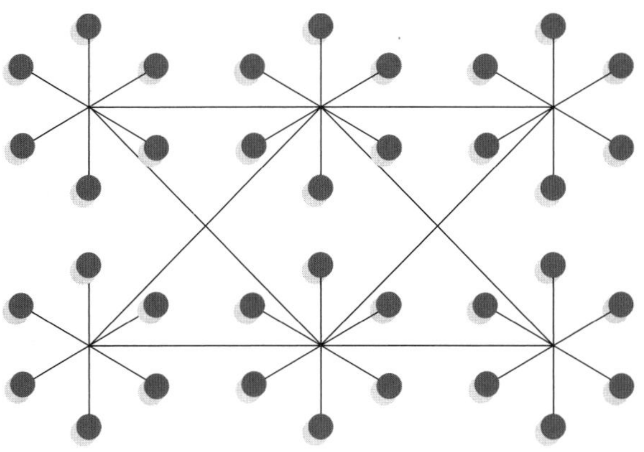

information to its partner companies so that it can focus on its specialty.

Virtual organizations create a network of collaborators that come together to pursue a specific opportunity. Once the opportunity has been realized, the collaborators usually disband and form new alliances to pursue new opportunities. Thus, virtual organizations are fluid, flexible, and constantly changing. Figure 7.13 illustrates a basic type of virtual organization.

**From the PERSPECTIVE OF...**

**A Home-Based Worker** What are the advantages and the disadvantages of working from a home office?

Technology plays a central role in allowing virtual organizations to form. Integrated computer and communication technology are the means by which the different collaborators are put together. To illustrate one example of how a virtual organization might work, suppose you head a large company.[20] It's Christmas season, and your company needs an additional 100 customer service representatives. Once the Christmas rush is over, these additional service representatives won't be needed, so it makes no sense to hire permanent employees.

Instead, you hire 100 people who work at home and have their own computers. The physical location of these virtual employees doesn't matter; they can be in Cleveland, Hong Kong, or Singapore. The virtual employees dial into the company's database and become an extension of the company. Whenever a customer calls, all information about that customer appears on the computer screen of the virtual employee handling the call; hence, the widely scattered employees can operate as if they are all at the same location. Once the Christmas rush is over, the collaboration is dissolved.

**Study Alert!**

Virtual organizations hold the dual promise of operational flexibility and cost minimization. Advances in global communication and Web technology have enabled an environment where business professionals can communicate in real time from all parts of the globe using sophisticated Web-conferencing equipment that's almost like being in the same room.

As outlined in Figure 7.14, virtual organizations have many potential benefits and challenges. Many people believe that some form of virtual organization is the wave of the future.

## >> Trends in Organization Structure

Several trends in organization structures have emerged over the last several decades. Beginning in the 1950s and 1960s, much attention was focused on the virtues of flat versus tall organization struc-

**Figure 7.14 • Benefits and Challenges of Transitioning to a Virtual Organization**

| Benefits | Challenges |
|---|---|
| Increases productivity. | Leaders must move from a control model to a trust method. |
| Decreases the cost of doing business. | New forms of communication and collaboration will be required. |
| Provides the ability to hire the best talent regardless of location. | Management must enable a learning culture and be willing to change. |
| Allows you to quickly solve problems by forming dynamic teams. | Staff reeducation may be required. |
| Allows you to more easily leverage both static and dynamic staff. | It can be difficult to monitor employee behavior. |
| Improves the work environment. | |
| Provides better balance for professional and personal lives. | |
| Provides competitive advantage. | |

**Flat Structure** Organization with few levels and relatively large spans of management at each level.

**Tall Structure** Organization with many levels and relatively small spans of management.

**Committee** Organization structure in which a group of people are formally appointed, organized, and superimposed on the line or line and staff structure to consider or decide certain matters.

tures. A **flat structure** has relatively few levels and relatively large spans of management at each level; a **tall structure** has many levels and relatively small spans of management (see Figure 7.15). A classic study in this area was conducted by James Worthy.[21] Worthy studied the morale of over 100,000 employees at Sears and Roebuck during a 12-year period. His study noted that organizations with fewer levels and wider spans of management offered the potential for greater job satisfaction. A wide span of management also forced managers to delegate authority and develop more direct links of communication—another plus. On the other hand, Rocco Carzo and John Yanouzas found that groups operating in a tall structure had significantly better performance than those operating in a flat structure.[22] Other studies have also shown conflicting results. Therefore, one cannot conclude that all flat structures are better than all tall structures, or vice versa.[23]

In general, Japanese organizations historically have had fewer middle managers and flatter structures than American organizations. For example, Toyota has had many fewer levels of management than has General Motors, Ford, or Chrysler. However, the downsizing many American organizations have experienced in the last three decades has resulted in flatter structures with wider spans of control. As organizations grow and meet with success, they tend to evolve into increasingly complex structures. How this occurs varies; frequently, a major cause is an increase in staff positions, especially at high levels. Many managers seem to feel a need for more staff and a more complex structure as the organization grows. They seem inclined to equate staff size with success.

More recently, many organizations have abandoned the more traditional line and staff structures in favor of horizontal structures and virtual organizations. All indications are that these trends will continue. As more and more employees become empowered, companies will put increased emphasis on managing through teams. Similarly, as communications technology continues to improve, many companies will evolve into virtual organizations.

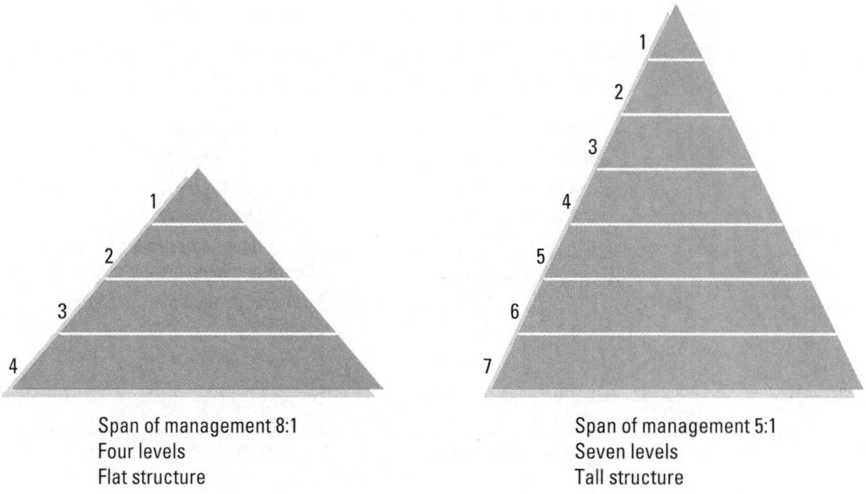

## >> Committees

Committees represent an important part of most traditional organization structures. A **committee** is a group of people formally appointed and organized to consider or decide certain matters. From a structural standpoint, committees are superimposed on the existing line, line and staff, or matrix structure. Committees can be permanent (standing) or temporary (ad hoc) and are usually in charge of, or supplementary to, the line and staff functions.

Teams are the counterpart to committees in nontraditional horizontal structures and virtual organizations. Because of their importance in today's organizations, the next chapter is devoted to understanding teams.

### USING COMMITTEES EFFECTIVELY

Managers can do many things to avoid the pitfalls and increase the efficiency of a committee. The first step is to define clearly its functions, scope, and authority. Obviously, the members must know the purpose of the committee to function effectively. If it is a temporary committee, the members should be informed of its expected duration. This will help avoid prolonging the life of the committee unnecessarily. Those responsible for establishing a committee should carefully communicate the limits of the committee's authority. This should be done very soon after the committee has been established.

**Figure 7.15 • Flat versus Tall Structures**

## Figure 7.16 • Methods of Selecting Committees

| Method | Advantages/Disadvantages |
|---|---|
| Appointment of chairperson and members | Promotes sense of responsibility for all. May result in most capable members. Members may not work well together. |
| Appointment of chairperson who chooses members | Will probably get along well. Lack of sense of responsibility by members. May not be most capable or representative. |
| Appointment of members who elect chairperson | Lack of sense of responsibility by chairperson. May not choose best chairperson for the job. Election of chairperson may lead to split in the committee. |
| Volunteers | Will get those who have greatest interest in the outcome or those who are least busy. Lack of responsibility. Potential for splits among committee members is great. |

**Study Alert!** An organization's board of directors carries the responsibility of corporate governance—that is, oversight on the leadership team to ensure that the interests of the organization's stakeholders (investors, customers, employees, and vendor partners) are represented in all business decisions. The recent failure of several large institutions (AIG, Lehman Brothers, Bear Stearns, General Motors, Washington Mutual, Wachovia, to name a few) have led to calls for greater scrutiny of who gets appointed to the board of directors and the degree to which they are held accountable for the organization's activities.

In addition, careful thought should go into the selection of the committee members and chairperson. Size is always an important variable; generally, committees become more inefficient as they grow in size. A good rule of thumb is to use the smallest group necessary to get the job done. It is more important to select capable members than representative members. It is also important to pick members from the same approximate organizational level. Members from higher levels may inhibit the actions and participation of the other members. Figure 7.16 lists several methods for selecting committee members and chairpersons and outlines advantages and disadvantages for each method.

## BOARDS OF DIRECTORS

A **board of directors** is really a type of committee that is responsible for reviewing the major policy and strategy decisions proposed by top management. A board of directors can be characterized as either an inside or an outside board. On an *inside board,* a majority of the members hold management positions in the organization; on an *outside board,* a majority of the members do not hold or have not held a position with the organization. While insiders who are members of a board ordinarily have other duties related to the strategic management process by virtue of their corporate position, the role the board plays as an entity should be basically the same for both types. Board members do not necessarily need to own stock; they should be chosen primarily for what they can and will contribute to the organization.

Although most boards of directors restrict their inputs to the policy and strategy level and do not participate in the day-to-day operations of the organization, their degree of involvement varies widely from board to board. For many years, boards were used primarily as figureheads, contributing little to the organization. However, this trend has been changing over the last several years. Recent lawsuits against boards of directors concerning their liabilities regarding the day-to-day operation of the organization have increased the risks of serving on boards.[24] Because of this, boards are becoming

**Board of Directors** Carefully selected committee that reviews major policy and strategy decisions proposed by top management.

# Thinking Critically 7.2

## >> A New Organization Structure

Yesterday, Adam Boyle was officially promoted to his new job as hospital administrator for Cobb General Hospital. Cobb General is a 600-bed hospital located in a suburban area of Cincinnati. Adam is extremely excited about the promotion but at the same time has some serious doubts about it.

Adam has worked at Cobb General for three years and had previously served as the associate administrator of the hospital. Although associate administrator was his official job title, he was really more of an errand boy for the former administrator, Mike Ambrosino. Because of Adam's educational background (which includes a master of hospital administration degree) and his enthusiasm for the hospital, Adam was offered the administrator's job last week after the hospital's board of directors had asked for Mike Ambrosino's resignation.

**Figure 7.17 • Organization Structure—Cobb General Hospital**

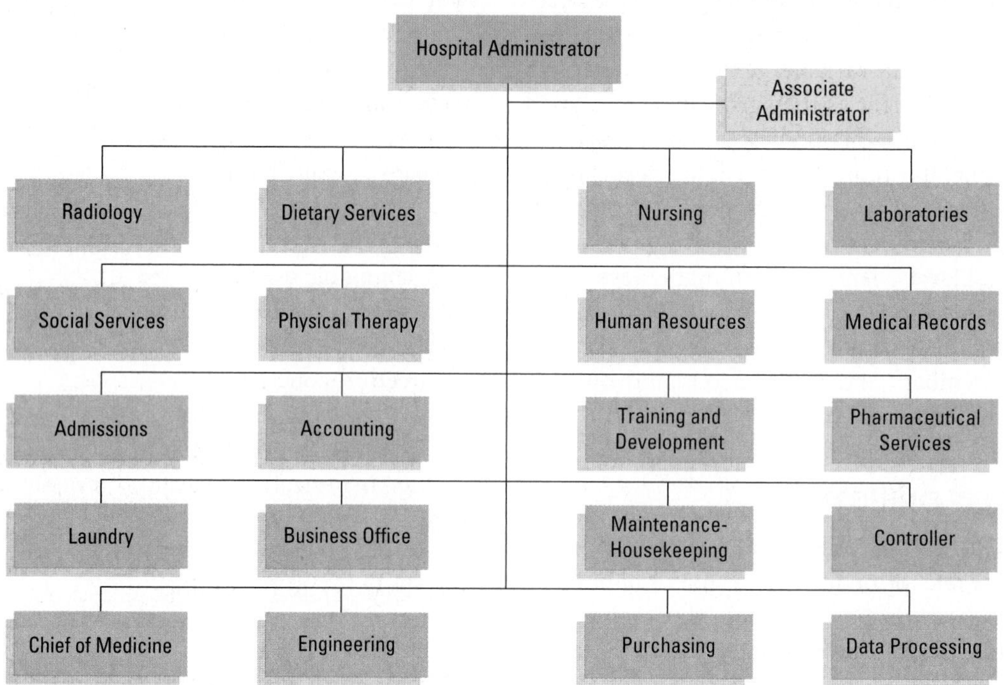


Adam is looking at the organization chart for the hospital, which had been pieced together over the years by Mike Ambrosino (see Figure 7.17). In reality, each time a new unit had been added or a new function started, Mike merely had the person report directly to him. Adam is worried about his ability to handle all the people currently reporting to him in his new position.

**QUESTIONS**

1. Do you think Adam has the necessary skills and experience for this position? Why or why not?
2. How would you describe Cobb General's current organization structure?
3. Do you agree with Adam's concern? Why?
4. How would you redraw the organization chart?

WHERE'S THE LINE?

At the height of his powers as the chairman and CEO of the Walt Disney Company, Michael Eisner's activities were, in theory at least, overseen by a board of directors that was reported to be independent, objective, and committed to ensuring that Eisner ran the company in an ethical and professional manner. In reality, Eisner had personal and professional relationships with many of the board members:

- Irwin Russell, Eisner's personal lawyer, negotiated Eisner's lucrative contract and had a professional duty of loyalty to Eisner simultaneous to his duty to shareholders. Yet Russell was also the chairman of Disney's compensation committee.
- Robert Stern was Eisner's personal architect and was beholden to Eisner for an immense amount of work from Disney, including designing the new animation building.
- Reveta Bowers was the principal of the prestigious Center for Early Education in West Hollywood, a school attended by Eisner's sons and the children of other Disney executives, who gave the school donations.
- Eisner had named Leo O'Donovan, a Jesuit priest and president of Georgetown University, to the board after Eisner's son Breck graduated from Georgetown. He gave Georgetown $1 million and his foundation financed a school scholarship.
- George Mitchell earned a $50,000 consulting fee in addition to his board stipend, and his law firm earned hundreds of thousands in legal fees representing Disney on various matters.

ETHICAL
MANAGEMENT
Is it ethical to have both personal and professional relationships with one's board of directors?


What's wrong with this picture? What should the Disney Company have done to ensure that the board could fulfill its obligation to shareholders?

*Source:* James B. Stewart, *The Disney War* (New York: Simon & Schuster, 2005).

## PROGRESS questions

13. What are the potential benefits and challenges of a virtual organization?
14. List three types of virtual organization.
15. Explain the difference between flat and tall structures. Which is better? Why?
16. Why are boards of directors becoming more active than they have in the past?

more active than they have been in the past. Moreover, some people now require liability insurance coverage before they will serve on a board of directors. An even more recent development is the tendency of shareholders to demand that the chairperson of the board be an outsider who is not employed in another capacity by the organization. Every diligent board of directors should address itself on behalf of the shareholders to this key issue: What is the standard of performance of the company's management—not what the company earned last year or this year, but what it *should* have earned?[25]

## >> Chapter Summary

Organization structure defines the boundaries of the formal organization and establishes the environment within which the organization operates. An appropriate organization structure helps ensure good performance, but the question as to whether a manager succeeds because of or in spite of an organization structure remains open for debate. This chapter has presented several different approaches to organization structure and offered different types of structure for your review. With all these options available, the key point to remember is that the organization structure should clearly establish who makes the decisions, how those decisions are made, and where responsibility for performance lies. In the next chapter we review how the management of the people who work within the organization structure can mean the difference between success and failure.

# For REVIEW >>

1. Explain the purpose of an organization chart.

   An organization chart uses a series of boxes connected with one or more lines to graphically represent the organization's structure. Each box represents a position within the organization, and each line indicates the nature of the relationships among the different positions. The organization chart not only identifies specific relationships but also provides an overall picture of how the entire organization fits together. As organizations become larger and more complex, it becomes increasingly difficult to represent all of the relationships accurately.

2. Describe factors and changes that affect an organization's structure.

   The size of the organization is a key determinant in how that organization is structured—a 50,000-employee company will look dramatically different from a 50-person company. The strategy that 50-person company adopts as the pathway to growth will also determine structure (and will hopefully be dynamic enough to modify that structure as the growth objectives of that strategy are achieved).

   Research studies have shown that the organization's external environment will also affect structure—stable industries (such as mining) tend to promote rigid structures (referred to as mechanistic), and dynamic industries (such as technology) tend to require very flexible structures (referred to as organic) as organizations reinvent themselves to keep up with changes in the marketplace.

   In recent years, technological advancements have produced two major changes in organization structure. First, outsourcing (in particular, offshoring) has enabled organizations to maintain smaller domestic structures as key functions are outsourced to specialist third-party vendors. Second, the rapid growth of Web-based commerce has promoted the growth of virtual organizations where departmental functions can be spread across the world and still interact in real time.

3. Define a contingency approach.

   A contingency approach to organizing acknowledges that there is no one best way to organize a company. All of the variables identified in Learning Outcome 2 should be assessed to determine the most appropriate structure for the situation. Because most of the relevant variables are dynamic, management should periodically analyze and appraise the organization's structure in light of any significant changes in key variables.

4. Identify the different types of departmentalization.

   Departmentalization involves grouping jobs into related work units:

   - Work functions. Units are grouped according to the nature of the work performed—typically production, marketing, finance, and human resources. Each of these basic functions may be broken down as necessary. For instance, the production department may be split into maintenance, quality control, engineering, manufacturing, and so on.
   - Product. All the activities needed to produce and market a product or service are usually under a single manager. This system allows employees to identify with a particular product and thus develop esprit de corps. It also facilitates managing each product as a distinct profit center.
   - Geographic. Organizations that maintain physically isolated and independent operations or offices are most likely to have departmentalization by geography, which permits the use of local employees or salespeople. This can create customer goodwill and an awareness of local needs.
   - Customer. An organization may be organized by customers served, such as wholesale versus retail or retail versus commercial.

- Time or shift. Organizations that operate production shifts around the clock may wish to monitor productivity and quality according to shift teams.
- Hybrid. A small company can use more than one type of departmentalization simultaneously and also change types in accordance with organizational needs as the company grows.

5. Describe the different types of organization structure, and explain why companies choose one structure over another.

The classic representation of an organizational hierarchy as a pyramid reflects the process of authority originating at the top of the organization and moving down in a line to senior leadership of key operating functions such as production, marketing, finance, and human resources. This line structure establishes authority through a clear chain of command and has the potential to promote rapid decision making (providing those function heads do not become bottlenecks in the communication process).

Adding staff specialists beneath those senior leaders creates a line and staff structure, where staff functions fulfill an advisory or supportive role (quality control, for example) and line functions fulfill a more direct role in the production, sales, and delivery of the organization's goods and services.

In a dynamic business environment, organizations will often create temporary committees or teams to manage short-term projects. These assignments promote a matrix structure where key personnel can receive cross-functional assignments (while maintaining their traditional line and staff responsibilities) to deliver on project objectives. This can serve to promote flexibility but can also cause confusion in the chain of command if project parameters are not clearly defined.

A relatively new type of structure is the horizontal structure (also called team structure). The pure form of a horizontal structure consists of two core groups. One group is composed of senior management responsible for strategic decisions and policies. The second group is composed of empowered employees working together in different process teams. The horizontal structure emphasizes customer satisfaction, rather than focusing on financial or functional goals. Information is processed at the local level by process teams. Local problems can often be resolved quickly by the process team, thus permitting the organization to operate with flexibility and responsiveness.

The most recent change in organization structure models has been the rise of the virtual organization, where companies leverage information technology to manage functional departments that may be spread across the globe. The capacity for real-time communication using e-mail and Web conferencing makes the geographic distance nothing more than a question of time zones.

6. Discuss the types and effective use of committees.

A committee is an organization structure in which a group of people is formally appointed, organized, and superimposed on the line or line and staff structure to consider or decide specific matters in the company. For committees to function effectively, the members must clearly understand the purpose and planned duration of the committee. In addition, those responsible for forming the committee should also clearly communicate the degree of authority with which the committee is empowered to operate. The number of committee members should draw an appropriate balance between adequate representation of the organizational functions affected by the committee and the need to achieve decisions without deadlocked deliberations.

# THE WORLD of Work >>

## KEVIN LEADS A PILOT PROJECT *(continued from page 141)*

Tony was impressed with Kevin's efforts on the strategic planning report. It was clear that Kevin had put a lot of time and effort into writing it, and Tony felt sure that the shift leader position was his for the taking. Kevin clearly understood the problem of increasing competition in the area, and some of his menu theme ideas had potential. At least, that's what Tony recalled feeling, right up until the last three pages of the report where Kevin took it upon himself to conclude that the organization of the Taco Barn unit model should be modified around functional responsibilities as opposed to operational hours. The biggest change, from what Tony read, was the replacement of the shift leader position with an assistant manager position for which Kevin, coincidentally, would be eligible to apply.

Tony's first reaction was one of anger and frustration at what he saw was a blatant attempt by Kevin to leap over the shift leader position into a new position of his own creation. Tony had served his time as a shift leader on his way up to unit manager, so why should Kevin be any different? However, as he reread Kevin's proposal, it did start to make a lot of sense, and Tony found himself agreeing with the underlying argument. The Taco Barn unit model was historical—the job titles originated with the first restaurant from years ago and things had certainly changed since then—so why couldn't they try something new? Tony forwarded Kevin's e-mail to Dawn with the recommendation for Kevin as the new shift leader, but in his message he specifically asked her to review Kevin's conclusions with the suggestion that they discuss the matter in more detail.

The next morning Tony received a response from Dawn. She liked the ideas proposed in Kevin's report and suggested that they run a pilot project in Tony's unit for three months. Any changes in title would be temporary, and there would be no salary adjustments, but she was definitely willing to give the new organization chart a chance.

Tony called Kevin into his office. "Congratulations Kevin, you are about to become our first temporary assistant unit manager!"

### QUESTIONS

1. What risks was Kevin taking in proposing the new organization structure?
2. What do you think would have happened if Tony hadn't supported Kevin's proposal?
3. What risks was Tony taking in endorsing Kevin's proposal to Dawn?
4. What should Kevin do now?

## Key Terms >>

board of directors 157

committee 156

contingency (situational) approach 148

customer departmentalization 150

departmentalization 148

flat structure 156

functional departmentalization 148

geographic departmentalization 150

horizontal structure 154

hybrid departmentalization 150

line and staff structure 152

line functions 152

line structure 151

matrix structure 153

mechanistic systems 143

organic systems 143

organization structure 142

outsourcing 147

product departmentalization 149

staff functions 152

tall structure 156

virtual organization 154

1. What purpose does an organization chart serve?
2. How does technology affect the structure of an organization?
3. What factors might prompt an organization to reverse a decision to outsource a business task?
4. What are the advantages and disadvantages of a line and staff structure?
5. How would an organization make the transition to a virtual structure?
6. How is a board of directors appointed?

# INTERNET In Action >>

1. You plan to start a consulting company that will meet the criteria of a truly virtual organization. You plan to avoid hiring any employees and to work exclusively with independent contractors around the globe on a project basis. Everyone, including you, will work out of home offices. Use Internet research to identify tools, templates, and/or vendors to help you put this new company together.
2. Identify the most recent list of most admired companies as selected by *Fortune* magazine. Select two companies from the top 10 and two companies from the bottom 10 on the list. Using Internet resources, determine how many outside directors and how many inside directors are serving each company.
   a. Do these companies have a majority of inside or outside directors?
   b. Are there any obvious differences in the composition of the boards of those companies from the top of the most admired list compared to those from the bottom of the list?
   c. If you were a shareholder of any of these companies, would you prefer to have more inside or outside directors? Why?

1. **Insourcing**

   Divide into teams of three or four students. For each team, a company of your choosing has decided, based on very negative internal or external customer feedback, to bring one of its outsourced business functions back in-house—*insourcing!* Identify the business function to be insourced, and propose a multistep plan to implement the initiative over the next 90 days.

2. **Organizing**

   Divide the class into two or three teams. Each team should select a company whose product is being sold in a highly competitive marketplace. On the assumption that the product has not been selling well against its competition, despite clear design and functionality advantages, it has been decided to reorganize the sales division. You can make any reasonable assumptions you think are necessary to complete the following tasks:

   a. Design what you think would be the best way to organize the sales (marketing) division of your company.
   b. Design an alternative structure for your division. Why do you prefer one structure over the other?
   c. Design a matrix structure for this situation (if you did not use one in question *a* or *b*). What would be the pros and cons of such a structure in this situation?

# Case 7.1

## >> Working from Home • In an industry sector famous for scams, Alpine Access really does want you to work from home.

After selling their traditional call center operation (read "cube farm") in 1997, Jim Ball and co-founder Steve Rockwood looked for ways to improve a profitable enterprise that came with too many headaches. With rampant employee turnover and high real estate costs, the obvious choice was to let their customer service agents work from home rather than commute every day to work in a sterile cube environment for minimum wage.

With no commuting costs, the founders reasoned, industry wage levels would be more attractive, and the flexible work arrangements would help reduce turnover and provide access to home-based workers with young children or older parents who would normally be excluded from traditional employment opportunities. In addition, lower operating costs allowed their new company, Alpine Access, to bid more competitively against those offshore call centers that had leveraged their low labor costs to price most domestic vendors out of the market.

Alpine's timing could not have been better. Increased awareness of environmental responsibility allowed the founders to promote the potential for reduced carbon emissions and traffic jams as their workers stayed in their homes. Customer frustration with willing but language-challenged overseas call reps was prompting many large companies, such as Dell Computers, Delta Airlines, and JP Morgan Chase, to bring their customer service departments back to the United States, and Alpine was ready and waiting to help them.

Fast-forward 13 years, and Alpine now has over 3,000 employees in 1,000 cities taking calls for clients such as America Online, Office Depot, and the Internal Revenue Service. Sales hit $53 million in 2009, and the company's ability to offer productive employment for home-based workers is enabling it to qualify for many of the employment performance agreements being promoted by the Obama administration's plan to get the country back to work. In January 2010 the company was awarded a $75,000 agreement by the Sherman Economic Development Corporation in Texas, as an incentive to hire 50 new full-time positions.

But what about the employees? The work-at-home sector is rife with employment scams to stuff envelopes or process medical claims (often requiring an up-front payment for "training" or "application processing"). How does Alpine keep a positive track record among such cynicism?

Starting pay is $8 to $12 an hour depending on experience and qualifications, and employees have access to benefits including a 401(k) plan into which Alpine pays a matching amount. At minimum wage levels, Alpine doesn't contribute to the cost of health care but does make available a health insurance plan that employees can purchase. Hours are flexible—up to a point. Employees must work 20 to 30 hours a week, and shift requests—early morning, evening, graveyard (10 P.M. to 6 A.M)—are subject to availability and frequent change depending on client needs.

Is Alpine a good company to work for? That depends on whom you ask. Review blogs and Web sites such as **www.jobvent.com** and **www.reviewopedia.com** offer mixed reviews, with some posters raving about the company and others claiming that they would sooner flip burgers than work for Alpine again.

What is clear is that a need is being served here. People who might struggle to work in a more traditional nine-to-five office or factory environment because of family and personal situations can find productive employment, and the lower operating costs achieved by not maintaining a call center location allows Alpine to compete against very low cost overseas outsourcers.

### QUESTIONS

1. In what ways do employees, customers, and shareholders benefit from the flexible work environment at Alpine Access?
2. Some corporate executives worry that home-based customer service agents will have too many distractions and too little supervision. Are those valid concerns? Why or why not?
3. What steps would an organization need to take to incorporate home-based customer service agents in its operation?
4. Would you work from home if you could? What would be the positives and negatives of that arrangement for you?

*Source:* Jennifer Alsever, "A Telecommuting Pioneer's Call Center Revolution," www.cnnmoney.com, February 23, 2010; Kathy Williams, "Performance Agreement Awarded to Alpine Access," Sherman, Texas, *Herald Democrat*, January 21, 2010; and "Alpine Access Launches Consulting Service," www.alpineaccess.com/static/blog/press-releases/alpine-access-launches-consulting-service.html.

# Case 7.2

## >> Dumping the Auto Dealers?

In May 2009, a national network of automobile dealers that can trace its origins back to the days of Henry Ford received harsh news as two of the "Big Three" U.S. car companies—Chrysler and General Motors (GM)—announced plans to terminate dealer contracts that for many had been in place for decades.

Chrysler, operating under Chapter 11 protection despite its summer 2007 purchase from Daimler Benz by equity group Cerberus Capital Management, L.P., struck the first blow by announcing in a letter from CEO Robert Nardelli on May 14 that "as an important part of our creation of a new company with Fiat, today we took a major step toward rightsizing our US dealer network and aligning it with the realities of a smaller network."

"Rightsizing" translated into the closure of 789 dealerships, or about 25 percent of its network.

GM followed with its own announcement on May 15 that about 1,100 dealers, or 18 percent of the company's network, would be closed as part of an overall strategy to reduce its network by 42 percent through dealer closings and brand re-alignments—the sale of Saab, Saturn, and Hummer and the closure of the Pontiac brand, leaving the four core brands Chevrolet, Cadillac, Buick, and GMC.

Chrysler elected to disclose the list of 789 dealerships that were losing their contracts with the announcement, since the dealers affected by the announcement received the news in letters delivered that morning by UPS. GM elected not to disclose its list, leading to a macabre "death watch" covered by local media stations as GM dealers waited to receive their notice of contract termination by the same method.

### Living on Borrowed Time

The apparent cruelty of such an unceremonious ending to decades long relationships masked the reality of an operational environment that was long overdue for change. In its earliest days, the concept of a dealer network enabled young car companies to guarantee outlets for the increasing number of cars (thanks to Ford's assembly line) that were coming out of their factories. To further sweeten the deal, the network territories or franchises were granted exclusively. This decision, combined with state franchise laws that condoned near-monopoly status for these dealerships (buyers cannot buy directly from the manufacturer and there are detailed limits on how close dealers can be located to each other in a local market), created a lucrative relationship that survived untouched for decades.

For the car manufacturers, the trade-off of dealing directly with customers was a network of dealers that would take whatever they were given in terms of new model designs and a sales channel that could always be manipulated with an increasingly confusing range of pricing incentives. Customers were, until the arrival of greater information availability through the Internet, left with the painful experience of negotiating for a car with a vendor that held all the cards and that seemed determined to squeeze every last nickel out of the deal.

The capacity to search databases for accurate information on dealer costs and option availability has transformed the car business into a commodity business. Critics argue that the Japanese carmakers—Toyota and Honda—saw this coming and made the transition to lean production factories that can switch assembly lines to different car models in hours rather than weeks. U.S. automakers still followed the "move-the-metal" philosophy of building the most profitable models and handing them to the dealers to convince customers to buy.

Not surprisingly, the dealers affected by these contract cancellations refused to go down without a fight. Many cried foul over increased pressure from Chrysler to merge its Dodge, Jeep, and Chrysler dealerships and take more inventory in the final days before bankruptcy (all at the dealers expense), only to have their dealer contract canceled three weeks later. Chrysler did not offer any form of an appeals process for the closures. GM said it had heard 856 appeals and granted 45.

When called before Washington lawmakers on the House Energy Committee's oversight subcommittee to defend their actions, executives from both companies defended the closures as being necessary to their restructuring and survival. Describing their dealer networks as a relic of rapid expansion from five decades ago, executives argued that continued support costs and incentive payments would be a prohibitive drain on efficient operations. In an argument that typically accompanies any layoffs or plant closures, Chrysler's vice president of North American Sales and Marketing, Steven J. Landry, stated that without the 789 closures "the stark reality is all 3,181 dealers will face elimination."

With a sales volume of only 10 million cars in 2009, down from a high of 17 million in 2005, it is obvious that these are dark times for the U.S. auto industry, but the question remains as to whether the capacity to unburden debt and legal obligations through the bankruptcy process will really change the management skills of the industry or simply bury its mistakes.

## QUESTIONS

1. If the dealer network was indeed a relic from five decades ago, why wait until now to fix it?
2. What is meant by the statement that "the car business is now a commodity business"?
3. How will these actions affect relations with the surviving dealerships?
4. Could this restructuring have been handled differently? How?

*Source:* Phil Mintz, "Nardelli: A Need to 'Rightsize' Dealers," *BusinessWeek*, May 14, 2009; "Kicking the Tyres," *The Economist*, May 22, 2009; Nick Bunkley, "Chrysler Dealers Make Case against Closings," *The New York Times*, May 23, 2009; and Jack Healey, "Back on Hill, Automakers Defend Dealer Closings," *The New York Times*, June 13, 2009.

# Case 7.3

## >> Restructuring U.S. Health Care

President Barack Obama ran for office with a commitment to tackle once and for all the unsustainable trajectory of health care spending. After decades of failed attempts to reform the U.S. health care system, including the much publicized Clinton plan overseen by now Secretary of State Hillary Clinton, the Obama administration appeared to have a better chance than most to force some form of workable consensus. The reason for the change? Simple demographics. America currently spends over $2.5 trillion per year for health care—an astronomical amount that represents 17.5 percent of the nation's gross domestic product (GDP). As the population ages, that expenditure is expected to increase to 48 percent of GDP by 2050. At those levels of spending, funds for education, defense, infrastructure, and welfare programs will have to be significantly curtailed or else the multitrillion-dollar deficit will continue to expand and place severe economic pressure on the U.S. economy and the value of the dollar.

### Using the Right Tools

From a business management perspective, the broken U.S. health care system was being presented as a series of operational challenges to be addressed in much the same manner as an organization would approach its operational efficiency with a strategic plan. There were, it was argued, clearly wasteful practices and operational inefficiencies that could be fixed to generate significant long-term cost savings. Of course, it will require equally significant capital investments up front to achieve those long-term savings. The biggest of these is health care information technology (HIT).

President Obama advocated allocating $20 billion to modernize HIT systems for health care providers that, after decades of mergers, consolidations, decouplings, and realignments, remain tied to inefficient proprietary systems that are often unable to communicate with their own internal systems, never mind other provider systems. Updating HIT on a common platform offering electronic health records (EHR) would, it was argued, reduce medical errors, reduce duplication of tests, and generate labor cost savings through the better alignment of administrative procedures such as patient admission and billing.

The size of this problem cannot be overestimated. In 1999, the Institute of Medicine estimated that preventable medical errors caused as many deaths as the crashes of 200 jumbo jets per year. Add to that the subsequent litigation and malpractice costs of those errors, and the price tag of $20 billion starts to look cheap at twice the price. However, selling the highly disruptive technology of common platform software to an industry that is already concerned over the potential move to a single provider system, like those offered in Canada and the United Kingdom, is much easier said than done. For all their inherent inefficiencies, the proprietary systems work well enough, and the procedures are so embedded in the operational policies of the total business model that there does not appear to be any opportunity for pilot projects to generate convincing data to pursue a systemwide initiative. If all that the health care providers see is an all-or-nothing option, they may well choose to do nothing with the argument that it is less disruptive to the rest of the system.

### Introducing Healthy Competition

In addition to tackling internal operational efficiencies, advocates of health care reform targeted what they saw as clear market irregularities that have contributed directly to the problem of escalating health care costs. In a 2008 survey, the American Medical Association (AMA) found that out of 314 metropolitan areas across the nation, 94 percent met the standard of a highly concentrated provider market, with two companies or even a single provider dominating the provision of health insurance coverage in that market. In 15 states, one insurer held half or more of the entire market, and in 7 states, a single insurer held 75 percent of the market or more. When challenged, the insurers argued that with 1,300 providers nationwide, the competition is more cutthroat than the AMA survey suggests, but a survey by the Kaiser Family Foundation revealed that premium price increases suggest that market domination does indeed lead to punitive price increases. Between 2000 and 2007, annual increases in premiums averaged around 9 percent, while health care spending increased only 6.7 percent. In the last decade, health insurance premiums have increased 120 percent compared to cumulative inflation of 44 percent and wage growth of only 29 percent over the same period.

Initial discussions on the subject of competitive pricing have centered on a commitment to information transparency, but the threat of a competing government plan in markets with only one or two providers in order to force competitive pricing almost made it into the legislation.

After an extremely contentious period of debate, health care reform became law in March 2010 with the passage of the Patient Protection and Affordable Care Act, followed shortly after by the Healthcare and Education Reconciliation Act. It remains to be seen whether the new legal framework will achieve the significant changes to which President Obama was committed or whether future administrations will undo much of the work with additional legislation.

QUESTIONS

1. What is the argument against a single provider system?
2. Is health care reform just a business management problem?
3. Assuming a hospital system is convinced of the cost savings of an HIT software package, how would you propose that it implements the technology?
4. Why would the subject of health care generate such contentious debate?

*Source:* Catherine Arnst, "Health Insurers Fight a Public Plan, but Rarely Each Other," *BusinessWeek,* July 21, 2009; "Heading for the Emergency Room," *The Economist,* June 25, 2009; Gerry Shih, "White House Official Links Health Care Plan to Fiscal Balance," *The New York Times,* July 23, 2009; "Healthcare Reform," *U.S. News and World Report,* August 2009; and Clayton M. Christensen and Jason Hwang, "A Disruptive Solution for Health Care," *BusinessWeek,* February 23, 2009.

CHAPTER 8

"I will pay more for the ability to deal with people than any other ability under the sun."

John D. Rockefeller

# ORGANIZING PEOPLE

LEARNING OUTCOMES

After studying this chapter, you will be able to:

1. Outline the human resource planning process.
2. Define *job analysis, job description, job specification,* and *skills inventory.*
3. Distinguish between different types of employment interviews.
4. Explain formal and informal work groups.
5. Define *groupthink.*
6. Discuss the concept of team building.

## THE WORLD OF WORK Kevin makes a suggestion

Tony had promoted Kevin to the shift leader position after Tanya had left Taco Barn. Kevin had gone one step further and proposed the creation of a new assistant unit manager position, which Dawn had approved as a pilot project. Kevin had proved to be a smart choice. He had done a great job on the scheduling project, and Tony was already grooming him for the management development program in anticipation of Dawn assigning Kevin to his own Taco Barn unit in the future.

Kevin was enthusiastic and constantly coming up with new ideas, and today was no exception. Tony was working on the produce order for the next day when Kevin knocked on the office door.

"Tony, do you have a couple of minutes?"

"Sure, Kevin, what do you need?"

"I'd like to run an idea by you about my crew. You know the scheduling project we worked on?"

"Yes," answered Tony, wondering where this conversation was headed.

"Well, they've been bitten by the bug, and now they want to work on some other projects as a team. To be honest, Tony, I know you gave me a lot of credit for that scheduling project, but they did most of the work. I think they've got some really good ideas for improving our food ordering and our inventory management. How would you feel about letting them meet for half an hour once or twice a week to work on their ideas? They'll have to come to you for budget approval if they want to spend any money, and I'll make sure that their work doesn't suffer. What do you think?"

Tony's first reaction was a brief panic that if his crew started coming up with all the new ideas, Dawn wouldn't have a reason for keeping him around, but he was impressed by Kevin's willingness to go to bat for his people and his support and confidence in their abilities.

"I think that's a great idea, Kevin," said Tony. "Ask them to pick a project, and give them a couple of weeks to work on it. Then we can look at what they come up with and see if it's worth putting it in front of Dawn for approval."

"Thanks, Tony—I think you'll be really surprised with what they come up with," said Kevin.

### QUESTIONS

1. Why would Tony's first reaction to Kevin's idea be one of panic?
2. Why is Kevin supporting his people in this manner? What's in it for him?
3. Do you think Tony is making a mistake here? Why or why not?
4. Would this idea work at your company? Why or why not?

## >> Staffing

Organizations run on the skills and efforts of people. The staffing function of management involves securing and developing people to perform the jobs created by the organizing function. The goal of staffing is to obtain the best available people for the organization and to develop the skills and abilities of those people. Obtaining the best available people generally involves forecasting personnel requirements and recruiting and selecting new employees. Developing the skills and abilities of an organization's employees involves employee development as well as the proper use of promotions, transfers, and separations. The staffing function is complicated by numerous government regulations that are covered in detail in Chapter 13. Furthermore, many of these regulations are subject to frequent change.

Unfortunately, many staffing activities have traditionally been conducted by human resource and/or personnel departments and have been considered relatively unimportant by line managers. However, securing and developing qualified personnel should be a major concern of all managers because it involves the most valuable asset of an organization: human resources.

## >> Job Analysis

**Job analysis** is the process of determining, through observation and study, the pertinent information relating to the nature of a specific job. The end products of a job analysis are a job description and a job specification. A **job description** is a written statement that identifies the tasks, duties, activities, and performance results required in a particular job. The job description should be used to develop fair and comprehensive compensation and reward systems. In addition, the accuracy of the job description can help or hinder recruiters in their efforts to attract qualified applicants for positions within the company. A **job specification** is a written statement that identifies the abilities, skills, traits, or attributes necessary for successful performance in a particular job. In general, a job specification identifies the qualifications of an individual who could perform the job. Job analyses are frequently conducted by specialists from the human resource department. However, managers should have input into the final job descriptions for the jobs they are managing.

**Job Analysis** The process of determining the pertinent information relating to the nature of a specific job.

**Job Description** A written statement that identifies the tasks, duties, activities, and performance results required in a particular job.

**Job Specification** A written statement that identifies the abilities, skills, traits, or attributes necessary for successful performance in a particular job.

**Skills Inventory** Consolidated information about an organization's current human resources.

### SKILLS INVENTORY

Through conducting job analyses, an organization defines its current human resource needs on the basis of existing or newly created jobs. A **skills inventory** consolidates information about the organization's current human resources. The skills inventory contains basic information about each employee of the organization, giving a comprehensive picture of the individual. Through analyzing the skills inventory, the organization can assess the current quantity and quality of its human resources.

Six broad categories of information that may be included in a skills inventory, along with examples for each category, are as follows:

1. *Skills:* Education, job experience, and training.
2. *Special qualifications:* Memberships in professional groups, and special achievements.
3. *Salary and job history:* Present salary, past salary, dates of raises, and various jobs held.
4. *Company data:* Benefit plan data, retirement information, and seniority.
5. *Capacity of individual:* Scores on tests and health information.
6. *Special preferences of individual:* Location or job preferences.

The primary advantage of a computerized skills inventory is that it offers a quick and accurate evaluation of the skills available within the organization. Combining the information provided by the job analysis and the skills inventory enables the organization to evaluate the present status of its human resources.

Specialized versions of the skills inventory can also be devised and maintained. One example would be the management inventory, which would separately evaluate the specific skills of managers, such as strategy development, experiences (e.g., international experience or language skill), and successes or failures at administration or leadership.

In addition to appraising the current status of its human resources, the organization must consider

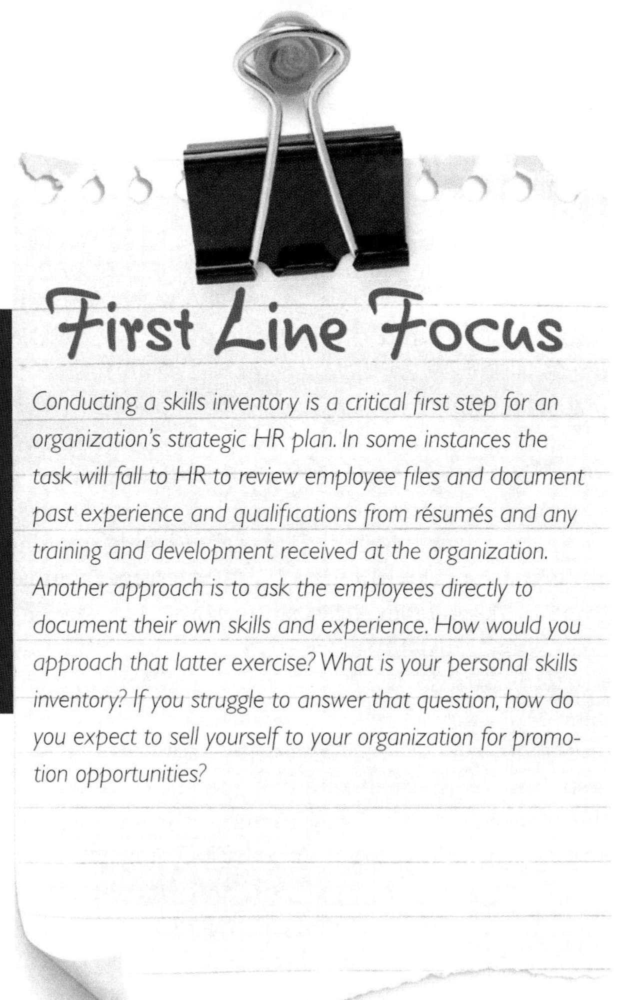


anticipated changes in the current workforce due to retirements, deaths, discharges, promotions, transfers, and resignations. Certain changes in personnel can be estimated accurately and easily, whereas other changes are more difficult to forecast.

SKILLS INVENTORY . . .
First Line Focus
Conducting a skills inventory is a critical first step for an organization's strategic HR plan. In some instances the task will fall to HR to review employee files and document past experience and qualifications from résumés and any training and development received at the organization. Another approach is to ask the employees directly to document their own skills and experience. How would you approach that latter exercise? What is your personal skills inventory? If you struggle to answer that question, how do you expect to sell yourself to your organization for promotion opportunities?

**Human resource planning (HRP)** involves getting the right number of qualified people into the right job at the right time. Put another way, HRP involves matching the supply of people—internally (existing employees) and externally (those to be hired)—with the openings the organization expects to have for a given time frame.

HRP involves applying the basic planning process to the human resource needs of the organization. Once organizational plans are made and specific objectives set, the HRP process attempts to define the human resource needs to meet the organization's objectives.

The first basic question addressed by the planning process is, Where are we now? Human resource planning frequently answers this question by using job analyses and skills inventories.

## FORECASTING

The second basic question the organization addresses in the planning process is, Where do we want to go? **Human resource forecasting** attempts to answer this question with regard to the organization's human resource needs. It is a process that attempts to determine the future human resource needs of the organization in light of the organization's objectives. Some of the many variables considered in forecasting human resource needs include sales projections, skills required in potential business ventures, composition of the present workforce, technological changes, and general economic conditions. Given the critical role human resources play in attaining organizational objectives, all levels of management should be involved in the forecasting process.

**Human Resource Planning (HRP)** Matching the internal and external supply of people with the openings the organization expects to have for a given time frame.

**Human Resource Forecasting** A process that attempts to determine the future human resource needs of an organization in light of the organization's objectives.

Human resource forecasting is presently conducted largely on the basis of intuition; the experience and judgment of the manager are used to determine future human resource needs. This assumes all managers are aware of the future plans of the total organization. Unfortunately, this is not true in many cases.

## TRANSITION

In the final phase of human resource planning, the transition, the organization determines how it can obtain the quantity and quality of human resources it needs to meet its objectives as reflected by the human resource forecast. The human resource forecast results in a statement of the organization's human resource needs in light of its plans and objectives. The organization engages in several transitional

activities to bring its current level of human resources in line with the forecast requirements. These activities include recruiting and selecting new employees, developing current or new employees, promoting or transferring employees, laying off employees, and discharging employees. Given the current trend of downsizing in many organizations, some human resource departments now maintain a replacement chart for each employee. This confidential chart shows a diagram of each position in the management hierarchy and a list of candidates who would be qualified to replace a particular person should the need arise. Generally, the coordination of all the activities mentioned earlier is delegated to a human resource or personnel department within the organization. Figure 8.1 shows the relationship between job analysis, skills inventory, human resource planning, recruitment, and selection.

**Recruitment** Process of seeking and attracting a supply of people from which qualified candidates for job vacancies can be selected.

## Figure 8.1 • Relationship between Job Analysis, Skills Inventory, Human Resource Planning, Recruitment, and Selection

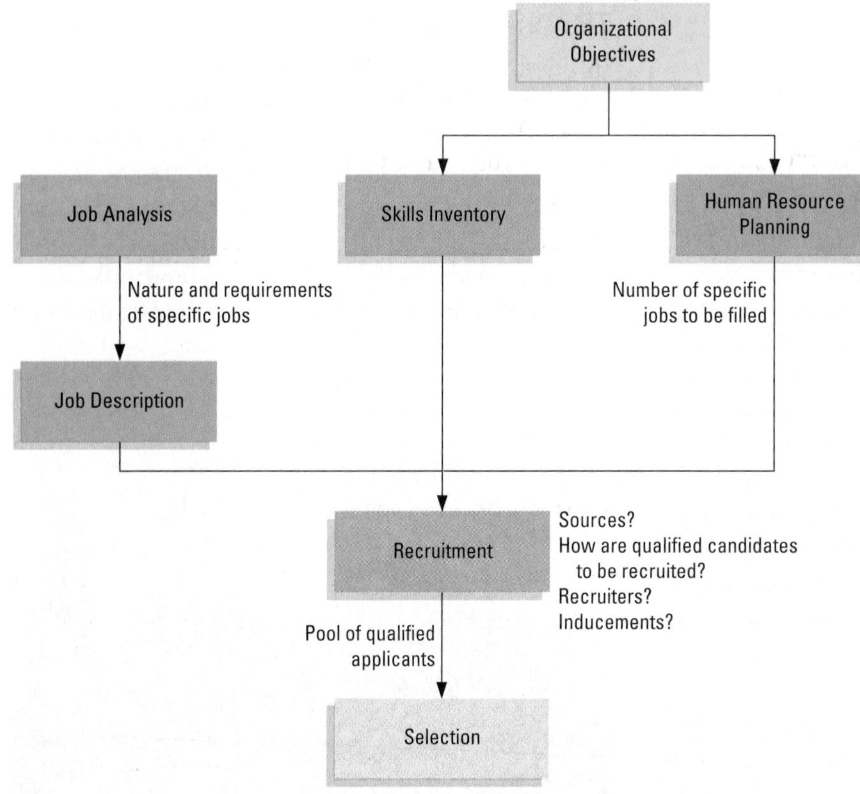


# >> Recruitment

**Recruitment** involves seeking and attracting a supply of people from which qualified candidates for job vacancies can be selected. The amount of recruitment an organization must do is determined by the difference between the forecasted human resource needs and the talent available within the organization. After the decision to recruit has been made, the sources of supply must be explored.

An organization that has been doing an effective job of recruiting employees has one of the best sources of supply for filling job openings: its own employees. Promotion from within is very popular with growing and dynamic organizations. If internal sources prove to be inadequate, external sources are always available. Though usually more costly and time consuming to pursue, such external sources as employment agencies, consulting firms, employee referrals, and employment advertisements can be valuable resources for an organization. Figure 8.2 summarizes the advantages and disadvantages of using internal and external sources for human resource needs.

One of the fastest-growing areas of recruitment is **temporary help** hired through employment agencies. The agency pays the salary and benefits of the temporary help; the organization pays the employment agency an agreed-on figure for the services of the temporary help. The use of temporary help is not dependent on economic conditions. When an organization is expanding, temporary employees are used to augment the current staff. When an organization is downsizing, temporary employees create a flexible staff that can be laid off easily and recalled when necessary. One obvious disadvantage of using temporary employees is their lack of commitment to the organization.

Unlike temporary agencies, which normally place people in short-term jobs at various companies, **employee leasing companies** and professional employer organizations (PEOs)

### Figure 8.2 • Advantages and Disadvantages of Internal and External Sources

| Source | Advantages | Disadvantages |
|---|---|---|
| **Internal** | • Company has a better knowledge of strengths and weaknesses of job candidate.<br>• Job candidate has a better knowledge of company.<br>• Morale and motivation of employees are enhanced.<br>• The return on investment that an organization has in its present workforce is increased. | • People might be promoted to the point where they cannot successfully perform the job.<br>• Infighting for promotions can negatively affect morale.<br>• Inbreeding can stifle new ideas and innovation. |
| **External** | • The pool of talent is much larger.<br>• New insights and perspectives can be brought to the organization.<br>• Frequently it is cheaper and easier to hire technical, skilled, or managerial employees from outside. | • Attracting, contacting, and evaluating potential employees is more difficult.<br>• Adjustment or orientation time is longer.<br>• Morale problems can develop among those employees within the organization who feel qualified to do the job. |

provide permanent staff at customer companies, issue the workers' paychecks, take care of personnel matters, ensure compliance with workplace regulations, and provide various employee benefits.[1] In addition, highly skilled technical workers, such as engineers and information technology specialists, are supplied for long-term projects under contract between a company and a technical services firm.

**From the PERSPECTIVE OF...**

**A Temp Agency Manager** In what ways is the recruitment process different for temporary positions?

## >> Selection

The selection process involves choosing from those available the individuals most likely to succeed in the job. The process is dependent on proper human resource planning and recruitment. Only when an adequate pool of qualified candidates is available can the selection process function effectively. The ultimate objective of the selection process is to match the requirements of the job with the qualifications of the individual.

**Temporary Help** Help that may augment the current staff or be laid off whenever necessary; hired through an agency that pays the benefits and salary of the help, while the organization pays the agency an agreed-on figure for its services.

**Employee Leasing Companies** Companies that provide permanent staff at customer companies, issue the workers' paychecks, take care of personnel matters, ensure compliance with workplace regulations, and provide various employee benefits.

### WHO MAKES THE DECISION?

The responsibility for hiring is assigned to different levels of management in different organizations. Often, the human resource or personnel department does the initial screening of recruits, but the final selection decision is left to the manager of the department with the job opening. Such a system relieves the manager of the time-consuming responsibility of screening out unqualified and uninterested applicants. Less frequently, the human resource or personnel department is responsible for both the initial screening and the final decision. Many organizations leave the final choice to the immediate manager, subject to the approval of higher levels

**Study Alert!**

The recruitment process should not be initiated with an employee resignation or termination. An effective company should always be looking for strong candidates, both internally and externally. A comprehensive training and development program, combined with a detailed succession plan, should help you identify and nurture future managers and leaders for your organization. Occasionally you may come across a stellar candidate before you have a suitable position for him or her. At that point serious consideration should be given to temporarily overstaffing a department if that's what it takes. The short-term cost incurred will have a long-term payoff in a valuable addition to your team.

**Tests** Methods for obtaining a sample of behavior that is used to draw inferences about the future behavior or performance of an individual.

**Aptitude Tests** Tests that measure a person's capacity or potential ability to learn.

**Psychomotor Tests** Tests that measure a person's strength, dexterity, and coordination.

**Job Knowledge Tests** Tests that measure the job-related knowledge possessed by a job applicant.

**Proficiency Tests** Tests that measure how well the applicant can do a sample of the work to be performed.

**Interest Tests** Tests that determine how a person's interests compare with the interests of successful people in a specific job.

**Psychological Tests** Tests that measure personality characteristics.

**Polygraph Tests** Tests that record physical changes in the body as the test subject answers a series of questions.

of management. In small organizations, the owner or the top manager often makes the choice.

An alternative approach is to involve peers in the selection decision. Traditionally, peer involvement has been used primarily with professionals and those in upper levels of management, but it is becoming more popular at all levels of the organization. With this approach, co-workers have an input into the final selection decision.

## SELECTION PROCEDURE

Figure 8.3 presents a suggested procedure for selecting employees. The preliminary screening and preliminary interview eliminate candidates who are obviously not qualified for the job. In the preliminary screening of applications, personnel data sheets, school records, work records, and similar sources are reviewed to determine characteristics, abilities, and the past performance of the individual. The preliminary interview is then used to screen out unsuitable or uninterested applicants who passed the preliminary screening phase.

**Figure 8.3 • Steps in the Selection Process**

| Steps in Selection Process | Possible Criteria for Eliminating Potential Employee |
|---|---|
| • Preliminary screening from application form, résumé, employer records, etc. | Inadequate educational level or performance/experience record for the job and its requirements. |
| • Preliminary interview | Obvious disinterest and unsuitability for job and its requirements. |
| • Testing | Failure to meet minimum standards on job-related measures of intelligence, aptitude, personality, etc. |
| • Reference checks | Unfavorable reports from references regarding past performance. |
| • Employment interview | Inadequate demonstration of ability or other job-related characteristics. |
| • Physical examination | Lack of physical fitness required for job. |
| • Personal judgment | Intuition and judgment resulting in the selection of a new employee. Inadequate demonstration of ability or other job-related characteristics. |

## TESTING

One of the most controversial areas of staffing is employment testing. **Tests** provide a sample of behavior that is used to draw inferences about the future behavior or performance of an individual. Many tests are available to organizations for use in the selection process.[2] Tests used by organizations can be grouped into the following general categories: aptitude, psychomotor, job knowledge and proficiency, interests, psychological, and polygraphs.

**Aptitude tests** measure a person's capacity or potential ability to learn. **Psychomotor tests** measure a person's strength, dexterity, and coordination. **Job knowledge tests** measure the job-related knowledge possessed by a job applicant. **Proficiency tests** measure how well the applicant can do a sample of the work to be performed. **Interest tests** are designed to determine how a person's interests compare with the interests of successful people in a specific job. **Psychological tests** attempt to measure personality characteristics. **Polygraph tests**, popularly known as *lie detector tests,* record physical changes in the body as the test subject answers a series of questions. By studying recorded physiological measurements, the polygraph examiner then makes a judgment as to whether the subject's response was truthful or deceptive.

Employment testing is legally subject to the requirements of validity and reliability. **Test validity** refers to the extent to which a test predicts a specific criterion. For organizations, the criterion is usually performance on the job. Thus, test validity generally refers to the extent to which a test predicts future job success or performance. The selection of criteria to define job success or performance is a difficult process, and its importance cannot be overstated. Obviously, test validity cannot be measured unless satisfactory criteria exist.

**Test reliability** refers to the consistency or reproducibility of the results of a test. Three methods are commonly used to determine the reliability of a test. The first method, called *test-retest,* involves testing a group of people and then retesting them later. The degree of similarity between the sets of scores determines the reliability of the test. The second method, called *parallel forms,* entails giving two separate but similar forms of the test. The degree to which the sets of scores coincide determines the reliability of the test. The third method, called *split halves,* divides the test into two halves to determine whether performance is similar on both halves. Again, the degree of similarity determines the reliability. All these methods require statistical calculations to determine the degree of reliability of the test.

### BACKGROUND AND REFERENCE CHECKS

Background and reference checks usually fall into three categories: personal, academic, and past employment. Contacting personal and academic references is generally of limited value, because few people will list someone as a reference unless they feel that that person will give them a positive recommendation. Previous employers are in the best position to supply the most objective information. However, the amount and type of information that a previous employer is willing to divulge varies. Normally, most previous employers will provide only the following information: yes or no to the question if this applicant worked there, the employee's dates of employment, and the position he or she held.[3]

If a job applicant is rejected because of information in a credit report or another type of report from an outside reporting service, the applicant must be given the name and address of the organization that developed the report. The reporting service is *not* required by law to give the person a copy of his or her file, but it *must* inform the person of the nature and substance of the information.

## >> Employment Interview

The employment interview is used by virtually all organizations as an important step in the selection process. Its purpose is to supplement information gained in other steps in the selection process to determine the suitability of an applicant for a specific opening in the organization. It is important to remember that all questions asked during an interview must be job-related. Equal employment opportunity legislation has placed limitations on the types of questions that can be asked during an interview.

**Test Validity** The extent to which a test predicts a specific criterion.

**Test Reliability** The consistency or reproducibility of the results of a test.

**Structured Interview** An interview conducted using a predetermined outline.

**Semistructured Interview** An interview in which the interviewer prepares the major questions in advance but has the flexibility to use techniques, such as probing, to help assess the applicant's strengths and weaknesses.

### TYPES OF INTERVIEWS

Organizations use several types of interviews. The **structured interview** is conducted using a predetermined outline. Through the use of this outline, the interviewer maintains control of the interview so that all pertinent information on the applicant is covered systematically. Structured interviews provide the same type of information on all interviewees and allow systematic coverage of all questions deemed necessary by the organization. The use of a structured interview tends to increase reliability and accuracy.

Two variations of the structured interview are the semistructured and the situational interview. In the **semistructured interview**, the interviewer

### [PROGRESS] ✓questions

1. What are the six broad categories of information that may be included in a skills inventory?
2. Explain the human resource planning (HRP) process.
3. Who makes the hiring decisions in an organization?
4. What are the six general categories of tests that organizations use in the selection process?

TEST-DRIVING EMPLOYEES?

You are hiring a night manager for one of your hotels. In a tough economy, you are not surprised at the large volume of applications you receive—many with no relevant experience in the industry and many who appear to be overqualified for the position. You identify a shortlist of 12 candidates for interviews.

The last interview candidate of the day is a man in his mid-50s (he discloses his age in the interview). He interviews well but presents nothing to make himself stand out from the other candidates. As you are wrapping up the interview, he turns to you and says:

"Look, I've been out of work for over a year now. Lots of interviews for positions that I know I'm qualified for, but I never get far enough to be able to provide the excellent references I have to show the value I can bring to your organization. I know my age works against me, but I really need this job. If it will make a difference, I will work for you for free for three months—call me an unpaid intern if you want—to prove my value."

What would you do and why?

ETHICAL
MANAGEMENT
Should you hire someone because they are willing to work for free to prove their worth?

prepares the major questions in advance but has the flexibility to use techniques, such as probing, to help assess the applicant's strengths and weaknesses. The **situational interview** uses projective techniques to put the prospective employee in action situations that might be encountered on the job. For example, the interviewer may wish to see how the applicant might handle a customer complaint or observe certain important decision-making characteristics. With either method interviewer bias must be guarded against.

**Unstructured interviews** are conducted without a predetermined checklist of questions. This type of interview uses such open-ended questions as, "Tell me about your previous job." Interviews of this type pose numerous problems, such as a lack of systematic coverage of information, and are susceptible to the personal biases of the interviewer. This type of interview, however, does provide a more relaxed atmosphere.

Organizations have used three other types of interviewing techniques to a limited extent. The **stress interview** is designed to place the interviewee under pressure. In the stress interview, the interviewer assumes a hostile and antagonistic attitude toward the interviewee. The purpose of this type of interview is to detect whether the person is highly emotional. In the **board (or panel) interview** two or more interviewers conduct the interview. The **group interview,** which questions several interviewees together in a group discussion, is also sometimes used. Board interviews and group interviews can involve either a structured or an unstructured format.

**Situational Interview** An interview in which the interviewer uses projective techniques to put the prospective employee in action situations that might be encountered on the job.

**Unstructured Interviews** Interviews conducted without a predetermined checklist of questions.

**Stress Interview** An interview during which the interviewee is placed under pressure.

**Board (Panel) Interview** An interview conducted by two or more people.

**Group Interview** Several interviewees are interviewed at once.

## PROBLEMS IN CONDUCTING INTERVIEWS

Although interviews have widespread use in selection procedures, they can pose a host of problems. The first and one of the most significant problems is that interviews are subject to the same legal requirements of validity and reliability as other steps in the selection process. Furthermore, the validity and reliability of most interviews are questionable. One reason seems to be that it is easy for the interviewer to become either favorably or unfavorably impressed with the job applicant for the wrong reasons.

Several common pitfalls may be encountered in interviewing a job applicant. Interviewers, like all people, have personal biases, and these biases can play a role in the interviewing process. For example, a qualified male applicant should not be rejected merely because the interviewer dislikes long hair on males.

Closely related is the problem of the **halo effect**, which occurs when the interviewer allows a single prominent characteristic to dominate judgment of all other traits. For instance, it is often easy to overlook other characteristics when a person has a pleasant personality. However, merely having a pleasant personality does not ensure that the person will be a qualified employee.

Overgeneralizing is another common problem. An interviewee may not behave exactly the same way on the job that she or he did during the interview. The interviewer must remember that the interviewee is under pressure during the interview and that some people naturally become nervous during an interview.

## CONDUCTING EFFECTIVE INTERVIEWS

Problems associated with interviews can be partially overcome through careful planning. The following suggestions are offered to increase the effectiveness of the interviewing process.

First, careful attention must be given to the selection and training of interviewers. They should be outgoing and emotionally well-adjusted people. Interviewing skills can be learned, and the people responsible for conducting interviews should be thoroughly trained in these skills.

Second, the plan for the interview should include an outline specifying the information to be obtained and the questions to be asked. The plan should also include room arrangements. Privacy and some degree of comfort are important. If a private room is not available, the interview should be conducted in a place where other applicants are not within hearing distance.

Third, the interviewer should attempt to put the applicant at ease. The interviewer should not argue with the applicant or put the applicant on the spot. A brief conversation about a general topic of interest or offering the applicant a cup of coffee can help ease the tension. The applicant should be encouraged to talk. However, the interviewer must maintain control and remember that the primary goal of the interview is to gain information that will aid in the selection decision.

**Halo Effect** Interviewer allowing a single prominent characteristic to dominate judgment of all other traits.

*Job interviews can vary as widely as the positions applied for, even within the same company. How would your preparation vary based on an interview at Sears' cosmetics department versus the juniors department?*

Fourth, the facts obtained in the interview should be recorded immediately. Generally, notes can and should be taken during the interview.

Fifth, the effectiveness of the interviewing process should be evaluated. One way to evaluate effectiveness is to compare the performance ratings of individuals who are hired against assessments made during the interview. This cross-check can serve to evaluate the effectiveness of individual interviewers as well as that of the overall interviewing program.

## PERSONAL JUDGMENT

The final step in the selection process is to make a personal judgment regarding which individual to select for the job. (Of course, it is assumed that at this point more than one applicant will be qualified for the job.) A value judgment using all of the data obtained in the previous steps of the selection process must be made in selecting the best individual for the job. If previous steps have been performed correctly, the chances of making a successful personal judgment improve dramatically.

The individual making the personal judgment should also recognize that in some cases, none of the applicants is satisfactory. If this occurs, the job should be redesigned, more money should be offered to attract more qualified candidates, or other actions should be taken. Caution should be taken against accepting the "best" applicant if that person is not truly qualified to do the job.

**Study Alert!**

The *halo effect* can come into play for lots of reasons: a pleasant personality, a shared work history (i.e., you both worked for the same company in the past), or a shared network of business colleagues. When there is an urgent need to fill the position, other factors can start to come into play: a local candidate versus a potential relocation, or an unemployed candidate who is immediately available versus a candidate who will be giving two weeks' notice. It requires discipline and a detailed job description to ensure that you are hiring Miss Right rather than Miss Right Now.

# Thinking Critically 8.1

## >> A Good Hire

Debbie Cornell is a human resources manager for a major retailer. She recruits and selects the associates who work in the store. Recently, she met with the electronics department manager, who needed an associate with experience in computer software. Finding someone with this specific knowledge had become more difficult in recent months, because of a new competitor down the street. The electronics manager told Debbie that she met a girl at his community college who was studying information systems. Debbie encouraged the manager to talk to the student to see if she would be interested in interviewing for the position.

Later that week, Melony Henshaw called Debbie about the job opening in the electronics department. She told Debbie that she had heard about the opening from the electronics manager. Debbie set up an interview for the next morning at 9:00 A.M. Debbie had a strong feeling that this would be a "good hire," based on their brief telephone conversation.

At 9:25 the next morning, Melony arrived for her interview. She came into Debbie's office wearing a T-shirt, flip-flops, and a nose ring. Against all her instincts, Debbie went through with the interview. During the interview, Melony presented herself as a creative and knowledgeable person. Debbie came away from her interview with Melony far more impressed than when she started.

Debbie decided to invite Melony to new employee orientation the following morning. She was still worried about Melony's behaviors from the day before—her lateness to the interview and her inappropriate dress. Still, the electronics department needed someone with Melony's expertise, and she was easily the best candidate.

The new employee orientation began at 9:00 A.M. the next day. The small group gathered in a meeting room, but Melony was nowhere to be found. After sending the orientation group to another meeting room to complete some paperwork, Debbie got a call—it was Melony. She told Debbie that she had overslept but could get to the store by 10:30 A.M.

**QUESTIONS**

1. If you were Debbie, what would you say to Melony?
2. What are the advantages and disadvantages of hiring Melony?
3. Would you treat Melony differently from the other newly hired employees? Why or why not?
4. Can Melony's behaviors be corrected? If so, how?

## >> Transfers, Promotions, and Separations

The final step in the human resource planning process involves transfers, promotions, and separations. A transfer involves moving an employee to another job at approximately the same level in the organization with basically the same pay, performance requirements, and status. Planned transfers can serve as an excellent development technique. Transfers can also be helpful in balancing varying departmental workload requirements. The most common difficulty relating to transfers occurs when a "problem" employee is unloaded on an unsuspecting manager. Training, counseling, or corrective discipline of the employee may eliminate the need for such a transfer. If the employee cannot be rehabilitated, discharge is usually preferable to transfer.

A promotion moves an employee to a job involving higher pay, higher status, and thus higher performance. The two basic criteria used by most organizations in promotions are merit and seniority. Union contracts often require that seniority be considered in promotions. Many organizations prefer to base promotions on merit as a way to reward and encourage performance. Obviously, this assumes the organization has a method for evaluating performance and determining merit. An organization must also consider the requirements of the job in question, not just the employee's performance in previous jobs. Success in one job does not automatically ensure success in another job. Both past performance and potential must be considered. This also reduces the probability that the Peter Principle effect will occur (i.e., that an employee will be promoted to her or his level of incompetence).

A separation involves either voluntary or involuntary termination of an employee. In voluntary separations, many organizations attempt to determine why the employee is leaving by using exit interviews. This type of interview provides insights into problem areas that need to be corrected in the organization. Involuntary separations involve terminations and layoffs. Layoffs occur when there is not enough work for all employees. Laid-off employees are called back if the workload increases. A termination usually occurs when an employee is not performing his or her job or has broken a company rule. Terminations should be made only as a last resort. When a company has hired an employee and invested resources in the employee, termination results in a low return on the organization's investment. Training and counseling often are tried before firing an individual. However, when rehabilitation fails, the best action is usually termination because of the negative impact a disgruntled or misfit employee can have on others in the organization.

# >> Understanding Work Groups and Teams

## FORMAL WORK GROUPS

Management establishes **formal work groups** to carry out specific tasks. Formal groups may exist for a short or long period of time. A task force is an example of a formal group. These groups have a single goal, such as resolving a problem or designing a new product.

A different type of formal work group is the *command,* or *functional, group*. This group consists of a manager and all the employees he or she supervises. Unlike a task group, the command group's work is ongoing and not confined to one issue or product.

**Formal Work Groups** Groups established by the management to carry out specific tasks.

**Informal Work Groups** Groups formed voluntarily by members of an organization.

## INFORMAL WORK GROUPS

**Informal work groups** are formed voluntarily by members of an organization. They develop from personal contacts and interactions among people. Groups of employees who lunch together regularly and office cliques are examples of informal work groups.

A special type of informal group is the *interest group*. Its members share a purpose or concern. For example, women executives might form a group to share ideas about issues that women in management face.

Work is a social experience. Employees interact while performing job duties in offices, factories, stores, and other workplaces. Friendships emerge naturally from these contacts. Informal groups sharing mutual interests fill important social needs. In earlier

## [PROGRESS] ✓questions

5. Explain the six most common types of interviews.
6. What is the halo effect?
7. What five things should you do to increase the effectiveness of the interviewing process?
8. "Terminations should only be made as a last resort." Do you agree with this statement? Why or why not?

STAYING CONFIDENTIAL

The company for which you are working is about to be restructured. Everyone knows that there will be some layoffs. You work for the director of human resources and have access to confidential information about the restructure, including the names of those scheduled to be laid off.

One day at lunch, a colleague mentions that her boss is about to take on a heavy debt in order buy a new house. It seems that he needs the space as his wife is due to have a third child in a few months' time.

You recognize the name as someone who has been identified to be let go.

ETHICAL
MANAGEMENT
What do you do when you know who's getting fired?


What are your choices here? Should you give this information to the director of human resources? Should you tell your colleague's boss before he buys the bigger house?

*Source:* "Ethical Dilemmas: St. James Ethics Centre," www.ethics.org.au.

centuries, such groups as extended families, churches, and small towns met these needs. Today, people socialize mostly with people they meet at work.

Informal work groups affect productivity, the morale of other employees, and the success of managers. They can be the result of—and can help create—a shared sense of loyalty. This is especially prevalent in high-risk occupations, such as firefighting and police work.

Informal work groups often develop in areas where employees work closely together (such as offices with cubicles) and among employees in the same field (such as accounting or graphic design). Employees may band together to share fears or complaints. In such cases, informal groups work against organization goals.

Studies have identified the power of informal work groups in organizations. The Hawthorne studies discovered that groups may set their own productivity levels and pressure workers to meet them. In one group, workers who produced more or less than the acceptable levels met with name-calling, sarcasm, ridicule, and, in some cases, a blow on the arm. The Hawthorne studies concluded that informal organizations with their own social systems exist within formal organizations.

In general, management does not recognize informal groups that revolve around friendships, interests, or shared working space and tasks. Yet an understanding of these groups can improve managers' work with formal groups. Employees join informal groups to meet a social need. They often gain great satisfaction from informal groups. Managers seek to duplicate this satisfaction in formal work groups.

**Group Norms** The informal rules a group adopts to regulate the behavior of group members.

## GROUP NORMS

**Group norms** are the informal rules a group adopts to regulate the behavior of group members. They may be extremely simple—a group that lunches together may maintain a rigid seating order. They may include expectations that group members will remain loyal to each other under any circumstances. Whatever the norms, group members are expected to hold to them. Members who break the rules often are shut out.

Norms don't govern every action in a group, only those important for group survival. For instance, a working group's norms would affect its productivity levels, operating procedures, and other work-related activities. Norms may not be written down or even spoken. Rather, group members use their actions to show new members how to behave.[4]

## GROUP BEHAVIOR

Think about the informal groups of friends and classmates you have belonged to at school or in your neighborhood. However they develop, informal work groups share similar types of behaviors. They include cohesiveness, conformity, and groupthink.

**Group Cohesiveness** **Group cohesiveness** is the degree of attraction among group members, or how tightly knit a group is. The more cohesive a group, the more likely members follow group norms. A number of factors affect the cohesiveness of informal work groups: size, success, status, outside pressures, stability of membership, communication, and physical isolation.[5]

Size is a particularly important factor in group cohesiveness. The smaller the group, the more cohesive it is likely to be. A small group allows individual members to interact frequently. Members of large groups have fewer chances to interact; therefore, these groups tend to be less cohesive.

Think about how two close friends operate when they study together. Because they know each other well and talk easily, they have no trouble working together. Now imagine three new people in the study session. Everyone might not agree on the best way to cover material. It may be hard to work with different people. This might cause the study group to fall apart.

Success and status affect group cohesiveness. The more success a group experiences, the more cohesive it becomes. Several factors contribute to a group's status. For instance, highly skilled work groups tend to have more status than less skilled groups. Like groups that meet their goals, high-status groups tend to be more cohesive than other informal work groups. These relationships are circular—success and status bring about cohesiveness, and cohesiveness brings about status and success.

Outside pressures, such as conflicts with management, can increase group cohesiveness. If a group sees management's requests as a demand or threat, it becomes more cohesive. In these situations, members may develop an "us against them" mentality.

A stable membership and easy lines of communication improve group cohesiveness. Long-standing members know each other well and are familiar with group norms. Employees who work in the same area socialize easily. In a production line, however, conversation is difficult and groups are less cohesive.

Finally, physical isolation from other employees may increase group cohesiveness. The isolation forces workers into close contact with each other and strengthens bonds.

**Group Conformity** **Group conformity** is the degree to which group members accept and follow group norms. A group generally seeks to control members' behavior for two reasons. First, independent behavior can cause disagreements that threaten a group's survival. Second, consistent behavior creates an atmosphere of trust that allows members to work together and socialize comfortably. Members are able to predict how others in the group will behave.

**Group Cohesiveness** The degree of attraction among group members, or how tightly knit a group is.

**Group Conformity** The degree to which group members accept and follow group norms.

Individual members tend to conform to group norms under certain conditions:

- Group norms are similar to personal attitudes, beliefs, and behavior.
- They do not agree with the group's norms but feel pressure to accept them.
- The rewards for complying are valued, or the sanctions imposed for noncompliance are devalued.

**Group Pressure and Conformity** Researchers have studied the influence of group pressure on individual members. One study of group conformity took place at a textile firm in Virginia.[6] A textile employee began to produce more than the group norm of 50 units per day. After two weeks, the group started to pressure this worker to produce less, and she quickly dropped to the group's level. After three weeks, all the members of the group were moved to other jobs except for this worker. Once again, her production quickly climbed to double the group norm (see Figure 8.4).

**Groupthink** When group members lose their ability to think as individuals and conform at the

**Figure 8.4 • Effect of Group Norms on a Member's Productivity**

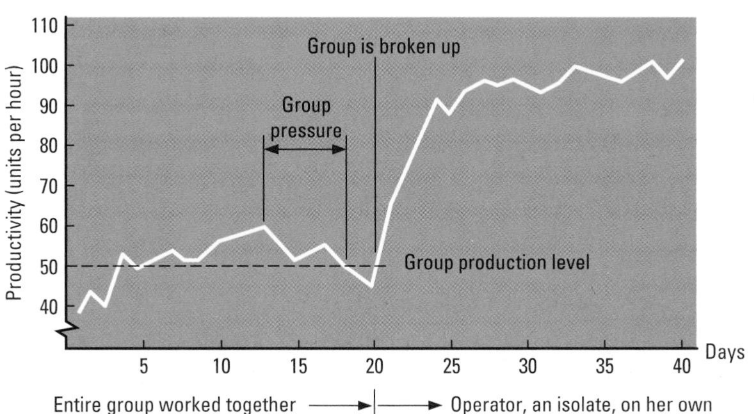

**Groupthink** Group members losing their ability to think as individuals and conforming at the expense of their good judgment.

**Linchpin Concept** Concept that managers are members of overlapping groups and link formal work groups to the total organization.

expense of their good judgment, **groupthink** occurs. Members become unwilling to say anything against the group or any member, even if an action is wrong.

Keeping a group together under any circumstance is a goal in itself. Groups with this goal believe that the group is indestructible and always right. Group members justify any action, stereotype outsiders as enemies of the group, and pressure unwilling members to conform. In business, groupthink is disruptive because it affects employees' ability to make logical decisions.[7]

## PROGRESS ✓questions

9. What are group norms?
10. What are the differences between formal and informal work groups?
11. What is the difference between group cohesiveness and groupthink?
12. Consider a group you work with in the organization you either currently work for or have worked for in the past. How would you describe the norms of that group? Explain.

*A group's ability or inability to work as a unit is key to any company's success. How can you be a team player?*

## THE IMPORTANCE OF TEAMS

Teams play an important part in helping an organization meet its goals. Groups have more knowledge and information than individuals. They make communicating and solving problems easier. This creates a more efficient and effective company.

The importance of managing groups effectively is becoming recognized in the business world. Employees must work closely to improve production and maintain a competitive edge. Changes in the workforce are bringing men and women from different backgrounds together. Managers must work with groups to overcome cultural and gender differences. These, and other factors, make managing work groups one of management's most important tasks.

## INFLUENCING WORK GROUPS

Studies at the Hawthorne plant, where researchers documented the existence of informal work groups, looked at the effects of various changes on workers' productivity. Researchers varied job factors, including the way workers were paid and supervised, lighting, the length of rest periods, and the number of hours worked. Productivity rose with each change.

This result led to the coining of the term *Hawthorne effect*. As you may remember from Chapter 1, the Hawthorne effect states that giving special attention to a group of employees changes the employees' behavior. The results of the studies show that when groups of employees are singled out for attention, they tend to work more efficiently.

## BUILDING EFFECTIVE TEAMS

Members of informal work groups often develop a shared sense of values and group loyalty. Formal groups rarely share these qualities because they are assigned rather than voluntary. Managers are responsible for developing shared values and group loyalty in formal work groups.

## Figure 8.5 • Linchpin Concept

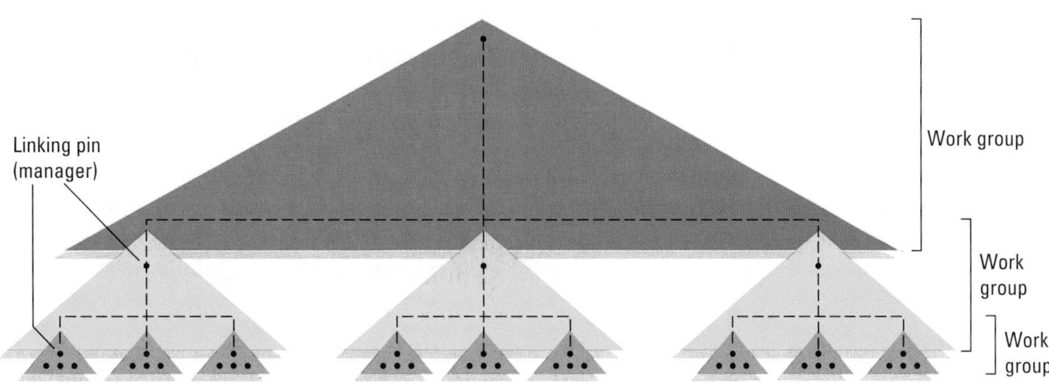


**From the** PERSPECTIVE OF...

**A Jury Foreperson** Our legal system is built on cases being decided by "a jury of your peers." As the foreperson of a group of 11 complete strangers, what challenges would you face in helping this new team arrive at a verdict?

The Linchpin concept is one way of describing management's role in work groups. The **Linchpin concept** holds that because managers are members of overlapping groups, they link formal work groups to the total organization. Managers improve communication and ensure that organizational and group goals are met. In other words, managers themselves are the linchpins (see Figure 8.5).

Building effective formal work groups often is called team building. **Team building** is the process of establishing a cohesive group that works together to achieve its goals.[8] A team will be successful only if its members feel that working conditions are fair to all. A team can fail, even in a supportive organization, if a manager does not encourage fair play.

The success of a group or team can be measured in the same way as the success of an organization. Successful organizations and groups meet their goals by using their resources well. Managers encourage teamwork by selecting group members carefully, creating a positive work environment, building trust, and increasing group cohesiveness. Figure 8.6 describes three steps to use in building productive teams.

### CREATING GROUPS

**Team Building** The process of establishing a cohesive group that works together to achieve its goals.

For a group to succeed, members must be able to perform the tasks assigned by management. Selecting the right individuals is key to the success of a group. The first step is to identify qualified people. Then management must make the group attractive to these individuals.

For most employees, a formal work group is attractive because it increases pay and offers some satisfaction. If employees see that joining a formal group can provide them with the same satisfaction that an informal group can, they are more likely to participate willingly.

Environment also can be important to the success of a group. An important requirement for meeting group goals is a suitable place to work. How the office is laid out and other physical factors will affect the group's ability to work together successfully.

## Figure 8.6 • Steps for Building Productive Teams

1. **Selecting Individuals**
   The first step in building an effective team is finding the right people. Group members need to have the right skills and the right personality fit.
2. **Building Trust**
   The second step is to build trust among group members and between the group and management.
3. **Encouraging Group Cohesiveness**
   Managers can improve group cohesiveness by keeping groups small, giving them clear goals, and rewarding them as a team.

Study Alert

The less time that a manager devotes to staffing a team and preparing its members to complete the project to which they are assigned, the more time gets used up in the forming and storming phases of development. The performing phase is the most productive stage of a team project, but without adequate training and preparation, it can take hours or even weeks of frustrating meetings to get there.

## BUILDING TRUST

Trust is essential among group members and between groups and management. A successful group effort means sharing responsibilities and making decisions together. Group members must feel that the entire group is willing and able to work together successfully to achieve goals. Without trust, groups can't set or stick to production norms.

Managers must have faith in their employees. They also must recognize the interests of the organization, the group, and the employees. Effective managers should become personally involved, take a real interest in group members, share information, and exhibit honesty.

## INFLUENCING GROUP COHESIVENESS AND CONFORMITY

Think about teams you have belonged to at school or summer camp. These successful teams often are highly competitive and eager to succeed. Effective work groups share these characteristics. Both types of groups also draw their primary satisfaction from a sense of accomplishment, which comes from a job well done.

Managers can affect formal group performance levels by studying the degree of group conformity. Formal groups must be cohesive and dedicated to high-performance norms in order to succeed. Managers can influence group cohesiveness by:

- Keeping groups small.
- Selecting group members carefully.
- Finding a good personality fit between new and old employees.
- Developing an office layout that improves communication.
- Creating clear goals.
- Inspiring group competition.
- Rewarding groups rather than individuals.
- Isolating groups from each other.

High individual performance with poor team performance is not what winning is about, either in sports or in business. Individuals must surrender their egos so that the end result is bigger than the sum of its parts. When this happens, the team works together like fingers on a hand.

## PHASES IN THE LIFE OF TEAMS

Effective work teams go through four phases of development: forming, storming, norming, and performing. Phase one *(forming)* occurs when the team members first come together. Uncertainty and anxiety are common feelings that members of the team experience. Therefore, the focus of the forming phase is for members of the team to get to know each other and have their questions answered. Phase two *(storming)* often involves a period of disagreement and intense discussion as members attempt to impose their individual viewpoints on the rest of the group. In phase three *(norming)*, the team develops the informal rules that enable it to regulate the behavior of the team members. In phase four *(performing)*, the team becomes an effective and high-performing team only if it has gone through the three previous phases.

## QUALITY CIRCLES

One type of formal work group is the quality circle. A *quality circle* is a group of employees, usually from 5 to 15 people, from a single work unit (such as a department) who share ideas on how to improve quality. The goal of a quality circle is to involve employees in decision making. Membership is almost always voluntary, and members share a common bond—they perform similar tasks.

Japan has used quality circles since the early 1960s. The idea arrived in the United States after executives from Lockheed Corporation visited Japan in the 1970s and saw the circles in action. Lockheed used quality circles to improve quality and save several million dollars.

Quality circles have benefits other than increasing employee participation.[9] They encourage communication and trust among members and managers. They are an inexpensive way to provide employees with training while giving them a sense of control over their work lives. Most important, however, they may solve problems that have been around for years. Quality circles create strong lines of communication. "Me" becomes "us" in a good quality circle.

## SELF-DIRECTED WORK TEAMS

Another type of formal work group is the *self-directed work team (SDWT)*. SDWTs are empowered to control the work they do without a formal supervisor.

Each SDWT has a leader who normally comes from the employees on the team. Most of these teams plan and schedule their work, make operational and personnel decisions, solve problems, set priorities, determine which employee does which work, and share leadership responsibilities.

### VIRTUAL WORK TEAMS

Virtual work teams were largely nonexistent a decade ago. Today, globalization, technology, and fast responses to customer needs have led organizations to establish virtual work teams. Virtual work teams are responsible for making or implementing important decisions for the business, mainly using technology-supported communication, with the team members working and living in different locations. It is likely that this form of work team over time will be more widely used.

13. Explain the Hawthorne effect.
14. List six ways in which managers can influence group cohesiveness.
15. Discuss the challenges in each of the four phases of development for effective work teams.
16. Explain the difference between a quality circle and a self-directed work team.

## >> Groups and Leaders

When an informal group selects a leader, members choose the person most capable of satisfying the group's needs. The group gives this leader authority and can take the authority away at any time. This leader needs strong communication skills, especially in setting objectives for the group, giving directions, and summarizing information.

To see how informal groups choose leaders, imagine a group of people shipwrecked on an island. The group's first goal is to find food, water, and shelter. The individual best equipped to help the group survive would naturally become the leader. Later, the group's goal might change to getting off the island. The original leader may no longer be the best person to help meet the new goal, and a new leader could emerge. The process may continue through several leaders.

### GAINING ACCEPTANCE

Managers assigned to formal work groups must work to gain acceptance as leaders. They generally do not have the same authority as leaders of informal groups. The formal authority granted by top management is no guarantee that a manager will effectively guide a group.

Think about how you respond to your teachers. You respect teachers who know their subject well, communicate information effectively, treat students with respect, and make fair judgments. Managers working with formal groups can use these same behaviors to gain the trust and respect of employees.

Managers must keep track of the changes within the organization that might affect the group. At times, they may have to modify group goals to meet new organizational goals. For example, an organization faced with strong competition may need to make decisions rapidly rather than rely on groups to come up with a solution. In these cases, managers must be ready to make immediate decisions for the group.

### ENCOURAGING PARTICIPATION

Building an effective team requires a nontraditional managerial approach. In a traditional organizational structure, managers direct the employees who work for them. As part of a team, however, managers encourage participation and share responsibility, acting more like a coach than a manager.

One way of encouraging team spirit is to provide the group with a vision. People who organize groups to support social causes often use this approach. For example, one person may rally a community around a project such as reclaiming a vacant lot for a park. In the business

## Thinking Critically 8.2

### >> Who is Telling the Truth?

Amanda Demuth manages a large retail store. She oversees a team that exceeds 30 employees and department managers. On Saturday mornings, she leads a shift meeting that meets near the store deli. Amanda leaves a standing order with her third shift deli leader to prepare doughnuts, coffee, and fresh fruit for these Saturday meetings. This meeting is part of the store culture; both associates and managers look forward to the meeting as a way to bond.

The deli that puts together the breakfast is made up of a small crew that works the third shift. The Friday night shift is made up of only two people, the deli leader and her assistant. The deli leader, Beverly Byrd, has worked at the store for a number of years and has a spotless work record. In fact, she volunteered to take over the third shift duties when the former leader retired. Guy Ashley is Beverly's assistant, and he is not a model employee. He has been disciplined on a number of occasions for tardiness and disrespectful behavior toward management.

Just before the latest meeting, Guy makes an announcement that causes a stir. He states that Beverly had left the restroom without washing her hands on several occasions during the third shift. Beverly immediately denies Guy's accusation.

**QUESTIONS**

1. If you were Amanda, what would be your immediate response to the situation?
2. What could be Guy's motivation for making such a statement?
3. After the meeting, what would you say to Beverly?
4. In this situation, what is the danger in making assumptions about who is telling the truth?

world, managers can offer team members the possibility of designing a state-of-the-art product or service.

Managers lead by example. Their attitude and performance become the standard for group norms. A manager who believes that a group must listen to and support all members might create a group of top managers who share this feeling. Employees who see managers functioning within a cohesive group are more likely to work effectively in groups themselves.

## >> Summary

Once management has identified and categorized the jobs to be performed in the organization and then developed an organization structure for the performance of those jobs, the next task is to hire and develop the people who will fill the jobs. In this chapter we have reviewed the importance of a carefully managed hiring process with detailed skills inventory (to determine the resources on hand and the positions to be filled) and a thorough interview process (to identify the best candidates from the applicant pool). In addition, we have considered the challenge for managers in hiring individuals who will ultimately work as a team within the organization, either within a specific department or as a group assigned to a specific project. In the next chapter we examine the importance of leadership as it relates to management and review the importance of an organizational culture that supports an environment in which effective management can take place.

1. Outline the human resource planning process.

   Human resource planning involves getting the right number of qualified people into the right job at the right time. As the term implies, the organization's supply of human resources (people)—internally (existing employees) and externally (those to be hired)—must be matched with the openings the organization expects to have for a given time frame.

   The first basic question addressed by the planning process is, Where are we now? By utilizing job analysis and skills inventories, the organization can assess its current human resource capability. When this information is compared to strategic plans and objectives, a forecast of future human resource needs can be calculated and a plan to recruit (or downsize) can be put into operation.

   With any planning process, there must be ongoing monitoring of key objectives to ensure that plan goals are met appropriately.

2. Define *job analysis, job description, job specification,* and *skills inventory.*
   - *Job analysis.* The process of determining, through observation and study, the relevant information relating to the nature of a specific job. The end products of a job analysis are a job description and a job specification.
   - *Job description.* A written statement that identifies the tasks, duties, activities, and performance results required in a particular job.
   - *Job specification.* A written statement that identifies the abilities, skills, traits, or attributes necessary for successful performance in a particular job.
   - *Skills inventory.* A detailed assessment of the organization's current human resources.

3. Distinguish between different types of employment interviews.
   - *Structured interview.* The interviewer uses a predetermined outline to gather the same type of information gathered on all interviewees, allowing systematic coverage of all questions deemed relevant to the job opening by the organization. The use of a structured interview tends to increase reliability and accuracy by minimizing interviewer improvisation.
   - *Semistructured interview.* An interviewer prepares the relevant questions in advance but also has the flexibility to probe interviewee responses with follow-up questions in order to assess the applicant's strengths and weaknesses. The option of follow-up questions requires that the interviewer be sufficiently trained to avoid any interview bias.
   - *Situational interview.* Rather than answering a list of questions, an interviewee is presented with a potential situation that might arise in the position for which he or she is applying. For example, an interviewer might want to see how the applicant would handle a customer complaint. Here again, the flexibility at the disposal of the interviewer demands appropriate training to avoid any interview bias.
   - *Unstructured interview.* No predetermined questions are prepared, and questions in the interview tend to be open-ended, such as, "Tell me where you see yourself in five years." While providing a more relaxed environment, unstructured interviews tend to be weak on systematic coverage of information and represent the highest risk of interview bias.
   - *Stress interview.* An interviewer will adopt a hostile attitude in the interview in order to detect how well the interviewee handles emotion.
   - *Board or panel interview.* Two or more interviewers conduct the interview. This type of interview is used if the position will report to more than one individual or if there is a concern that the applicant should be a good fit for the team.

*Continued on next page*

Continued from page 189

- *Group interview.* Several candidates are interviewed together in a group discussion, in either a structured or unstructured format—often as a means of identifying the finalists who will progress to individual interviews.

4. Explain formal and informal work groups.

   Formal work groups are established by management to carry out specific tasks, such as resolution of a process problem or designing a new product, service, or sales campaign. Since they are most often project-driven, formal groups may exist for a short or long period of time.

   Informal work groups are formed voluntarily by members of an organization. They develop from personal contacts and interactions among people. Groups of employees who lunch together regularly and office cliques are examples of informal work groups.

   Informal work groups affect productivity, the morale of other employees, and the success of managers. They can be the result of—and can help create—a shared sense of loyalty. This is especially prevalent in high-risk occupations, such as firefighting and police work. Informal work groups often develop in areas where employees work close together (such as offices with cubicles) and among employees in the same field (such as accounting or graphic design). Employees may band together to share fears or complaints. In such cases, informal groups work against organization goals.

5. Define *groupthink.*

   Groupthink occurs when group members lose their ability to think as individuals and conform at the expense of good judgment—members become unwilling to say anything against the group or any individual member, even if an action is wrong.

6. Discuss the concept of team building.

   Team building is the process of establishing a cohesive group that works together to achieve its goals. A team will be successful only if its members feel that working conditions are fair to all. A team can fail, even in a supportive organization, if a manager does not encourage fair play. The success of a group or team can be measured in the same way as the success of an organization. Successful organizations and groups meet their goals by using their resources well. Managers encourage teamwork by selecting group members carefully, creating a positive work environment, building trust, and increasing group cohesiveness.

**THE TACO BARN SURVIVES THE EXPERIMENT**
***(continued from page 171)***

When the two weeks were up, Kevin and his crew asked for an opportunity to present their ideas to Tony. They handed in not just a written report but a formal business presentation with PowerPoint slides and handouts supporting the business case for their ideas in considerable detail. Tony had to admit, he was impressed before he had even heard what they had to say.

The presentation took about 30 minutes, and everyone took part. They explained how they had come up with their ideas, where they had done the research to support their proposal, and how they had arrived at their final recommendations including proposed costs and potential savings to be achieved. Tony guessed that Kevin had told them that showing the material to Dawn would be the next step in the process, because their handouts had obviously been prepared with that end in mind—charts, spreadsheets, numbers, and all the supporting material.

At the end of the presentation Tony was so impressed that the only fitting response for him was to stand up and applaud his crew. The look of surprise and pride on their faces was priceless, and it took a moment for them to get over the shock. Then chaos broke out, and everyone started screaming and shouting about how nervous they had been, how uncertain they had been that he would like their ideas, and how much they appreciated the chance to do this, even if Dawn didn't take any of their suggestions.

Tony gave them a few minutes to blow off some steam, and then he spoke: "You have done a wonderful job here guys. I am really impressed with your creativity and your attention to detail. You've redesigned our ordering and modified the storeroom layout to make the deliveries easier. You've even worked out a better way to incorporate vendor specials into our menu that has the potential to save us a lot of money. I think Dawn is really going to be interested in that one."

Tony paused as the energy level bubbled over again. "So what other ideas do you and your team have, Kevin?"

**QUESTIONS**

1. Why didn't Tony come up with all these ideas? If they were obvious to his crew, surely they should have been obvious to him as the unit manager?
2. How do you think this project will change the atmosphere at Tony's Taco Barn?
3. Do you think Dawn will adopt some of these ideas? Why or why not?
4. Would you want the opportunity to be involved in a project like this? Why or why not?

## Key Terms >>

**aptitude tests 176**
**board (panel) interview 178**
**employee leasing companies 175**
**formal work groups 181**
**groupthink 184**
**group cohesiveness 183**
**group conformity 183**
**group interview 178**
**group norms 182**
**halo effect 179**
**human resource forecasting 173**
**human resource planning (HRP) 173**
**informal work groups 181**
**interest tests 176**
**job analysis 172**
**job description 172**
**job knowledge tests 176**
**job specification 172**
**linchpin concept 184**
**polygraph tests 176**
**proficiency tests 176**
**psychological tests 176**
**psychomotor tests 176**
**recruitment 174**
**semistructured interview 177**
**situational interview 178**
**skills inventory 172**
**stress interview 178**
**structured interview 177**
**team building 185**
**temporary help 175**
**tests 176**
**test reliability 177**
**test validity 177**
**unstructured interviews 178**

1. Describe the relationship between job analysis, skills inventory, and human resource planning.
2. Discuss some common pitfalls in interviewing.
3. Which is better, a structured interview or an unstructured one? Why?
4. Outline the conditions under which individual members of a group tend to conform to group norms.
5. Of the four phases of team development, which is the most important to the organization?
6. Discuss the advantages and disadvantages of virtual teams.

## INTERNET In Action >>

1. Research the term *skills inventory* on the Web. Identify tools, templates, and/or vendor organizations that could be utilized to help your organization implement a comprehensive employee skills assessment as part of an overall strategic HR plan.
2. Your company is moving to a new state to take advantage of growth opportunities and attractive tax incentives. You have been asked to work with HR to research the advantages and disadvantages of offering employee relocation packages. You must determine which options are available to offer to key personnel. Use Web-based research to identify tools, templates, and potential costs to the organization (both financial and employee relations).

**1. The Layoff**

Two years ago, your organization experienced a sudden increase in its volume of work. At about the same time, it was threatened with an equal employment opportunity suit that resulted in an affirmative action plan. Under this plan, additional women and minority members have been recruited and hired.

Presently, the top level of management in your organization is anticipating a decrease in volume of work. You have been asked to rank the clerical employees of your section in the event a layoff is necessary.

Below you will find biographical data for the seven clerical people in your section. Divide into two groups. Each group must rank the seven people according to the order in which they should be laid off; that is, the person ranked first is to be laid off first and so on. Each group will then present its rankings back to their peers, along with the justification for the assigned ranking of each employee.

*Burt Green:* White male, age 45. Married, four children; five years with the organization. Reputed to be an alcoholic; poor work record.

*Nan Nushka:* White female, age 26. Married, no children; husband has a steady job; six months with the organization. Hired after the affirmative action plan went into effect; average work record to date. Saving to buy a house.

*Johnny Jones:* Black male, age 20. Unmarried; one year with organization. High-performance ratings. Reputed to be shy—a "loner"; wants to start his own business some day.

*Joe Jefferson:* White male, age 24. Married, no children but wife is pregnant; three years with organization. Going to college at night; erratic performance attributed to work-study conflicts.

*Livonia Long:* Black female, age 49. Widow, three grown children; two years with the organization. Steady worker whose performance is average.

*Ward Watt:* White male, age 30. Recently divorced, one child; three years with the organization. Good worker.

*Rosa Sanchez:* Hispanic female, age 45. Six children; husband disabled one year ago; trying to help support her family; three months with the organization. No performance appraisal data available.

**Questions**

1. Which criteria did you use for ranking the employees?
2. What implications does your ranking have in the area of affirmative action?
3. How hard was it to reach consensus as a group in this exercise?
4. How would you feel if you were ranked in your organization in the same manner?

2. **The Life of a Team**

Divide into groups of four. Divide the four phases of team development—forming, storming, norming, and performing—between the group. Decide on a project for the team to work on. Based on that project, develop a plan to minimize the amount of productive time lost in the first three phases so that the team can start performing as quickly as possible. Time permitting, prepare a brief presentation to your fellow students on your proposal.

# Case 8.1

## >> NASA's Cultural Curse

When the space shuttle *Challenger* exploded 73 seconds after liftoff on the morning of January 28, 1986, the nation was shocked at the death of seven crew members, including high school teacher Christa McAuliffe. The official enquiry into the *Challenger* disaster by the Rogers Commission attributed the cause of the explosion to a malfunctioning O-ring seal on one of the solid rocket boosters (SRB). The commission also made note of "a serious flaw in the decision-making process leading up to the launch." Investigations revealed that concerns about the performance of the O-rings had been circulating within the space agency for months before the accident, but "NASA appeared to be requiring a contractor to prove that it was not safe to launch rather than proving it was safe."

*Continued on next page*

Continued from page 193

By the morning of January 28, the *Challenger* launch had been postponed (scrubbed) twice for weather concerns and equipment malfunctions. With unusually low temperatures forecast for the morning of the launch, engineers for Rockwell International, the prime contractor for the shuttle program, raised concerns about ice buildup on the SRBs, as did engineers for Morton Thiokol, the contractors responsible for the construction and maintenance of those SRBs. However, pressure to launch led NASA engineers to decide that secondary O-ring seals would engage if there were any problems with the first set of seals, and the launch proceeded with catastrophic results.

Seventeen years later, on Saturday, February 1, 2003, all seven members of the crew of the space shuttle *Columbia* died in an explosion over Texas upon reentering earth's atmosphere, just 16 minutes before the shuttle was due to land at Cape Canaveral in Florida.

In August 2003, the final conclusions of the Columbia Accident Investigation Board (CAIB)—based on the review of 30,000 documents and 200 formal interviews—attributed the cause of the explosion to a 10-inch hole in the shuttle's heat shield caused by a piece of insulating foam that broke off the external fuel tank shortly after takeoff. The hole in the heat shield in the shuttle's left wing caused the wing to melt upon reentry.

Seventeen years later, on Saturday, February 1, 2003, all seven members of the crew of the space shuttle Columbia died in an explosion over Texas upon reentering earth's atmosphere, just 16 minutes before the shuttle was due to land at Cape Canaveral in Florida.

The tragedy of a second shuttle disaster was worsened by overwhelming evidence that NASA managers were made aware of the loss of the insulating foam during takeoff at the beginning of the 16-day mission. Engineer requests to reposition spy satellites in order to get photographs of the extent of the damage were denied. Proposals to have the *Columbia's* sister shuttle *Atlantis* prepared for a rescue mission—in case the foam damage might prevent *Columbia* from returning safely—were also overruled.

Interview transcripts from the CAIB indicate that NASA management was perceived as being complacent about mission safety, with an operational attitude of "invulnerability." The pressure to keep the mission schedule on track appeared to carry a greater priority than making the tough judgment calls that might result in another launch delay. Interviews with engineers as well as administrative personnel from contractors noted the same belief that managers were more concerned about adherence to political pressure than raising any issues that might rock the boat. Lower-level engineers responded to this environment by making initial attempts to raise concerns but then conceding to managers in order to preserve their jobs.

When we compare the two tragedies, separated by 17 years and two separate third-party investigations, the similarity of issues is disheartening. Critics have argued that NASA appeared to learn very little from the *Challenger* disaster and that the price paid for that complacency and adherence to a groupthink mentality came with the *Columbia* disaster.

## QUESTIONS

1. What evidence of groupthink at NASA is offered in this article?
2. Why would managers be unwilling to listen to engineers?
3. Explain the phrase "adherence to political pressure."
4. What lessons should NASA managers seek to learn from these two tragic events?

*Source:* "The Future of NASA: Lost in Space," *The Economist,* August 28, 2003; John Schwartz and Matthew L. Wald, "Space Agency Culture Comes under Scrutiny," *The New York Times,* March 29, 2003; John Schwartz and Matthew L. Wald, "The Nation: NASA's Curse? 'Groupthink' Is 30 Years Old, and Still Going Strong," *The New York Times,* March 9, 2003; Claire Ferraris and Rodney Carveth, "NASA and the Columbia Disaster: Decision-Making by Groupthink?" Association for Business Communication, 2003 Convention, http://bama.ua.edu/~sprentic/672%20Ferraris%20&%20Carveth.pdf.

# Case 8.2

## >> The Promise of ROWE • ROWE takes flexible working practices to the extreme.

Imagine working in a job where you are empowered to work whenever and wherever you want with no hassle from your boss as long as the work gets done. For most of us, such fantasies are the stuff of daydreams on an afternoon coffee break on the Monday of yet another endless week of mind-numbing work. With ID badges tracking your every move and micromanagers demanding visibility at all times to ensure that you aren't slacking off somewhere, the thought of being trusted enough to act in the best interests of the organization and get the job done is strange to the point of being ridiculous.

However, there are a few organizations out there that have been crazy enough to give this idea a try. Electronics retailer Best Buy is credited with the first pilot project, and its name for the pilot has become the accepted term—ROWE, or results-only work environment—that supporters praise as "a radical experiment whose aim is to reshape the corporate workplace, achieve an unparalleled degree of work/life balance and redefine the very nature of work itself."

The basic premise of ROWE is that organizations change their approach to work. Instead of such nonproductive activities as commuting to and from the office; being visible in meetings with the right people; and managing your personal and vacation time to the hour in order to schedule doctor's appointments, parent-teacher conferences, school plays, and kids stricken with a flu bug, ROWE shifts the focus to the work itself. In other words, it's about *how* the work gets done rather than *where* or *when.*

While there are documented benefits to employees in this arrangement—better relationships with family and friends, increased loyalty to the company, and feeling more energized and focused at work—there is also a financial payoff to the organization. Increased loyalty reduces absenteeism, tardiness, and turnover. With an estimated per-employee turnover cost of $102,000 at Best Buy, it is estimated that once everyone in the 4,000-person headquarters made the transition over to the ROWE plan, the company was saving $13 million a year in replacement costs, in addition to an estimated increase in productivity of 35 percent from happier, less stressed employees.

In 2008, Gap Outlet, a division of clothing retailer Gap, Inc., in San Francisco, California, piloted a ROWE plan for "137 headquarters employees and executives in merchandising, design, production, finance, HR and IT." Like Best Buy, retail employees were not eligible to participate since stores need employees to be present to serve customers.

The company had already taken incremental steps toward work-life balance with no-meeting Friday afternoons, seminars on conducting meetings effectively, and laptops distributed so employees could work from home. ROWE seemed to be the next logical step. As Eric Severson, vice president of HR, commented: "We are in one of the worst commute cities and in one of the most expensive cities to live." In addition: "We have a 76 percent female workforce with an average age of 34." With an employee demographic greatly in need of workplace flexibility, Gap Outlet gave the pilot a year to produce results. In February 2009, a postpilot

*Continued on next page*

Continued from page 195

assessment documented a 21 percent increase in productivity and a 15 percent improvement in quality. As with the Best Buy pilot, turnover fell significantly—down 18 percent over 2008.

So if the numbers are there to back it up, why are so few companies willing to consider ROWE? Most managers seem to adhere to the old adage, "If you give them an inch, they'll take a mile." In other words, they fear that employees will run away and never show up for work. As a result, organizations have dabbled in flexible work arrangements (e.g., telecommuting, adjusting work schedules, and casual dress codes), but the fundamental expectation of documenting an eight- or nine-hour day doesn't change.

Best Buy is piloting a results-only work environment, described as 'a radical experiment whose aim is to reshape the corporate workplace, achieve an unparalleled degree of work/life balance and redefine the very nature of work itself'

The thought of an employee with enough autonomy to unplug his laptop and go fishing on a sunny afternoon or taking a conference call from the park is still too much of a culture shock for most. It seems that organizations are willing to leverage operational advantages from technology (Web conferences or company-issued Blackberrys so you are always reachable), but turning that around and granting employees some work-life balance with that same technology is asking too much for now.

**QUESTIONS**

1. Why would Best Buy and Gap Outlet consider such a radical employment policy?
2. What are the potential benefits and drawbacks of a ROWE program?
3. Consider your current job (or one you have held in the past). Would this kind of program work there? Why or why not?
4. Do you think such employment flexibility would improve your productivity and morale? Explain your answer.

*Source:* Michelle Conlin, "Smashing the Clock," BusinessWeek Online, December 11, 2006; Patrick J. Kiger, "Throwing Out the Rules of Work," *Workforce,* www.workforce.com/section/09/feature/24/54/28/; Adrienne Fox, "Gap Outlet: Second Retailer Adopts Result-Only Work Environment Strategy," *Society for Human Resource Management,* September 8, 2009.

# Case 8.3

## >> The "Gift of Time"

Proponents of employee wellness programs argue that healthy employees are productive, dedicated to the long-term success of the organization, and remain loyal to companies that show a broader interest in their overall well-being. Pragmatic financial analysts will also point out that the active promotion of wellness programs—specifically weight loss, exercise, quitting smoking, and counseling or therapeutic services—can equate to a sizable reduction in health insurance premiums for the organization.

However, research from the Corporate Executive Board (CEB) has shown that the provision of these wellness programs can be an inefficient use of resources when only 20 percent of employees take advantage of them. Having the services available offers a reassurance to employees, but numbers-driven organizations track utilization of those services as the indicator of success when in fact what employees would respond to most is simply the "gift of time." In fact, of the 50,000 global employees surveyed in the CEB study, more than 60 percent identified flexible schedules as the most important work-life practice their employer could provide.

In a 2006 study, 53 percent of employees felt they had a good work-life balance. By the first quarter of 2009, that number had fallen to only 30 percent. Why the steep decline? In an economic downturn, long-term job security becomes a primary concern, and for many employees, working harder and longer hours is seen as a way of reducing the odds of getting laid off, even though layoffs are usually a numbers game of labor dollars needed to hit a specific budget goal, rather than a direct attack on targeted employees. It's ironic that in such a pressurized environment, employees avoid wellness plans that could help them cope because of the fear of appearing as if they cannot cope with stress and should therefore be added to the layoff list.

Is there a way out of this vicious cycle? Managers at SCAN Health, Capital One, and BDO Seidman would argue that there is. Each company revisited the traditional model of management seniority equating to greater office square footage and examined the true cost to the bottom line of corporate real estate. Leveraging the technological capabilities of telecommuting from home offices with laptops and the ubiquitous Blackberrys has allowed companies to drastically reduce real estate costs. Capital One estimates a 20 percent reduction, even with the provision of up to $1,000 to each home-based manager for refurbishment of home office space.

How does this affect work-life balance? Eve Gelb, a project manager at SCAN Health, traded her hour-and-a-half commute to work in Los Angeles for a walk around the neighborhood before sitting down to work in her home office—same cardio workout, less stress. And as for fears of isolation from office news and gossip? On the days she does go into the office, she is able to connect with her fellow home-based managers in shared space more than she ever did when they were locked away in their offices.

### QUESTIONS

1. If telecommuting equates to hard real estate cost savings, why don't all companies do it?
2. Do you think companies would be as supportive if there weren't a real estate cost savings? Why or why not?
3. What problems does a home-based workforce present for a manager?
4. Assume that your job would allow you to telecommute. How would you propose that idea to your boss?

*Source:* Staff of the CEB, "The Increasing Call for Work-Life Balance," *BusinessWeek,* March 27, 2009; "Vive la Différence!" *The Economist,* May 7, 2009; David Leonhardt, "Financial Careers Come at a Cost to Families," *The New York Times,* May 27, 2009; and Michelle Conlin, "Telecommuting: Once a Perk, Now a Necessity," *BusinessWeek,* February 26, 2009.

CHAPTER 9

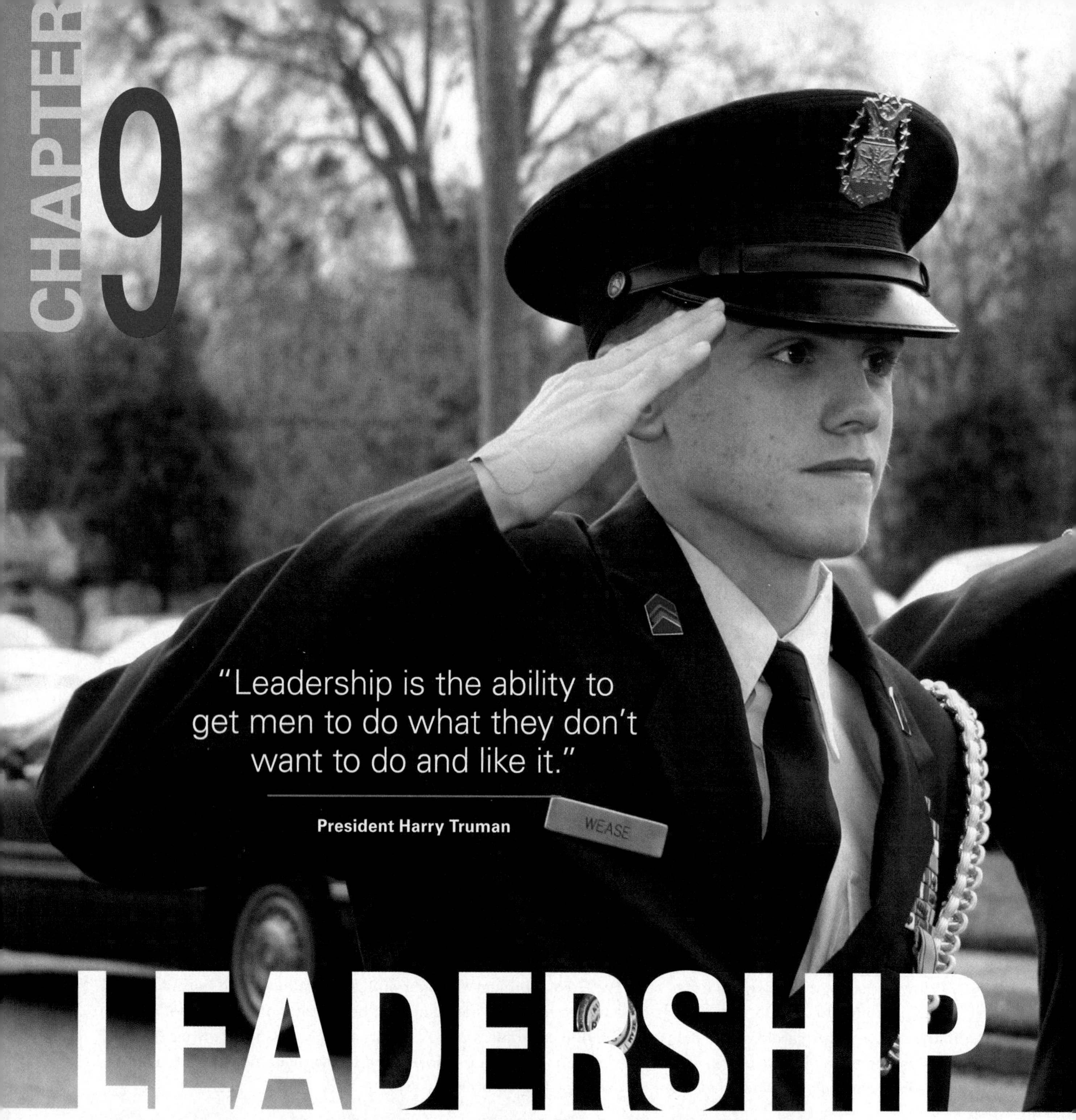

"Leadership is the ability to get men to do what they don't want to do and like it."

**President Harry Truman**

# LEADERSHIP AND CULTURE

**LEARNING OUTCOMES**

After studying this chapter, you will be able to:

1. Define *leadership, power,* and *authority.*
2. Discuss leadership as it relates to management.
3. Explain leadership attitudes.
4. Describe the differences between a Theory X and Theory Y manager.
5. Explain the differences between transactional, transformational, and charismatic leadership styles.
6. Identify strategies for effectively managing corporate culture.

## THE WORLD OF WORK Tony gets assigned to a project

Tony had put Kevin's name forward as a replacement for Tanya as shift leader at the Taco Barn. He had asked Kevin to write a report to support his application—a strategic plan for the next three to five years.

Kevin had gone above and beyond what Tony had asked by proposing the creation of an assistant manager role instead of a shift leader role, and Dawn had approved the idea as a pilot project. In fact, Dawn had been so impressed with the report idea that she asked Tony to come and see her at the regional offices.

"Tony, that idea of the strategic plan was very creative," said Dawn as they began their morning meeting.

"Thanks, Dawn—I really thought it would give Kevin a chance to show that he had some positive ideas to contribute—he's a really good team member, and with the right encouragement, I think he could go far with Taco Barn."

"Speaking of people who could go far with Taco Barn," continued Dawn, "you seem to have filled Jerry's shoes very well Tony—sales are up and your people are working well together. You've really hit the ground running."

Tony thought for a second and realized there was an opportunity here. "Thanks, Dawn. Jerry built a great crew, and he gave me some great advice before he took up his new position, "If it ain't broke, don't try to fix it", and I've tried to remember that." Tony did his best to look as serious as possible, even as the thought of his disastrous scheduling idea flashed across his mind—if only Dawn knew how close he had come to a mutiny over that one.

"Well," continued Dawn, "I think your unit is running well enough that we can pull you away for a week to work on a companywide project. What do you think?"

"Excellent," answered Tony. "My assistant unit manager can cover things, and I can check in on a regular basis if Kevin needs any help."

Dawn continued, "We're looking at developing a leadership development program for the future leaders of this organization—people like you and Kevin. We've been working with a team of consultants, and they've suggested that before we start putting the program together, we really need to survey our employees to get a sense of the type of leaders we currently have in the organization and the kind of organizational culture those leaders have created. Once we have that in place, then we can move on to looking at whether that culture and leadership style will take us to where we want to go in the future. What do you think?"

"Sounds great," responded Tony, wondering just how long the project would take and whether he could really answer those questions himself. What was his leadership style, and could he describe the culture of the Taco Barn organization?

**QUESTIONS**

1. From what you know of Tony so far, how would you describe his leadership style? Refer to pages 201 to 209 for some suggested classifications of different leadership styles.
2. How would you describe the organizational culture of Taco Barn?
3. Do you think the consultants' recommendation of an employee survey is a good idea? Why or why not?
4. List six questions that you think should be included in the survey.

# >> Power, Authority, and Leadership

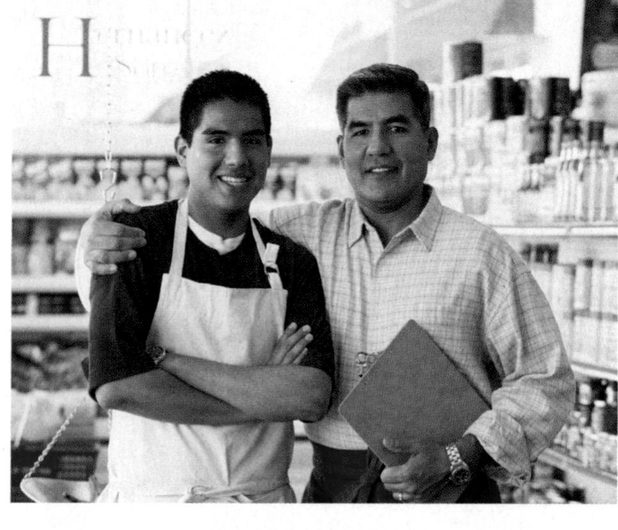

Before undertaking a study of leadership, a clear understanding must be developed of the relationships between power, authority, and leadership. **Power** is a measure of a person's potential to get others to do what he or she wants them to do, as well as to avoid being forced by others to do what he or she does not want to do. Figure 9.1 summarizes several sources of power in organizations. The use of or desire for power is often viewed negatively in our society because power is often linked to the concepts of punishment, dominance, and control.

Power can have both a positive and negative form. Positive power results when the exchange is voluntary and both parties feel good about the exchange. Negative power results when the individual is forced to change. Power in organizations can be exercised upward, downward, or horizontally. It does not necessarily follow the organizational hierarchy from top to bottom.

**Power** A measure of a person's potential to get others to do what he or she wants them to do.

**Authority** The right to issue directives and expend resources.

**Leadership** The ability to influence people to willingly follow one's guidance or adhere to one's decisions.

**Leader** A person who influences followers in setting and achieving objectives.

**Authority**, which is the right to issue directives and expend resources, is related to power but is narrower in scope. Basically, the amount of authority a manager has depends on the amount of coercive, reward, and legitimate power the manager can exert. Authority is a function of position in the organizational hierarchy, flowing from the top to the bottom of the organization. An individual can have power—expert or referent—without having formal authority. Furthermore, a manager's authority can be diminished by reducing the coercive and reward power in the position.

**Leadership** is the ability to influence people to willingly follow one's guidance or adhere to one's decisions. Obtaining followers and influencing them in setting and achieving objectives make a **leader**. Leaders use power in influencing group behavior. For instance, political leaders often use referent power. Informal leaders in organizations generally combine referent power and expert power. Some managers rely only on authority, while others use different combinations of power.

## Figure 9.1 • Sources of Power

| Organizational Sources | Basis |
|---|---|
| Reward power | Capacity to provide rewards. |
| Coercive power | Capacity to punish. |
| Legitimate power | Person's position in the organizational hierarchy. |
| **Personal Sources** | **Basis** |
| Expert power | The skill, expertise, and knowledge an individual possesses. |
| Referent power | The personal characteristics of an individual that make other people want to associate with the person. |

# >> Leadership and Management

Leadership and management are not necessarily the same but are not incompatible. Effective leadership in organizations creates a vision of the future that considers the legitimate long-term interests of the parties involved in the organization, develops a strategy for moving toward that vision, enlists the support of employees to produce the movement, and motivates employees to implement the strategy. Management is a process of planning, organizing, staffing, motivating, and controlling through the use of formal authority. In practice, effective leadership and effective management must ultimately be the same.

## >> Leader Attitudes

Douglas McGregor developed two attitude profiles, or assumptions, about the basic nature of people. These attitudes were termed *Theory X* and *Theory Y*; they are summarized in Figure 9.2. McGregor maintained that many leaders in essence subscribe to either Theory X or Theory Y and behave accordingly. A Theory X leader would likely use a much more authoritarian style of leadership than a Theory Y leader would. The real value of McGregor's work was the idea that a leader's attitude toward human nature has a large influence on how that person behaves as a leader.[1]

The relationship between a leader's expectations and the resulting performance of subordinates has received much attention. Generally, it has been found that if a manager's expectations are high, productivity is likely to be high. On the other hand, if the manager's expectations are low, productivity is likely to be poor. McGregor called this phenomenon the **self-fulfilling prophecy**.

### Figure 9.2 • Assumptions about People

**Theory X**

1. The average human being has an inherent dislike of work and will avoid it if possible.
2. Because of their dislike of work, most people must be coerced, controlled, directed, or threatened with punishment to get them to put forth adequate effort toward the achievement of organizational objectives.
3. The average human being prefers to be directed, wishes to avoid responsibility, has relatively little ambition, and wants security above all.

**Theory Y**

1. The expenditure of physical and mental effort in work is as natural as play or rest.
2. External control and the threat of punishment are not the only means for bringing about effort toward organizational objectives. Workers will exercise self-direction and self-control in the service of objectives to which they are committed.
3. Commitment to objectives is a function of the rewards associated with their achievement.
4. The average human being learns, under proper conditions, not only to accept but also to seek responsibility.
5. The capacity to exercise a relatively high degree of imagination, ingenuity, and creativity in the solution of organizational problems is widely, not narrowly, distributed in the population.
6. Under the conditions of modern industrial life, the intellectual potential of the average human being is only partially utilized.

### PROGRESS ✓questions

1. Define the terms *power, authority,* and *leadership.*
2. Explain the different expectations of Theory X and Theory Y managers.
3. Would you describe yourself as a Theory X or a Theory Y manager? Why?
4. Define the self-fulfilling prophecy of management.

## >> Framework for Classifying Leadership Studies

Many studies have been conducted on leadership. One useful framework for classifying these studies is shown in Figure 9.3. *Focus* refers to whether leadership is to be studied as a set of traits or as a set of behaviors. *Traits* refer to what characteristics the leader possesses, whereas *behaviors* refer to what the leader does. The second dimension—*approach*—refers to whether leadership is studied from a universal or contingent approach. The universal approach assumes there is one best way to lead regardless of the circumstances. The contingent approach assumes the best approach to leadership is contingent on the situation. Each of the studies shown in Figure 9.3 is discussed in the following sections.

**Self-Fulfilling Prophecy** The phenomenon of productivity being directly linked to managers' expectations.

## TRAIT THEORY

Early research efforts devoted to leadership stressed what the leader was *like* rather than what the leader did—a **trait theory** of leadership. Many personality traits (such as originality, initiative, persistence, knowledge, enthusiasm), social traits (tact, patience, sympathy, etc.), and physical characteristics (height, weight, attractiveness) have been examined to differentiate leaders.

**Trait Theory** A theory about leadership based on what the leader is like rather than what the leader does.

### Figure 9.3 • Framework for Classifying Leadership Studies

| | Approach | |
|---|---|---|
| **Focus** | **Universal** | **Contingent** |
| Traits | Trait theory | Fiedler's contingency theory |
| Behaviors | Leadership styles<br>Ohio State studies<br>Michigan studies<br>Managerial grid | Path-goal theory<br>Situational theory |

At first glance, a few traits do seem to distinguish leaders from followers. These include being slightly superior in such physical traits as weight and height and in a tendency to score higher on tests of dominance, intelligence, extroversion, and adjustment. But the differences seem to be small, with much overlap.

Thus, the research in this area has generally been fruitless—largely because the traits related to

### Figure 9.4 • Relationship between Styles of Leadership and Group Members

**Autocratic Style**

*Leader*

1. The individual is very conscious of his or her position.
2. He or she has little trust and faith in members of the group.
3. This leader believes pay is a just reward for working and the only reward that will motivate employees.
4. Orders are issued to be carried out, with no questions allowed and no explanations given.

*Group members*

1. No responsibility is assumed for performance, with people merely doing what they are told.
2. Production is good when the leader is present, but poor in the leader's absence.

**Laissez-Faire Style**

*Leader*

1. He or she has no confidence in his or her leadership ability.
2. This leader does not set goals for the group.

*Group members*

1. Decisions are made by whoever in the group is willing to do it.
2. Productivity generally is low, and work is sloppy.
3. Individuals have little interest in their work.
4. Morale and teamwork generally are low.

**Democratic Style**

*Leader*

1. Decision making is shared between the leader and the group.
2. When the leader is required or forced to make a decision, his or her reasoning is explained to the group.
3. Criticism and praise are given objectively.

*Group members*

1. New ideas and change are welcomed.
2. A feeling of responsibility is developed within the group.
3. Quality of work and productivity generally are high.
4. The group generally feels successful.

leadership in one case usually did not prove to be predictive in other cases. It can be said that traits may influence the capacity to lead. But these traits must be analyzed in terms of the leadership situation (described in detail later in this chapter).

## BASIC LEADERSHIP STYLES

Other studies dealt with the style of the leader. They found three basic leadership styles: autocratic, laissez-faire, and democratic. The main difference among these styles is where the decision-making function rests. Generally, the **autocratic leader** makes more decisions for the group; the **laissez-faire leader** allows people within the group to make all decisions; and the **democratic leader** guides and encourages the group to make decisions. More detail about each of the leadership styles is given in Figure 9.4. The figure implies that the democratic style is the most desirable and productive. However, current research on leadership, discussed later in this chapter, does not necessarily support this conclusion. The primary contribution of this research was identifying the three basic styles of leadership.

## OHIO STATE STUDIES

A series of studies on leadership was conducted at Ohio State University to find out the most important behaviors of successful leaders. The researchers wanted to find what a successful leader does, regardless of the type of group being led: a mob, a religious group, a university, or a business organization. To do this, they developed a questionnaire called the **Leader Behavior Description Questionnaire (LBDQ)**. Both the original form and variations of it are still used today.

From research with the LBDQ, two leader behaviors emerged consistently as being the most important: consideration and initiating structure. The term **consideration** refers to the leader behavior of showing concern for individual group members and satisfying their needs. The term **initiating structure** refers to the leader behavior of structuring the work of group members and directing the group toward the achievement of the group's goals.

Since the Ohio State research, many other studies have been done on the relationship between the leader behaviors of consideration and initiating structure and their resulting effect on leader effectiveness. The major conclusions that can be drawn from these studies are as follows:[2]

**Autocratic Leader** One who makes many decisions on behalf of the group.

**Laissez-Faire Leader** One who allows people within the group to make all decisions.

**Democratic Leader** One who guides and encourages the group to make decisions.

**Leader Behavior Description Questionnaire (LBDQ)** Questionnaire designed to determine what a successful leader does, regardless of the type of group being led.

**Consideration** The leader behavior of showing concern for individual group members and satisfying their needs.

**Initiating Structure** The leader behavior of structuring the work of group members and directing the group toward the achievement of the group's goals.

1. Leaders scoring high on consideration tend to have more satisfied subordinates than do leaders scoring low on consideration.
2. The relationship between the score on consideration and leader effectiveness depends on the group being led. In other words, a high score on consideration was positively linked with leader effectiveness for managers and office staff in a large industrial firm, whereas a high score on consideration was negatively linked with leader effectiveness for production foremen.
3. There isn't any consistent relationship between initiating structure and leader effectiveness; rather, the relationship varies depending on the group that is being led.

## UNIVERSITY OF MICHIGAN STUDIES

The Institute for Social Research of the University of Michigan conducted studies to discover principles contributing both to the productivity of a group and to the satisfaction derived by group members. The initial study took place at the home office of the Prudential Insurance Company in Newark, New Jersey.

Interviews were conducted with 24 managers and 419 nonmanagerial employees. Results of the interviews showed that managers of high-producing work groups were more likely to have the following characteristics:

1. To receive general rather than close supervision from their superiors.
2. To like the amount of authority and responsibility they have in their job.
3. To spend more time in supervision.
4. To give general rather than close supervision to their employees.
5. To be employee-oriented rather than production-oriented.

Supervisors of low-producing work groups had basically opposite characteristics and techniques. They were production-oriented and gave close supervision.

Rensis Likert, then director of the institute, published the results of his years of research in the book *New Patterns of Management*, which is a classic in its field.[3] Likert believes there are four patterns or styles of leadership or management employed by organizations. He has identified and labeled these styles as follows:

**Managerial Grid** A two-dimensional framework rating a leader on the basis of concern for people and concern for production.

***System 1:*** *Exploitative authoritative.* Authoritarian form of management that attempts to exploit subordinates.

***System 2:*** *Benevolent authoritative.* Authoritarian form of management, but paternalistic in nature.

***System 3:*** *Consultative.* Manager requests and receives inputs from subordinates but maintains the right to make the final decision.

***System 4:*** *Participative.* Manager gives some direction, but decisions are made by consensus and majority, based on total participation.

Likert used a questionnaire to determine the style of leadership and the management pattern employed in the organization as a whole. The results of his studies indicated that system 4 was the most effective style of management and that organizations should strive to develop a management pattern corresponding to this system.

## THE MANAGERIAL GRID

Robert Blake and Jane Mouton have also developed a method of classifying the leadership style of an individual.[4] The **Managerial Grid**, depicted in Figure 9.5, is a two-dimensional framework rating a leader on the basis of concern for people and concern for production. (Notice that these activities closely relate to the leader activities from the Ohio State studies—consideration and initiating structure.)

**PROMOTING**

You run the southeast region of a national photocopier company. Your sales manager, Deona Casel, has just given her two weeks' notice. The next person in line for the position based on seniority would be Gregory Bartell, one of your top salespeople, and he has expressed an interest in the position in his last two performance appraisals. However, in those appraisals, Greg categorized himself as a Theory X manager. He is aggressive and believes a team should be led with the approach of "my way or the highway." Deona was more of a Theory Y manager—she valued every member of her team and built an environment of trust and respect for each of their contributions.

You have invested a considerable amount of time and resources in training your sales team, and they have become one of the best teams in the company. Do you promote Greg?

ETHICAL
MANAGEMENT
Would you promote someone whose managerial style wasn't what you thought was best for the position?

## Figure 9.5 • The Managerial Grid

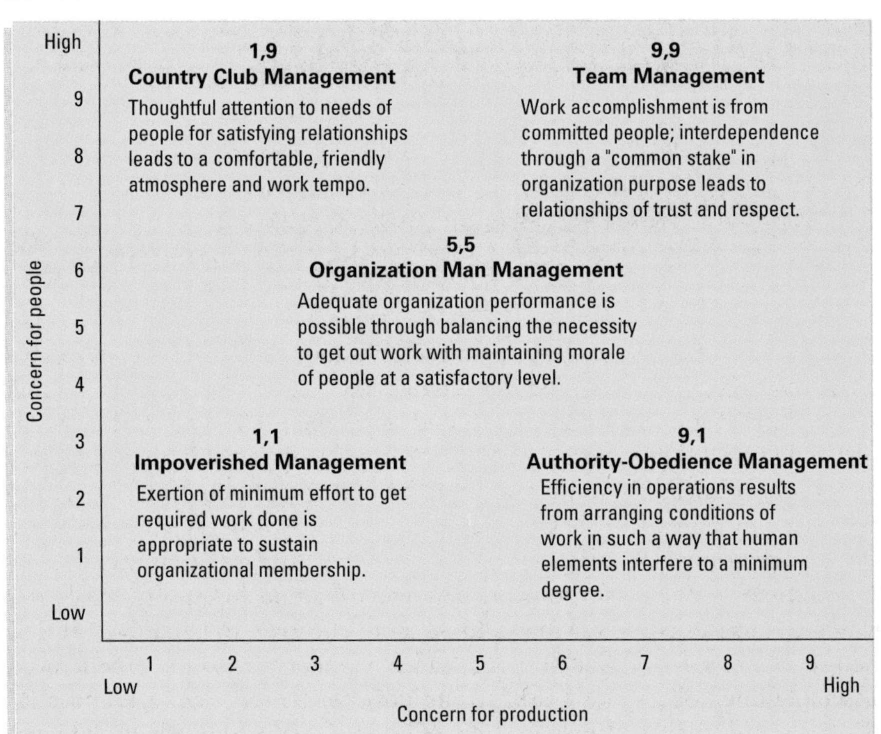


A questionnaire is used to locate a particular style of leadership or management on the grid.

Blake and Mouton identified five basic styles of management using the Managerial Grid. *Authority-obedience*—located in the lower-right-hand corner (position 9, 1)—assumes that efficiency in operations results from properly arranging the conditions at work with minimum interference from other people. The opposite view, *country club management*—located in the upper-left-hand corner (1, 9)—assumes that proper attention to human needs leads to a comfortable organizational atmosphere and workplace. *Team management*—in the upper-right-hand corner (9, 9)—combines a high degree of concern for people with a high degree of concern for production. The other two styles on the grid are *impoverished management* (1, 1) and *organization man management* (5, 5). The Managerial Grid is intended to serve as a framework for managers to learn what their leadership style is and to develop a plan to move toward a 9, 9 team management style of leadership.

## CONTINGENCY APPROACH TO LEADERSHIP

The leadership studies discussed so far are similar in that they did not specifically address the complex differences between groups (such as production workers versus accountants) and their influences on leader behavior. To imply that a manager should be employee-oriented rather than production-oriented (Michigan studies) or that the manager should exhibit concern for both production and people (Blake and Mouton) does not say much about what the manager should do in particular situations. Nor does it offer much guidance for daily leadership situations. As a result, research began to focus on the leadership style that is most effective in particular situations. This is called the **contingency approach to leadership**.

One of the first studies using the contingency approach was conducted by Fred Fiedler.[5] He studied the match between the leader's personality and the situation. Fiedler defined two basic leader personality traits: task and relationship motivation. Task-motivated leaders gain satisfaction from the performance of a task. Relationship-motivated leaders gain satisfaction from interpersonal relationships. Fiedler viewed task versus relationship as a leader trait that was relatively constant for any given person.

**Contingency Approach to Leadership** The leadership style that is most effective in particular situations.

A scale, called the *least preferred co-worker scale* (LPC), was used to measure whether a person is a task- or relationship-oriented leader. Respondents were asked to think of all the people they had worked with and select the person with whom they could work least effectively. The respondents then described their least preferred co-worker on the LPC. A person who described a least preferred co-worker in fairly favorable terms was presumed to be motivated to have close interpersonal relations with others; Fiedler classified these people as *relationship-motivated* leaders. On the other hand, people who rejected co-workers with whom they had difficulties were presumed to be motivated to accomplish or achieve the task; they were classified as *task-oriented* leaders.

Fiedler next turned to the situation in which the leader was operating. He placed leadership situations along a favorable-unfavorable continuum based on three major dimensions: leader-member relations,

## Figure 9.6 • Fiedler's Classification of Situations

| Situation | 1 | 2 | 3 | 4 | 5 | 6 | 7 | 8 |
|---|---|---|---|---|---|---|---|---|
| Leader-member relations | Good | Good | Good | Good | Poor | Poor | Poor | Poor |
| Task structure | Structured | Structured | Unstructured | Unstructured | Structured | Structured | Unstructured | Unstructured |
| Position power | Strong | Weak | Strong | Weak | Strong | Weak | Strong | Weak |
| | *Favorable for leader* | | | | | | *Unfavorable for leader* | |

**Leader-Member Relations** Degree to which others trust and respect the leader and the leader's friendliness.

**Task Structure** Degree to which job tasks are structured.

**Position Power** Power and influence that go with a job.

task structure, and position power. **Leader-member relations** refer to the degree others trust and respect the leader and to the leader's friendliness. This compares somewhat to referent power. **Task structure** is the degree to which job tasks are structured. For example, assembly-line jobs are more structured than managerial jobs. **Position power** refers to the power and influence that go with a job. A manager has more position power who is able to hire, fire, and discipline. Position power compares to coercive, reward, and legitimate power. Using these three dimensions, an eight-celled classification scheme was developed. Figure 9.6 shows this scheme along the continuum.

Figure 9.7 shows the most productive style of leadership for each situation. In both highly favorable and highly unfavorable situations, a task-motivated leader was found to be more effective. In highly favorable situations, the group is ready to be directed and is willing to be told what to do. In highly favorable situations, the group welcomes having the leader make decisions and direct the group. In moderately favorable situations, a relationship-motivated leader was found to be more effective. In situation 7 (moderately poor leader-member relations, unstructured task, and strong position power), the task and relationship styles of leadership were equally productive.

## CONTINUUM OF LEADER BEHAVIORS

Robert Tannenbaum and Warren Schmidt also contend that different combinations of situational elements require different styles of leadership. They suggest that there are three important factors, or forces, involved in finding the most effective leadership style: forces in the manager, the subordinate, and the situation. Furthermore, all these forces are interdependent.[6]

Figure 9.8 describes in detail the forces that affect leadership situations. Since these forces differ in strength and interaction in differing situations, one style of leadership is not effective in all situations.

In fact, Tannenbaum and Schmidt argue that there is a continuum of behaviors that the leader may

## Figure 9.7 • Leadership Style and Leadership Situations

| Situation | 1 | 2 | 3 | 4 | 5 | 6 | 7 | 8 |
|---|---|---|---|---|---|---|---|---|
| Leader-member relations | Good | Good | Good | Good | Poor | Poor | Poor | Poor |
| Task structure | Structured | Structured | Unstructured | Unstructured | Structured | Structured | Unstructured | Unstructured |
| Leader position power | Strong | Weak | Strong | Weak | Strong | Weak | Strong | Weak |
| | *Favorable for leader* | | | | | | *Unfavorable for leader* | |
| Most productive leadership style | Task | Task | Task | Relationship | Relationship | No data | Task or relationship | Task |

## Figure 9.8 • Forces Affecting the Leadership Situation

| Forces in the Manager | Forces in the Subordinates | Forces in the Situation |
|---|---|---|
| *Value system:* How the manager personally feels about delegating, degree of confidence in subordinates.<br>Personal leadership inclinations.<br>Authoritarian versus participative.<br>Feelings of security in uncertain situations. | *Need for independence:* Some people need and want direction, while others do not.<br>*Readiness to assume responsibility:* Different people need different degrees of responsibility.<br>*Tolerance for ambiguity:* Specific versus general directions.<br>*Interest and perceived importance of the problem:* People generally have more interest in, and work harder on, important problems.<br>*Degree of understanding and identification with organizational goals:* A manager is more likely to delegate authority to an individual who seems to have a positive attitude about the organization.<br>*Degree of expectation in sharing in decision making:* People who have worked under subordinate-centered leadership tend to resent boss-centered leadership. | *Type of organization:* Centralized versus decentralized.<br>*Work group effectiveness:* How effectively the group works together.<br>*The problem itself:* The work group's knowledge and experience relevant to the problem.<br>*Time pressure:* It is difficult to delegate to subordinates in crisis situations.<br>Demands from upper levels of management.<br>Demands from government, unions, and society in general. |

employ, depending on the situation (see Figure 9.9). These authors further conclude that successful leaders are keenly aware of the forces that are most relevant to their behavior at a given time. Successful leaders accurately understand not only themselves but also the other persons in the organizational and social environment, and they are able to behave correctly in light of these insights.

## PATH-GOAL THEORY OF LEADERSHIP

The **path-goal theory of leadership** attempts to define the relationships between a leader's behavior and the subordinates' performance and work activities. Leader behavior is acceptable to subordinates to the degree that they see it as a source of satisfaction now or as a step toward future satisfaction. Leader behavior influences the motivation of subordinates when it makes the satisfaction of their needs contingent on successful performance; and it provides the guidance, support, and rewards needed for effective performance (but that are not already present in the environment). The path-goal theory of leadership and the expectancy approach to motivation, which is described in the next chapter, are closely related in that

**Path-Goal Theory of Leadership** Relationship between a leader's behavior and the subordinates' performance and work activities.

## Figure 9.9 • Continuum of Leader Behaviors

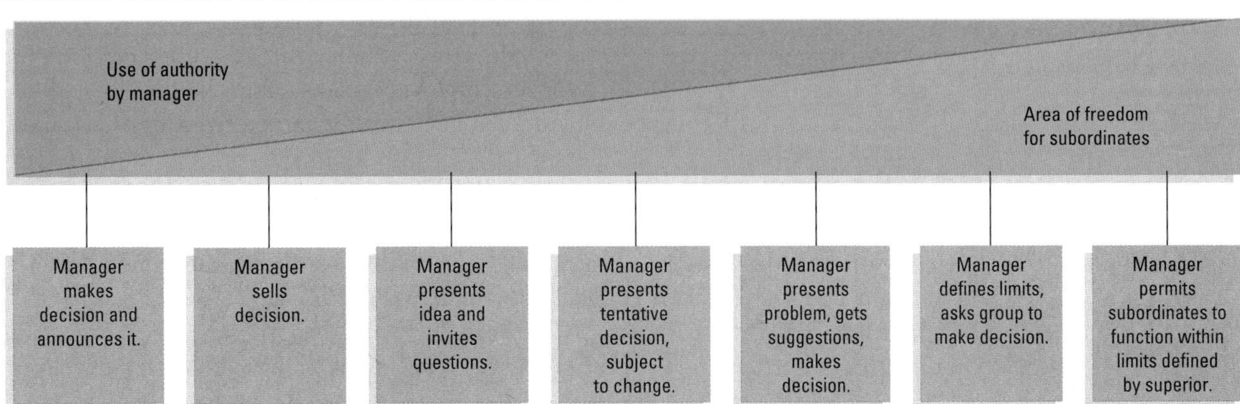

**Situational Leadership Theory** Leadership theory that states as the level of maturity of followers increases, structures should be reduced while emotional support should first be increased and then gradually decreased.

**Transactional Leadership** The approach that leaders engage in bargaining relationships with their followers.

**Transformational Leadership** Leadership style that cultivates employee acceptance of the group mission.

leader behaviors can either increase or decrease employee expectancies.

In path-goal theory, leader behavior falls into one of the four basic types: role classification, supportive, participative, and autocratic. *Role classification leadership* lets subordinates know what is expected of them, gives guidance as to what should be done and how, schedules and coordinates work among the subordinates, and maintains definite standards of performance. *Supportive leadership* has a friendly, approachable leader who attempts to make the work environment more pleasant for subordinates. *Participative leadership* involves consulting with subordinates and asking for their suggestions in the decision-making process. *Autocratic leadership* comes from a leader who gives orders that are not to be questioned by subordinates.

Under this theory, each leadership behavior results in different levels of performance and subordinate satisfaction, depending on the structure of the work tasks. Role clarification leads to high satisfaction and performance for subordinates engaged in unstructured tasks. Supportive leadership brings the most satisfaction to those who work on highly structured tasks. Participative leader behavior enhances performance and satisfaction for subordinates engaged in ambiguous tasks. Autocratic leadership behavior has a negative effect on both satisfaction and performance in both structured and unstructured task situations.

**Study Alert!** Situational leadership theory takes the most pragmatic approach to leadership. How you lead your department, your division, or your entire company should reflect the situation you are facing, both in terms of the business environment in which you are working and the mix of employees you are leading.

## SITUATIONAL LEADERSHIP THEORY

Paul Hersey and Kenneth Blanchard include maturity of the followers as an important factor in leader behavior.[7] According to the **situational leadership theory**, as the level of maturity of followers increases, structure (task)

**Figure 9.10 • Situational Leadership Theory**

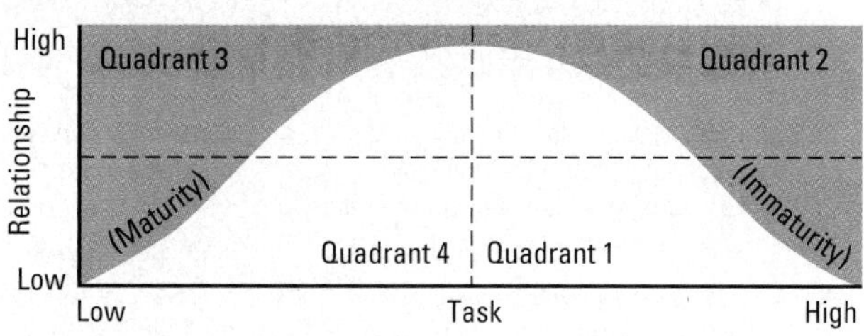


should be reduced while emotional support (relationship) should first be increased and then gradually decreased. The maturity level of the followers is determined by their relative independence, their ability to take responsibility, and their achievement-motivation level.

Figure 9.10 shows the cycle of the basic leadership styles that should be used by the leader, depending on the maturity of the followers. The situational leadership theory proposes that as the followers progress from immaturity to maturity, the leader's behavior should move from (1) high task–low relationships to (2) high task–high relationships to (3) low task–high relationships to (4) low task–low relationships.

## TRANSACTIONAL, TRANSFORMATIONAL, AND CHARISMATIC LEADERS

Another approach to the leadership analysis has been based on how leaders and followers influence one another. Under this method, leadership is viewed as transactional, transformational, or charismatic. **Transactional leadership** takes the view that leaders engage in an unemotional bargaining relationship with their followers—management is simply done "by the book." Under this approach, the leader (manager) tells employees what they need to do to obtain rewards and takes corrective action only when employees fail to meet performance objectives.

**Transformational leadership** involves cultivating employee acceptance of the group mission. The manager-employee relationship is one of mutual encouragement and is characterized by the leader's personality, inspiration, and consideration and the intellectual motivation between the leader and followers. Transformational leaders go beyond "management by the book" and transform not only the situation but also the followers.

**Charismatic leadership** presents a unique situation in which the leader and followers develop a

WHAT'S YOUR LEADERSHIP STYLE . . . ?

## First Line Focus

*Leadership research has endeavored to document and categorize leadership styles in the hope that successful behavior can be replicated by training future leaders. However, a leadership style is ultimately a personal choice that reflects your skill set and your values.*

*As Douglas McGregor captured in his Theory X and Theory Y research, how you feel about your employees will dictate how you lead them, and their performance will directly reflect your leadership style.*

*If you've never given any thought to your leadership style or the type of leader you aspire to be, consider your work experience and the leaders you have worked for in the past. Which ones would you like to emulate and why?*

**From the** PERSPECTIVE OF...

**An Internal Auditor** The auditing function of an organization requires attention to detail and compliance to rules and regulations. How can a leader be transformational in that environment?

relationship based directly on the personality of that leader, often in the face of a lack of any proven skills or experience. In contrast to the modern interpretation of "charismatic leadership" as a leader being polished and skilled at managing public relations, the traditional definition implies a specific set of circumstances. Charismatic leaders are often credited with heroic feats (turning around ailing corporations, revitalizing aging bureaucracies, or launching new enterprises) by achieving the following:[8]

1. Powerfully communicating a compelling vision of the future.
2. Passionately believing in their vision.
3. Relentlessly promoting their beliefs with boundless energy.
4. Putting forward creative outside-the-box ideas.
5. Inspiring extraordinary performance in followers by (a) expressing confidence in followers' abilities to achieve high standards and (b) building followers' trust, faith, and belief in the leader.

**Charismatic Leadership** Leadership style that can successfully influence employee behavior on the strength of the leader's personality or perceived charisma, without the formal power or experience to back it up.

## PROGRESS ✓questions

5. Define the following leadership styles: autocratic, laissez-faire, and democratic.
6. Summarize the findings of both the Ohio State and University of Michigan leadership studies.
7. Explain the path-goal theory of leadership.
8. Explain the differences between transactional, transformational, and charismatic leadership styles.

## >> Lessons from Leadership Studies

How can all these leadership theories be made relevant to the organization's need for effective managers? First, given the situational factors discussed in this chapter, it appears unlikely that a selection process will be developed to accurately predict successful leaders. The dynamic, changing nature of managerial roles further complicates the position. Even if the initial process could select effective leaders, the dynamics of the managerial situation might make the selection invalid. Further, contrary to the conclusions of many studies, most leadership training today seems to assume there is one best way to lead. In reality, most leadership remains situational. Successful leaders recognize that effective leadership requires drawing on a range of skills and techniques,

# Thinking Critically 9.1

## >> Changes in the Plastics Division

Jack Lamborn was vice president of the Plastics Division of Warner Manufacturing Company. Eleven years ago, Jack hired Jim Lewis as a general manager of the Plastics Division's two factories. Jack trained Jim as a manager and thought Jim a good manager, an opinion based largely on the fact that products were produced on schedule and were of such quality that few customers complained. In fact, for the past eight years, Jack had pretty much let Jim run the factories independently.

Jim believed strongly that his job was to see that production runs smoothly. He felt that work was work. Sometimes it was agreeable, sometimes disagreeable. If an employee didn't like the work, he or she could either adjust or quit. "Jim," said the factory personnel, "runs things. He's firm and doesn't stand for any nonsense. Things are done by the book, or they are not done at all." The turnover in the factories was low; nearly every employee liked Jim and believed that he knew his trade and that he stood up for them.

Two months ago, Jack retired, and his replacement, Chris Perlee, took over as vice president of the Plastics Division. One of the first things Chris did was call his key management people together and announce some major changes he wanted to implement. These included (1) bringing the operative employees into the decision-making process; (2) establishing a planning committee made up of three management members and three operative employees; (3) starting a suggestion system; and (4) as quickly as possible, installing a performance appraisal program agreeable to both management and the operative employees. Chris also stated he would be active in seeing that these projects would be implemented without delay.

After the meeting, Jim was upset and decided to talk to Shana Puetz, director of sales for the Plastics Division.

**Jim:** Chris is really going to change things, isn't he?

**Shana:** Yeah, maybe it's for the best. Things were a little lax under Jack.

**Jim:** I liked them that way. Jack let you run your own shop. I'm afraid Perlee is going to be looking over my shoulder every minute.

**Shana:** Well, let's give him a chance. After all, some of the changes he's proposing sound good.

**Jim:** Well, I can tell you our employees won't like them. Having them participate in making decisions and those other things are just fancy management stuff that won't work with our employees.

### QUESTIONS

1. What different styles of leadership are shown in this case?
2. What style of leadership do you think Chris will have to use with Jim?
3. Do you agree with Jim? Why or why not?
4. If "products were produced on schedule and were of such quality that few customers complained," why should there be any changes?

depending on the individual situation, not on a prescribed leadership model.

The effectiveness of any leadership style can often be determined by the environment or atmosphere of the organization itself. Are the employees happy and productive? Or are there problems with absenteeism and employee turnover? Do the employees feel valued? Do they contribute positive and creative ideas for the organization's future growth? Or do they "punch in and punch out," waiting for the next paycheck?

*How might the corporate cultures differ between an independent record store and a national chain?*

Leadership is a key determinant of the atmosphere or culture of an organization, and the future success or failure of that organization can rest on the degree to which that culture supports or challenges the organization's ability to move forward in a competitive market.

**Culture** The set of important understandings (often unstated) that members of a community share.

## >> Managing Corporate Culture

The word *culture* is derived in a roundabout way from the Latin verb *colere*, which means "to cultivate."[9] In later times, *culture* came to indicate a process of refinement and breeding in domesticating a particular crop. The modern-day meaning draws on this agricultural derivation: It relates to society's control, refinement, and domestication of itself. A contemporary definition of **culture** is "the set of important understandings (often unstated) that members of a community share in common."[10]

**Study Alert !**

"The way we do things around here" may capture the general meaning of a corporate culture, but understanding exactly how far that culture is embedded in the organization requires the documentation of unwritten rules and accepted behavioral practices. Drawing attention to the way things are done, and asking why they are done in a certain way, may prompt change in those rules and practices before they are even documented.

Culture in an organization compares to personality in a person. Humans have fairly enduring and stable traits that help them protect their attitudes and behaviors. So do organizations. In addition, certain groups of traits or personality types are known to have common elements. Organizations can be described in similar terms. They can be warm, aggressive, friendly, open, innovative, conservative, and so forth. An organization's culture is transmitted in many ways, including long-standing and often unwritten rules; shared standards regarding what is important; prejudices; standards for social etiquette and demeanor; established customs for relating to peers, subordinates, and superiors; and other traditions that clarify to employees what is and is not appropriate behavior. Thus, corporate culture communicates how people in the organization should behave by a value system conveyed through rites, rituals, myths, legends, and actions. Simply stated, **corporate culture** means "the way we do things around here."[11]

## CULTURAL FORMS OF EXPRESSION

Culture has two basic components: (1) substance, the meanings contained in its values, norms, and beliefs and (2) forms, the practices whereby these meanings are expressed, affirmed, and communicated to members.[12]

## HOW DOES CULTURE ORIGINATE?

There is no question that different organizations develop different cultures. What causes an organization to develop a particular type of culture? Many organizations trace their culture to one person who provided a living example of the major values of the organization. Robert Wood Johnson of Johnson & Johnson, Harley Procter of Procter & Gamble, Walt Disney of Walt Disney Company, Thomas J. Watson Sr. of IBM, and Phil Knight of Nike all left their imprints on the organizations they headed. Research indicates, however, that fewer than half of a new company's values reflect the values of the founder or chief executive. The rest appear to develop in response both to the environment in which the business operates and to the needs of the employees.[13] Four distinct factors contribute to an organization's culture: its history, environment, staffing, and entry socialization.[14]

**History** Employees are aware of the organization's past, and this awareness builds culture. Much of the way things are done is a continuation of how things have always been done. The existing values that a strong leader may have established originally are constantly and subtly reinforced by experiences.

The status quo is also protected by the human tendency to fervently embrace beliefs and values and to resist changes. Executives at Walt Disney Company reportedly pick up litter on the grounds without thinking because of the Disney vision of an immaculate Disneyland.

**Environment** Because all organizations must interact with their environments, the environment plays a role in shaping their culture. Deregulation of the telecommunications industry in the 1980s dramatically altered its environment. Before deregulation, the environment was relatively risk averse and noncompetitive. Increases in costs were automatically passed on to customers. As a result of deregulation, the environment changed overnight to become highly competitive and much more dynamic. No longer sheltered by a regulated environment, the cultures of the telecommunications companies were forced to change.

**Staffing** Organizations tend to hire, retain, and promote people who are similar to current employees in important ways. A person's ability to fit in can be important in these processes. This "fit" criterion ensures that current values are accepted and that potential challengers of how we do things are screened out. Adjustment has to be carefully managed. For example, when Bill George took over Medtronic, a leading producer of pacemakers, in 1991, he quickly found out that to survive in the rapidly growing high-tech health care business, he needed a change—but not at the expense of what had historically worked for the company. He opted for a merger with another company. The merger brought in new blood that was free-spirited and experimental in nature and teamed them with a highly disciplined, methodical existing culture. Though it was hard work, empowerment of people and a merger of cultures helped the company halve its development time and remain competitive in the industry.[15]

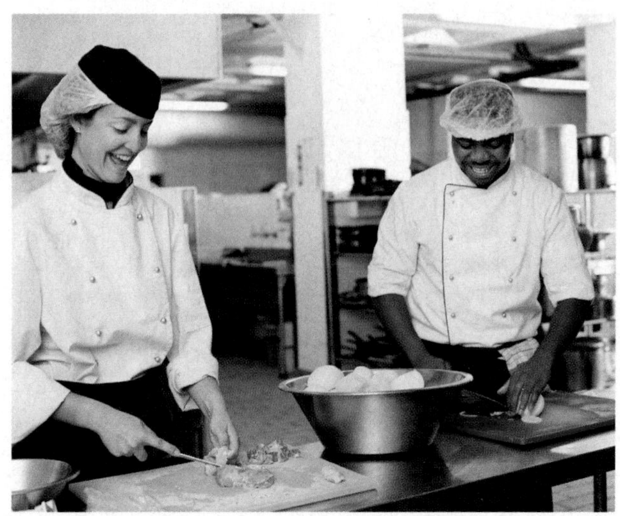

**Entry Socialization** While an organization's values, norms, and beliefs may be widely and uniformly held, they are rarely written down. The new employee, who is least familiar with the culture, is most likely to challenge it. It is therefore important to help the newcomer adopt the organization's culture. Companies with strong cultures attach great importance to the process of introducing and training new employees. This process is called **entry socialization.** Entry socialization not only reduces threats to the organization from newcomers but also lets new employees know what is expected of them. It may be handled in a formal or informal manner, as well as on an individual or group basis.

## STRONG AND WEAK CORPORATE CULTURES

A strong corporate culture is clearly defined, reinforces a common understanding about what is important, and has the support of management and employees. Such a culture contributes greatly to an organization's success by creating an understanding about how employees should behave. Figure 9.11 identifies the characteristics of a strong corporate culture.

**Figure 9.11 • Characteristics of a Strong Corporate Culture**

- Organizational members share clear values and beliefs about how to succeed in their business.
- Organizational members agree on which beliefs about how to succeed are most important.
- Different parts of the organization have similar beliefs about how to succeed.
- The rituals of day-to-day organizational life are well organized and consistent with company goals.

Weak cultures have the opposite characteristics. In a weak corporate culture, individuals often act in ways that are inconsistent with the company's way of doing things. Figure 9.12 summarizes characteristics of a weak culture.

**Corporate Culture** Value system for people in an organization and conveyed through rites, rituals, myths, legends, and actions.

**Entry Socialization** Adaptation process by which new employees are introduced and indoctrinated into the organization's culture.

9. Define the term *culture.*
10. Where does organizational culture originate?
11. Explain the four distinct factors that contribute to an organization's culture.
12. Summarize the characteristics of a weak organizational culture.

**Figure 9.12 • Characteristics of a Weak Corporate Culture**

- Organizational members have no clear values or beliefs about how to succeed in their business.
- Organizational members have many beliefs as to how to succeed but cannot agree on which are most important.
- Different parts of the organization have fundamentally different beliefs about how to succeed.
- Those who personify the culture are destructive or disruptive and don't build on any common understanding about what is important.
- The rituals of day-to-day organizational life are disorganized or working at cross-purposes.

## IDENTIFYING CULTURE

Researchers have identified seven characteristics that, taken together, capture the essence of an organization's culture:[16]

1. *Individual autonomy.* The degree of responsibility, independence, and opportunities for exercising initiative that individuals in the organization have.
2. *Structure.* The number of rules and regulations and the amount of direct supervision that are used to oversee and control employee behavior.
3. *Support.* The degree of assistance and warmth provided by managers to their subordinates.
4. *Identification.* The degree to which members identify with the organization as a whole rather than with their particular work group or field of professional expertise.
5. *Performance-reward.* The degree to which reward allocations (i.e., salary increases, promotions) in the organization are based on performance criteria.
6. *Conflict tolerance.* The degree of conflict present in relationships between peers and work groups, as well as the willingness to be honest and open about differences.
7. *Risk tolerance.* The degree to which employees are encouraged to be aggressive, innovative, and risk seeking.

Each trait should be viewed as existing on a continuum ranging from low to high.

A picture of the overall culture can be formed by evaluating the organization on these characteristics.

There are as many distinct cultures as there are organizations. Most can be grouped into one of four basic types, determined by two factors: (1) the degree of risk associated with the organization's activities and (2) the speed with which the organization and its employees get feedback indicating the success of decisions. Figure 9.13 shows a matrix of the four generic types of culture.[17]

**Figure 9.13 • Generic Types of Organization Culture**

| | | Degree of Risk: High | Degree of Risk: Low |
|---|---|---|---|
| Speed of Feedback | Rapid | Tough-person, macho culture | Work-hard, play-hard culture |
| | Slow | Bet-your-company culture | Process culture |

**Tough-Person, Macho Culture** The **tough-person, macho culture** is characterized by individualists who regularly take high risks and get quick feedback on whether their decisions are right or wrong. Teamwork is not important, and every colleague is a potential rival. In this culture, the value of cooperation is ignored; there is no chance to learn from mistakes. People who do best in this culture are those who need to gamble and who can tolerate all-or-nothing risks because they need instant feedback. Companies that develop large-scale advertising programs for major clients would be characterized by the tough-person, macho culture; these advertising programs are usually high budget with rapid acceptance or failure.

**Tough-Person, Macho Culture** Culture in which individuals take high risks and get quick feedback on whether their decisions are right or wrong.

**Work-Hard, Play-Hard Culture** Culture in which high activity is expected and employees are encouraged to take few risks and to expect rapid feedback.

**Bet-Your-Company Culture** Culture in which big-stakes decisions are required but considerable time passes before the results are known.

**Process Culture** Culture that involves low risk with little feedback, with employees focusing on how things are done rather than on the outcomes.

**Work-Hard, Play-Hard Culture** The **work-hard, play-hard culture** encourages employees to take few risks and to expect rapid feedback. In this culture, activity is the key to success. Rewards accrue to persistence and the ability to find a need and fill it. Because of the need for volume, team players who are friendly and outgoing thrive. Companies that are sales-based, such as real estate companies, often have a work-hard, play-hard culture.

**Bet-Your-Company Culture** The **bet-your-company culture** requires big-stakes decisions, with considerable time passing before the results are known. Pressures to make the right decisions are always present in this environment. Companies involved in durable goods manufacturing are often characterized by a bet-your-company culture.

**Process Culture** The **process culture** involves low risk coupled with little feedback; employees must focus on how things are done rather than on the outcomes. Employees in this atmosphere become cautious and protective. Those who thrive are orderly, punctual, and detail-oriented. Companies in regulated or protected industries often operate in this type of culture.

**Organizational Subcultures** In addition to its overall culture, organizations often have multiple subcultures. It is not uncommon for the values, beliefs,

*Stock trading is an example of a tough-person, macho culture work environment.*

## PROGRESS ✓questions

13. Which seven characteristics capture the essence of an organization's culture?
14. Explain the four basic types of organizational culture.
15. Think of the organization you currently work for (or one you have worked for in the past). Which of the four basic types of culture most accurately describes that organization? Provide an example to support your selection.
16. Define the term *organizational subculture.*

and practices to vary from one part of the organization to another. For example, newly acquired components of a company often have cultural differences that must be worked out over time. Global companies also tend to be faced with multiple cultures. Such factors as language, social norms, values, attitudes, customs, and religion naturally vary throughout the world.

**Study Alert!** Proactive organizations monitor their culture and are prepared to make necessary changes for the five reasons identified by Kennedy. However, in a corporate merger or takeover situation, change can be forced on you, as two cultures, often from formerly competing organizations, must blend into one.

The presence of different subcultures within an organization does not preclude the development of areas of commonality and compatibility.[18] For example, a company's emphasis on quality can be embedded in the local culture at sites throughout the world. At the same time, successful companies have learned to look at the compatibility of cultures when considering acquisitions, mergers, and new locations. Extreme cultural differences can make it very difficult for an acquisition or an expansion to be successful.

### From the PERSPECTIVE OF...

**A Fast-Food Manager** With an industry average employee turnover rate of over 200 percent every year, should a fast-food company even try to develop a corporate culture?

### KEEPING YOUR STAFF

You have just been notified by the owners of your organization that they have agreed to sell the company to an international corporation that is looking to diversify its business interests. The acquiring corporation has never operated in your market before, but it has obviously decided that it would be quicker to buy its way into the market rather than start a company to compete against you.

As part of the due diligence process for the sale, you get to spend a lot of time with key personnel from your soon-to-be new owner. You notice that it has a very distinct corporate culture—very macho and cutthroat with little interest in teamwork or cooperation. This is very different from the team-based culture of your company where the contributions of everyone are recognized and rewarded.

To minimize the risk of a mass exodus of personnel at the announcement of the sale, the official message is that this will be an "arm's-length strategic acquisition where your company will be left alone to continue its track record of success." You know that the real plan is for your company to be assimilated into the new operational culture as soon as possible. As soon as the news breaks, several members of your team ask you what you know about the new owners. What should you share with them?

ETHICAL
MANAGEMENT
What should you tell your employees about upper management?

## Thinking Critically 9.2

### >> The Way We Do Things

Fitzgerald Company manufactures a variety of consumer products for sale through retail department stores. For over 30 years, the company has held a strong belief that customer relations and a strong selling orientation are the keys to business success. As a result, all top executives have sales backgrounds and spend much of their time outside the company with customers. Because of the strong focus on the customer, management at Fitzgerald emphasizes new-product development projects and growth in volume. The company rarely implements cost reduction or process improvement projects, preferring instead to focus on building a culture that they call "customer-centric." By constantly seeking feedback from their customers, it believes it can increase business by delivering products that it knows (with hard data) its customers want.

Between 1989 and 1999, Fitzgerald's 10 percent share of the market was the largest in the industry. Profitability was consistently better than the industry average. However, in the last 10 years, the markets for many of Fitzgerald's products have matured, and Fitzgerald has dropped from market share leader to the number three company in the industry. Profitability has steadily declined since 2000, although Fitzgerald offers a more extensive line of products than any of its competitors. Customers are complaining that Fitzgerald's prices are higher than those of other companies.

In June 2009, Jeff Steele, president of Fitzgerald Company, hired Valerie Stevens of Management Consultants, Inc., to help him improve the company's financial performance. After an extensive study of Fitzgerald Company and its industry group, Valerie met with Jeff and said, "Jeff, I believe the Fitzgerald Company may have to substantially change its culture."

**QUESTIONS**

1. Describe, in general terms, the corporate culture at Fitzgerald Company.
2. What's wrong with a business philosophy based on the belief "that customer relations and a strong selling orientation are the keys to business success"?
3. What does Valerie mean when she says Fitzgerald Company may have to change its culture? What are some of the necessary changes?
4. Discuss the problems the company may encounter in attempting to implement changes.

## CHANGING CULTURE

Executives who have successfully changed organization cultures estimate that the process usually takes from 6 to 15 years.[19] Because organization culture is difficult and time-consuming to change, any attempts should be well thought-out.

Allan Kennedy, an expert on organization culture, believes only five reasons justify a large-scale cultural change:[20]

1. The organization has strong values that do not fit into a changing environment.
2. The industry is very competitive and moves with lightning speed.
3. The organization is mediocre or worse.
4. The organization is about to join the ranks of the very large companies.
5. The organization is small but growing rapidly.

Some organizations attempt to change their cultures only when they are forced to do so by changes in their environments or economic situations; others anticipate a necessary change. While massive cultural reorientation may be unreasonable in most situations, it is usually possible to strengthen or fine-tune the current situation. A statement of corporate mission consistently reinforced by systems, structures, and policies is a useful tool for strengthening the culture.

Because of the cost, time, and difficulty involved in changing culture, many people believe it is easier to change, or physically replace, the people. This view assumes most organizations promote people who fit the prevailing norms of the organization. Therefore, the easiest if not the only way to change an organization's culture is to change its people.

## >> Chapter Summary

We have seen in this chapter that leadership and management are not necessarily the same but are not incompatible. Effective leadership creates a vision of the future and builds an organizational culture that encourages all stakeholders in the organization to work together in the realization of that vision. In practice, that's easier said than done, since each stakeholder brings his or her unique perspective to the table. So the challenge lies in creating a culture that embraces those individual perspectives while conveying a consistent message to drive the organization forward. As we shall see in the next chapter, a critical component in meeting that challenge is making sure that the people in the organization stay motivated toward achieving that vision.

1. Define *leadership, power,* and *authority.*

   Leadership is the ability to influence people to willingly follow one's guidance or adhere to one's decisions. Power is a measure of a person's potential to influence, command, or apply force—to get others to do what he or she wants them to do, as well as avoid being forced by others to do what he or she does not want to do. Power can have both a positive and a negative form. Positive power results when the exchange is voluntary and both parties feel good about the exchange. Negative power results when the individual is forced to change.

   Authority is the legitimate use of power—the right to issue directives and use resources as indicated by that person's position in the organizational hierarchy.

2. Discuss leadership as it relates to management.

   Effective leadership in organizations creates a vision of the future that considers the legitimate long-term interests of the parties involved in the organization, develops a strategy for moving toward that vision, enlists the support of employees to produce the movement, and motivates employees to implement the strategy. Management is a process of planning, organizing, staffing, motivating, and controlling through the use of formal authority. In practice, effective leadership and effective management must ultimately be the same.

3. Explain leadership attitudes.

   The attitude or expectation that a leader brings to the management of an organization has been shown to directly influence the performance of the people in that organization. Referred to as the "self-fulfilling prophecy" by Douglas McGregor in his book *The Human Side of Enterprise,* it has been found that, in general, if the managers' expectations are high, productivity is likely to be high. On the other hand, if the managers' expectations are low, productivity is likely to be equally low.

4. Describe the differences between a Theory X and Theory Y manager.

   Theory X managers hold a distinct attitude or set of beliefs that their employees have an inherent dislike of work and will avoid it at all costs. As a result, those employees must be

*Continued on next page*

Continued from page 217

closely monitored and threatened with punishment in order to get the minimum level of productivity needed to achieve organizational goals.

Theory Y managers hold an opposing attitude: Employees take pride in their work and enjoy the opportunity to be creative in the resolution of organizational problems and challenges. As such, the responsibility of a manager is to create an environment in which those employees are able to flourish.

First proposed by Douglas McGregor in the 1960s, the concept of Theory X and Y managers captures the idea that the attitudes held by managers will directly affect their treatment of their employees and produce the precise outcomes that those managers expected—the self-fulfilling prophecy.

5. Explain the differences between transactional, transformational, and charismatic leadership styles.

   Transactional leaders engage in an unemotional bargaining relationship with their followers—management is simply done by the book. Employees are told what they need to do to obtain rewards and receive corrective feedback only when there is a perceived failure to meet performance objectives.

   Transformational leaders cultivate employee acceptance of the group mission. The manager-employee relationship is one of mutual encouragement and is characterized by the leader's personality, inspiration, and consideration and by the intellectual motivation between the leader and followers. Transformational leaders go beyond management by the book and transform not only the situation but also the followers.

   Charismatic leaders develop a relationship with followers based on personality, passion, and powerful communication. Whether or not the leader can provide any evidence of proven skills or experience becomes secondary to the compelling vision he or she promotes to inspire employees to be creative and push through previously held limitations.

6. Identify strategies for effectively managing corporate culture.

   Corporate culture communicates "the way we do things around here"—how people in the organization are expected to behave—by establishing a value system conveyed through rites, rituals, myths, legends, and actions. Culture has two basic components: (1) substance, the meanings contained in its values, norms, and beliefs, and (2) forms, the practices whereby meanings are expressed, affirmed, and communicated to members.

   Effective management of a corporate culture requires a clear understanding of what the company stands for—often expressed in a detailed mission statement—with a process for consistent reinforcement of that culture through systems, structures, and policies.

**TACO BARN GETS SOME SURPRISING FEEDBACK**
***(continued from page 199)***

Tony found that he enjoyed the leadership survey project much more than he thought he would. Working with other unit managers and regional managers allowed him to get a much better sense of the organization as a whole—lots of creative and talented people but a remarkable difference in overall unit performance. Some units were very well run and very profitable for the Taco Barn organization, but there were also some "problem children," with high employee turnover, poor financial performance, and, unfortunately, very poor customer service.

That difference in unit performance was directly reflected in the responses to the employee survey. Employees in smooth-running units seemed to be happy with their jobs and had a strong level of confidence in the company's direction. They felt that the company had a strong, customer-focused culture, and they felt valued as a part of the overall organizational team. However, employees in the struggling units took the opportunity to express their sense of frustration with the leadership and their feeling of isolation from any sense of culture within the Taco Barn family.

Tony felt fortunate that even though the respondents were anonymous, those employees who could be identified from their comments as being from his unit were very positive. He also felt sorry for the other members of the survey project whose employees didn't respond so positively.

Once the survey data were collected and analyzed, Dawn called a meeting to review what the data had to say about their region and about the Taco Barn organization as a whole.

"Okay folks, I think you would agree that we have some work to do here. We have some very happy employees and also some very unhappy ones. We honestly didn't expect the results to be all over the map like this. We don't appear to have a consistent leadership style, and we certainly don't have a clear organizational culture that the employees can identify with.

"You know that we are anticipating significant expansion in the coming years, and we can only achieve that if we start from a solid foundation. So where do we go from here? What's the right leadership style for Taco Barn, and what kind of culture should the Taco Barn family have?"

### QUESTIONS

1. Should the leadership team have been surprised by the survey results? Why or why not?
2. Should Taco Barn be pursuing a "right" leadership style? Why or why not?
3. If the Taco Barn doesn't have a clear sense of culture (as the survey results appear to indicate), where and how does it start to develop one?
4. What should the leadership of the Taco Barn organization do now?

## Key Terms >>

authority 200
autocratic leader 203
bet-your-company culture 214
charismatic leadership 209
consideration 203
contingency approach to leadership 205
corporate culture 213
culture 211
democratic leader 203
entry socialization 213
initiating structure 203
laissez-faire leader 203
leader 200
Leader Behavior Description Questionnaire (LBDQ) 203
leader-member relations 206
leadership 200
Managerial Grid 204
path-goal theory of leadership 207
position power 206
power 200
process culture 214
self-fulfilling prophecy 201
situational leadership theory 208
task structure 206
tough-person, macho culture 214
trait theory 202
transactional leadership 208
transformational leadership 208
work-hard, play-hard culture 214

1. Discuss the following statement: "Leaders are born, not made."
2. Explain what people mean when they use this statement: "Leaders lead by example." Do you believe it? Explain your answer.
3. How would you use the Managerial Grid to classify the leadership style of an individual?
4. Explain the path-goal theory of leadership.
5. How is corporate culture originated and maintained?
6. List the five reasons that justify a large-scale cultural change.

## INTERNET In Action >>

1. Research prominent business executives in the Web versions of business magazines and newspapers. Select two executives: one who has an *autocratic* leadership style and one who has a *democratic* leadership style. Provide evidence to support your assessment of each leadership style. To what extent did leadership style contribute to the success or failure of that executive's organization?
2. Research two companies in the same industry that appear to have different organizational cultures. Summarize those differences. Is one culture better than the other? What could they learn from each other?

## << Team IN ACTION

1. **Transformational Leaders**

   In a recent survey, 90 percent of your managers classified themselves as transformational. When employees were surveyed about those managers, only 30 percent classified them as transformational. Divide into groups of two or three, and propose an action plan to respond to this information. Is it a communication issue? An education issue? What should be done to get everyone on the same page?

2. **Cultural Change**

   Divide the class into groups of three or four students. Each team must select an organization that will need to change its culture if it is to thrive in the future. Develop a PowerPoint presentation to be delivered to your fellow students outlining the following:

   a. A brief assessment of the culture of your selected organization.

   b. A summary of how that culture needs to change.

   c. An explanation of why you think this change must occur.

   d. Clear suggestions as to how that change could be implemented.

# Case 9.1

## >> The Confidence Factor • Bank of America CEO Kenneth D. Lewis struggled to win back investor confidence after the acquisition of Merrill Lynch.

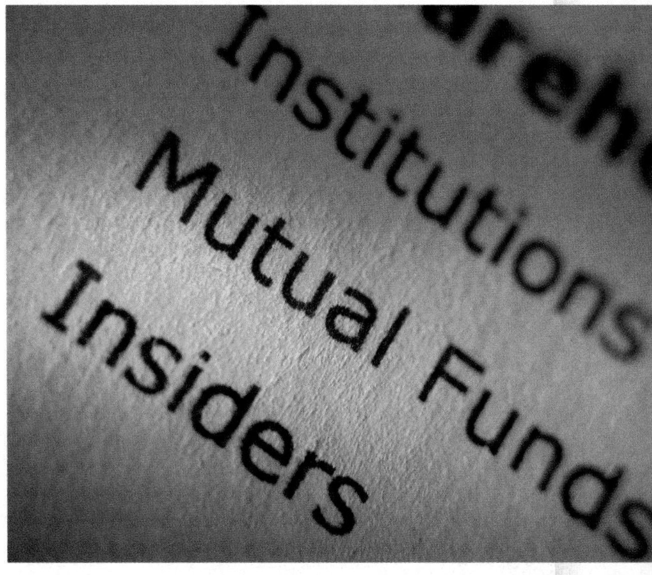


In August 2009, Bank of America (BoA) agreed to a settlement of $33 million to the Securities and Exchange Commission (SEC) without admitting or denying the accusations over misleading its shareholders about $5 billion in bonuses paid by Merrill Lynch, the brokerage company that BoA had acquired in 2008. The SEC accusations centered on a November 3 proxy statement in which BoA stated that Merrill had agreed not to pay year-end performance bonuses without BoA consent. In actuality, the SEC argued, there was documentation in place before the acquisition was even announced in September 2008, signed by the boards of both companies, authorizing the payment of up to $5.8 billion in year-end compensation.

The settlement marked yet another blow to Lewis's leadership of BoA in a series of missteps over the Merrill Lynch acquisition. Thrown together in 48 hours of frenetic negotiations in a period of considerable financial turmoil as another large Wall Street firm, Lehman Brothers, descended into bankruptcy and eventual collapse, the BoA-Merrill "marriage" suffered severe criticism ranging from "a shotgun wedding" to "an arranged marriage" and "doomed from the start." Without a doubt, the beginning of this new relationship was far from auspicious. Within three weeks of the closure of the deal in 2009, John Thain, Merrill's former CEO, was summarily dismissed after his own series of missteps. Accounts of lavish spending on office furniture and decorations, along with his aggressive lobbying for a $40 million bonus for closing the sale to BoA, did not apparently endear Thain to Lewis. The subsequent revelation of a $15.3 billion loss for Merrill's fourth quarter in 2008 that forced BoA to ask the government for an additional $20 billion of new capital and a guarantee of $118 billion on questionable Merrill assets (on top of the $25 billion granted in the October 2008 bailout) pretty much sealed Thain's future.

Defenders of Thain's record at Merrill Lynch argued that he succeeded in getting a good price for Merrill investors in the transaction—$29 a share for an overall valuation of $50 billion for the company at the time of the acquisition. Investors who elected to cash out on that deal would probably agree with that position. However, investors who held on in expectation of bigger and better things ahead saw the value of their new BoA shares fall by as much as 80 percent since then. Ironically, Lewis's savvy negotiation of a purchase price in shares rather than cash may be the only positive to come his way as a result of the Merrill deal.

The attraction of the Merrill Lynch deal, at first glance, was obvious—an attractive retail brokerage that could be counted on to promote BoA financial products, a solid brand identity, and a vast network of brokers known as "the thundering herd." Making the purchase at a time of financial uncertainty seemed to guarantee a fire-sale price that would pay off in long-term gains for Bank of America. The combined value of both companies at the time of the sale was $176 billion. Today, the combination has a market value closer to $40 billion. That severe devaluation, Thain's embarrassing departure, the "unexpected" fourth-quarter losses, and now the SEC settlement did, critics argue, irreparable damage to the reputation of a pragmatic, no-nonsense banker.

Lewis fought back valiantly against his critics on both the purchase of Countrywide Mortgage (under investigation for questionable lending practices) and Merrill Lynch. He claimed undue pressure from Ben Bernanke,

*Continued on next page*

Continued from page 221

the Federal Reserve chairman, to close the Merrill deal "for the good of the nation," and sought to spread responsibility for the apparent lack of due diligence on both acquisitions. At the BoA annual general meeting in April 2009, Lewis received a very clear message on the level of satisfaction with his performance. Shareholders reelected him to the board of directors, but they also voted to split his role as chairman and CEO, replacing him with Walter Massey as chairman.

On September 30, 2009, Lewis announced his intention to retire as chief executive at the end of the year. While his departure was widely anticipated, the announcement appeared to catch the board of directors off guard because there was no announcement of a successor to Lewis. After beginning as a low-level loan officer in 1969, Lewis left with pension benefits worth $53.2 million and an additional $81.8 million in stock and other compensation that he accumulated over his career. The appointment of his successor, Brian Moynihan, formerly president of BoA's consumer and small business banking, was announced on December 16, 2009.

QUESTIONS

1. Having just purchased Countrywide Mortgage, why would Bank of America want to take on another large acquisition at a time of such financial turmoil?
2. Why was an all-share deal rather than an all-cash deal for Merrill Lynch better for Bank of America?
3. Did Ken Lewis look out for the best interests of BoA's shareholders, or was he, as critics have claimed, just an "empire builder"? Defend your position.
4. Would Bank of America have been better off *not* buying Merrill Lynch? Why or why not?

*Source:* Louise Storey and Julie Creswell, "For Bank of America and Merrill, Love Was Blind," *The New York Times*, February 8, 2009; ."Changing Course," *The Economist*, April 30, 2009; Zachery Kouwe, "Bank of America Settles S.E.C. Suit over Merrill Deal," *The New York Times*, August 4, 2009; "No Gain, No Thain," *The Economist*, January 23, 2009; Elise Craig and Philip Mintz, "Bernanke Denies Bullying Bank of America," *BusinessWeek*, June 25, 2009; and Louise Storey and Eric Dash, "Bank of America Chief to Depart at Year's End," *The New York Times*, September 30, 2009.

# Case 9.2

## >> One of the Best Places to Work

SAS Institute (pronounced "Sass") is the largest privately held software company in the world in terms of prepackaged software, according to *Software Magazine*. Developing business analytics software for pharmaceutical companies, banks, retailers, and more, SAS generated revenues of $2.31 billion in 2009, and its software runs in 92 of the top 100 Global 500 companies. For a company of that size to still be privately held is significant enough, but SAS has found fame as a leader in providing a truly employee-friendly work environment.

Cofounded in 1976 by former North Carolina State University professor Jim Goodnight, SAS's focus on employee satisfaction and well-being was not part of the company's original vision. As Goodnight states: "In the early days, everyone was an owner, making it easier to spend more on ourselves." As an organization with more than 11,000 employees, 5,700 of whom work at the company's 300-acre Cary, North Carolina campus, it didn't take long for the employee-centric culture to take hold.

In 1981, when Goodnight heard about a key employee's decision to leave and become a stay-at-home mom, he hired an on-site day care provider and persuaded her to stay. Today there is an entire child care department staffed with 120 teachers and caregivers, looking after over 600 children each day. Employees in the child care department receive the same benefits as other SAS staffers.

In addition to first-class child care, the Cary campus also offers a fitness center, hiking and biking trails, an Olympic-size swimming pool, gourmet cafeterias, a company health care center, and such on-site conveniences as a car detailing service, hair salon, and ATMs.

The culture extends beyond the provision of an attractive benefits package. SAS encourages work-life balance by allowing employees to work a reasonable number of hours. Goodnight often says publicly that he believes employees should leave the office at 5 P.M. sharp to have dinner with their families. As its Web site proudly states: "If you treat employees as if they make a difference to the company, they will make a difference to the company."

Critics argue that SAS is an exception because the multibillionaire Goodnight can afford to be generous. In fact, Goodnight's leadership of an organization that appears consistently in *Forbes* magazine's top 10 places to work aligns this focus on employees with a much broader business strategy. The technology sector has proved to be notoriously cyclical (anyone remember the "dot-com boom and bust"?), and in good times companies have resorted to the blatant poaching of key employees by offering attractive benefit packages and stock options.

> If you treat employees as if they make a difference to the company, they will make a difference to the company.

Goodnight takes a much longer-term view. For a company that regularly spends over 20 percent of its revenues on research and development to stay ahead of the competition, taking the same approach to its human resources makes perfect sense. In the 2001–2002 economic downturn, for example, when layoffs were the name of the game in Silicon Valley, SAS increased hiring in those two years. Profits from the company stayed flat over that period, but since the company is privately held, the fallout was minimal. As Goodnight points out: "There were a lot of very good people out in the street looking for jobs. . . . We used that as a building time. Now, if we had been public, I'd probably be out of a job by now because we didn't increase profits."

The final testament on the SAS culture comes from the employees themselves. Annual turnover is consistently around 4 percent, far below the industry average. When surveyed in an internal poll, 87 percent of SAS employees said they opposed going public, even though for many of their colleagues in other companies, going public and cashing in stock options is the traditional road to wealth.

## QUESTIONS

1. CEO Jim Goodnight is adamant that remaining privately held rather than going public gives SAS a strategic advantage. In what way?
2. SAS's employee costs are obviously at the top end of the range for technology companies based on such an impressive benefits package. How can the company justify this expense in such a cost-conscious market?
3. If there is a direct link between employee satisfaction and low turnover (as Goodnight believes), why don't more companies follow SAS's example?
4. How would you sell the SAS employee-centric model to your company?

*Source:* John S. McClenahen, "Dr. Goodnight's Good Days," *IndustryWeek*, December 1, 2004; David A. Kaplan, "SAS: A New No. 1 Best Employer," *Fortune*, January 22, 2010; and Laurence Prusak and Don Cohen, "How to Invest in Social Capital," *BusinessWeek*, October 23, 2007.

# Case 9.3

## >> A New Style of "Patient-Centric" Leadership

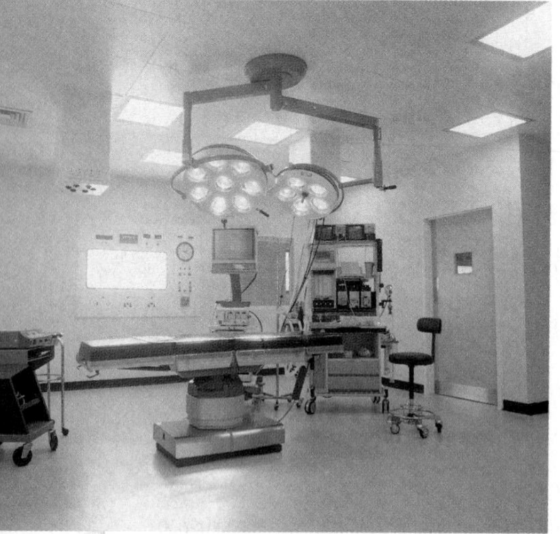

For a U.S.-based hospital system, the newest medical technology provides excellent material for an aggressive marketing campaign to position the organization as a leader is its local and regional markets. However, new technology is capital-intensive and places a huge burden on the bottom line; and since most testing procedures are governed by predetermined price agreements with insurance providers, the ability to pass on that increased capital expenditure is limited.

Mark McClellen of the Brookings Institution, an American think tank, argues that there is an overuse of technology. If a doctor orders a scan, the system will pay for it, without making a judgment as to whether or not it is really needed. For the doctor, that order for a scan may simply be a standard practice as a defense against a potential malpractice claim, rather than a direct patient need. "The root cause is not greed, but tremendous technological pressure imposed upon a fractured health system," says Thomas Lee of Partners Community Healthcare, a health provider in Boston.

Critics argue that in many cases the new equipment is only marginally better than the last version, and the resources diverted to this "technology-centric" approach deprive hospital systems of the capacity to serve other sectors of their market—specifically their poorer patient populations. Shivinder Singh, head of Fortis, a hospital chain based in New Delhi, India, advocates for a more "patient-centric" approach. "We got out of this arms race a few years ago," he says. While their scanners are not the newest, they are still "world class," and the cost savings allow Fortis to support a regional network of small hospitals to serve poorer rural populations, in addition to larger hospitals in major population centers to serve India's emerging middle class.

'The root cause is not greed, but tremendous technological pressure imposed upon a fractured health system'

Commitment to a patient-centric model means more than simply fighting off aggressive medical equipment salespeople. It demands a careful analysis of every new advance in medical technology to ensure that the additional costs provide sufficient cost-plus benefits to the institution and its patients. Every dollar spent on equipment carries an opportunity cost of a dollar not being spent somewhere else in the system. Without a clear understanding of the cost model for the entire system, the cost of new equipment is left to business managers to justify in terms of increased market share or column inches of media coverage gained through news stories about the new machines.

For Fortis and their primary competitor Apollo Hospitals, the requirement for detailed cost-benefit analysis has led to significant capital investments in fully integrated health information technology (HIT) and comprehensive electronic health records (EHR) for all their patients—capabilities that have featured very prominently in the Obama administration's calls for change in the U.S. health care system. In addition, better resource utilization results in 22 to 27 procedures per week in Fortis's operating rooms, compared with 4 to 6 per week in private clinics.

The fully integrated HIT system facilitates immediate availability of comprehensive patient information, even in the remotest rural hospitals in the Fortis system. This has reduced medical errors, and since the software also handles patient registration and billing, the system achieves significant labor cost savings.

Paul Yock, head of the bio-design laboratory at Stanford University, which develops medical devices, argues that medical technology giants have "looked at need, but been blind to cost." As President Obama's very public commitment to health care forces the nation to examine what many consider to be runaway health care spending, Yock thinks that the industry can learn a lot from the Indian approach.

Patients certainly seem to agree. With spending on health care in India expected to increase from $40 billion in 2008 to $323 billion by 2023, India's domestic health care needs provide reason enough for a new leadership approach. There has, however, been an unexpected boon to this patient-centric philosophy—medical tourism.

According to *Patients without Borders: Everybody's Guide to Affordable, World-Class Medical Tourism*, by Josef Woodman, overseas care can trim 60 to 80 percent, or more, off the price of major surgeries. One example lists the cost of a heart bypass operation in India as being 1/13th of the price for the same surgery in America.

U.S. health insurers appear to be more than willing to take advantage of this cost differential. Blue Cross Blue Shield's Companion Global Healthcare subsidiary has already signed partnership agreements with Bumrungrad International Hospital in Bangkok, Thailand, and Parkway Group Healthcare, owner of three hospitals in Singapore.

Jonathan Edelheit, president of the Medical Tourism Association, an industry group formed in 2007, is confident that convincing customers to receive treatment overseas will not be that hard. Even if the insurer chooses to waive all deductibles and copays, and picks up the tab for all travel costs for the patient and family members, it will still save tens of thousands of dollars.

However, this race to cut costs presents an interesting paradox for the nations that led the way in this new patient-centric approach to health care. If a rapid increase in medical tourism will draw domestic medical professionals into the population centers to provide care for these visiting international patients, what will become of the rural medical centers?

## QUESTIONS

1. Could this patient-centric model work in the United States? Why or why not?
2. If U.S. hospital systems adopt the same cost-benefit approach to new medical technology as the Indian hospitals, what will happen to the U.S. medical equipment industry?
3. Why is HIT such a key component of medical care?
4. Would you go overseas for a medical procedure? Why or why not?

*Source:* Saritha Rei, "Low Costs Lure Foreigners to India for Medical Care," *The New York Times*, April 7, 2005; Bruce Einhorn, "Outsourcing the Patients," *BusinessWeek*, March 13, 2008; Joshua Kurlantzick, "Medical Tourism: Sometimes, Sightseeing Is a Look at Your X-Rays," *The New York Times*, May 20, 2007; and "Lessons from a Frugal Innovator," *The Economist*, April 16, 2009.

CHAPTER 10
"Management is nothing more than motivating other people."
Lee Iacocca

# MOTIVATING PEOPLE

LEARNING OUTCOMES

After studying this chapter, you will be able to:

1 Define *motivation.*

2 Discuss the equity approach to motivation.

3 Explain the hierarchy of needs.

4 Discuss the expectancy approach to motivation.

5 Discuss the motivation-maintenance approach to motivation.

6 Define *job satisfaction* and *organizational morale.*

# THE WORLD OF WORK

## Employee of the month—again!

"And the employee of the month is . . ." Tony paused for dramatic effect. "Kelly Stevens!" The round of applause that followed was very unenthusiastic. Probably, Tony thought, because Kelly had been voted employee of the month three times in the last six months, and this was her fourth award.

That was one of the biggest challenges in running a single unit like this. The part-time staff weren't around enough to really make a memorable impact, and so the pool of candidates for the award typically ended up being the small core of full-time crew members. They had tried to modify the program a few months ago by recognizing specific examples of excellent customer service observed by the manager or shift leaders, but that had backfired when people started going out of their way to "create" opportunities for memorable service. The most blatant example, Tony recalled, had been when one of their new servers took orders from a table of eight. The orders were totally off the standard menu and had to be cooked to order using ingredients purchased very rapidly from the food market down the block! That was definitely service "above and beyond" the norm, but when the server charged them all standard prices, Tony had to step in and control their enthusiasm.

On the day after the employee of the month award, Tony called his staff into a brief meeting and proposed a new idea:

"I know everyone is working hard here, and the company is committed to rewarding you for that, but the employee of the month award doesn't work for such a small crew of full-timers. I'd like to explore some other ways of recognizing all your efforts—ways that include the part-time team members as well as the full-time ones. More importantly, I'm looking for ways to offer incentives that really mean something to you—not just the plaque on the wall and the designated parking space—something that you will enjoy receiving long after the award is given.

"Since you'll be the ones receiving the awards, I'd like you to propose some ideas for what those awards should be," continued Tony. "I'm not going to put you on the spot now for ideas, but I would like you to write some down and put them in the suggestion box in the break room. We'll give it a few days, and then we'll look at what everyone came up with. Okay?"

### QUESTIONS

1. Why does Tony feel that the employee of the month award isn't working?
2. What's the value in asking the Taco Barn employees for their ideas?
3. What ideas do you have for recognizing employee performance?
4. Consider the organization you currently work for or one you have worked for in the past. How did that organization recognize employee performance?

# >> Motivating Employees

Statements and questions such as the following are often expressed by managers: "Our employees are just not motivated. Half the problems we have are due to a lack of personal motivation. How do I motivate my employees?"

The problem of motivation is not a recent development. Research conducted by William James in the late 1800s indicated the importance of motivation.[1] James found that hourly employees could keep their jobs by using approximately 20 to 30 percent of their ability. He also found that highly motivated employees will work at approximately 80 to 90 percent of their ability. Figure 10.1 illustrates the potential influence of motivation on performance. Highly motivated employees can bring about substantial increases in performance and substantial decreases in such problems as absenteeism, turnover, tardiness, strikes, and grievances.

**Motivation** The concern with what activates human behavior, what directs this behavior toward a particular goal, and how this behavior is sustained.

**Equity Theory** Motivation theory based on the idea that people want to be treated fairly in relationship to others.

The word **motivation** comes from the Latin word *movere,* which means to move. Numerous definitions are given for the term. Usually included are such words as *aim, desire, end, impulse, intention, objective,* and *purpose.* These definitions normally include three common characteristics of motivation. First, motivation is concerned with what activates human behavior. Second, motivation is concerned with what directs this behavior toward a particular goal. Third, motivation is concerned with how this behavior is sustained.

Motivation can be analyzed using the following connecting sequence:

Needs → drives or motives → achievement of goals

In motivation, needs produce motives, which lead to the accomplishment of goals. Needs are caused by deficiencies, which can be either physical or psychological. For instance, a physical need exists when an individual goes without sleep for 48 hours. A psychological need exists when an individual has no friends or companions. Individual needs are explored in much greater depth later in this chapter.

**Figure 10.1 • Potential Influence of Motivation on Performance**

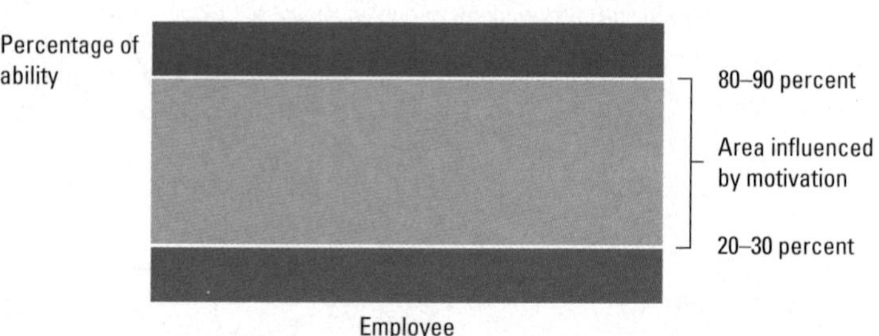


***Source:*** P. Hersey and K. H. Blanchard, *Management of Organizational Behavior: Utilizing Human Resources,* 4th ed., Prentice Hall, 1982.

A motive is a stimulus that leads to an action that satisfies the need. In other words, motives produce actions. Lack of sleep (the need) activates the physical changes of fatigue (the motive), which produces sleep (the action or, in this example, inaction).

Achievement of the goal satisfies the need and reduces the motive. When the goal is reached, balance is restored. However, other needs arise, which are then satisfied by the same sequence of events. Understanding the motivation sequence in itself offers a manager little help in determining what motivates employees. The approaches to analyzing motivation described in this chapter help provide a broader understanding of what motivates people. They include the following: scientific management, equity, hierarchy of needs, achievement-power-affiliation, motivation-maintenance, expectancy, and reinforcement.

# >> Importance of Trust in Management

The importance of trust in management by employees cannot be stressed enough as being absolutely essential for the success (or failure) for all motivational efforts. Without trust in management, all organizational efforts to motivate employees for improved performance are suspect. The presence of trust gives management credibility when asking for more productivity from employees.

# >> Equity Approach

**Equity theory** is based on the idea that people want to be treated fairly in relationship to others. **Inequity** exists when a person perceives his or her job inputs and rewards to be less than the job inputs and outcomes of another person. The important point to note in this definition is that it is the person's *perception* of

GETTING TO KNOW YOU . . .

# First Line Focus

*Motivating your team requires that you as their manager get to know them well enough to understand their needs and aspirations. For a small team this level of familiarity is relatively easy to achieve, and you can identify which of your team members is eager for career advancement, which one responds well to recognition, and which one prefers to be left alone to do the work to which he or she has been assigned.*

*However, as the number of people reporting directly to you grows alongside your advancement in the organization, maintaining that level of familiarity becomes much harder to achieve. It will be up to you to pass on the value of "getting to know your people" to your managers and their supervisors so that they can manage their teams in the same way. Without that level of knowledge, it won't be long before your organization resorts to the standard methods of employee recognition: employee of the month photographs on the wall and gift cards.*

inputs and rewards, not necessarily the actual inputs and rewards. Furthermore, the other person in the comparison can be an employee in the person's work group or in another part of the organization, which forms the employee's internal equity perception. Likewise, an employee may compare his or her inputs and rewards to others in similar jobs outside the company.

**Inputs** are what an employee perceives are his or her contributions to the organization (i.e., education, intelligence, experience, training, skills, and the effort exerted on the job). Outcomes are the rewards received by the employee (i.e., pay, rewards central to the job, seniority benefits, and status). Equity theory also suggests that the presence of inequity in a person creates tension in the person that is directly relative to the size of the inequity. Furthermore, the tension will motivate the person to achieve equity or reduce inequity. The strength of the motivation varies directly with the amount of inequity. A person might take several actions to reduce inequity:

1. Increase inputs on the job if his or her inputs are low relative to the other person. For example, a person might work harder to increase his or her inputs on the job.
2. Reduce inputs if they are high relative to the other person's inputs and to his or her own outcomes.
3. Quit the job.
4. Request a pay increase.

## [PROGRESS] ✓questions

1. What are the three common characteristics of motivation?
2. Why is trust in management so important for any motivational efforts?
3. What is equity theory?
4. Define the term *inputs.*

## >> Hierarchy of Needs

The **hierarchy of needs** assumes that individuals are motivated to satisfy a number of needs and that money can directly or indirectly satisfy only some of those needs. The need hierarchy is based largely on the work of Abraham Maslow.[2] The hierarchy of needs consists of the five levels shown in Figure 10.2.

The **physiological needs** are basically the needs of the human body that must be satisfied in order to sustain life. These needs include food, sleep, water, exercise, clothing, shelter, and so forth.

**Safety needs** are concerned with protection

**Inequity** Perception of a person that his or her job inputs and outcomes are less than the job inputs and outcomes of another person.

**Inputs** Employee's perception of his or her contributions to the organization (e.g., education, intelligence, experience, training skills, and the effort exerted on the job).

**Hierarchy of Needs** Theory that individuals are motivated to satisfy a number of needs and that money can directly or indirectly satisfy only some of these needs.

**Physiological Needs** Needs of the human body that must be satisfied in order to sustain life.

**Safety Needs** Protection against danger, threat, or deprivation.

# Thinking Critically 10.1

## >> An Informative Coffee Break

On a Monday morning, April 28, Cat Schwartz was given the news that effective May 1, she would receive a raise of 5 percent. This raise came two months before her scheduled performance appraisal. Her manager, Karen Watters, informed her that the basis for the raise was her performance over the past several months and her value to the company. She was told that this was an above-average increase.

On the next day, Tuesday, a group of Cat's co-workers were having their regular morning coffee break. The conversation slowly made its way around to salary increases. One member of the group shared that she had received a performance review in April, but she had yet to receive any indication of a salary increase. Cat made a comment about the amount of any such increases, specifically questioning the range of increase percentages. Another co-worker immediately responded by saying how surprised he was in getting an across-the-board 4 percent increase last Friday. Another co-worker confirmed that he too had received a similar salary increase. Shocked by this information, Cat pressed for information, only to learn that several people had received increases of "around" 4 to 5 percent. Confused and angry, Cat excused herself, went back to her office, and closed the door.

That evening, Cat wrestled with her conscience concerning the morning's discussion. Her first impression of her raise was that it had been given based on performance. She felt she was being singled out for recognition for her hard work and her value to the organization. Now she wasn't so sure. Several questions were bothering her:

1. Why did her boss present the raise to her as a merit increase when it was the same as everyone else's?
2. Did individual job performance really count for that much in salary increases in her department?
3. Did her boss hide the truth regarding the raise?
4. Can she trust her boss in the future?
5. Will future salary increases be averaged across the board too?

**QUESTIONS**

1. Do you think Cat is right to be this upset? Why or why not?
2. How do you think the information Cat discovered during that morning coffee break will affect her performance from now on?
3. How would you react if you were Cat? Why?
4. What can Karen Watters do to regain Cat's trust?

against danger, threat, or deprivation. Since all employees have (to some degree) a dependent relationship with the organization, safety needs can be critically important. Favoritism, discrimination, and arbitrary administration of organizational policies are all actions that arouse uncertainty and therefore affect the safety needs.

**Social Needs** The needs for love, affection, belonging—all are concerned with establishing one's position relative to others.

The third level of the hierarchy is composed of the **social needs**. Generally categorized at this level are the needs for love, affection, belonging—all are concerned with establishing one's position relative to others. Social needs are satisfied by the development of meaningful personal relations and by acceptance into meaningful groups of individuals. Belonging to organizations and identifying with work groups are means of satisfying these needs in organizations.

The fourth level is composed of the **esteem needs**. The esteem needs include both self-esteem and the

## Figure 10.2 • Hierarchy of Needs

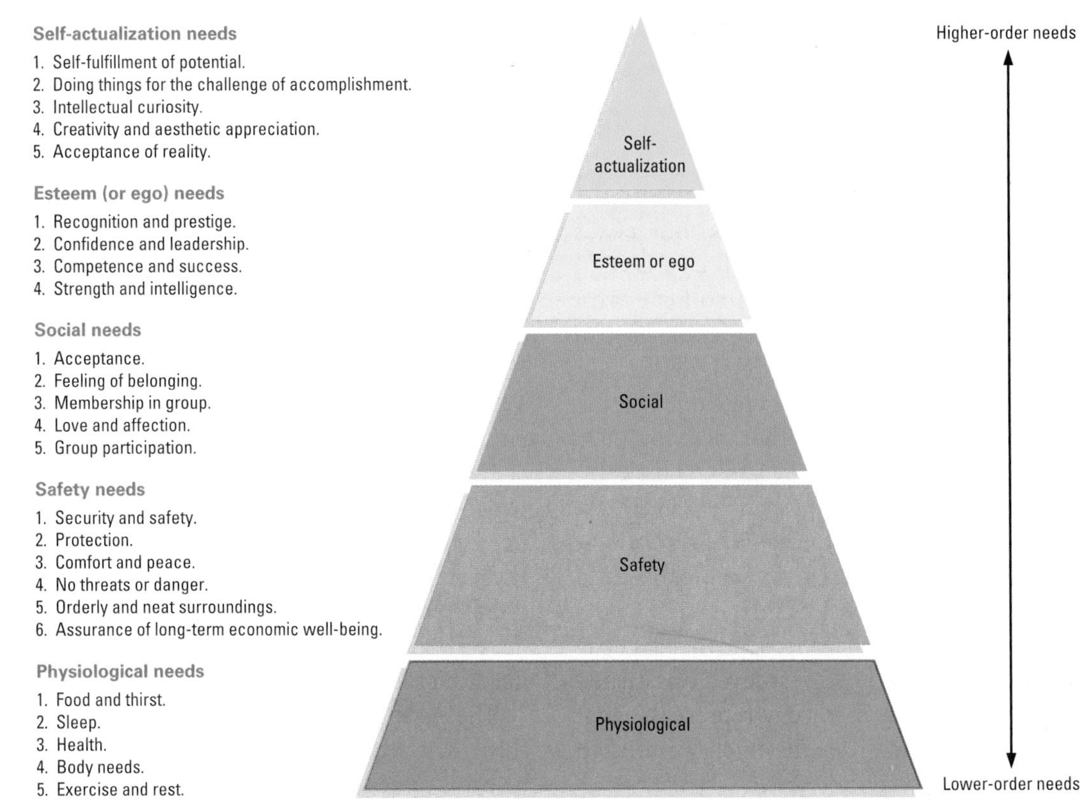


esteem of others. These needs influence the development of various kinds of relationships based on adequacy, independence, and the giving and receiving of indications of esteem and acceptance.

Self-actualization needs
1. Self-fulfillment of potential.
2. Doing things for the challenge of accomplishment.
3. Intellectual curiosity.
4. Creativity and aesthetic appreciation.
5. Acceptance of reality.
Esteem (or ego) needs
1. Recognition and prestige.
2. Confidence and leadership.
3. Competence and success.
4. Strength and intelligence.
Social needs
1. Acceptance.
2. Feeling of belonging.
3. Membership in group.
4. Love and affection.
5. Group participation.
Safety needs
1. Security and safety.
2. Protection.
3. Comfort and peace.
4. No threats or danger.
5. Orderly and neat surroundings.
6. Assurance of long-term economic well-being.
Physiological needs
1. Food and thirst.
2. Sleep.
3. Health.
4. Body needs.
5. Exercise and rest.
Self-actualization
Esteem or ego
Social
Safety
Physiological
Higher-order needs
Lower-order needs

The highest-order needs are the **self-actualization** or **self-fulfillment needs**—that is, the needs of people to reach their full potential in applying their abilities and interests to functioning in their environment. These needs are concerned with the will to operate at the best possible level. The need for self-actualization or self-fulfillment is never completely satisfied; one can always reach one step higher.

The hierarchy of needs adequately describes the general order or ranking of most people's needs. However, there are several other possibilities to be considered. First, although the needs of most people are arranged in the sequence shown in Figure 10.2, differences in the sequence can occur, depending on an individual's experience, culture, social upbringing, and numerous other personality aspects. Second, the strength or potency of a person's needs may shift back and forth under different situations. For instance, during

**Esteem Needs** Needs that influence the development of various kinds of relationships based on adequacy, independence, and the giving and receiving of indications of esteem and acceptance.

**Self-Actualization or Self-Fulfillment Needs** Highest-order needs involve people reaching their full potential in applying their abilities and interests to functioning in their environment.

*The span from the lowest to highest level in Maslow's hierarchy is fairly significant. Simple everyday activities can feel vastly different, depending on specific need requirements. Which needs do you feel are fulfilled in your own life?*

**Motivation-Maintenance** An approach to work motivation that associates factors of high-low motivation with either the work environment or the work itself; also known as the *two-factor* or *motivation-hygiene approach.*

bad economic times, physiological and safety needs might tend to dominate an individual's behavior; in good economic times, higher-order needs might dominate an individual's behavior.

The unconscious character of the various needs should be recognized. In addition, there is a certain degree of cultural specificity of needs. In other words, the ways by which the various needs can be met tend to be controlled by cultural and societal factors. For example, a particular culture may dictate one's eating habits, social life, and numerous other facets of life.

Finally, different methods can be used by different individuals to satisfy a particular need. Two individuals may be deficient in relation to the same physiological need; however, the way in which each chooses to satisfy that need may vary considerably.

As far as motivation is concerned, the thrust of the hierarchy of needs is that the lowest-level, unsatisfied need causes behavior. The hierarchy represents what Maslow thought was the order in which unsatisfied needs would activate behavior.

Many of today's organizations are applying the logic of the needs hierarchy. For instance, compensation systems are generally designed to satisfy the lower-order needs—physiological and safety. On the other hand, interesting work and opportunities for advancement are designed to appeal to higher-order needs. So the job of a manager is to determine the need level an individual employee is attempting to satisfy and then provide the means by which the employee can satisfy that need. Obviously, determining the need level of a particular person can be difficult. All people do not operate at the same level on the needs hierarchy. All people do not react similarly to the same situation.

Little research has been conducted to test the validity of the hierarchy of needs theory. Its primary value is that it provides a structure for analyzing needs and, as seen later in this chapter, is used as a basis for other theories of motivation.

## >> Achievement-Power-Affiliation Approach

While recognizing that people have many different needs, David C. McClelland developed the achievement-power-affiliation approach to motivation, which focuses on three needs: (1) need to achieve, (2) need for power, and (3) need for affiliation.[3] The use of the term *need* in this approach is different from the hierarchy of needs approach in that, under this approach, the three needs are assumed to be learned, whereas the needs hierarchy assumes that needs are inherent.

The *need for achievement* is a desire to do something better or more efficiently than it has been done before—to achieve. The *need for power* is basically a concern for influencing people—to be strong and influential. The *need for affiliation* is a need to be liked—to establish or maintain friendly relations with others.

McClelland's approach assumes that most people have developed a degree of each need, but the level of intensity varies among people. For example, an individual may be high in the need for achievement, moderate in the need for power, and low in the need for affiliation. This individual's motivation to work will vary greatly from that of another person who has a high

**PERKS FOR THE STAFF OR THE CUSTOMERS?**

After receiving some very disappointing responses to an employee satisfaction survey, you decide to implement an improved employee recognition award program as a way of encouraging superior performance. Instead of a photograph on the wall and a gift certificate, you decide to give the award winner a day off with pay and a designated parking space as close to the front of your store as possible (right next to the handicapped parking spots). You place a sign at the parking spot that states: "Reserved for our employee of the month."

The program is well received by the employees, and you hold a celebratory lunch to award the parking space and day off with pay for the first time. However, that afternoon you get paged to come to the customer service desk to speak with a customer who wishes to complain about your newly designated parking space: "Aren't your customers supposed to come first?" How would you answer your customer?

ETHICAL
MANAGEMENT
Should you put the happiness of your employees above that of your customers?

*The need for achievement is a powerful motivator for many employees. Is it a motivator you think you would respond to?*

need for power and low needs for achievement and affiliation. An employee with a high need for affiliation would probably respond positively to demonstrations of warmth and support by a manager; an employee with a high need for achievement would likely respond positively to increased responsibility. Finally, under this approach to motivation, when a need's strength has been developed, it motivates behaviors or attracts employees to situations where such behaviors can be acted out. However, this does not satisfy the need; it is more likely to strengthen it further. Figure 10.3 describes the achievement-power-affiliation approach to motivation.

## Figure 10.3 • Achievement-Power-Affiliation Needs

1. **The Need for Achievement**
   Other people are strongly motivated by the need for achievement. They are likely to be happiest working in an environment in which they can create something new.
2. **The Need for Power**
   Some people are strongly motivated by the need for power. They are likely to be happiest in jobs that give them control over budgets, people, and decision making.
3. **The Need for Affiliation**
   Some people are strongly motivated by the need for affiliation. These people usually enjoy working with other people. They are motivated by the prospect of having people like them.

## MOTIVATION-MAINTENANCE APPROACH

Another approach to work motivation was developed by Frederick Herzberg and is referred to by several names: the **motivation-maintenance**, two-factor, or motivation-hygiene approach.[4] Initially, the development of the approach involved extensive interviews with approximately 200 engineers and accountants from 11 industries in the Pittsburgh area. In the interviews, researchers used what is called the critical-incident method. It involved asking subjects to recall work situations in which they had experienced periods of high and low motivation. They were asked to recount specific details about the situation and the effect of the experience over time.

Analysis of the interviewees' statements showed that different factors were associated with good and bad feelings. The findings fell into two major categories. Those factors that were most frequently mentioned in association with a favorably viewed incident concerned the work itself. The factors were achievement, recognition, responsibility, advancement, and the characteristics of the job. But when subjects felt negatively oriented toward a work incident, they were more likely to mention factors associated with the work environment. These included status; interpersonal relations with supervisors, peers, and subordinates; technical aspects of supervision; company policy and administration; job security; working conditions; salary; and aspects of their personal lives that were affected by the work situation.

**Study Alert !**

Maslow's hierarchy of needs is based on the assumption that lower-level needs must be satisfied before higher-level needs can impact behavior. Maslow also believed that these needs were inherent rather than taught, so employee behavior in response to these needs was instinctive rather than premeditated. In contrast to Maslow's hierarchy of needs, McClelland proposed that different needs could coexist simultaneously and affect employee behavior based on individual situations.

**Job Enlargement** The practice of giving an employee more of a similar type of operation to perform.

**Job Rotation** The practice of periodically rotating job assignments within the organization.

**Job Enrichment** The practice of upgrading a job by adding motivators.

The latter set of factors was called *hygiene* or *maintenance* factors because the researchers thought that they are preventive in nature. In other words, they do not produce motivation but can prevent motivation from occurring. Thus, proper attention to maintenance factors is a necessary but not sufficient condition for motivation. The first set of factors was called *motivators.* The researchers contended that these factors, when present in addition to the maintenance factors, provide true motivation.

In summary, the motivation-maintenance approach contends that motivation comes from the individual, not from the manager. At best, proper attention to the maintenance factors keeps an individual from being highly dissatisfied but does not make that individual motivated. Both motivation and maintenance factors must be present in order for true motivation to occur. Figure 10.4 has examples of motivation and maintenance factors.

Job enrichment programs have been developed in an attempt to solve motivational problems by using the motivation-maintenance theory. Unlike **job enlargement**, which merely involves giving an employee more of a similar type of operation to perform, or **job rotation**, which is the practice of periodically rotating job assignments, **job enrichment** involves an upgrading of the job by adding motivators. Designing jobs that provide meaningful work, achievement, recognition, responsibility, advancement, and growth is the key to job enrichment.

As can be seen from Figure 10.5, the motivation-hygiene approach is very closely related to the hierarchy of needs approach to motivation and so is subject to many of the same criticisms.

## Figure 10.5 • Comparison of the Hierarchy of Needs with the Motivation-Maintenance Approach

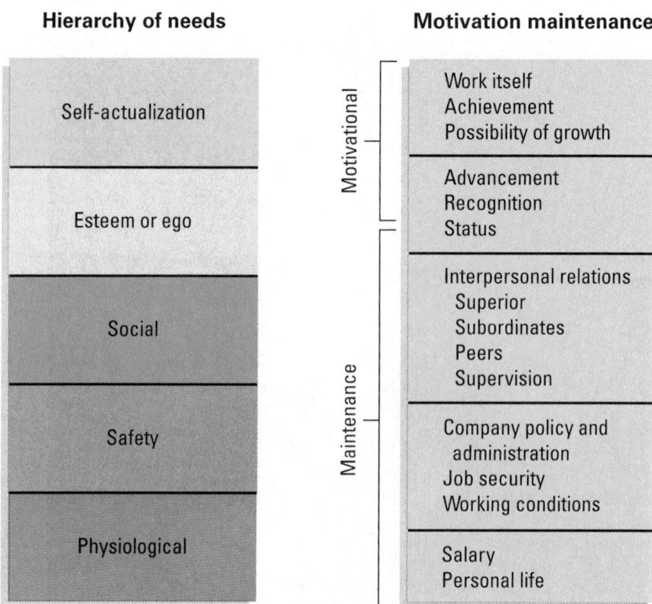


What does a manager do in using the maintenance-hygiene theory when the manager has an employee that is not performing well? First, all hygiene factors should be checked to ensure that they are satisfactory. Second, a motivation should be applied that meets the individual's needs and drives.

## Figure 10.4 • Motivation-Maintenance Factors

| Maintenance Factors (Environmental) | Motivator Factors (Job Itself) |
|---|---|
| Policies and administration | Achievement |
| Supervision | Recognition |
| Working conditions | Challenging work |
| Interpersonal relations | Increased responsibility |
| Personal life | Opportunities for advancement |
| Money, status, security | Opportunities for personal growth |

## EXPECTANCY APPROACH

The **expectancy approach**, from Victor Vroom's perspective, argues that employees will measure the

5. Why is self-actualization or self-fulfillment at the top of Maslow's hierarchy of needs?
6. How does McClelland's achievement-power-affiliation approach to motivation differ from Maslow's hierarchy of needs?
7. Explain the statement, "Proper attention to maintenance factors keeps an individual from being highly dissatisfied but does not make that individual motivated."
8. Explain the terms *job enlargement, job rotation,* and *job enrichment.*

## Figure 10.6 • Expectancy Approach

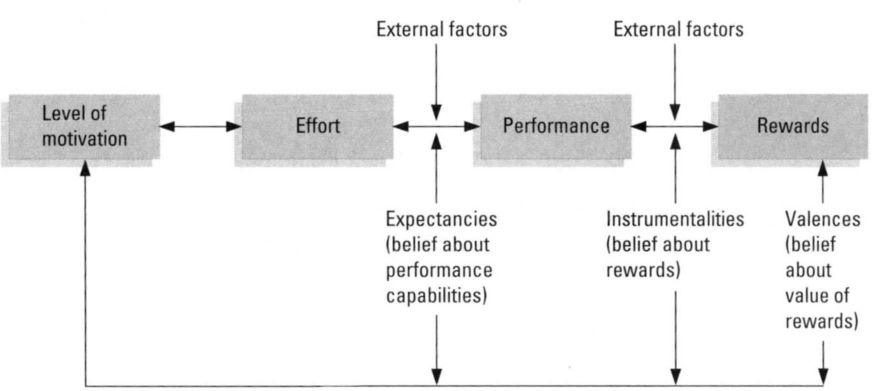


Study Alert

Herzberg's research was the first to propose the concept that addressing employee dissatisfaction would not automatically lead to increased employee satisfaction. Tackling the maintenance factors that prompt dissatisfaction would hopefully lead to less dissatisfaction, but since the issues that prompted employee satisfaction (motivators) were completely different, employees would not suddenly become completely satisfied with their work environment.

outcomes expected from their performance against how much effort they perceive is required to achieve that performance.[5] The degree to which that measurement is positive for the employee will determine that employee's motivation. For example, the opportunity for overtime is measured in the extra work required against the extra money in the paycheck—if the employee doesn't think it's enough, he or she will either not sign up for it or, if it's mandatory, do the minimum amount of work while on the overtime clock. Figure 10.6 outlines the expectancy approach to motivation.

The expectancy approach suggests that an employee's level of motivation depends on three basic beliefs: expectancy, instrumentality, and valence. **Expectancy** refers to the employee's belief that his or her effort will lead to the desired level of performance. **Instrumentality** refers to the employee's belief that achieving the desired level of performance will lead to certain rewards. **Valence** refers to the employee's belief about the value of the rewards. External factors are beyond the employee's control and often negatively influence expectancies and instrumentalities because they introduce uncertainty into the relationship. Company policies and efficiency of the equipment being used are examples of external factors.

The following example is intended to illustrate the expectancy approach. Assume John Stone is an insurance salesman for the ABC Life Insurance Company. John has learned over the years that he completes one sale for approximately every six calls he makes. John has a high expectancy about the relationship between his effort and performance. Since John is on a straight commission, he also sees a direct relationship between performance and rewards. Thus, his expectation that increased effort will lead to increased rewards is relatively high. Further, suppose that John's income is currently in a high tax bracket such that he gets to keep, after taxes, only 60 percent of his commissions. This being the case, he may not look on the additional money he gets to keep (the outcome) as being very attractive. The end result is that John's belief about the value of the additional money (valence) may be relatively low. Thus, even when the expectation of receiving the additional money is high, his motivation to do additional work may be relatively low.

Each of the separate components of the expectancy approach can be affected by the organization's practices and management. The expectancy that increased effort will lead to increased performance can be positively influenced by providing proper selection, training, and clear direction to the workforce. The expectancy that increased performance will lead to desired rewards is almost totally under the control of the organization. Does the organization really attempt to link rewards to performance? Or are rewards based on some other variable, such as seniority? The final component—the preference for the rewards being offered—is usually taken for granted by the

**Expectancy Approach** Motivation theory based on the idea that employees will measure the outcomes expected from their performance against how much effort they perceive is required to achieve that performance.

**Expectancy** Employee's belief that his or her effort will lead to the desired level of performance.

**Instrumentality** Employee's belief that attaining the desired level of performance will lead to desired rewards.

**Valence** Employee's belief about the value of the rewards.

**Positive Reinforcement** Provision of a positive consequence as a result of desirable behavior.

**Avoidance** Opportunity for a person to bypass a negative consequence by exhibiting a desirable behavior; also called *negative reinforcement.*

**Extinction** Absence of positive consequences or removal of previously provided positive consequences as a result of undesirable behavior.

**Figure 10.7 • Types of Reinforcement**

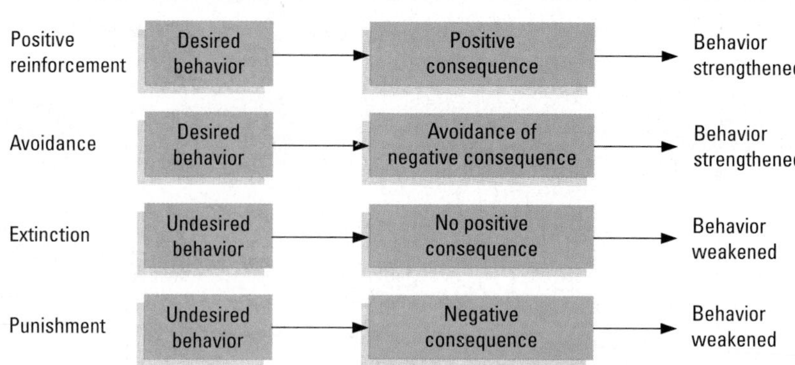


organization. Historically, organizations have assumed that whatever rewards are provided will be valued by employees. Even if this were true, some rewards are certainly more valued than others. Certain rewards, such as a promotion that involves a transfer to another city, may be viewed negatively. Organizations should solicit feedback from their employees concerning the types of rewards that are valued. Since an organization is going to spend a certain amount of money on rewards (salary, fringe benefits, and so on), it should try to get the maximum return from its investment.

## REINFORCEMENT APPROACH

Developed by B. F. Skinner, the general idea behind the reinforcement approach to motivation is that the consequences of a person's present behavior influence his or her future behavior.[6] For example, behavior that leads to a positive consequence is likely to be repeated, while behavior that leads to a negative consequence is unlikely to be repeated.

The consequences of an individual's behavior are called *reinforcement.* Basically, four types of reinforcement exist: positive reinforcement, avoidance, extinction, and punishment. They are summarized in Figure 10.7. **Positive reinforcement** involves providing a positive consequence as a result of desired behavior. **Avoidance**, also called *negative reinforcement,* involves giving a person the opportunity to bypass a negative consequence by exhibiting a desired behavior. Both positive reinforcement and avoidance can be used to increase the frequency of desired behavior.

**Extinction** involves providing no positive consequences or removing previously provided positive consequences as a result of undesirable behavior. In other words, behavior that no longer pays is less likely to be repeated. **Punishment** involves a negative consequence as a result of undesired behavior. Both extinction and punishment can be used to decrease the frequency of undesired behavior.

The current emphasis on the use of reinforcement theory in management practices is concerned with positive reinforcement. Examples include increased pay for increased performance, and praise and recognition when an employee does a good job. Generally, several steps are to be followed in the use of positive reinforcement. These steps include:

1. Select reinforcers that are strong and durable enough to establish and strengthen the desired behavior.
2. Design the work environment in such a way that the reinforcing events are contingent on the desired behavior.
3. Design the work environment so that the employee has the opportunity to demonstrate the desired behavior.

The key to successful positive reinforcement is that rewards must result from performance. Several suggestions for the effective use of reinforcement have been proposed. These include the following:

1. All people should not be rewarded the same. In other words, the greater the level of performance by an employee, the greater should be the rewards.
2. Failure to respond to an employee's behavior has reinforcing consequences.
3. A person must be told what can be done to be reinforced.
4. A person must be told what he or she is doing wrong.
5. Reprimands should not be issued in front of others.
6. The consequences of a person's behavior should be equal to the behavior.

In addition, positive reinforcement generally is more effective than negative reinforcement and punishment in producing and maintaining desired behavior.

**Figure 10.8 • The Relationship between Different Motivation Approaches**

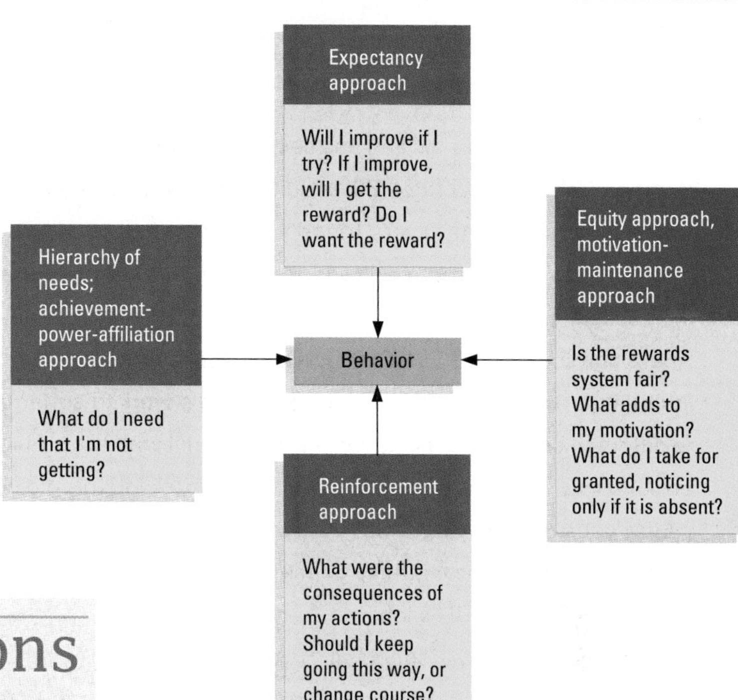
Expectancy approach
Will I improve if I try? If I improve, will I get the reward? Do I want the reward?
Hierarchy of needs; achievement-power-affiliation approach
What do I need that I'm not getting?
Behavior
Equity approach, motivation-maintenance approach
Is the rewards system fair? What adds to my motivation? What do I take for granted, noticing only if it is absent?
Reinforcement approach
What were the consequences of my actions? Should I keep going this way, or change course?

## PROGRESS ✓questions

9. What is the expectancy approach to motivation?
10. Explain the terms *instrumentality* and *valence.*
11. Explain the difference between positive reinforcement and avoidance.
12. What are the six key points to remember in the effective use of reinforcement?

## INTEGRATING THE APPROACHES TO MOTIVATION

There are many ways to look at motivation. Each approach emphasizes different contributors to motivation or sees the same contributors from a different perspective (see Figure 10.8). No single approach provides all the answers, so it is sometimes necessary to utilize more than one approach.

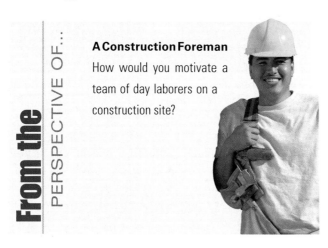

**From the PERSPECTIVE OF...**

**A Construction Foreman**

How would you motivate a team of day laborers on a construction site?

## JOB SATISFACTION

**Job satisfaction** is an individual's general attitude about his or her job. The five major components of job satisfaction are (1) attitude toward work group, (2) general working conditions, (3) attitude toward company, (4) monetary benefits, and (5) attitude toward supervision. Other major components that should be added to these five are the individual's attitudes toward the work itself and toward life in general. The individual's health, age, level of aspiration, social status, and political and social activities can all contribute to job satisfaction. Therefore, job satisfaction is an attitude that results from other specific attitudes and factors.

Job satisfaction is not synonymous with organizational morale. **Organizational morale** refers to an individual's feeling of being accepted by, and belonging to, a group of employees through common goals, confidence in the desirability of these goals, and progress toward these goals.

**Punishment** Negative consequence as a result of undesirable behavior.

**Job Satisfaction** An individual's general attitude about his or her job.

**Organizational Morale** An individual's feeling of being accepted by, and belonging to, a group of employees through common goals, confidence in the desirability of these goals, and progress toward these goals.

## Thinking Critically 10.2

### >> The Long-Term Employee

Bill Harrison is 57 years old and has been with Ross Products for 37 years. For the last 20 years, he has been a top-paid machine operator. Bill is quite active in community affairs and takes a genuine interest in most employee activities. He is very friendly and well liked by all employees, especially the younger ones, who often come to him for advice. He is extremely helpful to younger employees and never hesitates to help when asked. When talking with the younger employees, Bill never talks negatively about the company.

Bill's one shortcoming, as his supervisor Alice Jeffries sees it, is his tendency to spend too much time talking with other employees. This not only causes Bill's work to suffer but also, perhaps more importantly, hinders the output of others. Whenever Alice confronts Bill with the problem, Bill's performance improves for a day or two. It never takes long, however, for Bill to slip back into his old habit of storytelling and interrupting others.

Alice considered trying to have Bill transferred to another area where he would have less opportunity to interrupt others. However, Alice concluded she needs Bill's experience, especially since she has no available replacement for Bill's job.

Bill is secure in his personal life. He owns a nice house and lives well. His wife works as a librarian, and their two children are grown and married. Alice has sensed that Bill thinks he is as high as he'll ever go in the company. This doesn't seem to bother him since he feels comfortable and likes his present job.

**QUESTIONS**

1. What approach would you use to try to motivate Bill? Explain in detail what you would do.
2. Suppose Alice could transfer Bill. Would you recommend that she do it?
3. How do you think the other employees would respond if Alice fired Bill?
4. If Bill's behavior doesn't change, what are Alice's options?

Morale is related to group attitudes, whereas job satisfaction is more of an individual attitude. However, the two concepts are interrelated in that job satisfaction can contribute to morale and morale can contribute to job satisfaction.

### THE SATISFACTION-PERFORMANCE CONTROVERSY

For many years, managers have believed for the most part that a satisfied worker will automatically be a good worker. In other words, if management could keep all the workers "happy," good performance would automatically follow. Many managers subscribe to this belief because it represents the path of least resistance. Increasing employees' happiness is far more pleasant for the manager than confronting employees with their performance if a performance problem exists.

*J.M. Smucker, the company best known for Smucker's Jams and Jellies, is ranked as one of the best companies to work for. Execs have claimed that the fantastic smell in the factory contributes to well-above-average employee morale.*

Research evidence generally rejects the more popular view that employee satisfaction leads to improved performance. The evidence does, however, provide moderate support for the view that performance causes satisfaction. The evidence also provides strong indications that (1) rewards constitute a more direct cause of satisfaction than does performance and (2) rewards based on current performance cause subsequent performance.

Research has also investigated the relationship between intrinsic and extrinsic satisfaction and performance for jobs categorized as being either stimulating or nonstimulating.[7] The studies found that the relationship did vary, depending on whether the job was stimulating or nonstimulating. These and other studies further emphasize the complexity of the satisfaction-performance relationship. One relationship that has been clearly established is that job satisfaction does have a positive impact on turnover, absenteeism, tardiness, accidents, grievances, and strikes.[8]

In addition, recruitment efforts by employees are generally more successful if the employees are satisfied. Satisfied employees are preferred simply because they make the work situation a more pleasant environment. So even though a satisfied employee is not necessarily a high performer, there are numerous reasons for cultivating satisfied employees.[9]

A wide range of both internal and external factors affect an individual's level of satisfaction. The top portion of Figure 10.9 summarizes the major factors that determine an individual's level of satisfaction (or dissatisfaction). The lower portion shows the organizational behaviors generally associated with satisfaction and dissatisfaction. Individual satisfaction leads to organizational commitment, while dissatisfaction results in behaviors detrimental to the organization (turnover, absenteeism, tardiness, accidents, etc.). For example, employees who like their jobs, supervisors, and other job-related factors will probably be very loyal and devoted employees. However, employees who strongly dislike their jobs or any of the job-related factors will probably be disgruntled and will often exhibit these feelings by being late, absent, or by taking more covert actions to disrupt the organization.[10]

**Figure 10.9 • Determinants of Satisfaction and Dissatisfaction Growth**

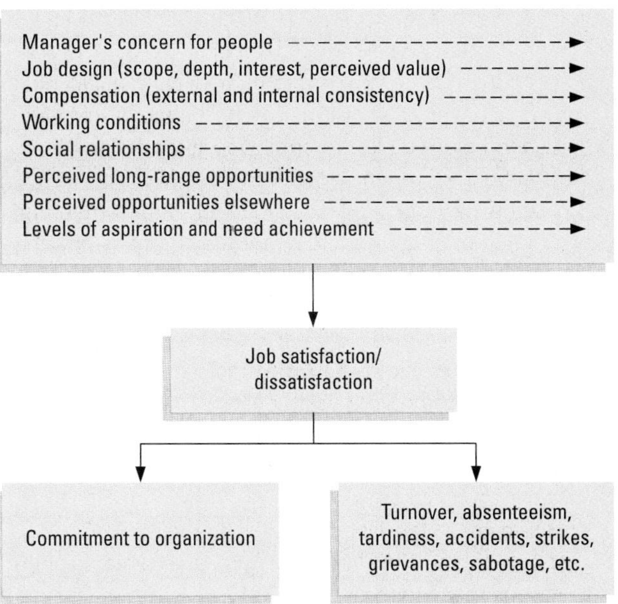


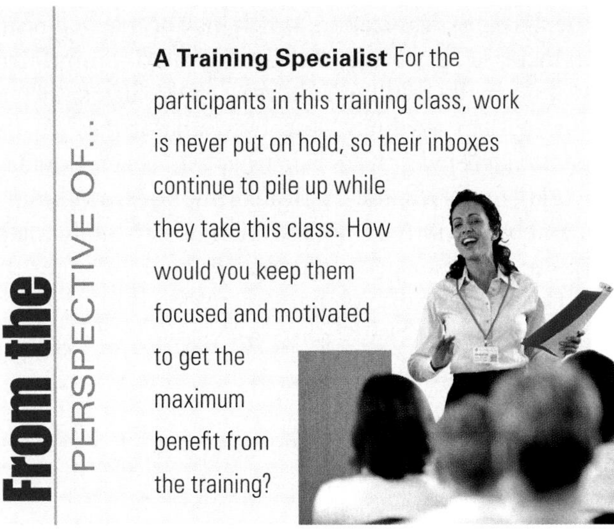


**A Training Specialist** For the participants in this training class, work is never put on hold, so their inboxes continue to pile up while they take this class. How would you keep them focused and motivated to get the maximum benefit from the training?

**PROGRESS ✓questions**

13. What are the five major components of job satisfaction?
14. Define the term *organizational morale.*
15. Consider the organization you currently work for or one you have worked for in the past. How would you describe the morale of that organization? Explain.
16. Explain the difference between satisfaction and motivation.

## A PROPORTIONAL RESPONSE

Denny Spisak is the human resource manager of ABC Industries, a small, privately owned, metal fabrication company. After three years of trying, Denny has finally convinced the owners of the company that a performance bonus incentive system, tied to specific cost and revenue targets, will help with employee productivity and help reduce the employee turnover problems they've been experiencing over the last year.

The new program is launched in an all-staff meeting, and the employees are told that if the company hits the cost and revenue targets, they will receive their bonus checks at the annual holiday party held on the last Saturday before Christmas.

The response from the ABC employees is very positive. They become very cost conscious and productivity increases dramatically. Several new process ideas are proposed that save the company tens of thousands of dollars in the first six months.

However, in the last quarter of the year, ABC's biggest competitor, XYZ Industries, drops its prices significantly and manages to steal two of ABC's largest clients. XYZ doesn't have better products or better service, but it offers prices that Denny is convinced are below XYZ's cost of production, just to win the business away from ABC. As a result, ABC misses its revenue targets for the year. The company grew at a rate of 8 percent instead of the planned 15 percent. Despite Denny's requests for the owners to consider the cost savings and new process ideas achieved by the employees, the owners decide that the incentive bonuses will not be paid out, and they cancel the holiday party as an additional cost saving measure.

ETHICAL
MANAGEMENT
Is it fair to cancel bonuses because the numbers weren't met—even though performance was better?


- Do you agree with the owners' decision not to pay out the bonuses? Why or why not?
- How do you think the employees will react?
- What could the owners have done to salvage the situation and maintain the increased levels of productivity and creativity at ABC Industries?

## >> Chapter Summary

Satisfaction and motivation are not identical. Motivation is a drive to perform, whereas satisfaction reflects the individual's attitude or happiness with the situation. The factors that determine whether an individual is satisfied with the job differ from those that determine whether the individual is motivated. Satisfaction is largely determined by the comfort offered by the environment and the situation. Motivation, on the other hand, is largely determined by the value of rewards and their effect on performance. The result of motivation is increased effort, which in turn increases performance if the individual has the ability and if the effort is properly directed. The result of satisfaction is increased commitment to the organization, which may or may not result in increased performance. This increased commitment will normally result in a decrease in problems, such as absenteeism, tardiness, turnover, and strikes. In the next chapter we review what happens when the ideal world of satisfied and motivated employees working in a smoothly running organization doesn't quite materialize and managers need to step in and monitor the performance of the company more closely.

1. Define *motivation.*

   Motivation is concerned with what activates human behavior, what directs this behavior towards a particular goal, and how this behavior is sustained. Organizations pay a lot of attention to motivation because evidence has shown that highly motivated employees can bring about substantial increases in performance and substantial decreases in such problems as absenteeism, turnover, tardiness, strikes, and grievances.

2. Discuss the equity approach to motivation.

   The equity approach to motivation is based on the idea that people want to be treated fairly in relationship to others. It is argued that employees monitor a balance of inputs (what they contribute to the organization, such as education, intelligence, experience, training, skills, and effort) against outcomes received from the organization, such as pay, benefits, seniority, and status. If an employee perceives an inequity between the inputs and outcomes or perceives that another employee is getting a better deal, this creates tension that prompts action to address the situation. Since the employee has no immediate control over outcomes, the action would focus on inputs—either increasing or decreasing them in accordance with the perceived inequity. If that doesn't help, more extreme action, such as demanding a pay raise or quitting the job altogether, could result.

3. Explain the hierarchy of needs.

   The hierarchy of needs, based largely on the work of Abraham Maslow, assumes that individuals are motivated to satisfy a number of needs and that money can directly or indirectly satisfy only some of those needs. Starting with basic physiological needs, such as food, water, sleep, and shelter, the hierarchy documents the change in needs as each preceding need is addressed—that is, as the physiological needs are addressed, safety needs become the primary concern. Once those are addressed, social needs (e.g., love, affection, and belonging) take precedence. With relationships starting to form, esteem needs (both self-esteem and the esteem of others) become important. At the top of the hierarchy is the highest-order need of self-actualization or self-fulfillment, where a person seeks to realize his or her full potential in applying skills and abilities to their maximum potential.

   As far as motivation is concerned, the lowest-level unsatisfied need drives behavior. For an organization seeking to motivate employees, this concept is critical. Offering opportunities to do creative and challenging work will only motivate those employees who have their lower-level needs met. Those who are concerned with physiological or safety needs would most likely respond to financial incentives rather than the opportunity for self-actualization.

4. Discuss the expectancy approach to motivation.

   The expectancy approach suggests that an employee's level of motivation depends on three basic beliefs: expectancy (the employee's belief that his or her effort will lead to the desired level of performance); instrumentality (the employee's belief that achieving the desired level of performance will lead to certain rewards); and valence (the employee's belief about the value of those rewards). Each separate component of the expectancy approach can be affected by the organization's practices and management. The desired level of performance must be clearly communicated, and the employee should be capable of performing to that level (through proper selection, training, and the provision of appropriate resources to do the job correctly). Rewards should be linked to performance, and the type of rewards available should be developed in consultation with employees to ensure that the rewards have value.

*Continued on next page*

Continued from page 241

5. Discuss the motivation-maintenance approach to motivation.

   Developed by Frederick Herzberg, the motivation-maintenance approach (also known as the motivation-hygiene or two-factor approach) separates the factors that motivate employees into two categories: the work itself (motivators) and the work environment (maintenance). Positive feedback from the employees typically concerned the work itself—achievement, recognition, responsibility, advancement, and the characteristics of the job itself. Since these factors clearly motivated employees to improve their performance, they were labeled "motivators."

   When negative feedback was received from employees during Herzberg's study, that feedback was most commonly associated with the work environment: interpersonal relations with supervisors, company policies, working conditions, and the impact the job was having on their personal lives. Herzberg labeled these factors as "maintenance" or "hygiene" factors because he believed they were preventive in nature. In other words, they do not produce motivation but can prevent motivation from occurring.

   In summary, the motivation-maintenance approach contends that motivation comes from the individual, not the manager. At best, proper attention to the maintenance factors keeps an individual from being highly dissatisfied, but does not make that individual motivated. Both motivation and maintenance factors must be present in order for true motivation to occur.

6. Define *job satisfaction* and *organizational morale.*

   Job satisfaction and organizational morale are interrelated. Job satisfaction refers to the individual's general attitude about the job. This mind-set may be positive or negative, depending on the five major components of job satisfaction: (1) attitude toward work group, (2) general working conditions, (3) attitude toward company, (4) monetary benefits, and (5) attitude toward supervision.

   Organizational morale refers to an individual's feeling of being accepted by and belonging to a group of employees through common goals, confidence in the desirability of those goals, and progress toward those goals. Morale is related to group attitudes, whereas job satisfaction is more of an individual attitude. However, job satisfaction can contribute to morale, and morale can contribute to job satisfaction.

**YOU CAN'T PLEASE EVERYONE** ***(continued from page 227)***

As promised, Tony gave his crew a few days to put forward some ideas for recognizing employee performance, and then he emptied the suggestion box from the break room. He was hoping for something simple and straightforward such as gift certificates or cash awards in their paychecks. Unfortunately, what he found in the suggestion box responses was not so simple.

Some wanted gift certificates from specific companies like grocery stores or electronic stores; others wanted certificates they could use at a store of their choice; others wanted certificates for specific services like a spa day or a car detailing; others just wanted the cash (either in their paychecks or in cold, hard cash); and some even wanted to keep the current employee of the month award, as long as Kelly Stevens didn't keep winning it! Some didn't ask for money at all—they wanted a day off with pay. Others felt that the award was more trouble than it was worth and suggested that the whole program be scrapped in favor of a big staff party at the end of the year or a minivacation paid for by Taco Barn.

As he read through all the suggestions, Tony started noticing a clear pattern. They were supposed to be anonymous suggestions, but Tony knew his people well enough to recognize a lot of the handwriting, and it was this that helped him identify the pattern. Those older employees with families and the younger single moms had fairly simple requests, such as gift certificates from the grocery store or cash in their paychecks. The younger, part-time employees, most of whom were still in school or college, wanted the gift certificates for the electronics store or to put more music on their iPods. Those with no kids or two incomes coming in wanted the treats like a spa day or their car detailed.

Tony was pleased on the one hand that they had put so much thought into their suggestions, but on the other hand he was disappointed to learn that the employee of the month award had meant so little to so many of his crew. He really did want them to be motivated by the chance to win these employee recognition awards, but how was he going to make sure that everybody got what he or she wanted?

**QUESTIONS**

1. Were the suggestions that Tony received really that surprising? Why or why not?

2. How do these suggestions relate to Abraham Maslow's hierarchy of needs?

3. Was it a good idea to create the expectation that the employees could pick their own award? Why or why not?

4. What should Tony do now?

## Key Terms >>

**avoidance 236**

**equity theory 228**

**esteem needs 231**

**expectancy 235**

**expectancy approach 235**

**extinction 236**

**hierarchy of needs 229**

**inequity 229**

**inputs 229**

**instrumentality 235**

**job enlargement 234**

**job enrichment 234**

**job rotation 234**

**job satisfaction 237**

**motivation 228**

**motivation-maintenance 232**

**organizational morale 237**

**physiological needs 229**

**positive reinforcement 236**

**punishment 237**

**safety needs 229**

**self-actualization or self-fulfillment needs 231**

**social needs 230**

**valence 235**

1. Explain the motivation sequence.
2. Which theory has greater applicability in today's business world: Maslow's hierarchy of needs or McClelland's achievement-power-affiliation? Why?
3. Discuss the satisfaction-performance controversy.
4. From a managerial standpoint, what are the real benefits of having satisfied employees?
5. Consider a job you currently hold or one you have held in the past. Using Herzberg's theory, document the motivator and maintenance factors in the job.
6. What elements would have to be present for you to be completely satisfied with your job?

# INTERNET In Action >>

1. Utilizing the search phrase "motivation in the workplace," find a selection of quotes and inspirational stories that could be used to support a planned employee recognition week at a company of your choice. Other than quotes and stories, what else would you propose doing to make the week meaningful to employees?
2. Visit the Web site for Outward Bound New Zealand at **www.outwardbound.co.nz.**
   a. What is the "Navigator Leadership Development Programme"?
   b. What kind of outcomes can you expect from the navigator course?
   c. How do past participants describe the experience?

## << Team IN ACTION

1. **Does Money Motivate?**

   You will be divided into two groups (or an equal number of smaller groups).

   Each group will be assigned one of the two following statements:

   a. Money is the primary motivator of people.

   b. Money is not the primary motivator of people.

   Prepare for a debate with another group on the validity of the statement that your group has been assigned. You will be debating a group that has the opposing viewpoint.

   At the end of the debate, answer the following questions:

   1. Summarize the key points of your viewpoint.
   2. Summarize the key points of the opposing group's viewpoint
   3. Did the information shared in the debate change your opinion? Why or why not?
   4. Your viewpoint was chosen for you according to the team to which you were assigned. How did the team members reach agreement in their debating viewpoint? Explain your answer.

2. **Motivation at Work**

   An employee satisfaction survey has revealed that company morale is at an all-time low. A tough economy, recent layoffs, and a pay freeze have shattered what used to be a fun place to work. Divide into three groups, and propose a 30-day motivation program for your company to improve employee morale. You may select the industry in which your company operates, but assume there are no funds budgeted for this program. Plan for 15 minutes, and then deliver a brief 5-minute presentation to your peers.

# Case 10.1

## >> Seagate Goes "Eco" • Team building costs $9,000 a head.

Plenty of companies try to motivate the troops, but few go as far as Seagate Technology.

For a company generating $10 billion a year in revenue, allocating $40 million to training and development of its employees may s eem reasonable, but allocating almost 5 percent ($1.8 million) of that budget to one event for 200 employees out of a worldwide total of 55,000 might raise some questions. Are these senior executives on a privileged retreat? Or the CEO's favorite hunting trip? In this case, neither is true.

Imagine 200 type-A engineers, PhDs, and MBAs all voluntarily competing in an event that's a cross between *Survivor* and *The Amazing Race,* and you start to get a sense of what "Eco Seagate," a weeklong team-building event in South Island, New Zealand, is all about.

The event is the vision of CEO Bill Watkins, who held the first Eco week in 2000. In 2009, over two thousand people applied for the event—some for the first time, and others had been trying to make the event since the beginning. Its purpose? To build "a collaborative, team-oriented company." He also thinks it teaches his people about priorities.

Watkins kicks off the event the same way every year: "Everyone here's going to die . . . at some point." They know they're here to build teams, but for Watkins there's as much to be learned about self-actualization as there is about collaboration. He continues: "Are you doing what you want to do in your life? Or are you just blowing through? I'm challenging your life right now. What would you do if you knew you couldn't fail? Would you take a trip around the world? Run a company? If you're not doing what you want, that's where I want you to go. This week is about doing what you want to do for every week of the rest of your life."

Volunteering for grueling mountain treks, bike rides, kayak races, and a Tyrolean zip line across a 200-foot-deep gorge may not be your idea of a typical employee motivation program. There are no employees of the month or designated parking spaces, and there are more power bars than gift certificates given out during Eco week. However, the impact of the event is uniquely personal. Some may be inspired to change their lives in a dramatic way. Others may leave great memories on South Island. A few may be prompted to leave altogether: Charlie Sander joined Seagate at the same time as Watkins. He was 49 when he ran his fourth and final Eco. "This particular Eco was about aspiring to goals," Sander remembers. "I had a dream to run my own company. By the end of the week, on the plane back, I decided this is the time."

In January 2009, after five years of a flat stock price, Watkins announced his resignation. Despite having its best ever year in revenues and profits for 2008, the economy was deemed to be so weak that a new direction was required. Watkins had already announced that things were so tough Eco Seagate 2009 was going to be canceled.

### QUESTIONS

1. Selecting 200 staffers at $9,000 per head is an expensive tab for a motivation event. What does Seagate hope to get for its investment?
2. Over 2,000 employees applied to be included in the 200. What does that say about the culture of Seagate?
3. Seagate spends over $40 million each year on training and development. Is that a worthwhile investment of funds? Why or why not?
4. Would you apply to take part in Eco Seagate? Why or why not?

*Source:* Sarah Max, "Seagate's Morale-a-thon," *BusinessWeek,* April 3, 2006; Jeffrey M. O'Brien, "Team Building in Paradise," *Fortune,* May 21, 2008; and Chris Nuttall, "On a Hard Drive for Team Spirit," *Financial Times,* January 28, 2008.

# Case 10.2

## >> Becoming a Chief Inspiration Officer • Employees want to know they're making a difference in people's lives, says Entergy's CEO.

Katrina gave his troops a chance to shine.

Wayne Leonard is the CEO of Entergy, America's third largest electric utility company, which serves Arkansas, Louisiana, Mississippi, and Texas. Leonard's actions during hurricanes Katrina and Rita offer an inspiring case study for people seeking to improve their leadership communications skills.

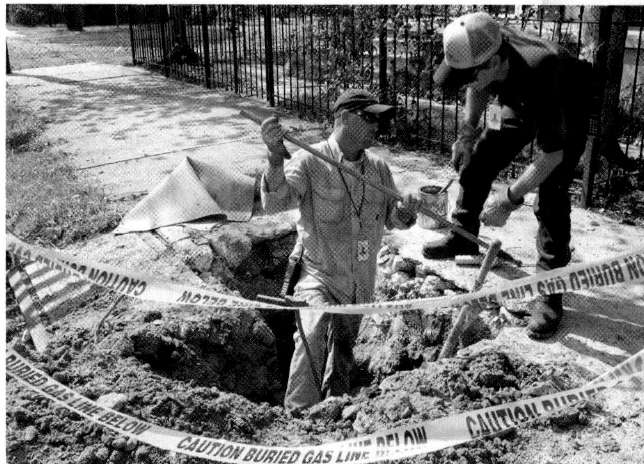


In August 2005, Katrina knocked out power to more than 1 million of Entergy's 2.7 million customers. Approximately 1,500 Entergy employees were displaced, and many of them saw their homes destroyed or severely damaged. One lineman and his friends were caught in rising water. They fled to an attic and used a two-by-four to break through the roof. The very next day, after being rescued, that lineman joined his fellow workers to turn the lights back on for Entergy's customers. His story wasn't unusual. It was common to see crews working 16-hour days for more than a week while they were unable to check on their own homes. By the end of the first week, power was restored to 550,000 people. And nearly everyone had power restored by the end of September—a remarkable achievement by all accounts.

### Simple Mission

Within a month of Katrina, hurricane Rita knocked out power to more than three-quarters of a million Entergy customers. The company was hit by two massive natural disasters in a row, and yet its employees showed devotion, commitment, and a level of teamwork that would be the envy of any corporation in America. CEO Wayne Leonard has consistently cultivated a culture based on a simple mission—to leave this world a better place than the company found it. In other words, for Entergy employees, their work represents more than a paycheck. If Entergy's displaced employees had viewed their role as just another job instead of a mission to provide hope to those in need, its customers might have remained in the dark a lot longer.

### Passion and Power

Entergy won numerous awards for its handling of the crisis, as did Leonard himself. It's easy to see why. Leonard wrote a string of emotional and optimistic e-mails to all his employees in the days and weeks after Katrina. The correspondence reflects the power of a mission consistently and passionately conveyed. Here are some excerpts:

In every man and woman's life, there is a defining moment. It is a brief intersection of circumstances and choices that define a person for better or worse, a life of unfilled potential or a life that mattered, that made a difference. It is true of individuals and it is true of business. We have great passion for the difference we make in other's lives. We provide a commodity that sustains life. But, more importantly, we provide the most precious commodity of all—hope.

The task before us is awesome, but not insurmountable. We will be challenged at every turn, but this is what has always defined Entergy. We are at our best when the challenge is greatest. . . . Our response to this crisis will make the people we call Entergy remembered and revered for all time. . . . We are bruised, but not broken. We are saddened, but not despondent. We are at that remarkable place in time where the hearts, minds, and souls of the good cross with challenge and opportunity to set the course of history. We define ourselves here and now for all to see, everywhere.

*Continued on next page*

Continued from page 247

Future generations will stand in awe at what you have endured and accomplished. Books will be written. Stories will be handed down. Some fall or spring day, the sun will be out, the temperature will be in the 70s, and you'll be sitting on the front porch content with the knowledge that you were not only there, but you stood tall and you didn't break or bend. Maybe it wasn't the life you envisioned, but in many ways it was better. Stronger, more courageous, more selfless than you ever even imagined you might be. You see things like this on television or in history books and ask, "How did they do it?" Now, you can tell them, because you did it. You were in the game. Maybe you were or maybe you weren't a "superstar" growing up. But I know this. You are now.

### "A Great Cause"

While some leaders motivate by fear and greed, Leonard believes the best motivation is appreciation. "It goes back to whether you believe people are basically good or not," Leonard says. "I know in my heart that people are basically good. People want to know that what they do makes a difference. And in our business, it does make a difference. We need to remind people of that fact and reinforce that message. When you show people that you really do appreciate them, they will do anything in the world for you when times get tough."

**QUESTIONS**

1. What is Entergy's mission?
2. "People want more than a paycheck." Explain this statement.
3. CEO Wayne Leonard "believes the best motivation is appreciation." How does Entergy's approach to motivation reflect that statement?
4. Think of the organization you currently work for or one you have worked for in the past. Does the organization's mission inspire you? Why or why not?

*Source:* Adapted from Carmine Gallo, "Viewpoint," *BusinessWeek*, April 20, 2006.

# Case 10.3

## >> Diagnosis: Low Employee Morale

The topic of health care features prominently in any conversation about employee motivation. The range and costs of medical benefits, and the increasing pressure to enforce employee wellness plans as a means of keeping benefit costs down, continue to be topics of debate—even more so with the health care reform legislation passed by the Obama administration in 2010.

Rarely, however, is consideration given to the employees who work in health care—from doctors and nurses to radiologists and lab technicians; from administrative staff to third-party vendors that staff call centers and store medical records. How are they motivated? Does their work environment require a different approach?

If the new legislation requires lower medical costs and lower reimbursement rates, critics are already speculating how long it will be before health care providers return to staff reductions in order to achieve those lower-cost targets. How will managers motivate employees in that environment?

Critics of the corporatization of health care argue that low employee morale on the front line of patient care can have terrible consequences. As one reader commented in *Healthcare Finance News:* "Increased patient workloads impact patient mortality and morbidity rates, placing employees (and health care organizations) at risk for litigation and that in and of itself creates an adverse working environment affecting employee morale."

Health care executives may well dismiss such commentary as someone with an ax to grind, but a December 2009 survey by the employment search company CareerBuilder reported some depressing statistics: "Twenty percent, or one in five, of the more than 350 health care employers reported low morale. Meanwhile, 38 percent of health care workers cited lack of motivation and nearly 25 percent reported no loyalty to their employers. . . . Nearly half of the health care workers surveyed cite increased stress on the job, and 50 percent noted an increase in their workload in the last six months."

Feelings of stress and frustration over being understaffed, overworked, and underpaid are not unique to health care, but in a service industry where the service provided is patient care, the negative feedback for poor service is immediate and direct, which only adds to low morale.

Health care organizations are taking cues from their commercial and industrial counterparts with flexible work schedules and incentive programs, but examples of companies that address the stress issue head-on are rare. The Fraser Health Authority in British Columbia, Canada, took the opportunity to promote employee wellness and "celebrate the success of our people, strengthen internal ties, and reward people for healthy behaviors." Over seven hundred employees participated in a virtual race from British Columbia to Panama by building walking teams and recording every step taken. In the first two weeks of the program, over 20 million steps were walked. Using an online template from a third-party vendor, participants were able to log their activity and leave messages for other teams (most motivational but a few couldn't resist a little trash talking to inspire their colleagues).

The trip to Panama was expected to take three months, but the response was so positive that teams reached their destination in two months. Project Director Wendy Creelman summarized the event: "The project goal was to demonstrate the need to care about our health, have fun and reduce stress in the workplace related to the health care industry."

Having fun is a theme shared by the Beryl Companies, a Texas-based company that provides call center services to hospitals and other health care organizations. To quote CEO Paul Spiegelman: "We have an executive whose official title is 'Queen of Fun and Laughter.' Her sole responsibility is to make sure that we stay true to our unique culture and that co-workers, lives stay in balance. The title doesn't sound serious, but her role is."

**QUESTIONS**

1. Why would the topic of health care feature prominently in any conversation about employee motivation?
2. Does the issue of patient care make low employee morale more important for health care organizations? Why or why not?
3. How would you describe the employee morale at your job or a job you have held in the past? What evidence can you offer to support that assessment?
4. Would hiring a "Queen of Fun and Laughter" work at your organization? Why or why not?

*Source:* Patty Enrado, "Healthcare Employers Battle Low Employee Morale," *Healthcare Finance News,* December 9, 2009; "Race to Panama Gets the Employees Active," www.welcoa.org/PDFs/Fraser_Health_Case_Study.pdf, retrieved 6/22/10; and Paul Spiegelman, "Happy Employees Make Thriving Companies," *The Washington Post,* February 19, 2010, www.entrepreneur.com.

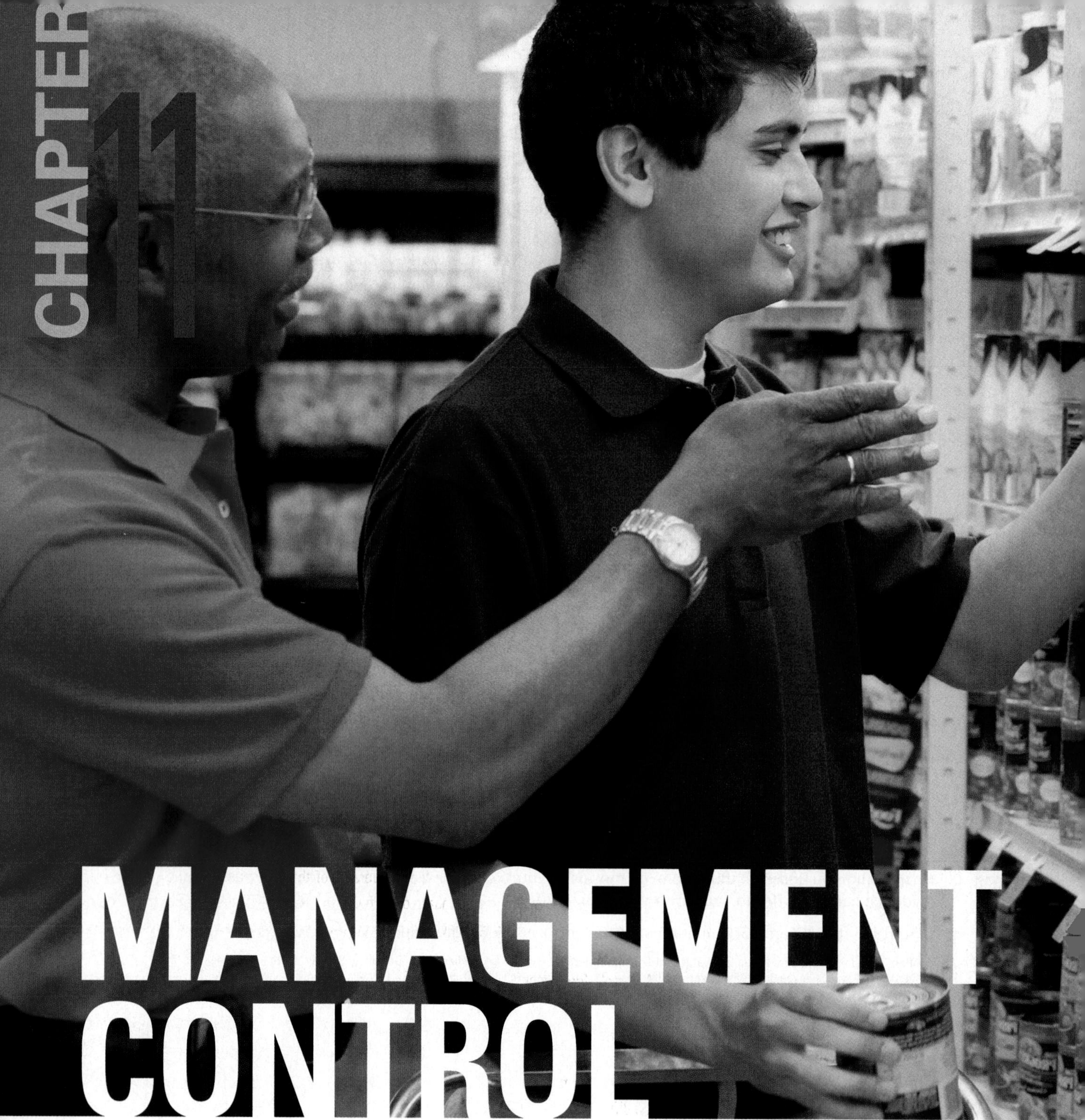

# CHAPTER 11

# MANAGEMENT CONTROL

"To persuade is more trouble than to dominate, and the powerful seldom take this trouble if they can avoid it."

**Charles Horton Cooley, American sociologist, 1864–1929**

After studying this chapter, you will able to:

1 Explain why management controls are necessary.

2 Discuss where control should reside in an organization.

3 Differentiate between preliminary, concurrent, and postaction controls.

4 Compare the four basic types of financial ratios.

5 Explain the determinants of performance.

6 Describe the major performance appraisal methods.

## THE WORLD OF WORK Managing by objective

When Tony had worked as a shift crew leader for Jerry Smith, his annual performance review had consisted of a brief meeting, a review of his successes for the year, and the notification of what his raise would be—usually a cost of living increase plus a little extra if the company was having a good year. For Tony, that had always been enough. Jerry was a good manager and always made himself available to his people, so there was never a need to have any major discussions about issues that had been stewing for a while. Jerry kept an open door policy, and if you needed to talk something over, you just asked for some time to sit down with him and work it through. That always worked both ways. If Jerry saw something that he didn't like, he would pull you aside and talk to you about it there and then, in private, without embarrassing you in front of your co-workers.

Now that Tony was the unit manager for this Taco Barn, he wanted to do things a little differently. It wasn't that Jerry's approach didn't work. He had been and still was a fantastic mentor to Tony, but, Tony thought, this was his crew now, and he wanted to put his stamp on things. Plus, the changes Tony had in mind weren't that dramatic. He felt strongly that several of the members of his unit crew had real potential and promising futures with the Taco Barn organization. He wanted them to start thinking of themselves in the same way, and he had begun to think that the annual performance reviews were a way to start that process. One of his business professors had talked about a process called management by objectives (MBO) where you worked with your people in the development of clear goals to be achieved each year. Tony thought that by helping his people work on specific goals, they could move that much closer to their potential both personally and professionally.

The reviews were always done on the anniversary of the worker's hire date with the company, and over the next two weeks, over a dozen of his full-time folks were due for their reviews—a perfect time to get going on this new approach, Tony thought. Kevin, Tony's assistant unit manager, was first on the list.

A week before the anniversary of Kevin's hire date with the company, Tony asked to meet with him after the lunch rush was over. They met on a regular basis, so Kevin saw no need to be nervous about the request, but Tony's opening question caught Kevin by surprise.

"Kevin, you know how happy we are with your work here at Taco Barn—both Dawn and I think you have a great future with the organization. For that reason, I'd like to do your performance review a little differently this year. I'd like you to come to your review meeting with some goals that you'd like to achieve over the coming year. They can be work-related and personal goals if you'd like. We'll incorporate those goals into a plan for the year and then review your achievement of those goals at next year's performance review. How does that sound?"

### QUESTIONS

1. Why does Tony think that incorporating MBO will be a positive move for his restaurant? Review page 262 for some guidance on this.
2. How do you think Kevin will respond to this request?
3. What challenges can you see in adopting the MBO approach?
4. If your boss made the same request of you as Tony is making of Kevin, how would you respond?

TACO BARN

# >> Controlling

The basic premise of organizations is that all activities will function smoothly; however, the possibility that this will not be the case gives rise to the need for control. **Control** simply means knowing what is actually happening in comparison to set standards or objectives and then making any necessary corrections. The overriding purpose of all management controls is to alert the manager to an existing or a potential problem before it becomes critical. Control is a sensitive and complex part of the management process.

**Control** Process of ensuring that organizational activities are going according to plan; accomplished by comparing actual performance to predetermined standards or objectives and then taking action to correct any deviations.

Controlling is similar to planning. It addresses these basic questions: Where are we now? Where do we want to be? How can we get there from here? But controlling takes place after the planning is completed and the organizational activities have begun. Whereas most planning occurs before action is taken, most controlling takes place after the initial action has been taken. This does not mean control is practiced only after problems occur. Control decisions can be preventive, and they can also affect future planning decisions.

# >> Why Practice Management Control?

As we just noted, management controls alert the manager to potentially critical problems. At top management levels, a problem occurs when the organization's goals are not being met. At middle and lower levels, a problem occurs when the objectives for which the manager is responsible are not being met. These may be departmental objectives, production standards, or other performance indicators. All forms of management controls are designed to give the manager information regarding progress. The manager can use this information to do the following:

1. *Prevent crises.* If a manager does not know what is going on, it is easy for small, readily solvable problems to turn into crises.
2. *Standardize outputs.* Problems and services can be standardized in terms of quantity and quality through the use of good controls.
3. *Appraise employee performance.* Proper controls can provide the manager with objective information about employee performance.
4. *Update plans.* Even the best plans must be updated as environmental and internal changes occur. Controls allow the manager to compare what is happening with what was planned.
5. *Protect the organization's assets.* Controls can protect assets from inefficiency, waste, and pilferage.

## THE CONTROL PYRAMID

The control pyramid provides a method for implementing controls in the organization.[1] The idea is to implement simple controls first and then move to more complex controls at a later time. The first area to be considered using this method would be *foolproof controls,* where the control deals with repetitive acts and requires little thought (e.g., turning off lights). Surprisingly, many of these acts and controls already exist in an organization's normal course of business. The second area to consider is *automatic control,* where a feedback loop can exist without much human interaction (e.g., regulation of plant temperature). These systems require monitoring, but the control can be machine- or computer-based. The third area is *operator control,* which requires a human response (e.g., a salesperson checking records). The key to this form of control is to make it meaningful for the controller. The fourth area is *supervisory control,* the layer that controls the person or persons implementing the controls (e.g., a department head checking an employee's reports). The organization must make sure that this form of control gets results and is not redundant. The fifth area is *informational control* (e.g., report summaries). This is the ultimate feedback loop,

## Figure 11.1 • The Control Pyramid

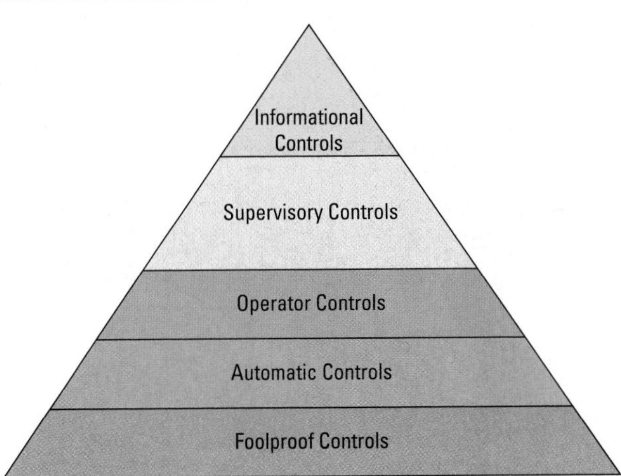


wherein the manager must pull together all the information provided by the other controls.[2] Seeing the process as a whole helps a manager get a feel for how interrelated the control process is and how it must be synchronized. Figure 11.1 shows how the different types of controls relate to each other.

### WHERE SHOULD CONTROL RESIDE?

For years, it was believed that control in organizations is a fixed commodity that should rest only in the hands of top management. This viewpoint naturally favored a highly centralized approach to decision making and controlling. However, as decentralized organizations have become more common, controls have been pushed farther and farther down the hierarchy. It is now recognized that where the controls reside is an important factor in how much control is desirable.

James Champy, author of *Reengineering Management,* believes the modern approach to control should involve more "enabling," or learning to control at lower levels.[3] Supporting this idea, Leon Royer, director of Learning Services at 3M, found that learning and enabling go hand in hand. Lower-level employees are valuable controllers if they are allowed to learn how to control.[4] The difficulty with enabling, however, is that it means senior management must be willing to relinquish control. One reason for pushing controls down in the organization is that the controllers are close to the actual situations that require control.

Evidence favors relatively tight controls as long as they are placed as far down in the organization as possible.[5] This approach has several advantages. First, it keeps higher-level managers from getting too involved in details. Second, it shows why the control is necessary. Third, it elicits commitment from lower-level managers. When controls are spread through many levels of an organization, caution must be taken to ensure that there are no disagreements about how the controls are distributed. In other words, managers at every level should clearly understand their authority and responsibility.

**Study Alert!**

In highly centralized organizations, control resides with the upper levels of management. This can lead to micromanagement and slow down the decision-making process. If managers and team leaders receive appropriate training on the value and implementation of control processes, lower-level control can promote greater operational flexibility.

## >> Types of Control

There are two categories of control methods: behavior control and output control. **Behavior** or **personal control** is based on direct, personal surveillance. The first-line supervisor who maintains a close personal watch over employees is using behavior control. **Output** or **impersonal control** is based on the measurement of outputs. Tracking production records and monitoring sales figures are examples of output controls.

Research shows that these two categories of control are not substitutes for each other in the sense that a manager uses one or the other.[6] The evidence suggests that output control occurs in response to a manager's need to provide an accurate measure of performance. On the other hand, behavior control is exerted when performance requirements are well known and personal surveillance is needed to promote efficiency and motivation. In most situations, organizations need to use a mix of output and behavior controls because each serves different organizational needs.

**Behavior or Personal Control** Control based on direct, personal surveillance.

**Output or Impersonal Control** Control based on the measurement of outputs.

**Preliminary Control** Method of exercising control to prevent a problem from occurring; also known as *steering control.*

## >> Methods of Control

In general, methods for exercising control can be described as *preliminary, concurrent,* or *postaction.*

### PRELIMINARY CONTROL METHODS

**Preliminary control** methods, sometimes called *steering control,* attempt to prevent a problem from occurring. Requiring prior approval for purchases of all items over a certain dollar value is an example. Budgets are probably the most widely used preliminary control devices. A **budget** is a statement of expected results or requirements expressed in financial or numerical terms. Budgets express plans, objectives, and programs of the organization in numerical terms. Preparation of the budget is primarily a planning function; however, its administration is a controlling function.

**Study Alert !** Preliminary control can be seen to be a preemptive or proactive action on the part of the management team. Putting measures in place in anticipation of a problem may seem pessimistic, but it's really a recognition of what can go wrong based on years of business experience

**Budget** Statement of expected results or requirements expressed in financial or numerical terms.

**Zero-Base Budgeting** Form of budgeting in which the manager must justify each area of a budget. Each year the activity is identified, evaluated, and ranked by importance.

Many different types of budgets are in use. Figure 11.2 outlines some of the most common ones. Some may be expressed in terms other than dollars. For example, an equipment budget may be expressed in numbers of machines; material budgets may be expressed in pounds, pieces, gallons, and so on. Budgets not expressed in dollars can usually be translated into dollars for inclusion in an overall budget.

While budgets are useful for planning and control, they are not without their dangers. Perhaps the greatest danger is inflexibility. This is a special threat to organizations operating in an industry with rapid change and high competition. Rigidity in the budget can also lead to ignoring organizational goals for budgetary goals. The financial manager who won't go $50 over budget to make $500 is a classic example. Budgets can hide inefficiencies. The fact that a certain expenditure has been made in the past often becomes justification for continuing the practice even when the situation has greatly changed. Managers may also "pad" budgets (build in extra cost items) because they anticipate that their budgets will be cut by superiors. Since the manager is never sure how severe the cut will be, the result is often an inaccurate, if not unrealistic, budget.

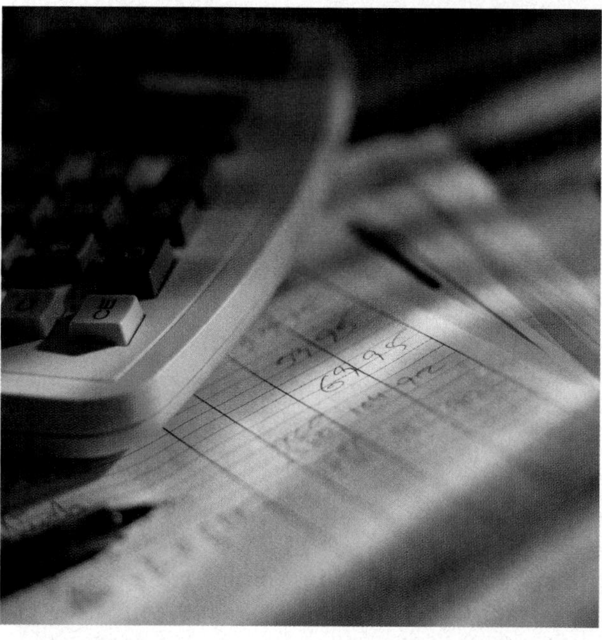

The answer to effective budget control may be to make the manager and any concerned employees accountable for their budgets. Performance incentives can be tied to budget control, accuracy, and fulfillment. In other words, if it is worth budgeting, it is worth budgeting right! Others believe budgets should also be tied not only to financial data but also to customer satisfaction. Budgeting for what it takes to satisfy the customer would be the rule of thumb for this logic. Managers can get so hung up on measuring themselves by sticking to their own sets of rules, focusing internally, and watching their budgets that they forget their customers.[7] Yet the customer is what business is all about. Generally managers meet on a periodic basis (usually monthly or quarterly) with accounting officials to discuss planned finances versus actual expenses.

## Figure 11.2 • Types and Purposes of Budgets

| Type of Budget | Purpose |
|---|---|
| Revenue and expense budget | Provides details for revenue and expense plans. |
| Cash budget | Forecasts cash receipts and disbursements. |
| Capital expenditure budget | Outlines specific expenditures for plant, equipment, machinery, inventories, and other capital items. |
| Production, material, or time budget | Expresses physical requirements of production, or material, or the time requirements for the budget period. |
| Balance sheet budget | Forecasts the status of assets, liabilities, and net worth at the end of the budget period. |

## ZERO-BASE BUDGETING

Zero-base budgeting was designed to stop basing this year's budget on last year's budget. **Zero-base budgeting** requires each manager to justify an entire budget request in detail. The burden of proof is on each manager to justify why any money should be spent. Under zero-base budgeting, each activity under a manager's discretion is identified, evaluated, and ranked by importance. Then each year every activity in the budget is on trial for its life and is matched against all the other claimants for an organization's resources.

**From the** PERSPECTIVE OF...

**A Finance Manager**

Budgets determine the resources available to a manager in running his or her department. How do you involve your employees in the budget process so they see the budget as a planning tool rather than a handicap?

1. What is the overriding purpose of all management controls?
2. Explain the five layers of the control pyramid.
3. What are the five most common types of operational budgets?
4. Explain zero-base budgeting.

## CONCURRENT CONTROL METHODS

**Concurrent controls**, also called *screening controls*, focus on things that happen as inputs are being transformed into outputs. They are designed to detect a problem as it occurs. Personal observation of customers being helped is an example of a concurrent control.

## DIRECT OBSERVATION

A store manager's daily tour of the facility and a company president's annual visit to all branches are examples of control by direct observation. Although time-consuming, personal observation is sometimes the only way to get an accurate picture of what is really happening. One hazard is that employees may misinterpret a superior's visit and consider such action interfering or eavesdropping. A second hazard is that behaviors change when people are being watched or monitored. Another potential inaccuracy lies in the interpretation of the observation. The observer must be careful not to read into the picture events that did not actually occur. Visits and direct observation can have positive effects when viewed by employees as a display of the manager's interest.

**Concurrent Controls** Controls that focus on a process as it occurs; designed to detect a problem as it occurs; also known as *screening controls*.

**Postaction Control** Control that is designed to detect an existing problem after it occurs but before it reaches crisis proportion.

## ELECTRONIC MONITORS

As we'll discuss in more detail in Chapter 12, electronic devices can be used to monitor what is going on. Examples include electronic cash registers that record items sold and when; video cameras that record employee and customer movements; phones that record how long each customer was engaged; and Internet programs that track where and how long an employee or customer is at certain Internet sites.

**Study Alert!**

Concurrent control is a "real-time" practice. Using procedures and mechanisms to manage events as they are unfolding offers greater responsiveness and the opportunity to minimize risk and/or damage to the organization.

## POSTACTION CONTROL METHODS

**Postaction control** methods are designed to detect existing problems after they occur but before they reach crisis proportions. Most controls are based on postaction methods.

## WRITTEN REPORTS

Written reports can be prepared on a periodic or an as-necessary basis. There are two basic types of written reports: analytical and informational. Analytical reports interpret the facts they present; informational reports present only the facts. Preparing a

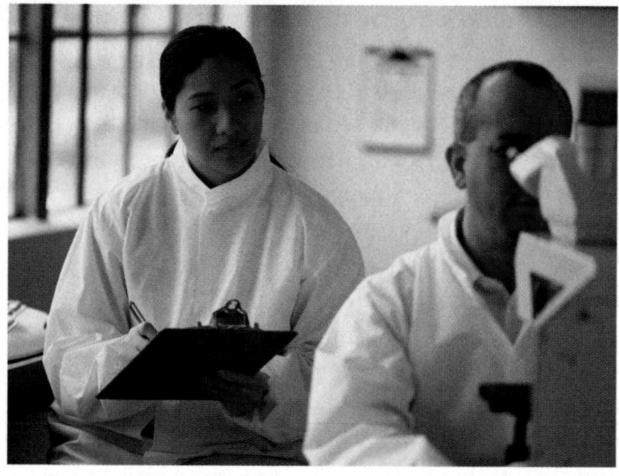

report is a four- or five-step process, depending on whether it is informational or analytical. The steps are (1) planning what is to be done, (2) collecting the facts, (3) organizing the facts, (4) interpreting the facts (this step is omitted with informational reports), and (5) writing the report.[8] Most reports should be prepared for the benefit of the reader and not the writer. In most cases, the reader wants useful information not previously available.

## FINANCIAL CONTROLS

In addition to using budgets as a preliminary control mechanism, many managers use other types of financial information for control purposes. These include balance sheets, income statements, and financial ratios. Regardless of the type of financial information used, it is meaningful only when compared with either the historical performance of the organization or the performances of similar organizations. For example, knowing that a company had net income of $100,000 last year doesn't reveal much by itself. However, when compared to last year's net income of $500,000 or to an industry average of $500,000, much more can be determined about the company's performance.

**Financial Ratio Analysis** Financial ratios can be divided into four basic types: profitability, liquidity, debt, and activity ratios. *Profitability ratios* indicate the organization's operational efficiency, or how well the organization is being managed. Gross profit margin, net profit margin, and return on investment (ROI) are all examples of profitability ratios. *Liquidity ratios* are used to judge how well an organization will be able to meet its short-term financial obligations. The current ratio (current assets divided by current liabilities) and the quick ratio (current assets minus inventories divided by current liabilities) are examples of liquidity ratios. *Debt* (sometimes called *leverage*)

### Figure 11.3 • Summary of Financial Ratio Calculations

| Ratio | Calculation | Purpose |
|---|---|---|
| **Profitability Ratios** | | |
| Gross profit margin | $\frac{\text{Sales} - \text{Cost of goods sold}}{\text{Sales}}$ | Indicates efficiency of operations and product pricing. |
| | $\frac{\text{Net profit after tax}}{\text{Sales}}$ | Indicates efficiency after all expenses are considered. |
| Return on assets (ROA) | $\frac{\text{Net profit after tax}}{\text{Total assets}}$ | Shows productivity of assets. |
| Return on equity (ROE) | $\frac{\text{Net profit after tax}}{\text{Stockholders' equity}}$ | Shows earnings power of equity. |
| **Liquidity Ratios** | | |
| Current ratio | $\frac{\text{Current assets}}{\text{Current liabilities}}$ | Shows short-run debt-paying ability. |
| Quick ratio | $\frac{\text{Current assets} - \text{Inventories}}{\text{Current liabilities}}$ | Shows short-term liquidity. |
| **Debt Ratios** | | |
| Debt to equity | $\frac{\text{Total liabilities}}{\text{Stockholders' equity}}$ | Indicates long-term liquidity. |
| Total debt to total assets | $\frac{\text{Total liabilities}}{\text{Total assets}}$ | Shows percentage of assets financed through borrowing. |
| **Activity Ratios** | | |
| Asset turnover | $\frac{\text{Sales}}{\text{Total assets}}$ | Shows efficiency of asset utilization. |
| Inventory turnover | $\frac{\text{Cost of goods sold}}{\text{Average inventory}}$ | Shows management's ability to control investment in inventory. |
| Average collection period | $\frac{\text{Receivables} \times 365 \text{ days}}{\text{Annual credit sales}}$ | Shows effectiveness of collection and credit policies. |
| Accounts receivable turnover | $\frac{\text{Annual credit sales}}{\text{Receivables}}$ | Shows effectiveness of collection and credit policies. |

*ratios* measure the magnitude of owners' and creditors' claims on the organization and indicate the organization's ability to meet long-term obligations. The debt to equity ratio and total debt to total assets ratio are two common debt ratios. *Activity ratios* evaluate how effectively an organization is managing some of its basic operations. Asset turnover, inventory turnover, average collection period, and accounts receivable turnover represent commonly used activity ratios.

As mentioned earlier, financial ratios are meaningful only when compared to past ratios and to ratios of similar organizations. Also, financial ratios reflect only certain specific information, and therefore they should be used in conjunction with other management controls. Figure 11.3 presents a summary of several financial ratio calculations.

**Sarbanes-Oxley Act of 2002** On July 30, 2002, President Bush signed into law the Sarbanes-Oxley Act of 2002. The Sarbanes-Oxley Act, which has been called the most dramatic change to federal securities laws since the 1930s, radically redesigned federal regulation of public company corporate governance and reporting obligations. The law also significantly tightens accountability standards for corporate directors and officers, auditors, securities analysts, and legal counsel. The purpose of the act is to prevent the kind of accounting and financial maneuvering that caused the meltdowns experienced at companies such as Enron and WorldCom. Figure 11.4 summarizes the major points of the law.

One major concern related to the Sarbanes-Oxley Act is its hefty compliance costs. A 2004 survey by Financial Executives International (FEI) reported that large public companies spent thousands of hours and an average of $4.4 million each to comply with the Sarbanes-Oxley Act.[9] The costs stem largely from a 66 percent increase in external costs for consulting, software, and other vendors and a 58 percent increase in the fees charged by external auditors. In response to concerns about the costs of complying for smaller businesses, the Securities and Exchange Commission delayed implementation of key sections of the act until 2007 for companies with less than $75 million in market capitalization.[10]

**Figure 11.4 • Major Points of the Sarbanes-Oxley Act of 2002**

The SEC will direct the NYSE and NASDAQ to prohibit listing any public company whose audit committee does not comply with a new list of requirements affecting auditor appointment, compensation, and oversight. The audit committee must consist solely of independent directors.

CEOs and CFOs must certify in each periodic report containing financial statements that the report fully complies with Sections 13(a) and 15(d) of the Securities Exchange Act of 1934 and that the information fairly presents the company's financial condition and results of operations.

Certifying officers will face penalties for false certification of $1,000,000 and/or up to 10 years' imprisonment for "knowing" violation and $5,000,000 and/or up to 20 years' imprisonment for "willing" violation.

No public company may make, extend, modify, or renew any personal loan to its executive officers or directors, with limited exceptions.

The act sets a deadline for insiders to report any trading in their companies' securities to within two business days after the execution date of the transaction.

Each company must disclose "on a rapid and current basis" additional information about the company's financial condition or operations as the SEC determines is necessary or useful to investors or in the public interest.

All annual reports filed with the SEC containing financial statements must include all material corrections identified by a public accounting firm.

The act creates several new crimes for securities violations, including:

- Destroying, altering, or falsifying records with the intent to impede or influence any federal investigation or bankruptcy proceeding.
- Knowing and willful failure by an accountant to maintain all audit or workpapers for five years.
- Knowingly executing a scheme to defraud investors in connection with any security.

## BALANCED SCORECARD

The balanced scorecard (BSC) system is a measurement and control system that is similar to management by objectives and based on the idea that financial measures alone do not adequately indicate how an organization or organizational unit is performing. BSC attempts to balance traditional financial measures with measures relating to customer service, internal processes, and potential for learning and innovation. The idea is to balance these four categories of measures on both the short and long term.

A significant advantage of the BSC is that it is based on participation and commitment at all levels within the organization. Under BSC, operational managers develop scorecards at every level in the organization so that each manager can see how his or her job duties relate to and contribute to the higher-level objectives and strategies. The key is that the scorecards at one level are derived from the scorecards at the next level up. Once the scorecards have been developed, managers and employees use them to periodically assess how they are doing and what, if any, corrective actions should be taken.[11]

## MANAGEMENT INFORMATION SYSTEMS

As discussed in Chapter 3, management information systems (MISs) are computerized systems designed to produce information needed for successful management of a process, department, or business. Usually, the information provided by an MIS is in the form of periodic reports, special reports, and outputs of mathematical simulations.[12]

**Audits** Method of control normally involved with financial matters.

**Management Audits** Audits that attempt to evaluate the overall management practices and policies of the organization.

**Break-Even Charts** Charts that depict graphically the relationship of volume of operations to profits.

## AUDITS

**Audits** can be conducted by either internal or external personnel. External audits are normally done by outside accountants and are limited to financial matters. Most are conducted to certify that the organization's accounting methods are fair, are consistent, and conform to existing practices. Internal audits are performed by the organization's own personnel.

An audit that looks at areas other than finance and accounting is known as a management audit. **Management audits** attempt to evaluate the overall management practices and policies of the organization. They can be conducted by outside consultants or inside staff; however, a management audit conducted by inside staff can easily result in a biased report.

## BREAK-EVEN CHARTS

**Break-even charts** depict graphically the relationship of volume of operations to profits. The break-even

### FUDGING THE NUMBERS

Andy Finn, the newly appointed vice president of a manufacturing company, has just been informed that a team of internal auditors from the corporate head office will be arriving in two days. He prepares his staff as best he can. The day before the auditors arrive, one of his assistants discovers some disturbing news. It appears, he says, that Matt Garcia, a 30-year veteran of the plant, has been systematically altering accounts for years. Month by month, Matt has been shipping products to customers without billing them—and then billing customers without shipping anything.

Andy is stunned. Seeking an explanation, he learns that the practice has nothing to do with fraud. Matt wasn't lining his own pocket. He was simply trying to be helpful. His goal was to smooth out the cyclical nature of the orders so that, month by month, the figures sent to the home office appeared level and consistent, with no peaks and valleys. Andy discovers that no money has been lost or gained: It all balances out in the end. And while the amount is not immense, the funds affected amount to perhaps 5 percent of the plant's annual earnings.

ETHICAL
MANAGEMENT
Is it ever okay
to tweak
accounts?

In one sense, Matt's adjustments have benefited Andy, who has already been complimented by his boss for his wise forecasts and for meeting his targets so accurately. But Andy also knows that if these practices were to come to light, Matt would be fired instantly—he himself, though ignorant of the practice until now, might have some tough explaining to do. After all, Matt has been fudging records and misstating corporate revenues to management, shareholders, and the IRS.

What should Andy do?

*Source:* Adapted from "Smoothing the Factory's Accounts," Institute for Global Ethics, www.globalethics.org/resources/dilemmas/smoothing.htm.

# Thinking Critically 11.1

## >> "Bird-Dogging" the Employee

Ace Electronics, Inc., is a small company located in Centerville. It is owned and operated by Al Abrams, a highly experienced electronics person who founded the company.

Ace's basic product is a walkie-talkie that is sold primarily to the U.S. military. The walkie-talkie units are relatively simple to produce; Ace merely purchases the parts—cables, wires, transistors, and so on—and assembles them with hand tools. Due to this moderate level of complexity, Ace employs semiskilled workers at low wage rates.

Although Ace has made a profit each year since it started production, Al Abrams was becoming increasingly concerned. Over the past six years, he had noticed a general decline in employee morale; furthermore, he had observed a decline in his employees' productivity and his company's profit margin.

As a result of his concern, Al asked his supervisors to keep a closer watch on the workers' hour-to-hour activities. In the first week, they discovered two workers in the restroom reading magazines. This "bird-dogging" technique, as management called it, or "slave driving," as the workers called it, failed to increase either production or productivity.

Al recognized that the lack of performance on the part of some employees was affecting the production of everyone. This phenomenon was caused by the balanced assembly line under which the walkie-talkies were assembled. If an employee next to a normally productive employee did not work fast enough, walkie-talkies would back up on the line. Instead of having a backup, however, the assembly line was usually readjusted to the production rate of the slower employees.

In addition, another situation developed to lower productivity and increase unit costs. Ace was required by the government to meet monthly production and delivery schedules. If it failed, a very substantial financial penalty could result. In recent years, the production and delivery schedule had become more difficult to meet. For the last eight months, Al had scheduled overtime to meet the production and delivery schedule and thus avoid the financial penalty. This overtime increased unit production costs and caused another problem: Many employees began to realize that if they worked more slowly at the beginning of the month, they could receive more overtime at the end of the month. Even the senior employees were slowing down to increase their overtime wages.

Al was very reluctant to fire employees, especially senior employees. Even if he was inclined to do so, it was difficult to catch employees slowing down or provide any reasonable evidence for such a rash action. Al was frustrated and perplexed.

**QUESTIONS**

1. Describe in detail the control dilemma at Ace Electronics.
2. Are Al Abrams and the employees getting the same feedback? Why or why not?
3. Al is avoiding a substantial financial penalty from the government by paying the overtime in order to meet delivery schedules. Does that justify the decision to pay the overtime? Why or why not?
4. What should Al do?

point (BEP) is the point at which sales revenues exactly equal expenses. Total sales below the BEP result in a loss; total sales above the BEP result in a profit.

Figure 11.5 shows a typical break-even chart. The horizontal axis represents output; the vertical axis represents expenses and revenues. Though not required, most break-even charts assume there are linear relationships and all costs are either fixed or variable. Fixed costs do not vary with output, at least in the short run. They include rent, insurance, and administrative salaries. Variable costs vary with output. Typical variable costs include direct labor and materials. The purpose of the chart is to show the break-even point and the effects of changes in output. A break-even chart is useful for showing whether revenue and costs are running as planned.

**Performance** Degree of accomplishment of the tasks that make up an employee's job.

## First Line Focus

ANALYSIS PARALYSIS . . .

*The ability to accurately forecast and document the operation of an organization from the preliminary, concurrent, and postaction perspectives is critical to effective management. However, the data generated by these policies and procedures are of limited value until managers actually "pull the trigger" and make decisions based on that data. The analysis stage of any new project is vital in developing as accurate a picture as possible of the current situation and in forecasting anticipated outcomes based on the collected data; but until the management team moves to the selection and implementation stages, the organization runs the risk of analysis paralysis, where data are reviewed, re-reviewed, and reviewed yet again without any key decisions being made.*

5. Explain the following ratios: productivity, liquidity, debt, and activity.
6. Describe the five steps in the written report process.
7. Explain the balanced scorecard (BSC) system.
8. Define the term *break-even point.*

### Figure 11.5 • Break-Even Chart

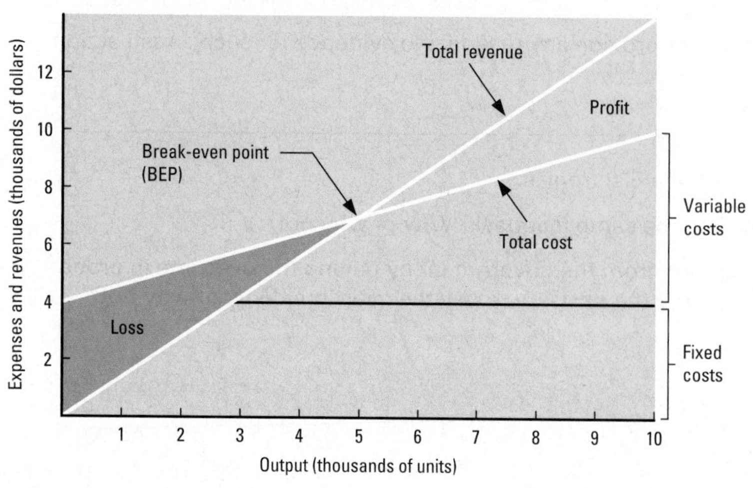


# >> Appraising Performance

## UNDERSTANDING PERFORMANCE

**Performance** refers to the degree of accomplishment of the tasks that make up an employee's job. It reflects how well an employee is fulfilling the requirements of the job. Often confused with effort, which refers to energy expended, performance is measured in terms of results. Because many organizations have become very results-oriented in the last decade, more and more emphasis is being placed on managing performance.

## DETERMINANTS OF PERFORMANCE

Job performance is the net effect of an employee's effort as modified by abilities, role perceptions, and results produced. This implies that performance in a given situation can be viewed as resulting from the interrelationships among effort, abilities, role perceptions, and results produced.

**Effort**, which results from being motivated, refers to the amount of energy an employee uses in performing a job. **Abilities** are personal characteristics used in performing a job. Abilities usually do not fluctuate widely over short periods of time. **Role perception** refers to the direction in which employees believe they should channel their efforts on their jobs. The activities and behavior employees believe are necessary in the performance of their jobs define their role perceptions. The results produced are usually measured by standards created by the degree of achievement of management-directed objectives.

## PERFORMANCE APPRAISAL PROCESS

Performance appraisal systems that are directly tied to an organization's reward system provide a powerful incentive for employees to work diligently and creatively toward achieving organizational objectives. When properly conducted, performance appraisals not only let employees know how well they are presently performing but also clarify what needs to be done to improve performance.[13]

**Performance appraisal** is a process that involves (1) determining and communicating to employees how they are performing their jobs and (2) establishing a plan for their improvement. Some of the more common uses of performance appraisals are to make decisions related to merit pay increases, promotions, layoffs, and firings. For example, the present job performance of an employee is often the most significant consideration for determining whether to promote the person. While successful performance in the present job does not necessarily mean an employee will be an effective performer in a higher-level job, performance appraisals do provide some predictive information.

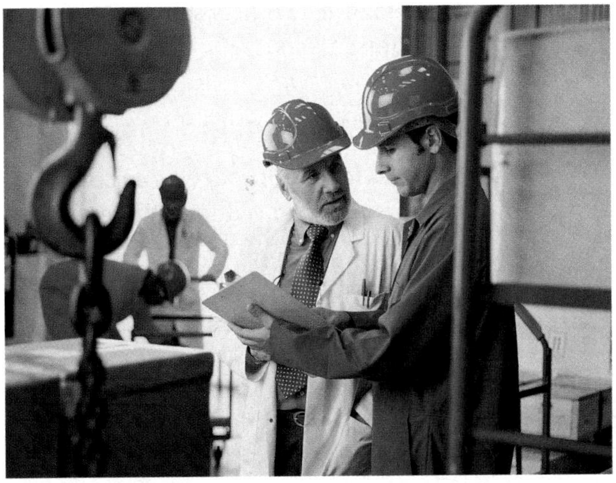

Performance appraisal information can also provide needed input for determining both individual and organizational training and development needs. For example, it can be used to identify individual strengths and weaknesses. The data can then be used to help determine the organization's overall training and development needs. For an individual employee, a completed performance appraisal should include a plan outlining specific training and development needs.

**Effort** Result of being motivated; the amount of energy an employee uses in performing a job.

**Abilities** Personal characteristics used in performing a job.

**Role Perception** Direction in which employees believe they should channel their efforts on their jobs.

**Performance Appraisal** Process that involves (1) determining and communicating to employees how they are performing their jobs and (2) establishing a plan for their improvement.

Another important use of performance appraisals is to encourage performance improvement. In this regard, performance appraisals are used as a means of communicating to employees needed changes in behavior, attitude, skill, or knowledge. This type of feedback clarifies for employees the job expectations the manager holds. Often, this feedback must be followed by coaching and training by the manager to guide an employee's work efforts.

**Study Alert!**

Effective performance appraisal requires active participation from both the manager and the employee. The manager must be fully prepared with documented examples of positive behavior and any areas for improvement that should be addressed. The employee should be open to the feedback and be prepared to discuss plans for addressing any areas for improvement as well as opportunities to further develop his or her value to the organization.

To work effectively, performance appraisals must be supported by documentation and a commitment by management to make them fair and effective. Typical standards for the performance appraisal process are that it be fair, be accurate (facts, not opinions, should be used), include as much direct observation as possible, be consistent, and contain as much objective documentation as possible. The amount and types of documentation necessary to support decisions made by management vary, but the general rule of thumb is to provide enough varied documentation to allow anyone evaluating the performance of an employee to generally come to the same conclusion as the manager.

An additional concern in organizations is how often to conduct performance appraisals. No real consensus exists on this question, but the usual answer is as often as necessary to let employees know the kind of job they are doing and, if performance is not satisfactory, the measures they must take to improve. For many employees, this cannot be accomplished through one annual performance appraisal. Therefore, it is recommended that for most employees, informal performance appraisals should be conducted two or three times a year in addition to the annual performance appraisal.

## >> Performance Appraisal Methods

An early method of performance appraisal used in the United States was described as follows:

> On the morning following each day's work, each workman was given a slip of paper informing him in detail just how much work he had done the day before, and the amount he had earned. This enabled him to measure his performance against his earnings while the details were fresh in his mind.[14]

**Production Standards Approach** Performance appraisal method most frequently used for employees who are involved in physically producing a product; basically a form of objective setting for these employees.

This method of performance appraisal was effective in that it gave immediate feedback and tied pay to performance. Since then, the number and variety of performance appraisal methods have dramatically increased. The following sections describe the performance appraisal methods used in businesses today.

### GOAL SETTING, OR MANAGEMENT BY OBJECTIVES

Management by objectives (MBO) was discussed in Chapter 3 as an effective means for setting objectives. In addition to being a useful method for directing the organization's objective-setting process, management by objectives can also be used in the performance appraisal process. The value of linking the MBO program to the appraisal process is that employees tend to support goals if they agree the goals are acceptable and if they expect to be personally successful in their efforts. Employee acceptance (by giving the employee a stake in the MBO process) is certainly a powerful motivator for considering the MBO process. The typical MBO process consists of following steps:

*The production standards approach would work for this employee. Name some industries for which that standard of measurement might prove problematic.*

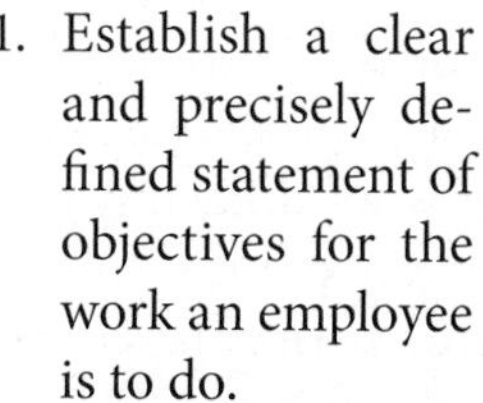

1. Establish a clear and precisely defined statement of objectives for the work an employee is to do.
2. Develop an action plan indicating how these objectives are to be achieved.
3. Allow the employee to implement this action plan.
4. Appraise performance based on objective achievement.
5. Take corrective action when necessary.
6. Establish new objectives for the future.

If an employee is to be evaluated on the objectives set in the MBO process, several requirements must be met. First, objectives should be quantifiable and measurable; objectives whose attainment cannot be measured or at least verified should be avoided if possible. Objectives should also be challenging, yet achievable, and they should be expressed in writing and in clear, concise language. Figure 11.6 lists sample objectives that meet these requirements.

### PRODUCTION STANDARDS

The **production standards approach** to performance appraisal is most frequently used for employees who

**Figure 11.6 • Sample Objectives**

To answer all customer complaints in writing within three days of receipt of complaint.
To reduce order-processing time by two days within the next six months.
To implement the new computerized accounts receivable system by August 1.

## Figure 11.7 • Frequently Used Methods for Setting Production Standards

| Method | Areas of Applicability |
|---|---|
| Average production or work | When tasks performed by all employees are the same or approximately the same. |
| Performance of specially selected employees | When tasks performed by all employees are basically the same, and it would be cumbersome and time-consuming to use the group average. |
| Time study | Jobs involving repetitive tasks. |
| Work sampling | Noncyclical types of work in which many different tasks are performed and there is no set pattern or cycle. |
| Expert opinion | When none of the more direct methods (described above) applies. |

are involved in physically producing a product and is basically a form of objective setting for these employees. It involves setting a standard or an expected level of output and then comparing each employee's performance to the standard. Generally, production standards should reflect the normal output of an average person. Production standards attempt to answer the question of what is a fair day's output. Several methods can be used to set production standards. Figure 11.7 summarizes some of the more common methods.

An advantage of the production standards approach is that the performance review is based on highly objective factors. Of course, to be effective, the standards must be viewed by the affected employees as being fair. The most serious criticism of production standards is a lack of comparability of standards for different job categories.

## ESSAY APPRAISAL

The **essay appraisal** method requires the manager to describe an employee's performance in written account form. Instructions are often provided to the manager as to the topics to be covered. Typical essay appraisal instructions might be, "Describe, in your own words, this employee's performance, including quantity and quality of work, job knowledge, and ability to get along with other employees. What are the employee's strengths and weaknesses?"

The primary problem with essay appraisals is that their length and content can vary considerably (depending on the manager), and the method can be very subjective (whereas objective measures are more defensible). For instance, one manager may write a lengthy statement describing an employee's potential and saying little about past performance; another manager may concentrate on the employee's past performance. Thus, essay appraisals are difficult to compare. The writing skill of a manager can also affect the appraisal. An effective writer can make an average employee look better than the actual performance warrants.

## CRITICAL-INCIDENT APPRAISAL

The **critical-incident appraisal** method requires the manager to keep a written record of incidents, as they occur, involving job behaviors that illustrate both satisfactory and unsatisfactory performance of the employee being rated. As they are recorded over time, the incidents provide a basis for evaluating performance and providing feedback to the employee.

The main drawback to critical-incident appraisal is that the manager is required to jot down incidents regularly, which can be a burdensome and time-consuming task. Also, the definition of a critical incident is unclear and may be interpreted differently by different managers. Some believe this method can lead to friction between the manager and employees when the employees think the manager is keeping a "book" on them.

**Essay Appraisal** Appraisal method by which the manager describes an employee's performance in written narrative form.

**Critical-Incident Appraisal** Appraisal method by which the manager keeps a written record of incidents, as they occur, involving job behaviors that illustrate both satisfactory and unsatisfactory performance of the employee being rated.

**Graphic Rating Scale** Appraisal method by which the manager assesses an employee on such factors as quantity of work, dependability, job knowledge, attendance, accuracy of work, and cooperativeness.

## GRAPHIC RATING SCALE

With the **graphic rating scale** method, the manager assesses an employee on such factors as quantity of work, dependability, job knowledge, attendance, accuracy of work, and cooperativeness. Graphic rating scales include both numerical ranges and written descriptions. Figure 11.8 gives an example of some of the items that might be included on a graphic rating scale that uses written descriptions.

## Figure 11.8 • Sample Items on a Graphic Rating Scale Evaluation Form

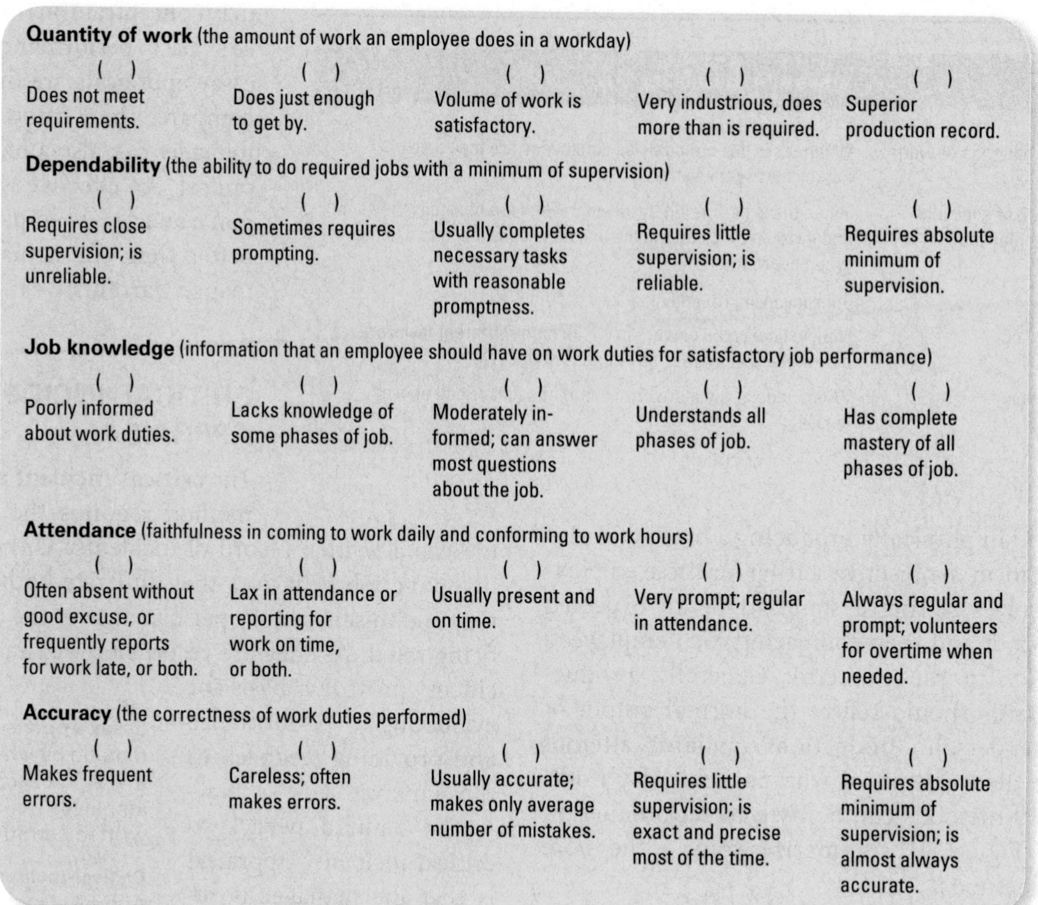

**Quantity of work** (the amount of work an employee does in a workday)

| ( ) | ( ) | ( ) | ( ) | ( ) |
|---|---|---|---|---|
| Does not meet requirements. | Does just enough to get by. | Volume of work is satisfactory. | Very industrious, does more than is required. | Superior production record. |

**Dependability** (the ability to do required jobs with a minimum of supervision)

| ( ) | ( ) | ( ) | ( ) | ( ) |
|---|---|---|---|---|
| Requires close supervision; is unreliable. | Sometimes requires prompting. | Usually completes necessary tasks with reasonable promptness. | Requires little supervision; is reliable. | Requires absolute minimum of supervision. |

**Job knowledge** (information that an employee should have on work duties for satisfactory job performance)

| ( ) | ( ) | ( ) | ( ) | ( ) |
|---|---|---|---|---|
| Poorly informed about work duties. | Lacks knowledge of some phases of job. | Moderately informed; can answer most questions about the job. | Understands all phases of job. | Has complete mastery of all phases of job. |

**Attendance** (faithfulness in coming to work daily and conforming to work hours)

| ( ) | ( ) | ( ) | ( ) | ( ) |
|---|---|---|---|---|
| Often absent without good excuse, or frequently reports for work late, or both. | Lax in attendance or reporting for work on time, or both. | Usually present and on time. | Very prompt; regular in attendance. | Always regular and prompt; volunteers for overtime when needed. |

**Accuracy** (the correctness of work duties performed)

| ( ) | ( ) | ( ) | ( ) | ( ) |
|---|---|---|---|---|
| Makes frequent errors. | Careless; often makes errors. | Usually accurate; makes only average number of mistakes. | Requires little supervision; is exact and precise most of the time. | Requires absolute minimum of supervision; is almost always accurate. |

**Checklist Appraisal** Appraisal method by which the manager answers yes or no to a series of questions concerning the employee's behavior.

The graphic rating scale is subject to some serious weaknesses. One potential weakness is that managers are unlikely to interpret written descriptions in the same manner because of differences in background, experience, and personality. Another potential problem relates to the choice of rating categories. It is possible to choose categories that have little relationship to job performance or omit categories that have a significant influence on job performance.

### CHECKLIST

With the **checklist appraisal** method, the manager answers yes or no to a series of questions concerning the employee's behavior. Figure 11.9 lists some typical questions. The checklist can also have varying weights assigned to each question.

Normally, the scoring key for a checklist appraisal is kept by the human resource department; the manager is generally not aware of the weights associated with each question. But because the manager can see the positive or negative connotation of each question, bias can be introduced. Additional drawbacks to the checklist method are that it is time-consuming to assemble the questions for each job category; a separate listing of questions must be developed for each job category; and the checklist questions can have different meanings for different managers.

## Figure 11.9 • Sample Checklist Appraisal Questions

| | Yes | No |
|---|---|---|
| 1. Does the employee lose his or her temper in public? | ___ | ___ |
| 2. Does the employee play favorites? | ___ | ___ |
| 3. Does the employee praise people in public when they have done a good job? | ___ | ___ |
| 4. Does the employee volunteer to do special jobs? | ___ | ___ |

## RANKING METHODS

When it becomes necessary to compare the performance of two or more employees, ranking methods can be used. Three of the more commonly used ranking methods are alternation, paired comparison, and forced distribution.

**Alternation Ranking** In the alternation ranking method, the names of the employees to be evaluated are listed down the left side of a sheet of paper. The manager is then asked to choose the most valuable employee on the list, cross that name off the left-hand list, and put it at the top of the column on the right side of the paper. The manager is then asked to select and cross off the name of the "least valuable" employee from the left-hand column and move it to the bottom of the right-hand column. The manager then repeats this process for all the names on the left-hand side of the paper. The resulting list of names in the right-hand column gives a ranking of the employees from most to least valuable.

**Paired Comparison Ranking** The paired comparison ranking is best illustrated with an example. Suppose a manager is to evaluate six employees. The names of the employees are listed on the left side of a sheet of paper. The manager then compares the first employee with the second employee on a chosen performance criterion, such as quantity of work. If the manager thinks the first employee has produced more work than the second employee, she or he places a check mark by the first employee's name. The first employee is then compared to the third, fourth, fifth, and sixth employees on the same performance criterion. A check mark is placed by the name of the employee who produced the most work in each of these paired comparisons. The process is repeated until each employee has been compared to every other employee on all the chosen performance criteria. The employee with the most check marks is considered to be the best performer. Likewise, the employee with the fewest check marks is the lowest performer. One major problem with the paired comparison method is that it becomes unwieldy when comparing large numbers of employees.

**Forced Distribution** Forced distribution requires the manager to compare the performances of employees and place a certain percentage of employees at various performance levels. It assumes the performance level in a group of employees is distributed according to a bell-shaped, or "normal," curve. Figure 11.10 illustrates how the forced distribution method works.

**Figure 11.10 • Forced Distribution Curve**

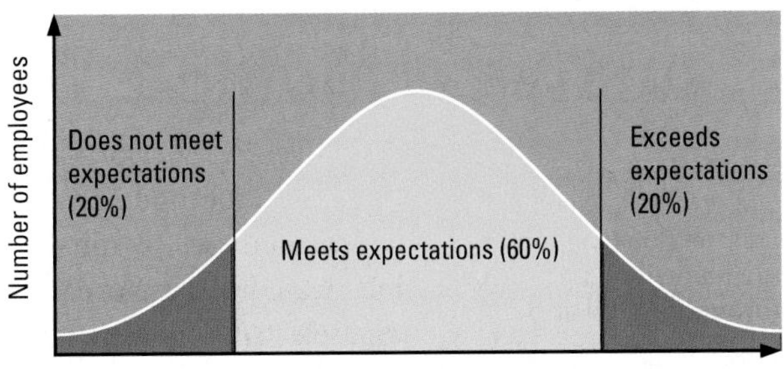


The manager is required to rate 60 percent of the employees as meeting expectations, 20 percent as exceeding expectations, and 20 percent as not meeting expectations.

One problem with forced distribution is that for small groups of employees, a bell-shaped distribution of performance may not be applicable. Even where the distribution approximates a normal curve, it is probably not a perfect curve. This means some employees will probably not be rated accurately. Also, ranking methods differ dramatically from the other methods in that one employee's performance evaluation is a function of the performance of other employees in the job.

## MULTIRATER ASSESSMENT (OR 360-DEGREE FEEDBACK)

The final method of performance appraisal is called **multirater assessment** or **360-degree feedback**. Typically, an employee's performance appraisal is conducted by his or her manager. With multirater assessment, the process of evaluation is expanded to other individuals who have knowledge of the employee's work performance. These individuals can come from inside the organization (co-workers, supervisors, and subordinates) as well as outside (customers and vendor partners).

**Multirater Assessment or 360-Degree Feedback** Method of performance appraisal that uses input from an employee's managers, peers, customers, suppliers, or colleagues.

In addition to the above, the person that is being evaluated does a self-evaluation using the same form that the evaluators use. When all the questionnaires are completed, a circle (360 degrees) of evaluations exists. Normally the questionnaires are rather lengthy. The human resource department compiles the results of the questionnaires and provides the results to the employee who is being evaluated. The employee gets to see how his or her opinion differs from those of the group doing the assessment.[15]

# >> Selecting a Performance Appraisal Method

**Leniency** Performance appraisal error of grouping of ratings at the positive end of the scale instead of spreading them throughout the scale.

**Central Tendency** Performance appraisal error that results in most employees being evaluated similarly as doing average or above-average work.

**Recency** Performance appraisal error that results when evaluations are based on work performed most recently, generally work performed one to two months before evaluation.

Whatever performance appraisal method an organization uses, it must be job-related. Therefore, before selecting a performance appraisal method, job analyses must be conducted and job descriptions written. Normally, job analyses are performed by trained specialists with the organization's human resource department or by outside consultants. Figure 11.11 summarizes the information a job analysis provides.

Job analysis involves not only determining job content but also reporting the results of the analysis. One product of a job analysis is a job description, a formal written document, usually one to three pages long, that should include the following:

- Date written
- Job status (full-time or part-time)
- Job title
- Supervision received (to whom the jobholder reports)
- Supervision exercised (who reports to this employee)
- Job summary (a synopsis of the job responsibilities)
- Detailed list of job responsibilities
- Principal contacts (inside and outside the organization)
- Competency or position requirements
- Required education or experience
- Career mobility (position or positions employee may qualify for next)

After a job description is written, the most appropriate performance appraisal method can be determined.[16]

**Figure 11.11 • Information Provided by Job Analysis**

| Area of Information | Contents |
|---|---|
| Job title and location within company | |
| Organizational relationship | A brief explanation of the number of persons supervised (if applicable) and the job title(s) of the position(s) supervised; a statement concerning supervision received. |
| Relation to other jobs | Describes and outlines the coordination required by the job. |
| Job summary | Condensed explanation of the content of the job. |
| Information concerning job requirements | Varies greatly from job to job and from organization to organization; typically includes information on such topics as machines, tools, and materials; mental complexity and attention required; physical demands; and working conditions. |

# >> Potential Errors in Performance Appraisals

Several common errors have been identified in performance appraisals. **Leniency** is the grouping of ratings at the positive end of the performance scale instead of spreading them throughout the scale. **Central tendency** occurs when performance appraisal statistics indicate that most employees are evaluated similarly as doing average or above-average work. **Recency** occurs when performance evaluations are based on work performed most recently, generally work performed one to two months before evaluation. Leniency, central tendency, and recency errors make it difficult, if not impossible, to separate the good performers from the poor performers. In addition, these errors make it difficult to compare ratings from different managers. For example, it is possible for a good performer who is evaluated by a manager committing central tendency errors to receive a lower rating than a poor performer who is rated by a manager committing leniency errors.

Another common error in performance appraisals is the *halo effect*.[17] This occurs when managers allow a single prominent characteristic of an employee to influence their judgment on each separate item in the performance appraisal. This often results in the employee receiving approximately the same rating on every item.

Personal preferences, prejudices, and biases can also cause errors in performance appraisals. Managers with biases or prejudices tend to look for employee behaviors that conform to their biases. Appearance, social status, dress, race, and sex have influenced many performance appraisals. Managers have also allowed first impressions to influence later

*Appearance, age, dress, race, and sex have unfortunately influenced many performance appraisals. Name a better way to evaluate employees.*

judgments of an employee. First impressions are only a sample of behavior; however, people tend to retain these impressions even when faced with contradictory evidence.

## >> Conducting Effective Performance Appraisals

A promising approach to conducting effective performance appraisals is to improve the skills of managers. Suggestions on the specific training managers should receive are often vague, but they usually emphasize that managers should be given training to observe behavior more accurately and judge it fairly.

### [PROGRESS] ✓questions

9. Define *performance appraisal.*
10. List the six steps of the MBO process.
11. List three of the more commonly used ranking methods.
12. Explain the four most common errors in the performance appraisal process.

More research is needed before a definitive set of topics for manager training can be established. However, at a minimum, managers should receive training in (1) the performance appraisal method(s) of the company, (2) the importance of the manager's role in the total appraisal process, (3) the use of performance appraisal information, and (4) the communication skills necessary to provide feedback to the employee.

General dos and don'ts of the performance appraisal process can help managers not only prevent but also reduce the errors that always seem to plague the process. The dos include the following:

1. Base performance appraisal on job performance only and not other factors unrelated to the job.
2. Use only those rating scales that are relevant to the job itself and are indicators of objective performance and attainment.
3. Sincerely work at the appraisal interview process.
4. Be problem-solving-oriented.

The don'ts include the following:

1. Don't criticize. Be proactive.
2. Carefully avoid the halo effect and leniency errors.
3. Don't dominate conversations about performance. Encourage employees to speak and to address issues in the evaluation process themselves.
4. Avoid general prescriptions to fix performance. Always present concrete and realizable objectives. Performance goals are the foundation of productivity.

## >> Providing Feedback Through the Appraisal Interview

After one of the previously discussed methods for developing an employee's performance appraisal has been used, the results must be communicated

## Thinking Critically 11.2

### >> The College Admissions Office

Steve Phillips was hired to replace Mary Ann Nicks as administrative assistant in the admissions office of Claymore Community College. Before leaving, Mary Ann had given a month's notice to the director of admissions, hoping this would allow ample time to locate and train her replacement. Mary Ann's responsibilities included preparing and mailing transcripts at the request of students, mailing information requested by people interested in attending the college, answering the telephone, assisting students or potential enrollees who came to the office, and general supervision of clerical personnel and student assistants.

After interviewing and testing many people for the position, the director hired Steve, mainly because his credentials were good and he made a favorable impression. Mary Ann spent many hours during the next 10 days training Steve. He appeared to be quite bright and seemed to quickly pick up the procedures involved in operating a college admissions office. When Mary Ann left, everyone thought Steve would do an outstanding job.

However, little time had elapsed before people realized that Steve had not caught on to his job responsibilities. Steve seemed to have personal problems that were severe enough to stand in the way of his work. He asked questions about subjects that Mary Ann had covered explicitly; he should have been able to answer these himself if he had comprehended her instructions.

Steve appeared to constantly have other things on his mind. He seemed to be preoccupied with such problems as his recent divorce, which he blamed entirely on his ex-wife, and the distress of his eight-year-old daughter, who missed her father terribly. His thoughts also dwelled on his search for peace of mind and some reasons for all that had happened to him. The director of admissions was aware of Steve's preoccupation with his personal life and his failure to learn the office procedures rapidly.

**QUESTIONS**

1. Could Mary Ann have done anything differently here? Why or why not?
2. What would you do at this point if you were the director of admissions?
3. Do you think Steve should keep his job? Why or why not?
4. Describe how you might effectively use a performance appraisal in this situation.

to the employee. Unless this interview is properly conducted, it can and frequently does result in an unpleasant experience for both manager and employee. Following are some of the more important factors influencing success or failure of appraisal interviews:

- The more employees participate in the appraisal process, the more satisfied they are with the appraisal interview and with the manager and the more likely they are to accept and strive to meet performance improvement objectives.
- The more a manager uses positive motivational techniques (e.g., recognizing and praising good performance), the more satisfied the employee is likely to be with the appraisal interview and with the manager.
- The mutual setting by the manager and the employee of specific performance improvement objectives results in more improvement in performance than does a general discussion or criticism.
- Discussing and solving problems that may be hampering the employee's current job performance improve the employee's performance.

**From the** PERSPECTIVE OF...

**A Credit Union Branch Manager**

When your branch is the training center for new staff members that are then assigned to other branches in your market, what objectives would you have in delivering performance appraisals?

- Areas of job performance needing improvement that are most heavily criticized are less likely to be improved than similar areas of job performance that are less heavily criticized.
- The more employees are allowed to voice their opinions during the interview, the more satisfied they will be with the interview.
- The amount of thought and preparation employees independently devote before the interview increases the benefits of the interview.
- The more the employee perceives that performance appraisal results are tied to organizational rewards, the more beneficial the interview will be.

The interviewer must also be aware that many employees are skeptical about the appraisal process because of its potential association with punishment. Research has shown that this most often happens because the employee does not trust the manager's motivation; the feedback is unclear; the employee does not respect the manager's judgment; the feedback is inconsistent with the opinions of others; and the employee has had negative past experiences with the evaluation, appraisal, or feedback process. Most of these problems can be overcome by simply accentuating the positive as the basis for the interview, feedback, and correction processes.[18]

## >> Developing Performance Improvement Plans

Earlier in this chapter, we stated that a completed performance appraisal should include a performance improvement plan. This important step is often ignored. However, managers must recognize that an employee's development is a continuous cycle of setting performance goals, providing training necessary to achieve the goals, assessing performance as to the accomplishment of the goals, and then setting new, higher goals. A performance improvement plan consists of the following components:

1. *Where are we now?* This question is answered in the performance appraisal process.
2. *Where do we want to be?* This requires the evaluator and the person being evaluated to mutually agree on the areas that can and should be improved.
3. *How does the employee get from where he or she is now to where he or she wants to be?* This component is critical to the performance improvement plan. Specific steps to be taken must be agreed on. The steps may include the training the employee will need to improve his or her performance and should also include how the evaluator will help the employee achieve the performance goals.

### [PROGRESS] ✓questions

13. Describe the four areas of training needed by managers before conducting performance appraisals.
14. What are the four "dos" of the appraisal process?
15. What are the corresponding "don'ts" of the process?
16. Describe at least five of the important factors that can influence the success or failure of performance appraisal.

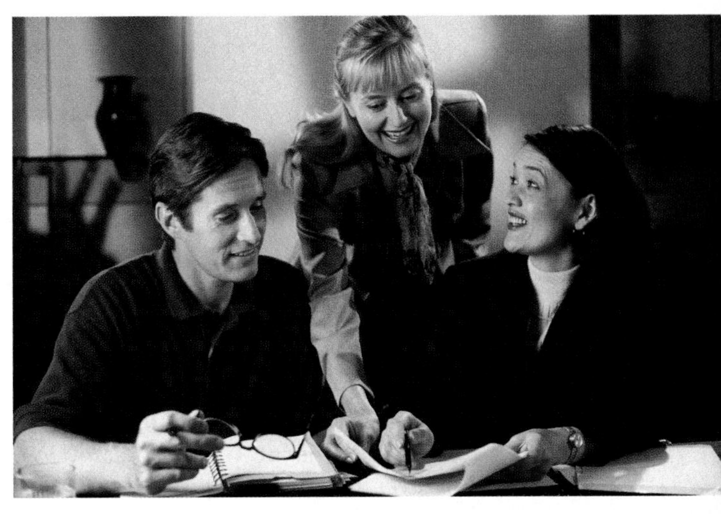

INSIDER KNOWLEDGE

You are in the middle of the monthly meeting with the area account manager for ABC Corporation, the company that produces one of the key components in your best-selling product. He suddenly asks if he can tell you something "off the record." You are understandably curious and answer, "Sure." He then proceeds to tell you that his company is about to raise prices on your key component by 25 percent because it has inside information that its competitor is experiencing production problems with its component and would be unable to take additional orders from ABC customers who chose to switch vendors in response to the 25 percent price increase.

Based on this information, your account manager strongly advises you to place a large order to beat the 25 percent price increase.

Would you place a large order? Why?

If ABC's competitor then announced a new version of its product that was much better than ABC's component, what would you do?

ETHICAL
MANAGEMENT
Should you act on information that you're not supposed to know?


Would you suspect that your area account manager had set you up? Why or why not?

What if the 25 percent price increase never came? What would you do then?

## >> Chapter Summary

The responsibility of managers to control the running of the organization simply means that they should know what is happening in comparison to established standards or performance objectives and then make any corrections where necessary. With clearly established standards in place, the control mechanisms can serve as an early warning system to alert managers when a problem exists or, even better, before a problem occurs. To be effective and comprehensive in their coverage of the organization, control mechanisms must address both the work performance of the personnel in the organization and the systems and processes required to produce the product or service that the organization delivers to its customers. In the next chapter we review the importance of managing both the design and the control of those systems and processes.

1. Explain why management controls are necessary.

   Management controls alert a manager to an existing or potential problem before it becomes critical. Control is accomplished by comparing actual performance to predetermined standards or objectives and then taking action to correct any deviation from the standard.

2. Discuss where control should reside in an organization.

   The traditional organization pyramid would suggest that control resides at the top levels of the organization with a highly centralized approach to decision making. However, as the need for continued growth has forced organizations to become more decentralized, controls have been pushed farther and farther down the hierarchy. While this transition has been tougher on senior executives who perceive it as a loss of control, research from top-performing organizations has shown that control is best positioned as close to the actual situations that require control as possible (as long as employees are appropriately trained to handle that responsibility).

3. Differentiate between preliminary, concurrent, and postaction controls.

   Preliminary control methods, sometimes called steering controls, attempt to prevent a problem from occurring. Requiring prior approval for purchases of all items over a certain dollar value is an example. Budgets are probably the most widely used preliminary control devices. Concurrent controls, also called screening controls, focus on things that happen as inputs are being transformed into outputs. They are designed to detect a problem as it occurs. Personal observation of customers being served is an example of a concurrent control. Postaction control methods are designed to detect existing problems after they occur but before they reach crisis proportions. Most controls are based on postaction methods.

4. Compare the four basic types of financial ratios.

   Financial ratios can be divided into four basic types: profitability, liquidity, debt, and activity. Profitability ratios indicate the organization's operational efficiency or how well the organization is being managed. Gross profit margin, net profit margin, and return on investment (ROI) are examples of profitability ratios. Liquidity ratios are used to judge how well an organization will be able to meet its short-term financial obligations. The current ratio (current assets divided by current liabilities) and the quick ratio (current assets minus inventories divided by current liabilities) are examples of liquidity ratios. Debt (sometimes called leverage) ratios measure the magnitude of owners' and creditors' claims on the organization and indicate the organization's ability to meet long-term obligations. The debt to equity ratio and total debt to total assets ratio are two common debt ratios. Activity ratios evaluate how effectively an organization is managing some of its basic operations. Asset turnover, inventory turnover, average collection period, and accounts receivable turnover represent commonly used activity ratios.

5. Explain the determinants of performance.

   Job performance is the net effect of an employee's effort as modified by abilities, role perceptions, and results produced. This implies that performance in a given situation can be viewed as resulting from the interrelationships among effort, abilities, role perceptions, and results produced. Effort, which results from being motivated, refers to the amount of energy an employee uses in performing a job. Abilities are personal characteristics used in performing a job. Abilities usually do not fluctuate widely over short periods of time. Role perception refers to the direction in which employees believe they should channel their efforts on their jobs. The activities and behavior employees believe are necessary in the performance of their jobs define their role perceptions. The results produced are usually measured by standards created by the degree of achievement of management-directed objectives.

6. Describe the major performance appraisal methods.

   Performance refers to the degree of accomplishment of the tasks that make up an employee's job. It reflects how well an employee is fulfilling the requirements of the job. The process of appraising that performance provides employees with a clear picture of how well they are currently doing and what needs to be done to improve performance. There are several methods available to managers:

   - *Management by objectives (MBO).* Measurable goals or objectives are agreed with the employee with a plan and deadline for achievement. At deadline, performance is appraised and corrective action taken if needed. If goals are achieved successfully, new goals are agreed with the employee with a new plan and deadline.
   - *Production standards.* An expected level of output is set (usually based on an average), and performance is measured against that standard.
   - *Essay appraisal.* The manager describes the employee's performance in essay form. This method presents challenges with the subjectivity of the manager and the comparability of assessments across the organization.

*Continued on next page*

Continued from page 271

- *Critical-incident appraisal.* A manager is required to keep a written record of incidents of both positive and negative employee performance as they occur. Managers tend to see this as a very time-consuming task.
- *Graphic rating scale.* A manager assesses an employee on such factors as quantity of work, dependability, job knowledge, attendance, accuracy of work, and cooperativeness. Scales can include both numerical and written descriptions, but they are subject to the same issue of managerial subjectivity as the essay appraisal.
- *Checklist appraisal.* A manager answers yes or no to a series of questions concerning the employee's behavior. The respective weighting assigned to each question is normally kept by the human resources department to minimize the possibility of manager bias. One major weakness of this method is the time required to develop a checklist for each job category.

## THE WORLD of Work >>

**KEVIN GETS SOME GOALS *(continued from page 251)***

Kevin took a few days to think about Tony's question. The first day had been taken up with worrying about what was really going on here. Kevin had never been asked to do this in any of his other jobs. His annual review had always been the same—a brief chat with the boss; here's what you're doing well; here's something you could improve on; keep up the good work; and here's your pay raise. Simple and predictable, thought Kevin.

Now Tony wanted goals and, more than that, goals for which Kevin would be held accountable over the next year. What was Tony looking for? Was he looking for Kevin to learn Spanish (something they had talked about because of their growing Latino customer base), or finally finish his bachelor's degree, or maybe take some more management training courses that the company was always offering at the regional meetings?

Suddenly, Kevin realized how excited he was at the prospect of committing to doing something new over the next year, and committing to it in writing rather than just talking about it. He started to make a list of what he wanted to do, taking the extra time to make notes for Tony on how the restaurant would benefit if it gave him the time off to do them or, better yet, if it was willing to help him cover the costs of doing them. Before he knew it, Kevin had two pages of ideas. Some of them would take longer than a year to achieve, but many of them could be started right away and be done a lot sooner, which would allow Kevin to show progress toward his goals long before the next annual review. The management courses could be taken at the regional meeting next month, and the local college started Spanish classes for beginners every other month. "I wonder if Tony realized what he was letting himself in for when he started this," Kevin said to himself.

**QUESTIONS**

1. Kevin had no problem coming up with ideas for personal and professional goals. Do you think he'll get to do them all? Why or why not?
2. Do you think Tony is expecting this kind of response from every one of his people? Why or why not?
3. What challenges will Tony face if everyone is as creative as Kevin in choosing goals?
4. What can Tony do to manage this situation?

## Key Terms >>

abilities 261

audits 258

behavior or personal control 253

break-even charts 258

budget 254

central tendency 266

checklist appraisal 264

concurrent controls 255

control 252

critical-incident appraisal 263

effort 261

essay appraisal 263

graphic rating scale 263

leniency 266

management audits 258

multirater assessment or 360-degree feedback 265

output or impersonal control 253

performance 260

performance appraisal 261

postaction control 255

preliminary control 253

production standard approach 262

recency 266

role perception 261

zero-base budgeting 254

1. Describe the two categories of control methods.
2. Where should control reside in an organization? Explain your answer.
3. Explain how a manager would use a break-even chart.
4. Outline the major points of the Sarbanes-Oxley Act of 2002.
5. Identify at least three uses of performance appraisal information.
6. Outline at least three factors that influence the success or failure of performance appraisal interviews.

1. Research the use of the balanced scorecard (BSC), and answer the following questions:
   a. What are the advantages and disadvantages of BSC?
   b. Provide an example of a company that uses BSC, and document the success achieved with its use.
   c. Find an example of a scorecard, and summarize the measures and targets used.
   d. How would you introduce BSC in your company? Develop a scorecard that lists the key measures for your company.
2. Visit the Web site **http://work911.com/performance/particles/stupman.htm**, and review the top 10 things that managers do to mess up performance appraisals. Answer the following questions:
   a. Which of the top 10 things is easiest to fix? Why?
   b. Which of the top 10 is the hardest to fix? Why
   c. Explain the statement: "Appraisal is about improvement, not blame."
   d. Why do managers seem to have such difficulties with performance appraisal?

1. **Debating Centralized versus Decentralized Control**

Divide the class into two groups (or an even number of smaller groups). Group A will speak in support of highly centralized control mechanisms. Group B will speak in support of decentralized control mechanisms (giving control to lower-level employees). Review the control pyramid in Figure 11.1, and develop a case in support of your assigned position. Your instructor may allow you to gather additional information through library or Internet research. Summarize your argument points in outline form, and be prepared to debate classmates who take the other side of the argument. Once the debates are completed, answer the following questions:

**Questions**

1. Summarize the key points of your argument.
2. Summarize the key points of the opposing group's argument.
3. Did the information shared in the debate change your opinion? Why or why not?
4. Your viewpoint was chosen for you according to the team to which you were assigned. How did the team members reach agreement in their debating viewpoint? Explain your answer.

2. **The Secret Shopper**

Josh was a successful manager for a major retailer. He worked in a small store that had enjoyed a steady growth in sales over the past three years. Josh also had an excellent assistant manager in his current location, Justin Baxtron. Josh had come to rely on Justin's support to carry out his plans. Josh's performance caught the interest of his district manager, Evelyn Noble, who recommended him for an opening at a larger location. Josh was naturally interested in the opportunity to work in a store with a larger staff and greater sales. He was also attracted by the chance to earn a significant raise.

Evelyn recognized Josh's talents, and she wanted him to take over the store. She warned Josh that the larger store was not performing up to its potential. She believed that the location had two major problems. One, it was selling less merchandise per square foot than the average store. Two, the location had a serious problem with employee morale. She told Josh that he would definitely have his work cut out for him.

Evelyn wanted Josh to come into the new job with his "eyes wide open," and she suggested that Josh visit the store as if he were a "secret shopper." Josh thought this was a great idea, as it would allow him to see how the store associates and department managers behaved in their normal routine. He noticed many problems with the store in only a few minutes. He encountered a number of aisles with new stock piled on the floor that needed shelving. He observed a number of employees gathered in the electronics section, watching a basketball game. Josh also overheard (salaried) department managers complaining about their work schedule. He was embarrassed to see a band of shoplifters operating in plain sight.

Divide the class into two groups—A and B:
Group A: How should Josh address the operational issues in the store?
Group B: How should Josh address the employee issues in the store?

*Source*: Submitted by R25—how should this be listed??

# Case 11.1

## >> Bob Iger Makes His Mark

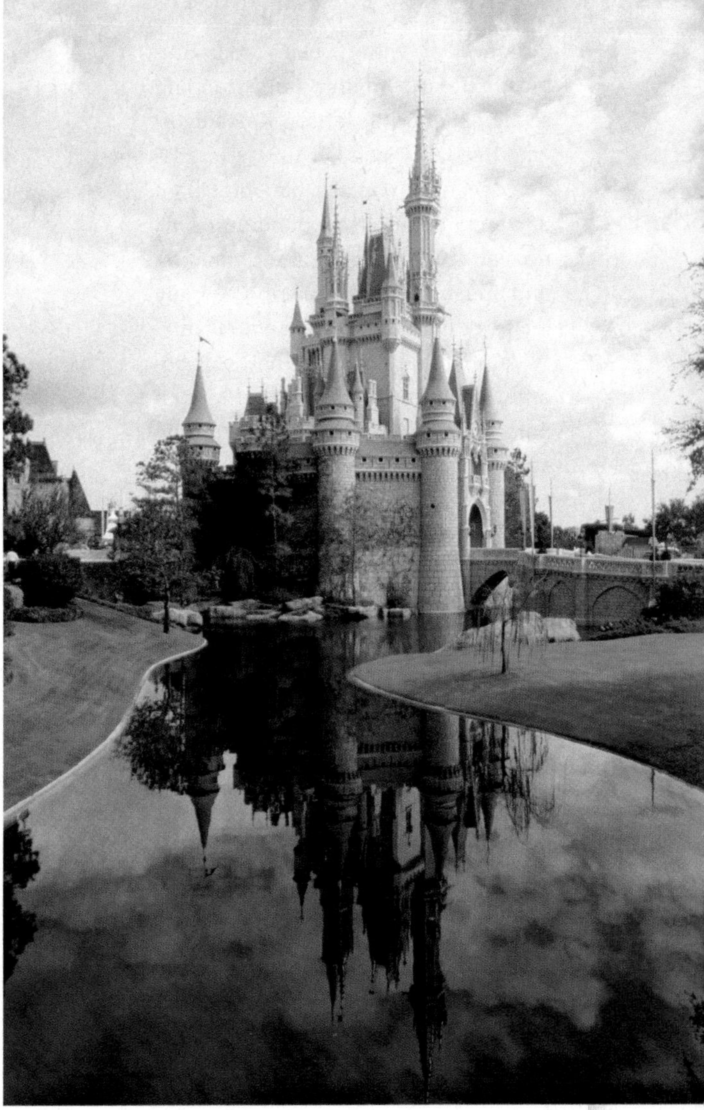

Appointed as president and chief operating officer of the Walt Disney Company in 2000, Robert "Bob" Iger succeeded Michael Eisner as chief executive officer in March 2005. The last days of Eisner's tenure as CEO had been extremely contentious, prompting former board members Roy E. Disney (Walt's nephew) and Stanley Gold to call for Eisner's resignation under a "Save Disney" campaign. Analysts expected Iger to launch his tenure by cleaning house and bringing in his own executive team. He has certainly tipped Eisner's centrally planned company on its end, hacking away at the bureaucracy and unshackling a group of veteran executives to plot their own courses. However, rather than throwing Eisner's people out just because he could, Iger has kept the team largely intact, and by surrounding himself with smart people and letting them get on with it, Iger has recreated a can-do culture at Disney.

Even so, to this day, Iger won't speak ill of Eisner. "I think fondly of Michael. I learned a lot from him," he says. "In a way, he founded the modern Walt Disney."

What Iger tactfully leaves unsaid is that during the final years of Eisner's otherwise brilliant two-decade run, Disney lost its animating spirit. To say the culture was poisonous doesn't begin to capture the company's dysfunction. Eisner left behind a place where division chiefs were afraid to make decisions—the last thing the company needed when such rivals as News Corp. and Viacom Inc. were boldly staking out territory on the Web.

Iger recognized that the problem wasn't the people running the show. It was the work environment—and he set about changing it. One of the first things Iger did was make the Monday morning meetings less autocratic. Where Eisner held court, Iger encouraged a conversation. And he made a point of visiting the troops—for example, spending half a day at Buena Vista Games Inc. talking to game developers in town for a brainstorming session. Iger also reached out to former Disney people who can help him chart a new strategic direction.

If Eisner struggled to rise above the petty and personal, Iger sees the big picture. He doesn't dump on people's ideas. Eisner famously wrote, "Where's my wow?" on subordinates' proposals he didn't like. And where Eisner got involved in every aspect of the creative process, from the color of the carpets at the theme park hotels to Tuesday morning script sessions, Iger let his people take the lead.

The acquisition of Pixar in 2006 for $7.4 billion in stock brought the creative team of John Lasseter and Ed Catmull to Disney's animation unit, and it also brought Steve Jobs to the Disney board as the single largest

*Continued on next page*

Continued from page 275

shareholder in the company. Rather than battle the famous Jobs ego, Iger gave Lasseter's team a free hand to revive animation, supporting them in their decisions to lay off 160 people and reassign executives.

February 2009 brought a distribution deal with Dreamworks Studios, strengthening a long-standing relationship with Jeffrey Katzenberg who had left Disney in 1994 after Eisner declined to make him president of the company in recognition of his revival of Disney's feature animation unit and, ironically, brokering a highly lucrative distribution deal with Pixar.

August 2009 brought news of another deal—the acquisition of Marvel Entertainment for $4 billion. With the support and approval of Stan Lee, the creator of many of Marvel's core characters, Iger brought a rich archive of future franchises to leverage Disney's undisputed talent at merchandising characters through multiple channels, including movies, Web sites, video games, live shows, and theme park attractions. Existing contractual relationships with competitors (Universal Studios owns distribution rights to the *Hulk* and has them for park attractions linked to Marvel characters in Orlando; Sony owns rights to *Spider-Man;* News Corporation owns rights to *X-Men*) and the potential for copyright lawsuits from surviving relatives of many of the character originators make the Marvel deal far more complex than the acquisition of Pixar. However, Iger once again took a hands-off approach, leaving it to John Lasseter to reassure Marvel's talented employees that their creative legacy and culture would be safe in Disney's hands.

The problem wasn't the people running the show. It was the work environment. One of the first things Iger did was make the Monday morning meetings less autocratic, more of a conversation. And he made a point of visiting the troops, and former Disney people to help him chart a new strategic direction.

QUESTIONS

1. How is Bob Iger's approach to managerial control different from Michael Eisner's?
2. Iger had the chance to start with a new leadership team, but he chose to keep Eisner's team almost intact. From a control perspective, was that the right decision? Why or why not?
3. "Iger let his people take the lead." How do you balance that approach with managerial control?
4. Do you think Iger's approach will be successful? Why or why not?

*Source:* Ronald Grover, "Entertainment: How Bob Iger Unchained Disney," *BusinessWeek*, February 5, 2007; Richard Siklos, "Big Changes in the Cast at Disney," *Fortune*, November 13, 2009; "Of Mouse and X-Men," *The Economist*, September 3, 2009; and Ronald Grover, "Disney to Buy Marvel for $4bn," *BusinessWeek*, August 31, 2009.

# Case 11.2

## >> Fear of Firing • The threat of litigation is making companies skittish about axing problem workers.

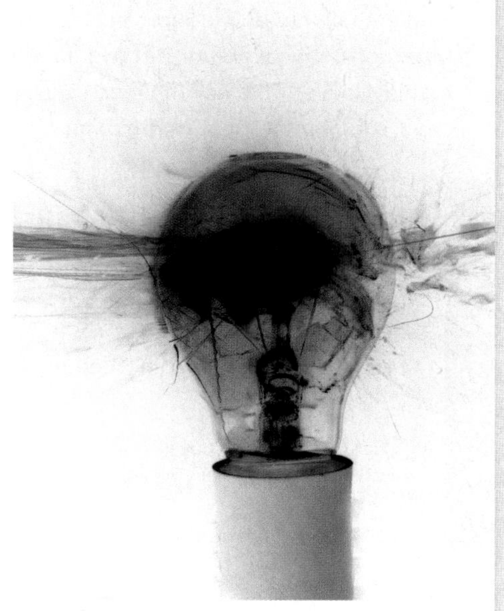

Would you have dared fire Hemant K. Mody? In February, the longtime engineer had returned to work at a GE facility in Plainville, Connecticut, after a two-month medical leave. He was a very unhappy man. For much of the prior year, he and his superiors had been sparring over his performance and promotion prospects. According to court documents, Mody's bosses claimed he spoke disparagingly of his co-workers, refused an assignment as being beneath him, and was abruptly taking days off and coming to work late. But Mody was also 49, Indian born, and even after returning from leave, he continued to suffer a major disability: chronic kidney failure that required him to receive daily dialysis. The run-ins resumed with his managers, whom he had accused flat out of discriminating against him because of his race and age. It doesn't take an advanced degree in human resources to recognize that the situation was a ticking time bomb. But Mody's bosses were fed up. They fired him in April. The bomb exploded in July 2006. Following a six-day trial, a federal court jury in Bridgeport, Connecticut, found GE's termination of Mody to be improper and awarded him $11.1 million, including $10 million in punitive damages. But the award wasn't for discrimination. The judge found those claims so weak that Mody wasn't allowed to present them. Instead, jurors concluded that Mody had been fired in retaliation for complaining about bias. GE sued to have the award overturned but was only able to get the award reduced by $5 million in 2007. Unfortunately, Mody never saw any of the 2006 jury award; he died in April 2007 of a heart attack.

> Mody's bosses claimed he spoke disparagingly of his co-workers, refused an assignment as being beneath him, and was abruptly taking days off and coming to work late.

If this can happen to GE, a company famed for its rigorous performance reviews, with an HR operation that is studied worldwide, it can happen anywhere. The result: Many companies today are gripped by a fear of firing. Terrified of lawsuits, they let unproductive employees linger, lay off coveted workers while retaining less valuable ones, and pay severance to nonperformers and even crooks in exchange for promises that they won't sue. The fear of firing is particularly acute in the HR and legal departments. They don't directly suffer when an underperformer lingers in the corporate hierarchy, but they may endure unpleasant indirect consequences if that person files a lawsuit.

When Mody signed GE's job application in 1998, the form said his employment was "at will" and "the Company may terminate my employment at any time for any reason." Well, not exactly. The notion that American workers are employed "at will"—meaning, as one lawyer put it, you can be fired if your manager doesn't like the color of your socks—took root in the laissez-faire atmosphere of the late 19th century and, as an official matter, is still the law of the land in every state, save Montana. For most American workers now, their status as at-will

*Continued on next page*

Continued from page 277

employees has been transformed by a succession of laws growing out of the civil rights movement in the 1960s that bar employers from making decisions based on such things as race, religion, sex, age, and national origin. This is hardly controversial. Even the legal system's harshest critics find little fault with rules aimed at ensuring that personnel decisions are based on merit. Most freely acknowledge that it is much easier to fire people in the United States than it is in, say, most of Western Europe. Mass layoffs, in fact, are a recurring event on the American corporate scene. Yet even in these situations, RIFs, or "reductions in force," are carefully vetted by attorneys to assess the impact on employees who are in a legally protected category. These days the majority of American workers fall into one or more such groups. Mody, for example, belonged to three because of who he was (age, race, and national origin) and two more because of things he had done (complained of discrimination and taken medical leave). That doesn't mean such people are immune from firing. But it does mean a company will have to show a legitimate, nondiscriminatory business reason for the termination, should the matter ever land in court.

QUESTIONS

1. Why are many companies afraid of terminating unproductive employees?
2. Why do supervisors bear much of the blame when HR says someone can't be shown the door?
3. Can managers really fire employees "at will"?
4. GE was successful in getting the amount of the award reduced, but was the size of the award really its first concern?

*Source:* Michael Orey, "Fear of Firing," BusinessWeek Online, April 27, 2007; "Judge Cuts $12 Million Award in GE Case," www.abcmoney.co.uk/news/242007150976.htm#, retrieved 3/29/10; and Steve Bruce, "Fear of Firing: How to Handle HR's Least-Liked (and Most Dangerous) Task," *HR Daily Advisor*, April 8, 2008.

# Case 11.3

## >> Trials and Tribulations • FDA warns J&J on poor management of drug trials for a second time.

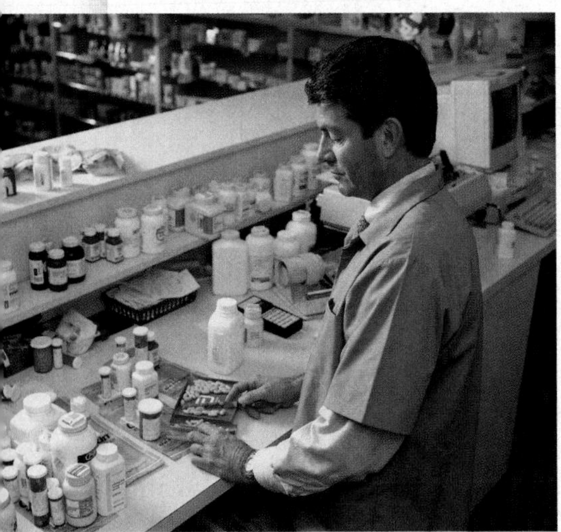

In a warning letter dated August 10, 2009, the Center for Drug Evaluation and Research, part of the U.S. Food and Drug Administration (FDA), accused Johnson & Johnson Pharmaceuticals (J&J) of failing to properly manage two human tests of its antibiotic drug candidate *ceftobiprole* (which will be marketed as Zeftera or Zevtera). The FDA letter did not identify the drug by name, but J&J later confirmed the identity of the drug in the press release response to the letter that endeavored to reassure investors that the problems related to only a "handful" of trial sites. The letter represented the second delay of approval for the drug, with similar problems being cited in both instances.

The letter identified four areas of "alleged deficiency" in J&J's management of the trials:

- Failure to ensure proper monitoring of the clinical investigations, which resulted in "deficiencies in record-keeping with respect to case histories and drug accountability by clinical investigators participating in the above-referenced studies."

- Failure to ensure that an investigation was conducted in accordance with the general investigational plan and protocols, as specified in the Investigational New Drug (IND) application for ceftobiprole (e.g., study monitors failed to ensure that planned trial blinding procedures were followed correctly at one site).
- Failure to secure investigator compliance with the investigator plan and applicable FDA regulations (e.g., all patients should have begun dosing on the same day as randomization; this did not happen at one site).
- Failure to ensure that only investigators qualified by training and experience were selected as appropriate experts for the trials—for example, one doctor was chosen despite a prestudy monitoring visit documenting that the investigator was "not recommended" due to lack of compliance in completing regulatory documents, lack of diligence in study start-up procedures, and an inadequate patient population.

Further evidence documented such basic errors as not making sure patients were storing the drug properly when using it at home, failing to document some doses given to patients, not conducting thorough examinations of all patients, and enrolling some patients who failed to meet J&J's own eligibility criteria for the study.

The approval delays may have a dramatic impact on J&J's financial performance in the future. A forecast by Decision Resources, a leading research advisory firm for pharmaceutical and health care issues, in December 2006 estimated the sales of ceftobiprole could reach $500 million by 2015, making it a "category killer" in the highly competitive market for antibacterial drugs. The attraction of the drug is that it can be used to treat methicillin-resistant *Staphylococcus aureus* (MRSA), an infection typically acquired in hospitals that can result in contracted infections or pneumonia (extending hospital stays by as many as 26 days) or death.

In order to gain a competitive foothold in this lucrative market, Johnson & Johnson licensed the drug from a Swiss company, Basilea Pharmaceutica Ltd., but as a result of the delays, both companies are now in litigation.

**QUESTIONS**

1. Given that this is the second delay for Johnson & Johnson in these drug trials, what does this say about its management controls?
2. Of the four areas of alleged deficiency, which one represents the greatest management challenge to correct? Why?
3. What will be the consequences for these trials and for the organization if Johnson & Johnson fails to correct these errors?
4. If you were assigned to manage this project now, what would be your first step?

*Source:* Peter Mansell, "FDA Warns J&J over Ceftobiprole Trial Violations," August 19, 2009, http://pharmatimes.com/, retrieved August 20, 2009; "By 2015, J&J/Basilea's Ceftobiprole Will Achieve Sales of Nearly US$500 Million for Treating Hospital-Acquired Infections," release issued December 13, 2006, www.decisionresources.com, retrieved August 20, 2009; Marley Seaman, "FDA Warns Johnson & Johnson on Antibiotic Trials," Associated Press, August 19, 2009; and FDA, "Inspections, Compliance, Enforcement, and Criminal Investigations: Johnson & Johnson Pharmaceutical Research & Development, LLC 8/10/09," www.fda.gov/ICEC/EnforcementActions/WarningLetters/ucm177398.htm, retrieved August 20, 2009.

CHAPTER 12

"Just because it can be counted doesn't mean it counts and just because it counts doesn't mean it can be counted."

Albert Einstein

# OPERATIONS CONTROL

LEARNING OUTCOMES

After studying this chapter, you will able to:

1 Understand the basic requirements for controlling operating costs.

2 Define *quality* from the perspective of an operations manager.

3 Explain the concept of total quality management (TQM).

4 Define the following terms: *continuous improvement, kaizen, six sigma, lean manufacturing,* and *quality at the source.*

5 Understand the difference between *raw material, in-process,* and *finished-goods* inventory classifications.

6 Explain the concept of just-in-time (JIT) inventory.

## THE WORLD OF WORK Taco Barn goes Japanese

Kevin's success with the MBO project gave Tony an idea.

"If one employee could be that insightful and creative in planning his own future, how many new ideas could we come up with if we gave every employee the chance to contribute ideas? Not just a simple suggestion box (which usually gathered more gum wrappers than employee suggestions) but a real plan to improve the restaurant based on the ideas of the employees who work here—the folks who cook the food, serve the food, and listen to our customers?"

On his next regular lunch meeting with his mentor and former boss Jerry Smith, Tony put the idea forward for Jerry's feedback.

"I think it's a great idea, Tony," said Jerry. "You've got a bright group over there, and I'm sure they'll surprise you with some really creative ideas. In fact, I just came back from a leadership conference where they had a presentation on this very topic. It's a philosophy called 'kaizen,' and it comes from Japanese companies that commit to continuously reinventing their operations, even when they're already the market leader in their industry. Toyota has become a global car company as a direct result of its kaizen practices."

Tony figured he would have to go back and do some Web searching on Toyota and its kaizen processes, but never one to miss an opportunity, he decided to take full advantage of Jerry's recent conference trip.

"That sounds really interesting, Jerry. What else did you pick up at the conference?"

"They had this great exercise that might help you get your group into the spirit of being creative," continued Jerry. "It's called 'stand in the circle'—you get your team to stand in a circle drawn on the floor. They each have a pad with at least 30 lines on it. You then give them 30 minutes to come up with 30 ideas to improve the company. They can be as wild and crazy as they want, but the ideas have to be improvements on the way things are currently done. The 30-minute time limit is supposed to help focus their energy. Then you meet as a group, review the ideas, and decide, as a group, which ones will be implemented and how soon that will be done. The instructor made us do the exercise on the experience we were having at our hotel. You would be amazed how many ideas we generated. A couple of people even asked for extra paper!"

Tony thought this over for a while and decided, "I think that might just work for us—thanks, Jerry!"

**QUESTIONS**

1. How did Kevin's performance on the MBO project inspire Tony to consider kaizen?
2. If the employee suggestion box only collects gum wrappers, why should this exercise be any different?
3. What kind of ideas do you think Tony's team will come up with?
4. Would this exercise work at your company? Why or why not?

## >> Operations Control

There are two aspects to an effective operating system: design and control. These aspects are related in that after a system has been designed and implemented, day-to-day operations must be controlled. With respect to efficient operation, the system processes must be monitored; quality must be ensured; inventories must be managed; and all these tasks must be accomplished within cost constraints. In addition to ensuring that things do not get out of control, good operations control can be a substitute for resources. For example, good quality control can reduce scrap and wasted materials, thus cutting costs. Similarly, effective inventory control can reduce the investment costs in inventories.

**Variable Overhead Expenses** Expenses that change in proportion to the level of production or service.

**Fixed Overhead Expenses** Expenses that do not change appreciably with fluctuations in the level of production or service.

Effective operations control is attained by applying the basic control concepts to the operations function of the organization. Operations controls generally relate to one of three areas: costs, quality, or inventories.

## >> Controlling Operations Costs

Ensuring that operating costs do not get out of hand is one of the primary jobs of the operations manager. The first requirement for controlling costs is to understand the organization's accounting and budgeting systems. Operations managers are primarily concerned with costs relating to labor, materials, and overhead. Figure 12.1 describes the major components of each of these costs. **Variable overhead expenses** change with the level of production or service. **Fixed overhead expenses** do not change appreciably with the level of production or service.

Normally, operations managers prepare monthly budgets for each major cost area. Once these budgets have been approved by higher levels of management, they are put into effect. By carefully monitoring the ensuing labor, material, and overhead costs, the operations manager can compare actual costs to budgeted costs. The methods used to monitor costs naturally vary, but typically they include direct observation, written reports, break-even charts, and so on.

Usually a cost control system indicates only if a particular cost is out of control; it does not address the question of *why* it is out of control. For example, suppose an operations manager determines from

**Figure 12.1 • Budget Costs: The Basis for Cost Control**

| Type of Cost | Components |
|---|---|
| Direct labor—variable | Wages and salaries of employees engaged in the direct generation of goods and services. This typically does not include wages and salaries of support personnel. |
| Materials—variable | Cost of materials that become a tangible part of finished goods and services. |
| Production overhead—variable | Training new employees, safety training, supervision and clerical, overtime premium, shift premium, payroll taxes, vacation and holiday, retirement funds, group insurance, supplies, travel, repairs and maintenance. |
| Production overhead—fixed | Travel, research and development, fuel (coal, gas, or oil), electricity, water, repairs and maintenance, rent, depreciation, real estate taxes, insurance. |

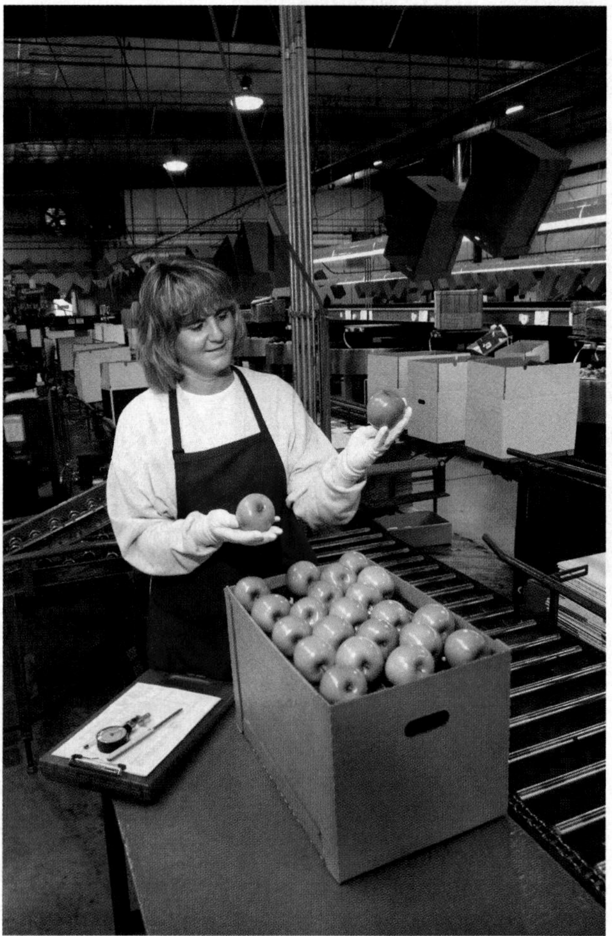

the monthly cost report that the labor costs on product X are exceeding budget by 20 percent. The manager must then attempt to determine what is causing the cost overrun. The causes could be many, including unmotivated employees, several new and untrained employees, low-quality raw materials, or equipment breakdowns. The wise manager not only investigates the cause but also plans for prevention. The logical conclusion of a monitoring process is the implementation of prevention measures.[1]

Determining the cause may require only a simple inspection of the facts, or it may call for an in-depth analysis. Whatever the effort required, the operations manager must ultimately identify the source of the problem and then take the necessary corrective action. If the same cost problems continue to occur, chances are the manager has not correctly identified the true cause of the problem or the necessary corrective action has not been taken.

**Figure 12.2 • The Dimensions of Design Quality**

| Dimension | Meaning |
|---|---|
| Performance | Primary product or service characteristics |
| Features | Added touches; bells and whistles; secondary characteristics |
| Reliability/durability | Consistency of performance over time; probability of failing; useful life |
| Serviceability | Ease of repair |
| Aesthetics | Sensory characteristics (sound, feel, look, and so on) |
| Reputation | Past performance and other intangibles (perceived quality) |

## >> Quality Management

**Quality** is a relative term that means different things to different people. The consumer who demands quality may have a different concept from the operations manager who demands quality. The consumer is concerned with service, reliability, performance, appearance, and so forth. The operations manager's primary concern is that the product or service specifications be achieved, whatever they may be. For the operations manager, quality is determined in relation to the specifications or standards set in the design stages. Thus, the design quality refers to the inherent value of the product or service in the marketplace.[2] Figure 12.2 lists the six common dimensions of design quality.

The quality of an organization's goods and services can affect the organization in many ways. Some of the most important of these areas are (1) loss of business, (2) liability, (3) costs, and (4) productivity.[3] The reputation of an organization is often a direct reflection of the perceived quality of its goods or services. In today's legalistic environment, an organization's liability exposure can be significant and the associated costs can be high. Higher-quality goods and services generally have less liability exposure than lower-quality goods and services. In addition to liability costs, quality can affect other costs, including scrap, rework, warranty, repair, and replacement. Productivity and quality are often closely related.[4] Poor-quality equipment, tools, parts, or subassemblies can cause defects that hurt productivity. Similarly, high-quality equipment, tools, parts, and subassemblies can boost productivity.

**Quality** The degree or grade of excellence specified; for the operations manager, quality is determined in relation to the specifications or standards set in the design stages.

Because of the many different ways quality can affect an organization, it is often difficult to determine precisely the costs associated with different quality levels. Also, it must be realized that consumers and customers are willing to pay for quality only up to a point. In response, many firms have instituted a total customer response program in which quality in the workplace is transferred to dealings with customers. To implement the program, firms must (1) develop a new attitude toward customers, (2) reduce management layers so that managers are in contact with customers, (3) link quality and information systems to customer needs and problems, (4) train employees in customer responsiveness, (5) integrate customer responsiveness throughout the entire distribution channel, and (6) use customer responsiveness as a marketing tool.[5]

**Study Alert!** Operating costs are forecast as part of the budget process. Effective management requires identification of variances from those budgeted costs as quickly as possible so that corrective action can be taken.

### QUALITY ASSURANCE

For years, the responsibility for quality in almost all organizations rested with a quality control department.[6] The idea under this approach was to identify and remove defects or correct mistakes before they got to the customer. Some systems emphasized finding and correcting defects at the end of the line; others focused on detecting defects during the production process. Both approaches focused on only the production part of the process; they gave little or no consideration to the design of the products or services or to working with suppliers. Suppliers were usually treated as adversaries.

Today's quality management emphasizes the prevention of defects and mistakes rather than finding and correcting them. The idea of "building in" quality as opposed to "inspecting it in" is known as *quality assurance.* This approach views quality as the responsibility of all employees rather than the exclusive domain of a quality control department. Furthermore, suppliers are treated as partners.

While there have been many individuals who have championed the prevention approach to quality, W. Edwards Deming is perhaps most responsible. Deming was a statistics professor at New York University in the 1940s who went to Japan after World War II to assist in improving quality and productivity. While he became very revered in Japan, Deming remained almost unknown to U.S. business leaders until the 1980s when Japan's quality and productivity attracted the attention of the world. Figure 12.3 presents a list compiled by Deming of 14 points he believed are needed to achieve quality in any organization. The underlying philosophy of Deming's work in this area is that the cause of poor quality and low productivity is the system and not the employees. He also stressed that it is management's responsibility to correct the system so that the desired results can be achieved.

**Study Alert!**

Quality is a relative term that means different things to different people. However, for an organization to build in quality to a production or service process, an agreed quality standard must be identified and measured so that compliance to that standard can be monitored and variances from that standard can be addressed in a timely manner.

## Figure 12.3 • Deming's 14 Points

1. Create and publish to all employees a statement of the aims and purposes of the company or other organization. The management must demonstrate constantly their commitment to this statement.
2. Learn the new philosophy, top management and everybody.
3. Understand the purpose of inspection, for improvement of processes and reduction of cost.
4. End the practice of awarding business on the basis of price tag alone.
5. Improve constantly and forever the system of production and service.
6. Institute training.
7. Teach and institute leadership.
8. Drive out fear. Create trust. Create a climate for innovation.
9. Optimize toward the aims and purposes of the company the efforts of teams, groups, and staff.
10. Eliminate exhortations for the workforce.

11a. Eliminate numerical quotas for production. Instead learn and institute methods for improvement.

11b. Eliminate management by objective. Instead learn the capabilities of processes and how to improve them.

12. Remove barriers that rob people of pride of workmanship.
13. Encourage education and self-improvement for everyone.
14. Take action to accomplish the transformation.

## TOTAL QUALITY MANAGEMENT

Total quality management (TQM) is a management philosophy that emphasizes "managing the entire organization so that it excels in all dimensions of products and services that are important to the customer."[7] TQM, in essence, is an organizationwide emphasis on quality as defined by the customer. Under TQM, everyone from the CEO on down to the lowest-level employee must be involved. TQM can be summarized by the following actions:[8]

1. Find out what customers want. This might involve the use of surveys, focus groups, interviews, or some other technique that integrates the customer's voice in the decision-making process.

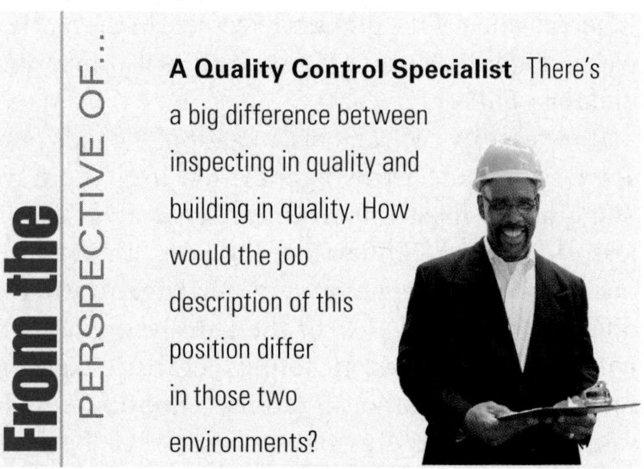

From the
PERSPECTIVE OF...
A Quality Control Specialist There's a big difference between inspecting in quality and building in quality. How would the job description of this position differ in those two environments?

2. Design a product or service that will meet (or exceed) what customers want. Make it easy to use and easy to produce.
3. Design a production process that facilitates doing the job right the first time. Determine where mistakes are likely to occur, and try to prevent them. When mistakes do occur, find out why so that they are less likely to occur again. Strive to mistake-proof the process.
4. Keep track of results, and use those results to guide improvement in the system. Never stop trying to improve.
5. Extend these concepts to suppliers and to distribution.

As stated previously, TQM is an organizationwide emphasis on quality as defined by the customer. It is not a collection of techniques but a philosophy or way of thinking about how people view their jobs and quality throughout the organization.

## PROGRESS ✓questions

1. Compare the two aspects to an effective operating system.
2. Why is quality a relative term?
3. Explain the term *total quality management* (TQM).
4. Which one of the 14 points that Deming believed are needed to achieve quality in an organization is the most important? Why?

## IMPLEMENTING TQM

Today's managers are bombarded with advice and literature telling them how to implement TQM. Three of the most popular approaches for implementing TQM are the Deming method, the Juran method, and the Crosby method, each named after the person who championed the respective approach. These three men, W. Edwards Deming, Joseph M. Juran, and Philip Crosby, are known as the "quality gurus." The Deming method emphasizes statistical quality control through employee empowerment. The Juran method emphasizes the reformulation of attitudes, comprehensive controls, and annual objective reviews. The Crosby method emphasizes conformance to requirements and zero defects. All three approaches are sound; however, the best approach for implementing TQM is to custom-tailor the process for each application. In a study conducted by Frank Mahoney, the following initiatives were those most often cited by senior executives who had successfully implemented TQM.[9]

1. Demonstrate top-down commitment and involvement push.
2. Set *tough* improvement goals, not just stretch goals.
3. Provide appropriate training, resources, and human resource backup.
4. Determine critical measurement factors; benchmark and track progress.
5. Spread success stories, especially those about favorable benchmarking; always share financial progress reports.
6. Identify the costs of quality and routes to improvement; prove the case that quality costs decline with quality progress.
7. Rely on teamwork, involvement, and all-level leadership.
8. Respect the gurus, but tailor every initiative for a good local fit.
9. Allow time to see progress, analyze the system's operation, reward contributions, and make needed adjustments.
10. Finally, recognize that the key internal task is a culture change and the key external task is a new set of relationships with customers and suppliers.

Although it would seem to make good sense to transform an organization in the direction of total quality management, there is still resistance from the traditionalists. Figure 12.4 compares traditional organizations with those using TQM. The most often cited barriers to adopting TQM are (1) a lack of

**Figure 12.4 • Comparison of Traditional Organizations with Those Using TQM**

| Aspect | Traditional | TQM |
|---|---|---|
| Overall mission | Maximize return on investment | Meet or exceed customer satisfaction |
| Objectives | Emphasis on short term | Balance of long term and short term |
| Management | Not always open; sometimes inconsistent objectives | Open; encourages employees' input; consistent objectives |
| Role of manager | Issue orders; enforce | Coach, remove barriers, build trust |
| Customer requirements | Not highest priority; may be unclear | Highest priority; important to identify and understand |
| Problems | Assign blame; punish | Identify and resolve |
| Problem solving | Not systematic; by individuals | Systematic; by teams |
| Improvement | Erratic | Continual |
| Suppliers | Adversarial | Partners |
| Jobs | Narrow, specialized; much individual effort | Broad, more general; much team effort |
| Focus | Product oriented | Process oriented |

**Continuous Improvement** Ongoing effort to make improvements in every part of the organization relative to all its products and services.

**Kaizen** "Good change"; a process of continuous and relentless improvement.

**Quality at the Source** The philosophy of making each employee responsible for the quality of his or her own work.

consistency of purpose on the part of management, (2) an emphasis on short-term profits, (3) an inability to modify personnel review systems, (4) mobility of management (job hopping), (5) lack of commitment to training and failure to instill leadership that is change-oriented, and (6) excessive costs.[10]

## SPECIFIC APPROACHES FOR IMPROVING QUALITY

*Continuous improvement, kaizen, quality at the source, six sigma,* and *lean manufacturing* are all terms that have particular relevance to TQM. Each approach is discussed in this section.

**Six Sigma** Examination and improvement of the entire production or service system; literally, in statistical terms, six standard deviations from the mean.

**Lean Manufacturing** A systematic approach to identifying and eliminating waste and non-value-added activities.

**Continuous improvement** in general refers to an ongoing effort to make improvements in every part of the organization relative to all its products and services.[11] With regard to TQM, it means focusing on continuous improvement in the quality of the processes by which work is accomplished. The idea here is that the quest for better quality and better service is never ending.

**Kaizen** is a philosophy for improvement that originated in Japan and that has recently enjoyed widespread adoption throughout the world. Many people consider kaizen and continuous improvement to be one and the same; others consider kaizen to be a subset of or a particular type of continuous improvement. The word *kaizen* comes from two Japanese words: *kai,* meaning "change," and *zen,* meaning "good."[12] Hence, kaizen literally means "good change," and in today's context it describes a process of continuous and relentless improvement. Kaizen is not based on large technical leaps but on the incremental refining of existing processes. Kaizen is basically a system of taking small steps to improve the workplace. It is based on the belief that the system should be customer-driven and involve all employees through systematic and open communication. Under kaizen, employees are viewed as the organization's most valued asset. This philosophy is put into practice through teamwork and extensive employee participation. In summary, kaizen applies the principles of participatory management toward incremental improvement of the current methods and processes. Kaizen does not focus on obtaining new and faster machines but on improving the methods and procedures used in the existing situation.

**Quality at the source** refers to the philosophy of making each employee responsible for the quality of his or her work.[13] In effect, this approach views every employee as a quality inspector for his or her own work. A major advantage of this approach is that it removes the adversarial relationship that often exists between quality control inspectors and production employees. It also encourages employees to take pride in their work.

**Six sigma** is both a precise set of statistical tools and a rallying cry for continuous improvement.[14] Six sigma was pioneered by Motorola during the 1980s and literally means, in statistical terms, six standard deviations from the mean. The philosophy of six sigma is that in order to realize the very high level of quality demanded by six sigma (most processes traditionally have used three sigma), the entire

# Thinking Critically 12.1

## >> Production Problems

Braddock Company of Sea Shore City fabricates stamped metal parts used in the production of wheelbarrows. Braddock fabricates two basic styles of wheelbarrow trays: One is for a deep, 4-cubic-foot construction model, and the other is for a shallow, 2-cubic-foot homeowner's model. Braddock's process is simple. Raw metal sheets are picked up from inventory (Braddock presently maintains about 7 days' worth of the large metal sheets for the construction model and about 10 days' worth of the smaller sheets for the homeowner's model) and fed into a large machine that bends and shapes the metal into the desired tray. The trays are then inspected and packaged, 10 to a box, for shipping.

In the past few days, Braddock has been experiencing quality problems with both tray styles. Undesirable creases have been forming in the corners following the stamping operation. However, the problem with the construction model tray is more pronounced and appeared almost three full days before it did on the homeowner's model.

Several incidents have occurred at Braddock during the past week that Hal McCarthy, the operations manager, thinks may have a bearing on the problem. Shorty McCune, a machine operator and labor activist, was accused of drinking on the job and released a few days before the problem began. Since his release, Shorty has been seen in and around the plant talking to several other employees. About two weeks ago, Braddock also began receiving raw metal from a new supplier because of an attractive price break.

The only inspection the company performs is the postfabrication inspection.

**QUESTIONS**

1. What do you think is causing Braddock's problem?
2. Why is the problem more pronounced on the construction model than on the homeowner's model?
3. How can Braddock eliminate its problem?
4. What systems or processes should Braddock put in place to make sure this doesn't happen again?

production or service system must be examined and improved. Customer focus and data-driven rigor are at the heart of six sigma. Six sigma addresses the question, "What does the customer want in the way of quality?" The answer to this question is then translated into statistical terms and rigorously analyzed.

Although it's most often thought of as applying to manufacturing processes, six sigma can be applied to any business process where the quality of the result may be quantified and the results of each process tracked.[15] Processes such as shipping, pickup and delivery of goods, order taking, and credit management readily lend themselves to six sigma.

**Lean manufacturing** is a systematic approach to identifying and eliminating waste and non-value-added activities.[16] The essence of lean manufacturing is to look at the entire production or service process to eliminate waste or unnecessary activities wherever possible.

**Study Alert!**

Six sigma received broader acceptance outside of Motorola with the development of professional certification based on the martial arts' colored belt sequence, starting with a white belt and rising to the level of master black belt six sigma.

**Reengineering** Searching for and implementing radical change in business processes to achieve breakthroughs in costs, speed, productivity, and service; also called *business process engineering.*

**ISO 9000** A set of quality standards for international business with the major objective of promoting the development of standardization and facilitating the international exchange of goods and services.

All the above terms—continuous improvement, kaizen, quality at the source, six sigma, and lean manufacturing—are approaches for improving the quality of the product or service offered. These approaches are not mutually exclusive but are complementary; the differences are that each offers a different emphasis. It should also be pointed out that each approach can be applied in such nonmanufacturing environments as service, education, and government.

As stated earlier, TQM is an organizationwide emphasis on quality as defined by the customer. It is not a collection of techniques but a philosophy or way of thinking about how people view their jobs and quality through the organization.

## REENGINEERING

Some people confuse the concept of reengineering with TQM. **Reengineering**, also called *business process engineering,* is "the search for and implementation of radical change in business processes to achieve breakthrough results in costs, speed, productivity, and service."[17] Unlike TQM, reengineering is not a program for making marginal improvements in existing procedures. Reengineering is rather a onetime concerted effort, initiated from the top of the organization, to make major improvements in processes used to produce products or services. The essence of reengineering is to start with a clean slate and redesign the organization's processes to better serve its customers.

## OTHER QUALITY STANDARDS

While TQM is a highly effective, organizationwide philosophy about quality, there are other techniques and approaches that organizations may adopt to encourage quality. Most of these can be used alone or in conjunction with TQM. Quality circles were discussed in Chapter 8. Three additional approaches are discussed below.

**ISO 9000** **ISO 9000** is a set of quality standards created in 1987 by the International Organization for Standardization (ISO) in Geneva, Switzerland. ISO is currently composed of the national standards bodies of over 175 countries with the major objective of promoting the development of standardization and facilitating the international exchange of goods and services. The American National Standards Institute (ANSI) is the member body representing the United States in the ISO.

Originally the ISO published five international standards designed to guide internal quality management programs and to facilitate external quality assurance endeavors. The original 1987 standards were slightly revised in 1994. In essence, ISO 9000:1994 outlined the quality system requirements necessary to meet quality requirements in varying situations. ISO 9000:1994 focused on the design and operation processes, not on the end product or service. ISO 9000:1994 required extensive documentation in order to demonstrate the consistency and reliability of the processes being used. While ISO issues the standards, it does not regulate the program internally; regulation is left to national accreditation organizations such as the U.S. Register Accreditation Board (RAB). RAB and other such boards then authorize registrars to issue ISO 9000 certificates.

New ISO 9000 standards were implemented beginning in fall 2000. The new standards emphasize international organization and in-house performance, rather than engineering, as the best way to deliver a product or service. In essence, the new ISO 9000:2000 focuses more on continuous improvement and customer satisfaction. ISO 9000:2000, like its predecessor, is really a series of interrelated standards. In ISO 9000:2000 there are three interrelated standards. ISO 9000:2000 deals with fundamentals and vocabulary; ISO 9001:2000 states the requirements for the new system; and ISO 9004:2000 provides guidance for implementation. Because ISO 9001:2000 represents the heart of the new standards, this entire set of standards is sometimes referred to as ISO 9001:2000, as opposed to ISO 9000:2000.[18]

**ISO 14000** Sparked by the success of ISO 9000, ISO developed a similar series of international standards for environmental management. **ISO 14000** is a series of voluntary international standards covering environmental management tools and systems.[19] While many countries have developed environmental management system standards, these standards are often not compatible. The goal of ISO 14000 is to provide international environmental standards that are compatible. Similar to ISO 9000, which does not prescribe methods to integrate quality processes into an organization, ISO 14000 does not prescribe environmental policies. ISO 14000 does provide an international standard for environmental management systems so that organizations will have a systematic framework for their environmental activities. ISO 14000 focuses heavily on strategic issues such as setting goals and developing policies. ISO 14000 certification requires compliance in four organizational areas:[20] (1) implementation of an environmental management system, (2) assurance that procedures are in place to maintain compliance with laws and regulations, (3) commitment to continual improvement, and (4) commitment to waste minimization and prevention of pollution.

Although the ISO 14000 series will ultimately include 20 separate standards covering everything from environmental auditing to environmental labeling to assessing life cycles of products, ISO 14001 is the first standard released. ISO 14001, "Environmental Management Systems–Specification with Guidance for Use," is the standard companies will use to establish their own environmental management systems. As of December 31, 2004, 90,569 companies in 127 countries had been certified for ISO 14001.[21] This represents an increase of 37 percent over the previous year.

**Zero Defects** The name *zero defects* is somewhat misleading in that this approach doesn't literally try to cut defects or defective service to zero. Such an approach would obviously be very cost ineffective in many situations. A **zero-defects program** attempts to create a positive attitude toward the prevention of low quality. The objective of a zero-defects program is to heighten awareness of quality by making everyone aware of his or her potential impact on quality. Naturally, this should lead to more attention to detail and concern for accuracy.

Most successful zero-defects programs have the following characteristics:

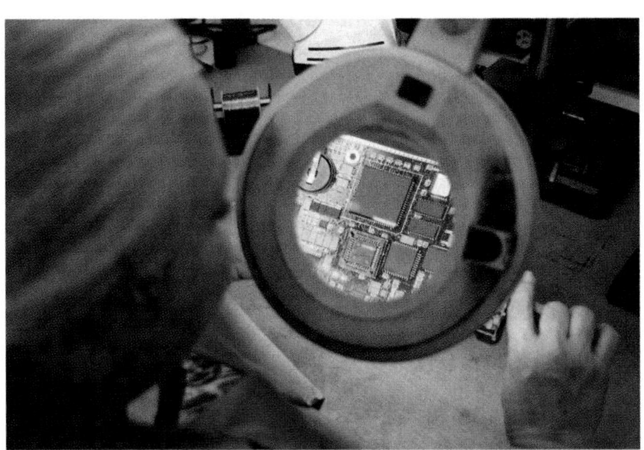

## [PROGRESS] ✓questions

5. Compare the perspectives of the quality gurus?
6. Explain the term *kaizen*.
7. What are the key differences between ISO 9000 and ISO 14000?
8. Explain the term *zero defects*.

1. Extensive communication regarding the importance of quality (e.g., signs, posters, contests, and so on).
2. Organizationwide recognition (e.g., publicly granting rewards, certificates, and plaques for high-quality work).
3. Problem identification by employees (e.g., employees pointing out areas where they think quality can be improved).
4. Employee goal setting (e.g., employees participating in setting quality goals).[22]

**ISO 14000** Addition to the ISO 9000 to control the impact of an organization's activities and outputs on the environment.

**Zero-Defects Program** Method of increasing quality by increasing everyone's impact on quality.

## THE MALCOLM BALDRIGE NATIONAL QUALITY AWARD

In 1987, the U.S. Congress passed the Malcolm Baldrige National Quality Improvement Act. The purpose of this legislation was to inspire increased

CUTTING CORNERS

Kaufman's Bakery, a family-owned business, had been baking and selling fine baked goods and breads to retail and wholesale customers since 1948. Because of its reputation for selling tasty products and using only quality ingredients in production, Kaufman's was highly respected by its customers and other stakeholders. However, with customers tightening their belts in this tough economy, sales had been falling over the last year and the bakery was facing financial difficulties. With tougher lending policies, the bank was unwilling to discuss modifying the bakery's line of credit, and it was getting harder and harder to meet payroll every two weeks.

Teresa Taggart started as a baker with the company when she was still in college. With her leadership ability and increasing understanding of the business, she was soon promoted to lead baker, assistant production manager, and, recently, production manager.

Teresa's promotion coincided with the arrival of Beth Kaufman, the granddaughter of the bakery founder and the new company CEO. Beth had already started putting her stamp on the bakery—several long-term employees had been laid off in favor of younger, less experienced people, and Beth had started enforcing the rule book to the letter, down to timing coffee breaks and requiring everyone to clock in and out. Teresa felt more micromanaged than she ever had under Beth's father Bob. He understood the need for strict controls, but Kaufman's

ETHICAL
MANAGEMENT
What do you do when cutting costs compromises product quality?

had good people who had worked for them for many years, and Teresa felt they should be trusted rather than controlled.

Teresa's greatest concern was Beth's decision to cut costs by using lesser quality ingredients and not changing the prices of Kaufman's products. Suppliers were already noticing the difference, and Teresa was convinced that customers were starting to notice as well.

**QUESTIONS**

1. What do you think about the situation Teresa faces?
2. What are Teresa's options in this situation?
3. What would you do if you were Teresa?

*Source:* Adapted from an idea suggested by R28—how should this be cited??

efforts by U.S. businesses to improve the quality of their products and services. The **Malcolm Baldrige Award** is named after the late Malcolm Baldrige, who was a successful businessman and a former U.S. secretary of commerce. The award is administered by the National Institute of Standards and Technology and can only be awarded to businesses located in the United States. The purpose of the award is to encourage efforts to improve quality and to recognize the quality achievements of U.S. companies. A maximum of two awards may be given annually in each of five categories: manufacturing, service, small business (500 or fewer employees), education, and health care. Education and health care were added as categories in 1999. In October 2004, President Bush signed legislation that expands the Baldrige Award to include nonprofit and government organizations.

## TYPES OF QUALITY CONTROL

Quality control relating to the inputs or outputs of the system is referred to as **product quality control** (sometimes called *acceptance control*). Product quality control is used when the quality is being evaluated with respect to a batch of products or services that already exists, such as incoming raw materials or finished goods. Product quality control lends itself to acceptance sampling procedures, in which some portion of a batch of outgoing items (or incoming materials) is inspected to ensure that the batch meets specifications with regard to the percentage of defective units that will be tolerated in the batch. With acceptance sampling procedures, the decision to accept or reject an entire batch is based on a sample or group of samples.

**Process quality control** concerns monitoring quality while the product or service is being produced. Process control relates to the control of the equipment and processes used during the production process. Under process control, periodic samples are taken from a process and compared to a predetermined standard. If the sample results are acceptable, the process is allowed to continue. If the sample results are not acceptable, the process is halted and adjustments are made to bring the machines or processes back under control.

ARE YOU VISIBLE . . . ?

## First Line Focus

*The policies and procedures of an effective operations control program can generate mountains of data to reassure managers that they are truly on top of everything that is going on in their organization. However, all those reports and numbers cannot compensate for your visible presence on the factory floor, in the call center, or out on the showroom floor.*

*Many managers develop a comfort level with reports and data analytics without ever leaving their offices to take the pulse of their department once in a while. You may be able to measure employee satisfaction in a survey, but you won't get a real sense of employee morale if you fill your daily calendar with meetings and conference calls and never leave your office. Promoting an "open door policy" to encourage your people to come and see you is one thing, but getting out there and talking to your people in their workspace is much more effective.*

**Acceptance sampling** is a method of predicting the quality of a batch or a large group of products from an inspection of a sample or group of samples taken from the batch. Acceptance sampling is used for one of three basic reasons:

1. The potential losses or costs of passing defective items are not great relative to the cost of inspection; for example, it would not be appropriate to inspect every match produced by a match factory.
2. Inspection of some items requires destruction of the product being tested, as is the case when testing firecrackers.
3. Sampling usually produces results more rapidly than does a census.

Acceptance sampling draws a random sample of a given size from the batch or lot being examined. The sample is then tested and analyzed. If more than a certain number (determined statistically) are found to be defective, the entire batch is rejected, as it is deemed to have an unacceptably large percentage of defective items. Because of the possibility of making an incorrect inference concerning the batch, acceptance sampling always involves risks. The risk the producer is willing to take of rejecting a good batch is referred to as the *producer's risk.* The risk of accepting a bad batch is referred to as the *consumer's risk.* Obviously, one would desire to minimize both the producer's risk and the consumer's risk. However, the only method of simultaneously lowering both these risks is to increase the sample size, which also increases the inspection costs. Therefore, the usual approach is to decide on the maximum acceptable risk for both the producer and the consumer and design the acceptance sampling plan around these risks.

**Malcolm Baldrige Award** Recognition of U.S. companies' quality achievements.

**Product Quality Control** Quality evaluation of a batch of existing products or services; related to inputs or outputs of the system; also called *acceptance control.*

**Process Quality Control** Quality evaluation while the product or service is being produced.

A **process control chart** is a time-based graphic display that shows whether a machine or a process is producing output at the expected quality level. If a significant change in the variable being checked is detected, the machine is said to be out of control. Control charts do not attempt to show why a machine is out of control, only whether it is out of control.

The most frequently used process control charts are called *mean* and *range charts.* Mean charts (also called *X-charts*) monitor the mean or average value of some characteristic (dimension, weight, etc.) of the items produced by a machine or process. Range charts (also called *R-charts*) monitor the range of variability of some characteristic (dimension, weight, etc.) of the items produced by a machine or process.

The quality control inspector, using control charts, first calculates the desired level of the characteristic being measured. The next step is to calculate statistically the upper and lower control limits, which determine by how much the characteristic can vary from the desired level before the machine or process is considered to be out of control. Once the control chart has been set up, the quality control inspector periodically takes a small sample from the machine or process outputs. Depending on the type of chart being used, the mean or range of the sample is plotted on the

**Acceptance Sampling** Statistical method of predicting the quality of a batch or a large group of products by inspecting a sample or group of samples.

**Process Control Chart** Time-based graphic display that shows whether a machine or process is producing items at the expected quality level.

## Figure 12.5 • Mean Chart

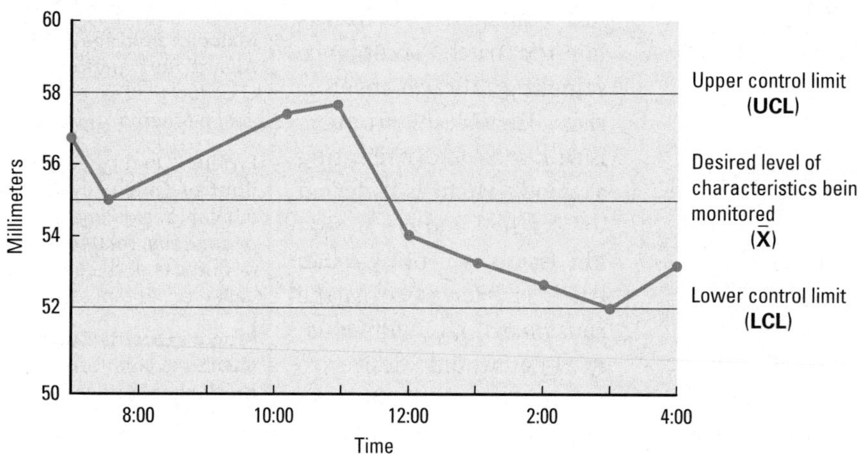


**Inventories** Quantities of raw materials, in-process goods, or finished goods on hand; serves as a buffer between different rates of flow associated with the operating system.

**Just-in-Time Inventory Control (JIT)** Inventory control system that schedules materials to arrive and leave as they are needed; also known as *zero inventory systems, stockless systems,* or *kanban systems.*

control chart. By plotting the results of each sample on the control chart, it is easy to identify quickly any abnormal trends in quality. Figure 12.5 shows a sample mean chart. A range chart looks like a mean chart; the only difference is that the range, as opposed to the mean, of the characteristic being monitored is plotted.

A mean or range chart used by itself can easily lead to false conclusions. For example, the upper and lower control limits for a machined part might be 0.1000 millimeter and 0.0800 millimeter, respectively. A sample of four parts of 0.1200, 0.1100, 0.0700, and 0.0600 would yield an acceptable mean of 0.0900; yet every element of the sample is out of tolerance. For this reason, when monitoring variables, it is usually desirable to use mean and range charts simultaneously to ensure that a machine or a process is under control.

### [PROGRESS] ✓questions

9. What was the purpose of the Malcolm Baldrige National Quality Improvement Act?
10. Explain the difference between *product* quality control and *process* quality control.
11. How would a manager use acceptance sampling?
12. Explain the difference between mean and range charts.

# >> Inventory Control

Inventories serve as a buffer between different rates of flow associated with the operating system. **Inventories** are generally classified into one of three categories, depending on their location within the operating system: (1) raw material, (2) in process, or (3) finished goods. Raw material inventories serve as a buffer between purchasing and production. In-process inventories are used to buffer differences in the rates of flow through the various production processes. Finished-goods inventories act as a buffer between the final stage of production and shipping.

Inventories add flexibility to the operating system and allow the organization to do the following:

1. Purchase, produce, and ship in economic lot sizes rather than in small jobs.
2. Produce on a smooth, continuous basis even if the demand for the finished product or raw material fluctuates.
3. Prevent major problems when forecasts of demand are in error or when unforeseen slowdowns or stoppages in supply or production occur.

If it were not so costly, every organization would attempt to maintain very large inventories to facilitate purchasing, production scheduling, and distribution. However, many costs are associated with carrying inventory. Potential inventory costs include such factors as insurance, property taxes, storage costs, obsolescence costs, spoilage, and the opportunity cost of the money invested in the inventory. The relative importance of these costs depends on the specific inventory being held. For example, with women's fashions, the obsolescence costs are potentially high. Similarly, the storage costs for dangerous chemicals may be high. Thus, management must continually balance the costs of holding the inventory against the costs of running short of raw materials, in-process goods, or finished goods.

## JUST-IN-TIME INVENTORY CONTROL

**Just-in-time inventory control (JIT)** was pioneered in Japan but has become popular in the United States. JIT systems are sometimes referred to as *zero*

# Thinking Critically 12.2

## >> The Purchasing Department

The buyers for a large airline company were having a general discussion with the manager of purchasing in her office Friday afternoon. The inspection of received parts was a topic of debate. The company employed an inspector who was supposedly responsible for inspecting all aircraft parts, in accordance with FAA regulations. However, the inspector had not been able to check those items purchased as nonaircraft parts because he was constantly overloaded. Furthermore, many of the aircraft parts were not being properly inspected because of insufficient facilities and equipment.

Apparently, several parts had recently been rejected six months or more past the standard 90-day return period. One recent example of the type of problem being encountered was the acceptance of a batch of plastic forks that broke easily when in use. The vendor had shipped over 100 cases of the defective forks. Unfortunately, all the purchase order specified was "forks." Another example was the acceptance of several cases of plastic cups with the wrong logo. The cups were put into use for in-flight service and had to be used because no other cups were available. A final example was the discovery that several expensive radar components in stock were found to be defective and with expired warranty. These components had to be reordered at almost $900 per unit.

It was apparent that the inspection function was inadequate and unable to cope with the volume of material being received. Purchasing would have to establish guidelines as to what material should or should not be inspected after being processed by the material checker. Some of the buyers thought the material checker (who was not the inspector) should have more responsibility than simply checking quantity and comparing the packing sheet against purchase orders. Some believed the checker could and should have caught the obvious errors in the logo on the plastic cups. Furthermore, if the inspector had sampled the forks, they would have been rejected immediately. As for the radar tubes, they should have been forwarded by the inspector to the avionics shop for bench check after being received. Such a rejection delay was costing the company a considerable amount of money, since most of the items were beyond the standard 90-day return period. The current purchasing procedures stated that the department using the parts was responsible for the inspection before the part was placed in stock. Some buyers thought the inspector should be responsible for inspection of all materials received, regardless of its function or usage. It was pointed out, however, that several landing gears had been received from the overhaul-repair vendor and tagged by the inspector as being acceptable. These gears later turned out to be defective and unstable and had to be returned for repair. This generated considerable discussion concerning the inspector's qualifications, testing capacity, workload, and responsibility for determining if the unit should be shop-checked.

Much of the remaining discussion centered around what purchasing should recommend for the inspection of material. One proposal was that everything received be funneled through the inspection department. Another proposal was that all material be run through inspection except as otherwise noted on the purchase order. Other questions were also raised. If purchasing required all material to be inspected, would additional inspection personnel have to be hired? Who would be responsible for inspection specifications? Furthermore, who should determine what items should be shop-checked?

The meeting was finally adjourned until the following Friday.

*Continued on next page*

Continued from page 293

QUESTIONS

1. Why is the inspection of received parts such a concern for the airline?
2. What do you think of the current system of inspection?
3. Do you think the inspector is at fault? Explain.
4. What would you suggest happen at the meeting next Friday?

*inventory systems*, *stockless systems*, or *kanban systems*. JIT is actually a philosophy for production to ensure that the right items arrive and leave as they are needed. Traditionally, incoming raw materials are ordered in a few relatively large shipments and stored in warehouses until needed for production or for providing a service.

Under JIT, organizations make smaller and more frequent orders of raw materials. JIT depends on the elimination of setup time between the production of different batches of different products. JIT can be viewed as an operating philosophy whose basic objective is to eliminate waste. In this light, waste is "anything other than the minimum amount of equipment, materials, parts, space, and workers' time which are absolutely essential to add value to the product or service."[23]

The JIT philosophy applies not only to inventories of incoming raw materials but also to the production of subassemblies or final products. The idea is not to produce an item or a subassembly until it is needed for shipment. JIT is called a *demand pull system* because items are produced or ordered only when they are needed (or pulled) by the next stage in the production process. Figure 12.6 summarizes the benefits of JIT. One potential hazard is that the entire production line can be shut down if the needed parts or subassemblies are not available when needed. JIT has been successfully implemented by many American companies, including Hewlett-Packard, Motorola, Black & Decker, General Motors, Ford, Chrysler, General Electric, Goodyear, and IBM.[24]

Despite the popularity of JIT in American business, it is not a quick fix for all the quality and operations problems a company may face. In fact, JIT may take many years to really catch hold in a company. Beginning in the early 1960s, it took Toyota over 20 years to fully implement the concept.[25] Although JIT was a key to Toyota's lean production system, it also exposed many defects in the inventory system, because JIT enables easier detection of defective inventory. Fixing these forms of defects (finding where and how the defects occurred) is sometimes time-consuming and difficult to accomplish.

## Figure 12.6 • Benefits of JIT Systems

1. Inventory levels are drastically lowered.
2. The time it takes products to go through the production facility is greatly reduced. This enables the organization to be more flexible and more responsive to changing customer demands.
3. Product/service quality is improved and the cost of scrap is reduced because defective parts and services are discovered earlier.
4. With smaller product batches, less space is occupied by inventory and materials-handling equipment. This also allows employees to work closer together, which improves communication and teamwork.

Tom Peters offers a new twist on JIT. He believes that instead of using JIT just to assist suppliers in improving their products (i.e., resulting in fewer defective parts), a company can push JIT forward in the distribution channel to actively seek out opportunities to assist customers (by using some variant of JIT as a marketing strategy) and link them to the company's processes. In other words, by examining and solving customers' problems by supplying them with exactly what they need, the company not only improves its quality control but also builds ties to its customer base.[26]

## TRACKING INVENTORY

Before computers, tracking inventory was a tedious and time-consuming task. It was difficult to keep accurate inventory records. Employees recorded every sale and purchase, and a bookkeeper would subtract all sales and add all purchases at the end of the week. This determined how much inventory remained in stock. However, employees often forgot to record transactions. Bookkeepers frequently made mistakes computing figures. Both kinds of errors made it difficult for businesses to know how much inventory they actually had in stock.

**Bar Code and RFID Technology** Technology continues to improve inventory tracking. The universal packaging *bar codes* (i.e., patterns of bars and spaces that an electronic scanner recognizes) are now being enhanced with radio frequency identification (RFID) technology. Bar coding has reduced errors in tracking inventory. When a company purchases or sells an item, an employee scans the item's bar code. A computer program recognizes the information contained in the bar code and automatically adds or subtracts the item from inventory. RFID technology utilizes radio waves to allow identification *tags* to be read from increasing distances outside of the sight of the reader.

The full potential of RFID is still being uncovered. Using an integrated circuit allows for the storage and processing of far more information in the tag than that reflected in a traditional bar code. Incorporating a small battery power source in the tag allows that information to be broadcast over great distances, allowing international shipments to be tracked in real time rather than at key staging points (e.g., warehouse, customs check, and recipient delivery). In the shipment of fresh produce, for example, the ripening of that produce can be monitored using the RFID tags to avoid spoilage.

**Physical Inventory** Process of counting the number of units a company holds in stock.

**Physical Inventory** Even if computers track inventory, managers need to take physical inventory. A **physical inventory** involves actually counting the number of units of inventory a company holds in stock. Most businesses perform a physical inventory once or twice a year.

Managers need to conduct physical inventories because actual inventory is often different from the level of inventory tracked. The discrepancy may reflect errors or unauthorized withdrawals, including theft. Managers who do not adjust their inventory occasionally may experience shortages.

**Study Alert!** JIT can have a significant financial impact on an organization. Smaller deliveries of raw materials or subassemblies on an as-needed basis can save an organization from having to keep millions of dollars of capital tied up in inventory stock that may, if left too long, expire or become outdated if a "new and improved" alternative is developed.

## INDEPENDENT VERSUS DEPENDENT DEMAND ITEMS

**Independent demand items** are finished goods or other end products. For the most part, independent demand items are sold or shipped out as opposed to being used in making another product. Examples of independent demand environments include most retail shops, book publishers, and hospital suppliers.[27] **Dependent demand items** are typically subassemblies or component parts that will be used in making some finished product. In these cases, the demand for the items depends on the number of finished products being produced. An example is the demand for wheels for new cars. If the car company plans to make 1,000 cars next month, it knows it must have 5,000 wheels on hand (allowing for spares).[28] With independent demand items, forecasting plays an important role in inventory stocking decisions. With dependent demand items, inventory stocking requirements are determined directly from the production plan.

**Independent Demand Items** Finished goods or end products ready to be sold or shipped.

**Dependent Demand Items** Subassembly or component parts used to make a finished product; their demand is based on the number of finished products being produced.

**ABC Classification System** Method of managing inventories based on their total value.

## ABC CLASSIFICATION SYSTEM

One of the simplest and most widely used systems for managing inventories is the ABC approach. The **ABC classification system** manages inventories based on the total value of their usage per unit of time. In many organizations, a small number of products or materials, group A, account for the greatest dollar value of the inventory; the next group of items, group B, accounts for a moderate amount of the inventory value; and group C accounts for a small amount of the inventory value. Figure 12.7 illustrates this concept. The dollar value reflects both the cost of the item and the item's usage rate. For example, an item might be put into group A through a combination of either low cost and high usage or high cost and low usage.

Grouping items in this way establishes appropriate control over each item. Generally, the items in group A are monitored very closely; the items in group B are monitored with some care; and the items in group C are checked only occasionally. Items in group C are usually not subject to the detailed paperwork of items in groups A and B. In an automobile service station, gasoline would be considered a group A item and monitored daily. Tires, batteries, and transmission fluid would be group B items and might be checked weekly or biweekly. Valve stems, windshield wiper blades, radiator caps, hoses, fan belts, oil and gas additives, car wax, and so forth would be group C items and might be checked and ordered only every two or three months.[29]

**Figure 12.7 • ABC Inventory Classification**

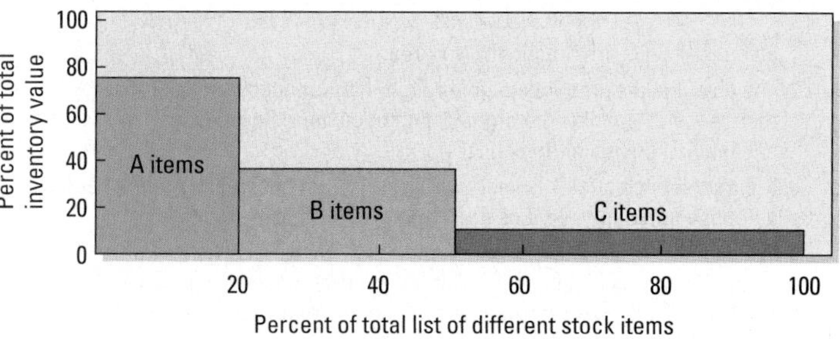


One potential shortcoming of the ABC method is that although the items in group C may have very little cost or usage value, they may be critical to the operation. It is possible, for instance, for an inexpensive bolt to be vital to the production of a costly piece of machinery. One way to handle items such as this is to designate them as group A or B items regardless of their cost or usage value. The major advantage of the ABC method is that it concentrates on controlling those items that are most important to the operation.

With computer technology and information systems becoming increasingly commonplace in small and medium-size firms, the ABC method can be computerized and categories can be monitored or changed with greater skill and accuracy. An additional value of computerizing the operation and control of the classification system is the power it brings to ordering cycles and stock control.

## SAFETY STOCKS

Most organizations maintain **safety stocks** to accommodate unexpected changes in demand and supply and allow for variations in delivery time. The optimal size of the safety stock is determined by the relative costs of a stock-out of the item versus the costs of carrying the additional inventory. The cost of a stock-out item is often difficult to estimate. For example, the customer may choose to go elsewhere rather than wait for the product. If the product is available at another branch location, the stock-out cost may be simply the cost of shipping the item from one location to another.

**From the PERSPECTIVE OF...**

**A Production Manager** Producing too much of a finished product can leave unsold inventory on the shelves, which represents a significant financial drain on the company and the potential for future losses if that inventory has to be sold off at a discount. With which departments should the production manager communicate to make sure this doesn't happen?

### THE ORDER QUANTITY

Most materials and finished products are consumed one by one or a few units at a time; however, because of the costs associated with ordering, shipping, and handling inventory, it is usually desirable to purchase materials and products in large lots or batches.

When determining the optimal number of units to order, the ordering costs must be balanced against the cost of carrying the inventory. *Ordering costs* include such things as the cost of preparing the order, shipping costs, and setup costs. The capacity to order online has reduced the ordering costs for many organizations. *Carrying costs* include storage costs, insurance, taxes, obsolescence, and the opportunity costs of the money invested in the inventory. The smaller the number of units ordered, the lower the carrying costs (because the average inventory held is smaller) but the higher the ordering costs (because more orders must be placed). The optimal number of units to order, referred to as the **economic order quantity (EOQ),** is determined by the point at which ordering costs equal carrying costs, or where total cost (ordering costs plus carrying costs) is at a minimum.

**Safety Stocks** Inventory maintained to accommodate unexpected changes in demand and supply and allow for variations in delivery time.

**Economic Order Quantity (EOQ)** Optimal number of units to order at one time; determined by the point at which ordering costs equal carrying costs, or where total cost (ordering costs plus carrying costs) is at a minimum.

The greatest weakness of the EOQ approach is the difficulty in accurately determining the actual carrying and ordering costs. However, research has shown that the total costs associated with order sizes that are reasonably close to the economic order quantity do not differ appreciably from the minimum total costs associated with the EOQ.[30] Thus, as long as the estimated carrying and ordering costs are in the ballpark, this approach can yield meaningful results. Variations of this basic model have been developed to take into account such things as purchase quantity and other special discounts.

13. Compare the three categories of inventory classification.
14. Explain the difference between *dependent* and *independent* demand items.
15. Explain the advantages offered by RFID tags.
16. How do you calculate the economic order quantity when placing purchase orders for materials or products?

## >> Chapter Summary

After an operating system has been designed and implemented, it must be monitored on a daily basis to ensure quality and operational efficiency. To do that, managers must have a clear sense of what product (or service) quality means to their organization, and they must be able to control every element of the process, including minimizing waste in the production process and controlling the cost of the inventory needed to supply materials to that process. In the next chapter we step back from these operational management issues and examine the legal framework within which managers must operate and consider some of the ethical challenges they may face in their work.

BIG BROTHER

Your company has recently made a sizable investment in radio frequency identification (RFID) technology to help it better manage inventory control and product shipment to customers. By attaching RFID tags to product containers, you can now accurately record item quantities in the warehouse (helping to reduce the chance of items being out of stock). With the appropriate transmission signal on your delivery trucks, you can track the shipments on the way to customers and provide an accurate delivery time—all this with a wafer-thin electronic chip embedded in the tag.

As an added bonus from the RFID equipment vendor for this substantial order, your company has also been provided with new employee ID tags that also have a wafer-thin electronic chip embedded inside them. The company announced the move as a new building security measure without mentioning that the technology allows the location of every employee on-site to be tracked in real time.

ETHICAL
MANAGEMENT
Should management be able to track your every move?


**QUESTIONS**

1. How comfortable are you with this ability to track your location?
2. Do you see the RFID tag as an invasion of your privacy? Why or why not?
3. How do you think the employees would react if they knew about this capability?

1. Understand the basic requirements for controlling operating costs.

   Operations managers need a detailed budget that outlines fixed and variable costs in key areas—usually labor, material, and overhead expenses. With budgeted costs in place, actual costs can then be compared to budget as they are incurred. However, a cost control system only indicates when a particular cost is over budget; it does not address the question of why it is over budget—that requires further investigation, resolution, and the implementation of prevention measures to ensure that the cost remains in line with budget in the future.

2. Define *quality* from the perspective of an operations manager

   For the operations manager, quality is determined in relation to the specifications or standards set in the design stage. Design quality is commonly stated in six dimensions: performance, features, reliability and durability, serviceability, aesthetics, and reputation.

3. Explain the concept of total quality management (TQM).

   Total quality management (TQM) is a management philosophy that emphasizes "managing the entire organization so that it excels in all dimensions of products and services that are important to the customer." TQM, in essence, is an organizationwide emphasis on quality as defined by the customer. Under TQM, everyone from the CEO on down to the lowest-level employee takes responsibility for the quality of the product or service being delivered to the customer.

4. Define the following terms: *continuous improvement, kaizen, six sigma, lean manufacturing,* and *quality at the source.*
   - Continuous improvement refers to an ongoing effort to make improvements in every part of the organization. It means focusing on continuous improvement in the quality of the processes by which work is accomplished. The idea here is that the quest for better quality and better service is never ending.
   - Kaizen (meaning "good change" in Japanese) shares the same philosophy as continuous improvement—a process of relentless improvement through a series of small, incremental steps rather than large technical leaps.
   - Six sigma was pioneered by Motorola during the 1980s and literally means, in statistical terms, six standard deviations from the mean. In order to realize the very high level of quality demanded by six sigma (most processes traditionally have used three sigma), the entire production or service system must be examined and improved.
   - Lean manufacturing is a systematic approach to identifying and eliminating waste and non-value-added activities. In the same manner as continuous improvement, the quest is never ending.
   - Quality at the source refers to the philosophy of making each employee responsible for the quality of his or her work. A major advantage of this approach is that it removes the adversarial relationship that often exists between quality control inspectors and production employees by viewing every employee as a quality inspector for his or her own work.
5. Understand the difference between raw material, in-process, and finished-goods inventory classifications.
   - Raw material inventory is the quantity of components or ingredients that the organization has on hand (or in the warehouse) for the manufacturing process. This inventory serves as a buffer between purchasing and production.
   - In-process inventory is the quantity of partially completed components or recipes that the organization has on hand. Depending on the product, organizations may keep partially assembled units in storage to minimize the production time of finished products once orders are received. This inventory serves as a buffer in the rates of flow through the various production processes.
   - Finished-goods inventory is the quantity of completed units or products assembled and ready for shipment. This inventory acts as a buffer between the final stage of production and shipping.
6. Explain the concept of just-in-time (JIT) inventory.

   JIT is a philosophy for production to ensure that the right items arrive and leave as they are needed. Traditionally, incoming raw materials are ordered in a few relatively large shipments and stored in warehouses until needed for production or for providing a service. Under JIT, organizations make smaller and more frequent orders of raw materials. JIT depends on the elimination of setup time between the production of different batches of different products. JIT can be viewed as an operating philosophy whose basic objective is to eliminate waste. In this light, waste is "anything other than the minimum amount of equipment, materials, parts, space, and workers' time which are absolutely essential to add value to the product or service."

# THE WORLD of Work >>

**KAIZEN POWER—HANDLE WITH CARE!** ***(continued from page 281)***

Tony followed Jerry's instructions to the letter and got his team together to "stand in the circle." At first there were a few laughs and a few comments about "square dancing" and who didn't shower that morning, but once the group figured out that Tony was serious about the exercise, they got down to business. It took a while for them to start filling up their pads, but soon the competitive spirit started to kick in. Just as Jerry had predicted, a couple of them even asked for extra paper (which earned them several boos and comments from the team members who were still working on their first page).

When the exercise was complete, the team met to review their ideas, and Tony was literally overwhelmed by the range and imagination of the ideas they presented. He had given them fairly basic instructions and encouraged them to go as "far out into left field" as they wanted to find their ideas. Now he was beginning to have second thoughts because they had really taken him at his word. Ideas to change the theme of the restaurant entirely, to automate the restaurant, to bring in a live DJ, and to start featuring flamenco dancers during dinner were among the more routine ones. The obvious ones included a pay raise for the staff (which Tony explained wasn't a new idea, just a regular request!), new menu items, lower menu prices, and even higher menu prices.

Altogether the exercise generated close to two thousand ideas. When they had read all the ideas through, Kevin commented, "Wow, Tony, I guess you should be careful what you ask for, eh?"

Then Tony got the question he had been dreading as soon as he had seen the size of the list: "Okay Tony, which one are we going to implement first?"

**QUESTIONS**

1. Is a list of "close to two thousand ideas" a successful outcome for Tony? Or has he created a monster here?
2. What do you think the reaction of the employees would be if none of the ideas were implemented?
3. If Tony encouraged his team to go as "far out into left field" as they wanted, how many of these new ideas are going to be practical? Why?
4. Where do you think Tony should start first? Why?

## Key Terms >>

**ABC classification system 296**
**acceptance sampling 291**
**continuous improvement 286**
**dependent demand items 296**
**economic order quantity (EOQ) 297**
**fixed overhead expenses 282**
**independent demand items 296**
**inventories 292**
**ISO 14000 289**
**ISO 9000 288**
**just-in-time inventory control (JIT) 292**
**kaizen 286**
**lean manufacturing 286**
**Malcolm Baldrige Award 291**
**physical inventory 295**
**process control chart 291**
**process quality control 291**
**product quality control 291**
**quality 283**
**quality at the source 286**
**reengineering 288**
**safety stocks 297**
**six sigma 286**
**variable overhead expenses 282**
**zero-defects program 289**

1. Name the three major categories of costs that usually concern operations managers from a control standpoint. Give an example from each category.
2. Explain the difference between *fixed* and *variable* overhead expenses.
3. Compare and contrast the six common dimensions of design quality. Provide an example of each dimension.
4. Which is more important: knowing *when* a process is out of control or *why* it is out of control? Explain your choice.
5. If quality means different things to different people, how can you measure it?
6. Define *six sigma* and *lean manufacturing*. How are they related?

## INTERNET In Action >>

1. Visit the Web site for the Malcolm Baldrige National Quality Award (MBNQA) at **www.quality.nist.gov**, and answer the following questions:
   a. How did the MBNQA come into existence?
   b. Why would organizations consider applying for the MBNQA?
   c. What are the three stages of the award process?
   d. Review the MBNQA recipients for the last three years, and compare how their commitment to quality led to success in the Baldrige award program.
2. Visit the Web site for the International Organization of Standardization at **www.iso.org.** Under the "ISO Standards" link, locate the "Management Standards" for ISO 9000 and ISO 14000, and review the "Quality Management Principles."
   a. What are the benefits to an organization in adopting these principles?
   b. Which principle presents the greatest challenge to an organization? Why?
   c. How would you implement these principles in your organization?

1. **Kaizen**

   Divide the class into two groups (A and B), and then organize each group into teams of three to four students. Group A, take 5 minutes to list 10 things that your university or college could do to improve the campus parking situation. Stop after 10 minutes and review your list. Then take 10 minutes to come up with another 10 improvements. Group B, follow the same process with ideas to improve the student registration process for your university or college. Be prepared to report your ideas back to your class.

   **Questions**

   1. How long did it take you to come up with your first 10 improvement ideas?
   2. What were the major challenges in coming up with the second 10 improvement ideas?
   3. Which topic, parking or registration, generated the most improvement ideas? Why was that?
   4. What do you think you would find if you applied this exercise to other areas of your institution?

2. **Inventory Control**

   After a detailed financial audit and a reengineering study from an outside consultant, it has been determined that your widget manufacturing company is carrying too much inventory of raw materials, widgets in process, and finished widgets. These high inventory levels represent a significant financial burden on the company, and they are starting to affect liquidity (the amount of money that the company has on hand to pay its bills). Divide into three groups—raw materials, in process, and finished product—and take 20 minutes to come up with a plan of action for addressing this problem. Be prepared to present your proposal to your class.

# Case 12.1

## >> Toyota Stumbles • The world's biggest carmaker went wrong.

How quickly things can change. When Toyota Motor Corporation dislodged General Motors (GM) as the world's biggest carmaker in the middle of 2008, many critics were ready to pronounce the death of the American automobile industry. And yet, only 18 months later, company president Akido Toyoda, grandson of legendary Toyota founder Sakichi Toyoda, was being asked to appear before a congressional committee and explaining in a *Washington Post* editorial: "We have not lived up to the high standards you have come to expect from us. I am deeply disappointed by that and apologize. As the president of Toyota, I take personal responsibility."

To understand the extent of this apparent fall from world supremacy, we need to go back to the 1950s when engineer Taiichi Ohno developed a set of operating practices that evolved two decades later into the "Toyota Production System" (TPS). Incorporating principles of automation *(jidoka),* continuous improvement (kaizen), and just-in-time manufacturing (later termed *lean manufacturing*), Ohno's ideas not only changed the automobile industry but also changed late 20th century manufacturing practices around the world. Toyota was renowned for an obsessive attention to detail and a frugality that prompted managers to label photocopiers with the cost per copy to discourage overuse and to turn down the heat in employee dormitories during working hours.

As the benchmark for production quality, Toyota developed levels of customer loyalty that were the envy of its competition. Toyota owners fervently believed that the company was in a class of its own, and for this reason, the recent failures seem to have damaged the mystique of the brand that much more. From November 2009, the company was forced to recall nearly nine million vehicles for problems with "uncontrolled acceleration" and "braking issues" linked by U.S. regulators to 51 deaths—problems that are expected to cost Toyota more than $2 billion in repairs and lost sales in 2010 alone. In addition, the company is facing over 100 class action and 30 individual lawsuits in the United States and Canada.

> A relentless drive for growth, combined with an apparent managerial arrogance based on decades of supremacy as the world's best combined to create a willingness to transform an obsession with quality into an obsession with cost reduction.

Inevitably, analysts, critics, and lawyers are looking for the reasons behind this dramatic change in the fortunes of this formerly renowned corporation. Finding that information has proved difficult given the traditional

*Continued on next page*

Continued from page 303

reticence of the Japanese culture. What seems clear is that a relentless drive for growth, combined with an apparent managerial arrogance based on decades of supremacy as the world's best, created a willingness to transform an obsession with quality (the famous TPS) into an obsession with cost reduction that would make the executives at Walmart proud.

In 2000, Toyota produced 5.2 million cars. By 2009, it had the capacity to produce 10 million. Between 1995 and the end of 2009, Toyota doubled the number of overseas plants and manufacturing facilities in North America, Asia, and Europe in an effort to improve market responsiveness, manage currency issues with a strong yen, and sidestep potential trade disputes about car exports from Japan. At the same time, the company was pushing a program dubbed "CCC21" (Construction of Cost Competitiveness for the 21st Century) that was reputed to have cut $10 billion from global operating costs in only six years. However, it is how those savings were achieved that many critics now feel was the turning point for Toyota.

Rather than staying true to the principles of kaizen—incremental continuous improvement alongside an obsessive commitment to product quality—designers pressured suppliers to cut procurement costs and modified designs to minimize installation times and "time to market" periods, allowing Toyota to get a new model to the market in 12 months rather than the industry average of 24 to 36 months. However, CCC21 then evolved into "aggressive CCC21," and cost reductions started to require things like less expensive plastic in vehicle interiors and thinner padding for car headliners—changes that started to make the cars look "cheaper" according to U.S.-based service technicians.

It wasn't long before problems arose. Between 2003 and 2010 the National Highway Traffic Safety Administration (NHTSA) opened eight investigations of unintended acceleration of Toyota vehicles. The company responded by blaming drivers for incorrect installation of interior floor mats, but several of the pending lawsuits allege that the company knew about the problems long before the issue exploded in 2009 and led to Akido Toyoda's 2010 confession in his testimony before a congressional committee: "I feel the pace at which we have grown may have been too quick. . . . Priorities became confused, and we were not able to stop, think, and make improvements as much as we were able to before."

Unfortunately for Toyota, the company's problems are coming at a time when U.S. automakers are emerging from their near collapse with a much improved reputation for product quality and a growing competence in creative vehicle design. How long it will take Toyoda and his successors to turn around the global giant that Toyota has become remains to be seen. What is clear is that the company now has a severely tarnished reputation to address, and it seems unlikely that its former prominence as a paragon of automobile quality will ever be regained.

## QUESTIONS

1. What factors led to Toyota's leadership position in automobile quality?
2. What was the purpose of CCC21?
3. What evidence does the case present of Toyota's managerial arrogance?
4. What should Toyota do now?

*Source:* Bill Saporito, "Behind the Troubles at Toyota," *Time*, February 11, 2010; Alan Ohnsman, Jeff Green, and Kae Inoue, "The Humbling of Toyota," *BusinessWeek*, March 11, 2010; and "Losing Its Shine," *The Economist*, December 12, 2009.

# Case 12.2

## >> A Dynamo Called Danaher • The Rales brothers' sprawling conglomerate makes everything—especially money.

Danaher Corporation is not nearly as big, famous, or influential as such conglomerates as General Electric, Berkshire Hathaway, or 3M. It owns such a mundane and sprawling portfolio of sleepy, underloved industrial businesses—companies that make dental surgery implements, multimeters, drill chucks, servomotors, and wrenches, just to name a few—that it seems deliberately assembled to be as unsexy as possible. But despite its low profile, Danaher is probably the best-run conglomerate in America. It's clearly the best performing: Over 20 years, it has returned a remarkable 25 percent to shareholders annually, far better than GE (16 percent), Berkshire Hathaway (21 percent), or the Standard & Poor's 500-stock index (12 percent).

The Washington, D.C., company is the brainchild of the obsessively private brothers Steven M. and Mitchell P. Rales. They have turned Danaher from a mere acquisition vehicle into a true-blue, cash-producing, publicly owned industrial manufacturer. In the process, the Rales brothers have become two of the richest people in the United States, worth more than $2 billion apiece.

Think of Danaher as the anti-Berkshire Hathaway. Warren Buffett runs his empire like a benevolent curator. These "conglomerateurs" have built their portfolio not by buying undervalued companies and holding them but by imposing on them the "Danaher Business System." DBS, as it's called, is a set of management tools borrowed liberally from the famed Toyota Production System. In essence, it requires every employee, from the janitor to the president, to find ways every day to improve the way work gets done. Such quality improvement programs and lean manufacturing methods have been standard practice for manufacturers for years. The difference at Danaher: The company started lean manufacturing in 1987, one of the earliest U.S. companies to do so, and it has maintained a cultish devotion to making it pay off. Even before a deal is done, the DBS team, made up of managers throughout the company steeped in training, works with the acquisition target to inject a heavy dose of Danaher DNA. For employees at the newly acquired companies, it can be a jarring experience. It wouldn't be at all unusual for a Danaher manager clutching a clipboard, a tape measure, and a stopwatch, in a search for wasted motion, to tick off how many steps a data analyst has to take to get to the copier. Danaher also isn't afraid to swing the ax; it has, at times, bought certain product lines and closed the rest of a company.

It wouldn't be at all unusual for a manager clutching a clipboard, a tape measure, and a stopwatch, in a search for wasted motion, to tick off how many steps a data analyst has to take to get to the copier.

Danaher's portfolio—with more than 600 subsidiary companies—reflects a move away from its hand tool legacy to more technologically advanced products. The newest of its four units, accounting for 23 percent of sales, specializes in medical technologies. It includes Sybron, a dental equipment maker, and Leica Microsystems, which makes high-end microscopes for pathology labs. Its most profitable division, professional instrumentation, includes Fluke, known to engineers for products such as multimeters. Fluke was purchased in 1998 for

*Continued on next page*

Continued from page 305

an all-stock deal worth $625 million. Danaher put Fluke through its DBS program and bought 20 other companies to support Fluke's technology. Since then, Danaher's electronic-testing segment sales have increased by 120 percent.

The company's industrial tools division, though it only accounts for about 14 percent of sales, houses Danaher's most well-known brand, Craftsman hand tools. The rest of Danaher's business comes from industrial technologies, including machinery components and product-ID devices, such as Accu-Sort package scanners.

Danaher has continued to prosper through the economic downturn. In September 2009, the company announced the purchase of the life sciences instrumentation business of MDS, Inc., for $1.1 billion, alongside a restructuring program that cut 3,300 jobs and closed 30 facilities, generating an expected $220 million in annual cost savings. In a deviation from its normal practice of acquisition and DBS reorientation, Danaher announced a joint venture in March 2010 with Cooper Industries, PLC. The new fifty-fifty ownership company will blend Cooper's portfolio of power tool products, wireless technologies, and hand tools with Danaher's mechanic's hand tools businesses. The joint venture is expected to generate over $1.2 billion in revenue.

QUESTIONS

1. How is Danaher able to generate such large profits on "such a mundane and sprawling portfolio of sleepy, underloved industrial businesses"?
2. What is lean manufacturing?
3. Do you think that Danaher's use of the kaizen philosophy has greater effect when it is selecting the companies to purchase or when it owns the companies? Explain your answer.
4. Consider the organization you currently work for or one you have worked for in the past. How easy would it be to introduce the kaizen philosophy in that organization? Explain your answer.

*Source:* Brian Hindo, "Managing: A Dynamo Called Danaher," BusinessWeek Online, February 19, 2007; Alex Davidson, "Danaher: Acquisition Machine," *Forbes*, December 20, 2007; and "Cooper Industries, Danaher to Form Tool Venture," Associated Press, March 26, 2010.

# Case 12.3

## >> Five Million Lives

In summer 2009 President Barack Obama made a very public commitment to health care reform. Driven by forecasts of escalating costs and an ageing population that will lead health care costs to absorb a growing percentage of the U.S. gross national product (GNP), the Obama administration launched a plan to overhaul health care in the shadow of a failed attempt under the Clinton administration and a general perception that there were too many vested interests—provider networks and insurance companies—with powerful lobbyists to achieve any real change. Supporters argue that change is long overdue. With 50 million uninsured people in one of the wealthiest nations in the world and prohibitive cost levels for medical treatment, they argue that change must be a matter of *when,* not *if.*

One organization that has been working for years to lead and support for change in health care is the Institute for Healthcare Improvement (IHI). Founded in 1991, IHI is a non-profit organization that seeks to apply the best practices used in other industries—such as TQM, lean manufacturing, and process innovation—to the health care field.

In recent years, IHI has focused on the over 15 million incidents of medical harm that occur in U.S. hospitals each year. People that go to the hospital to get well often suffer unintended harm, such as surgical errors, bedsores, or hospital-acquired infections (the most frequent of which is methicillin-resistant *Staphylococcus aureus,* or MRSA). Such incidents of harm can add tens of thousands of dollars to the cost of patient care and, according to the Centers for Disease Control and Prevention, an estimated 100,000 people die each year from such incidents.

In December 2004, IHI launched the "100,000 Lives Campaign," calling on hospitals to make a public pledge to the implementation of six key life-saving interventions in an attempt to reduce preventable deaths in U.S. hospitals each year. Over an 18-month period, over 3,000 hospitals (which exceeded the original target of 2,000 hospitals) enrolled in the campaign, enlisting almost 75 percent of the total U.S. hospital beds in this national effort. Implementation of the interventions, combined with other national and local improvement efforts, was directly attributed to the reduction of inpatient deaths by an estimated 122,000 during the period of the campaign.

The six recommended interventions were evidence-based and explicitly action-oriented in order to emphasize the need for change:

- *Deploy rapid response teams:* At the first sign of patient decline—and before a catastrophic cardiac or respiratory event.
- *Deliver reliable, evidence-based care for acute myocardial infarction:* To prevent deaths from heart attack.
- *Prevent adverse drug events:* By reconciling patient medications at every transition point in care.
- *Prevent central line infections:* By implementing a series of independent, scientifically grounded steps.
- *Prevent surgical site infections:* By following a series of steps, including reliable, timely administration of correct perioperative antibiotics.
- *Prevent ventilator-associated pneumonia:* By implementing a series of interdependent, scientifically grounded steps.

Success stories from IHI's 100,000 Lives Campaign included the Dominican Hospital in Santa Cruz, California, that reduced the rate of hospital-acquired infections to near zero after adopting IHI's methods, and Albany Memorial Hospital where a 15 percent reduction in patient mortality was achieved in 2006.

In December 2006, IHI endeavored to build on the success of the 100,000 Lives Campaign with the subsequent "5 Million Lives Campaign," a two-year national initiative whose aim was to protect patients from five million incidents of medical harm. The new campaign doubled the number of recommended interventions from 6 to 12, including a direct call to "Get Boards on Board," calling for hospital boards of directors to support and enable improvements that lead to safer patient care. In 2007 IHI reported that over 4,000 hospitals had enrolled in the 5 Million Lives Campaign, and in 2008, 65 hospitals reported being free of ventilator-acquired pneumonia (VAP) for a year.

## QUESTIONS

1. Visit the IHI Web site at **www.ihi.org**, and summarize a success story from the 5 Million Lives Campaign.
2. Why should the involvement of boards of directors be considered a critical intervention?
3. Of the six life-saving interventions from the IHI 100,000 Lives Campaign, which one presents the greatest management challenge? Why?
4. If you held a management position in a hospital, how would you present the IHI 5 Million Lives Campaign to your board of directors?

*Source:* "5 Million Lives Campaign: The Wisconsin Node," www.metastar.com/web/default.aspx?tabid=108, retrieved August 20, 2009; "The Five Million Lives Campaign," www.ihi.org, press release, December 12, 2006, retrieved August 20, 2009; L. R. Peterson, D. M. Hacek, D. Rolland, and S. E. Brossette, "Detection of a community infection outbreak with virtual surveillance," *Lancet,* vol. 362, November 8, 2003; and Jessie Scanlon, "Innovation: Donald Berwick: Curing the Healthcare System," *BusinessWeek,* November 17, 2008.

CHAPTER 13

"There is one and only one social responsibility of business—to use its resources and engage in activities designed to increase its profits so long as it stays within the rules of the game, which is to say, engages in open and free competition without deception or fraud."

**Milton Friedman, economist (1912–2006)**

# STAYING LEGAL AND ETHICAL:

## ETHICAL AND SOCIAL RESPONSIBILITIES

After studying this chapter, you will be able to:

1 Discuss the legal environment of business.

2 Explain the appropriate legislation governing operational and employment practices in a business.

3 Discuss an organization's code of ethics.

4 Explain an ethical dilemma.

5 Classify and measure an organization's social responsibility.

6 Understand the steps involved in conducting a social audit.

## THE WORLD OF WORK

### Taco Barn becomes socially responsible

Tony was beginning to dread the regional meetings. Lately, every meeting produced a major policy change for the organization that usually had a direct impact on his responsibilities as a unit manager. He appreciated that the leadership team was trying to stay ahead of a very aggressive growth plan for Taco Barn in a very competitive market, but a simple meeting to review seasonal menu items once in a while wouldn't hurt, would it?

As soon as Tony walked into the conference room, he realized that this meeting would be no exception—Dawn obviously had major news to share. The walls were covered with full color posters showing fresh produce, farms, people from various countries around the world, and newspaper columns blown up to poster size on one specific topic: how businesses are becoming more socially responsible.

The meeting started 15 minutes late—probably so that folks could take the time to read the posters, thought Tony—but Dawn wasted no time in getting right to the point:

"Starting next month, we are launching a major repositioning initiative to portray Taco Barn as a more socially responsible organization. You've all seen what the competition has been doing: healthier menu choices, recyclable packaging materials, and supporting local farmers and vendors in their food purchases. It's time that we got on the same page before these guys start to steal our customers.

"I realize that you've all been making individual strides in this area in your own units, but we want to approach this as an organizationwide initiative to show both the sincerity of our commitment to this and the extent to which the entire organization is behind it," continued Dawn. "We're not looking for a few pet projects or public relations exercises here, guys. We want to show real creativity and innovation in approaching this issue so that we have a strong message to share with our customers and our stakeholders. The plan is to give a lot of coverage to this in our annual report next quarter, so we have to get going. Go back to your units, and get your teams involved in this. We're starting with a full social audit and will reconvene in two weeks to start brainstorming some ideas. Remember: Full involvement from everyone in the company is expected."

On the drive back to his restaurant, Tony thought about how his team would react to this new project.

#### QUESTIONS

1. What is a social audit and how is it done? Refer to page 322 for guidance on this.
2. Is Taco Barn simply following a trend here, or is there evidence that this is a real commitment on the part of the organization? Explain your answer.
3. How will these new rules affect Tony's job as a unit manager?
4. How do you think your organization (or an organization you have worked for in the past) would react to this kind of policy change?

## >> The Legal Environment of Business

Prospective investors and business partners assess businesses on the profitability of their operations—how operating costs are controlled, how sales revenue is generated, how much market share is owned, how competitors are handled, and, most importantly, how much profit is generated by the company. What is most commonly taken for granted is that the company operates in full compliance with all relevant legislation governing that business—both in terms of the operating practices and the employment practices. Such practices should ensure that the executives of the company operate a safe and healthy work environment for their employees and produce safe and effective products or services for their customers.

For managers, this responsibility of legal compliance must be a top priority. Being found to be out of compliance by any regulatory authority can bring severe financial consequences, ranging from increased operating costs, penalties, and PR damage to complete closure of the organization in extreme circumstances.

In this chapter, we review the most important elements of legal and ethical business practices, with the understanding that with a topic worthy of several stand-alone courses, this review will not be comprehensive. By definition, *legal compliance* is the domain of legal professionals, and for managers the responsibility lies with enforcement rather than creation. For example, as a manager, it is unlikely that you would be involved in the creation of the legal entity that is the corporation or limited liability company (LLC) that employs you. Expecting you to have detailed knowledge of the intricacies of corporate law would be unreasonable. In addition, as a manager you may be responsible for maintaining productive relationships with vendor partners, but if a contract dispute should arise with one of those vendors, expecting you to be familiar with the inner workings of the Uniform Commercial Code (UCC) laws governing commercial contracts would be equally unreasonable. Our objective here is to review the legal framework that governs the day-to-day operations of your company. To do this, we will separate the environments into operating and employment, as indicated in Figure 13.1.

**Figure 13.1 • Overlap of Operating and Employment Environments**

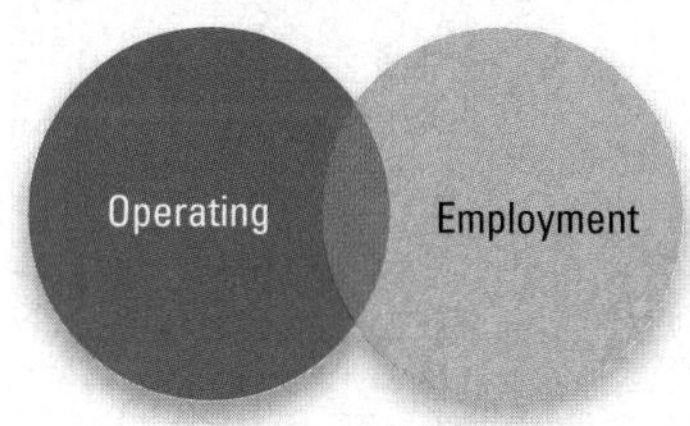


### OPERATING ENVIRONMENT

Concern for employee health and workplace safety is a surprisingly young phenomenon in the United States. Mass-production techniques of the early 20th century provided more than enough evidence of the dangers of working with fast-moving machinery as factory owners experimented with assembly-line speeds to maximize worker productivity. However, prior to 1970, there were only two key pieces of legislation designed to address workplace safety. The 1863 Safety Appliance Act required the presence of safety equipment in factories making railroad equipment, and in 1910 the Federal Bureau of Mines was established to enforce mine safety protocols in response to a series of highly publicized mine explosions.

**Occupational Safety and Health Act, 1970** On December 29, 1970, President Richard Nixon signed the first piece of federal legislation to govern workplace safety and employee health. Effective on April 28, 1971, the act created the Occupational Safety and Health Administration (OSHA) as an agency of the Department of Labor, with the authority to both set and enforce workplace health and safety standards.[1] With the declared intent "to assure so far as possible every working man and woman in the Nation safe and healthful working conditions and to

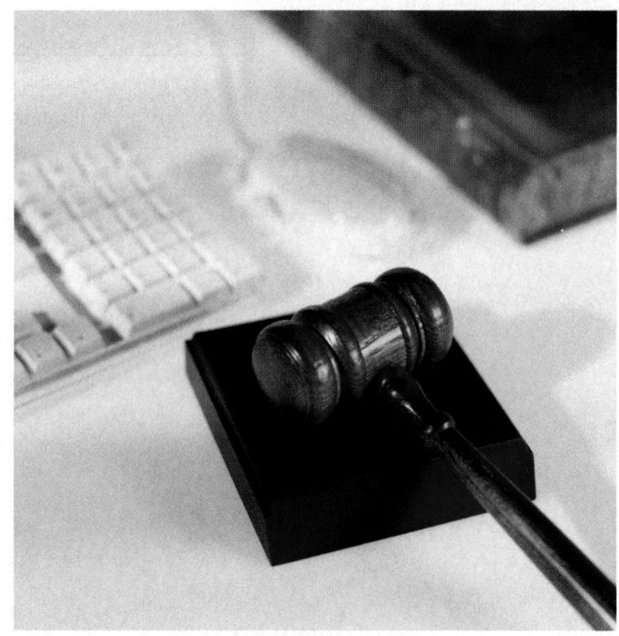

preserve our human resources,"[2] the act focuses on basic mechanical and chemical hazards (e.g., electrical, chemical, fires, explosions, machines, hazardous waste, infectious diseases, and falls), strict reporting requirements for work-related incidents, and the protection of employees from retaliation when notifying OSHA of workplace concerns. The act also encourages states to adopt and enforce their own occupational safety and health plans. As of 2007, 26 states have OSHA-approved plans that cover most private-sector employees as well as state and local government workers.[3]

**Sarbanes-Oxley Act of 2002** Named after sponsors U.S. Senator Paul Sarbanes and U.S. Representative Michael G. Oxley, the Sarbanes-Oxley Act (SOX) is regarded by supporters as a long-overdue piece of legislation requiring greater control and accountability in the financial management of publicly held corporations. Critics of the act complain that it burdens businesses with increased paperwork and reporting responsibilities in much the same way as OSHA, with very little improvement in operational efficiency.

Enacted in response to a series of major accounting scandals in the 1990s (Enron, WorldCom, HealthSouth, Tyco, Adelphia, to name a few), the legislation was designed to implement new standards of financial reporting in order to restore public confidence in capital markets trading stocks based on apparently falsified accounting reports.

Praised by President George W. Bush as including "the most far-reaching reforms of American business practices since the time of Franklin D. Roosevelt,"[4] SOX contains 11 different "titles" establishing specific mandates on corporate fraud, penalties for white-collar crime, conflicts of interest, and enhanced corporate responsibility. Two key changes in the legislation can be traced directly back to the accounting scandals that preceded it:

1. *Corporate responsibility.* Title III mandates that the "principal officers" of the company (typically the chief executive officer and the chief financial officer) must certify their company's quarterly financial reports with their signature. This mandate was a direct response to claims made by Kenneth Lay of Enron, Bernard Ebbers of WorldCom, and Richard Scrushy of HealthSouth that they knew nothing of the highly suspect accounting practices adopted by their companies to inflate financial reporting numbers and, conveniently, keep the stock price elevated.
2. *Auditor independence.* Title II consists of nine separate sections establishing new standards of external auditor independence, including new auditor approval requirements, auditor reporting requirements, and specific restrictions on auditing companies providing such nonaudit services as consulting for the same client. This change is directly attributable to the extreme conflict of interest for Arthur Andersen acting as both auditor and consultant for Enron. Once revealed, the conflict led to the eventual collapse of Andersen, even though the work for Enron was managed by only one partnership out of hundreds within the organization.

The issue of auditor independence was seen as sufficiently critical to prompt the establishment of a brand new regulatory body—the Public Accounting Oversight Board (PCAOB)—in Title I of SOX, with nine sections mandating licensure for all auditing companies and new processes and procedures for compliance audits.

**Study Alert!**

Why should it be the manager's responsibility to oversee compliance to legislation? Isn't it better to delegate that responsibility to the people in each department?

What does this mean for a business manager on a daily basis? One word—*paperwork*. Critics of SOX argue that the enforcement of greater financial responsibility has been applied too broadly when the evidence clearly points to large public corporations with complex organizational holdings as being the primary candidates for fraudulent behavior. Applying the legislation to all publicly held corporations of $75 million revenue or more, it is argued, placed an unfair burden on smaller companies that lacked the centralized resources to meet all the new reporting requirements. A 2006 study found that companies with revenues exceeding $5 billion spent 0.06 percent of revenue on SOX compliance, whereas companies with less than $100 million in revenue spent 2.55 percent.[5]

## [PROGRESS] ✓questions

1. What are the primary areas of focus for OSHA?
2. Why would states have additional occupational health and safety rules?
3. Why was SOX enacted?
4. What was the biggest change mandated by SOX?

**From the PERSPECTIVE OF...**

**An OSHA Compliance Officer** You are an inspector responsible for enforcing regulations to protect the health and safety of employees, and your inspections often result in higher operating costs for organizations. Bringing those costs back in line can mean employee layoffs. How do you balance your duties?

## EMPLOYMENT ENVIRONMENT

**Fair Labor Standards Act, 1938** At the time of writing this chapter, unemployment in the United States stands at greater than 10 percent of the eligible working population, and academics and economists alike continue to debate whether the American economy is recovering from a recession or a depression. Some jobs, they argue, have been lost for good, never to return. Instead, full-time positions will be replaced with temporary or part-time positions, as employers remain skeptical over the long-term stability of the economy. In addition, temporary and part-time positions help keep benefit costs down.

In this context, it is hard to imagine that the key piece of legislation protecting the rights and wages of workers dates back as far as 1938, when the Fair Labor Standards Act (FLSA) was enacted to prohibit child labor, establish a minimum wage, and, for the first time, guarantee "time and a half" for overtime work in certain industries.[6]

Companies are subject to FLSA on the basis of the two following tests:

1. The *enterprise-employer coverage test,* where "two or more employees are sufficiently engaged in interstate commerce or in the production, handling, or selling of goods or materials moved or produced for interstate commerce" and "the employer has gross annual sales of not less than $500,000, unless working in an enterprise not subject to this dollar-value test" (such as hospitals and nursing homes).
2. The *individual employee coverage test,* where the employee's own actions involve the handling or production of goods in interstate commerce.

Numerous amendments to this legislation have been passed over the years as the government has endeavored to respond to inequitable treatment of workers by their bosses. The most common amendment has been to increase the national minimum wage from $1.00 per hour in 1955, to $7.25 per hour by summer 2009. Examples of other amendments include:

- The Portal-to-Portal Act of 1947 defined the precisely constituted work time for which employees should expect to be compensated. Travel to and from work was classified as a normal requirement of work and was therefore exempt from compensation.
- The Equal Pay Act of 1963 amended FLSA to make it illegal to pay employees lower wages based on their gender.
- The Family Medical Leave Act of 1993 provided eligible employees up to 12 weeks of unpaid, job-protected leave for specific family and medical reasons.

- The Small Business Job Protection Act of 1996 increased the federal minimum wage to $5.15 an hour, but in doing so, the legislation also separated tipped employees as a detached class that would be exempt from future minimum wage increases, with the minimum wage for this new class frozen at $2.13 per hour. However, state employment laws that granted higher minimum wage levels remained in effect.
- In 2004, controversial changes were made to the definition of an "exempt" employee (exempt from overtime entitlement for hours worked beyond the standard 40 per week). For many blue-collar supervisors, the new "fair pay" changes reclassified them as "executives," without any increase in salary, and made them ineligible for overtime pay.

**Social Security Act, 1935** The Social Security Act and its multiple amendments encompass several social welfare and insurance programs. Funded by mandated payroll taxes (paid by both the employee and the employer) under the Federal Insurance Contributions Act (FICA), the main part of the insurance program is most commonly referred to as OASDI (old age, survivors, and disability insurance) or RSDI (retirement, survivors, and disability insurance), with the largest portion of the program geared toward the payment of retirement benefits.

The economic viability of the RSDI has been under considerable scrutiny in recent years as the change in population demographics creates an economy where there will be more people drawing retirement benefits from the program than workers contributing to it through payroll taxes. Precisely how the long-term liquidity of the program will be maintained remains to be resolved, but employers and employees alike are bracing for increased payroll taxes to address the expected financial shortfall in RSDI funds.

In addition to RSDI, the social welfare agenda that began with President Franklin D. Roosevelt's New Deal in the 1930s has produced other legislation that affects how businesses are managed today:

- *Federal Unemployment Tax Act (FUTA), 1935.* FUTA imposes an employer tax of 6.2 percent on the first $7,000 of gross earnings (pretax) of each worker per year to cover the costs of administering unemployment insurance and job service programs in all states. When combined with credits for state unemployment taxes paid, the effective tax rate for FUTA may be reduced to only 0.8 percent for employers.
- *Taft-Hartley Act, 1947.* Formally known as the Labor-Management Relations Act, this legislation amended the 1935 National Labor Relations Act (the Wagner Act). The amendments added a list of "unfair labor practices" as a means of limiting the actions of labor unions. Specific practices that were prohibited included wildcat strikes, solidarity or political strikes, closed shops (mandatory union membership), and jurisdictional strikes in response to the assignment of work to nonunion workers. The legislation also empowered federal courts to enforce collective bargaining agreements, and to deliver strikebreaking injunctions when threatened strikes "imperiled the national health or safety."
- *Civil Rights Act, 1964.* As a landmark piece of social legislation, the influence of the Civil Rights Act went far beyond addressing discrimination in the business world, as it extended voting rights, outlawed segregation in schools and discrimination in public facilities, and overturned the "Jim Crow" state and local laws that endorsed a "separate but equal" status for black Americans. Title VII mandated the creation of the Equal Employment Opportunity Commission (EEOC) as an independent federal agency to enforce laws against discrimination in the workplace.
- *Age Discrimination in Employment Act (ADEA), 1967.* Building on the mandates of the 1964 Civil Rights Act, ADEA prohibited employment discrimination against persons 40 years or older.
- *Employee Retirement Income Security Act (ERISA), 1974.* ERISA established minimum standards for the administration of private pension plans after a series of disclosures in the 1960s revealed that many large public corporations in the United States had underfunded pension plans for their employees. ERISA does not mandate that employers establish pension plans for their employees—it regulates how that plan should be administered once established, including the provision of "vesting" status for employees. It is argued that the creation of the 401(k) employee-sponsored plans created by a 1978 amendment to the Internal Revenue Code was prompted by the less-than-positive information that was revealed after the ERISA requirement for more detailed reporting came into effect.
- *Consolidated Omnibus Budget Reconciliation Act (COBRA), 1985.* Despite its intimidating title, COBRA mandated, among other things, that an insurance plan be established to provide health insurance coverage to employees leaving employment (irrespective of whether that departure was voluntary or involuntary). The provision of the continued coverage is enforced through the denial of tax deductions to employers for group health plan costs if those plans do not include COBRA coverage options.

## First Line Focus

**I'M NOT A LAWYER, BUT . . .**

*The legal environment in which you manage will depend on your industry sector and the prevailing legislation governing that sector at the federal, state, county, and city levels. Compliance to that legislation is the domain of the legal experts, and unless you are a lawyer with suitable board certifications, it would be inappropriate to put yourself in a position where you are making legal judgments that could carry heavy financial consequences if you are found to be out of compliance. Assume that observance of and full compliance with all appropriate legislation is built into your organization's policies and procedures manual. Your job as a manager is to enforce those policies and procedures on a daily basis and to seek outside counsel (legal if necessary) if and when you are presented with a situation that isn't explicitly addressed in the manual.*

## [PROGRESS] ✓questions

5. Explain the two tests that determine an employee's coverage under FLSA.
6. What does RSDI do?
7. Which legislation amended the 1935 National Labor Relations Act? What was the outcome of those amendments?
8. What was the stated purpose of "Jim Crow" laws?

- *Americans with Disabilities Act (ADA), 1990.* Prohibiting discrimination on the basis of disability, ADA is a wide-ranging civil rights law with five distinct titles mandating protections for disabled individuals in specific circumstances:

  Title I, Employment, prohibits discrimination against a qualified individual with a disability.

  Title II, Public Entities (and public transportation), mandates access (including physical access) to all programs and services at the local and state levels, including the provision of transportation services.

  Title III, Public Accommodations (and commercial facilities), prohibits discrimination against the "full and equal enjoyment" of goods, services, facilities, or accommodations of any public place on the basis of disability. This requirement has generated significant litigation as private clubs, religious organizations, and historical sites have sought exemptions to the construction demands required to guarantee access.

  Title IV, Telecommunications, mandates the provision of functionally equivalent services: TTY (teletypewriter) and TDD (telecommunications device for the deaf).

  Title V, Miscellaneous Provisions, includes prohibition of any attempt at retaliation or coercion against anyone seeking to exercise their rights under ADA.

As you can see, there are numerous legal obligations that companies must manage in order to serve the needs of their employees and their customers. Failure to comply with these obligations can result in severe penalties that can extend as far as the dissolution of the company. However, what happens in the absence of legislation to enforce appropriate behavior? If the employee or customer has no legal recourse to enforce specific behavior from a company, why should companies be expected to "do the right thing"? To examine this question, we must move beyond legal requirements and consider the concept of ethical business practices.

**Ethics** A set of moral principles or values that govern behavior.

**Code of Ethics** A document that outlines the principles of conduct to be used in making decisions within an organization.

## >> Ethics and Social Responsibility

Individuals make personal decisions about what they believe is right or wrong. These decisions are based on their ethics. **Ethics** are a set of moral principles or values that govern behavior. All individuals develop their own set of ethical rules, which help them decide how to behave in different situations.

Like individuals, businesses develop ethics to help them enforce a uniform code of conduct. These ethics reflect a company's beliefs about which actions are appropriate and fair.

The role of ethics in management decisions is difficult. Management issues often are emotionally charged, and many types of ethical problems may arise in business situations. What should managers do if they are aware of unethical practices in their businesses? Should they blow the whistle and risk their jobs? Should they quit and allow unethical practices to continue? Should they ignore the practices? These are only a few of the difficult ethical decisions managers face.[7]

## >> Codes of Ethics

To help managers know how to respond ethically to different business situations, many companies have developed codes of ethics. A **code of ethics** is a document that outlines the principles of conduct to be used in making decisions within an organization. Most corporations in the United States have codes of ethics.

### CONTENT OF ETHICAL CODES

Codes of ethics are formal documents that are shared with all employees. Some of the areas they cover include the following:

- Honesty
- Adherence to the law
- Product safety and quality
- Health and safety in the workplace
- Conflicts of interest
- Employment practices
- Selling and marketing practices
- Financial reporting

## TOO BIG TO FAIL

Your employer, American International Group (AIG), received almost $180 billion in federal bailout dollars in the belief that the collapse of AIG would have a catastrophic effect on the U.S. financial markets: The company was "too big to fail." Poor management choices had led the company to depend heavily on revenue from insuring investors against defaults on financial bonds backed by risky subprime mortgages (up to trillions of dollars of policy coverage). With the collapse of the housing market, investors filed claims on those insurance policies with AIG, and the company quickly discovered that it had insufficient financial resources to meet all those claims.

You are responsible for signing off on bonuses for AIG executives in the amount of $165 million, with the top seven executives of the company each receiving more than $4 million. News of the bonus payments creates a public outcry over the payment of millions of dollars to executives who have driven the company into near bankruptcy.

ETHICAL
MANAGEMENT
Should companies be allowed to pay out bonuses with borrowed money?

### QUESTIONS

1. Supporters of the bonus structure at AIG argue that failure to pay the bonuses will result in the departure of senior executives to AIG's competitors? Is this a valid defense? Why or why not?
2. The AIG collapse was blamed on one division of the company—the credit default swap department. Executives in the other departments that contributed positive revenue to AIG's bottom line feel strongly that they earned their bonuses. Do they have a case?
3. Your boss encourages you to try and convince the executives to forgo their bonuses for the good of the company and its reputation. How would you go about doing that?
4. Is it possible to resolve this issue to the satisfaction of both the taxpayers who bailed out AIG and the senior executives? Why or why not?

*Source:* Gretchen Morgenson, "Behind Insurer's Crisis: Blind Eye to a Web of Risk," *The New York Times*, September 28, 2008; Sharona Coutts, "AIG Bonus Scandal," *ProPublica*, March 18, 2009; and "Op-Ed: Dear AIG: I Quit!" *The New York Times*, March 25, 2009.

- Pricing, billing, and contracting
- Trading in securities while using confidential information
- Acquiring and using information about competitors
- Security
- Payments to obtain business
- Political activities
- Protection of the environment

Merely establishing a code of ethics does not prevent unethical behavior. To be effective, codes of ethics must be enforced. In fact, ethical codes that are not enforced probably do more harm than good.

## BEHAVING ETHICALLY

Despite the prevalence of media stories to the contrary, businesspeople make ethical decisions as a matter of standard practice. These decisions have important consequences for both individuals and their companies. Behaving unethically can hurt, or even end, a businessperson's career. It can cause a company to lose millions of dollars or go out of business altogether. Behaving ethically helps employees gain the trust of the people with whom they work. It can also help businesses gain the trust of customers, suppliers, and others.

## BEHAVING HONESTLY

In many situations, the ethical course of action is clear-cut. Ethical employees never steal from their employers. They never lie about the hours they work. They never falsify documents. Employees who engage in any of these actions threaten their careers. They also risk causing severe damage to their employers.

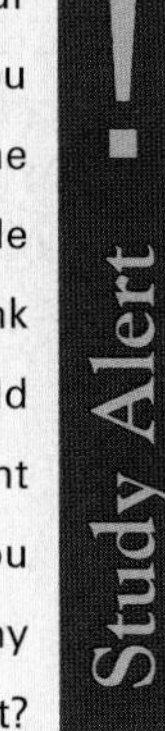

Study Alert!

Think about your organization (or one you have worked for in the past). Does it have a code of ethics? Do you think a code of ethics would help you make the right business decision if you needed to refer to it? Why or why not?

**Employee Theft** Employers trust their employees not to steal from them. Employees who behave ethically do not violate that trust.

Dishonest employees steal from their employers in a variety of ways. Some embezzle money or steal supplies or inventory from their employers. Some accept bribes from people who want to do business with their company. Others submit false expense accounts.

**Lying About Hours Worked** Employees who behave ethically are honest about the hours they work. Employees who work at home, for example, accurately report how long they work. They do not take advantage of the fact that their managers cannot check to see if they are actually at their desks.

Ethical employees also show up at work unless they are ill or need to be away from their jobs for a legitimate reason. They do not pretend to be sick in order to stay home when they should be at work.

**Falsifying Records** One of the worst ethical lapses an employee can commit is falsifying records. This can cause very grave damage to a company's reputation. It can even cause people to become ill or die. A manager at a pharmaceutical company, for example, who falsifies records documenting the side effects of the drugs the company produces can cause people who take the drug to die. A production supervisor who falsifies documents to indicate that computer parts were checked can cause his company to sell defective products. Years of excellent corporate performance can be wiped out by these kinds of unethical actions.

### Figure 13.2 • Solving Ethical Dilemmas

1. Have you defined the problem accurately?
2. How would you define the problem if you stood on the other side of the fence?
3. Whom could your decision or action injure? Can you discuss the problem with the affected parties before you make your decision?
4. Are you confident that your position will be as valid over a long period of time as it seems now?
5. Could you disclose without qualm your decision or action to your boss, your CEO, the board of directors, your family, and society as a whole?

### Figure 13.3 • Ethical Problems in the Business World

1. **Normal Interactions between Business Acquaintances**
   Many interactions between people doing business together are considered a normal part of doing business. Managers often take clients out to lunch or invite them to play golf, for example. These kinds of interactions help businesspeople get to know each other.
2. **Questionable Interactions between Business Acquaintances**
   Some interactions between business acquaintances are questionable. A manager who sends a client an expensive gift, for example, could be seen as trying to bribe the client into doing business with his or her company. Businesses often provide their employees with guidelines on the types of gifts they consider acceptable.
3. **Illegal Interactions between Business Acquaintances**
   Paying bribes to attract business is unethical and illegal. Managers who engage in this kind of activity could face legal action and go to jail.

## DEALING WITH ETHICAL DILEMMAS

Ethical dilemmas are situations in which the ethical course of action is not clear. Such situations arise regularly in the business world. Consider the following examples:

1. Your boss informs you confidentially that one of your friends is going to be fired. Your friend is about to buy a house. Should you warn your friend that he is about to be fired, even though you promised your boss that you would not?
2. Your colleague has been violating your company's code of ethics by accepting expensive gifts from a salesperson who does business with your company. Should you notify your supervisor?
3. One of your employees has not been performing her job properly. You know that she has been having serious personal problems, and you have tried to be understanding. However, your entire staff is suffering because of poor performance by this key team member. What should you do?

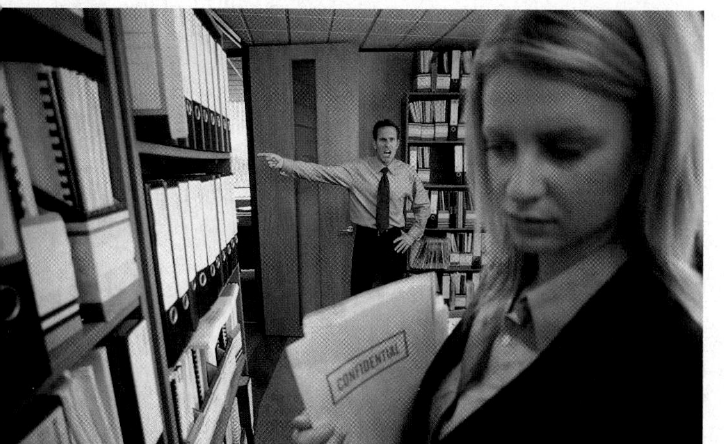


One way of approaching ethical dilemmas like these is to answer the series of questions shown in Figure 13.2. Talking to people you trust can also help you develop solutions to ethical problems. Figure 13.3 explains some of the ethical problems in business.

# >> Laws Relating to Ethics in Business

Over the years, various laws have been enacted that directly relate to the issue of ethics in business. These laws apply to competitive behavior, corporate governance, consumer protection, and environmental protection.

## COMPETITIVE BEHAVIOR

Since the late 19th century the federal government has regulated companies to make sure that they do not engage in anticompetitive behavior. All companies operating in the United States must abide by these laws. Enforcement of these laws is handled by the Antitrust Division of the Justice Department and by the Federal Trade Commission.

**The Sherman Act** The Sherman Antitrust Act of 1890 makes it illegal for companies to monopolize trade. Under the law, mergers can be prohibited if the new company that results from the merger will control too large a share of the market. The purpose of the law is to ensure that companies remain able to compete fairly.

**The Clayton Act** The Clayton Act of 1914 makes it illegal to charge different prices to different wholesale customers. This means that a manufacturer of steel, for example, cannot charge one price to General Motors and another price to Chrysler. The act also bans the practice of requiring a customer to purchase a second good. Manufacturers of computer hardware, for example, cannot require customers to purchase software as well.

**The Wheeler-Lea Act** The Wheeler-Lea Act of 1938 bans unfair or deceptive acts or practices, including false advertising. Under the act, businesses must inform consumers of possible negative consequences of using their products. Labeling of cigarette packages is an example of the kind of disclosure required by the Wheeler-Lea Act.

**The Foreign Corrupt Practices Act** The Foreign Corrupt Practices Act (FCPA) of 1977 was introduced in order to place more effective controls over the practice of paying bribes or other less obvious forms of payment to foreign officials and politicians by American publicly traded companies as they pursued international growth.

[PROGRESS] questions

9. What are ethics?
10. What is a code of ethics?
11. Does establishing a code of ethics prevent unethical behavior? Why or why not?
12. What is an ethical dilemma, and what challenges does it present in a business environment?

## CONSUMER PROTECTION

Several laws protect consumers in the United States against unethical and unsafe business practices. These laws cover food and drugs, other manufactured products, and loans.

**Study Alert!** Why is it necessary to legally enforce ethical business conduct?

**Food and Drugs** The Federal Food, Drug, and Cosmetic Act of 1938 bans the sale of impure, improperly labeled, falsely guaranteed, and unhealthful foods, drugs, and cosmetics. The law is enforced by the Food and Drug Administration (FDA), which has the power to force manufacturers to stop selling products it considers unsafe.

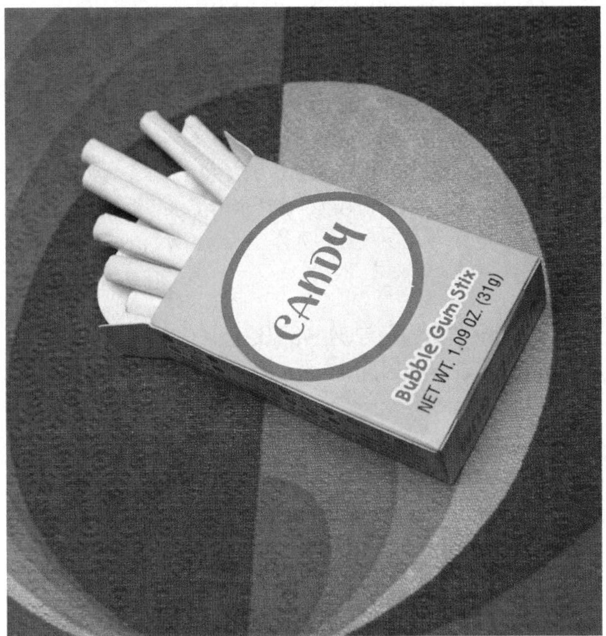


*In September 2009, the FDA banned candy cigarettes in order to keep kids from perceiving smoking as "cool."*

**Consumer Products** The Consumer Product Safety Commission (CPSC) was established in 1972. It establishes minimum product safety standards on consumer products. If a product is found to be defective, the Consumer Product Safety Commission has the authority to force the manufacturer to recall the product. For example, in 1999 the CPSC recalled a quarter of a million Nike water bottles. The bottles were recalled because the cap was not attached properly, possibly causing users to choke.

**Intellectual Property** Ownership of tangible ideas, such as inventions, books, movies, and computer programs, that gives creators of the intellectual property the exclusive right to market and sell their work.

**Loans** A series of laws protect U.S. consumers against unfair lending practices. Under the Truth in Lending Act of 1968, creditors are required to let consumers know how much they are paying in finance charges and interest. The Equal Credit Opportunity Act of 1975 prohibits creditors from making credit decisions on the basis of discriminatory practices.

## ENVIRONMENTAL PROTECTION

Since the late 1960s, environmental protection has been an important social and economic issue in the United States. This concern has been reflected in the many laws designed to protect the environment.

**The National Environmental Policy Act of 1969** The key piece of legislation in environmental protection is the National Environmental Policy Act of 1969. This law created the Environmental Protection Agency (EPA), whose mission is to protect human health and safeguard the air, water, and land.

Since 1969, many environmental laws affecting businesses have been passed. These laws include the Clean Air Act, the Toxic Substances Control Act, and the Clean Water Act. All these laws are enforced by the EPA.

**The Clean Air Act of 1970** The Clean Air Act of 1970 is the comprehensive federal law that regulates air emissions. The original act set maximum air pollution standards for each of the 50 states. In 1990, the act was amended to deal with problems of acid rain, ground-level ozone, stratospheric ozone depletion, and toxic substances in the air.

**From the PERSPECTIVE OF...**

**A Whistle-Blower** Employees who choose to speak out or "go public" with evidence of unethical or illegal corporate behavior are called *whistle-blowers.* They often see themselves as being torn between their obligations to their employer and their obligations to their family and to the community as a whole. What kinds of obligations are they referring to?

**The Toxic Substances Control Act of 1976** The Toxic Substances Control Act of 1976 was enacted to give the EPA the ability to track the 75,000 industrial chemicals currently produced in or imported into the United States. The EPA screens these chemicals and can require reporting or testing of those that may pose an environmental or human health hazard.

**The Clean Water Act of 1977** The Clean Water Act of 1977 gives the EPA the authority to set standards on the type and quantity of pollutants that industries can put into bodies of water. The law makes it illegal to discharge any pollutant into navigable waters unless a permit is obtained.

## ETHICAL STANDARDS AND CULTURE

Standards of business ethics differ around the world. This means that business practices that are acceptable in one country may be considered unethical in others.

Business managers working in foreign countries must be aware of these different ethical standards. They must set guidelines for their companies on how to operate both within their own culture and in other cultures.

## CORPORATE GIFT GIVING

Gift-giving customs differ around the world. In some cultures, gifts are expected; failure to present them is considered an insult. In Japan, for example, lavish gift giving is an important part of doing business. Gifts are usually exchanged at the first meeting.

In the United States, government officials are not allowed to accept expensive gifts from businesses. Regardless of local practices, American managers operating abroad must abide by the standards set in the United States.

## INTELLECTUAL PROPERTY

**Intellectual property** refers to ownership of tangible ideas, such as inventions, books, movies, and computer programs. In many

# Thinking Critically 13.1

## >> The Deported Patient

In 2000, a drunk driver of a stolen van crashed into a van in which Luis Jimenez was a passenger, killing two other people and leaving Jimenez a paraplegic with the cognitive ability of a fourth grader. Jimenez was treated at Martin Memorial Medical Center in Florida where, over the next three years, he received medical care amounting to $1.5 million. As an undocumented immigrant from Guatemala with no medical insurance, Jimenez was in no position to pay this bill. As a recipient of Medicare reimbursement funds, the hospital was required, under federal law, to provide emergency care to all patients regardless of their ability to pay until the patient could be stabilized and discharged to an appropriate long-term care facility.

The hospital was unable to find an appropriate facility, because Jimenez's immigration status made him ineligible for government reimbursement of his medical expenses. Hospital administrators then approached the government of Guatemala about providing long-term care for him and received confirmation that such care would be provided. On the morning of July 10, 2003, a private charter flight arranged by the hospital at a cost of $30,000 transported Jimenez back to Guatemala. After a brief hospital stay, Jimenez was discharged into the care of his 73-year-old mother in a remote mountaintop village.

Jimenez's family sued the hospital for damages plus $1 million to cover the lifetime cost of his care, claiming that he had been wrongfully deported against his wishes. The hospital claimed that based on the documentation from the Guatemalan government, the transfer was a "repatriation," rather than a deportation, and that it was acting on the patient's request to return home, even though Jimenez's cousin and legal guardian, Montejo Gaspar had been working to stop the transfer.

In July 2009 a jury in Stuart, Florida, ruled that the hospital had acted reasonably in transporting the patient back to his native country. This case has brought considerable media attention and polarized the debate over the care and support of undocumented immigrants. An appeal of the ruling is planned.

**QUESTIONS**

1. The jury found that Martin Memorial Medical Center did not act unreasonably in sending Jimenez back to Guatemala, but did the hospital administrators act in an ethical manner? Why or why not?
2. Who were the stakeholders in this case?
3. Jimenez's supporters argued that the hospital was deliberately avoiding its obligation to provide medical care to a patient. Supporters of the hospital argue that it was unreasonable to expect it to provide care for a patient who had no means to pay and had no legal status in the United States. What do you think?
4. How could the hospital have handled this case differently?

*Source:* Deborah Sontag, "Jury Rules for Hospital That Deported Patient," *The New York Times,* July 28, 2009; Laura Wides-Munoz, "Fla. Hospital Defends Secretly Deporting Patient," Associated Press, July 23, 2009; and "Editorial: Close the 'Weird' Loophole," *Palm Beach Post,* July 28, 2009.

countries, including the United States, creators of intellectual property have the exclusive right to market and sell their work. These rights are guaranteed through patent, trademark, and copyright laws. Such protection ensures that only the creators of intellectual property profit from their work.

Intellectual property protection is very important to business. Without such laws, a computer company could market a best-selling game created by another computer company. A pharmaceutical company could manufacture and sell drugs developed by another drug company.

**Social Responsibility** The obligation that individuals or businesses have to help solve social problems.

**Stakeholders** The people—employees, customers, suppliers, and the community—who are affected by the actions of a business.

Although the United States has tough laws governing intellectual property, enforcing those laws is a problem, particularly in the software industry. In 1999, the Justice Department, the FBI, and the Customs Service began cracking down on piracy and counterfeiting of computer software and other products in the United States.

Rules concerning intellectual property rights differ in some countries. In China and India, for example, the government does not enforce such rights. As a result, some Chinese companies copy and sell foreign computer programs. Some publishers in India reprint foreign textbooks, selling them as if they had published them themselves. In the United States, someone who engages in this practice is guilty of plagiarism and can be sued in a court of law.

## >> Social Responsibility

**Social responsibility** refers to the obligation that individuals or businesses have to help solve social problems. Most companies in the United States exhibit some sense of social responsibility.[8]

Businesses' concept of their role in society has changed dramatically over the past century. Views toward social responsibility evolved through three distinct schools of thought: profit maximization, trusteeship management, and social involvement.

### PROFIT MAXIMIZATION

In the 19th and early 20th centuries, business owners in the United States believed that their role was simply to maximize the profits their companies earned. Dealing with social problems was not considered a legitimate business activity.

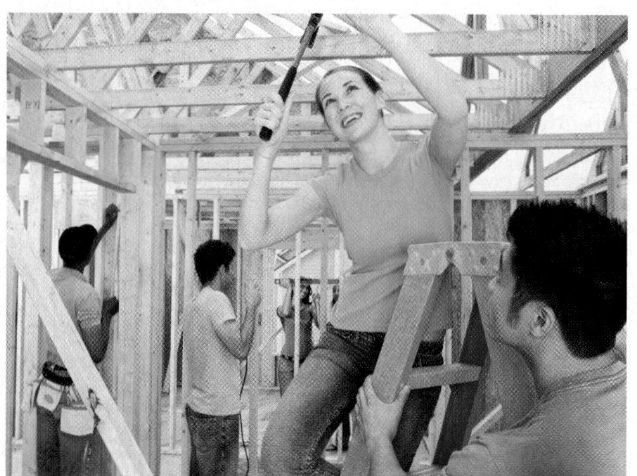

### TRUSTEESHIP MANAGEMENT

Thinking about the role of business changed in the 1920s and 1930s, when a philosophy known as *trusteeship management* became popular. This philosophy recognized that owners of businesses had obligations to do more than just earn profits. They also had obligations to their employees, their customers, and their creditors. Most businesspeople continued to hold this view until the 1960s.

### SOCIAL INVOLVEMENT

During the 1960s, many people began to believe that corporations should use their influence and financial resources to address social problems. They believed corporations should help solve problems such as poverty, crime, environmental destruction, and illiteracy.

According to this view, businesses should be responsible corporate citizens, not just maximizers of profit. Businesses have obligations to all the people affected by their actions, known as stakeholders. **Stakeholders** include a company's employees, customers, suppliers, and the community.

Since the 1960s, corporations have increasingly demonstrated their commitment to social change. One example of this commitment is the increased diversity in the workplace. Over the past 50 years, most corporations have made efforts to diversify their workforces by hiring and promoting more women and minorities. Many businesses also have established workshops to help their employees understand people from different backgrounds.

### MEASURING SOCIAL RESPONSIBILITY

Corporations demonstrate their sense of social responsibility in various ways. Performance in each area is measured as part of a social audit.

**Philanthropy and Volunteerism** One way a company demonstrates its sense of social responsibility is by contributing time and money to charitable, cultural, and civic organizations. Corporate philanthropy, or efforts to improve human welfare, can take many forms. Computer giant Compaq (now merged with Hewlett-Packard), for example, provides technology, product, and cash contributions to organizations throughout the United States. It also has planted seedlings in Australia, supported an institute for people with disabilities in India, and refurbished a school in Brazil. All these activities reflect the company's sense of social responsibility.

Some companies grant employees paid time off to participate in charitable activities. Many high-tech companies, for example, allow their employees to volunteer for the U.S. Tech Corps, which sends employees from technology companies to work in public schools. Other corporations encourage volunteerism by allowing employees time off to donate blood, participate in food and clothing drives, or raise money for such causes as the United Way.

Many corporations also donate money by matching charitable donations made by their employees. In this way companies both encourage employee giving and make their own contributions to philanthropic causes.

**Environmental Awareness** Another way companies demonstrate their sense of social responsibility is by limiting the damage their operations cause to the environment. They do so by creating production processes that are as environmentally friendly as possible.

Businesses also can affect the environment by establishing policies that reduce pollution. Many organizations now actively track their "carbon footprint" (the amount of carbon dioxide, or $CO_2$, their operations produce in the environment) and encourage customers to participate in reducing that footprint. Air Canada, for example, partners with a carbon-offset company called Zerofootprint to allow customers to mitigate the environmental impact of their travel.[9] Using biodegradable products also helps protect the environment.

**Sensitivity to Diversity and Quality of Work Life** One of the most important ways a company can demonstrate its sense of social responsibility is through its workforce. Socially responsible businesses maintain ethnically diverse workforces that reflect the societies in which they operate. McDonald's, for example, has created a diverse work environment. At least 70 percent of McDonald's restaurant management and 25 percent of the company executives are minorities and women.

Companies also can demonstrate their social responsibility by adopting policies that contribute to the quality of life of their workers. Flexible work hours, for example, allow workers to better meet their families' needs. On-site day care centers make life easier for employees with young children.

## ACTIONS NECESSARY TO IMPLEMENT SOCIAL RESPONSIBILITY

The biggest obstacle to organizations assuming more social responsibility is pressure by financial analysts and stockholders who push for steady increases in earnings per share on a quarterly basis. Concern about immediate profits makes it difficult to invest in areas that cannot be accurately measured and still have returns that are long run in nature. Furthermore, pressure for short-term earnings affects corporate social behavior; most companies are geared toward short-term profit goals. Budgets, objectives, and performance evaluations are often based on short-run considerations. Management may state a willingness to lose some short-term profit to achieve social objectives. However, managers who sacrifice profit and seek to justify these actions on the basis of corporate social goals may find stockholders unsympathetic.

Organizations should also carefully examine their cherished values, short-run profits, and others to ensure that these concepts are in tune with the values held by society. This should be a constant process, because the values society holds are ever changing.

Organizations should reevaluate their long-range planning and decision-making processes to ensure that they fully understand the potential social consequences. Plant location decisions are no longer merely economic matters. Environmental impact and job opportunities for disadvantaged groups are examples of other factors to consider.

Organizations should seek to aid both governmental agencies and voluntary agencies in their social efforts. This should include technical and managerial help as well as monetary support. Technological knowledge, organizational skills, and managerial competence can all be applied to solving social problems.

**Study Alert!**

Are there business advantages to being socially responsible? Or is it just a public relations exercise to keep stakeholders happy?

Organizations should look at ways to help solve social problems through their own businesses. Many social problems stem from the economic deprivation of a fairly large segment of our society. Attacking this problem could be the greatest social effort of organizations.

Another major area in which businesses are active is corporate philanthropy. Corporate philanthropy

TAKING ADVANTAGE?

You are the line manager for a team of people in your company in the finance sector. One of your key staff members is excellent at her job and is known for her ability to generate a high amount of income for the company—none of your other staff members comes close to her in terms of this.

You are aware that your company's competitors have made attempts to headhunt this staff member, which she has so far rejected, much to your relief as your department is heavily reliant on her abilities and you are paid bonuses based on your department's profitability.

However, you are certain that this staff member is submitting fraudulent expense claims, sometimes several hundred or thousands of dollars more than she has actually spent—a tiny fraction of the profits she is generating but fraudulent nonetheless.

ETHICAL
MANAGEMENT
Is it fair for the top-performing employee to "reward" herself?


### QUESTIONS

1. Should the high amount of income this staff member generates for the company justify "looking the other way" over these fraudulent expense claims? Why or why not?
2. What would your action be if she weren't such a star performer? Why?
3. How would you go about bringing this to the attention of your boss?
4. Do you think the company would terminate this employee? Why or why not?

*Source:* Adapted from "Ethical Dilemmas: How Much Should Valuable People Get Away with Things?" St. James Ethics Centre, www.ethics.org.au.

**Social Audit** A method used by management to evaluate the success or lack of success of programs designed to improve the social performance of the organization.

involves donations of money, property, or work by organizations to socially useful purposes. Many companies have directed their philanthropic efforts toward education, the arts, and the United Way. Contributions can be made directly by the company, or a company foundation can be created to handle the philanthropic program.

## CONDUCTING A SOCIAL AUDIT

One method of measuring the success of a firm is to conduct a social audit. A **social audit** allows management to evaluate the success or lack of success of programs designed to improve the social performance of the organization. Rather than looking exclusively at economic and financial measures, the social audit can be a beginning point for encouraging environmental and social strategies that really work.

One suggested method for accomplishing the social audit and reacting to the information includes the following steps:

1. Examine social expectations, sensitivity, and past responses.
2. Examine and then set social objectives and meaningful priorities.
3. Plan and implement strategies and objectives in each program area.
4. Set budgets for resources necessary for social action, and make a commitment to acquire them.
5. Monitor accomplishments or progress in each program area.

To ensure that stockholders, stakeholders, and the general public know about the commitment and accomplishments of social programs, most large corporations publish their successes in their annual reports. These firms make social responsibility an integral part of their mission statements. True commitment goes beyond the self-serving and selective nature of public relations. Most experts agree that socially responsible firms will eventually be rewarded by their markets and stakeholders.

13. What is social responsibility?
14. What are the three schools of thought from which social responsibility was developed?
15. Explain the terms *philanthropy* and *volunteerism*.
16. List the five steps of a social audit.

# Thinking Critically 13.2

## >> Shameless Exploitation in Pursuit of the Common Good

Newman's Own was supposed to be a tiny boutique operation—parchment labels on elegant wine bottles of antique glass. We expected train wrecks along the way and got, instead, one astonishment followed by another astonishment followed by another. . . . A lot of the time we thought we were in first gear we were really in reverse, but it didn't seem to make any difference. We anticipated sales of $1,200 a year and a loss, despite our gambling winnings, of $6,000. But in these 20 years we have earned over $175 million, which we've given to countless charities. How to account for this massive success? Pure luck? Transcendental meditation? Machiavellian manipulation? Aerodynamics? High colonics? We haven't the slightest idea.

In 1978, Paul Newman and A. E. Hotchner decided that rather than just distribute Paul's own salad dressing at Christmas to neighbors, they would offer it to a few local stores. Freewheeling, irreverent entrepreneurs, they conceived of their venture as a great way to poke fun at the mundane method of traditional marketing. Much to their surprise, the dressing was enthusiastically received. What had started as a lark quickly escalated into a full-fledged business, the first company to place all-natural foods in supermarkets. From salad dressing to spaghetti sauce, to popcorn, and to lemonade, Newman's Own became a major player in the food business. The company's profits were originally donated to medical research, education, and the environment and eventually went to the creation of the eight Hole in the Wall Gang camps for children with serious illnesses, serving over 13,000 children per year.

**QUESTIONS**

1. What makes Newman's Own such a positive example of corporate social responsibility?
2. What other products are now included in the Newman's Own line?
3. If the organization used only all-natural ingredients and did not donate its after-tax profits to charity, would it still be held in such high regard? Why or why not?
4. Provide an example of something that your organization (or an organization you have worked for in the past) could do to be more socially responsible. Explain your answer.

*Source:* www.newmansown.com; and P. Newman and A. E. Hotchner, *Shameless Exploitation in Pursuit of the Common Good: The Madcap Business Adventure by the Truly Oddest Couple* (New York: Random House, 2003).

## >> Chapter Summary

In this chapter we have reviewed the legal environment in which managers must operate on a daily basis. Extensive legislation provides detailed guidance on how managers must ensure a safe and healthy workplace for their employees and how those employees must be managed in a fair and equitable manner. For business decisions that fall outside of the realm of prevailing legislation, we have considered what is involved in ensuring that employees "do the right thing" for the company and all its stakeholders—employees, customers, vendor partners, community partners, and city, state, and federal agencies.

In the next chapter we draw our journey to a close by considering what the future holds for the management profession.

# For REVIEW >>

1. Discuss the legal environment of business.

   Effective managers must have a clear understanding of their businesses—how operating costs are controlled, how sales revenue is generated, how much market share is owned, how competitors are handled, and, most importantly, how much profit is generated by the company. There is an equally important responsibility to ensure that the company operates in full compliance with all relevant legislation governing that business—both in terms of the operating practices and the employment practices. Such practices should ensure that the executives of the company operate a safe and healthy work environment for their employees and produce safe and effective products or services for their customers.

   This responsibility of legal compliance must be a top priority. Being found to be out of compliance by any regulatory authority can bring severe financial consequences, ranging from increased operating costs, penalties, and PR damage to complete closure of the organization in extreme circumstance.

2. Explain the appropriate legislation governing operational and employment practices in a business.

   The business world is obligated to be compliant with dozens of pieces of legislation that are designed to enforce appropriate commercial behavior. The legislation has been enacted to ensure that companies operate a safe and healthy work environment for their employees and produce safe and effective products or services for their customers.

3. Discuss an organization's code of ethics.

   A code of ethics is a document that outlines the principles of conduct to be used in making decisions within an organization. The purpose of the code is to guide employees in "doing the right thing" when faced with an ethical dilemma in their work environment. If the code is sufficiently detailed, the decision should be straightforward.

4. Explain an ethical dilemma.

   Ethical dilemmas are situations in which the ethical course of action is not clear. Often the choice presented to a manager may be between two rights rather than a "right or wrong" choice. In this context, managers must be able to define the problem accurately; see both sides of the problem; develop a clear understanding of the likely outcomes of each decision choice; and defend the choice to senior leaders in the organization if called upon to do so. If the manager is unable to accomplish the preceding list, he or she should seek additional input before making a decision.

5. Classify and measure an organization's social responsibility.

   In the absence of a widely accepted template for measuring social responsibility, corporations demonstrate their activities in different ways. They may emphasize their philanthropic work by documenting the amount of money donated to which causes or the number of work hours donated to nonprofit organizations by their employees. Other corporations emphasize environmental awareness by promoting their efforts to minimize their carbon footprint by developing production processes that are as environmentally friendly as possible. They may also emphasize their commitment to diversity and quality of work life by promoting their diverse employee populations and flexible working practices that allow employees to manage work and family responsibilities in a balanced manner. Most organizations will seek to promote efforts in all three areas simultaneously as part of a focused public relations campaign—especially if the media find evidence to the contrary and there is a need to do some "damage control."

6. Understand the steps involved in conducting a social audit.

   A social audit allows management to evaluate the success or lack of success of programs designed to improve the social performance of the organization. Rather than looking exclusively at economic and financial measures, the social audit can be a beginning point for encouraging environmental and social strategies that really work. Social audits review the organization's past performance on environmental and social issues; set specific objectives and metrics; plan and implement strategies based on those objectives; allocate resources to fund and support those strategies; and monitor performance according to the selected metrics.

## THE WORLD of Work >>

**IT COSTS MONEY TO BE SOCIALLY RESPONSIBLE**
***(continued from page 309)***

The social audit of Taco Barn operations revealed that the company was more involved in socially responsible activities than most people thought. The company was an active recycler at every restaurant and at the regional and national headquarters. Donation of surplus food to community food banks was widespread and well coordinated. The company kept track of how many pounds of food were being donated and how many meals were being provided to the homeless based on those donations.

Opportunities for improvement were identified in the area of stakeholder relationships—both in how Taco Barn worked with its suppliers on building its socially responsible message into every aspect of the company's operation and in how the company supported the local business community in purchasing supplies from local vendors.

On these issues Dawn chose to look to the unit managers, including Tony, for ideas on how they could get more involved in their local communities. On the weekly conference calls that took place between the regional meetings, several of Tony's fellow unit managers had raised concerns about the impact of this new policy on their profit margins:

"It's going to cost me real money to be socially responsible—buying local produce in smaller quantities is going to cost a lot more than getting it from our wholesaler. Are our customers really going to care where we buy our tomatoes?"

Tony had already made up his mind on that question, and the answer was a definite yes!

When he had reviewed this new initiative at his staff meeting, the response from his people had been overwhelming. The younger crew members were thrilled and many commented that "it was about time." The older crew members also spoke up about how much their lives were going to improve now that they could give straight answers to customers who asked that very question: Where did Taco Barn buy its tomatoes? Was it from a local farm, or were they shipped in? What else did Taco Barn buy locally?

The only concern they expressed was whether or not the company was making a serious commitment here or was it just a short-term initiative? Tony had asked the same question of Dawn Williams, and his mentor Jerry Smith, and he had been happy with the response he received from them:

"Tony, it's a whole new business world out there. Our customers are expecting more from us, and we fully intend to deliver on those expectations."

**QUESTIONS**

1. Are the unit managers' concerns about increased costs valid? Why or why not?
2. How do you think Tony's crew members would react if the company did go back on this new commitment to social responsibility?
3. What options does Taco Barn have in managing the increase in costs from this new initiative?
4. Based on the information shared in this case, do you think Taco Barn will follow through on all these commitments? Why or why not?

## Key Terms >>

code of ethics 314

ethics 314

intellectual property 318

social audit 322

social responsibility 320

stakeholders 320

## Think << AND DISCUSS

1. Why did it take until 1970 for federal legislation protecting employee health and workplace safety to be implemented?
2. Critics of Sarbanes-Oxley argue that it penalized smaller businesses without bringing about any real change for large corporations. Do you agree or disagree? Why?
3. Which is the most important piece of employment legislation? Why?
4. The Social Security Act of 1935 was enacted to provide for citizens in their retirement or if their circumstances changed through disability or death of a spouse or dependent. Why would this legislation affect the daily operation of a business?
5. Identify the laws that deal with ethical issues in business.
6. What are the three ways in which corporations can demonstrate a sense of social responsibility?

## INTERNET In Action >>

1. Locate the Web site for the Ethics Resource Center (ERC). Does the center offer any training programs in ethics? If so, what types of programs are available? Does the site offer links to other ethical organizations? If so, list two companies that have their code of ethics linked from the ERC site.
2. Locate the Web site for the Ethics and Compliance Officers Association (ECOA). ECOA makes a public commitment to three key values. What are they? How does the mission of ECOA differ from that of ERC?
3. Locate the Web site for the Center for Business Ethics (CBE). Find the research publications page, and identify the most recent research report released by CBE. Briefly summarize the ethical issue discussed in the report. Do you agree or disagree with the conclusions reached in the report? Explain your answer.

1. **Where Do You Stand?**

Divide the class into groups (a maximum of six), and each group select one of the following situations. Decide how you would respond. Be prepared to justify your position in a class discussion and to share how you arrived at your decision.

***Situation 1: Family versus Ethics***

Jim, a 56-year-old middle manager with children in college, discovers that the owners of his company are cheating the government out of several thousand dollars a year in taxes. Jim is the only employee in a position to know this. Should Jim report the owners to the Internal Revenue Service at the risk of endangering his own livelihood, or should he disregard the discovery to protect his family's livelihood?

***Situation 2: The Roundabout Raise***

When Joe asks for a raise, his boss praises his work but says the company's rigid budget won't allow any further merit raises for the time being. Instead, the boss suggests the company "won't look too closely at your expense accounts for a while." Should Joe take this as authorization to pad his expense account because he is simply getting the money he deserves through a different route, or should he not take this roundabout "raise"?

***Situation 3: The Faked Degree***

Bill has done a sound job for over a year; he got the job by claiming to have a college degree. Bill's boss learns Bill actually never graduated. Should his boss dismiss him for a false résumé? Should he overlook the false claim, since Bill is otherwise conscientious and honorable and dismissal might ruin Bill's career?

***Situation 4: Sneaking Phone Calls***

Helen discovers that a co-worker makes about $100 a month in personal long-distance telephone calls from an office telephone. Should Helen report the employee or disregard the calls, since many people make personal calls at the office?

***Situation 5: Cover-Up Temptation***

José discovers that the chemical plant he manages is creating slightly more water pollution in a nearby lake than is legally permitted. Revealing the problem will bring negative publicity to the plant, hurt the lakeside town's resort business, and scare the community. Solving the problem will cost the company well over $100,000. It is unlikely that outsiders will discover the problem. The violation poses no danger whatever to people; at most, it will endanger a small number of fish. Should José reveal the problem despite the cost to his company, or should he consider the problem as a mere technicality and disregard it?

***Situation 6: Actual Salary***

Dorothy finds out that the best-qualified candidate for a job really earned only $18,000 a year in his last job, not the $28,000 he claimed. Should Dorothy hire the candidate anyway, or should she choose someone considerably less qualified?

2. **Who Are We?**

Divide the class into groups of three or four students. Each group selects an organization—one that a group member works for or has worked for in the past. In 15 minutes, develop an ethics charter or statement that provides clear guidance to employees and introduces a new employee to the organization's standard of ethical business practices. Be prepared to present and discuss your statement with your classmates.

*Source:* Roger Rickles, *The Wall Street Journal*. Copyright © 1983 by Dow Jones & Co., Inc., via Copyright Clearance Center.

# Case 13.1

## >> In-House Corporate Cops: The Rise of Ethics and Compliance Officers

Recent surveys by search firm Hudson Highland Group and the Ethics Resource Center have found that between 31 and 52 percent of U.S. workers have witnessed co-workers operating unethically. But that could change. One by-product of the scandals is growth in the ranks of ethics and compliance officers. A professional group for in-house corporate cops, the Ethics and Compliance Officer Association (ECOA), based in Waltham, Massachusetts, began with 19 founding members in 1992, grew to 600 three years ago, and has since doubled to 1,250. For the unethical these days, says Keith T. Darcy, ECOA executive director, "There are no secrets and no places to hide." Companies are finding improprieties very expensive. "The greatest threat to any publicly traded company is a well-publicized scandal," says Zachary W. Carter, a former U.S. attorney for the Eastern District of New York and former judge in the criminal court of New York, who now sits on the board of Marsh & McLennan. The insurance brokerage giant agreed in early 2005 to pay $850 million to settle allegations of price-fixing and collusion leveled by New York State Attorney General Eliot Spitzer who, ironically, managed to derail his own political career with a widely publicized scandal in 2008.

### Principle-Based Approach

But backers of aggressive corporate self-policing, say ethics officers, must be free to scrutinize everything in a company. Only then could they stand in the way of another Enron, argues Lee S. Richards III, an independent examiner at software company CA (formerly Computer Associates), which was caught up in a $2.2 billion accounting scandal that culminated in a 12-year prison sentence and $8 million fine for former CA chief executive Sanjay Kumar. Inside ethics officers "are in a position to prevent scandals of all sizes and shapes," adds Richards. He says they must have senior status in their companies, be able to look into "every nook and cranny," and take problems over the CEO's head to the board, if needed.

### Strict Rules

Ethics officers run training programs that spell out what's acceptable in dealings both internally and outside. They advise on ethical quandaries, such as when gifts are appropriate. And they monitor hotlines set up so whistle-blowers can draw attention to wrongdoing. "The rules are strict, and I don't apologize for that," says Susan E. Shepard, a former prosecutor and former commissioner of investigation for New York City who joined Nortel Networks as chief ethics and compliance officer in 2005. Nortel brought her on after it ousted CEO Frank Dunn and a clutch of other executives in 2004 amid disclosures of financial misreporting. Much of the dishonesty occurs at lower levels. Shepard tells of thefts in 2003 at Nortel in which equipment worth more than $1 million was stolen from a company lab affected by layoffs. Employees walked out the door with the gear, unchallenged. When her staff early last year reviewed an investigation of the thefts, she was stunned that controls on taking equipment out were still lax. That's not so anymore, the ethics chief says. In another case, a Nortel staffer was leaking company information to her husband, who worked for a competitor; the staffer has been canned. "When intellectual property is your product, you have to protect it," Shepard says.

### QUESTIONS

1. Why are companies "finding improprieties very expensive"?
2. What is the mission of ECOA?
3. What kind of stature should an ethics officer hold within an organization?
4. Research and summarize an example of unethical corporate behavior other than the ones given here.

*Source:* Joseph Weber, "Legal Affairs," *BusinessWeek,* February 13, 2006; "One in Three Workers Witness Ethical Misconduct Despite Clearly Communicated Guidelines," Hudson Highland Survey on Workplace Ethics, 2005; and Michael J. de la Merced, "Accounting Scandal Brings 12-year Sentence," *International Herald Tribune,* November 3, 2006.

# Case 13.2

## >> TerraCycle: Forget Recycle—Up-Cycle!

After being dismissed as tree huggers for decades, proponents of environmentally conscious business practices—green business—now see their proposals taking hold. Packaging companies proudly promote their post-consumer recycled content; paper and printing companies include their preconsumer content of scraps and test copies; and the 2010 Winter Olympics medals were made out of recycled electronics. However, the challenge of recycling is to continue finding ways to use waste materials in order to keep them out of landfills. Every old television, rubber tire, or newspaper saved from a landfill dump is a positive move, but success continues to be measured in small percentages, with the larger percentage representing millions of tons of garbage clogging the landfills.

What if you could take a nonrecyclable material and repurpose it into a new product, giving it a new retail life and saving it from the landfill? Welcome to the world of "up-cycling." In Trenton, New Jersey, a young company named TerraCycle is leading the way in this new world with over 100 products made from people's trash using an innovative program called "Sponsored Waste."

With its community-based "TerraCycle Brigades" in schools and charities, the company purchases its raw materials from recycling drives. Stonyfield Farm yogurt pots go for 3 cents each, and Capri Sun and Kool Aid drink pouches, Oreo cookie wrappers, Lays potato chip bags, and Clif Energy Bar wrappers all earn 2 cents each. If this sounds like a fun little PTA project, think again. TerraCycle Brigades have a membership of over eight million people, collecting 19 different products that are currently turned into 106 different up-cycled products. Drink pouches become pencil cases, lunch boxes, tote bags, and homework folders; cookie wrappers become backpacks, messenger bags, and even a kite. Over half the products are currently available at major retailers like Walmart, Target, Home Depot, OfficeMax, Petco, and Whole Foods Market.

What if you could take a nonrecyclable material and repurpose it into a new product, giving it a new retail life and saving it from the landfill? Welcome to the world of "up-cycling."

Founded in 2001 by a 19-year-old Princeton University freshman named Tom Szaky (pronounced "zackie"), TerraCycle's first product was an organic fertilizer created from worm poop. Manufacturing that worm poop required business practices that have become part of the TerraCycle lore—raising $20,000 to build a worm "gin," where tons of waste could be delivered to worms that would devour the waste and produce their own body weight in casings (poop) every 24 hours; and having to retrieve food waste bins from Princeton's dining halls after they had been sitting in the summer heat for days and were full of maggots—all to produce an organic fertilizer that was more effective, more environmentally conscious, and, more importantly for a new business venture, cheaper than the leading competitor's product, MiracleGro.

*Continued on next page*

Continued from page 329

The worm poop fertilizer gave way to a worm poop "tea" (allowing the company to buy worm poop from someone else) that could be sprayed on plants. With no money in the bank, packaging the tea required bottles and sprayers, and this was the turning point for TerraCycle. Using recycled soda bottles (initially retrieved from dumpsters and recycling bins before it was pointed out to Szaky that this was illegal), donated waste sprayer tops from bottle manufacturers, and shipped in donated misprinted boxes from packaging companies, the future path of the company was set.

The company has grown into a "detritivore" that diverts nonrecyclable waste away from the landfills into a profitable second retail life while teaching children about environmental awareness through their Terracycle Brigades. For Szaky, the journey is just beginning: "for me, the goal isn't growth for growth's sake, but rather to reduce—or even eliminate—the very substance on which our business is based: waste."

QUESTIONS

1. Why is up-cycling seen as an improvement over recycling?
2. Doesn't up-cycling just let manufacturers off the hook? They can continue to produce nonrecyclable materials and let companies like TerraCycle fix the problem for them? What do you think?
3. Critics of TerraCycle's business practices accuse it of greenwashing by taking materials straight from the original manufacturers rather than just from recycle drives. Is that a fair criticism? Why or why not?
4. Think of your company (or a company you have worked for in the past). How could your organization up-cycle?

*Sources:* Tom Szaky, *Revolution in a Bottle: How Terracycle Is Redefining Green Business* (New York: Portfolio, 2009); Natalie Hope McDonald, "Splendor in the Grass," *New Jersey Monthly,* December 20, 2007; Bo Burlingham, "The Coolest Little Start-Up in America," *Inc Magazine,* July 1, 2006; and Loren Feldman, "Garbage Mogul Makes Millions from Trash," cnnmoney.com, March 25, 2009.

# Case 13.3

## >> Pfizer: Going "Off-Label"

On September 2, 2009, Kathleen Sebelius, the secretary of Health and Human Services for the Obama administration, announced in a Washington news conference that pharmaceutical giant Pfizer had agreed to a $2.3 billion settlement over illegal promotion of its pain reliever Bextra. The agreement with the Justice Department extended to other brands in addition to Bextra, with $1.3 billion of the settlement representing a criminal penalty for Bextra, and $1 billion for civil fines in relation to three other drugs: Geodon, an antipsychotic medicine; Zyvox, an antibiotic; and Lyrica, an epilepsy medicine. The settlement also included a guilty plea for Pfizer unit Pharmacia & Upjohn to a single felony count of violation of the Food, Drug and Cosmetic Act for its promotion of Bextra. The settlement established a new record for prosecutors, far exceeding the $1.4 billion fine against Eli Lilly in January 2009 for illegal promotion of Zyprexa, an antipsychotic medicine.

Pfizer's conduct in aggressively promoting Bextra consisted of encouraging doctors to prescribe the drug for situations other than the Federal Drug Administration's approval as a pain reliever—what is referred to as going "off-label." The FDA had approved Bextra to relieve arthritis pain (at 10 milligrams a day) and menstrual pain (at 40 milligrams a day), but the Justice Department found evidence of the prescription of the drug at eight times the approved starting dose for migraine patients, and as a pre- and postsurgery pain reliever for knee operations.

The case against Pfizer had originated with a *qui tam* complaint under the Federal False Claims Act (FCA). *Qui tam* complaints, roughly translated as "one who sues for the king," are actions in which a private citizen (a "relator") brings an action on behalf of the government. Originating in English common law (hence the reference to the king), these lawsuits are most commonly referred to as whistle-blower lawsuits and fall under the protection of the FCA—legislation that was first enacted during the Civil War as the "informer's law" in an attempt to control the provision of poor-quality mules, rations, and ammunition by unscrupulous defense contractors. Originally enacted into law in 1863, the FCA was strengthened in a series of amendments in 1986 that granted treble the damages to be paid, granted protection to the whistle-blower from any retaliation from his or her employer, and increased the share of the damages paid to the whistle-blower.

'In the Army, I was expected to protect people at all costs. At Pfizer I was expected to increase profits at all costs, even when sales meant endangering lives.'

In this case, the relator, or whistle-blower, was West Point graduate John Kopchinski, who after leaving the army in 1992 was hired by Pfizer as a pharmaceutical sales representative. The evidence he compiled included e-mails and sales scripts outlining precisely how sales reps were expected to encourage doctors to broaden their use of Bextra (reps received a $50 bonus for each doctor who prescribed Bextra as standard care for surgery patients). Under the FCA rules, Kopchinski will receive $51.5 million of the money recovered by the Justice Department in addition to a portion of any other funds returned to various states involved in the settlement.

In a statement distributed by his attorneys at the Washington firm Phillips & Cohen, Kopchinksi commented: "In the Army, I was expected to protect people at all costs. At Pfizer I was expected to increase profits at all costs, even when sales meant endangering lives. I couldn't do that."

Ironically, the four-year investigation comes after Pfizer voluntarily pulled Bextra from the market in 2005 after concerns over the risks of heart attacks and strokes escalated following the removal of Merck's Vioxx drug a year earlier. Merck eventually settled about 50,000 lawsuits from Vioxx patients for a total of $4.85 billion. In October 2009, Pfizer announced the settlement of about 7,000 lawsuits from Bextra patients for $894 million. The statement settlement represented about 92 percent of the outstanding Bextra claims.

## QUESTIONS

1. As a pharmaceutical sales manager, how would you justify off-label promotion of one of your medicines to your sales reps?
2. With such multibillion-dollar settlements becoming frequent in the pharmaceutical industry, why would large companies like Pfizer continue to push their drugs beyond the FDA-approved uses?
3. What message is the Justice Department trying to send here?
4. Whistle-blowers who file complaints on behalf of the government *(qui tam)* are entitled to a portion of the damages. Whistle-blowers who file complaints as individual employees of corporations are not. Is that ethical? Why or why not?

*Source:* Carrie Johnson, "In Settlement: A Warning to Drugmakers," *The Washington Post,* September 3, 2009; Gardiner Harris, "Pfizer Pays $2.3 Billion to Settle Marketing Case," *The New York Times,* September 3, 2009; and Scott Hensley, "Pfizer Whistleblower Tells His Bextra Story," NPR's Health Blog, September 3, 2009, www.npr.org/blogs/health/2009/09/pfizer_whistleblower_tells_his.html.

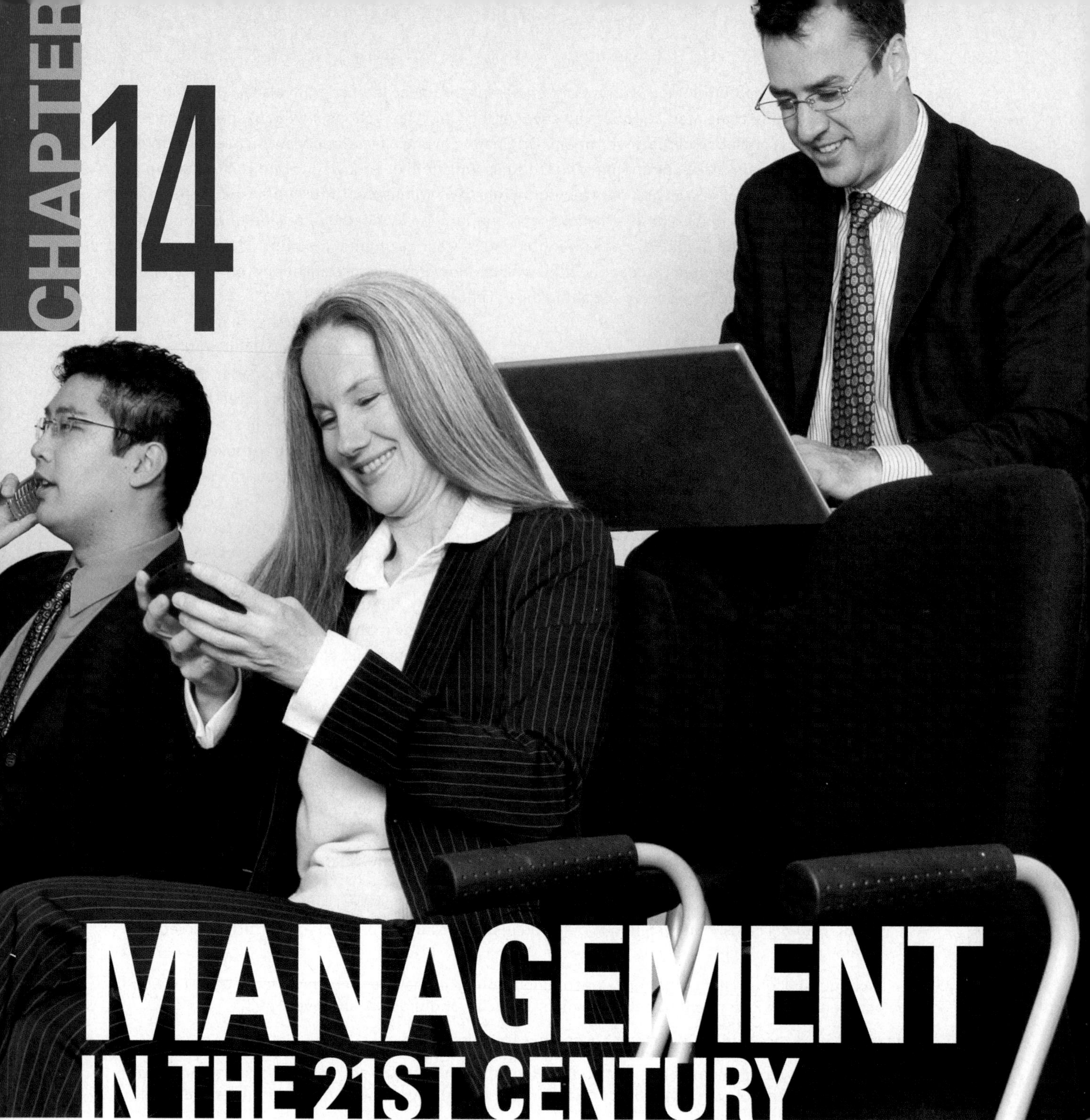


# MANAGEMENT IN THE 21ST CENTURY

"If you've spent any time inside large organizations, you know that expecting them to be strategically nimble, restlessly innovative, or a highly engaging place to work—or anything else than merely efficient—is like expecting a dog to do the tango."

**Gary Hamel, *The Future of Management***

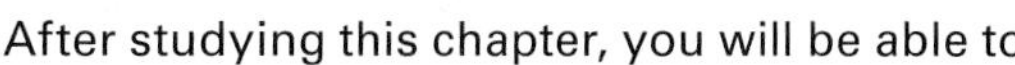

After studying this chapter, you will be able to:

1. Identify how technology affects the managerial role.
2. Review the challenges of managing a virtual team.
3. Identify the challenges of managing a mature workforce.
4. Explain the role of change in operational management.

## THE WORLD OF WORK Tony looks back

The e-mail from HR came as a complete surprise. Annual performance review? Had it really been a year already? "Where did the time go?" thought Tony. "It wasn't that long ago that I was wondering if I would ever make unit manager, and here I am up for my first review."

When he reported to Jerry Smith, performance reviews hadn't been such a big event. Jerry was great about giving regular feedback: what you were doing well, what you should be improving, and, most importantly for Jerry, asking how you were doing and if you needed anything. Plus, at that level of the organization, pay raises were small, rare, and usually applied to job titles rather than individual employees. Keeping your job was a sign you were doing good work.

This was different. As a unit manager, Tony was eligible for a bonus based on unit and corporate performance measures, and his individual performance was assessed against key performance indicators (KPIs), such as food costs, labor costs, revenue, and customer satisfaction scores. That had all been explained to Tony when he took the job after Jerry was promoted to regional manager. Tony's regional manager, Dawn Williams, had taken the time to ensure that he knew exactly what was expected of him and his team before he signed his employment agreement.

What had surprised Tony was the document attached to the e-mail from HR. It was titled "Employee Self-Appraisal," and asked him to summarize how he felt he had done this year, and then to submit the completed document to his supervisor before the performance appraisal meeting.

### QUESTIONS

1. How often do you receive feedback in your job? Is it helpful? Explain your answer.
2. Why would the supervisor want to see a self-appraisal before the meeting?
3. How would you rate Tony's performance this year? What has he done well? Where does he need to improve?
4. How would you rate your performance in your job this year? What have you done well? Where do you need to improve?

As we saw in Chapter 1, there is little doubt that significant changes occurred in the 20th century in all facets of American organizations and the manner in which those organizations are managed. From a management perspective, what changes are likely to occur as we move further into the 21st century?

The authors of the book *Beyond Workplace 2000* made some interesting projections as to what organizations and management might look like in the 21st century.

- Most American companies will find that they no longer can gain a competitive advantage from further improvements in quality, service, cost, or speed, since the gap between rivals on these traditional measures of performance will all but close.
- Every American business and every employee who works for an American business will be forced to become agile, flexible, and highly adaptive, since the product or service they will provide and the business processes they will employ will be in a constant state of change.
- Every American company will be forced to develop a much better understanding of what it does truly well and will invest its limited resources in developing and sustaining superiority in that unique knowledge, skill, or capability.
- Organizational structures will become extremely fluid. No longer will there be departments, units, divisions, or functional groups in most American businesses. There will only be multidisciplinary and multiskilled teams, and every team will be temporary.
- There will be a meltdown of the barrier between leader and follower, manager and worker. Bosses, in the traditional sense, will all but disappear. While there will be a few permanent leaders external to work and project teams, these people will act more as coordinators of team activities than as traditional leaders.[1]

Other, even more recent, projections about organizations and management in the future reinforce the central theme that future organizations will be more fluid and less rigid than in the past.[2]

Looking back on these predictions from 2010, one thing for certain is that the rate of change has continued to accelerate, and both organizations and managers will be required to adapt to these changes in the future. This chapter identifies four key areas that will dominate the future of management in the coming years: the growth of technology, the continued rise in virtual management, the ever-increasing pace of change, and the need to manage a noticeably different workforce.

## >> The Growth of Technology

It wasn't that long ago that many of the phrases and terms we now take for granted were brand new in our business vocabulary. The term *cyberspace* wasn't coined until the mid-1980s, and *e-commerce* (the abbreviated form of "electronic commerce") hasn't been around that long either—it was only as recently as 1994 that the first banner ad was placed on one of those newfangled Web sites everyone was talking about at the time.

In the two decades since the prefix *e-* started taking over our lives, technology has totally transformed our world. The world of business, and the role of a manager in business, has changed beyond all recognition. We now conduct business B2B (business to business), B2C (business to consumer), and even C2C (consumer to consumer) through electronic marketplaces such as eBay. Technology has condensed both time and space in the life of a manager:

- Complex calculations can now be processed in seconds.
- Information can be sent to multiple recipients anywhere in the world at the stroke of a computer key via e-mail.
- Vast amounts of information can be accessed through various search engines that can track down more data on a topic than you could ever use.
- *Google* is now a verb, even though the original selection of the name for the search engine was a spelling mistake (the original spelling was reputed to be "googol," a mathematical term representing $10^{100}$—1 followed by 100 zeroes—but the domain

name *google.com* was available and so an urban legend was born).

- Bricks-and-mortar stores have been replaced by "clicks-and-mortar" online vendors who may never see a customer in person. The largest book vendor in the world, Amazon.com, has no retail outlets at all.
- Traditional vendors now devote as many resources to their Web presence as they do to their physical storefront presence, and their marketing campaigns now emphasize organic search rankings and social networking campaigns on Facebook and Twitter over direct mail and radio or TV spots.
- Smartphones now carry more functionality than a room full of computers, and if the law attributed to Intel cofounder Gordon Moore holds true, the computing capacity of integrated circuits will continue to double every two years (more commonly quoted as 18 months) for the foreseeable future.

## [PROGRESS] ✓questions

1. Define the term *cyberspace*.
2. What is electronic commerce?
3. What is Moore's law, and who is Moore?
4. Explain the terms *B2B*, *B2C*, and *C2C*.

In the workplace, technology has pushed the development of management processes built around information rather than raw materials. One example of an information management process is enterprise resource planning (ERP), which involves the interconnection of all the functional departments of an organization on one common framework that is designed to give everyone in the organization instant access to the information they need to make key decisions in managing the organization's efficient performance. Developed from materials resource planning (the management of raw materials through a production process), ERP offers the promise of improved efficiency through the deliberate elimination of waste and rework. With current and accurate data available for all key decision points, the company is no longer required to commit significant resources based on projections—it can use hard data.

For customers, ERP technology has advanced into customer relationship management (CRM) technology, which promised the capacity for organizations to track every interaction or "touch point" with their customers, and for customers to know the whereabouts of their order in the manufacturing and/or delivery process at any time, in real time.

In addition, technology has pushed the customer further away from the company. Online e-commerce transactions now allow customers to purchase goods and services from an organization without ever speaking to or meeting with an employee. Customer service pages on Web sites and automated voice mail menus (assuming you can find a number for the organization on the Web site) manage interactions as transactions rather than opportunities to engage your customers in a dialog. If you do succeed in reaching someone, it's likely that representative is sitting in a cube on the other side of the world.

**Study Alert!**

How has technology affected the work you perform in your job? How would your productivity change if you were asked to perform without a computer? Would you be able to do your job without e-mail, spreadsheets, or Internet searches?

Satisfaction surveys can be completed using pop-up dialog boxes on the Web site, and your purchase history and buying profile can be documented, stored, analyzed, and fed back to you as "recommended items" using increasingly sophisticated mathematical algorithms.

# Thinking Critically 14.1

## >> How Twitter Is Changing the Business World

Launched in 2006, *Twitter* is a free social networking and microblogging service that enables users to send and receive *tweets*—brief, text-based messages with a maximum of 140 characters. Functioning in the same manner on the Web as short message service (SMS) texting does on mobile phones, tweets are displayed on the author's profile page and viewed by "followers." Access to that profile page can be restricted to specific friends or, typically, left as open access.

On February 5, 2010, Sun Microsystems CEO Jonathan Schwartz, who had succeeded Sun cofounder Scott McNealy as CEO in 2006, announced his widely anticipated resignation in a tweet in the form of a haiku (a form of Japanese poetry): "Financial crisis/stalled too many customers/CEO no more." The takeover of Sun Microsystems by Oracle in 2009 had sealed Schwartz's fate, but his unique use of a tweet as a resignation letter illustrated the extent to which Twitter has entered the mainstream business culture.

Critics of the service argue that it represents nothing more than another frustrating intrusion into your life, like text messages and e-mails, and while there are million-plus followers for celebrities like Oprah and Ashton Kutcher, there are far more small groups of a dozen or more folks keeping in touch on a wide range of subjects. Yes, some are doing nothing more than providing details of what they ate for breakfast this morning, but as the service has grown, the emphasis has moved from minute-by-minute thoughts and updates to a greater emphasis on sharing information. Although 140 characters isn't a lot of room, if it can link you to a 10,000-word article or an event or a new blog posting, the broader goal of *communication* is served. In contrast to the breadth and depth of Google's ever-expanding search universe, and the promise of smarter searching with increasingly sophisticated algorithms, Twitter offers efficiency and immediacy—you follow the people you like and follow up on their suggestions.

New uses for the service continue to emerge. In May 2009 an anticommunist uprising in Moldavia was organized via Twitter. In the January 2010 earthquake in Haiti, names of survivors were relayed to frantic families around the world, and fund-raising efforts reached millions of dollars in only a few days as a direct result of the availability of Twitter.

How does the world of business benefit from this new service? Many large companies have embraced the phenomenon with multiple corporate Twitter accounts that encourage direct dialogue with customers and prospects about products and services. This serves multiple goals—further endorsing your brand, building brand loyalty, and promoting the transparency of your company (provided you are seen to respond proactively to customer tweets). This is just the beginning, however. We have yet to see the full impact of the immediacy of this service in the business world. For example, Angie's List and *Consumer Reports* may give you detailed assessments of contractors and products on a Web site or a printed report, but what if you could get an assessment of the work done by a plumber as soon as his truck leaves the driveway of a customer who just used his company?

**QUESTIONS**

1. "Twitter offers efficiency and immediacy." Why is that important?
2. Is the 140-character limit an obstacle to the future growth of Twitter? Why or why not?
3. How can a company benefit from a corporate Twitter account?
4. Are there any disadvantages to a corporate Twitter account?

*Source:* Brandon Bailey, "Sun Microsystems Says Farewell via Twitter Haiku," *San Jose Mercury News*, February 5, 2010; David Carr, "Why Twitter Will Endure," *The New York Times*, January 1, 2010; and Steven Johnson, "How Twitter Will Change the Way We Live," *Time*, June 5, 2009.

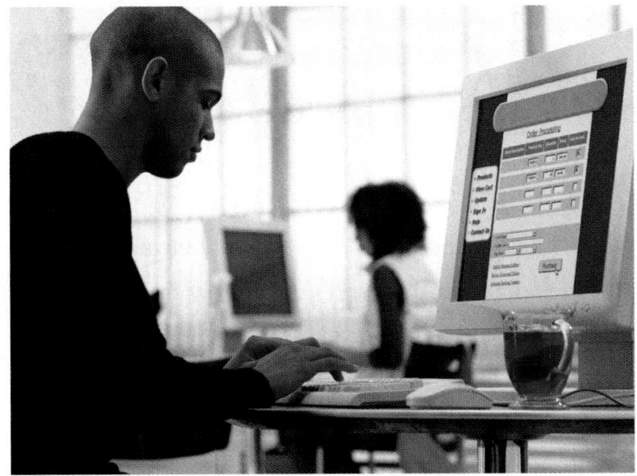

## >> Virtual Management

Technological advancement has produced a business environment in which the traditional organizational framework of functional departments dispersed by geographic location has been replaced by a complex network of suppliers, partners, and collaborators who interact in the delivery of the organization's products and/or services from vast distances over an electronic platform. For managers, this presents a unique set of challenges:

**From the** PERSPECTIVE OF...

**A Telecommuter** How do you adjust to a company's culture if you're never in the office? What are the advantages and disadvantages of working from a remote office or home office?

1. How do you manage a team that may be spread across 50 states or 20 countries?
2. The technology may be there to support conference calls or webinars or videoconferences, but how do you build a team when the team members never meet in person?
3. Outsourcing offers tremendous cost savings when you take advantage of lower labor costs in other countries, but how much of your proprietary information are you willing to share with this "partner" in order to make this new relationship work?
4. If your company has grown on the basis of a high-quality product that you designed and manufactured in-house, and you must now transfer that production overseas in order to maintain your profit margins, how do you know you can maintain that quality working through a third-party vendor?

As we reviewed in Chapter 7, a *virtual organization* is one in which business partners and teams work together across geographic or organizational boundaries by means of information technology.[3] The attractions of this type of organization are both operational and financial. Having people on the ground in all your markets without carrying the overhead of fully staffed corporate offices can keep you connected to the ever-changing needs of your global customer base at a much lower cost. If you can keep those people employed as "independent contractors" without the expense of employer taxes, Social Security, or employee benefits, the cost savings can be even greater. Technology has made all of this possible, provided you can embrace an organizational structure that is dramatically different from the traditional pyramid model.

Managing a team that may only meet face to face across a conference table once or twice a year presents a series of challenges for a manager. The traditional command-and-control model of management is built on visibility, by which you keep a regular eye on your people and notify them immediately if they step out of line in any way. However, if your team is scattered across the globe, your interactions are going to be by e-mail or voice mail with regularly scheduled conference calls or videoconferences to keep everyone updated. Project management software and the increased popularity of wiki workspaces, where multiple people have access to the same project document, can keep the momentum of the team moving forward, but such a dynamic work environment can often change the role of a manager

### [PROGRESS] ✓questions

5. What is a virtual organization?
6. What are some of the challenges managers face in a virtual organization?
7. How would you manage a virtual team?
8. Can the technology of videoconferences replace the human interaction of meeting with stakeholders in person? Why or why not?

# Thinking Critically 14.2

## >> Virtual Organization Creates Virtual Convention

The Real Estate Cyberspace Society (RECS) was founded in 1996 in Boston as a completely virtual organization. The for-profit society developed a system for delivering audiotapes and newsletters to help real estate professionals who were interested in using technology and the Internet to improve their business. After September 11, 2001, the society's staff accurately predicted that member and exhibitor participation would decline at traditional in-person events. Leveraging its online experiences, the society's leaders decided to produce an online convention in April 2002. The event was highly successful with some 22,000 real estate professionals attending across five days. The attendees registered for the convention, listened to speakers, networked, and visited exhibitor booths—all online.

In April 2004, the convention was extended from five to seven days, and 42,000 real estate professionals attended. During the seven days of the convention, participants could go to the exposition and view the exhibits at any time and have live chats with exhibitors. Each day four national speakers were showcased. Attendees could listen to these speakers and print out their handouts at any time during the scheduled 24-hour day. The convention also featured three keynote speakers. Participants unable to attend the keynote sessions live could retrieve slides, hear the talk, and get the handouts online at their own convenience.

**QUESTIONS**

1. How is it possible to attend an entire convention online?
2. Visit the Real Estate Cyberspace Society at **www.recyber.com.** How has the organization of the convention changed since it was first created?
3. What are the four key advantages that RECS offers its members?
4. Would you attend an online convention in your industry? Why or why not?

*Source:* John M. Peckham III, "Virtual Society, Virtual Convention," *Association Management*, December 2004, p. 55.

**Study Alert!**

Think of the company you work for (or one you have worked for in the past). Are there any examples of virtual management in current operating practices? If so, what are they? If not, where could the company take advantage of this technology?

from autocratic leader to democratic facilitator. Corporate policies and procedures can ensure standardized business practices, but it's up to the manager to build a cohesive team among people who assess and react to each other's performance in e-mail messages and conference calls rather than observed behavior in the office or on the factory floor. Offline conversations between workers are now handled with "back-channel" e-mails, and disagreements can generate lengthy e-mail trails copied to multiple participants who may or may not be directly involved in the issue (and a few blind-copied, or "bcc," people just to be safe).

Setting an expected standard of behavior and enforcing that standard are much more difficult if you cannot observe that behavior. A virtual environment requires a greater degree of trust in the professionalism of your people and places a greater emphasis on making the right hire from the outset.

WORKING FROM HOME

Six months ago, your company made a dramatic restructuring of job designs. When the lease for the corporate headquarters came up for renewal, the company reduced the amount of square footage it was leasing and invested the savings in better IT equipment to allow employees to telecommute (i.e., work from home). You were able to put a desk and chair in the corner of your living room, and with a new laptop and Internet connection paid for by the company, your home office was up and running in no time.

The change in your work life has been amazing. With no commuting time and no interruptions, you can get your work done in half the time, and with the growing availability of Wi-Fi spots around your town, you can work at the coffee shop, the bookstore, and even in the local park if the weather's good. Best of all, the extra free time is allowing you to take on some projects as a freelancer on consulting sites like Sologig and eLance. Life is good!

ETHICAL
MANAGEMENT
What are the risks of cutting your hours as a telecommuter?


**QUESTIONS**

1. What would prompt your company to make such a dramatic restructuring of job designs?
2. If you're able to get your assigned work done in half the time, does that automatically make the remaining time yours to work independently? Why or why not?
3. What do you think your boss would say if she found out?
4. When the company announces yet another round of restructuring, you are notified that it will be conducting an audit of all telecommuting positions. Now what will you do?

# >> The Silver Tsunami: Managing a Mature Workforce

Any strategic planning initiative requires an organization to project what the future holds in store. Inflation, deflation, new products, new competitors, economic recession—all these factors will have a direct impact on the fortunes of the company and the choices that company must make if it is to survive over the long term. Much of that projection is data-driven, and much of it is also guesswork. Ask a group of oil traders what the price of oil will be per barrel next year, and they will answer in a range from $25 per barrel to $125 per barrel, all based on their interpretation of the same market data.

One external factor that managers can be sure of is the "age wave," or "silver tsunami," that is on its way. The global workforce is aging rapidly, and by reviewing social demographic census data, we can predict fairly accurately when businesses will start to feel the effects of this trend. By 2012, one in three American workers will be over the age of 50. China, which enforced a one-child-per-family policy in the 1970s to control population growth, is facing the same trend of an aging workforce, with no young workers coming through to fill all the vacancies created as workers reach retirement age.

Management research and training over the last three decades has focused on employee retention as a cost-saving mechanism—keeping trained workers is much more cost effective than constantly training new hire replacements. This silver tsunami will require a different perspective, forcing managers to learn how to address the needs of older workers rather than developing succession plans for when those older workers retire.

This leads us to the question: How different are the needs and expectations of mature workers likely to be? Eric Lesser with IBM's Institute for Business Value identified six strategies for addressing the challenges of a mature workforce:[4]

- *Retain valued employees through developing alternative work arrangements.* This can include modified work schedules as well as modified work environments. ASDA, the United Kingdom's largest retailer (and a subsidiary of Walmart), is already gaining experience with the silver tsunami, with 19 percent of its workforce over 50 years of age. ASDA offers modified work schedules such as "Benidorm leave" (three months unpaid leave between January and March, which Americans would probably refer to as "snowbird leave"), and "grandparent leave" (a week of unpaid leave after the birth of a grandchild). The payoff for this flexibility? Absenteeism rates that are less than a third of the company's average. Abbott Laboratories took a similar approach by allowing veteran employees to work four-day weeks or take an additional 25 days of vacation time per year.

BMW tried a different approach by staffing a production line exclusively with the same mature workers that they anticipate will dominate its workforce in the near future. At first, the "pensioner's line" was less productive, but with a few ergonomic modifications such as adjustable tables, new chairs, and magnifying lenses, the "mature line" was able to match the productivity levels of the rest of the factory.

- *Provide opportunities for workers to continually update their skills.* Corporate training programs tend to front-load training in the early years of service with an organization, which means that many mature workers haven't received training for several years. Skills training can be equipment-technology-based or focus on the soft skills of team building, mentoring, or interpersonal skills. Allowing work veterans to pursue these training schedules as a cohort also serves to build trust and camaraderie.
- *Facilitate the coexistence of multiple generations in the workforce.* Generation gaps in the workforce can present barriers and create stereotypes on both sides, where young employees are resented for not having "paid their dues" and mature workers are dismissed as being "past it." Exposing mature workers to new skills as a combined group will help remove those barriers.
- *Help ensure that mature workers are able to effectively use technology in the workplace.* Mature workers may express more nervousness with new equipment and technology, but research has shown that their diligence in learning the ins and outs of the new equipment far exceeds their younger counterparts, who make it a matter of personal pride to "figure out" the new equipment without reading the user manual or calling tech support.

In addition to retaining workers, managers will also need to target mature workers in their recruitment processes to ensure sufficient resources are on hand to maintain production capacity:

- *Redirect recruiting and sourcing efforts to include mature workers.* Danish supermarket group Netto is experimenting with stores that are exclusively staffed with employees over 45 years of age. The Walt Disney Company targets mature workers for staffing their attractions at peak season because of the lower absenteeism that ASDA identified and the greater scheduling flexibility they offer (specifically no child care issues or minimum earning requirements).
- *Attracting mature workers does not have to be limited to entry-level positions.* Building on the scheduling flexibility of temporary or project-based personnel, pharmaceutical companies, such as Procter & Gamble and Eli Lilly, have supported "Yourencore.com," a contracting agency that recruits scientists and engineers for part-time, short-term contracts, with the promise that they are "accelerating innovation through proven experience."[5]

One economic factor that looks destined to support organizations and their managers through this age wave is the recent economic recession. As workers have seen their retirement accounts decline in value and the equity in their homes evaporate, postponing retirement has become a matter of financial necessity.

## PROGRESS ✓questions

9. Where did this silver tsunami come from?
10. Why should managers be concerned about the age of their workers?
11. What alternative work arrangements could be proposed for a mature workforce?
12. What types of skills would mature workers need to consider updating?

# >> Managing Change

The concept of change in a business environment is no longer considered in terms of "if," but rather "when," and "how much and how quickly." The ability to manage people and steer an organization through

ADDING VALUE . . .

## First Line Focus

*As we have seen in the chapters of this book, effective management demands control over operational policies and procedures. Organizations achieve efficiency and year-on-year growth through the development of systems that establish and maintain quality in every aspect of those organizations—from manufacturing to sales and marketing of the product or service you deliver to your customers. Managers play a vital role in the day-to-day oversight of those systems, but if you aspire to add real value to your organization in the future, learn to be comfortable with change. Accelerating technological growth on a global scale is rewriting many of the business rules we are taught in college, and organizations can no longer count on a period of rest and respite when they achieve a dominant position in their market. The days of "resting on your laurels" are long gone, and truly effective managers must be able to question everything, all the time. Just because your current product design or service delivery model is beating the competition doesn't mean that the situation won't change in 30, 60, or 90 days from now, so be prepared to go back to the drawing board and change that product or policy or procedure now, before your competitors change it for you.*

periods of significant change is seen as an absolute requirement for any rising executive, and change management now earns its own course in most business degree programs.

Unfortunately, even though there is a general acceptance that change is a constant force in business, many change initiatives continue to fail spectacularly. By spectacularly, we mean serious damage inflicted to the point of carnage with divisions sold or closed, assets disposed of at bargain prices, layoffs by the thousands with surviving employees left in a state of shock and extreme paranoia, and corporate brands irreparably harmed.

If this seems to make no sense, consider the driving force for change—efficiency and improved profitability. This has a tendency to sell change initiatives on the basis of the numbers without full consideration as to *how* the change will be implemented. Merging two former competitors will generate promised cost savings and economies of scale with no concern for how two opposing cultures will suddenly find a way to work together. Harvard Business School Professor John Kotter identified eight common errors that succeed in derailing many change initiatives—and these were errors shared by small and large businesses alike:[6]

**Study Alert !**

By 2012, one in three American workers will be over the age of 50. As a young leader, how would you manage a workforce where the average age was much higher than yours?

- Allowing too much complacency
- Failing to create a sufficiently powerful guiding coalition
- Underestimating the power of vision
- Undercommunicating the vision by a factor of 10 (or 100 or even 1,000)
- Permitting obstacles to block the new vision
- Failing to create short-term wins
- Declaring victory too soon
- Neglecting to anchor changes firmly in the corporate culture

As you can see, these errors are not complex in nature, but they are surprisingly easy to make. For future managers, the pressure to drive change will only increase as continued growth and profitability are sought on a global platform rather than a domestic one. If we can generate such carnage in our

### PROGRESS ✓questions

13. How are change initiatives sold "on the basis of the numbers"?
14. Which is more important: how the change will benefit the company or how the change will be implemented? Explain your answer.
15. Which of Kotter's eight mistakes is the toughest to fix? Why?
16. Summarize a change initiative in which you were involved at your company. How did it turn out in the end?

**Study Alert!**

If change is such a constant force in business, why do so many change initiatives fail so spectacularly? What are some ways that leadership can improve change in the workplace? What are the benefits to positive change experiences for employees?

own sandbox, the potential for damage to be inflicted with international or global mergers is downright scary.

In his 1997 book *The Innovator's Dilemma,* Clayton M. Christensen (a Harvard colleague of Kotter's) acknowledged the many reasons why companies can stumble: "Bureaucracy, arrogance, tired executive blood, poor planning, short-term investment horizons, inadequate skills and resources, and just plain bad luck."[7] He then proposed that what should really be keeping managers up at night was the potential for "disruptive technologies" to destroy a company's future prospects. Whether it's Ford's Model T bringing an abrupt end to the horse-drawn carriage industry, digital photography replacing film photography, or flash drives replacing disk drives, these new technologies appear to come out of nowhere and catch the traditional market leaders completely by surprise.

If we combine this potential with an increasing pace of technological advancement, the management of change now becomes a matter of undertaking major rather than minor initiatives if a company is to have any hope of holding on to its market position for long enough at the very least to recover its investment and at best to generate a profit on that investment.

**From the PERSPECTIVE OF...**

**A Senior Employee** I've worked for this company for 15 years and plan to work for a few more yet. Plus, if I go, who will replace me? These machines can be temperamental, and they don't teach you the tricks and techniques to keeping them running in a training class—you pick that stuff up over time.

## >> Conclusion: Where Do We Go from Here?

How many years do you have to serve before you can be considered to be an experienced or *veteran* manager? If you had asked that question as recently as 10 years ago, you would have received an answer that required you to think in decades rather than years. Today, the pace of change in business has become so fast that managers can look at their

**INFORMATION IS POWER**

You manage the Web services department of a small IT company. Your department is responsible for helping clients with the design and content of their Web sites and the promotion of those Web sites through search engine optimization (SEO). Your clients typically earn top page rankings and their businesses see significant increases in Web traffic and sales revenue as a result of your work.

One of your clients recently started paying his invoices late. Instead of paying in 10 days to take advantage of an early payment discount, invoices are now going unpaid for 120 days or more. The client's company appears to be doing okay, and he just purchased a brand new sports car. Your director, however, is concerned that too much money is being taken out of the client's business, and he instructs you to suspend the client's account and "undo all the work we did for him since the last paid invoice, since he hasn't paid us for it."

You have all the access information for the client's Web site hosting company, but you're not sure this is the right way to address the issue of nonpayment with the client. Should you "undo all the work"? Why or why not?

ETHICAL
MANAGEMENT
How do you deal with a client who owes money for services already rendered?

organizations and see dramatic changes occurring in months as opposed to years. Managers now consider themselves to be veterans after surviving a new product implementation, a companywide layoff, or the ever-popular merger with a former competitor. New products and new divisions can appear and old divisions can disappear in the blink of an eye. Just when you think you have the competition on the run, it comes up with a new product that puts it years ahead of you in the marketplace, or, even worse, a new competitor shows up with a product that makes your best-selling product obsolete! Welcome to management in the 21st century. The breakneck pace of change will make your head spin, but if you can rise to the challenge and grasp every opportunity to deliver inventive solutions with the help of a motivated and creative team of people who look to you for guidance and leadership, we can guarantee that you will never be bored!

## For REVIEW >>

1. Identify how technology affects the managerial role.

   Technology can be seen as a mixed blessing for managers. It can present tools with tremendous potential to improve quality, efficiency, and speed of response in business transactions. However, each improvement becomes the new benchmark for competitors to aim for, which then requires companies to find the next improvement.

2. Review the challenges of managing a virtual team.

   Managing people is essentially a humanistic function. You are responsible for their successful performance against organizational targets and quotas. For many managers, that job is made easier by having those people where you can keep an eye on them. Unfortunately the needs of modern commerce no longer support that ideal. With employees spread across the globe, management is now more about delegation of tasks and responsibilities and supporting your people in the successful performance of their jobs. Personal interaction may be less frequent, but we now have multiple mechanisms for frequent communication—some pestered employees might argue that there are too many mechanisms.

3. Identify the challenges of managing a mature workforce.

   As demographics change, managers will see a distinct shift in the profile of their employees. Mature workers will outnumber younger workers. This means the emphasis will shift from older workers teaching skills to the new kids before retiring, to companies finding ways to keep their mature workers around as long as is mutually beneficial for both parties. The career path will shift from steady promotion up the ranks of the organization before retirement to a later stage where mature employees may elect to step back from high-visibility senior positions and fill advisory or training roles to help the company maximize its intellectual knowledge.

4. Explain the role of change in operational management.

   The concept of change in a business environment is no longer considered in terms of "if," but "when" and "how much and how quickly." The ability to manage people and steer an organization through periods of significant change is now seen as an absolute requirement for any effective business executive. In practical terms, this means that every element of a company's operation must be managed with the expectations that nothing is taken for granted and that managers can never become complacent about their success. Every established policy and procedure should be reexamined and every assumption questioned on a regular basis to ensure that the company is always performing at its absolute maximum potential.

# THE WORLD of Work >>

## TONY LOOKS FORWARD *(continued from page 333)*

The self-appraisal process had, Tony thought, been very useful in preparing for his performance evaluation meeting with Dawn. At the end of his first year as manager of this Taco Barn, Tony felt proud of the work that he had done and grateful for the support of his team, Jerry Smith (his former boss), and Dawn. He felt that it had been a group effort, and he went great lengths to stress that as he reviewed his performance over the past year and as he responded to Dawn's comments about how happy she was with his unit's performance.

After reviewing Tony's past performance, Dawn moved on to his goals and objectives for the year ahead. The metrics for unit performance were the same—labor and food cost targets, revenue and average check targets, and, Tony's favorite, customer satisfaction scores from Taco Barn patrons and "mystery diners" that the corporation hired to inspect the "customer experience" at its restaurants on a regular basis. The goals included a couple of aggressive targets—the company referred to them as "stretch targets"—for lower labor costs and higher average check size. However, with the team he had in place and Kevin as his assistant manager, Tony was confident that they could hit them, and the bonus plan up for grabs for those units that did hit the targets would make the extra effort worthwhile.

Then Dawn caught Tony by surprise with some straightforward questions: "What about you, Tony? How can we support your development over the next year? Do you have any specific goals or objectives in mind?"

At first, Tony wasn't sure how to respond. "Don't I have enough to do with all those unit targets?" he thought. "And now you want me to take on a self-improvement project too?" Then it hit him—Dawn wasn't looking to give him more work. She was making sure that he had the opportunity to improve his value to the organization. From that perspective, he saw it as an investment *in* him rather than another demand *on* him.

"Well," Tony said, "I'd like to learn Spanish; I'd like to get more involved in the chamber of commerce to raise our profile in the local community; but mostly I've been thinking a lot lately about going back to college and finishing my degree. Can Taco Barn help me do that?"

**QUESTIONS**

1. What performance metrics do you have to meet in your job?
2. Which of those metrics have stretch targets attached to them?
3. Why would Tony be surprised by a question about personal goals from his boss?
4. How would you respond to Dawn's question? What personal goals would you like to pursue?

## Think << AND DISCUSS

1. How has technological growth affected the role of a manager?
2. What are the challenges involved in running a virtual business?
3. What are the advantages and disadvantages of operating an exclusively e-commerce business (one that has no retail locations)?
4. Just because services like Facebook and Twitter are available, should every business use them? Why or why not?
5. Given a choice between young employees and more mature employees, which group would be easier to manage? Explain your answer.
6. If we acknowledge that change is a fact of business life, how do we prepare for that?

## INTERNET In Action >>

1. Research the customer support function of an online vendor you use regularly. Answer the following questions:
   a. How does a customer locate the customer support function?
   b. What support functions are available? E-mail, live chat, telephone, Web-based FAQs?
   c. Can you rate the usefulness of an FAQ article? In what way?
   d. What other support services are available for this vendor?
   e. How would you rate your support experience with the vendor?
   f. What would you do to improve the support function?
2. High frequency and high touch: In recognition of the growing prominence of social networking, many companies are incorporating frequent and targeted messages to customers and prospects as part of their sales and marketing strategies. Review the business services that Facebook and Twitter have to offer, and propose a social networking campaign for your organization (or an organization you have worked for in the past).

1. **For and Against**

   Divide the class into two groups, and prepare arguments *for* and *against* the following position: "Corporations are obligated to incorporate any cost-saving technology, in order to satisfy the expectations of shareholders. Any negative impact on the overall customer service experience should be ignored." Be prepared to present your case to your fellow students.

2. **A Declaration of Independence**

   Review Whole Foods Market's "Declaration of Independence" at **www.wholefoodsmarket.com/company/declaration.php.** Divide into groups of three or four, and select an organization that one of the group members either works for currently or has worked for in the past. Based on your knowledge of the organization and some additional research, create a new "corporate philosophy statement" for the organization with the same tone and style as the "Declaration of Independence" for Whole Foods Market. Be prepared to present your statement to your classmates.

# Case 14.1

## >> AOL–Time Warner: Happily Never After • The biggest merger of its day was doomed to fail.

When the proposed merger of America Online (AOL) and Time Warner was announced on January 10, 2000, the deal was perceived as both stunning in its size (a combined value of $350 billion) and historic in its significance. The near hysterical excitement over the potential of new opportunities offered by the Internet gave AOL a stock price valued at twice that of Time Warner, even though AOL was generating only half the sales of its more "traditional" counterpart in the magazine, movie, and cable business.

The deal, it was argued, represented the classic win-win scenario. AOL cofounder Steve Case led a company at the forefront of a hyperactive world of digital media. He could deliver the e-mail users and the Web site visitors (the highly prized "eyeballs" for advertisers). At the time it seemed that AOL was announcing a new advertising deal every day. What Case needed was content to make sure his customers would have a reason to visit their AOL accounts several times a day, taking in a few ads with each visit.

For Time Warner chairman and chief executive Gerald M. Levin, there was increasing criticism that the content-rich company was bogged down in its own past glories and struggling to make the move forward into this exciting new world of digital media on the World Wide Web, despite an earlier announcement of a $500 million capital investment in new technology.

From a strategic management perspective, both companies were dealing with a make-or-buy decision—either invest the dollars to build divisions from the ground up or make strategic acquisitions to bring the expertise in-house. Case was savvy enough to realize that the high valuation of AOL stock gave him a window of opportunity to make a purchase using stock as the currency. Levin, whose stock had remained static during these crazy days of Internet speculation, was facing the prospect of a partnership rather than an outright purchase.

Promoted as a merger of equals, the deal was really an acquisition of Time Warner by AOL, and in hindsight the deal was doomed to failure from the outset. Struggling with its own internal challenges as the company endeavored to handle exponential growth (and Wall Street expectations of even greater growth in the future), AOL didn't have the time to develop a stable culture and operating practices to introduce into this new relationship. Time Warner, on the other hand, had a well-established traditional business philosophy that analysts dismissed as "old school" and "dinosaur management" in this new era. In other words, merging the two companies would be like trying to mix oil and water.

By January 2010, the corporate marriage had ended in a divorce that many analysts had considered an inevitability. The AOL–Time Warner merger was now the stuff of business school case legend, and after job losses in the thousands, subsequent investigations by the Securities and Exchange Commission (SEC) and the Justice Department over inflated earnings statements, and multiple executive restructurings, the companies went their separate ways with a combined value of less that $50 billion—one-seventh of their stated value a decade earlier.

QUESTIONS

1. Why were Case and Levin facing a make-or-buy decision?
2. Who stood to gain the most from the deal—AOL or Time Warner? Explain your answer.
3. If AOL were really purchasing Time Warner, why would it refer to the transaction as a *merger?*
4. Was the merger doomed to fail? Or could the situation have been handled differently?

*Source:* Tim Arango, "How the AOL-Time Warner Merger Went So Wrong," *The New York Times*, January 11, 2010; Josh Quittner, "Why AOL-Time Warner Wasn't Doomed to Failure," *Time*, May 28, 2009; Daniel Ohrent et al., "AOL-Time Warner Merger: Happily Ever After?" *Time*, January 24, 2000; and Alec Klein, *Stealing Time* (New York: Simon & Schuster, 2003).

# Case 14.2

## >> Putting the Money to Better Use: Pepsi Skips the 2010 SuperBowl

For decades, the Super Bowl of the National Football League has provided a venue for global brands to reach 100 million strong audiences in a single event. Typically, advertising spots reach premium prices (reported to be $3 million for 30 seconds in 2010 at Super Bowl XLIV between the Indianapolis Colts and the New Orleans Saints) and provide an opportunity for "signature," or "event," ads to be launched. Ever since Apple's "1984" ad was attributed with breaking new ground for Super Bowl advertisements, interest in which company will advertise and how it will communicate its message in this venue has never really waned. The caliber of ads has varied considerably from the "Bud-weis-er" frogs to Pepsi's adolescent lust over supermodel Cindy Crawford drinking a can of soda.

In 2010 Pepsi, a Super Bowl advertiser for the previous 23 years, elected to sit out Super Bowl XLIV and leave the market open for rival Coca Cola. Was this an admission that its advertising agency had failed to come up with a suitable event ad that year? Or perhaps an acknowledgment that spending $3 million for 30 seconds (Pepsi typically purchases multiple 30-second spots, spending $33 million on the 2009 Super Bowl) would be perceived as wasteful in such dire economic times?

*Continued on next page*

Continued from page 347

For a company with a product that many health advocates criticize as essentially carbonated sugar water, selling "the sizzle more than the steak" has been a matter of corporate policy since the organization was formed, and the savvy marketing of the "Pepsi Generation" has become the stuff of business legend. However, Pepsi's move seems to represent an acknowledgment that mass-market advertising toward a large audience population may not be as effective as targeted campaigns toward a more focused demographic—quality over quantity. On that basis, the multimillion-dollar ad not spent on the Super Bowl was replaced with a heavily promoted social media campaign for a new "Pepsi Refresh" initiative from the company's Web site. With a commitment to donate $20 million in grant funding, Pepsi elected to promote projects in six categories: health, arts and culture, food and shelter, the planet, neighborhoods, and education. The campaign encouraged people to visit the Web site **www.refresheverything.com** and to follow the projects through Facebook and Twitter to vote on submitted project ideas and propose ideas of their own. The $20 million will be distributed on a planned schedule—each month up to 32 grants will be awarded, with up to two $250,000 grants for large organizations and smaller grants in denominations of $50,000, $25,000, and $5,000 for smaller groups and individual projects.

Mass-market advertising toward a large audience population may not be as effective as targeted campaigns toward a more focused demographic

Pepsi certainly succeeded in grabbing media attention with the decision to opt out of the traditional Super Bowl advertising circus, but critics remained skeptical of its motives. The idea of encouraging a strong social message for the organization, and involving customers more directly in that conversation, was seen as an effective alignment with new social media trends. However, launching a campaign with such a strong social and environmental message, it was argued, could have been more successful with an advertisement for a captive audience of 100 million Super Bowl watchers. In addition, allowing Frito-Lay (another division of parent company PepsiCo) to continue with its $5 million "Crash the Super Bowl" contest for Doritos snack chips suggested that the "refresh everything" campaign was restricted to Pepsi rather than the whole organization.

It remains to be seen whether leaving the market open for traditional advertisers, like Coca Cola and Anheuser Busch's Budweiser, and taking an environmental high road with a social media campaign will pay off for Pepsi. If Pepsi returns in force to the 2011 Super Bowl, or other organizations decide to launch their own campaigns, we guess we'll have our answer.

## QUESTIONS

1. Why do you think Pepsi didn't choose the Super Bowl to launch such a fundamentally different campaign?
2. Does the fact that a sister division of PepsiCo (Doritos) will continue its traditional Super Bowl ad campaign weaken the Pepsi message here? Why or why not?
3. What happens if this new approach doesn't work?
4. Do you expect other companies to follow Pepsi's example? Why or why not?

*Source:* Ariel Schwartz, "Pepsi Ditches the Super Bowl; Embraces Crowd-Sourced Philanthropy Instead," *Fast Company*, January 4, 2010; Sean Gregory, "Behind Pepsi's Choice to Skip This Year's Super Bowl," *Time*, February 3, 2010; and Stuart Elliott, "An Advocacy Ad Elevates Interest in All the Ads," *The New York Times*, February 5, 2010.

# Case 14.3

## >> Managing the Needs of a Graying Workforce

In the 1976 science fiction movie *Logan's Run,* an idyllic future for the human race of the 23rd century has been achieved after an ecological disaster with one major societal change: life ends after age 30 in a ceremonial ritual. (Ironically, in a planned 2012 remake of the movie, the termination age has been reduced to 21.) In a similar vein, the movie *Children of Men* portrays a world in which the human race has lost the capacity to reproduce and features television commercials for suicide drugs for those unwilling or unable to face what the future holds for them. In the literary world, Christopher Buckley's *Boomsday* follows the fortunes of a blogger activist named Cassandra Devine, whose call for ritual mass euthanasia in the same manner as *Logan's Run* incites a global debate.

Dramatic and far-fetched? Absolutely, but beneath the artistic license of storytelling lies a real demographic shift: The global working population is getting older, and managers face hard choices in learning to meet the needs of that new "graying" workforce. With health insurance providers pricing benefit plans according to the age profile of your company's workforce, a graying employee population can quickly become an expensive cost item to cover.

The enforcement of mandatory retirement ages has always managed this problem in the past, allowing older workers to be handed over to Medicare membership rolls. However, as we have seen in this chapter, companies now have a vested interest in keeping senior employees around, and if the government chooses to fix an anticipated funding shortfall for Social Security and Medicare by extending retirement ages, companies will be faced with a higher average age for their employee population and correspondingly higher benefit plan premiums.

The solution? First, change your perspective on the issue: "The maturing workforce is often seen as an issue to be dealt with instead of a great opportunity to be leveraged," says Lorrie Foster, director of research working groups at the Conference Board. "The skills and knowledge mature workers possess can be utilized to great advantage by a company that knows itself well."

Whether you treat your employees as human resources, human capital, or simply as a percentage of operating expenses, the future of employee management will look very different from today. Older workers may have greater medical needs, but they are as committed to wellness and prevention as their younger counterparts in the company. They may elect to "ratchet back" from high-stress positions with extensive corporate responsibilities, but a true learning organization will recognize the knowledge resource that each long-serving employee represents and find a new employment model to ensure that resource can still contribute to the future growth of the organization.

### QUESTIONS

1. In what ways would the needs of a mature workforce differ from those of younger employees? Provide three examples.
2. What can an organization do to emphasize the importance of employee wellness?
3. What challenges would a young manager face in managing an older employee who has chosen to step down to a less responsible role?
4. How can an organization leverage the skills and knowledge of its mature employees?

*Source:* "Managing the Mature Workforce," The Conference Board, Report 1369, September 2009; Schumpeter, "The Silver Tsunami," *The Economist,* February 6, 2010; Ken Dychtwald, Tamara J. Erickson, and Robert Morison, *Workforce Crisis: How to Beat the Coming Shortage of Skills and Talent* (Boston: Harvard Business School Press, 2006); and Christopher Buckley, *Boomsday* (Twelve/Hachette Book Group, 2007).

Appendix

# Appendix: A Brief History of Management Thought

| Date | Primary work | Management Theory/ Proposition | Example |
|---|---|---|---|
| **1776** | Adam Smith: An Enquiry into Nature and Causes of the Wealth of Nations | Division of Labor/ Specialization | Using the example of a pin factory, Smith documented 18 distinct operations in the manufacture of a simple pin and offered as an alternative a simple set of tasks that he showed would increase productivity by 24,000% |
| **1911** | Frederick Winslow Taylor: The Principles of Scientific Management | Industrial efficiency | Believed in the 'one best way' to perform a task that was identified through detailed analysis and systematic observation of work performance. Preferred 'scientific management' to 'rule-of-thumb' performance standards |
| **1911** | Frank & Lillian Gilbreth:<br>Motion Study (1911)<br>Fatigue Study (1916)<br>Applied Motion Study (1917) | Developed time and motion study in industrial production, starting with bricklaying—among the first to use motion picture films to study motion and work methods. | Frank's major area of interest was the time and motion studies. Lillian's primary field was psychology and her work emphasized concern for the worker—specifically in the areas of fatigue, boredom, and employee morale. |
| **1916** | Henry L. Gantt:<br>"Work, Wages & Profits" (1916)<br>"Organizing for Work" (1919) | Contemporary of Taylor's, focused on Industrial efficiency through the effective scheduling of production. | Created the Gantt chart for the planning and controlling of work based on two principles—the amount of time needed to complete a task, and the amount of work to be done in that time period. |
| **1916** | Henri Fayol:<br>General and Industrial Management | Proposed five primary functions of management:<br>Planning<br>Organizing<br>Commanding<br>Coordinating<br>Controlling | Identified 6 types of operations, 9 levels of organization, and 14 principles of management. |
| **1918** | Mary Parker Follett:<br>The New State | Social worker and consultant who proposed groundbreaking theories in organizational behavior decades before her male contemporaries. | Advocated for the 'soft' theories of management that later became known as the 'human relations' movement. Her worked was echoed by Elton Mayo and Chester Barnard. |
| **1933** | Elton Mayo:<br>The Human Problems of an Industrialized Civilization | Attributed with founding The Human Relations Movement after his involvement in The Hawthorne Studies | In contrast to the industrial efficiency of scientific management, Mayo and his contemporaries argued that workers had social needs that directly impacted their work performance. |
| **1938** | Chester Barnard:<br>Functions of the Executive | Argued that the long-term survival of an organization was based on two criteria—efficiency and effectiveness | In a similar vein to Follett, he argued that authority was achieved by treating subordinates with respect and that performance was achieved through both tangible incentives and persuasion. |

| | | | |
|---|---|---|---|
| **1945** | Peter Drucker: Concept of the Corporation (A study of General Motors) 1954: The Practice of Management | Austrian-born journalist and business consultant credited with coining the term 'knowledge worker' in recognition of the growing importance of intellectual capacity over technical skill. | Credited with establishing the study of management as a profession, and advocating for the importance of the management function in effective organizational performance. |
| **1960** | Douglas McGregor: The Human Side of Enterprise | Proposed 'Theory X and Theory Y' as opposing managerial philosophies. | Argued that managers created an environment that was directly reflective of their beliefs about their employees. |
| **1979** | Philip Crosby: Quality is Free | Initiated the 'zero defects' program as quality control manager of the Pershing missile program. | Succeeded in reducing the overall rejection rate by 25%. Formed Philip Crosby & Associates at the beginning of the TQM boom in North America. |
| **1982** | Peters & Waterman: In Search of Excellence | Two McKinsey consultants who identified a group of 36 companies that had exhibited excellent performance over a 20-year period, based on six measures of financial success. | Became the best-selling management book of its time, based on a simple model of 8 characteristics including 'sticking to the knitting' and maintaining 'simultaneous loose-tight' properties. |
| **1986** | W. Edwards Deming: Out of the Crisis | Proposed 14 points for management effectiveness | Promoted Statistical Process Control (SPC) and both product and service quality as the key to cost control, increased productivity, and eventual market share growth. |
| **1994** | Collins & Porras: Built to Last: Successful Habits of Visionary Companies | Following the Peters & Waterman approach, studied 18 'visionary' companies. | Promoted the 'Big Hairy Audacious Goal' (BHAG)—a compelling, decades-long goal used to focus the entire organization on future performance. |
| **2001** | Jim Collins: Good to Great: Why some companies make the leap.... and others don't. | Follow-up study by Collins and a team of researchers that identified 11 'great' companies'. | Argued that 'good is the enemy of great', and promoted the notion of the 'hedgehog concept', where organizations identify the one big thing they are best at. |
| **2002** | Bossidy & Charan: Execution: The Discipline of Getting Things Done. | Larry Bossidy, CEO of Honeywell International, and Ram Charan, Management Consultant, advocate for the importance of getting things done as a key ability/skill for any manager. | Argued that: "Execution is a systematic process of rigorously discussing hows and whats, tenaciously following through, and ensuring accountability". |
| **2003** | Clayton Christenson: The Innovator's Dilemma | Harvard Business School Professor who argued that a company's successes can become obstacles in the face of changing markets and technologies. | Proposed the idea of 'disruptive technologies', such as the internet, that can dramatically change a business environment beyond anything envisioned in a company's strategic plan. |

## A

**ABC Classification System** Method of managing inventories based on their total value. 296

**Abilities** Personal characteristics used in performing a job. 261

**Absolute Advantage** The ability to produce more of a good than another producer with the same quantity of inputs. 99

**Acceptance Sampling** Statistical method of predicting the quality of a batch or a large group of products by inspecting a sample or group of samples. 291

**Aptitude Tests** Tests that measure a person's capacity or potential ability to learn. 176

**Audits** Method of control normally involved with financial matters. 258

**Authority** Legitimate exercise of power; the right to issue directives and expend resources; related to power but narrower in scope. 121, 200

**Autocratic Leader** One who makes many decisions on behalf of the group. 203

**Avoidance** Opportunity for a person to bypass a negative consequence by exhibiting a desirable behavior; also called negative reinforcement. 236

## B

**Balance of Trade** Difference between the value of goods a country exports and the value of goods it imports. 101

**Behavior or Personal Control** Control based on direct, personal surveillance. 253

**Bet-Your-Company Culture** Culture in which big-stakes decisions are required but considerable time passes before the results are known. 214

**Board (Panel) Interview** An interview conducted by two or more people. 178

**Board of Directors** Carefully selected committee that reviews major policy and strategy decisions proposed by top management. 157

**Break-Even Charts** Charts that depict graphically the relationship of volume of operations to profits. 260

**Budget** Statement of expected results or requirements expressed in financial or numerical terms. 254

**Business Strategies** Strategies that focus on how to compete in a given business; also known as competitive strategies. 75

## C

**Central Tendency** Performance appraisal error that results in most employees being evaluated similarly as doing average or above-average work. 266

**Centralization** Little authority is delegated to lower levels of management. 125

**Charismatic Leadership** Leadership style that can successfully influence employee behavior on the strength of the leader's personality or perceived charisma, without the formal power or experience to back it up. 209

**Checklist Appraisal** Appraisal method by which the manager answers yes or no to a series of questions concerning the employee's behavior. 264

**Closed System** An organization that has no interaction with its external environment. 14

**Code of Ethics** A document that outlines the principles of conduct to be used in making decisions within an organization. 314

**Combination Strategies** Strategies by which an organization simultaneously employs different strategies for different parts of the company. 75

**Committee** Organization structure in which a group of people are formally appointed, organized, and superimposed on the line or line and staff structure to consider or decide certain matters. 156

**Communication** The act of exchanging information. 26

**Conceptual Skills** Skills that help managers understand how different parts of a company relate to one another and to the company as a whole. 6

**Concurrent Controls** Controls that focus on a process as it occurs; designed to detect a problem as it occurs; also known as screening controls. 255

**Consideration** The leader behavior of showing concern for individual group members and satisfying their needs. 203

**Contingency (Situational) Approach** The process of assessing relevant variables that affect an organization's structure and then choosing the most appropriate structure for the situation. 148

**Contingency Approach to Leadership** The leadership style that is most effective in particular situations. 205

**Contingency Plans** Plans that address the what-ifs of a manager's job and that get the manager in the habit of being prepared and knowing what to do if something does go wrong. 53

**Continuous Improvement** Ongoing effort to make improvements in every part of the organization relative to all its products and services. 286

**Control** Process of ensuring that organizational activities are going according to plan; accomplished by comparing actual performance to predetermined standards or objectives and then taking action to correct any deviations. 252

**Corporate Culture** Value system for people in an organization that is conveyed through rites, rituals, myths, legends, and actions. 213

**Corporate Strategies** Strategies that address which businesses an organization will be in and how resources will be allocated among those businesses; also known as grand strategies. 74

**Critical-Incident Appraisal** Appraisal method by which the manager keeps a written record of incidents, as they occur, involving job behaviors that illustrate both satisfactory and unsatisfactory performance of the employee being rated. 263

**Culture** The set of important understandings (often unstated) that members of a community share. 211

**Customer Departmentalization** Organizational units that are defined by customers served. 150

## D

**Data Processing** Capturing, processing, and storing data. 64

**Decentralization** A great deal of authority is delegated to lower levels of management. 125

**Decision Making** In its narrowest sense, the process of choosing from among various alternatives. 56

**Decision Process** Process that involves three stages intelligence, design, and choice. 56

**Defensive or Retrenchment Strategies** Strategies by which a company reduces its operations. 74

**Democratic Leader** One who guides and encourages the group to make decisions. 203

**Departmentalization** Arrangement of jobs into related work units. 148

**Dependent Demand Items** Subassembly or component parts used to make a finished product; their demand is based on the number of finished products being produced. 296

**Diversification** Process by which a company engages in a variety of operations. 101

## E

**E-mail** Electronic mail; the system of sending and receiving messages over an electronic communications system. 32

**Economic Order Quantity (EOQ)** Optimal number of units to order at one time; determined by the point at which ordering costs equal carrying costs, or where total cost (ordering costs plus carrying costs) is at a minimum. 297

**Effort** Result of being motivated; the amount of energy an employee uses in performing a job. 261

**Embargo** A ban on exports to or imports from a foreign country. 103

**Employee Leasing Companies** Companies that provide permanent staff at customer companies, issue the workers' paychecks, take care of personnel matters, ensure compliance with workplace regulations, and provide various employee benefits. 175

**Empowerment** Form of decentralization in which subordinates have authority to make decisions. 125

**Entry Socialization** Adaptation process by which new employees are introduced and indoctrinated into the organization's culture. 213

**Equity Theory** Motivation theory based on the idea that people want to be treated fairly in relationship to others. 228

**Essay Appraisal** Appraisal method by which the manager describes an employee's performance in written narrative form. 263

**Esteem Needs** Needs that influence the development of various kinds of relationships based on adequacy, independence, and the giving and receiving of indications of esteem and acceptance. 231

**Ethics** A set of moral principles or values that govern behavior. 314

**Evaluation Phase** Third phase in strategic management, in which the implemented strategic plan is monitored, evaluated, and updated. 79

**Exception Principle** Principle that managers should concentrate on matters that deviate significantly from normal and let subordinates handle routine matters; also called management by exception. 127

**Expectancy** Employee's belief that his or her effort will lead to the desired level of performance. 235

**Expectancy Approach** Motivation theory based on the idea that employees will measure the outcomes expected from their performance against how much effort they perceive is required to achieve that performance. 235

**Exports** Goods and services that are sold abroad. 100

**External Environment** Everything outside the organization, with a focus on the external factors that affect the organization's business. 81

**Extinction** Absence of positive consequences or removal of previously provided positive consequences as a result of undesirable behavior. 236

## F

**Fixed Overhead Expenses** Expenses that do not change appreciably with fluctuations in the level of production or service. 282

**Flat Structure** Organization with few levels and relatively large spans of management at each level. 156

**Fordism** An economic model that features mass production, low prices, above-average wages, and workers becoming customers; named after Henry Ford. 10

**Foreign Intermediary** A wholesaler or agent that markets products for companies wanting to do business abroad. 106

**Formal Organization** Organization structure that defines the boundaries of the organization and within which the organization operates. 120

**Formal Plan** A written, documented plan developed through an identifiable process. 50

**Formal Work Groups** Groups established by the management to carry out specific tasks. 181

**Formulation Phase** First phase in strategic management, in which the initial strategic plan is developed. 79

**Free Trade Area** A region within which trade restrictions are reduced or eliminated. 104

**Functional Departmentalization** Categorization of organization units in terms of the nature of the work. 148

**Functional Plan** Plan that originates from the functional areas of an organization, such as production, marketing, finance, and personnel. 50

**Functional Strategies** Strategies that deal with the activities of the different functional areas of the business. 76

**Functions of Management** Elements of management that include planning, organizing, commanding, coordinating, and controlling. 13

## G

**Geographic Departmentalization** Organizational units that are defined by territories. 150

**Grapevine** Informal channels of communication within an organization. 32

**Graphic Rating Scale** Appraisal method by which the manager assesses an employee on such factors as quantity of work, dependability, job knowledge, attendance, accuracy of work, and cooperativeness. 263

**Group Cohesiveness** The degree of attraction among group members, or how tightly knit a group is. 183

**Group Conformity** The degree to which group members accept and follow group norms. 183

**Group Interview** Several interviewees are interviewed at once. 178

**Group Norms** The informal rules a group adopts to regulate the behavior of group members. 182

**Groupthink** Group members losing their ability to think as individuals and conforming at the expense of their good judgment. 184

**Growth Strategies** Strategies by which the organization tries to expand, as measured by sales, product line, number of employees, or similar measures. 74

## H

**Halo Effect** Interviewer allowing a single prominent characteristic to dominate judgment of all other traits. 179

**Hawthorne Effect** Phenomenon that employees respond positively to the attention paid to them by the researchers. 13

**Hierarchy of Needs** Theory that individuals are motivated to satisfy a number of needs and that money can directly or indirectly satisfy only some of these needs. 229

**Horizontal Structure** Organization structure consisting of two groups: the first composed of senior management responsible for strategic decisions and policies and the second composed of empowered employees working together in different process teams; also known as team structure. 154

**Human Relations Skills** Skills that managers need to understand and work well with people. 6

**Human Resource Forecasting** A process that attempts to determine the future human resource needs of an organization in light of the organization's objectives. 173

**Human Resource Planning (HRP)** Matching the internal and external supply of people with the openings the organization expects to have for a given time frame. 173

**Hybrid Departmentalization** Use of multiple types of departmentalization within the organization. 150

## I

**Implementation Phase** Second phase in strategic management, in which the strategic plan is put into effect. 79

**Imports** Goods and services purchased abroad. 100

**Independent Demand Items** Finished goods or end products ready to be sold or shipped. 296

**Inequity** Perception of a person that his or her job inputs and outcomes are less than the job inputs and outcomes of another person. 229

**Informal Organization** Aggregate of the personal contacts and interactions and the associated groupings of people working within the formal organization. 120

**Informal Work Groups** Groups formed voluntarily by members of an organization. 181

**Initiating Structure** The leader behavior of structuring the work of group members and directing the group toward the achievement of the group's goals. 203

**Inputs** Employee's perception of his or her contributions to the organization (e.g., education, intelligence, experience, training skills, and the effort exerted on the job). 229

**Instrumentality** Employee's belief that attaining the desired level of performance will lead to desired rewards. 235

**Intellectual Property** Ownership of tangible ideas, such as inventions, books, movies, and computer programs, that gives creators of the intellectual property the exclusive right to market and sell their work. 318

**Interest Tests** Tests that determine how a person's interests compare with the interests of successful people in a specific job. 176

**International Trade** The exchange of goods and services by different countries. 98

**Interpersonal Communication** An interactive process between individuals that involves sending and receiving verbal and nonverbal messages. 27

**Intranet** A private, corporate, computer network that uses Internet products and technologies to provide multimedia applications within organizations. 34

**Intuitive Approach** Decision-making process that relies on hunches and intuition. 58

**Inventories** Quantities of raw materials, in-process goods, or finished goods on hand; serves as a buffer between different rates of flow associated with the operating system. 292

**ISO 14000** Addition to the ISO 9000 to control the impact of an organization's activities and outputs on the environment. 289

**ISO 9000** A set of quality standards for international business with the major objective of promoting the development of standardization and facilitating the international exchange of goods and services. 288

## J

**Job Analysis** The process of determining the pertinent information relating to the nature of a specific job. 172

**Job Depth** Freedom of employees to plan and organize their own work, work at their own pace, and move around and communicate as desired. 121

**Job Description** A written statement that identifies the tasks, duties, activities, and performance results required in a particular job. 172

**Job Enlargement** The practice of giving an employee more of a similar type of operation to perform. 234

**Job Enrichment** The practice of upgrading a job by adding motivators. 234

**Job Knowledge Tests** Tests that measure the job-related knowledge possessed by a job applicant. 176

**Job Rotation** The practice of periodically rotating job assignments within the organization. 234

**Job Satisfaction** An individual's general attitude about his or her job. 237

**Job Scope** Number of different types of operations performed on the job. 121

**Job Specification** A written statement that identifies the abilities, skills, traits, or attributes necessary for successful performance in a particular job. 172

**Just-in-Time Inventory Control (JIT)** Inventory control system that schedules materials to arrive and leave as they are needed; also known as zero inventory systems, stockless systems, or kanban systems. 292

## K

**Kaizen** "Good change"; a process of continuous and relentless improvement. 286

## L

**Laissez-Faire Leader** One who allows people within the group to make all decisions. 203

**Law of Comparative Advantage** Axiom that producers should produce the goods they are most efficient at producing and purchase from others the goods they are less efficient at producing. 99

**Leader** A person who influences followers in setting and achieving objectives. 200

**Leader Behavior Description Questionnaire (LBDQ)** Questionnaire designed to determine what a successful leader does, regardless of the type of group being led. 203

**Leader-Member Relations** Degree to which others trust and respect the leader and the leader's friendliness. 206

**Leadership** The ability to influence people to willingly follow one's guidance or adhere to one's decisions. 200

**Lean Manufacturing** A systematic approach to identifying and eliminating waste and non-value-added activities. 286

**Leniency** Performance appraisal error of grouping of ratings at the positive end of the scale instead of spreading them throughout the scale. 266

**Level of Aspiration** Level of performance that a person expects to attain; determined by the person's prior successes and failures. 57

**Licensing Agreement** An agreement that permits one company to sell another company's products abroad in return for a percentage of the company's revenues. 106

**Linchpin Concept** Concept that managers are members of overlapping groups and link formal work groups to the total organization. 184

**Line and Staff Structure** Organization structure that results when staff specialists are added to a line organization. 152

**Line Functions** Functions and activities directly involved in producing and marketing the organization's goods or services. 152

**Line Structure** Organization structure in which authority originates at the top and moves downward in a line and in which all organizational units are directly involved in producing and marketing the organization's goods or services. 151

**Long-Range Objectives** Objectives that go beyond the current fiscal year and that must support and not conflict with the organizational mission. 53

**Long-Range Plans** Plans that span at least 3 to 5 years; some extend as far as 20 years into the future. 51

## M

**Malcolm Baldrige Award** Recognition of U.S. companies' quality achievements. 291

**Management** The process of deciding the best way to use an organization's resources to produce goods or provide services. 5

**Management Audits** Audits that attempt to evaluate the overall management practices and policies of the organization. 258

**Management by Objectives (MBO)** A philosophy based on converting organizational objectives into personal objectives. It assumes that establishing personal objectives elicits employee commitment, which leads to improved performance. 54

**Management Information Systems (MISs)** Integrated approach for providing interpreted and relevant data that can help managers make decisions. 63

**Managerial Grid** A two-dimensional framework rating a leader on the basis of concern for people and concern for production. 204

**Matrix Structure** Hybrid organization structure in which individuals from different functional areas are assigned to work on a specific project or task. 153

**Maximax Approach** Decision-making approach that involves selecting the alternative whose best possible outcome is the best of all possible outcomes for all alternatives; also known as the optimistic or gambling approach. 61

**Maximin Approach** Decision-making approach that involves comparing the worst possible outcomes for each alternative and selecting the one that is least undesirable; also known as the pessimistic approach. 61

**Mechanistic Systems** Organizational systems characterized by a rigid delineation of functional duties, precise job descriptions, fixed authority and responsibility, and a well-developed organizational hierarchy through which information filters up and instructions flow down. 143

**Middle Management** Managers responsible for implementing and achieving organizational objectives and for developing departmental objectives and actions. 5

**Mission** Basic purpose or purposes of the organization; why the organization exists; also known as purpose. 79

**Motivation** The concern with what activates human behavior, what directs this behavior toward a particular goal, and how this behavior is sustained. 228

**Motivation-Maintenance** An approach to work motivation that associates factors of high-low motivation with either the work environment or the work itself; also known as the two-factor or motivation-hygiene approach. 232

**Multinational Corporation (MNC)** Business that maintains a presence in two or more countries, has a considerable portion of its assets invested in and derives a substantial portion of its sales and profits from international activities, considers opportunities throughout the world, and has a worldwide perspective and orientation. 107

**Multirater Assessment or 360-Degree Feedback** Method of performance appraisal that uses input from an employee's managers, peers, customers, suppliers, or colleagues. 265

## N

**North American Free Trade Agreement (NAFTA)** Treaty that allows businesses in the United States, Mexico, and Canada to sell their products anywhere in North America without facing major trade restrictions. 104

## O

**Objectives** Statements outlining what a manager is trying to achieve. 53

**Open System** An organization that interacts with its external environment. 14

**Operations or Tactical Planning** Short-range planning that concentrates on the formulation of functional plans; done primarily by middle- to lower-level managers. 51

**Optimizing** Selecting the best possible alternative. 57

**Optimizing Approach** Decision-making process that includes the following steps: recognize the need for a decision; establish, rank, and weigh criteria; gather available information and data; identify possible alternatives; evaluate each alternative with respect to all criteria; and select the best alternative. 56

**Organic Systems** Organizational systems having less formal job descriptions, greater emphasis on adaptability, more participation, and less fixed authority. 143

**Organization** A group of people working together in some concerted or coordinated effort to attain objectives. 120

**Organization Structure** The framework that defines the boundaries of the formal organization and within which the organization operates. 142

**Organizational Morale** An individual's feeling of being accepted by, and belonging to, a group of employees through common goals, confidence in the desirability of these goals, and progress toward these goals. 237

**Organizing** Grouping activities, assigning activities, and providing the authority necessary to carry out the activities. 120

**Output or Impersonal Control** Control based on the measurement of outputs. 253

**Outsourcing** Practice of subcontracting certain work functions to an outside organization. 147

## P

**Parity Principle** Principle that authority and responsibility must coincide. 127

**Path-Goal Theory of Leadership** Relationship between a leader's behavior and the subordinates' performance and work activities. 207

**Perception** The mental and sensory processes an individual uses in interpreting information received. 27

**Performance** Degree of accomplishment of the tasks that make up an employee's job. 260

**Performance Appraisal** Process that involves (1) determining and communicating to employees how they are performing their jobs and (2) establishing a plan for their improvement. 261

**Physical Inventory** Process of counting the number of units a company holds in stock. 295

**Physiological Needs** Needs of the human body that must be satisfied in order to sustain life. 229

**Policies** Broad, general guides to action that constrain or direct the attainment of objectives. 54

**Polygraph Tests** Tests that record physical changes in the body as the test subject answers a series of questions. 176

**Position Power** Power and influence that go with a job. 206

**Positive Reinforcement** Provision of a positive consequence as a result of desirable behavior. 236

**Postaction Control** Control that is designed to detect an existing problem after it occurs but before it reaches crisis proportion. 255

**Power** Ability to influence, command, or apply force; a measure of a person's potential to get others to do what he or she wants them to do, as well as to avoid being forced by others to do what he or she does not want to do. 121, 200

**Preliminary Control** Method of exercising control to prevent a problem from occurring; also known as steering control. 253

**Principle of Bounded Rationality** Assumption that people have the time and cognitive ability to process only a limited amount of information on which to base decisions. 57

**Problem Solving** Process of determining the appropriate responses or actions necessary to alleviate a problem. 56

**Procedure** Series of related steps or tasks expressed in chronological order for a specific purpose. 54

**Process Control Chart** Time-based graphic display that shows whether a machine or process is producing items at the expected quality level. 291

**Process Culture** Culture that involves low risk with little feedback, with employees focusing on how things are done rather than on the outcomes. 214

**Process Quality Control** Quality evaluation while the product or service is being produced. 291

**Product Departmentalization** Placement of all activities necessary to produce and market a product or service under one manager. 149

**Product Quality Control** Quality evaluation of a batch of existing products or services; related to inputs or outputs of the system; also called acceptance control. 291

**Production Standards Approach** Performance appraisal method most frequently used for employees who are involved in physically producing a product; basically a form of objective setting for these employees. 262

**Professional Manager** Career person who does not necessarily have a controlling interest in the enterprise for which he or she works. 14

**Proficiency Tests** Tests that measure how well the applicant can do a sample of the work to be performed. 176

**Psychological Tests** Tests that measure personality characteristics. 176

**Psychomotor Tests** Tests that measure a person's strength, dexterity, and coordination. 176

**Punishment** Negative consequence as a result of undesirable behavior. 237

## Q

**Quality** The degree or grade of excellence specified; for the operations manager, quality is determined in relation to the specifications or standards set in the design stages. 283

**Quality at the Source** The philosophy of making each employee responsible for the quality of his or her own work. 286

**Quotas** Restrictions on the quantity of a good that can enter the country. 103

## R

**Recency** Performance appraisal error that results when evaluations are based on work performed most recently, generally work performed one to two months before evaluation. 266

**Recruitment** Process of seeking and attracting a supply of people from which qualified candidates for job vacancies can be selected. 174

**Reengineering** Searching for and implementing radical change in business processes to achieve breakthroughs in costs, speed, productivity, and service; also called business process engineering. 288

**Responsibility** Accountability for the attainment of objectives, the use of resources, and the adherence to organizational policy. 121

**Risk-Averting Approach** Decision-making approach that involves choosing the alternative with the least variation among its possible outcomes. 61

**Role** Set of behaviors associated with a particular job. 5

**Role Perception** Direction in which employees believe they should channel their efforts on their jobs. 261

**Rules** Require specific actions to be taken or not to be taken in a given situation. 55

## S

**Safety Needs** Protection against danger, threat, or deprivation. 229

**Safety Stocks** Inventory maintained to accommodate unexpected changes in demand and supply and allow for variations in delivery time. 297

**Satisficing** Selecting the first alternative that meets the decision maker's minimum standard of satisfaction. 57

**Scalar Principle** Principle that authority in the organization flows through the chain of managers one link at a time, ranging from the highest to the lowest ranks; also called chain of command. 128

**Scientific Management** Philosophy of Frederick W. Taylor that sought to increase productivity and make the work easier by scientifically studying work methods and establishing standards. 8

**Self-Actualization or Self-Fulfillment Needs** Highest-order needs involve people reaching their full potential in applying their abilities and interests to functioning in their environment. 231

**Self-Fulfilling Prophecy** The phenomenon of productivity being directly linked to managers' expectations. 201

**Semantics** The science or study of the meanings of words and symbols. 27

**Semistructured Interview** An interview in which the interviewer prepares the major questions in advance but has the flexibility to use techniques, such as probing, to help assess the applicant's strengths and weaknesses. 177

**Senior Management** The highest level of management; establishes the goals, or objectives, of the organization, decides which actions are necessary to meet those goals, and decides how to use the organization's resources. 5

**Short-Range Objectives** Objectives that are derived from an in-depth evaluation of long-range objectives and then set to help achieve the long-range objectives. 53

**Short-Range Plans** Plans that generally cover up to one year. 51

**Situation of Certainty** Situation that occurs when a decision maker knows exactly what will happen and can calculate the precise outcome for each alternative. 58

**Situation of Risk** Situation that occurs when a decision maker has reliable but incomplete information. 61

**Situation of Uncertainty** Situation that occurs when a decision maker has very little or no reliable information on which to evaluate the different possible outcomes. 61

**Situational Interview** An interview in which the interviewer uses projective techniques to put the prospective employee in action situations that might be encountered on the job. 178

**Situational Leadership Theory** Leadership theory that states as the level of maturity of followers increases, structures should be reduced while emotional support should first be increased and then gradually decreased. 208

**Six Sigma** Examination and improvement of the entire production or service system; literally, in statistical terms, six standard deviations from the mean. 286

**Skills Inventory** Consolidated information about an organization's current human resources. 172

**Social Audit** A method used by management to evaluate the success or lack of success of programs designed to improve the social performance of the organization. 322

**Social Needs** The needs for love, affection, belonging—all are concerned with establishing one's position relative to others. 230

**Social Responsibility** The obligation that individuals or businesses have to help solve social problems. 320

**Span of Management** Number of subordinates a manager can effectively manage; also called span of control. 129

**Stability Strategies** Strategies by which the organization maintains its present course (status quo strategies). 74

**Staff Functions** Functions that are advisory and supportive in nature; designed to contribute to the efficiency and maintenance of the organization. 152

**Stakeholders** The people—employees, customers, suppliers, and the community—who are affected by the actions of a business. 320

**Strategic Alliance** An agreement by which companies pool resources and skills in order to achieve common goals. 106

**Strategic Business Unit (SBU)** Distinct business that has its own set of competitors and can be managed reasonably independently of other businesses within the organization. 83

**Strategic Management** Formulation, proper implementation, and continuous evaluation of strategic plans; determines the long-run directions and performance of an organization. The essence of strategic management is developing strategic plans and keeping them current. 76

**Strategic Planning** Top-level, long-range planning. 51

**Strategy** Outline of the basic steps that management plans to take to achieve an objective or a set of objectives. 74

**Stress Interview** An interview during which the interviewee is placed under pressure. 178

**Structured Interview** An interview conducted using a predetermined outline. 177

**Supervisory Management** Managers responsible for the day-to-day operations of an organization and who supervise operative employees; considered the first level of management. 5

**SWOT** An acronym for strengths, weaknesses, opportunities, and threats. Business managers evaluate the performance of their department or the entire company using a SWOT analysis. 81

## T

**Tall Structure** Organization with many levels and relatively small spans of management. 156

**Tariff** Government-imposed tax on goods imported into a country. 103

**Task Structure** Degree to which job tasks are structured. 206

**Team Building** The process of establishing a cohesive group that works together to achieve its goals. 185

**Technical Skills** Specific abilities that people use to perform their jobs. 6

**Temporary Help** Help that may augment the current staff or be laid off whenever necessary; hired through an agency that pays the benefits and salary of the help, while the organization pays the agency an agreed-on figure for its services. 175

**Test Reliability** The consistency or reproducibility of the results of a test. 177

**Test Validity** The extent to which a test predicts a specific criterion. 177

**Tests** Methods for obtaining a sample of behavior that is used to draw inferences about the future behavior or performance of an individual. 176

**Theory X** Managerial belief that most employees don't like to work and will only work at the required level of productivity if they are forced to do so under the threat of punishment. 14

**Theory Y** Managerial belief that employees can be trusted to meet production targets without being threatened and that they will often seek additional responsibilities because they enjoy the satisfaction of being creative and increasing their own skills. 14

**Tough-Person, Macho Culture** Culture in which individuals take high risks and get quick feedback on whether their decisions are right or wrong. 214

**Trait Theory** A theory about leadership based on what the leader is like rather than what the leader does. 202

**Transaction-Processing Systems** Systems that substitute computer processing for manual record-keeping procedures. 64

**Transactional Leadership** The approach that leaders engage in bargaining relationships with their followers. 208

**Transformational Leadership** Leadership style that cultivates employee acceptance of the group mission. 208

## U

**Unity of Command Principle** Principle that an employee should have one, and only one, immediate manager. 127

**Unstructured Interviews** Interviews conducted without a predetermined checklist of questions. 178

## V

**Valence** Employee's belief about the value of the rewards. 235

**Variable Overhead Expenses** Expenses that change in proportion to the level of production or service. 282

**Virtual Organization** Temporary network of independent companies—suppliers, customers, and even rivals—linked by information technology to share skills, costs, and access to one another's markets. 154

## W

**Work-Hard, Play-Hard Culture** Culture in which high activity is expected and employees are encouraged to take few risks and to expect rapid feedback. 214

## Z

**Zero-Base Budgeting** Form of budgeting in which the manager must justify each area of a budget. Each year the activity is identified, evaluated, and ranked by importance. 254

**Zero-Defects Program** Method of increasing quality by increasing everyone's impact on quality. 289

# References


## Chapter 1

1 Henry Mintzberg, "The Manager's Job: Folklore and Fact," *Harvard Business Review*, March–April 1990, 163–76.
2 Ibid.
3 See Robert L. Katz, "The Skills of an Effective Administrator," *Harvard Business Review*, September–October 1987, 90–102.
4 *Scientific Management: Address and Discussions at the Conference on Scientific Management at the Amos Truck School of Administration and Finance* (Norwood, MA: Plimpton Press, 1912), 32–35.
5 John F. Mee, *Management Thought in a Dynamic Economy* (New York: New York University Press, 1963), 411.
6 John F. Mee, "Seminar in Business Organization and Operation" (unpublished paper, Indiana University, Bloomington, IN), 5.
7 Daniel Wren, *The Evolution of Management Thought*, 2nd ed. (New York: Ronald Press, 1979), 136–40.
8 Karel Williams, Colin Haslam, and John Williams, "Ford versus 'Fordism': The Beginning of Mass Production?" *Work, Employment & Society* 6, no. 4 (1992): 517–55.
9 "The Assembly Line and the $5 Day" was developed by Tom Hopper for the Michigan Historical Museum, http://www.michigan.gov/hal.
10 Bruce Pietrykowski, "Fordism at Ford: Spatial Decentralization and Labor Segmentation at the Ford Motor Company, 1920–1950," *Economic Geography* 71 (1995): 383–401.
11 Daniel A. Wren, "Henri Fayol as Strategist: A Nineteenth Century Corporate Turnaround," *Management Decision* 39, no. 5–6 (2001): 475–87; and Daniel A. Wren, Arthur G. Bedeian, and John D. Breeze, "The Foundations of Henri Fayol's Administrative Theory," *Management Decision* 40, no. 9 (2002): 906–18.
12 For a detailed description of the Hawthorne studies, see Fritz G. Roethlisberger and William J. Dickson, *Management and the Worker* (Cambridge, MA: Harvard University Press, 1939).
13 For example, see Alex Carey, "The Hawthorne Studies: A Radical Criticism," *American Sociological Review*, June 1967, 403–16.
14 Richard A. Johnson, Fremont E. Kast, and James E. Rosenzweig, *The Theory of Management Systems* (New York: McGraw-Hill, 1963), 3.
15 Douglas McGregor, *The Human Side of Enterprise* (New York: McGraw-Hill, 1960).

## Chapter 2

1 For additional information, see Mandy Thatcher, "The Grapevine: Communication Tool or Thorn in Your Side?" *Strategic Communication Management*, August 2003, 30–34.
2 For more information, see Darlene Fichter, "Making Your Intranet Live Up to Its Potential," *Online*, January–February 2006, 51–53.
3 Jon Perlow, "New in Labs: Stop Sending Mail You Later Regret," http://gmailblog.blogspot.com/2008/10/new-in-labs-stop-sending-mail-you-later.html.
4 J. Finney, "Six Secrets of Top Performers," *Communication World*, May–June 2008, 23–27.
5 "Las Vegas History: 10 Records Vegas Holds," http://www.vegas.com/lounge/centennial/records.html.

## Chapter 3

1 J. J. Hemphill, "Personal Variables and Administrative Styles," in *Behavioral Science and Educational Administration* (Chicago: National Society for the Study of Education, 1964), chap. 8.
2 A. L. Comrey, W. High, and R. C. Wilson, "Factors Influencing Organization Effectiveness: A Survey of Aircraft Workers," *Personnel Psychology* 8, no. 2 (1955): 245–57.
3 For a discussion of these studies, see John A. Pearce II, Elizabeth B. Freeman, and Richard D. Robinson Jr., "The Tenuous Link between Formal Strategic Planning and Financial Performance," *Academy of Management Review*, October 1987, 658–73; and Mike Schraeder, "A Simplified Approach to Strategic Planning," *Business Process Management Journal* 8, no. 1 (2002): 11–21.
4 Anthony Raia, *Managing by Objectives* (Glenview, IL: Scott Foresman, 1974), 38.
5 Herbert A. Simon, *The New Science of Management Decision* (New York: Harper & Row, 1960), 2.
6 Herbert A. Simon, *Model of Man* (New York: John Wiley, 1957), 198.
7 George S. Odiorne, *Management and the Activity Trap* (New York: Harper & Row, 1974), 142–44.
8 Ibid., 128–29; and George S. Odiorne, *The Change Resisters* (Englewood Cliffs, NJ: Prentice Hall, 1981), 15–25.
9 Irving Lorge, David Fox, Joel Davitz, and Martin Brenner, "A Survey of Studies Contrasting the Quality of Group Performance and Individual Performance, 1930–1957," *Psychological Bulletin*, November 1958, 337–72; Frederick C. Miner Jr., "Group versus Individual Decision Making: An Investigation of Performance Measures, Decision Strategies, and Process Losses/Gains," *Organizational Behavior and Human Performance*, February 1984, 112–24; and Alan S. Blinder and John Morgan, "Are Two Heads Better Than One? Monetary Policy by Committee," *Journal of Money, Credit, and Banking*, October 2005, 789.
10 M. E. Shaw, "A Comparison of Individuals and Small Groups in the National Solution of Complex Problems," *American Journal of Psychology*, July 1932, 491–504; Lorge et al., "A Survey of Studies"; and W. E. Watson, K. Kumar, and L. K. Michaelson, "Cultural Diversity's Impact on Interaction Process and Performance: Comparing Homogeneous and Diverse Task Groups," *Academy of Management Journal*, June 1993, 590–602.
11 M. Wallach, N. Kogan, and D. J. Bem, "Group Influence on Individual Risk Taking," *Journal of Abnormal and Social Psychology*, August 1962, 75–86; and N. Kogan and M. Wallach, "Risk Taking as a Function of the Situation, the Person, and the Group," in *New Directions of Psychology*, vol. 3, ed. G. Mardler (New York: Holt, Rinehart & Winston, 1967).
12 D. G. Meyers, "Polarizing Effects of Social Interaction," in *Group Decision Making*, ed. H. BranStatter, J. Davis, and G. Stock-Kreichgauer (New York: Academic Press, 1982).
13 Daniel D. Wheeler and Irving L. Janis, *A Practical Guide for Making Decisions* (New York: Macmillan, 1980), 17–36.

## Chapter 4

1 George A. Steiner, *Top Management Planning* (New York: Macmillan, 1969), 237.
2 Michael E. Porter, *Competitive Strategy: Techniques for Analyzing Industries and Competitors* (New York: Free Press, 1980).
3 Ibid., 37–38.
4 Patricia Braus, "What Does 'Hispanic' Mean?" *American Demographics*, June 1993, 46–49, 58.
5 Peter F. Drucker, *The Practice of Management* (New York: Harper & Row, 1954), 51.
6 Arthur A. Thompson Jr., John E. Gamble, and A. J. Strickland III, *Strategy: Core Concepts, Analytical Tools, Readings* (Burr Ridge, IL: McGraw-Hill/Irwin, 2006), 85.
7 Porter, *Competitive Strategy*.
8 George A. Steiner, John B. Miner, and Edmond R. Gray, *Management Policy and Strategy*, 2nd ed. (New York: Macmillan, 1982), 189.

## Chapter 5

1 L. Kemeny, "Banana Wars Slips into the Courts," *Sunday Times*, November 5, 2000.
2 "European Commission Enlargement," http://ec.europa.eu/enlargement/index_en.htm (accessed July 28, 2009).

## Chapter 6

1 Harold Koontz and Cyril O'Donnell, *Management: A Systems and Contingency Analysis of Managerial Functions*, 6th ed. (New York: McGraw-Hill, 1976), 274.
2 Chester L. Barnard, *Functions of the Executive* (Cambridge, MA: Harvard University Press, 1938), 114–15.
3 Gareth R. Jones, *Organizational Theory* (Reading, MA: Addison-Wesley, 1995), 9.
4 Thomas J. Peters and Robert H. Waterman Jr., *In Search of Excellence* (New York: Harper & Row, 1982), 313.

5 Mary Parker Follett, *Freedom and Co-ordination* (London: Management Publication Trust, 1949), 1–15 (the lecture reproduced in *Freedom and Co-ordination* was first delivered in 1926); and Barnard, *Functions of the Executive*, 163.
6 John Tschol, "Empowerment: The Key to Customer Service," *American Salesman*, November 1997, 12–15.
7 John H. Dobbs, "The Empowerment Environment," *Training & Development*, February 1993, 53–55.
8 Robert B. Shaw, "The Capacity to Act: Creating a Context for Empowerment," in *Organizational Architecture: Designs for Changing Organizations*, ed. David A. Nadler, Marc S. Gerstein, and Robert B. Shaw (San Francisco: Jossey-Bass, 1992), 169.
9 Renee Beckhams, "Self-Directed Work Teams: The Wave of the Future?" *Hospital Material Management Quarterly*, August 1998, 48–60.
10 Herbert M. Engel, *How to Delegate* (Houston, TX: Gulf, 1983), 6.
11 Michael Hammer and James Champy, *Reengineering the Corporation* (New York: Harper Business, 1993), 168, 180–81.
12 Ibid., 180–81.
13 L. F. Urwick, *The Elements of Administration* (New York: Harper & Row, 1943), 46.
14 Henri Fayol, *General and Industrial Management* (London: Sir Isaac Pitman & Sons, 1949), 36; first published in 1916.
15 Sir Ian Hamilton, *The Soul and Body of an Army* (London: Edward Arnold, 1921), 229.
16 V. A. Graicunas, "Relationship in Organization," *Bulletin of the International Management Institute* (Geneva: International Labour Office, 1933); reprinted in *Papers on the Science of Administration*, ed. L. Gulick and L. F. Urwick (New York: Institute of Public Administration, 1937), 181–87.
17 L. F. Urwick, "Scientific Principles and Organizations," *Institute of Management Series* No. 19 (New York: American Management Association, 1938), 8.
18 For a brief discussion of such situations, see Leslie W. Rue, "Supervisory Control in Modern Management," *Atlanta Economic Review*, January–February 1975, 43–44.
19 L. F. Urwick, "V. A. Graicunas and the Span of Control," *Academy of Management Journal*, June 1974, 352.
20 Carolyn Hirshman, "Share and Share Alike," *HR Magazine*, September 2005, 52–57.
21 Brian Gill, "Flextime Benefits Employees and Employers," *American Printer*, February 1998, 70; and Leah Carlson, "Firms Balance Workplace Flexibility and Business Demands," *Employee Benefit News*, April 1, 2005, 1.
22 http://www.workingfromanywhere.org/ (accessed November 8, 2005).
23 Hirshman, "Share and Share Alike."


## Chapter 7


1 Alan Filley and Robert House, *Managerial Process and Organizational Behavior* (Glenview, IL: Scott Foresman, 1969), 443–55.
2 A. D. Chandler, *Strategy and Structure* (Cambridge, MA: MIT Press, 1962).
3 Some relevant research includes J. Child, "Organization Structure, Environment, and Performance: The Role of Strategic Choice," *Sociology* 6 (1972): 1–22; R. Rumelt, *Strategy, Structure, and Economic Performance* (Boston: Harvard Business School, Division of Research, 1974); and Stephen P. Robins, *Organization Theory: Structure, Design, and Application* (Englewood Cliffs, NJ: Prentice Hall, 1990).
4 Tom Burns and G. M. Stalker, *The Management of Innovation* (London: Tavistock Institute, 1962).
5 Paul Lawrence and Jay Lorsch, "Differentiation and Integration in Complex Organizations," *Administrative Science Quarterly*, June 1967, 1–47; and Paul Lawrence and Jay Lorsch, *Organization and Environment* (Homewood, IL: Richard D. Irwin, 1969), originally published in 1967 by Division of Research, Graduate School of Business Administration, Harvard University.
6 Joan Woodward, *Industrial Organization: Theory and Practice* (London: Oxford University Press, 1965).
7 Edward Harvey, "Technology and the Structure of Organizations," *American Sociological Review*, April 1968, 247–59.
8 "Outsourcing Trends to Watch in '05," *Fortune*, March 21, 2005, C1–C10.
9 Michelle V. Rafter, "Promise Fulfilled," *Workforce Management*, September 2005, 51–54.
10 "Outsourcing Trends to Watch in '05."
11 Michael Corbett, "The Outsourcing Solution," *Fortune Small Business*, September 2005, 115.
12 Laure Edwards, "When Outsourcing Is Appropriate," *Wall Street & Technology*, July 1998, 96–98; and Laure Edwards, "Outsourcing: What's In, What's Out," *Employee Benefits*, October 6, 2003, 39.
13 Ibid.
14 Kathleen Madigan and Michael J. Mandel, "Outsourcing Jobs: Is It Bad?" *BusinessWeek*, August 25, 2003, 36.
15 David Cleland and William King, *Systems Analysis and Project Management*, 3rd ed. (New York: McGraw-Hill, 1983), 187.
16 Cliff McGoon, "After Downsizing . . . Then What?" *Communication World*, May 1994, 16–19.
17 Ronald K. Chung, "The Horizontal Organization: Breaking Down Functional Silos," *Business Credit*, May 1994, 21–24; and Barbara Crawford-Cook, "Breaking Down Silos," *Canadian HR Reporter*, May 31, 2004, 11–12.
18 Joyce Chutchian-Ferranti, "Virtual Corporation," *ComputerWorld*, September 1999, 33.
19 Ibid., 37.
20 This example is drawn from Samuel E. Bleecker, "The Virtual Organization," *Futurist*, March–April 1994, 9.
21 James Worthy, "Organization Structure and Employee Morale," *American Sociological Review* 15 (1956): 169–79.
22 Rocco Carzo Jr. and John Yanouzas, "Effects of Flat and Tall Organization Structure," *Administrative Science Quarterly* 114 (1969): 178–91.
23 Dan R. Dalton, William D. Todor, Michael J. Spendolini, Gordon J. Fielding, and Lyman W. Porter, "Organization Structure and Performance: A Critical Review," *Academy of Management Review*, January 1980, 49–54.
24 Richard M. Miller, "The D&O Liability Dilemma," *Chief Executive*, November–December 1988, 34–39; and Pamela W. Mason, "Portfolio D&O Insurance Can Leave Outside Directors in the Cold," *Venture Capital Journal*, October 1, 2005, 1.
25 Harold Geneen, *Managing* (Garden City, NY: Doubleday, 1984), 259.


## Chapter 8


1 Jane Ester Bahls, "Employment for Rent," *Nation's Business*, June 1991, 36.
2 For a detailed description of a large number of tests, see Robert A. Spics and Barbara S. Meke, eds., *The Sixteenth Mental Measurements Yearbook* (Lincoln, NE: Buros Institute–University of Nebraska Press, 2005).
3 See Edward C. Andler, *The Complete Reference Checking Handbook: The Proven (and Legal) Way to Prevent Hiring Mistakes* (New York: AMACOM, 2003).
4 David Greathatck and Timothy Clark, "Displaying Group Cohesiveness, Humour and Laughter in the Public Lectures of Management Gurus," *Human Relations*, December 2000, 15.
5 Lester Coch and John R. P. French Jr., "Overcoming Resistance to Change," *Human Relations*, 1948, 519–20.
6 Chris Bones, "Group-Think Doesn't Unite, It Divides," *Human Resources*, October 2005, 24.
7 See Paul E. Brauchle and David W. Wright, "Fourteen Team-Building Tips," *Training and Development Journal*, January 1992, 32–36. Also see Mahmoud Salem, Harold Lazarus, and Joseph Cullen, "Developing Self-Managing Teams: Structure and Performance," *Journal of Management Development* 11 (1992): 24–32.
8 Helene F. Uhlfelder, "It's All about Improving Performance," *Quality Progress*, February 2000, 49–53.


## Chapter 9


1 For another view on Theory X and Theory Y, see T. C. Carbone, "Theory X and Theory Y Revisited," *Managerial Planning*, May–June 1981, 24–27. See also Michael P. Bobie and William Eric Davis, "Why

So Many Newfangled Management Techniques Quickly Fail," *Journal of Public Administration Research and Theory*, July 2003, 239.
2 Victor H. Vroom, "Leadership," in *Handbook of Industrial and Organizational Psychology*, ed. Marvin D. Dunnette (Skokie, IL: Rand McNally, 1976), 1531.
3 Rensis Likert, *New Patterns of Management* (New York: McGraw-Hill, 1961).
4 Robert R. Blake and Jane Srygley Mouton, *The New Managerial Grid* (Houston, TX: Gulf Publishing, 1978); and Robert R. Blake and Jane S. Mouton, "How to Choose a Leadership Style," *Training and Development Journal*, February 1982, 38–45.
5 Fred E. Fiedler, *A Theory of Leadership Effectiveness* (New York: McGraw-Hill, 1967).
6 Robert Tannenbaum and Warren Schmidt, "HBR Highlights: Excerpts from How to Choose a Leadership Pattern," *Harvard Business Review*, July–August 1986, 131.
7 Paul Hersey and Kenneth Blanchard, "Life-Cycle Theory of Leadership," *Training and Development Journal*, June 1979, 94–100. See also George William Yeakey, "Hersey and Blanchard's Situational Leadership Theory: Applications in the Military" (PhD dissertation, Nova Southeastern University, 2002).
8 Excerpted from Jane M. Howell and Bruce J. Avolio, "The Ethics of Charismatic Leadership," *Academy of Management Executives* 6, no. 2 (1992).
9 Roy Wagner, *The Invention of Culture*, rev. ed. (Chicago: University of Chicago Press, 1981), 21.
10 Vijay Sathe, "Implications of Corporate Culture: A Manager's Guide to Action," *Organizational Dynamics*, Autumn 1983, 6.
11 Terrence E. Deal and Allan A. Kennedy, *Corporate Cultures: The Rites and Rituals of Corporate Life* (Reading, MA: Addison-Wesley, 1982), 4.
12 Harrison M. Trice and Janice M. Beyer, "Studying Organizational Cultures through Rites and Ceremonials," *Academy of Management Review* 9, no. 4 (1984): 645.
13 "The Corporate Culture Vultures," *Fortune*, October 17, 1983, 72.
14 Stephen P. Robbins, *Essentials of Organizational Behavior* (Englewood Cliffs, NJ: Prentice Hall, 1984), 174–76.
15 Ron Stodghill, "One Company, Two Cultures," *BusinessWeek*, January 22, 1996, 88.
16 Robbins, *Essentials of Organizational Behavior*, 171. © 1984; reprinted by permission of Prentice Hall, Inc.
17 This section is drawn from Deal and Kennedy, *Corporate Cultures*, 107, 129–35.
18 Arthur A. Thompson Jr. and A. J. Strickland III, *Strategic Management: Concepts and Cases*, 13th ed. (New York: McGraw-Hill/Irwin, 2003), 423.
19 "The Corporate Culture Vultures," 70.
20 Ibid.

## Chapter 10

1 Cited in Paul Hersey and Kenneth H. Blanchard, *Management of Organizational Behavior: Utilizing Human Resources*, 4th ed. (Englewood Cliffs, NJ: Prentice Hall, 1982), 4.
2 Abraham H. Maslow, *Motivation and Personality*, 2nd ed. (New York: Harper & Row, 1970).
3 David C. McClelland, *The Achievement Motive* (New York: Halsted Press, 1976).
4 Frederick Herzberg, Bernard Mausner, and Barbara Snyderman, *The Motivation to Work* (New York: John Wiley & Sons, 1959).
5 Victor H. Vroom, *Work and Motivation* (New York: John Wiley & Sons, 1967).
6 B. F. Skinner, *Science and Human Behavior* (New York: Macmillan, 1953); and B. F. Skinner, *Beyond Freedom and Dignity* (New York: Knopf, 1972).
7 Charles N. Greene, "The Satisfaction–Performance Controversy," *Business Horizons*, October 1972, 31. Also see D. R. Norris and R. E. Niebuhr, "Attributional Influences on the Job Performance–Job Satisfaction Relationship," *Academy of Management Journal*, June 1984, 424–31.
8 Greene, "The Satisfaction–Performance Controversy," 40.
9 John M. Ivancevich, "The Performance to Satisfaction Relationship: A Causal Analysis of Stimulating and Nonstimulating Jobs," *Organizational Behavior and Human Performance* 22 (1978): 350–64.
10 Donald P. Schwab and Larry L. Cummings, "Theories of Performance and Satisfactions: A Review," *Industrial Relations*, October 1970, 408–29.

## Chapter 11

1 J. M. Juran, *Managerial Breakthrough*, rev. ed. (New York: McGraw-Hill, 1995), 203–5.
2 Ibid.
3 James Champy, *Reengineering Management* (New York: Harper Business, 1995), 130; and James Champy, "Ambition: Root of Achievement," *Executive Excellence*, March 2000, 5–6.
4 Champy, *Reengineering Management*, 130.
5 Timothy J. McMahon and G. W. Perritt, "Toward a Contingency Theory of Organizational Control," *Academy of Management Journal*, December 1973, 624–35.
6 William G. Ouchi and Mary Ann Maguire, "Organizational Control: Two Functions," *Administrative Science Quarterly*, December 1975, 559–71; and William G. Ouchi, "The Transmission of Control through Organizational Hierarchy," *Academy of Management Journal*, June 1978, 174–76.
7 Champy, *Reengineering Management*, 140.
8 C. W. Wilkinson, Dorothy Wilkinson, and Gretchen Vik, *Communicating through Letters and Reports*, 9th ed. (Homewood, IL: Richard D. Irwin, 1986).
9 "Sarbanes-Oxley Act Improves Investor Confidence, But at a Cost," *The CPA Journal*, October 2005, 19.
10 Deborah Solomon, "Corporate Governance: At What Price? Critics Say the Cost of Complying with Sarbanes-Oxley Is a Lot Higher Than It Should Be," *Wall Street Journal*, October 17, 2005, R3.
11 William Stratton, Raef Lawson, and Toby Hatch, "Scorecarding as a Management Coordination and Control System," *Cost Management*, May–June 2004, 36–42.
12 James A. Seen, *Information Technology in Business*, 2nd ed. (Englewood Cliffs, NJ: Prentice Hall, 1998), 615; and Raymond McLeod Jr., *Management Information Systems*, 4th ed. (New York: Macmillan, 1990), 30.
13 Patricia M. Buhler, "The Performance Appraisal Process," *Supervision*, November 2005, 14–17.
14 Frederick W. Taylor, *Scientific Management* (New York: Harper & Row, 1911), 52.
15 See for instance Arthur Morgan, "360 Degree Feedback: A Critical Enquiry," *Personnel Review*, 2005, 663–82. Also see Roger Siler, "Getting Results with 360 Assessments," *Law Enforcement Technology*, September 2005, 148–56.
16 Noel Amerpohl, "Who Writes Your Job Description?" *Pro*, October–November 2005, 8–11.
17 See John W. Rogers, "Halo Effect," *Forbes*, September 26, 2005, 246.
18 Linda Henman, "Putting the Praise in Appraisals," *Security Management*, August 2005, 28–32.

## Chapter 12

1 Y. S. Chang, George Labovitz, and Victor Rosansky, *Making Quality Work* (New York: Harper Business, 1993), 65.
2 Richard B. Chase, F. Robert Jacobs, and Nicholas J. Aquilano, *Operations Management for Competitive Advantage*, 11th ed. (New York: McGraw-Hill/Irwin, 2006), 322.
3 William J. Stevenson, *Production/Operations Management*, 4th ed. (Burr Ridge, IL: Richard D. Irwin, 1993), 99.
4 Ibid., 100.
5 Tom Peters, *Thriving on Chaos* (New York: Knopf, 1987), 118–19.
6 Parts of this section were drawn from Stevenson, *Production/Operations Management*, 101.
7 Chase, Jacobs, and Aquilano, *Operations Management for Competitive Advantage*, 320.
8 Stevenson, *Production/Operations Management*, 104–5.
9 Adapted from Francis X. Mahoney and Carl G. Thor, *The TQM Trilogy* (New York: AMACOM, 1994), 132–37. Excerpted by permission of the publisher. All rights reserved.
10 Ibid., 134.

11 Richard B. Chase and Nicholas J. Aquilano, *Production and Operations Management: A Life Cycle Approach*, 6th ed. (Homewood, IL: Richard D. Irwin, 1992), 196; other parts of this section were drawn from this source.
12 Vivienne Walker, "Kaizen: The Art of Continual Improvement," *Personnel Management*, August 1993, 36–38.
13 Stevenson, *Production/Operations Management*, 105.
14 Erik Einset and Julie Marzano, "Six Sigma Demystified," *Tooling and Production*, April 2002, 43.
15 Ken Cowman, "Six Sigma: What, Where, When, Why and How," *Materials Management and Distribution*, October 2005, 69.
16 Esther Durkalski, "Lean Times Call for Lean Concepts," *Official Board Markets*, October 26, 2002, 38.
17 Thomas B. Clark, "Business Process Reengineering" (working paper, Georgia State University, November 1997), 1.
18 http://www.iso.org/iso/iso_catalogue/catalogue_tc/catalogue_detail.htm?csnumber=41014 (accessed July 6, 2010).
19 Ibid.
20 Ibid.
21 Ibid.
22 Chase and Aquilano, *Production and Operations Management*, 654–55.
23 Nicholas J. Aquilano and Richard B. Chase, *Fundamentals of Operations Management* (Homewood, IL: Richard D. Irwin, 1991), 586.
24 Norman Gaither, *Production and Operations Management*, 5th ed. (Fort Worth, TX: Dryden Press, 1992), 377.
25 Jeremy Main, *Quality Wars* (New York: Free Press, 1994), 115.
26 Peters, *Thriving on Chaos*, 117.
27 Chase and Aquilano, *Production and Operations Management*, 481.
28 Stevenson, *Production/Operations Management*, 585.
29 Chase, Jacobs, and Aquilano, *Operations Management for Competitive Advantage*, 611.
30 John F. Magee, "Guides to Inventory Policy: I. Functions and Lot Size," *Harvard Business Review*, January–February 1956, 49–60.

## Chapter 13

1 Nicholas A. Ashford, *Crisis in the Workplace: Occupational Disease and Injury* (Cambridge, MA: MIT Press, 1976).
2 29 United States Code 651(b).
3 "All about OSHA," U.S. Department of Labor, OSHA 3302-06N, 2006, 8.
4 Elisabeth Bumiller, "Bush Signs Bill Aimed at Fraud in Corporations," *The New York Times*, July 31, 2003.
5 Advisory Committee on Smaller Public Companies, Securities and Exchange Commission, April 23, 2006.
6 29 United States Code 207.
7 See Dennis W. Organ, "Business Ethics 101?" *Business Horizons*, January–February 2003, 1–2.
8 For additional information, see Ronald Paul Hill, Debra Stephens, and Iain Smith, "Corporate Social Responsibility: An Examination of Individual Firm Behavior," *Business and Society Review*, September 2003, 339–64.
9 "Environment," http://www.aircanada.com/en/environment/index.html?src=hp_ql (accessed July 5, 2010).

## Chapter 14

1 Joseph H. Boyett and Jimmie T. Boyett, *Beyond Workplace 2000* (New York: Penguin Books, 1995), xiii–xiv.
2 Peter Senior, "Where Organization and Management May Be Headed," *Consulting to Management*, June 2004, 50–56.
3 Joyce Chutchian-Ferranti, "Virtual Corporation," *Computer-World*, September 1999, 33.
4 Schumpeter, "The Silver Tsunami," *The Economist*, February 6, 2010, 74.
5 Eric Lesser, "Managing an Aging Workforce," IBM Institute for Business Value, CEO Forum Group, 2006.
6 http://www.yourencore.com.
7 John P. Kotter, *Leading Change* (Boston: Harvard Business School Press, 1996).
8 Clayton M. Christensen, *The Innovator's Dilemma* (Boston: Harvard Business School Press, 1997), introduction.

## Chapter 1

**Opener:** BananaStock/PictureQuest; **p. 4:** © Construction Photography/Corbis; **p. 5:** © Beathan/Corbis; **p. 8:** Corbis/PictureQuest; **p. 9:** Bloomberg/Getty Images; **p. 10:** © Stockbyte/Getty Images; **p. 11 (left):** © Eric Audras/Photoalto/PictureQuest; **p. 11 (middle):** © Eric Audras/Photoalto/PictureQuest; **p. 11 (right):** © Eric Audras/Photoalto/PictureQuest; **p. 13:** Courtesy of AT&T Archives and History Center; **p. 14:** © Mike Powell/Getty Images; **p. 21:** Jonathon Ross/Cutcaster; **p. 22:** 3M logo used with permission from 3M; **p. 23:** Brooklyn Production/Corbis.

## Chapter 2

**Opener:** © Ant Strack/Corbis; **p. 28 (left):** Christopher Robbins/Getty Images; **p. 28 (right):** Skip Nall/Getty Images; **p. 30 (top):** © Brand X Pictures/PunchStock; **p. 30 (bottom):** © Brand X Pictures/PunchStock; **p. 31:** © Ryan McVay/Photodisc/Getty Images; **p. 35:** Dimitri Vervitsiotis/Getty Images; **p. 36:** Brand X; **p. 37:** © Lars Niki; **p. 42:** Getty Images; **p. 43:** Burke/Triolo/Brand X Pictures/JupiterImages; **p. 45:** iStock Exclusive/Getty Images.

## Chapter 3

**Opener:** © Polka Dot Images/Masterfile; **p. 51 (top):** © Ariel Skelley/Getty Images; **p. 51 (bottom):** © Andersen Ross/Getty Images; **p. 52:** © Rommel/Radius Images; **p. 54:** Royalty-Free/Corbis; **p. 55:** Stockbyte/Getty Images; **p. 59 (left):** McGraw-Hill Companies; **p. 59 (right):** Getty Images; **p. 60:** The McGraw-Hill Companies, Inc./John Flournoy, photographer; **p. 61:** Polka Dot Images/JupiterImages; **p. 62:** The McGraw-Hill Companies, Inc./Jill Braaten, photographer; **p. 64:** Thomas Northcut/Getty Images; **p. 68:** © Getty Images; **p. 69:** GM logo used with permission from GM; **p. 71:** Tetra Images/Getty Images.

## Chapter 4

**Opener:** © Lars A. Niki; **p. 74:** Steve Cole/Getty Images; **p. 75:** © Anderson Ross/Getty Images; **p. 76:** Bloomberg/Getty Images; **p. 77:** S. Solum/PhotoLink/Getty Images; **p. 83:** Big Cheese Photo/JupiterImages; **p. 86:** Royalty-Free/Corbis; **p. 91:** Ryan McVay/Getty Images; **p. 92:** The McGraw-Hill Companies, Inc./Christopher Kerrigan, photographer; **p. 94:** © Digital Vision/PunchStock.

## Chapter 5

**Opener:** Getty Images/Rubberball; **p. 98:** Joseph Sohm/Visions of America/Corbis; **p. 99:** Royalty-Free/Corbis; **p. 100 (top):** Royalty-Free Corbis; **p. 100 (bottom):** Getty Images; **p. 101 (top, left):** © The McGraw-Hill Companies, Inc./John Flournoy, photographer; **p. 101 (top, right):** Andrew Ward/Life File/Getty Images; **p. 101 (bottom):** Blend Images/Getty Images; **p. 102 (top):** PhotoLink/Getty Images; **p. 102 (bottom):** Noel Hendrickson/Getty Images; **p. 103:** © Henri Conodul/Iconotec.com; **p. 106:** Author's Image/PunchStock; **p. 107:** Eric Audras/Photoalto/PictureQuest; **p. 108:** © Digital Vision/PunchStock; **p. 110:** © Flying Colours Ltd/Getty Images; **p. 114:** Sony logo used with permission from Sony Electronics, Inc.; **p. 115:** Siemens logo used with permission from Siemens; **p. 117:** Digital Vision.

## Chapter 6

**Opener:** © Veer; p. 120: Ryan McVay/Getty Images; **p. 122:** © Helen King/Corbis; **p. 124:** © Jon Silla; **p. 126:** © Image Source/PunchStock; **p. 127:** © Jetta Productions/Walter Hodges/Getty Images; **p. 130:** BananaStock/JupiterImages; **p. 131:** BananaStock/PictureQuest; **p. 136:** © Pixtal/SuperStock; **p. 137:** Getty Images; **p. 139:** © Comstock Images/PictureQuest.

## Chapter 7

**Opener:** BananaStock/PictureQuest; **p. 143:** Cultura/Getty Images; **p. 147:** © Digital Vision/PunchStock; **p. 149 (top):** © John A. Rizzo/Getty Images; **p. 149 (bottom):** © Jim Craigmyle/Corbis; **p. 150:** The McGraw-Hill Companies, Inc./Rick Brady, photographer; **p. 155:** BananaStock/JupiterImages; **p. 157:** © Royalty-Free/Corbis; **p. 165:** BananaStock/JupiterImages; **p. 166:** © Royalty-Free/Corbis; **p. 168:** AFP/Getty Images.

## Chapter 8

**Opener:** Ryan McVay/Getty Images; **p. 173:** Comstock/PunchStock; **p. 175:** Big Cheese Photo/JupiterImages; **p. 177:** © Digital Vision; **p. 179:** © AP Photo/Paul Sakuma; **p. 181:** Getty Images/Image Source; **p. 182:** CDC/Cade Martin; **p. 184 (top):** © BananaStock/PunchStock; **p. 184 (bottom):** © Image Source/Corbis; **p. 185:** Brand X Pictures; **p. 187:** Image100/Corbis; **p. 193:** Ilene MacDonald/Alamy; **p. 195:** © San Jose Mercury News; **p. 197:** © Lars A. Niki.

## Chapter 9

**Opener:** © The McGraw-Hill Companies, Inc./Kefover/Opatrany; **p. 200:** Ariel Skelley/AGE fotostock; **p. 201:** Eric Audras/Photoalto/PictureQuest; **p. 203:** Don Hammond/Design Pics/Corbis; **p. 206:** © Blend Images/AGE fotostock; **p. 209:** Ryan McVay/Getty Images; **p. 211 (top):** © Royalty-Free/Corbis; **p. 211 (bottom):** © Ryan McVay/Getty Images; **p. 212 (left):** © Robert Holmes/Corbis; **p. 212 (right):** © BananaStock/PunchStock; **p. 214:** Ryan McVay/Getty Images; **p. 215:** © Creatas Images/JupiterImages; p. 221: Brand X Pictures.

## Chapter 10

**Opener:** Comstock Images/Corbis; **p. 228:** © Stockbyte/PunchStock; **p. 229:** © CMCD/Getty Images; **p. 231 (left):** © Dirk Lindner/Corbis; **p. 231 (right):** moodboard/Corbis; **p. 233:** © Randy Faris/Corbis; **p. 236:** © Digital Vision; **p. 237:** Brand X/Fotosearch; **p. 238:** © AP Photo/Lisa Poole; **p. 239:** © Photodisc/PunchStock; **p. 246:** Seagate logo used by permission of Seagate; **p. 247:** Getty Images; **p. 248:** © Comstock/PunchStock.

## Chapter 11

**Opener:** Blend Images/Alamy; **p. 252 (top):** JupiterImages/Creatas/Alamy; **p. 252 (bottom):** © Digital Vision/PunchStock; **p. 254:** Stockbyte/Getty Images; **p. 255:** Ryan McVay/Getty Images; **p. 256:** © Ryan McVay/Getty Images; **p. 258:** Inti St. Clair/Digital Vision/Getty Images; **p. 261:** © Flying Colours Ltd/Getty Images; **p. 262:** Royalty-Free/Corbis; **p. 267 (top):** Jim Arbogast/Getty Images; **p. 267 (bottom):** © BananaStock/Alamy; **p. 269 (top):** Comstock Images/PictureQuest; **p. 269 (bottom):** Royalty-Free/Corbis; **p. 275:** © Carl & Ann Purcell/Corbis; **p. 277:** Ingram Publishing/SuperStock; **p. 278:** Royalty-Free/Corbis.

## Chapter 12

**Opener:** Royalty-Free/Corbis; **p. 283:** © Thinkstock/Corbis; **p. 284:** Digital Vision/PunchStock; **p. 285:** altrendo images/Getty Images; **p. 289 (left):** John A. Rizzo/Getty Images; **p. 289 (right):** Courtesy of NIST, National Institute of Standards and Technology; **p. 294 (top):** © Creatas/PunchStock; **p. 294 (middle):** © Ingram Publishing/Superstock; **p. 294 (bottom):** © Burke/Triolo Productions/Brand X Pictures/Getty Images; **p. 295:** Jack Hollingsworth/Getty Images; **p. 297:** © PunchStock/Digital Vision; **p. 303:** Masterfile (Royalty-Free Division); **p. 305:** C Squared Studios/Getty Images; **p. 306:** © PunchStock/Stockbyte.

## Chapter 13

**Opener:** U.S. Navy photo by Mass Communication Specialist 2nd Class Justin Stumberg; **p. 310:** © Stockbyte/Getty Images; **p. 312:** © Ingram Publishing/AGE Fotostock; **p. 316:** © 2007 Getty Images, Inc.; **p. 317:** Wendy Idele/Getty Images; **p. 318 (top):** © Stockdisc/PunchStock; **p. 318 (bottom):** © David J. Green – people/Alamy; **p. 320:** © Getty Images/Photodisc; **p. 329:** Terracycle logo used by permission of Terracycle; **p. 330:** © Comstock/Alamy.

## Chapter 14

**Opener:** © Beathan/Corbis; **p. 334 (top):** Jules Frazier/Getty Images; **p. 334 (bottom):** © David Cook/www.blueshiftstudios.co.uk/Alamy; **p. 335:** © image 100/PunchStock; **p. 337 (top):** Getty Images; **p. 337 (bottom):** BananaStock/JupiterImages; **p. 342:** Image Source/Getty Images; **p. 346:** Nick Koudis/Getty Images; **p. 347:** © Comstock; **p. 349:** BananaStock/JupiterImages.

Text Credits

## Chapter 1

Figure 1.3: Mintzberg's 10 managerial roles reprinted by permission of *Harvard Business Review* from "The Manager's Job: Folklore and Fact," *Harvard Business Review*, March–April 1990, pp. 163–76. Copyright © 1990 by the Harvard Business School Publishing Corporation. All rights reserved.

## Chapter 2

"Six secrets of top performers" from John Finney, *Communication World*, May–June 2008, pp. 23–27.

Adaption of "Finder, Minder & Grinder: The Charges and Rebuttal" from G. Yemen and M. N. Davidson, University of Virginia Darden School Foundation, 2005.

"Compensation and Benefits Review/Sage" adapted from Cindy Fruitrail and Valerie Wedin, "Creating Better Health Care Consumers: A Case Study," *Compensation and Benefits Review* 38, no. 5 (October 2006): pp. 40–45.

## Chapter 3

Excerpt of "Areas for establishing objectives in most organizations" from Anthony Raia, *Managing by Objectives* (Glenview, IL: Scott Foresman: 1974), p. 38. Copyright © 1974 Anthony Raia. Used with permission.

"How the Chips Fall" copyright © 2010 Institute for Global Ethics®. All rights reserved. The Institute for Global Ethics®, a 501(c)(3) non-profit, provides ethics training, membership, and online downloadable resources. Founded by Dr. Rushworth M. Kidder (1990). Visit our web site at www.globalethics.org.

Emotional attachments that can hurt decision makers from Odiorne, *Management and the Activity Trap* (New York: Harper & Row, 1974), pp. 142–44.

## Chapter 4

Mercy Hospital text adapted from A. M. Zuckerman, "Affiliate, Merge, or Stay Independent?" *Healthcare Financial Management*, August 2008, pp.118–20.

## Chapter 6

Excerpt from T. Forester and P. Morrison, *Computer Ethics: Cautionary Tales and Ethical Dilemmas in Computing*, 2nd ed., pp. 233–36. Copyright © 1993, Massachusetts Institute of Technology. Used by permission of The MIT Press.

## Chapter 7

Figure 7.11: Matrix structure from David Cleland and William King, *Systems Analysis and Project Management*, 3rd ed., 1983. Reproduced with permission of The McGraw-Hill Companies, Inc.

## Chapter 8

Figure 8.5: Linchpin figure from Renis Linkert, *New Patterns of Management*, 1961, p. 104.

## Chapter 9

Managerial grid from Robert R. Blake and Jane Srygley Mouton, *The New Managerial Grid*®, 1978, p. 11. Reprinted with permission.

Figure 9.2: "Assumptions about people" from D. McGregor and W. Bennis, *The Human Side of Enterprise*: 25th Anniversary Printing, 1989.

Figure 9.9: Leadership grid reprinted by permission of *Harvard Business Review* from Robert Tannenbaum and Warren H. Schmidt, "How to Choose a Leadership Pattern," *Harvard Business Review*, May–June 1973. Copyright © 1973 by the Harvard Business School Publishing Corporation. All rights reserved.

## Chapter 11

Figure 11.1: Control pyramid from J. Juran, *Managerial Breakthroughs*, 2nd ed., 1995, p. 205.

## Chapter 12

Figure 12.2: Dimensions of design quality from Richard B. Chase, F. Robert Jacobs, and Nicholas J. Aquilano, *Operations Management for Competitive Advantage*, 11th ed., 2006.

Figure 12.3: "The 14 Points" from W. Edwards Deming, *Out of the Crisis*, pp. 23–24. Copyright © 2000 Massachusetts Institute of Technology. Used by permission of The MIT Press.

Figure 12.4: Comparisons of traditional/TQM organizations from William J. Stevenson, *Production and Operations Management*, 4th ed., 1992, p. 107. Reproduced with permission of The McGraw-Hill Companies, Inc.

Figure 12.7: ABC Inventory classification from Richard B. Chase, F. Robert Jacobs, and Nicholas J. Aquilano, *Operations Management for Competitive Advantage*, 11th ed., 2002. Reproduced with permission of The McGraw-Hill Companies, Inc.

## Chapter 13

Figure 13.2: Reprinted by permission of *Harvard Business Review* from L. Nash, "Ethics Without the Sermon," *Harvard Business Review* 59, 1981, p. 78. Copyright © 1981 by the Harvard Business School Publishing Corporation. All rights reserved.

Excerpt from *The Wall Street Journal* by Roger Ricklefs, 1983. © Dow Jones.

## Chapter 14

Excerpt from John M. Peckham III, "Virtual Society, Virtual Convention," *Association Management*, December 2004, p. 55. Copyright © 2004 John M. Peckham III.

Eric Lesser, "Managing an aging workforce," IBM's Institute for Business Value, CEO Forum Group. Copyright © 2006. Used by permission of Institute for Business Value.

Whole Foods link courtesy of Whole Foods Market. "Whole Foods Market" is a registered trademark of Whole Foods Market IP, L.P.

# Index

## D



## E



## F

## G



## H



## I



## J

## K



## L



## M

## N



## O



## P